Business Connections

Information Technology in Action

Laura Elizabeth Pinto

Janice Lynn Ellerby

PEARSON
Prentice Hall

Toronto

National Library of Canada Cataloguing in Publication

Pinto, Laura Elizabeth
Business connections : information technology in action / Laura Elizabeth Pinto, Janice Lynn Ellerby.

Includes bibliographical references and index.
For use in grades 11 and 12.
ISBN 0-13-111349-6

1. Business—Data processing. 2. Information storage and retrieval systems—Business. 3. Information technology. I. Ellerby, Janice Lynn II. Title.

HF5548.2.P55 2003 650'.0285 C2003-900276-4

Editors	Marg Bukta, Geraldine Kikuta
Production Coordinator	Zane Kaneps
Production Manager	Theresa Thomas
Cover and Text Design	Alex Li
Cover Image	Alex Li
Page Layout	David Cheung Design Inc.
Illustrations	Paul Howalt/Three in a Box Kevin Cheng/Supercat Illustration David Cheung Design Inc.
Photo Research/Permissions:	Karen Hunter, Elizabeth Kelly, Michaele Sinko
Literary Permissions	Jane McWhinney
Indexer	May Look
Publisher	Reid McAlpine
Product Manager	David LeGallais
Project Developer	Doug Panasis

Every effort has been made to obtain permission and provide suitable credits. The authors and editors would be pleased to learn of any error or omission, so that corrections may be made to future printings.

The publisher has taken care to meet or exceed industry specifications for the manufacturing of textbooks. The spine and the endpapers of this sewn book have been reinforced with special fabric for extra binding strength. The cover is a premium, polymer-reinforced material designed to provide long life and withstand rugged use. Mylar gloss lamination has been applied for further durability.

Printed and bound in Canada
3 4 5 TCP 07 06 05 04

Table of Contents

CHAPTER 3

Working in Project Teams 47

CHAPTER 4

Computing Fundamentals 74

CHAPTER 5

CHAPTER 6

CHAPTER 7

Delivering With Impact 171

CHAPTER 8

Got the Message? Electronic Communication 203

CHAPTER 9

The Internet and E-Commerce 233

CHAPTER 10

Business in a Wired World 272

CHAPTER 13

Table of Acronyms and Initialisms

ABM	automated banking machine
ACM	Association for Computing Machinery
AMA	American Management Association; *also* American Medical Association
APA	American Psychological Association
ARPANET	Advanced Research Projects Agency Network
ASCII	American Standard Code for Information Interchange
ASP	Application Service Providers
ATM	automated teller machine
AUPs	acceptable use policies
B2B	Business to Business
B2C	Business to Consumer
BA	Bachelor of Arts
BIOS	basic input-output system
BMP	Bitmap
CASPIAN	Consumers Against Supermarket Privacy Invasion and Numbering
C2C	Consumer to Consumer
CA	certification authority
CAD	Computer Aided Design
CAM	Computer Aided Manufacturing
CBT	computer-based training
CGI	Common Gateway Interface
CIAC	Computer Incident Advisory Capability
CPRN	Canadian Policy Research Network
CPU	central processing unit
CRM	Customer Relationship Management
CRT	cathode ray tubes
CSS	Cascading Style Sheet
DNS	domain name system
DoS	Denial of Service
DSL	Digital Subscriber Line
DSS	decision support system
DTP	desktop publishing
DVD	digital versatile disks
EDI	electronic data interchange
EIM	enterprise instant messaging
EMS	Electronic Meeting System
EPS	Encapsulated Postscript
ERM	Enterprise Resource Management
FAT	file allocation table
FOI	freedom of information
FTP	file transfer protocol
GAAP	Generally Accepted Accounting Principles
GDP	Gross Domestic Product
GIF	Graphics Interchange Format
GUI	graphical user interface
HRDC	Human Resources Development Canada
HRM	Human Resources Management
HTML	hypertext markup language
HTTP	hypertext transfer protocols
ICT	information communications technology
IEEE	Institute for Electrical and Electronics Engineering
IFF	Interchange File Format
IP	Internet protocol
IRC	Internet Relay Chat
ISDN	Integrated Services Digital Network
ISO	International Standards Organization
ISP	Internet Service Provider
IT	information technology
ITAC	Information Technology Association of Canada
JPEG/JPG	Joint Photographic Experts Group
KDD	knowledge discovery in databases
LAN	local area network

LCD	liquid crystal display
MA	Master of Arts
MAC	Macintosh
MAN	metropolitan area network
MBA	Master of Business Administration
m-commerce	mobile commerce
MCS	multipoint communication systems
MICR	magnetic ink character recognition
MIDI	Musical Instrument Digital Interface
MIS	management information systems
MLA	Modern Language Association of America
MP3	MPEG Audio Layer Three
MPEG	Moving Pictures Experts Group
MTSO	Mobile Telephone Switching Office
MVNO	mobile virtual network operators
NAFTA	North American Free Trade Agreement
NIC	network interface card
NOS	networking operating system
NSFNet	National Science Foundation High-Speed Network
OCR	optical character recognition
OS	operating system
P2P	peer-to-peer; *also* person to person
PCS	personal communication services
PDA	personal digital assistant
PHP	PHP: Hypertext Preprocessor
PIN	personal identity number
PNG	Portable Network Graphic
POP3	Post Office Protocol
PR	public relations
R&D	Research and Development
RAM	random access memory
RIM	Research in Motion
ROM	read only memory
RSI	repetitive strain injury
SHRC	Software Human Resource Council of Canada
SLC	subscriber loop carrier
SME	subject matter expert
SMIL	Synchronized Multimedia Integration Language
SMTP	Simple Mail Transfer Protocol
SOHO	small office, home office
SPSS	Statistical Package for the Social Sciences™
SQL	Structured Query Language
SSL	secure sockets layer
TCP/IP	transmission control protocol/Internet protocol
TGA	Targa Graphics Adapter
TIFF/TIF	Tagged-Image File Format
UPC	Universal Product Code
URL	Uniform Resource Locator
USB	Universal Serial Bus
W3C	World Wide Web Consortium
WAN	wide area network
WAP	wireless application protocols
WBS	work breakdown structure
WiFi	wireless fidelity
WWW	World Wide Web
WYSIWYG	What You See Is What You Get
XML	Extensible Markup Language

Acknowledgements

Special thanks to the family and friends who were so supportive of this project: Brone Pinto, Robert C. Pinto, Rob Pinto, Kristen Hawkeswood, Adam Mock, Win-man, Finnegan, and Veronika Badikonis. I would also like to acknowledge Mandy Thomson, Madeline Dennis, Eija Forster, Cheryl Rosenthal, Noel Hurley, William Wellington, and Lennox Borel for mentoring me and providing so many opportunities for personal and professional growth over the years. Finally, I want to thank my co-author Janice Ellerby for (once again) making this such a great experience.

Laura Pinto, Toronto, 2003

I would like to take this opportunity to thank my husband, Rick, for his continued support, encouragement, unconditional love, and understanding. To my family, my thanks for understanding why I haven't always been around.

Janice Ellerby, Barrie, 2003

The authors would also like to thank our editor, Marg Bukta, for her tireless efforts, and Doug Panasis who helped bring this project to life. A special thank you goes to Ivan Saari for his tremendous contributions to the finished product.

Reviewers

The authors and publisher would like to thank the following reviewers for their valuable insights and suggestions:

Anna Battista, Father Michael Goetz Secondary School, Mississauga, ON

Bob Baran, Centre for Information Resources and Technology (CIRT), London District Catholic School Board, London, ON

Chris Bradford, Central Commerce Collegiate, Toronto, ON

Linda Brown, Clarke Secondary School, London, ON

Dean Brunetti, Westdale Secondary School, Hamilton, ON

Art Cseresnyes, Westdale Secondary School, Hamilton, ON

Tim Hawes, Ottawa-Carleton District School Board, Ottawa, ON

Jaye Herbert, Sir Frederick Banting Secondary School, London, ON

Jeff Lethbridge, Clarkson Secondary School, Mississauga, ON

Bob Martin, Cairine Wilson Secondary School, Orleans, ON

Zenobia Omarali, Business Studies Consultant, Toronto District School Board, Toronto, ON

Ivan Saari, Mackenzie High School, Deep River, ON

Linda Vandeven, Catholic Central High School, London, ON

Anthony Viola, Sir Allan MacNab Secondary School, Hamilton, ON

Wendy Warner, Lambton Central Collegiate-Vocational Institute, Petrolia, ON

Assessment Consultant

Avanell Scherer, former Business Studies and Information Technology Consultant, Hamilton-Wentworth District School Board

INTRODUCTION

Information Technology in Business

[Information technology] is profoundly changing economies, markets, and industry structures; products and services and their flow; consumer segmentation, consumer values and consumer behaviour; jobs and labour markets. But the impact may be even greater on societies and politics, and, above all, the way we see the world and ourselves in it.

Peter F. Drucker, "Beyond the Information Revolution," *The Atlantic Monthly*, October 1999, p. 47.

Information technology has changed our daily lives in big ways as well as subtle ones. Over the past 20 years it has completely transformed the way business operates, from changing the nature of individual jobs, to opening new markets, to increasing communication channels, and even to affecting the way organizations are structured. *Business Connections: Information Technology in Action* is designed to explore the ways that information technology affects business, as well as to provide you with the practical technology skills to pursue further education or a career in business. This textbook will provide you with the information necessary to make connections between the theory and the practical aspects of business in today's ever-changing environment.

Business Connections is designed to be a real-world, practical guide to applying information technology effectively in a business environment. It can be used in both PC and Mac environments and can accommodate a variety of software applications. To achieve this, applications categories (as opposed to specific programs) are described, and the details and nuances of specific software are left for the learner to explore.

Many paths are available to achieve these skills. Figure A illustrates the strands you will explore and their relationship to one another. Each of these strands has been selected for the important role it plays in preparing you for the world of information technology in business.

Figure A

Structure and Scope of *Business Connections*

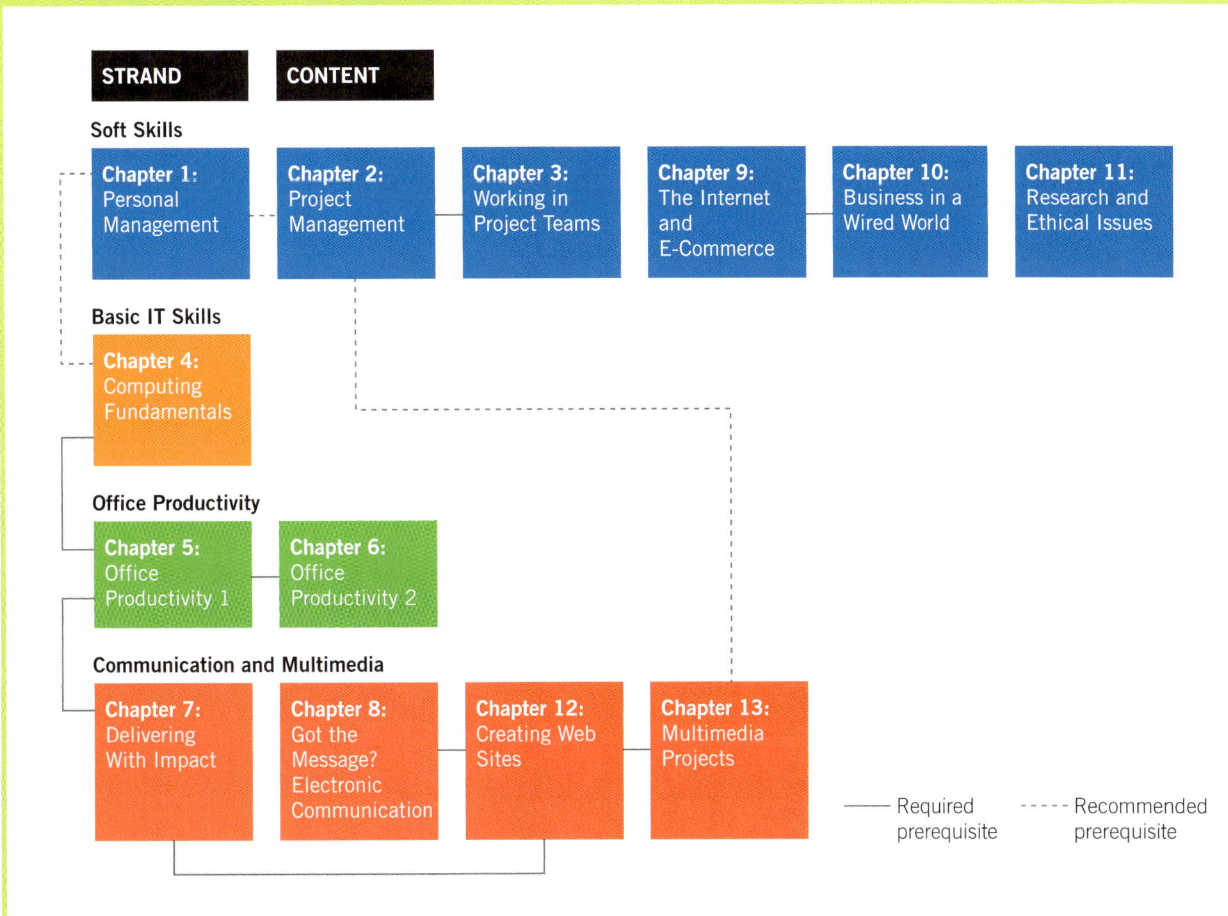

PROJECT-BASED APPROACH

Specific, authentic projects will be used to allow you to apply a skills set that will prepare you for further study or work in information technology. To make this experience as realistic as possible, chapters in this book have been organized around projects — allowing for the immediate application of theory into practice. By the end of the course, you will have had the opportunity to experience many different information technology applications and concepts, resulting in a strong foundation of important skills and competencies that can be displayed in a personal portfolio.

TEXT FEATURES

Throughout the text, you will recognize a number of common features that provide consistent supplements to and real-world applications of content.

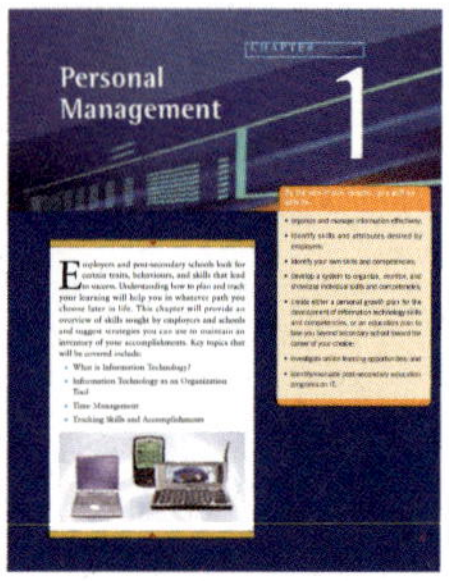

Chapter Opener: The chapter opener provides a summary of key themes and lists the major sections that will be covered.

Ready, Set, Go! These readiness exercises allow you to self-test your knowledge and help you to see where you need to catch up before you proceed. Note that not all chapters will require this.

Chapter Project: Chapter projects allow you to apply concepts as they appear in the text in a "project-based" fashion.

Get Connected: Throughout the content, this feature refers you to the *Business Connections* site at www.pearsoned.ca/businessconnections, where you can explore related content on the World Wide Web.

Digi-Know: These "fun facts" extend the content.

Getting IT: These end-of-section questions allow you to test your understanding of the content.

IT in Action: The IT in Action feature introduces you to businesses or individuals who use information technology and explains how they apply it.

Career Perspective: A variety of vignettes encourage you to explore career applications and options in information technology.

On the Case: Case studies allow you to apply and explore ideas contained in the text. These provide jumping-off points for activities, which may be questions, research, presentations, or projects.

It's a Wrap: At the end of each chapter, you will answer questions that challenge you to understand, apply, and communicate content under three categories: *Know It! Do It!* and *Analyze It!*

CHAPTER 1

Personal Management

By the end of this chapter, you will be able to:

- organize and manage information effectively;
- identify skills and attributes desired by employers;
- identify your own skills and competencies;
- develop a system to organize, monitor, and showcase individual skills and competencies;
- create either a personal growth plan for the development of information technology skills and competencies, or an education plan to take you beyond secondary school toward the career of your choice;
- investigate online learning opportunities; and
- identify/evaluate post-secondary education programs on IT.

Employers and post-secondary schools look for certain traits, behaviours, and skills that lead to success. Understanding how to plan and track your learning will help you in whatever path you choose later in life. This chapter will provide an overview of skills sought by employers and schools and suggest strategies you can use to maintain an inventory of your accomplishments. Key topics that will be covered include:

- What Is Information Technology?
- Information Technology as an Organization Tool
- Time Management
- Tracking Skills and Accomplishments

Use this exercise to assess your information technology skill levels on the computer. Try to complete it without referring to software manuals or asking others for assistance.

- Key your name and address using word-processing software and proper keyboarding technique. Change the font, and bold and italicize your name. Double-space the text. Change the margins of your document to 2 inches (5 cm) on each side, and set the page orientation to landscape. Indent the first line and add a bullet to the second line. Save the document using the name "ReadyCH-1."
- Input the following numbers into the first column of a spreadsheet: 112, 455, 239, 876. Change the number format to currency and the font to 20-point size. Increase the width of the column. Use a spreadsheet function to calculate the sum of the numbers, then create a bar graph to represent the numbers. Ensure the graph has a title and a legend. Save the document using the name "SetCH-1."
- Create a database with fields to represent a personal address book (e.g., first name, last name, telephone number, e-mail address, etc.). Input records for two of your friends or acquaintances and sort the database alphabetically by last name. Save the database using the name "GoCH-1."
- Create a slide show presentation with three slides: a title page, a slide that describes your work in this assignment, and another slide that describes the information technology skills you demonstrated in this assignment. Save the slide show using the name "Present."
- If your class has Internet access, create an e-mail message for your teacher and indicate the subject as "Ready, Set, Go." Attach the four files you created above, then send this to your teacher and copy yourself.
- Electronically, in point form, list the specific skills you demonstrated in this assignment.

Introduction to Chapter Projects

It is intended that the chapter projects introduced at the beginning of each chapter be completed as you work through the chapter. You are not expected to know the content or concepts at the beginning; rather, the projects act as a roadmap for learning, letting you "test drive" concepts in an authentic manner. Your teacher will provide you with assessment and evaluation criteria.

CHAPTER PROJECT 1

Create a growth plan for you to develop information technology skills and competencies. Your growth plan should:

- reflect the results of an information technology self-assessment (you may use the results of the *Ready, Set, Go!* assignment or the *IT Self-Assessment Tool* handout from your teacher); and
- identify key skills and education required, based on a summary of five detailed advertisements for entry-level jobs that require the use of information technology found in your local newspaper or on the Internet.

The plan should include the following sections:

- information technology skills you need to acquire, based on your self-assessment and the information gathered from job advertisements;
- ways to acquire those skills, either through tutorials, courses offered locally or online, or other methods (you will learn about some of these options throughout this chapter);
- a timeline for completion that indicates when you hope to achieve that skill or competency;
- strategies to track skills as you achieve them (you will learn about this later in the chapter when you study competencies and portfolios); and
- an explanation of how often you will update your growth plan and how or where you will update it.

CHAPTER PROJECT 11

Create an education plan that will provide you with a possible path to follow from high school to post-secondary education, and finally to an entry-level job in an information technology-related career. Be sure your education plan includes information technology skills and competencies that you will need to pursue the career you have chosen. Your education plan should include:

- an *Environmental Scan*, which is an introductory section that summarizes career areas requiring post-secondary education in information technology. You should:
  - include a description of at least two continuing education programs (information is available in your local library, your guidance office, and on the Internet) related to employment in the information technology sector in which you have an interest,
  - describe projected growth in the number of jobs available and summarize it in this section (some information is included in this chapter, but you may get

CHAPTER PROJECT 11 (continued)

  additional information from your local library, guidance department, or the Internet), and
  - locate 10 related job advertisements from your local newspaper or the Internet and identify the skills and education they require;

- a section that describes the components of post-secondary information technology programs in your community or province based on the information you gathered in the step above;
- three Web sites (or other electronic sources) you have located that provide advice on how to plan careers, prepare a résumé, and/or apply for jobs;
- a *Self-Assessment* section in which you describe your own current information technology competency levels based on the the *IT Self-Assessment Tool* handout from your teacher;
- a *Personal Learning and Growth Plan* that identifies priority areas for your own further development (you can use skills you do not yet possess from the *IT Self-Assessment Tool* handout);
- an *Action Plan* that outlines how you will achieve each of the priority areas you identified (ways to acquire those skills may include this course, as well as the education programs you researched earlier in the assignment);
- a *Timeline* that includes each stage of your education plan, specifically identifying when you will engage in certain types of education;
- an *Assessment Plan* that describes how you will know when you meet the learning objectives you have identified (e.g., being able to get a certain job, pass a certification exam, or do a certain type of electronic project on your own would allow you to demonstrate your learning); and
- a one-paragraph *Conclusion* that summarizes the information contained in your report.

1.1 What Is Information Technology?

From how we conduct our daily lives, to economic growth, to employment, computers and other information technologies play an increasingly vital role in Canada. The information technology sector accounted for 1.6% of Canada's Gross Domestic Product (GDP) in 2000 (slightly more than the agricultural sector), by generating revenues of over $25 billion. Over 155 000 people are employed directly by the information technology industry, and thousands more indirectly (Hewlett-Packard and Microsoft 2001). Most of us rely on a variety of information technologies for many aspects of our daily routine. What, then, is **information technology**?

Alone, the meanings of the terms *information* and *technology* are clear and easy to define. Information is knowledge, facts, and news, while technology is scientific knowledge applied to practical uses. Information technology, however, is more complex in meaning. On one level, information technology is used to describe all those technologies (computers, electronics, telephones, etc.) that allow us to store, transmit, reproduce, process, manipulate, and transform data. On another level, information technology is the term used to describe the broader subject area that covers all aspects (human and technological) of both managing and processing information. To distinguish between these two meanings, we will use the short form "IT" whenever we refer to the latter. Information technology (IT), then, has two main aspects:

- the electronic tools that help people to manage information (such as computers, communication networks, the Internet, and so on); and
- the relationship between technology and people's lives.

Sometimes, the term information and communications technology (ICT) is used interchangeably with IT. This term is a bit more specific, since it points out the importance of IT as a communications tool.

Figure 1.1 illustrates the spectrum of IT, from people-oriented issues to machine-oriented ones. People-oriented issues concern the interaction and information exchange between individuals, groups, and information technology, and the impact of that technology on people's lives. By contrast, machine-oriented issues relate to how information technology equipment works.

GETTING IT

1. Define *information technology.*
2. Describe three ways in which information technology affects your daily life.
3. Comment on the notion of the spectrum of information technology as displayed in Figure 1.1. Do you agree or disagree with the way it presents the concept of IT? Why or why not?

Figure 1.1
The Spectrum of IT

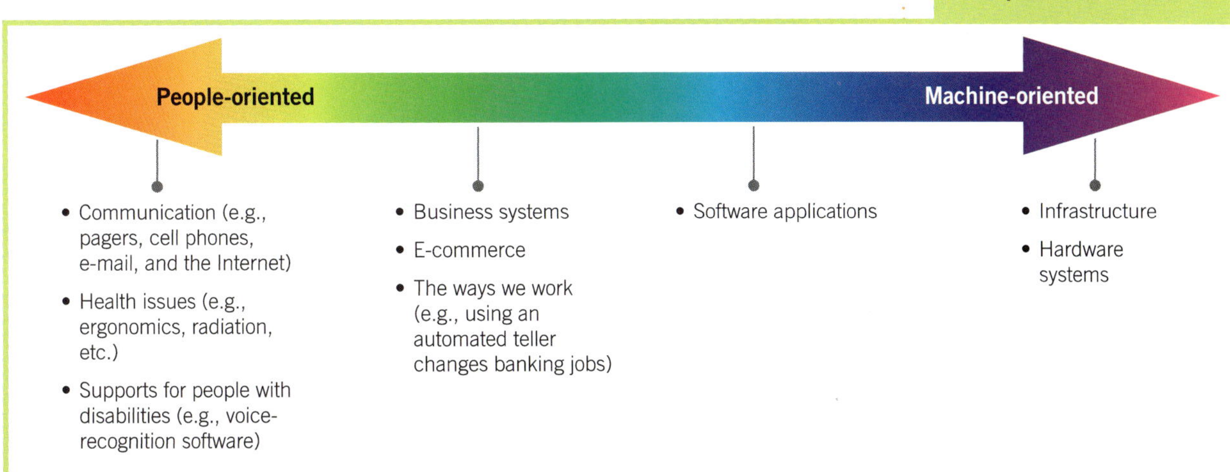

1.2 Information Technology as an Organization Tool

Users of information technology find that many programs or utilities are available to help them get organized. This section will examine how we can use functions to organize and store data.

One of the primary concerns with information technology is **storage**, or the place to save files and retain files so that they can be retrieved later. Computers have limited memory with which to function. When you "boot up" or turn on a computer, the **basic input-output system (BIOS)** — essential programs that contain the instructions to start the computer and facilitate the transfer of data and control instructions between the computer and other hardware, such as the printer – loads from the hard drive into the computer's **random access memory (RAM)**, or main memory. One of these essential programs is the **operating system (OS)**, which is the master control program for the computer. RAM, however, is volatile — the data stored in RAM disappear when you turn the computer off. To prevent losing your work when you turn off the computer, you must store it elsewhere.

Storage is also much less expensive than memory (RAM), so computer manufacturers and software developers have created ways to transfer necessary information from your permanent storage to RAM when programs and functions are required. On the downside, however, the speed at which data transfer from permanent storage to RAM is slower than if they were all held in RAM during operation.

Application files, or **programs**, are typically stored on a computer's hard drive or, in the case of a networked organization, on the file server. Computer users access these application files to perform the required tasks.

Storage is most commonly discussed as it relates to where people store files. Data files can be saved on any of a number of storage devices. The size of a storage device is typically measured in megabytes (Mb, millions of bytes) or gigabytes (Gb, billions of bytes). A **byte** is a unit of measurement for computer storage. One byte is equal to one character, number, or letter.

Computer storage terms can be very confusing. Figure 1.2 illustrates terminology related to electronic storage.

Figure 1.2
Electronic Storage Terminology

Term	Abbreviation	Bytes (approximately)
Kilobyte	K or Kb	1000 (one thousand)
Megabyte	M or Mb	1 000 000 (one million)
Gigabyte	G or Gb	1 000 000 000 (one billion)
Terabyte	T or Tb	1 000 000 000 000 (one trillion)

A variety of storage devices are available to meet different needs. Figure 1.3 shows some common storage devices. New methods for storing data are continually emerging. Figure 1.4 provides information on some common storage devices currently used.

Figure 1.3
Assorted Storage Devices

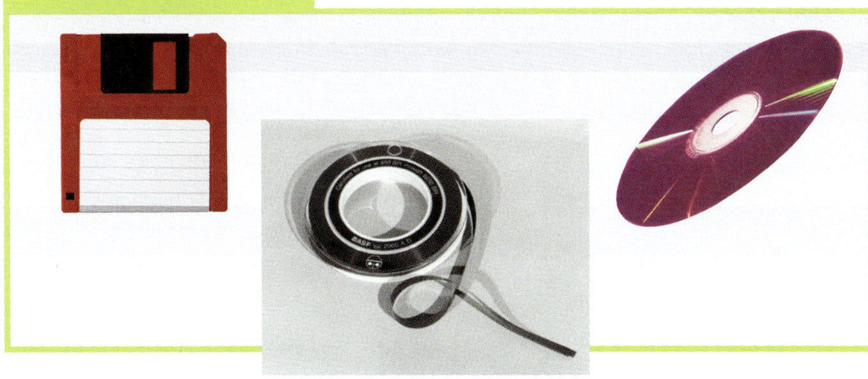

Figure 1.4
Characteristics of Selected Common Storage Devices

Storage Device	Storage Size	Description
3.5" Floppy Disk	1.44 Mb (IBM) 1.2 Mb (Macintosh)	Works with a computer's floppy disk drive to save files. Insufficient storage space for large multimedia files.
Hard Disk	20 Gb and up	Is the most important storage device. It is easy to access, since it requires no user intervention and is usually the default setting. Formatted to store files randomly for retrieval.
Removable Hard Disk	100 Mb to 2 Gb	Requires special disk drive installed on your system to store and read data. Examples include ZIP and JAZ disks.
Magnetic Tape	Up to 100 Gb	Used primarily for storage of files that do not have to be accessed frequently, e.g., system backups or archived files.
CD-ROM	Up to 800 Mb (more than 550 floppy disks)	Is ideal to store program files, multimedia files with large audio and graphic components, encyclopedias, and photos.
CD-R and CD-RW	Up to 800 Mb	Are a "write once" storage medium (you cannot erase or change files once burned into the CD-R). CD-RWs allow full read/write capabilities and are more expensive than CD-Rs.
DVD-ROM	Up to 17 Gb	Store a wide variety of files, from movies to audio and video. Digital Versatile Disks (DVD) drives can also read CDs.

1.2.1 Organizing Your Files

Once you have chosen the location for your files, you must save them and be able to locate them later. This process is known as **file management.** When you choose the *Save As* command from the File menu in most application programs, you are starting the process of transferring your work from RAM into permanent storage. A typical Save As box is shown in Figure 1.5. Each file is comprised of two parts:

- a file name; and
- an extension.

Figure 1.5

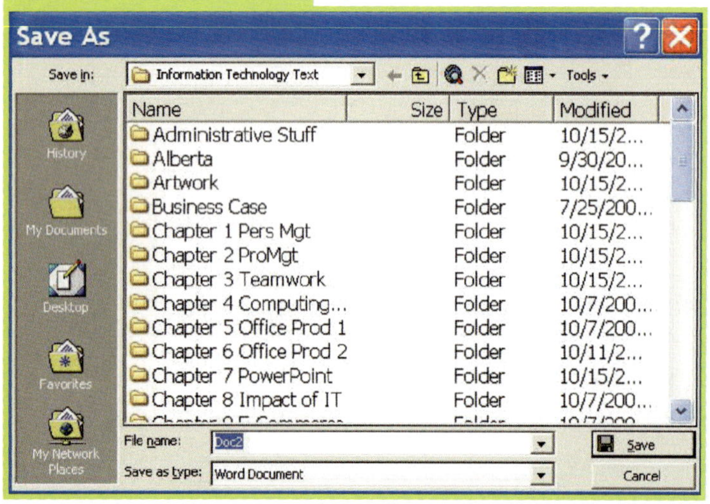

Save As is used when you first save a file so that you can assign a unique file name to your information. Subsequently, select Save to save your work because the file name has already been assigned.

The **file name** is the unique name you assign to your work. In the Windows® OS, it can be up to 250 characters in length, but this is not practical. You cannot choose a file name that already exists on the disk, otherwise you risk writing over the existing file. Typically, file names cannot contain the characters shown in Figure 1.6.

Windows programs typically add a period and an **extension** to a file name to identify the type of file it is. The extension is determined by the application in which you create the file. For example, a Microsoft® Excel spreadsheet has a .xls extension, Microsoft® Word documents end in .doc, WordPerfect® in .wpd, and CorelDRAW® in .cdr.

File names should be easily recognized by the user. For example, you would not name all your homework assignments homework 1, homework 2, etc. Instead, a file name of "geo hw pg 12–13 June 10" would help you easily identify a June 10 homework assignment for Geography on pages 12–13 of your textbook.

Figure 1.6
Characters To Be Avoided in File Names

Character	Symbol
Forward slash	/
Back slash	\
Greater than	>
Less than	<
Asterisk	*
Question mark	?
Quotation mark	"
Pipe symbol	|
Colon	:
Semicolon	;

If you were to save all your files for all your school subjects in random order on one disk, they could easily get confused. Saving files so that they are easy to use requires some organization on your part. Most students find it easier to organize their written work in different binders for different subjects when they go to class — or at the very least, to place dividers in one binder to separate notes. File management is essentially the same process.

On a disk, whether it is a 3.5" floppy disk or a hard disk drive on your personal computer, you can create folders in which to store related files. When you access the Save As command, it usually defaults to the My Documents folder in Windows. Within that window, you can click on the Create New Folder icon to create a folder within My Documents to store your Geography work, for example. Within that folder, you can create other folders for each of Assignments, Homework, Projects, and Notes, where you can arrange your work. This type of file structure, called a **hierarchy**, is shown in Figure 1.7. Be sure to organize your folders to reflect the way you think — so that you can follow your logic to retrieve documents. This process makes finding your files much quicker and easier when you go looking for them.

As important as saving files is, it is equally important to do periodic "house cleaning" with your file storage. In spite of the fact that storage is relatively inexpensive, you should:

- delete old files and previous versions of current documents and files;
- uninstall programs that are not being used; and
- empty the Recycle Bin from time to time.

These files take up space and reduce the speed at which your computer can find and load files you need.

When you remove unwanted files from your hard disk, it is advisable to perform a Disk Cleanup if you are using Windows. This program performs two main tasks: it eliminates temporary and archived files that may not be needed and it empties the Recycle Bin. Once these files are removed, **defragmenting** the hard disk is recommended. This process reorganizes the files on the hard disk so that unnecessary gaps are eliminated in the storage area. Files are rearranged so that they are stored together, not fragmented wherever the disk could find space when you saved them originally. This speeds up the data retrieval and storage process, making the computing more efficient. Figure 1.8 illustrates how data are organized both before and after defragmentation. Notice how condensed the data are after defragmentation.

Figure 1.7
Hierarchy of Folders

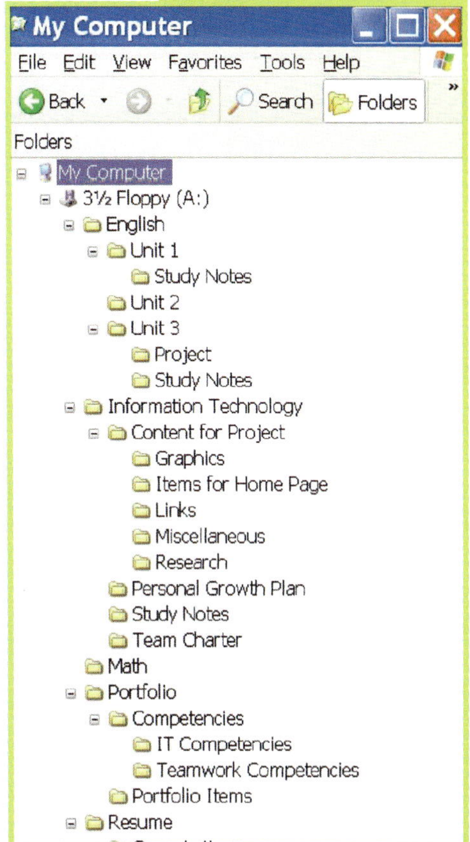

Figure 1.8
Data Organization

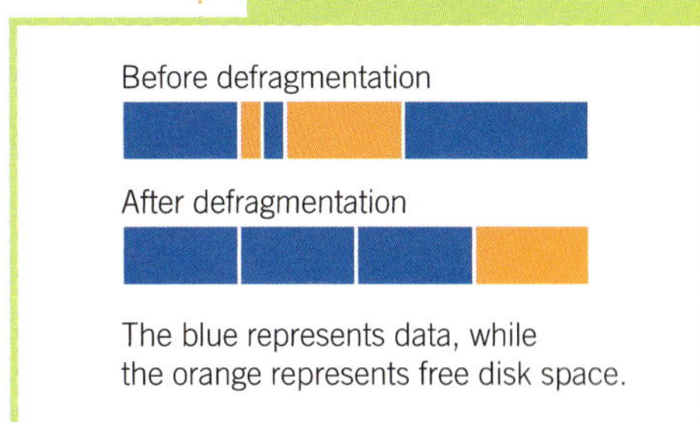

The blue represents data, while the orange represents free disk space.

GETTING IT

1. Explain the difference between RAM and storage.
2. Describe some of the benefits of storage over RAM.
3. Identify the main media used for storing files on your computer system.
4. Describe how a person should name files for ease of recognition and retrieval.
5. List the parts of a file name. Explain an extension and how it can help you to identify your files on a disk.
6. Describe how a person can use folders on a disk to aid in the storage and retrieval process.
7. Explain how defragmenting a disk works. List the benefits of defragmenting a disk.

1.3 Time Management

Time management is a vital skill not only at school and in your career, but throughout your life. Stephen Covey, the author of *The 7 Habits of Highly Effective People* and a guru who writes about many business practices, has discovered that the hardest concept for people to grasp is "putting first things first." His organization, the Covey Leadership Center, has developed a system for helping people with this — a method of scheduling priorities using a Time Management Matrix (see Figure 1.9). To use it, take all the things on your "to do" list and place them in the appropriate quadrant of the matrix. The first things that should be done are those in Quadrant I (important and urgent); next, things in Quadrants II and III should be addressed, with Quadrant IV last. This matrix helps with the effective prioritization of tasks and responsibilities.

According to Covey, the problem with most busy people is that everything seems urgent and important. To manage time effectively, people need to take a step back, prioritize what needs to be done, and work out their tasks accordingly.

An article by David Beardsley quotes an instructor for the Covey Institute: "If you are a fire fighter and you spend each day putting out fires, you're not doing your job properly. Most fire fighters realize their responsibility is to prevent fires from occurring" (Beardsley 1998). The point is that to do all the things that *seem* urgent, we cut other important things out of our day, like planning time and recreation/relaxation. By keeping a "to do" list organized according to the four quadrants, you can prioritize tasks so that attention is given to those that need it. Also, keeping such a list allows you to see what sorts of things are coming up in the future and to plan your time around them.

Beardsley offers a few additional tips:

- Set aside about half an hour a week to do some time management. Update your "to do" lists, process loose papers or mail, and think about upcoming events during this time.
- Keep certain kinds of lists, for example, one for projects (such as school projects, or any large undertakings), and "waiting for" lists to remind you to follow up on issues that are unresolved or information you are waiting for.
- Keep a calendar to ensure that things you need to do are finished on time.
- Remember the **two-minute rule**: anytime you are confronted with an action that takes less than two minutes to complete, do it immediately.

digiknow

According to the National Association of Professional Organizers, the average North American will be interrupted 73 times a day.

(Chi Ro Newsletter March 8, 2002)

Figure 1.9
Time Management Matrix

	Urgent	Not Urgent
Important	***Quadrant I Activities*** • Crises • Pressing problems • Studying for test within the next two weeks • Homework • Deadline-driven projects	***Quadrant II Activities*** • Preparation • Studying for an exam two months away • Planning • Recreation
Not Important	***Quadrant III Activities*** • Interruptions, phone calls not related to activities in Quadrant I or II • Mail, reports • Meetings	***Quadrant IV Activities*** • Trivia, busy work • Certain phone calls • Time wasters • "Escape" activities (such as surfing the Internet) • Irrelevant mail • Television

Excerpted from *The 7 Habits of Highly Effective People*, © 1989 Stephen R. Covey. The Time Management Matrix phrase and model are trademarks of Franklin Covey Co., www.franklincovey.com. Used with permission. All rights reserved.

GETTING IT

1. Explain what Covey means by prioritization.
2. Explain the benefits of using the time management matrix proposed by Covey.
3. Explain why recreation and relaxation activities are included in this list.

1.4 Tracking Skills and Accomplishments

Tracking skills and accomplishments has many benefits. In addition to boosting your self-esteem, this information can also assist you in pursuing further education and jobs. Imagine going into a job interview knowing precisely what your three greatest skills are – and being able to show the potential employer where you have demonstrated those skills.

Competencies and portfolios are used hand-in-hand to provide a way to label certain skills, and then to showcase them in one place. The following sections will explain these concepts and walk you through ways to use them to your advantage.

Get Connected

To learn more about Employability Skills, visit the student section of the *Business Connections* Web site at www.pearsoned.ca/businessconnections. Follow the link to the Conference Board of Canada Web site and click on Employability Skills. Using the online self-assessment tools, conduct a self-assessment in the area of your choice. Based on this self-assessment, record the skill areas that you need to improve upon and include them in your "growth plan."

1.4.1 Competencies

In ancient Rome, the government practised a form of competency profiling to define the characteristics of a "good Roman soldier." More and more organizations are adopting a similar, competency-based approach to defining jobs. Most large North American organizations (including companies, non-profit organizations, and governments) have defined specific lists of **competencies** (skills, behaviours, and traits) that they look for and expect in employees. The intent is to build a work force that is capable, motivated, and flexible, to achieve results in today's dynamic business environment. It has been found that one major difference between top-rated organizations and those that are less successful is their focus on *how* results are achieved (through competencies), not *what* is achieved.

Some definitions of competencies compiled by the Public Service Commission of Canada include:

- Competencies are general descriptions of the abilities necessary to perform successfully in areas specified. Competency profiles synthesize skills, knowledge, attributes and values, and express performance requirements in behavioural terms.
- They are building blocks which must be assembled and used in a variety of combinations and in a variety of circumstances to determine the skill sets needed within a given function or field of expertise.

Competencies are the characteristics of an individual that underlie performance or behaviour at work.

The different types of competencies can be illustrated as different levels of an iceberg (see Figure 1.10). The competencies above the water line (comprised of skills and knowledge) are easy to see. The deeper levels of behavioural competencies (comprised of traits, values, motives, and so on) are less visible but equally important.

Figure 1.10
The Iceberg Model

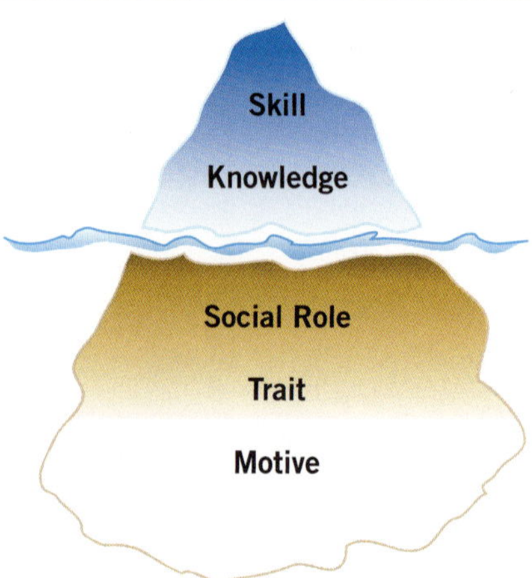

Skill: An ability to do something well (e.g., business planning)

Knowledge: Useable information in a particular area (e.g., in-depth understanding of a technical area)

Social Role: An image an individual projects to others (e.g., viewing oneself as teacher and coach)

Trait: A typical way of behaving (e.g., being a good listener)

Motive: Natural and constant thoughts in a particular area that determine outward behaviour (e.g., wanting to continuously achieve and make things better)

Throughout this course, you will be asked to keep an inventory of the skills and competencies you have developed, and evidence of how and when you demonstrated them. For example, think about the competencies that a Web designer would demonstrate in his or her daily work. For each completed Web site, there are IT competencies related to using Web authoring and graphics software. In addition, the designer probably demonstrates strong writing and editing skills in order to create error-free site content. Finally, the designer demonstrates good interpersonal communication skills in effectively working with clients, both in terms of getting the job and then ensuring that the Web sites created reflect what the clients have ordered.

GETTING IT

1. Describe how individuals and companies use competencies.
2. Based on what you have read about competencies and their uses, how would you present your competencies in writing so that a reader would understand what competencies you possess?
3. Explain how you might use your inventory of competencies when applying for a job. Be specific in your response.

digiknow

Software Experimentation and Learning

The survey that follows was conducted with 800 office workers in six of Canada's major urban business centres. With a sample of this size, the results are considered accurate to within ±3.5 percentage points, 19 times out of 20, of what they would have been had the entire office worker population been polled. However, individual city samples of 200 have a margin of error of ±7.1%, 19 times out of 20.

When it comes to software, workers like to experiment. Eighty percent of workers experiment with new features of the software they use at work rather than using the same features and not experimenting. When they want to learn new features in software applications, half just experiment on their own (50%), while one-fifth (19%) ask friends or colleagues, 13% read books or manuals and 12% find on-line help. Only 6% take a training course to learn more about software applications. Montreal workers are more likely to experiment on their own (59%) than workers in other major Canadian centres (47%).

1.4.2 Portfolio Development

Being able to show a potential employer what you are capable of producing before they hire you can provide you with a strong competitive advantage. Some employers and post-secondary schools require candidates to provide portfolios upon application. A **portfolio** is a collection of materials that showcase an individual's skills or talents over time. Usually, portfolios contain a variety of selected work samples and often include reflection and self-assessment. Ideally, they are linked to competencies, and specific items contained in the portfolio showcase the achievement of certain sets of competencies. Portfolios can have several purposes:

- documenting individual or group achievement;
- assessing growth over time;
- showcasing an individual's or a group's best work; and
- informing parents, post-secondary schools, and prospective employers of an individual's capabilities and progress.

ON THE CASE

Canadians Are Relentless Learners

In 2002, the Canadian Policy Research Network (CPRN) released "Working and Learning in the Information Age: A Profile of Canadians" (Livingstone 2002). Because work and technology change at such a rapid pace, Canadians need to engage in lifelong learning to succeed in an increasingly information-based world. Though some learning takes place through courses ("formal learning"), a great deal of learning takes place informally: learning on the job, self-teaching, reading, and other self-directed activities. The CPRN study found that Canadian adults spend an average of 15 hours per week engaged in informal learning activities related to their careers, household duties, volunteer work, and general interests. Of that time, an average of six hours is directly related to their paid employment. At the same time, enrolments in courses for adults have been consistently increasing over the past several decades.

Technological advances relating to education, such as computer-based training (CBT) and Internet courses (often called e-learning), have met with high demand and make learning more accessible. This trend is expected to continue, and more and more opportunities will be available to quench Canadians' thirst for learning. In the past, many Canadians were unable to enrol in college or university courses because the campuses were too far away or the timing of courses was inconvenient. Today, anyone with a computer, a browser, and an Internet connection can take courses from around the world in virtually any subject at any time of day! More importantly, tools such as chat features, Web cams, audio streaming, and discussion boards break down the barriers and allow students and teachers to collaborate.

Questions

1. Explain the difference between formal and informal learning. Give examples of each.
2. Describe what you think would be the most common informal learning strategies that people use. Why did you select these?
3. How many hours per week do you devote to informal learning?
4. Follow the links on the *Business Connections* Web site at www.pearsoned.ca/businessconnections to locate three available Internet courses. What subjects did you view? What features or functions were used or advertised to help students learn?
5. Explain why you would or would not take a CBT or an e-learning course.

Get Connected

Visit one of the portfolio Web sites through the link located at www.pearsoned.ca/businessconnections. Comment on the contents of the online portfolios of creative professionals in the advertising and marketing fields that are available for viewing. What skills and competencies do they demonstrate? Would potential clients or employers perceive these as effective? Why or why not?

Portfolios are as diverse in their presentation as the people whose work they showcase. Traditionally, individuals have maintained their portfolios on hard copy (anything from artwork, to business reports, to sculpture) in binders, folders, or filing cabinets like those shown in Figure 1.11. The key is to organize the contents in a logical order and to keep the portfolio tidy. More recently, individuals have started to maintain **electronic portfolios**, either online through a Web page or stored on a CD-ROM. Electronic portfolios offer tremendous potential for creativity through multimedia, graphics, hyperlinks, and animation. They are also less expensive to reproduce and more accessible to audiences.

Items included in any portfolio showcase what the individual is capable of creating. By analyzing the quality of work and level of achievement, a potential employer or school can determine what competencies the owner of the portfolio possesses. As you work through this course, you will be asked to maintain your own portfolio and to link each item in it to the skills and competencies it demonstrates. Your teacher will help you to determine which format to use to create and maintain your portfolio.

Figure 1.11
Portfolio Organizers

Describe how you would organize your portfolio and explain why.

GETTING IT

1. Describe the different purposes of portfolios.
2. Competencies are demonstrated within the work you include in your portfolio. Often, a cover page is used on portfolio items to make this connection. Identify the information you think such a cover page should include. Explain why.
3. In your opinion, what are the advantages of keeping an electronic portfolio instead of a paper-based version? What are the disadvantages?

IT In Action

Transferable Skills Lead to Career Variety

Few people are fortunate enough to experience a lifetime of careers before they turn 35 years old. Steve Bocska has focused on developing his project management and information technology skills and has applied them to a number of careers — from authoring a book, to writing and producing plays, to designing and producing video games.

"Technology allowed me to have two careers at once while going to school," explains Steve from his home in Vancouver, BC. While working on his Master of Business Administration (MBA) degree at the University of Victoria, Steve was applying his project management skills as a video game designer and producer at Disney, as well as teaching MBA courses online. "My information technology skills allowed me to get these jobs, and my project management skills helped me to succeed in them."

Before doing his MBA, Steve had already done quite a bit. He graduated with a Bachelor of Arts (BA) degree in geography and then a Master of Arts (MA) degree in planning. At that time, Steve had no idea where his career would take him. "I didn't plan on being involved in the video game industry early on. It just evolved!" After graduation, Steve worked on long-term strategic plans for the Towns of Kingsville, ON, and Sidney, BC, and the City of Colwood, BC, before moving on to business planning. From that experience, he made his move into project management when he applied for a position at Disney and enrolled in the MBA program part-time. His first video game there took two years of work, from the initial game design to production, testing, and, finally, the release of the game. Most of his information technology skills were self-taught, motivated by personal interest and needs related to projects on which he was working.

Steve is passionate about the projects he takes on. "I'm always excited at the process of creation — working on a project from start to finish — and then moving on to something completely different," he explains. "I have been able to do this for several video game companies over the years in producing short videos, and producing live stage performances. It never gets boring."

Though Steve plans to continue to perfect his project management skills in the video game industry, he is always looking for new and different projects. His skill set and varied experience will leave many doors open for him to pursue virtually any path he chooses.

Questions

1. To what other industries could Steve transfer his skills? Explain.
2. Identify the sorts of items you would expect to see in Steve's portfolio. Explain why.
3. Based on your reading of the Conference Board of Canada's Employability Skills 2000+ at www.pearsoned.ca/businessconnections, list three/four skills you think are most characteristic of Steve. Why?

CAREER PERSPECTIVE 1

The Competitive World of IT

"The shortage of IT workers has been a chronic and critical problem for the information technology industry," Gaylen Duncan, the Information Technology Association of Canada's (ITAC) president and chief executive officer, was quoted as saying in *The Globe and Mail* (Weber 2002). According to a study conducted by ITAC in 2002, the shortage of skilled workers will result in project delays, customer dissatisfaction, and lost sales. In addition to the problem of finding new graduates with information technology skills, the study revealed that information technology workers are also difficult to keep, with over half of all employees in the sector reporting that they would leave their employer if offered a new job for less than a 20% higher salary. About 69% of graduates looking for information technology work reported finding employment within 90 days of graduation.

Questions

1. Explain why you think Canada is experiencing a shortage of information technology workers.
2. Describe what organizations can do to keep employees, aside from increasing salaries.
3. Many Canadians are unemployed but want to work. Identify and record the concrete steps they can take to capitalize on this worker shortage.

CAREER PERSPECTIVE 2

Survey reveals motivation behind IT job hoppers

By Jack Kapica
For *The Globe and Mail,* September 4, 2001.

Career development, not a large salary, motivates information-technology workers to change jobs, a new survey has found.

In a study of computer systems design, insurance carriers, and architectural and engineering services, the Software Human Resource Council of Canada found that more than one-third of IT employees left their last job to develop their careers, while less than half that number changed jobs to earn a higher salary.

(continued)

But it appears that IT is still a man's world. According to the study, women represented as little as 13% to 36% of IT employees in the three industries surveyed.

In the labour force as a whole, women represent 46% of all employed persons.

The study, called the IT Employees Survey and released Wednesday in Ottawa, was conducted by Statistics Canada on behalf of Human Resources Development Canada and the SHRC, an industry trade association.

Results showed that 36% of IT employees in the computer systems design industry and 39% in the insurance industries left for career-development reasons.

On an interesting note, the survey found that those who change careers have become a major pool of new talent. In the three industries surveyed, a third of IT workers had begun their careers in industries other than IT.

More than 80% of the respondents to the survey were under the age of 35. In the labour force as a whole, 38% of workers are under the age of 35.

Education plays an important role in salaries, too. In the computer systems and design industry, university graduates were paid much more than workers with college training. University graduates were paid 20% to 25% more than those college graduates, the survey found.

Computer programmers, the survey noted, change jobs significantly more often than typical Canadians. In all three industries surveyed, programmers had been in their current jobs for only 3.5 to 4.5 years.

Nationally, the average Canadian worker has been in his or her job for a little less than eight years.

Questions

1. From the study, identify the main motivation for IT workers to change jobs. Does this surprise you? Why or why not?
2. Identify the category of workers that changes jobs most often.
3. If you were an employer, would you be pleased about the results of the survey or not? Explain.
4. How long does the average Canadian hold a job?
5. List the advantages and disadvantages of changing jobs often.

IT's A Wrap

Key Terms in This Chapter

basic input/output system (BIOS) (p. 6)
byte (p. 6)
competencies (p. 12)
defragmenting (p. 9)
electronic portfolio (p. 15)
extension (p. 8)
file management (p. 8)
file name (p. 8)
gigabyte (p. 6)
hierarchy (p. 9)
information technology (p. 4)
kilobyte (p. 6)
megabyte (p. 6)
operating system (OS) (p. 6)
portfolio (p. 13)
program (p. 6)
random access memory (RAM) (p. 6)
storage (p. 6)
terabyte (p. 6)
two-minute rule (p. 10)

1. **a.** Choose a format for the portfolio you plan to use to showcase your work from this course. Explain how often you will update it, how you will organize it, and why you have chosen this organization method.

   b. Update your portfolio to include examples of work from this chapter.

2. Use Employability Skills 2000+ at www.pearsoned.ca/businessconnections to begin a competency list you will update throughout the course. Develop a strategy to cross-reference portfolio items to the competencies they demonstrate.

Know It!

3. Describe a machine-oriented problem you have experienced with information technology.
4. Describe three situations involving people-oriented problems related to information technology.
5. Explain how and why organizations use competencies.
6. Differentiate between storage and memory.
7. Describe situations in which you would want to use a 3.5" floppy disk and a 100-Mb removable hard disk.

Do It!

8. Devise a file system for saving your work for the term or semester. In a diagram, indicate the names of the electronic folders you plan to use. Trade diagrams with a partner, and provide constructive feedback. What did your partner do well? Can you offer any suggestions?
9. In addition to the storage options described on page 7, locate additional ways to store electronic data through computer magazines, catalogues, or the Internet.
10. Using the time management matrix on page 11, organize your activities for the next week. Which quadrant is the most heavily filled? How can you use your completed matrix?
11. Complete at least one module of the free computer-based courses linked to the student site at www.pearsoned.ca/businessconnections. Describe how it compares with a classroom course. Do you prefer computer-based or face-to-face learning? Why?

IT's A Wrap (continued)

Analyze It!

12. According to the survey conducted by Ipsos-Reid described on page 13, a majority of workers prefer to experiment on their own with new software features. Identify the advantages and disadvantages that this experimentation might have for an employer.

13. Consider the case study on page 14; what criteria would you use to select an e-learning course?

14. Explain why employers place such a strong emphasis on their employees' ability to learn.

CHAPTER

Project Management

2

By the end of this chapter, you will be able to:

- understand and apply the project management methodology;
- create a project plan that includes a workplan; and
- identify and use tools to manage complex projects while maintaining team productivity.

The transition to e-business depends on successful project management. More than ever, this success is directly tied to effective involvement of business executives and the speed at which decisions and actions are taken. Today's project management best practices must act as the catalyst for communication and decision-making right up to the board room level.

—William Smillie, *Partner Program and Project Management Services,* PricewaterhouseCoopers, LLP

Project management is widely recognized as the new frontier in modern organizations. It is an approach to doing work that more and more employers are demanding of their employees. Moreover, its simple and logical principles can assist you in developing good work habits that will lead to success.

Each chapter in this book begins with a project that requires you to apply project management principles for its completion. This chapter will provide a foundation of project management skills that includes these topics:

- Projects and Project Management
- The Project Manager's Skill Set
- Strategic Planning
- Overview of the Project Life Cycle
- Workplanning
- Tools of the Trade: Technology to Facilitate Project Management
- Team Productivity

Introduction to Chapter Projects

Recall that the chapter projects are introduced at the beginning of the chapter and are to be completed as you work through the chapter. Your teacher will provide you with assessment and evaluation criteria.

CHAPTER PROJECT 1

Use the course outline provided by your teacher at the beginning of the course as a guide to create a workplan for this or any other course in which you are currently enrolled. Your workplan should break down all the tasks you will have to undertake to finish the course. Either electronically or by hand, create a Gantt chart or flowchart that represents each task, deliverable, and milestone as these concepts are introduced in the chapter.

CHAPTER PROJECT 11

Your teacher will assign you a semester-long project. It will either be a school project, a community project, or a case project from the *Project Assignment Bank* available from your teacher. For that project, create a project plan that includes:

- purpose;
- objectives;
- evaluation measures;
- scope;
- work breakdown structure (including tasks, deliverables, and milestones); and
- a Gantt chart or flowchart.

2.1 Projects and Project Management

Many things that you use in your everyday life — software, video games, vehicles, buildings, and city streets — started with a project plan that was developed using a project management methodology. A **project** is a process undertaken to achieve a specific goal that has a defined scope and outcomes, can be accomplished within a specific time frame, utilizes human effort and a limited set of resources (time, money, equipment, etc.), and is characterized by a sequence of activities.

A project is intended to come to an end and have a finite life — that is, once it is finished, the project team does not need to continue. The end product of the project, however, usually has a long, or indefinite, life. For example, if the project is designing a software application, that project is over once the application goes on sale. The product (the software application) continues to exist and be used long after the project is finished. It might resurface as a separate project, however, if a new version needs to be created.

Project management is the approach used to manage non-repetitive work within the constraints of time, cost, and performance targets. Project management provides a focus on deliverables (specific outcomes that can be measured). It provides:

- the "what" (describing the end product and how it works);
- the "when" (a schedule of when work will be done); and
- the "with what" (who will do the work and how much it will cost).

Examples of projects include:

- the design and creation of a new piece of software, such as a video game or word-processing program;
- extensive renovation on a house;
- building a highway or bridge;
- creating a Web site;
- the planning and execution of a specific event, such as a fundraising sports tournament or an awards ceremony;
- the design and creation of a new product, such as a soft drink, toothpaste, shampoo, or piece of equipment;
- the planning and execution of a specific advertising campaign for a new or existing product or service; and
- the modification of a computer information system to perform a new function, such as adding a service charge to a bank's central computer system.

2.1.1 Where Do Projects Come From?

A project always originates from a need. If something is lacking within an organization, someone within that organization will identify the deficiency and suggest a way to solve it. Often senior managers will address the deficiency and initiate the process. In other instances, a strategic plan or business plan will create a new need, which becomes the project. Sometimes, employees see a need to improve a process or a program, and they propose projects. Regardless of who identifies the need, a project:

- is characterized by a specific outcome;
- is achieved in a set period of time; and
- does not continue past that time.

digiknow

A stakeholder is any person, group, or organization (internal and external to the project manager's organization) whose interests must be considered throughout the project. Stakeholders may include end users, customers, employees, financial contributors, security departments, or others affected by the project.

2.1.2 How Do Project Managers Fit In?

Project managers are responsible for meeting the *performance, schedule,* and *cost* constraints of the project (see Figure 2.1). Using the resources of the organization, the project manager must see that a certain goal is met. Performance refers to the outcome of the project and how effectively it meets the desired objectives. Scheduling refers to setting out the time line for a project and ensuring that deadlines are met. Cost refers to the resource allocation for the project, including the financial cost and opportunity cost of all resources involved.

Within those constraints, project managers have a number of responsibilities, as outlined in Figure 2.2.

Figure 2.1
The Three Project Constraints

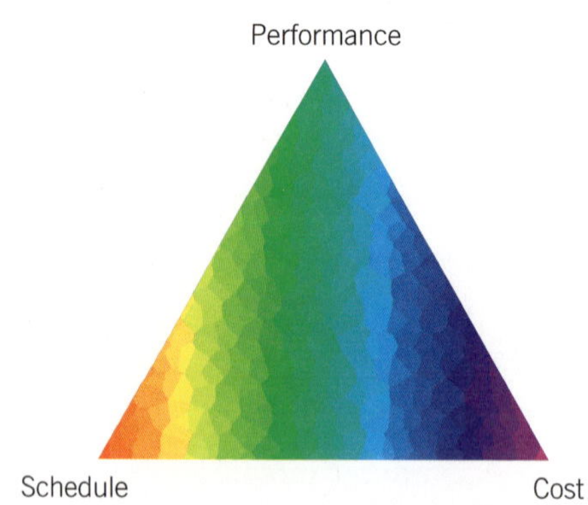

The three project constraints are represented as a triangle since each of them have equal influence on a project.

Figure 2.2
Project Manager's Responsibilities

Responsibility	Description
Project design	• proposing the idea • identifying the goal • defining the tasks • scheduling the tasks
Tactical planning	• creating time lines that include all tasks • assigning tasks to individuals • planning for potential problems and risk
Team management	• leading the project team through the process efficiently
Stakeholder interface	• working with the persons, departments, or organizations that the end product affects • planning for potential problems and risk
Resource allocation	• taking available resources (money, materials, time, and people) and budgeting them into a reasonable project plan

GETTING IT

1. Give an example of a project you have completed. Explain how you know it was a project. How did you get started with this project?
2. Describe the job of a project manager in your own words.
3. You are the Student Council president for your school. Convince the principal that you can meet performance, schedule, and cost constraints to run the upcoming Valentine's Day Dance.

digiknow

A Brief History of Project Management

The discipline of project management began approximately 40 years ago as a way to ensure that engineering projects followed a proven procedure. Many different methodologies have been brought forward throughout its history, and these have been based on the needs of those managers creating them and the "fashionable" business principles of the day. Similarly, different methodologies have been developed for different industries. The Project Management Institute has compiled much of this information and history into a document called *The Project Management Body of Knowledge* and offers best practices to help people manage projects effectively.

IT In Action

Radical Entertainment Inc.

Based in Vancouver, BC, Radical Entertainment Inc. has been a leading developer of digital, interactive entertainment since it opened its doors in 1991. Radical creates such products as video games for well-known publishers such as Fox Interactive, Microsoft, and others.

"Creativity and independence among our project teams is one of the keys to our success," explains Danielle Michael, Director of Business Development. Clearly, the staff at Radical agree — it was ranked the #1 Place to Work in BC by *BC Business Magazine* and Wattson Wyatt in 2002. Organized into six project teams with an administration and support department, the over 185 permanent staff at Radical rely on communication and collaboration, in addition to technology, to accomplish results. Unlike many other project-based organizations, Radical tries to keep project teams together beyond the life cycle of a project to leverage group strength for future projects. Their philosophy is that when team members work well together and complement one another's skills, they should continue to build on their achievements. Though Radical strives for this, it is not always possible.

Developing a video game (or any multimedia application) requires expertise on the part of individual team members. In addition, since video games take one to two years (or more) to create, commitment to the project is essential. Each team is led by a Producer, who is responsible for managing the work and liaises with clients (such as Fox or Microsoft). A Project Manager and/or an Associate Producer assist(s) the Producer with co-ordination and workflow. Other team members fulfil roles in product design, animation, testing, graphic design, and programming. Teams also often rely on other teams; for instance, a single technology team at Radical is responsible for creating the electronic tools necessary to develop and build games.

Good project planning and collaboration are essential for Radical's teams to successfully deliver a quality product on time and on budget to publishers. Radical has a game development process as a foundation; however, the process is open and flexible so that individual teams can customize their process for their unique needs and culture. This allows the teams to develop processes that fit the unique needs of their projects. This is part of the organization's commitment to flexibility and leads to efficiency among teams. Though teams have reporting and quality requirements, how they gather and track information is up to them.

While most teams use Microsoft® Project to plan and manage their work, other teams have established their own creative solutions. One team maintains an Intranet Web site that is updated daily to reflect meetings, team communication, and project and task status. Other teams use traditional, low-tech white boards with sticky notes.

Ms. Michael explains that people at Radical have used their creativity to develop team processes, "and if they work, they become formalized."

Questions

1. Create a chart that shows the advantages and disadvantages of working in a project team as Radical's employees do, instead of alone.
2. Describe the tools or processes Radical's employees use when working together.
3. Explain how the project manager's skill set (Figure 2.3) relates to this organization.
4. Follow the link at www.pearsoned.ca/businessconnections to learn more about Radical Entertainment Inc. Locate news about the company based on recent press releases. Record this information in your notes.

2.2 The Project Manager's Skill Set

To perform their roles effectively, project managers must possess a variety of skills (see Figure 2.3). These skills can be divided into two categories: interpersonal skills, and organization and planning skills. Each of the categories is equally essential to a project manager's success. Without the ability to communicate with and motivate others, a project manager will get little accomplished. Similarly, without careful planning and organization, a project will not succeed.

Get Connected

To learn more about project management, visit www.pearsoned.ca/businessconnections. List the resources that this site provides for project managers. Explain how you might use it.

Figure 2.3
The Project Manager's Skill Set

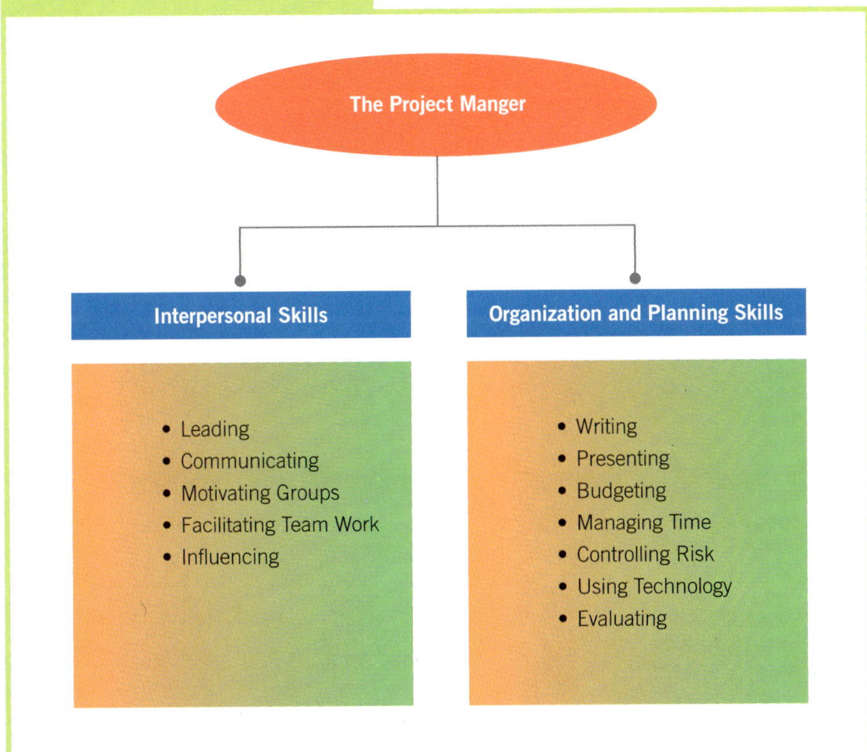

2.2.1 Interpersonal Skills

Because much of a project manager's day-to-day job consists of working with the project team, good interpersonal skills are a necessity. There are three major groups that a project manager must interact with:

- the project team;
- the end user (an individual or organization that will use the product); and
- colleagues, co-workers, and other departments within the organization that are involved, directly or indirectly, with the project.

A project manager must first take the lead in initiating and managing the project. The ability to communicate effectively with the project team and the end user(s) is crucial to completing the project. As the team's leader, the project manager must also be able to:

- motivate group members to work together so that they can complete their tasks effectively and on time;
- facilitate group work to obtain high productivity from the group members; and
- exert a positive influence during the process to ensure that personal and group objectives are met.

2.2.2 Organization and Planning Skills

Though essential, interpersonal skills alone do not make an effective project manager. Virtually all projects begin with proposals. A project manager must be able to articulate his or her vision for a project in writing and be able to present it effectively. Without these skills, a project will not get off the ground.

Any successful project must be planned carefully, with clear objectives and outcomes that are understood by all parties involved. Crucial areas of planning for project managers include:

- budgeting money, time, and other resources;
- establishing and meeting deadlines;
- scheduling team members for various tasks within the project; and
- identifying and controlling risk.

A project manager must use the project management methodology to perform these functions. To be most efficient, many project managers use technological tools to help them budget, plan, and organize. There is a great deal of technology available to assist project managers. They must be able to identify the appropriate technology, adapt it to their projects, and use the technology to its fullest potential. Refer to Figure 2.10 on pages 41–44 for examples of some of these forms of technology.

GETTING IT

1. Which are your strong skills—interpersonal skills or organization and planning skills? Provide specific examples to support your answer. How could you improve the weaker category?
2. Identify two examples of project risks that a project manager might encounter. What problems would they pose? How could the project manager plan to overcome them?

3. Explain why team management is an important aspect of the project manager's job.
4. Refer to the Employability Skills 2000+ at www.pearsoned.ca/businessconnections. What specific skills would be relevant to project managers?

2.3 Strategic Planning

Today, most organizations (including businesses, governments, and non-profit or public sector) create strategic plans. A **strategic plan** is a document that serves as a roadmap by identifying where an organization wants to be in the future and specific steps that will be undertaken to get there. Though strategic plans vary, they usually contain the following components:

- a list of long-term goals for the organization (usually including a vision of how the organization will look or what it will be doing in the future);
- an analysis of competing organizations;
- an evaluation of the organization's resources (financial, location, knowledge, and employees) to determine its strengths and weaknesses; and
- identification of actions that will be undertaken (including which people or departments will undertake them, when they will be completed, and how they will be evaluated) to reach the long-term goals.

Organizations engage in strategic planning for several reasons. First, strategic planning is a tool for decision making. Anyone in the organization who has to make a decision can simply refer to the strategic plan to determine if the decision fits in with the organization's vision. Second, the strategic plan helps an organization co-ordinate its resources to be able to best use them toward a common goal. Third, a strategic plan serves as a target, linking with the organization's mission and vision and giving focus to its aspirations.

Often, people confuse strategic plans with project plans and workplans (these are discussed in Section 2.5). A strategic plan is unique in that it is extremely goal oriented and lacks details — instead, it focuses on the "big picture," using a time frame of three to five years. By contrast, project plans and workplans are concerned with detailed steps, and generally focus on a shorter time span.

Some organizations function in reactive mode. This means they change their plans, products, advertising, etc. in response to something that happened in the market or with a competitor. Strategic planning goes far beyond that.

Strategic planning changes the way organizations and their employees think about and do their work. It requires that all employees and divisions

Get Connected

The Government of Canada has information about strategic planning on its Web site. You can view the site through the link at www.pearsoned.ca/businessconnections. Follow the government index under "Business Information by Sector." Explain why you think the government provides advice to Canadian businesses about strategic planning. List the specific information that the site provides.

in the organization (even in very large corporations) work toward a coherent vision that considers external events in planning, but looks toward a long-term common goal.

GETTING IT

1. Define *strategic planning.*
2. Describe the components of a strategic plan.
3. Explain the benefits of having a strategic plan.

2.4 Overview of the Project Life Cycle

Because project management is a methodology, it comprises a framework. This framework, explained in more detail in the sections that follow, is used to describe the process of a project through to completion. Specific tasks need to be accomplished within each of the stages to ensure that the project is effectively and efficiently completed.

2.4.1 Stages in the Project Life Cycle

Project managers throughout North America follow the fundamental framework of the project life cycle (see Figure 2.4). Every basic project management model requires the manager to first plan the work, then work the plan. Though models proposed by different theorists and organizations vary with respect to the names of the stages, the model we will examine is proposed by the Project Management Institute. Each of the stages in the project life cycle will be described in detail in its own section. The descriptions in Figure 2.5 provide a brief overview meant to serve as an introduction and general overview.

Figure 2.4
The Project Life Cycle

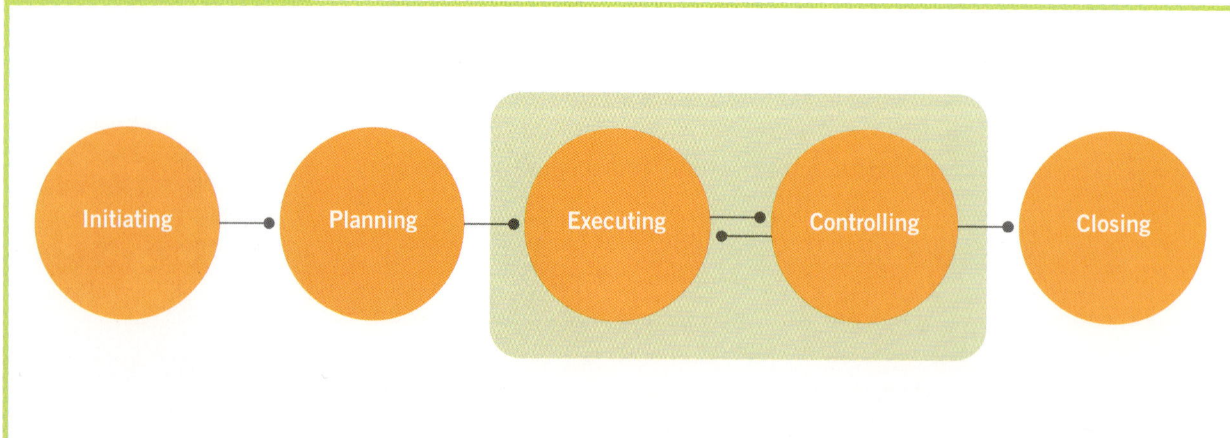

Figure 2.5
Stages in the Project life Cycle

1. Project Initiating	2. Project Planning	3. Project Execution and Control	4. Project Closing
This first stage consists of the formulation of the project idea.	During this stage, the project manager creates a detailed plan of steps necessary for the project's completion.	Sometimes shown as two separate stages, execution and control consist of overseeing the project as the project team is completing it.	This stage includes documenting the completion of each task, ensuring the project is on time and on budget, and making necessary changes. Closing involves wrapping up all aspects of the project.
The end product and purpose of the project are defined during this stage, and the objectives and the scope are identified. A project manager is assigned to lead the project and a project team to complete the work is identified.	The end product is described in detail within a project plan that includes a work breakdown structure (WBS) that identifies each task that needs to be performed by the project team to complete the project. This results in a schedule. Costs and other resources needed to complete the project are defined. Risks are identified, together with strategies to minimize and overcome them. A project quality plan identifies the level of quality desired and how it will be evaluated. Finally, a project communication plan explains who will receive information about the status and how often.	The project is monitored and the completion of tasks and milestones is tracked. Project status is reported regularly.	Evaluation and assessment of the final product takes place, including feedback from all people involved. Documents and reports about the processes used in completing the project are created and archived, including recommendations for future projects with lessons learned from the experience.
A proposal for the project is completed.	A project plan provides a detailed roadmap for the project.	Updates are provided as per the communication plan, indicating progress against the project plan.	Evaluation documents and a record of what was done well and what requires improvement are completed.

ON THE CASE

Project You

For Microsoft's Adam Rauch, 31, it was a choice between building on a strength and starting something new. He joined Microsoft as the first project manager for Visual Basic®, a software language now used by 3 million programmers. He led the product team through the launch and a major revision. He became a rising star. Then it was time for yet another revision. Rauch decided to let work start without him. He jumped to a new project. "I wanted a new challenge," he explains.

For Universal Creative's Tawny Halbert, 25, it was a choice between work that was glamorous and work that she enjoyed. She had spent eight months on the project team that created Dante's Peak, a high-profile attraction at Universal Studios Hollywood Theme Park. Now it was time to settle on her next assignment. Would she help build the highly anticipated Terminator 2 exhibit, or a simple buffet restaurant within the park? She chose the restaurant because the project would be completed in one year rather than the three it would take to create T2.

"I like shorter projects," Halbert says. "Being out on the site and dealing with people is more rewarding than sitting in my cubicle doing paperwork. Plus, shorter projects leave you open to more opportunities. It's hard to be on a three-year project and watch all those opportunities pass you by."

Leadership expert, Harvard Professor, and author, John Kotter says, "You need to figure out what skills will be relevant in the future and to map out projects to develop those skills." Susan Campbell, a change consultant and the author of *From Chaos to Confidence: Survival Strategies for the New Workplace* (Simon & Schuster 1995) could not agree more. "The workplace of the future is going to be organized according to jobs that need doing, and that means a project-oriented workplace," she argues. "Even if you never show it to anybody, open a file called My Ongoing, Ever-Expanding Résumé of Projects I've Done. There will be a time when you need it."

These stories raise some obvious questions:

- How do you figure out which projects you should join?
- Where and when do you look for your next project?
- How do you document the results of your work?

Answering these and other questions is a project in and of itself. This article will help you with questions about your most important project — you.

Which Projects Are Best for Me?

Here's a simple question that remarkably few people can answer: If you could work on any project, which would it be? There's no right answer, of course. But finding projects that are right for you means thinking hard about four related questions:

- How much can I learn?
- How much can I contribute?
- How important is the project?
- Who is the leader?

Most career experts put a premium on learning. Of course, if you're always learning, you're seldom leading — that is, demonstrating the expertise you already have. "It's a balancing act," says Harvard's Kotter. "If a project has visibility, you'd better make sure that you're contributing, not just learning. But if the stakes aren't that high, then join it for the learning opportunity. Your odds of getting into trouble are lower."

How Do I Document My Success?

These days, switching projects often means switching project leaders, which raises lots of tough questions about getting the recognition (and developing the reputation) you deserve. Sure, previous project leaders know you do great work. But, how do you know whether your track record has travelled along to your new project?

"It's all about visibility," says change consultant Susan Campbell. "You want to be viewed as a person who likes to do a great job."

The way to develop the reputation that you are successful in what you undertake is to make sure that other people agree your project was a success. And that means arriving at a clear definition of achievement, before your project starts.

The second step is to find ways to share these results with the people who matter.

Author and consultant Kevin Cashman, the founder and president of LeaderSource, a consulting firm based in Minneapolis, likes that approach. "If you market what you've done, it can seem like self-promotion," he says. "But if you market what you can do, it feels more like a service." That's why Cashman recommends a two-step regimen: document your achievements as they happen, and record the skills you're developing on a regular basis.

Susan Campbell agrees. "You should create a new résumé every month," she argues. "Write down what matters: the problems you've solved, how much money you've saved the company, the real results you've achieved. It's not something for you to send to prospective employers. But if you keep all your accomplishments fresh in your mind, it will be easier to sell yourself in conversations."

Where Are All These Projects Taking Me?

We said it at the outset: the traditional career path has disappeared. But what's taking its place? Are we on the road to nowhere? Or can you create direction from a series of projects?

Some people don't think so. "I don't have a seven-year plan in mind," says Microsoft's Rauch. "I just want to work on cool technology with great people."

(Adapted from an article by Eric Matson that appeared in *Fast Company Magazine*, Issue 12, January 1998, page 192.)

Questions

1. Summarize the main message that the author of this article was attempting to convey.
2. Based on this article, does project management interest you? Why or why not?
3. Select one project that is profiled in the article and describe that project's purpose, objectives, and scope.
4. The article states that "sometimes the best projects are those you create for yourself." What does that statement mean? Describe a project you would like to initiate sometime in your life. How would you go about it?
5. The article talks about the importance of documenting your success. How is the advice in the article similar to that on the use of competency lists and portfolios for this course?

Figure 2.6
Sizing Projects

Project Variables	Small Project	Medium Project	Large Project
Length	3–12 months	1–2 years	2–5+ years
Budget	$250 000–$1 000 000	$1 000 000–$5 000 000	Over $5 000 000
Team Size	1–5 full-time team members	6–25 full-time team members	26–50 full-time team members
Difficulty	Low–medium technological challenge	Medium–high technological challenge	High technological challenge
Project Management	Part-time project manager	Part- or full-time project manager	Full-time project manager

The criteria shown are used to classify projects industry wide. A project classified as "small" in this framework might be a large undertaking for an individual or small company.

GETTING IT

1. Describe the stages in the project life cycle.
2. Explain how a project proposal differs from a project plan.
3. Describe how a project is monitored.
4. Identify the activities that take place during project closing.
5. Explain how each stage in the project life cycle is connected.
6. In what stage would the team members meet to discuss what they did well and what they need to improve? Why?
7. In what stage would the project manager prepare a report to say which tasks are not finished on time? Why?

2.5 Workplanning

Planning the project should be a team effort that involves all members. The project manager cannot possibly gather all the information about the project alone and needs to rely on team members as subject and work experts. The team must break down the final outcome into a series of steps or tasks that must be accomplished to finish the project — almost a checklist to show what needs to be completed on what day. This helps the project manager and the team know at any given point if they are on schedule or not. As well, the team can use the project plan as a roadmap to guide and co-ordinate their activities, making sure efforts are not duplicated and team members know what their peers are working on.

2.5.1 Components of a Workplan

A **task** is an activity or event that has a well-defined start and end or duration and produces a measurable result or end product. More simply stated, it is something that needs to be done to move toward the completion of a project and is stated using a verb. Examples of tasks include *holding* a team meeting, *calling* a supplier, *receiving* an order of materials, and *testing* a pilot version of software. A project plan is made up of many tasks.

A **deliverable** is a report or the product of one or more tasks that must be delivered to satisfy the requirements of either managers or the end user. Unlike tasks, deliverables are stated using nouns. Often deliverables are used as checkpoints by the team throughout the project's development to ensure that quality is sufficient and things are running on schedule. As a result, deliverables must be measurable; that is, people need to be able to evaluate them for quality and completeness. Though the final product is the ultimate deliverable, a series of interim deliverables must be produced throughout the project development. Each of these is tested to ensure that it works and that everyone is satisfied. If the deliverable is not satisfactory, the project manager must devise a plan to make changes or improvements.

Milestones are important events that provide feedback to the project team on the progress of the project. Essentially, they are deliverables evaluated by an *outside* source such as the organization that commissioned the project. At these significant points along the course of a project, there is evaluation and, sometimes, payment for progress to that point. Milestones must be approved before a project team can move to the next task. They are defined as meaningful achievements and are represented in software with a project task duration of 0. Milestones should be specific, measurable, visible, and frequent during a project. They can include reviews, documentation and phase dates, flight test dates, and significant design releases. Examples of milestones for development of a video game are: background for all levels of game completed, animation for main character completed, a version of game ready for formal testing, and testing of game completed.

The **baseline** is a snapshot in time of a project plan (made up of the tasks, deliverables, and milestones) against which project progress can be measured.

To create a workplan, all tasks (e.g., phone calls, software tests, meetings) are listed. Then, each task is stated as a verb (e.g., *designing* graphics, *animating*, *testing* a Web site). All the tasks have to be put into sequence based on when they are due, and deliverables and milestones have to be added. For each task, a start date and an end date need to be assigned, as well as who is responsible for completing it. Tasks, deliverables, and milestones also need to be identified.

These are assembled into a work breakdown structure (WBS) — a task-oriented "family tree" of activities that organizes, defines, and graphically displays the total work needed to complete a project. Three of the most common ones are:

- *The Gantt chart.* A Gantt chart (see Figure 2.7) is a graphical representation that shows the life of the project using lines and symbols. A legend identifies what each symbol represents, and often specific details are included for each task, milestone, and deliverable. Project management software will usually automatically generate a Gantt chart for each project, based on the information entered in the input table. Alternately, these can be hand-drawn on graph paper or created using spreadsheet or word-processing software.

Figure 2.7
Gantt Chart

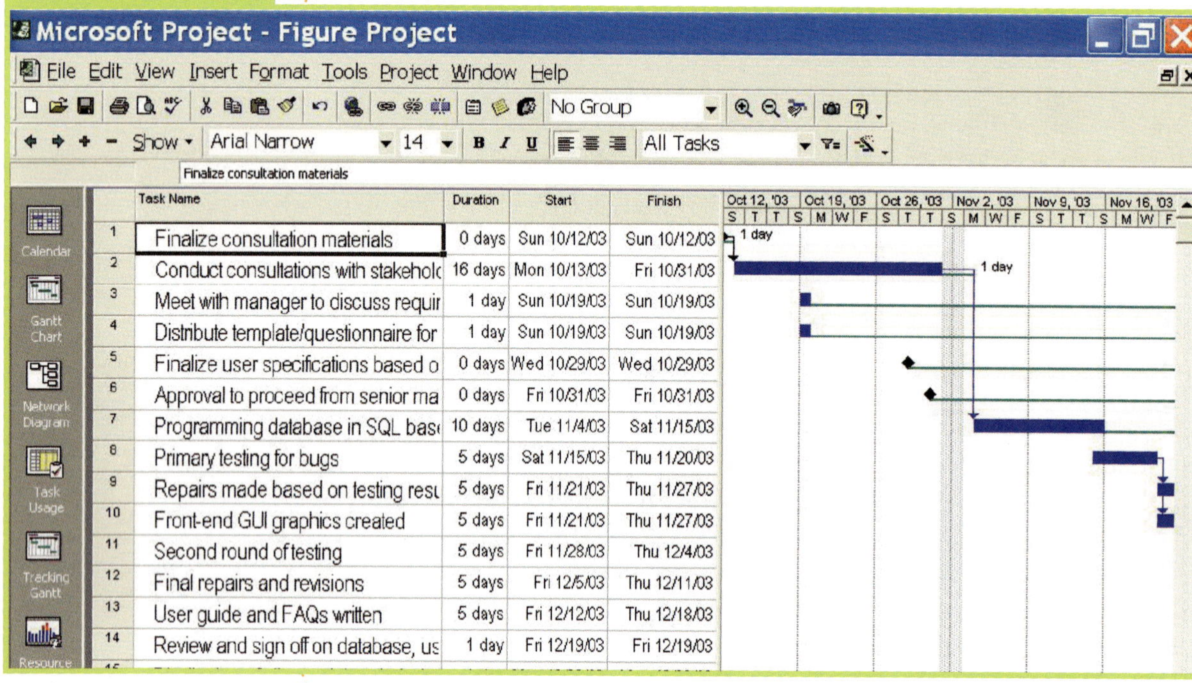

- *Flowchart.* A flowchart is also a sequential, graphical representation of tasks, deliverables, and milestones. It is extremely useful to visualize the sequence of tasks, deliverables, and milestones for a project in the order in which they need to be completed. Generally, flowcharts use a series of symbols and arrows to illustrate progress. They can be created using specialized flowchart software or, more simply, the draw tools found in common spreadsheet and word-processing software. When creating a very basic flowchart, you can use rectangular text boxes to represent tasks, arrows to illustrate the sequence of tasks, and diamonds to represent decisions to be made (see Figure 2.8). Refer to Chapter 12, Section 12.4.3 for more details and the use of special symbols for creating flowcharts.

Figure 2.8
Flowchart

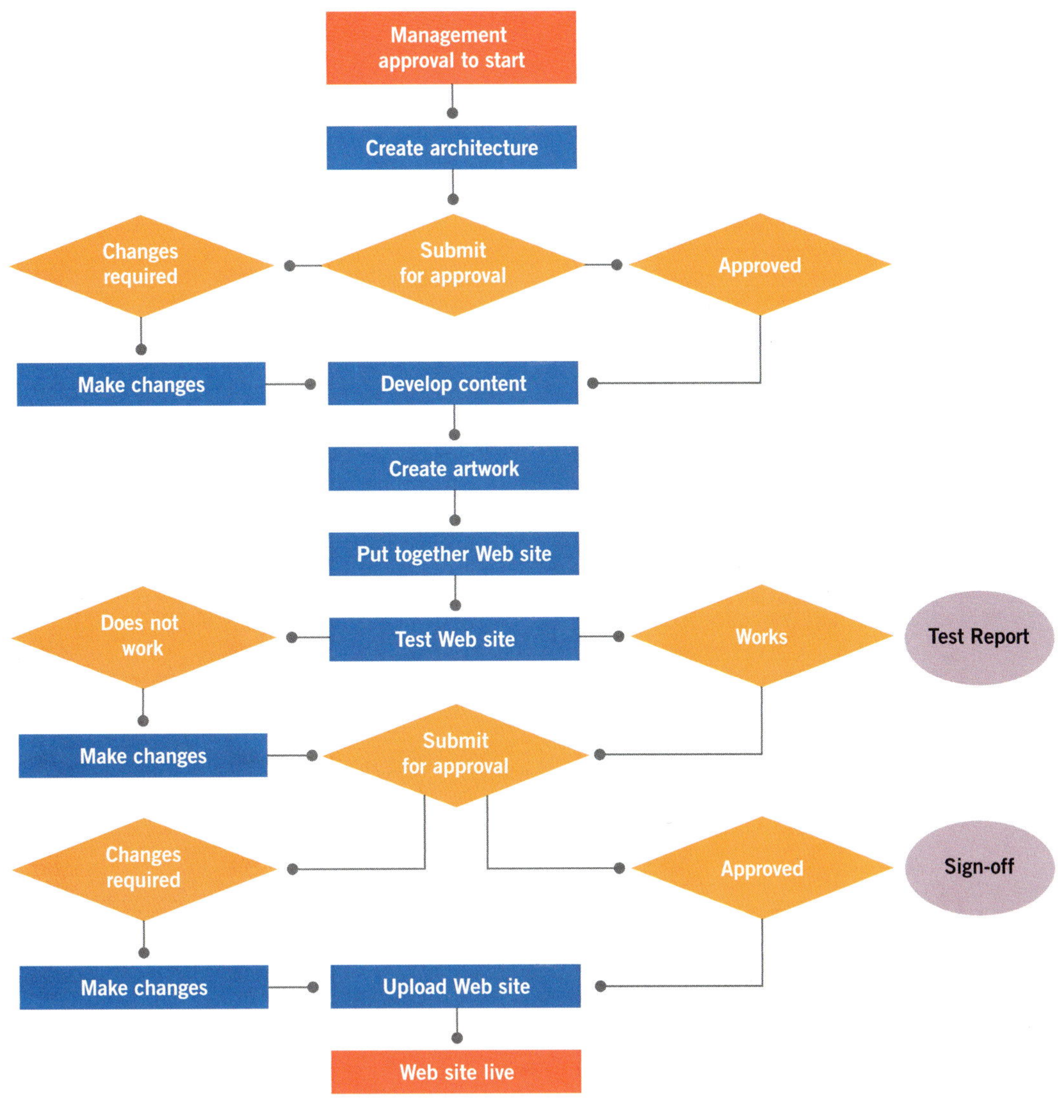

- *Table or matrix*. Using word-processing software or a spreadsheet, you can set up a table to represent the project's workplan (see Figure 2.9). Usually, column headings include deliverable, task, milestone, responsibility, start date, and end date.

Figure 2.9
Workplan—Customized Database

Task, Deliverable, or Milestone	Completion Date	Responsibility (initials)
October 2003		
Finalize consultation materials.	October 12	SH
Conduct consultations with stakeholders to determine needs.	Ongoing throughout month	LP & SH to lead
Meet with manager to discuss requirements and agree upon deliverables.	October 19	LP with NI & SH
Distribute template/questionnaire for input on user features: • All members of management • 20% of all users (random sample) • Quality Service Priority Improvement leads	October 19	NI & SH to lead
Finalize user specifications based on findings.	October 29	SH
Obtain approval to proceed from senior management.	October 31	All
November 2003		
Program the database in SQL based on user specifications.	November 1–15	NI
Do a primary test for bugs.	November 15–20	SH
Make repairs based on testing results.	November 20–25	NI
Create front-end GUI graphics.	November 20–25	SH
Perform the second-round test.	November 25–30	NI
December 2003		
Repairs and revise.	December 1–7	SH& NI
Write user guide and FAQs.	December 1–7	LP
Review and sign off on database, user guide, and FAQs by (senior management).	December 10	LP
Distribute all materials to helpdesk.	December 11	LP
Conduct a workshop to train helpdesk.	December 12	NI & SH
January 2004		
Launch database live on Intranet.	January 2	NI
Send communication package (memo, user guide, FAQs) to all users.	January 3	NI

GETTING IT

1. Differentiate between tasks, milestones, and deliverables using an example.
2. Identify the two common methods of graphically displaying the work needed to complete a project. Describe their use and advantages.
3. Explain how a project is monitored.
4. Describe the activities that take place during project closing.
5. Think about the work that you have to complete to earn a credit for this course and create a list of tasks, milestones, and deliverables. Then create either a flowchart, a workplan, or a Gantt chart to represent the sequence and timing for these tasks. If you are completing Chapter Project I, this is a part of your project.
6. If you are working on Chapter Project II, use the information from this section to create a list of tasks, deliverables, and milestones for the project assigned to you. Next, create either a flowchart, a workplan, or a Gantt chart to represent the sequence and timing.

ON THE CASE

It is hard to imagine what a complete project plan looks and feels like without seeing one. These pages are samples from a project plan for a service called "E-Nanny for Dogs." Review the entire project plan at www.pearsoned.ca/businessconnections and respond to the questions below electronically or in your notebook.

Questions

1. Explain how this project plan is consistent with the project management methodology.
2. Describe three specific ways that the author of the plan could use it.
3. Based on what you have learned about project plans in this chapter, identify two strengths and two weaknesses of this project plan.

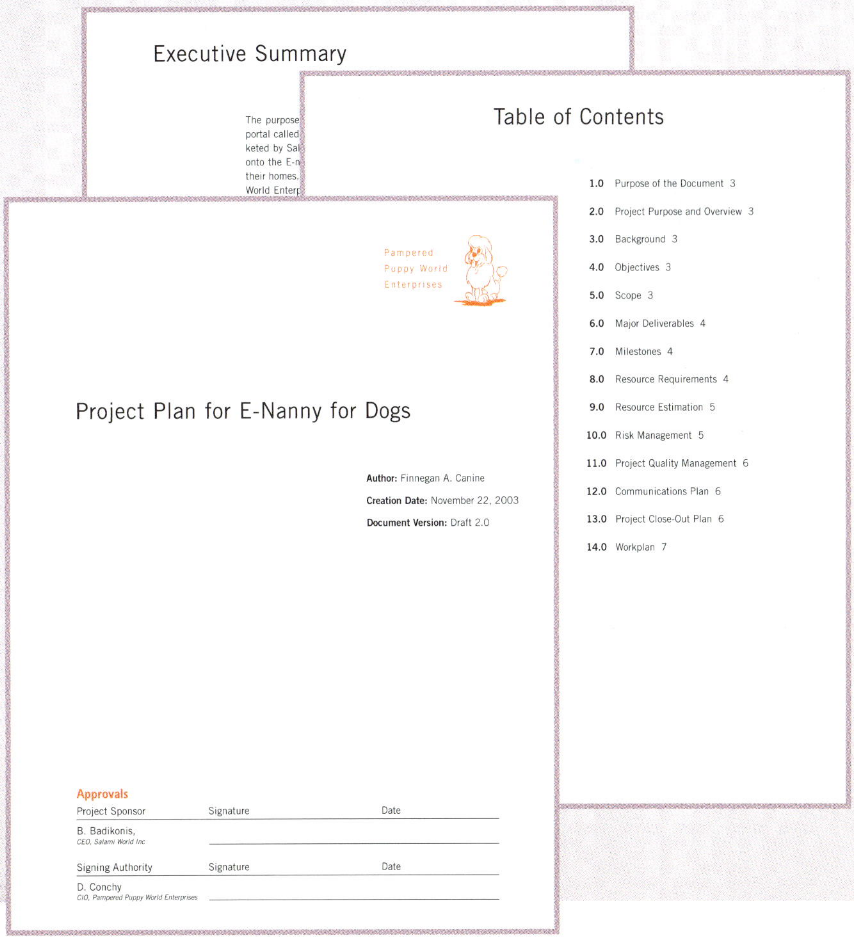
Executive Summary

The purpose
portal called
keted by Sal
onto the E-n
their homes.
World Enter

Table of Contents

Pampered Puppy World Enterprises

Project Plan for E-Nanny for Dogs

Author: Finnegan A. Canine
Creation Date: November 22, 2003
Document Version: Draft 2.0

Approvals

Project Sponsor	Signature	Date
B. Badikonis, CEO, Salami World Inc		
Signing Authority	Signature	Date
D. Conchy, CIO, Pampered Puppy World Enterprises		

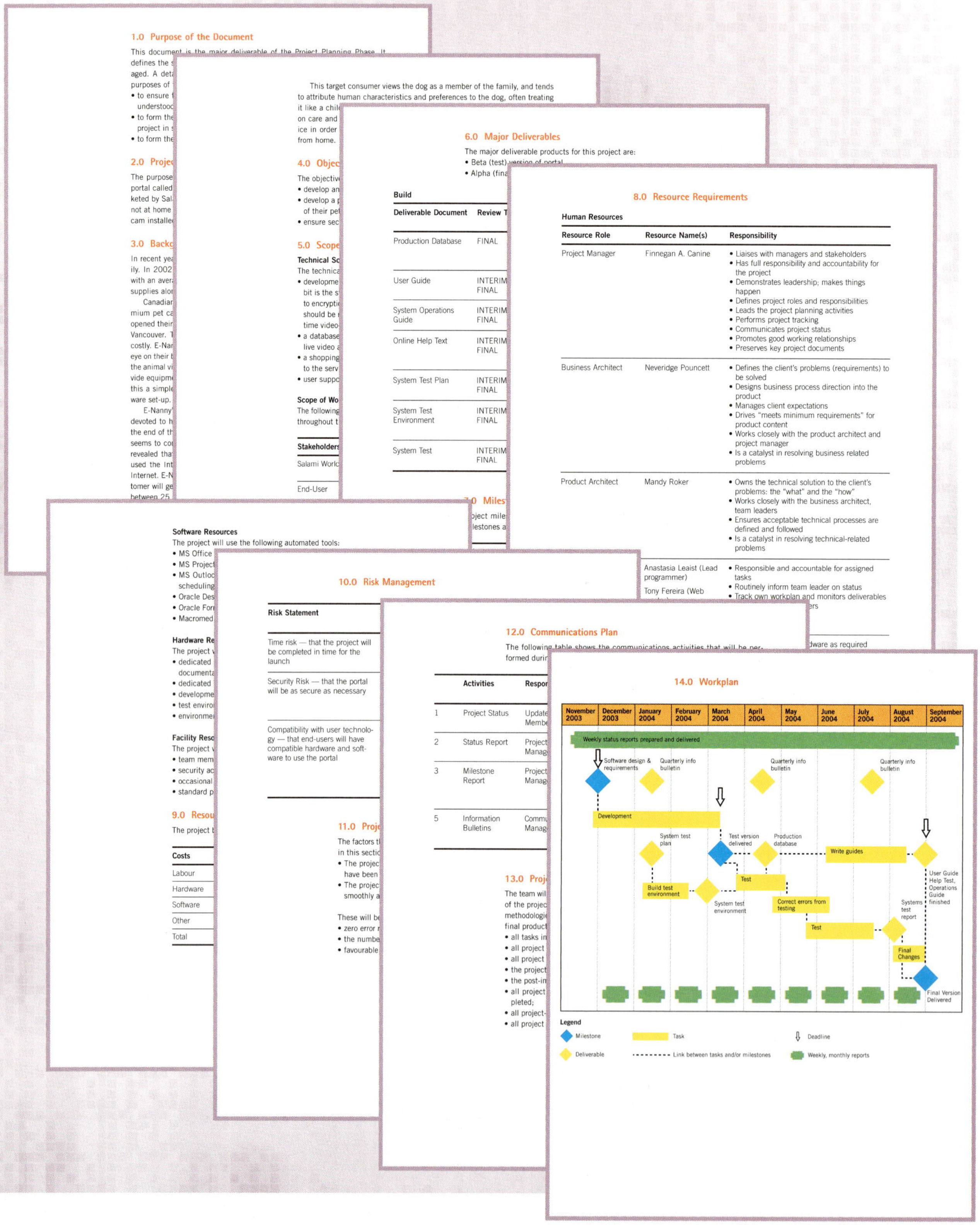
1.0 Purpose of the Document
This target consumer views the dog as a member of the family, and tends to attribute human characteristics and preferences to the dog, often treating
6.0 Major Deliverables
The major deliverable products for this project are:
Build
Deliverable Document
Production Database FINAL
8.0 Resource Requirements
Human Resources
Resource Role | Resource Name(s) | Responsibility
Project Manager | Finnegan A. Canine | Liaises with managers and stakeholders; Has full responsibility and accountability for the project; Demonstrates leadership; makes things happen; Defines project roles and responsibilities; Leads the project planning activities; Performs project tracking; Communicates project status; Promotes good working relationships; Preserves key project documents
Business Architect | Neveridge Pouncett | Defines the client's problems (requirements) to be solved; Designs business process direction into the product; Manages client expectations; Drives "meets minimum requirements" for product content; Works closely with the product architect and project manager; Is a catalyst in resolving business related problems
Product Architect | Mandy Roker | Owns the technical solution to the client's problems: the "what" and the "how"; Works closely with the business architect, team leaders; Ensures acceptable technical processes are defined and followed; Is a catalyst in resolving technical-related problems
Software Resources
The project will use the following automated tools:
10.0 Risk Management
Risk Statement
Time risk — that the project will be completed in time for the launch
Security Risk — that the portal will be as secure as necessary
Compatibility with user technology — that end-users will have compatible hardware and software to use the portal
12.0 Communications Plan
Activities
1 Project Status
2 Status Report
3 Milestone Report
5 Information Bulletins
14.0 Workplan
November 2003
December 2003
January 2004
February 2004
March 2004
April 2004
May 2004
June 2004
July 2004
August 2004
September 2004
Weekly status reports prepared and delivered
Software design & requirements
Quarterly info bulletin
Development
System test plan
Test version delivered
Production database
Write guides
Build test environment
Test
System test environment
Correct errors from testing
User Guide Help Test, Operations Guide finished
Systems test report
Final Changes
Final Version Delivered
Legend
Milestone
Task
Deadline
Deliverable
Link between tasks and/or milestones
Weekly, monthly reports

2.6 Tools of the Trade: Technology to Facilitate Project Management

Technology helps project managers and project teams to organize the many, often interdependent, tasks of a project, to allocate who's doing the work, to keep track of progress (or lack thereof), and to know how much the project is costing. Technology is designed to impose structure on potential chaos, make sense out of complexity, and help to plan, analyze, and communicate the status of a project to team members and stakeholders.

Some software packages and technology tools are stand-alone programs, while others do most or part of the job but are assisted by additional software packages for areas of risk analysis, sub-project integration, charting, and other relevant issues.

Reasons for selecting one software package over another depend on the size and complexity of projects. Small projects (less than 100 tasks and 25 resources) could be handled without specialized software. Medium-sized projects, which may contain 1000 tasks and several hundred resources, may benefit from the use of specialized software. Larger projects have more tasks or more sub-projects and resources, and are generally handled with the assistance of project management software. Another factor that affects choices is the location of team members. When team members work at different sites or in different cities, technology can be essential to allow for meetings, collaboration, and immediate sharing of information over great distances. Figure 2.10 below summarizes some of the common technologies and software that many project teams rely upon in planning and executing their projects.

Figure 2.10
Common Project Technologies and Software

Type of Tool	Examples	Benefits	Shortcomings
Office Productivity Software: includes word-processing, database, and spreadsheet applications	• Microsoft® Office • ClarisWorks® • AppleWorks® • Corel® WordPerfect® Suite	• Most individuals have this type of software. • The software is powerful enough to generate a variety of documents quickly. • This software allows for collaboration on written documents.	• Software does not allow for real-time collaboration. • Software must be compatible for individuals to view documents. • Software is not specialized for unique, project-based functions (e.g., Gantt chart).
E-mail Software: allows messages to be sent via the Internet among individuals	• Microsoft® Outlook Express • Hotmail®	• There are no compatibility issues on e-mail messages. • Most companies and many individuals already have this type of software. • It is a relatively fast way to transmit information. • It allows for electronic attachments.	• This software does not allow for real-time communication. • It relies primarily on written information (though video messaging is coming into favour).

Figure 2.10 (continued)
Common Project Technologies and Software

Type of Tool	Examples	Benefits	Shortcomings
Teleconferencing and Conference Calls	• PolyCom SoundPoint and SoundStation phones	• This technology allows team members to connect from remote locations by calling to a central number. • Real-time communication is possible. • Only a telephone is necessary to connect.	• The platform or service to connect all members can be costly. • The technology does not allow collaboration on written work.
Project Management Software: integrates components of word processing, spreadsheet, database, scheduling, and control. Special functions allow for automatic creation of Gantt charts, flowcharts, resource plans, etc.	• Microsoft® Project (see Figure 2.7) • Primavera Systems' Sure-Trak Project Manager • Symantec Corporation's Time Line	• Specialized applications allow users to generate a variety of reports and representations of information after entering data only once. • Tasks are entered into an input table, and graphical representations (such as Gantt charts) are automatically generated. • Software has specialized features for tracking and communication.	• This software is costly to purchase. • Training may be required to use software effectively. • The software requires an understanding of project management terminology and processes.
Intranet: a network that looks very much like the Internet, but is restricted to users on a specific network Users navigate through the Intranet, using a browser (such as Netscape or Internet Explorer)	N/A	• Easy to use. • Information can be posted relatively easily for all members of the team to access.	• A network environment and a firewall are required to screen out users who are not supposed to access the site.
Extranet: an intranet that has been opened to external access for selected user groups (e.g., partners, customers, suppliers, etc.) through restricted access (e.g., passwords)	• Aventail® EX-1500™ Appliance • Saturno Extranet • InfoStreet Extranet Package	• Technology provides a safe way to allow transactional business-to-business activities. • Instant transactions and communicating project status to stakeholders in real time can save time and money. • Allowing external parties to have access to information can strengthen relationships.	• Sending private information securely over public networks requires more security and technical considerations. • External users need to be compatible with the system.

Figure 2.10 (continued)
Common Project Technologies and Software

Type of Tool	Examples	Benefits	Shortcomings
Time Management Software: specialized software that allows users to track their activities in a calendar, and automatically schedule group meetings	• TimeKeeper • Microsoft® Outlook	• All members of a group can see one another's schedules. • Meetings can be scheduled automatically. • It is often linked to e-mail software. • Software generates a variety of reports that illustrate how the group is using time.	• Capabilities beyond scheduling and viewing calendars are limited.
Newsgroups: Internet-based discussion forums that allow individuals to communicate by posting messages on a board and responding to the messages of others	• Usenet	• They allow for collaboration and communication. • Discussions remain on the site for future reference.	• Real-time discussions need to be scheduled and moderated. • Sign-in protocols may need to be set up to ensure only certain users have access.
Internet Relay Chat (IRC) and Instant Messaging: an Internet application that allows for real-time discussion among subscribers	• Windows® Messenger • ICQ	• Application allows for real-time discussion and collaboration. • Documents can be instantly sent through these services.	• Individuals need to be online to receive instant messages. • To participate, members need to install the software. • It does not create a permanent record of discussions. • If using an Internet-based service, there is little confidentiality.
Facsimile (fax machine): technology that transmits scanned images of documents over a telephone line, either as a stand-alone machine or an application on a PC	• HotSend • Windows® Fax Messenger	• Machine is relatively inexpensive to purchase and use. • It is easy to use. • Most organizations already have the technology available.	• Only written or graphic documents can be transmitted. • The quality of transmission varies depending on the machines sending and receiving information.
Videoconferencing: the use of digital video technology over a dedicated phone or cable line to simulate face-to-face meetings. Often, includes the use of a whiteboard (a separate area of the videoconferencing screen) to allow those attending the meeting to share information by drawing or keying information	• Avistar Conference software • Bitfield Video Communication System Software • Intel VideoPhone equipment	• Team members from a variety of locations can interact in a way that is very similar to face-to-face meetings (including real-time collaboration).	• Equipment is extremely costly to purchase or rent. • If videoconferencing is taking place in several locations, the equipment needs to be compatible (e.g., in Northern Canada, fibre-optic equipment is not available). • Individuals need training on how to communicate effectively via the technology.

Figure 2.10 (continued)
Common Project Technologies and Software

Type of Tool	Examples	Benefits	Shortcomings
Web cam: a low-resolution camera attached to a PC that transmits live images of participants over the Internet.	• Microsoft NetMeeting®	• Equipment is inexpensive and easy to purchase and install. • It allows for real-time communication and, depending on the software, possible whiteboard collaboration (similar to a chalkboard, this allows groups to share an online board to post comments, drawings, etc.).	• It requires sufficient Internet bandwidth. • The quality of transmission is uneven; sometimes images are jerky or delayed. • Individuals may need training on how to effectively communicate with this technology. • Software is necessary to conduct Web cam meetings. A moderator is needed to cue people when it is their turn to communicate.

2.7 Team Productivity

Productivity refers to the efficient use of resources, including time and technology, by individuals and teams. In project management, emphasis is placed on the ability to use all resources efficiently. Part of the project manager's challenge is to keep track of team productivity — in other words, to make sure that all team members are completing what they need to complete on time and within the resources allocated. Many electronic tools can be used to help monitor and assess actual productivity in relation to the project plan (which includes resources allocated to the project). These include:

- tracking features in project management software;
- e-mail to communicate the status of projects;
- reports generated by word-processing software;
- notations in scheduling software; and
- updates on newsgroups or Intranet sites.

GETTING IT

1. Identify the types of project management-related technologies you have used. How have you used them?
2. Given that you will be completing a project for this course, determine the types of software you plan to use. Explain why you have selected them. How will you use them?
3. Which of the technologies described in Figure 2.10 would be most appropriate for each of the four stages in the project life cycle?

CAREER PERSPECTIVE

Help Wanted: Project Manager

The following advertisement appeared on *The Globe and Mail*'s Workopolis Web site on October 16, 2002.

Project Manager, Software - Ref #269

Department: Project Management
Position Type: Full Time

- Key Responsibilities: Develop the project strategy, plans and schedules ensuring that all the necessary components and deliverables will be met
- Plans, organizes, leads, and monitors the activities of the project team
- Prepares the management deliverables — "Project Management Plan," requests for change, etc. — and seeks approval when necessary
- Notifies the Product Management and/or the Client representative of discrepancies in planning and submits recommendations to resolve these issues
- Takes action on issues of non-compliance
- Keeps the lines of communication open among all project stakeholders
- Tracks the deliverables, milestones, and any decisions made regarding requests for changes and outstanding items
- Provides status on schedule and main issues on a regular basis
- Logs the Outstanding Items and ensures prompt resolution of issues
- Deals with the other project management centres, marketing, manufacturing, and product management on various project matters

Qualifications:

- 5 to 10 years of experience in project management
- Leadership, communication and negotiation skills and a team player
- PMP designation and Wireless Industry experience an asset

Questions

1. In what ways does this job advertisement reflect the project management methodology described in this book?
2. Would you be interested in this type of position? Why or why not?
3. What do you think "PMP designation" means? Test your hypothesis using the Internet.
4. If you were to give advice to someone who wants this position in the future, what would you tell her or him to do to prepare?

IT's A Wrap

Key Terms in This Chapter

baseline (p. 35)
deliverable (p. 35)
milestone (p. 35)
productivity (p. 44)
project (p. 23)
project management (p. 23)
project manager (p. 24)
strategic plan (p. 29)
task (p. 35)

1. Create a list of competencies you have acquired through your work in this chapter.
2. Update your portfolio to include examples of your work from this chapter.

Know It!

3. Give an example of a project.
4. What are the specific features that make your example a project?
5. Describe the role of the project manager in an organization.
6. Explain how deliverables, milestones, and tasks are similar and how they differ.

Do It!

7. Create a time management matrix that reflects the tasks you face over the next few months.
8. Suppose you were the project manager for your next school dance. Identify several risks associated with your project and what you would do to be prepared for them.
9. You have been assigned the project of publishing a new monthly newspaper for your school, which includes establishing the format, the content, and the production, within a limited budget. Create a list of tasks, deliverables, and milestones for that project. Identify any technologies and software you plan to use.
10. Make a chart of the types of software available for your use as a project manager, and indicate how and why you would use each.

Analyze It!

11. Do you think every organization should have a strategic plan? Why or why not?
12. Explain the ways you could see yourself using the project management methodology in your life today.
13. Identify the methods and criteria you would use to assess the usefulness of software for a project. Some people think that creating a project plan is very logical. Others think it is too much work up front. Respond to these opinions.

CHAPTER

3 Working in Project Teams

By the end of this chapter, you will be able to:

- create a project team charter;
- understand various workplace environments, organizational structures and designs, virtual enterprises, and their characteristics;
- describe and exhibit good communication skills;
- identify different types of teams in the workplace and how they operate;
- identify and use tools to evaluate and enhance team productivity; and
- apply best practices to address conflict in a team environment to resolve problems.

With increased global competition and fast-paced technological changes, the workplace has changed a great deal over the past 20 years and will continue to evolve in the 21st century. Many people have compared the **Information Revolution** created by information technology with the Industrial Revolution of the late 1700s and early 1800s. The Information Revolution has caused a shift from manual labour to information processing — allowing for greater flexibility in the way we work but also necessitating work in teams. In addition to strong technical skills, workers also need strong collaboration skills as the workplace increasingly relies on project teams to accomplish objectives. This chapter will help you to develop the teamwork skills used in modern organizations by addressing the following topics:

- Workplaces and Organizations in the IT World
- Working in Teams
- Communication
- Conflict

Introduction to Chapter Project

Recall that the Chapter Project is introduced at the beginning and is to be completed as you work through the chapter. Your teacher will provide you with assessment and evaluation criteria.

CHAPTER PROJECT

A project team charter is a simple document that many teams develop before they start a project. It is similar to a contract in that it explains the roles and expectations of each member, outlines the processes that team members will follow, and is signed by all team members to signify their agreement with the content. The team, rather than an individual, should create the charter. By the end of the chapter, your project team will create and sign a project team charter. As you work through the chapter, take notes of items you think should be included in your team's charter for the project you will complete for this course. Sections of this project charter will include:

1. Project Team Mission
The mission consists of three parts:

- *Background*: the situation that exists before the start of this project;
- *Purpose*: the reasons for needing the project team; and
- *Benefits*: the benefits that will accrue as a result of the team's successful completion of the project goal.

2. Project Team Goal
The project team goal defines, in a single sentence, what will be accomplished, incorporating in it an event that signifies project completion. Make the goal realistic and attainable.

3. Project Team Roles
The specific roles and expectations of each team member should be clearly identified so that each member knows her or his responsibilities.

4. Conflict Resolution Plan
The strategies and processes the group will follow to address conflict or disagreement must be identified.

5. Productivity Measures
The electronic tools that will be used to measure team productivity (i.e., whether the team is accomplishing their goals on time and using their time efficiently) must be identified. The way(s) in which the tools will be used should also be described.

6. Team Signatures
Each team member will sign the charter to indicate that he or she understands and agrees with its contents.

3.1 Workplaces and Organizations in the IT World

Twenty-five years ago, few individuals owned or knew how to use computers. Manufacturing relied heavily on manual labour. Today, computers are commonplace in almost all workplaces and are necessary to perform a variety of jobs. In fact, clerical workers now outnumber factory workers. Factories are increasingly automated, and employees in those environments rely on computers for certain functions of their jobs. As a result of the accessibility and power of computers, the way organizations and individuals do their jobs has changed. Moreover, organizations have had to change their various structures to make the most of technologies and new types of products and services and to meet employees' needs.

digiknow

According to the National Association of Professional Organizers, in 1850 only 4% of North Americans made a living through handling information. Today, information processing accounts for more than half of our Gross Domestic Product (GDP) (GDP refers to units of economic output).

3.1.1 The Workplace

When we think about careers, we often imagine working for large companies. The truth is that corporate settings are only one of several types of work environment.

Figure 3.1

In Canada today, more employees work in offices than in factories or on farms.

The **workplace setting** is the location where employees conduct their day-to-day work. Several models of workplace settings are common. A **corporate workplace setting** is a central location where employees of an organization (not necessarily a corporation) come together to work. Examples include Ottawa's Parliament buildings, any fast-food restaurant, or the Scotia Plaza in Toronto. This is the traditional workplace setting — for decades men and women across the world have gone to work, put in their workday, and then headed home. In the past, there was no other option — all the equipment one would need to do the job was at work. People could not afford to have most office equipment at home. Moreover, mail- or hand-delivery was the only option available to pass on finished products to co-workers or supervisors. Little by little, this traditional model has become less rigid as increasingly people are able to work in other places, collaborating and sharing information through electronic channels.

Over the past several decades, as communication technology and information technology have become smaller and more affordable, more and more home offices are appearing. Nicknamed **SOHO** (the acronym for "small office, home office"), a home office is space within a private residence where an occupant conducts day-to-day work. Generally, a home office (see Figure 3.2) is equipped with a telephone, a fax, and a computer with Internet access and a printer. Depending on the nature of the work, additional hardware might be necessary (e.g., scanners, Web cams, video or audio equipment). Though many home offices belong to entrepreneurs (i.e., people who run their own businesses), more and more large organizations are allowing their employees to **telecommute** or work from home too.

Get Connected

To find out more about SOHOs, visit www.pearsoned.ca/businessconnections. After you view the various sites, summarize the information you have found by listing three to five key points (e.g., advice for people with SOHOs, tips for success, etc.). Explain how this information would be helpful to a new entrepreneur.

Telecommuting opens up wonderful job possibilities for people who live in remote parts of Canada and would otherwise be unable to have certain types

Figure 3.2

In a two-column chart, identify the benefits and the drawbacks of working in a SOHO.

of jobs without relocating. Individuals can complete their work, e-mail it to colleagues, clients, or supervisors, and conduct meetings and communicate by telephone, e-mail, and video conferencing. Proponents also point out that this arrangement is very environment friendly since workers do not have to commute.

Another workplace setting exists that falls between a home office and a corporate setting. A **cooperative** is a shared workspace maintained by a group of independent individuals (often entrepreneurs). This is an economical way to have a workspace that contains a variety of equipment that one person alone would not necessarily be able to afford. By renting office space together and sharing equipment they already own, members of a cooperative can have access to pieces of technology that other cooperative members already have. As well, members can combine their skills and market themselves as a full-service "package" to potential clients. To find out how this works, read the *IT in Action* case below.

IT In Action

Elance Online

Elance Online is an innovative concept that brings together freelance workers and organizations or individuals who want to purchase services. Elance is organized in the form of a cooperative. Individuals who have a service to provide (such as Web design, graphic design, data entry, project management, tutoring, etc.) join the cooperative by creating a service profile and paying a monthly subscription fee (similar to a membership fee). Space is available online to post a profile and an electronic portfolio that showcase the freelancer's abilities and expertise. In addition to the monthly fee, freelancers pay a 5% commission on their earnings to Elance.

At the same time, organizations that need work done post the projects they have available. A freelancer who has paid the membership fee can browse through the available work and bid for relevant jobs electronically. **"Bidding"** refers to attempting to secure available work by submitting a quote for the fee expected to the organization that has posted the work. Then, the organization selects one freelancer to take on the job. Elance points out that not always the lowest bid wins!

Questions

1. Name and briefly describe two types of jobs that are available for bid currently on one of the cooperative Web sites that you locate in Get Connected.
2. List the advantages and disadvantages of this type of service for freelance workers. For companies and individuals purchasing services.
3. Identify the criteria that organizations can use to evaluate which freelancers to select.
4. Visit a second cooperative Web site on the *Business Connections* student site. What do both cooperatives have in common? How are they different?

Get Connected

Visit www.pearsoned.ca/businessconnections to examine two Web sites of cooperatives.

ON THE CASE

The Virtual Enterprise

As information and communications technologies overcome the barriers of time and distance, it becomes possible for organizations to work together in new ways. A **virtual enterprise** is an arrangement in which a number of corporations or organizations combine their specialties to create a product or deliver a service. Virtual enterprises form quickly in response to new opportunities, then dissolve just as quickly when the need ceases (Hardwick et al. 1996). Characteristically, the organizations that comprise such an enterprise are distributed geographically and their work is coordinated via electronic communications.

Many smaller organizations can profit from this type of arrangement, which can give them the benefits of the resources of a large organization while they retain the agility and independence of a small one.

According to David Skyrme (1995 and 1999), the following conditions need to be addressed by virtual enterprises:

1. Each partner must have some distinctive added value to bring to the group.
2. Partners must develop a high degree of mutual trust and understanding. As a result, the same individuals and organizations tend to work together often.
3. Projects should be the focus of the virtual enterprise.
4. Terms of reference for the roles and responsibilities of each member need to be defined up-front, to ensure that each partner can commit the necessary resources to the enterprise.
5. Individuals in coordination roles (similar to the role of a project manager) are necessary to plan and monitor all aspects of the projects.

In fact, many successful projects and organizations have adopted this model. First Virtual Communications, an international corporation with offices in France, the United States, China, and Japan, participates in virtual enterprises in two ways. To begin with, this organization specializes in multimedia network products, such as video collaboration tools, that enable PCs to become high-quality communications platforms, thus providing an infrastructure for virtual enterprises. Moreover, it also operates as a virtual enterprise itself, focusing on its core competencies to quickly come up with innovations and bringing them to life by building powerful partnerships with other organizations that have the expertise to see them through (Gebauer and Segev 1998).

In the book publishing industry, virtual enterprises are common. For example, a publisher may choose to contract a packager to create a new book. The packager then partners with a freelance author in another city or country to create a manuscript that is then sent (usually electronically) to an editor who prepares the manuscript for publishing. Another partner would be brought in to typeset and print the book. Copies of the book are then sent to a distribution company (usually contracted by the publisher) that partners with retailers to sell the book. Finally, retailers sell the books to customers.

ON THE CASE (continued)

As new communication technologies continue to emerge, we can expect to see more and more virtual enterprises. They allow organizations to involve themselves in projects they could never do alone, while building strong partnerships that lead to successful projects and to more business opportunities.

Questions

1. Identify the conditions that need to be addressed by a virtual enterprise.
2. List well-known companies you can think of that have a virtual enterprise model. Describe the model that they use. To answer this question, visit the Web sites of several large, well-known companies to determine if they participate in virtual enterprise. Alternatively, you can use a search engine.
3. Suppose you wanted to form a virtual enterprise for Web-based or multimedia applications. Identify possible external partners in your community or province that use information technology for virtual enterprise purposes.
4. Create a criteria sheet that lists the qualities or characteristics you would look for in selecting or identifying partners for your virtual enterprise.

3.1.2 Organizational Design and Structure

An organization is much like a jigsaw puzzle — many small pieces fit together to create an overall picture. **Organizational structure** refers to the way in which all the pieces of the organization fit together. The International Standards Organization (ISO) defines organizational structure as "the pattern of responsibilities, authorities, and relationships that control how people perform their functions and how they interact with one another" (Praxiom Research Group Limited 2002). Many forms of organizational structure exist, with different types of organizations requiring different arrangements of the "jigsaw puzzle pieces" to best achieve their desired results. **Organizational design**, on the other hand, refers to the decisions and assumptions that lead to a specific organizational structure, including processes for how parts of the organization work together, ways in which information flows, and how technology is integrated.

Organizational structure is expressed through an organization chart (often called simply an "org chart") — a visual picture that shows all the positions in that organization (see Figures 3.3 and 3.4 on pages 55 and 56). If you were to compare the organization charts of an entity over many years, you would probably see the names and number of departments change, but the basic shape of the design would most likely be the same.

The basic forms of organizational structure are:

- ***Bureaucratic/hierarchical.*** This organizational structure is based on a very formal system of authority. Employees have very specific lines of management hierarchy they have to follow to have decisions made and requests approved. Hierarchies are vertical structures (if you were to draw a picture of this type of structure, it would be very tall). You might have a president, who has four vice-presidents reporting to her or him, each of whom has six managers reporting to them, and finally 20 employees, each reporting to a manager. This is the most traditional type of structure.
- ***Horizontal.*** The opposite of bureaucratic/hierarchical, a horizontal organizational structure indicates that many individuals report to one supervisor, but there are few layers of management. If you were to draw a picture of the horizontal structure, it would be much wider than the hierarchical structure and not nearly as tall.
- ***Centralized.*** A centralized organizational structure is one in which power and control for decision making are at the top of the organization (i.e., at the level of the president or vice-president).
- ***Decentralized.*** A decentralized organizational structure is one in which power and control are delegated to lower levels of the organization, and employees toward the "bottom" of the organization chart have the authority to make decisions.

In recent years, organizations have moved to a flatter, horizontal organizational structure. This shift is the result of several factors. First, having fewer layers of management is more cost-effective for any organization. Second, the impact of information technology on the type and volume of work that one individual can perform has eliminated the need for certain types of positions. For example, voice mail systems and word-processing software/computer technology reduce the need for a layer of administrative employees to answer phones, take messages, and deal with correspondence. Similarly, anyone in an organization can manipulate the vast amounts of information stored in databases or even on spreadsheets to create meaningful data. This eliminates the need to employ individuals to sift through information and disseminate bits to different people.

Organizations can have elements of hierarchical or horizontal structure and can be either centralized or decentralized, as described above. Layered on top of those characteristics of organizations, the "pieces of the puzzle" that make up the organization can be organized in several ways. The two most common ways are division-/department-based and matrix-/project-based.

- *Division- or department-based organization.* Departments operate on their own as business units and work without much interaction. See Figure 3.3 for a manufacturing example. Departments can be based on job function (e.g., human resources, marketing, finance), on geography (e.g., eastern region, western region), by product (e.g., hardware, software, training, service), by process (e.g., shipping, receiving, manufacturing), or by customer (e.g., consumer, industrial, government).

  For instance, Bank of Montreal follows this type of organizational design: marketing, human resources, and finance are centralized functions. These three functions make decisions for Bank of Montreal branches and employees across Canada. Each region of Canada (eastern, central, western) is organized as its own department and executes the decisions made centrally.

Figure 3.3
Division- or Department-Based Organization Chart

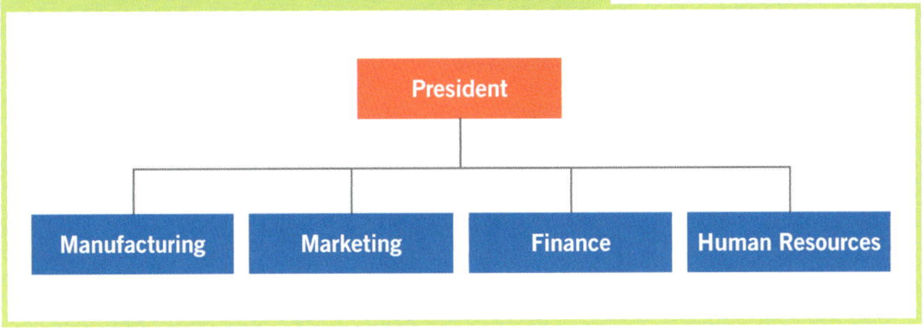

- *Matrix- or project-based organization.* Department managers exist, but employees belong to more than one department and move around to perform their specialized tasks as the need arises. This organizational structure is often used in project-based work (though it is quite common in large, complex organizations that are not project based). For example, a number of employees in a software company might be programmers and work in the same location. Similarly, graphic artists, animators, and testers work for the company too. When a project comes up, one or two people from each group will be pulled together, based on their expertise and skill, to form a team that will be in place for only that project's duration. Each employee's "boss" will vary from project to project, and a person might report to several supervisors at once if she or he is working on several projects at the same time. This form of organization has a tendency to be more horizontal than the divisional model, simply because of the nature of the reorganization necessary.

The consulting group Monday (formerly the management consulting division of PricewaterhouseCoopers) is a matrix-based organization. This company provides advice to organizations undertaking large projects (such as new products or internal reorganization). Monday employs thousands of individuals whose expertise ranges from finance to human resources, benefits, research, law, marketing, and public relations. When a new project is taken on, a project manager reviews the needs of the client and then assembles a team that includes individuals from each of the groups. For the duration of the project those individuals report to the project manager. Once the project is over, each person will be assigned to a new project team and may work with entirely different people for a different project manager. A matrix-based organization chart appears in Figure 3.4.

Figure 3.4
Matrix- or Project-Based Organization Chart

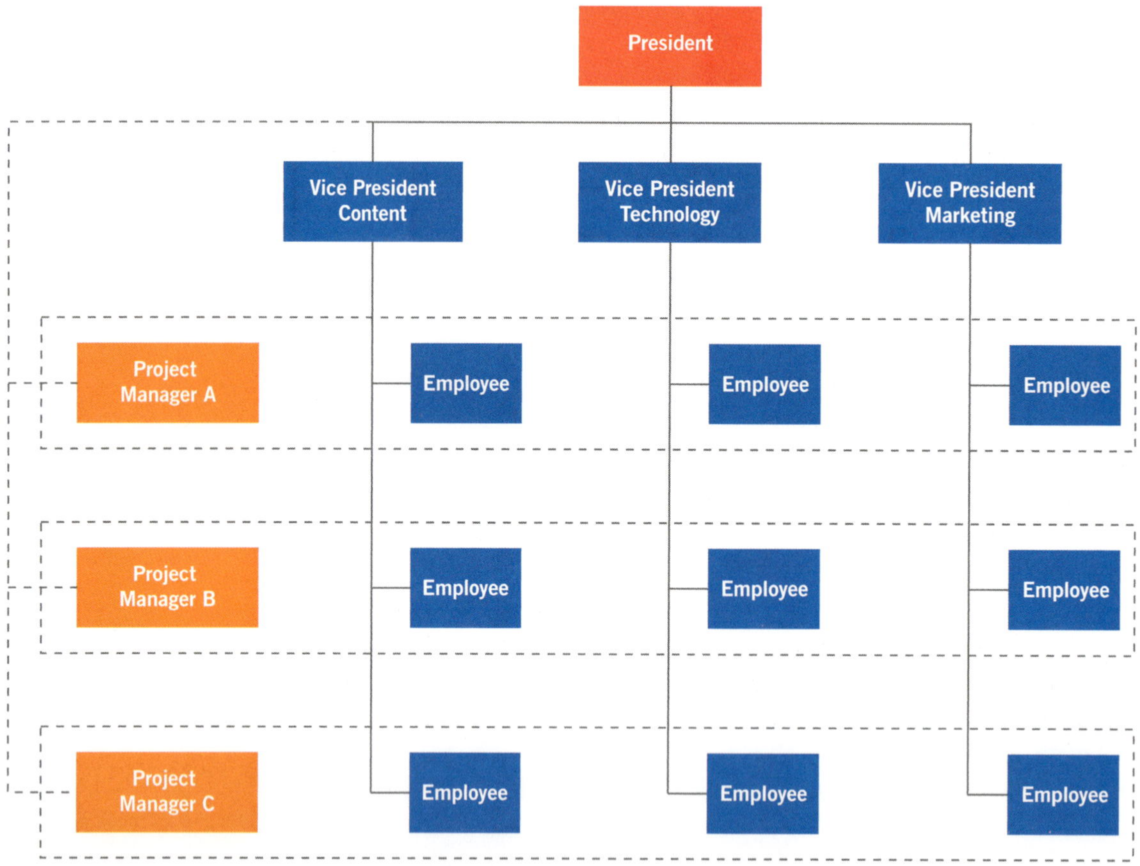

Notice that project managers assemble teams from each of the functional areas (technology, content, and marketing) for specific projects. The individual employees are accountable to both the project managers (as indicated by the dotted box) and to the vice presidents (as indicated by the solid line).

Source: adapted from David D. Van Fleet, *Contemporary Management* (Boston: Houghton Mifflin, 1988), p. 271.

GETTING IT

1. Differentiate among the terms *workplace, organizational structure,* and *organizational design.*
2. Use the Internet to find the organization charts for two well-known organizations and identify the type of structure and design they possess.
3. Draw an organization chart that represents the staff at your school. Based on your drawing, what type of organizational design would you classify it as? Is the structure horizontal or hierarchical? Explain.
4. Having learned about different options for organizational structure and design, create an innovative, new organization chart for your school. Explain the reasons for your new design.

3.2 Working in Teams

A **team** is a collection of people who regularly interact in pursuit of a common goal. Most people either love working in teams or hate it. However, the reality is that, in most jobs, some degree of teamwork is unavoidable. Teamwork can also be extremely effective and rewarding when all the team members are properly equipped to work together and perform their jobs.

3.2.1 Project Teams

In the modern workplace, people are required to work in teams on a regular basis. In particular, project management requires groups of individuals to complete specific projects as a team. Outlined in Figure 3.5 are some advantages and disadvantages of working in teams.

Project teams are specific groups formed to plan and execute projects. Project teams should be assigned early, kept intact, and located near the work, if applicable, in contiguous spaces. The project team consists of those who work on the project and usually report to a project manager. Generally, each member is assigned to a team because he or she possesses a certain skill that is essential to the completion of the project. For instance, a software project team would require a software designer, several programmers, possibly a graphic artist, a tester (or quality assurance specialist), and a project manager.

Figure 3.5

Advantages and Disadvantages of Working in Teams

Advantages of Working in Teams	Disadvantages of Working in Teams
• Promotes innovation and creativity	• Requires interaction that may result in too much time off-task
• Improves the quality of decision making	• Success depends on all team members being responsible
• Gains members' commitment to tasks	• Results in time lost because of numerous meetings
• Exerts control or discipline on members	• Conflicts may result from differences in personality or leadership style
• Promotes interaction among members that satisfies the affiliation needs of individuals	
• Provides more information to all involved through the contribution of individuals	

Figure 3.6

Describe how working as part of a team on a school project has benefited you.

ON THE CASE

Working in Teams

The survey that follows was conducted with 800 office workers in six of Canada's major urban business centres between May 2 and May 11, 2001. With a sample of this size, the results are considered accurate to within ±3.5 percentage points, 19 times out of 20, of what they would have been had the entire office worker population been polled. However, individual city samples of 200 have a margin of error of ±7.1%, 19 times out of 20.

Toronto, ON — A survey released today, conducted by Ipsos-Reid and sponsored by Microsoft Canada Co., shows that fully three-quarters of office workers (75%) in six of Canada's leading economic centres say that sharing information with their co-workers has become more important over the last five years. The survey also revealed that:

- On average, 5.2 hours each week are spent in meetings.
- Workers in larger organizations (500 employees or more) spend much more time on average in meetings than those in smaller (less than 50 employees) or medium organizations (50–499 employees) — 6.9 hours versus 3.8 and 4.6 hours, respectively.
- Montreal workers spend less time each week in meetings (3.8 hours) than their counterparts in other major urban centres (5.7 hours).
- Most workers (91%) report that they collaborate with others in their organization on the same documents or electronic files (52% frequently and 39% sometimes).
- Collaboration is even more common among workers in larger organizations (60% frequently collaborate versus 42% in smaller organizations and 53% in medium organizations).

Almost all workers (96%) agree that "fast and easy access to information is a critical part" of their job. Furthermore, more than half (57%) say that the need to work in teams as opposed to working individually has increased over the last five years. Further highlighting the need to share information, a quarter (26%) of workers say that job sharing in their organization has increased over the same time period.

Excerpt from Public Release Date: May 31, 2001.

Questions

1. Explain what the implications of working in teams are to you as a potential employee, given the degree to which today's careers require teamwork.
2. Describe the specific steps you can take to improve and demonstrate your ability to work in a team environment.
3. Give examples of group work and of skills you have demonstrated by taking part in teams, either through your schoolwork, clubs, or athletics.

Depending on the organization and the nature of the work, several different types of teams can exist. They are described in Figure 3.7 below.

Figure 3.7
Types of Teams

Type	Role Definition	Communication	Goal	Example
Crew	Prescribed, well-defined	Well-defined	Common, short-term	Disaster clean-up group
Task force or project team	Vague definition with room for interpretation	Not defined or loosely defined	Common, can be short- or long-term	Video game or software design team
Standing team or department	Similar for all team members	As needed	Multiple goals, ongoing over the long term	Product management team (e.g., Oreo cookie product line), English Department teachers

Source: From information in Theresa Kline, *Remaking Teams: The Revolutionary Research-Based Guide That Puts Theory Into Practice* (San Francisco, CA: Jossey-Bass/Pfeiffer, 1999).

digiknow

The term **synergy** is used to describe the situation where the combined output of a group is greater than the sum of the outputs of the individuals that compose the group. Groups that exhibit synergy will therefore accomplish more than the individuals could have accomplished on their own.

3.2.2 Team Productivity

All organizations are concerned with ensuring that teams are productive — that they use their time efficiently and meet their objectives on time. Chapter 2 described a variety of electronic tools that can be used along with principles of project management for team members to work together effectively. A variety of other tools are available to help teams increase their productivity, leading to greater success in the work they do.

Team productivity software applications in the form of **groupware** (software that can have more than one user collaborating simultaneously) are available. Examples of groupware include Microsoft® Exchange, Electronic Meeting System (EMS) published by the Marshall Institute, Team Focus™ published by Executive Development Inc., and Teamware™ Dolphin. These tools help teams through features such as:

- instant messaging;
- organization tools that allow team members to identify issues, problems, or tasks that need to be addressed;
- "polling" or survey features that allow team members to vote on issues;
- tools to develop meeting agendas and keep minutes (summary notes on what happened at a meeting);
- conflict resolution tools that walk team members through steps; and

- message boards that allow team members to post their thoughts, ideas, and responses on pre-defined topics.

These types of tools provide "one-stop shopping" for teams to maintain records of their information. More importantly, they encourage collaboration and communication — particularly important for teams that work in different offices or cities. These tools do not replace other software applications (such as e-mail, project management, and office productivity software), but enhance them by providing new and different features.

3.2.3 Stages in Team Development

As teams first meet and form, a specific process is generally followed before they are able to work productively. Research has indicated that newly formed groups behave in a different way from mature ones. By understanding the process of group development, a project manager or team member can predict what is likely to happen and take steps to improve the group's work. The stages listed below and in Figure 3.8 are:

Figure 3.8
Stages in Team Development

- *Form*. In the formative stage, group members get to know each other and talk about the purpose of the group, what is expected of each member, and what each can contribute. Group members are also "testing the waters" to see what sort of boundaries exist and what sort of behaviour is acceptable.
  Members' personalities, experiences, impressions, and goals will affect how well a group comes together. Having members come up with written group objectives and goals is an effective tactic during this stage.
- *Storm*. The storming stage is a period of high tension while groups elaborate on their goals and activities, structure themselves, and focus on obstacles in the way of their goals. As well, members begin to clarify and understand each other's personal styles.
- *Norm*. The norming stage focuses on the integration of the group. During this stage, members become coordinated as a working group. Members will acquire some sort of "team spirit" or sense of belonging. Successful completion of this stage will hold the group together to accomplish its goal.
- *Perform*. The performing stage begins when the group begins to work efficiently toward its goals. At this time, members are able to creatively handle disagreements and/or problems. Group structure in this stage is stable.

3.2.4 Team Member Roles and Types

Much of a group's activities take place in meetings or through informal group discussion. These are situations in which team members define their roles and take on certain behaviours. Group behaviours fit into one of two broad categories: initiators or responders. Within each of these categories lie a number of roles members assume. People tend to vary their behaviours and roles within a team or group, depending on the situation. Though someone may primarily be an initiator, they may also sometimes act as a responder.

Initiators are people who speak up first. They initiate discussion by contributing knowledge of facts, experiences, or opinions. Some common types of initiator are:

- *Idea-Generators* come up with ideas and suggestions, offering them willingly to the group for evaluation. Idea-generators can be useful in suggesting lists of alternatives and creative solutions to questions posed, but responders are necessary to stimulate evaluation of these ideas.

- *Experts and Back-Seat Drivers* "know it all" and are eager to demonstrate their knowledge. Experts can be beneficial if they actually have expertise or knowledge about the issue being discussed. They can contribute valuable information to generate solutions. However, these same individuals can derail a good idea with their overpowering "knowledge" if others pay too much attention to their ideas.

- *Storytellers* have a story for every problem or situation. More often than not, these stories are long and not necessarily relevant to the situation or problem being considered. In most cases, storytellers simply waste time. On occasion, the stories can be of value and help the group accomplish a goal based on an individual's past experience.

- *Ideologists* state theories of how things ought to be under ideal circumstances. Their comments may stimulate ideas from others.

- *Stars* brag about their past experiences that vaguely relate to the issues being discussed. These individuals are more concerned with "looking good" in the group's eyes than solving problems or making progress.

Responders, unlike initiators, listen to what's being said by initiators and respond to them by evaluating and/or commenting on information. Some common types of responders are:

- *Active Listeners* ask questions about, probe, re-state, and clarify statements made by others. They constantly ensure that they have correctly interpreted messages sent by others and often keep notes. Provided they are not taking too much of the group's time, active listeners are extremely beneficial for group progress.

- *Devil's Advocates* ask "what if" questions in response to any suggestion. Devil's advocates can be very useful in helping to evaluate a situation by stimulating thought about the comments made by others. When made without preconceived judgement or criticism, a devil's advocate's comments can be useful to the group and should be encouraged.

- *Defeatists* are convinced nobody's ideas will work, or that the comments of others are unrealistic. Defeatists can be a dangerous negative influence, so their comments should be tactfully kept to a minimum.

- *Axe-Grinders* relate any comments or problems made by others to their pet peeve, whether it has to do with the group or not. They use the group's time to complain about issues that bother them. Axe-grinders should be encouraged to make positive rather than negative contributions.

- *Aggressors* are out to get others in the group. They react to the statements of others in a personal way and will often attack the sender of a message instead of the message itself. Their behaviour can be very destructive to a group.

For groups to work effectively, there must be an even balance of initiators and responders. When groups are working together well, members switch back and forth between initiating and responding. There is constant dialogue, evaluation, and communication. If member roles are out of balance, one of two situations will occur. When there are too many initiators, competition develops. Everyone has ideas they want to pursue and the group becomes too divided to make up its mind. When there are too many responders, the group becomes quiet and generally cannot make up its mind. The team's leader or facilitator must maintain this balance by leading the communication process.

Other roles are disruptive to the goals of group work:

- *Clowns* try to entertain the group by joking around. They may know the purpose of the group but do not take it seriously. Instead of contributing, they make statements to draw attention to themselves. Clowns are dangerous because they can get the group off-track and waste its time. Generally, clowns are neither initiators nor responders.

- *Dominators* try to use group time to meet their own agendas. They are more interested in running things than in hearing or solving group problems and concerns, and attempt to take over discussions and change the topic to their own issues. Like clowns, dominators can get the group off-track and waste group time discussing issues that are only relevant to themselves.

- *Hitchhikers* are just "along for the ride" and rarely contribute to the group. They sit quietly through meetings, often doodling and daydreaming. They will do the absolute minimum in contributing to completing group tasks. Hitchhikers may just be lazy, or bored, or uninterested in the goal.

GETTING IT

1. Identify and explain the evidence that shows that teamwork is increasingly important in today's workplace.
2. Describe the three types of teams in today's workplace settings.
3. Explain how understanding the stages in team development can help you to be a more effective team member.
4. A number of team member roles and types have been identified in this section. Select the one that most reflects how you function in a team. Explain why you think this characterizes your behaviour. Do you think you contribute well to a team in this role?
5. List the steps you can take to improve your ability to work in a team.
6. Describe how team productivity tools work.

3.3 Communication

Communication may be the most important skill that contributes to the success of individuals and teams. Team members need to articulate their needs and the status of their work to others, and at the same time need to know what their colleagues are doing to ensure that all the pieces of the project are fitting together well.

Figure 3.9

Facial expressions and hand gestures can also send messages in the communication process.

3.3.1 Basic Concepts of Communication

Communication is a two-way process. It involves sending a message *and* receiving one. It can be defined as an interpersonal process of sending and receiving symbols with messages attached to them. A project manager's job often focuses around the need to communicate with other parties. As well, effective communication can minimize conflicts and eliminate problems before they occur.

IT In Action

Vitesse Canada Inc. and Malkam Cross Cultural Training

Sharpening One's Soft Skills

Ottawa's Vitesse (re-skilling) Canada Inc. and Malkam Cross Cultural Training have teamed up to develop a soft skills training workshop for new Canadian high-tech professionals.

"They (Vitesse) were discovering on the soft skills side many people who were eminently qualified in hard skills were having difficulty moving into and staying employed because of soft skills deficits," said Kathleen Thomas, Malkam's employment program coordinator. "If you don't have soft skills, you're not able to, for instance, work as a team member. And almost everything is done as a member of a team or work group. Not much work is done in isolation," said Thomas.

Vitesse is launching its two-day pilot workshop — Canadian Workplace Practices — at the end of August. "It'll be very intensive. There will be ways to enhance their ability to work in teams, to understand and work within culturally diverse situations, to understand management structures, and there will be strategies for ESL (English as a second language) speakers," said Doug Francis, director of program development, Vitesse.

Soft skills are required in just about any profession, but Francis said they are particularly key to high-tech professionals right now because "there seems to be more people right now with the requisite hard skills that employers can choose from.

"But once they've had a chance to take these people in or to interview them, I think it's the soft skills that really round out the package and decide who employers will stick with, who they will promote within their organization, who will make good team leaders, and who will move into eventual project manager (positions)."

Excerpt from *Computing Canada*, August 24, 2001, vol. 27, no. 18, p. 25.

Questions

1. Hypothesize what you think the article means by "soft" skills and "hard" skills. Compare your response with that of another student.
2. List three soft skills and three hard skills that you require to be successful as a student. Why do students need these?
3. Explain how team members' soft skills can contribute to the success of a project.

3.3.2 Listening

Listening is the most important communication skill. People are naturally drawn to good listeners. The person who is talking knows that the true listener believes what they have to say is important. By not listening, individuals can miss important information or not perceive forthcoming problems based on what the other person is saying. Listening is based on the intention to do one of four things:

- understand someone;
- enjoy someone;
- learn something; or
- give help or support.

Just being quiet while someone talks is called "pseudo-listening." Everyone is a pseudo-listener sometimes (listening but not really hearing/concentrating on the topic). However, the more a person engages in real listening, the more effective he or she will be personally and professionally.

Active listening is the ideal way to listen. Clearly, listening doesn't mean sitting still without speaking. An active listener must ask questions and get feedback to fully appreciate what is being said. The goal of an active listener is to participate in what is being said — to focus on clarifying and enhancing the information that is being passed along.

Get Connected

Understanding your personal communication style can help you improve the ways that you deal with others. Find out your communication style at www.pearsoned.ca/businessconnections. What did your result summary tell you? Do you think it was accurate?

3.3.3 Disclosure and Expression

Disclosure is simply communicating information about yourself. It is the second basic communication skill. Being able to disclose and express information, such as observations, thoughts, feelings, and needs, will ensure that team members get the information they need from one another to get the job done and eliminate miscommunication through assumptions.

3.3.4 Meetings: You Cannot Avoid Them, but You Can Make Them Worthwhile

To plan, share information, and sometimes celebrate achievements or project completion, all teams participate in meetings. Despite the amount of time most people spend in meetings, few actually have the skills to conduct meetings effectively. And because time is such a valuable resource, using meeting time efficiently is of key importance to an organization and a team.

An effective meeting is one that has a specific purpose that all attendees are aware of and a schedule (called an agenda) to follow, so as to achieve the intended outcomes. Generally, meetings fall into one of four categories:

ON THE CASE

Tips for Effective Communication

The American Management Association (AMA) first published the following "10 Commandments of Good Communication" in the 1955 edition of the *AMA Management Handbook* as a foundation for building effective communication skills — and they have stood the test of time. These guidelines, however, are specific to North American etiquette. Communicating with individuals and groups from other cultures requires knowledge of their customs and unique communication methods.

1. Clarify your ideas before communicating. Think through the message, and consider who will be receiving and/or affected by it.
2. Examine the purpose of each communication. Prepare your message around the objective.
3. Consider the total physical and human setting. Make sure that the timing and setting (location) are appropriate for what is being said.
4. Consult with others when planning communication. Those who were involved in planning the communication will be more supportive of it.
5. Be aware of the overtones of your message. Your tone of voice, expression, and body language will affect the way the listener will perceive the message.
6. Take every opportunity to communicate something of help or value to the listener. Try looking at things from the listener's point of view.
7. Follow up on communication. Ask questions and encourage feedback from others to help you.
8. Communicate for tomorrow as well as today. Remember that postponing an unpleasant communication will only make it worse. Communicate messages as soon as possible.
9. Make sure your actions support your words. Follow through with any promises you make.
10. Be a good listener at all times.

Questions

1. The passage above indicates that it focuses on the North American communication style. In a small group, discuss the characteristics of North American communication. Record points on which you agree.
2. Use your favourite search engine or the links on www.pearsoned.ca/businessconnections to locate a site that describes the communication style of another culture. How does it differ from that of North America?
3. Explain the ways that messages could get mixed up if a North American were trying to communicate a message with someone from the culture you researched.

- *Specific information meetings*: time allotted to share information that is relevant to the project;
- *Decision-making meetings*: time allotted to come to consensus as a group about an issue that affects the project;
- *General information meetings*: time allotted for general information exchange or updates on individuals' progress; and
- *Celebratory meetings*: meetings held to celebrate the completion of a project, to recognize the outstanding work of an individual, or to congratulate one another on an achievement.

Most of the literature and research on effective meetings have resulted in similar sets of criteria for holding effective meetings. Common recommendations for holding meetings in North America are:

- Prepare an agenda (schedule) in advance and distribute it to all attendees.
- Select a "chairperson" to host the meeting and move through the agenda.
- Time all segments and keep speakers on track.
- Take notes (called "**minutes**") that summarize the discussion that took place and distribute them to all attendees afterward as a record of what was discussed and decided upon. Be sure to include "action items" to remind members of what they committed to do.
- End all meetings on time.

Be aware that different cultures and countries have different protocols and expected behaviours for meetings.

GETTING IT

1. In your own words, define and describe *effective communication.*
2. Identify and record the steps you can take to improve your listening skills.
3. List the different types of meetings that exist. How do they differ?
4. Prepare a poster that highlights the attributes that would make a meeting successful.
5. Define *agenda.*
6. Define *minutes.*
7. Describe the role of the chairperson.

3.4 Conflict

We have all experienced differences of opinion at one time or another. Regardless of where you work or with whom, you are bound to experience conflict at one time or another when working collaboratively. The ability to resolve **conflict** as a team can make or break a project.

3.4.1 Dealing With Conflict

Usually, conflict is a result of one of two things: either differences in ideas about performance (e.g., when team members disagree on how work should be done or who should do it) or differences in strongly held beliefs (e.g., personal values that surface during the course of work or the vision of what outcomes should be). Conflict, when not resolved, can reduce productivity or even halt a team's work. As well, it can make the workplace unpleasant for the team. The best strategy is to deal with conflict directly, as soon as it arises, because conflict has a way of bubbling over when it is not addressed. Figure 3.10 below identifies a process for dealing with conflict constructively.

Figure 3.10
A Process for Dealing with Conflict

I. Explore
- Clarify critical issues by listening to others and having a frank discussion.
- Identify who is involved in the conflict and who is affected by it.
- Assess sources of conflict.
- Anticipate possible disagreements before they boil over.

II. Look for Areas of Agreement
- Review the purpose of the team and its goals.
- Focus on what you agree upon.

III. Determine How the Conflict Affects the Team's Work
- Determine specific ways in which the conflict affects the team's work.
- Determine specific ways in which the conflict affects the final product.
- If the conflict does not affect the work or final product, members should agree to disagree and end the process at this stage.

IV. Resolve
- Determine the best approach for the conflict at hand (*see Figure 3.11: Conflict Resolution Approaches*)
- Carry out the plan.
- Monitor progress.
- Reflect and learn from the experience.

A number of approaches can be taken to resolve conflict. Different approaches are suitable for different situations. Figure 3.11 summarizes some effective strategies to deal with conflict, as well as the most appropriate situations in which they should be used.

Figure 3.11
Conflict Resolution Approaches

Approaches	Behaviour	Appropriate Situation or Justification
Avoidance and/or Agreeing to Disagree	Non-confrontational; ignores or passes over issues; may deny the issue is a problem	Differences too minor to bother with; attempts at solution might damage relationships, creating bigger problems
Accommodation	Agreeable; non-assertive; cooperates even at the expense of personal goals	Not worth risking damage to relationships, which would create bigger problems
Win/Lose	Confrontational, aggressive, and assertive; must win at any cost	Possible legal threat, could injure someone; potential conflict with personal values
Compromising	Important all parties achieve basic goals and maintain good relationships; aggressive but cooperative	No one perfect solution
Problem Solving	Both parties' needs are viewed as legitimate and important; high respect for mutual support; assertive and cooperative	When parties openly discuss issues, a mutually beneficial solution can be found without anyone making major concessions

Adapted from Robert B. Maddux, *Successful Negotiation*, 3rd edition (Menlo Park, CA: Crisp Publications Inc., 1995), p. 68.

GETTING IT

1. Conflict is inevitable in any team. Explain what you can do as a team member to help overcome conflict that arises.
2. Explain how effective conflict resolution can contribute to team productivity.

CAREER PERSPECTIVE 1

But you need experience to get experience!

By Bonnie Busby

Many recent technology graduates have written to me about their difficulties in finding employment in their field. Indeed, it is extremely frustrating to have the education and training required for a job and yet be passed over due to one's lack of experience. This is especially frustrating given media reports about shortages of skilled workers.

The experience requirement is an obstacle that almost all recent graduates face. However, you can overcome this challenge with patience, perseverance, and some creativity.

To be successful in your job search, focus on entry-level opportunities. Doing some research is also helpful: compile a list of companies you would be interested in working for, and then visit their Internet sites.

Companies that hire new graduates or students will typically advertise this on their site. HRDC (Human Resources Development Canada) is also an excellent source of information.

Find out about technology career fairs happening in your area. They take place in most major cities on a regular basis. They provide great opportunities to meet representatives from organizations that are currently recruiting technology professionals.

Finally, consider options outside of regular full-time employment. You might also want to consider contacting temporary staffing agencies in your area to get the valuable experience you need to land a full-time job.

Volunteering your time, though not lucrative at the moment, can pay off in the long run by providing you with valuable experience that you can put on your résumé.

Being as flexible and creative as possible will enable you to accumulate the experience that employers are looking for!

Excerpt from an article by the same title that appeared in *The Globe and Mail* on May 28, 2001.

Questions

1. Explain the "experience requirement" and why it is a problem for graduates.
2. Make a list of the creative ways (those listed in the article and others you can think of) to get experience without a job.
3. Aside from salary, state what you are looking for in the first job you get upon completing your education.
4. Consider your skills and competencies, personality, strengths, and weaknesses. Name the type of organization you think you would work best in. Why?
5. Describe the methods the article suggests to look for jobs.
6. Based on what you learned throughout the chapter as well as the advice in the article, identify the options for new graduates outside of regular, full-time employment.

CAREER PERSPECTIVE 2

Wanted: a good personality. Experts say IT skills rank second to good business skills.

By Jack Kazmierski

The number one challenge facing IT directors is the skills shortage, according to UK-based Xephon, an IT research and publishing company. Xephon's conclusions are based on discussions with members of IBEX, an informal association of senior IT professionals from enterprises worldwide, including two from Canada, who participated in the company's third annual "IT Plans" survey.

However, Mark Lillycrop, director of research for Xephon said there was not a lack of workers to fill IT positions. "On the contrary, there's a good supply of technical people coming out of school," he said. "However, the problem is they don't have enough practical business skills."

Julie Kaufman, research manager at IDC Canada in Toronto, agreed. "IT skills come second," she stated. "What's most important is personality and business acumen. People with an eagerness to learn can be taught technical skills. Personality, on the other hand, is something you're either born with or not," she said.

What makes finding workers with the right mix of personality and technical and business skills even more challenging is the number of companies competing for this limited resource, said Lillycrop.

Excerpt from an article of the same title in *Computing Canada*, September 29, 2000, vol. 26, no. 20, p. 28.

Questions

1. Did the message of this article — that personality and "soft skills" are in demand as much as technological skills — surprise you? Why or why not?
2. Write a paragraph that describes what you would recommend to jobseekers to address this problem.
3. In your opinion, which set of skills, soft skills versus technological skills, is more difficult to acquire? Why?
4. Many people highlight their education and technical skills in their résumé when they apply for jobs. Explain how a job seeker might communicate soft skills to a potential employer.

IT's A Wrap

Key Terms in This Chapter

active listening (p. 66)
bidding (p. 51)
bureaucratic/hierarchical structure (p. 54)
centralized structure (p. 54)
communication (p. 64)
conflict (p. 69)
cooperative (p. 51)
corporate workplace setting (p. 50)
decentralized structure (p. 54)
disclosure (p. 66)
division-/department-based organization (p. 55)
groupware (p. 60)
horizontal structure (p. 54)
Information Revolution (p. 47)
initiator (p. 62)
listening (p. 66)
matrix-/project-based organization (p. 55)
minutes (p. 68)
organizational design (p. 53)
organizational structure (p. 53)
project team (p. 58)
responder (p. 63)
SOHO (p. 50)
synergy (p. 60)
team (p. 57)
telecommute (p. 50)
virtual enterprise (p. 52)
workplace setting (p. 50)

1. Create a list of competencies you have acquired through your work in this chapter.
2. Update your portfolio to include examples of your work from this chapter.

Know It!

3. Describe ways that workplace settings have evolved as a result of less expensive, more user-friendly software.
4. Explain how electronic productivity tools contribute to more efficient teamwork.
5. Describe the stages of team development.
6. Define *active listening* and explain how it can contribute to successful team functioning.

Do It!

7. Explain what you can do as a team member to ease the team development process.
8. Create a one-page guide to running effective meetings based on what you learned in this chapter.
9. Think about a recent conflict or disagreement you have experienced. Analyze how you addressed each of the phases in handling the situation. What strategies did you use? How did you implement your solution? What was effective? How could you have improved?

Analyze It!

10. Project team charters take time and effort to create. Do you think that creating one is a worthwhile use of time? Explain.
11. With a partner, select a specific workplace setting (such as a hospital, travel agency, or bank) and investigate the specific hardware and software requirements in that setting. Share your findings with the class.
12. Reflect on a team situation in which you were involved that worked well. What team member roles and types did people play? Explain why it was effective.

CHAPTER 4

Computing Fundamentals

On completion of this chapter, you will be able to:

- identify and describe the components of a workstation and a network, and the features of operating systems;
- describe what information technology looks like in a business setting;
- summarize and describe a variety of issues that relate to the use of information technology in business;
- demonstrate correct procedures when using information technology; and
- solve a variety of problems relating to networks in a business environment.

As you sit at your computer workstation and complete the tasks assigned by your teacher for this course, do you take for granted that all equipment and software will work as expected? Many of us do. In fact, few people really consider what is taking place every time they key in a document, browse the Internet, or print out a project that is due in the next class.

This chapter will provide an overview of the technical aspects of your computer workstation and of networking, as well as things you should consider as you work in a computerized environment. The following areas will be discussed:

- Workstation Components
- Connecting Computers Together
- System Software
- Interacting with Your Computer Environment

Introduction to Chapter Projects

Recall that the Chapter Projects are introduced at the beginning and are to be completed as you work through the chapter. Your teacher will provide you with assessment and evaluation criteria.

CHAPTER PROJECT I

Computer equipment is constantly being upgraded and designed to enhance overall user effectiveness and efficiency. As a student of technology, it is vitally important for you to be as up to date as possible with the changes in this area.

This chapter project requires you to investigate the development of new hardware and system software during the past 12 months. You should focus on the new technological advances being made and the impact they will have on overall organization effectiveness and efficiency. As part of your analysis, prepare your assessment of how outdated equipment could affect overall business planning and operations.

CHAPTER PROJECT II

One of the jobs of a network administrator is to develop plans to map equipment and arrange it for a business. Your project for this chapter requires you to assume that role. As part of this assignment, you must interview the owner or manager of a local business to determine:

- the level of computer use in the business;
- how the equipment is configured;
- what type of network topology is being used;
- how the information flows throughout the business; and
- what requirements the owner or manager has or what changes he or she would like to see to the network.

As you read through this chapter, prepare notes that will assist in the preparation of a plan to improve the overall design of the system. This plan should:

- incorporate a diagram that shows what data are required within the organization and where the data must travel; and
- detail the current configuration and any recommendations you have to change the configuration to make it more efficient.

Present your completed plan to the business.

4.1 Workstation Components

When a PC is connected to a network, it is referred to as a **workstation**. A typical computer workstation comprises hardware that performs one of the following functions:

- *input*: providing data and commands for further processing;
- *processing*: handling each instruction to perform a specific task;
- *output*: displaying the results of the processing in a way that makes sense to humans; or
- *storage*: keeping copies of the files for later retrieval.

Each component performs very specific functions, as you will see. In the pages that follow, we will examine the functions of the various hardware components before seeing how they can be linked in networks.

4.1.1 Input

A computer is essentially an automated productivity tool that requires the user to provide the input with which to perform the various functions for which it is programmed. This section will examine the various methods of inputting data and commands into a computer that allow us to maximize productivity on the job.

Figure 4.1a
QWERTY Keyboard

Figure 4.1b
RIM BlackBerry

Figure 4.1c
Folding Keyboard

- *Keyboard*. The keyboard is probably the most common form of input device. As you press the keys on the board, a plunger connects the electrical wires beneath the keys to send an electrical impulse to the processor. The processor determines, according to the software that is running, what action to take as a result of your pressing the key. It could display a letter or number or other symbol on a screen, or activate a command in the software. The signal can be sent along a cable attached to the back of your computer or by an infrared signal (like your TV remote control) to the computer's processor, depending on how your computer is configured.

  Most keyboards use the QWERTY key arrangement (Figure 4.1a) even though it was originally conceived to prevent the jamming of keys on a typewriter over 100 years ago. This keyboard arrangement has been modified somewhat with the inclusion of function keys and a numeric keypad to allow for input of commands and numeric data in a more efficient manner.

  Computer workstations are not the only devices in the modern office that utilize keyboards to input data. Hand-held devices called **PDAs (personal digital assistants)** that are used to store information such as appointments and addresses might have keyboards built into them (e.g., the BlackBerry by RIM, Figure 4.1b). Other PDAs, such as those for Palm Pilots, have detachable or folding keyboards (Figure 4.1c).

- *Pointing devices*. The second most common form of input device is the mouse or other similar pointing device. The **mouse** is used to give the computer commands, to respond to prompts from software (e.g., "Do you want to save the changes to Chapter 4, Computing Fundamentals?"), or to position the cursor on the screen. The most common form of mouse has a ball that rolls along the underside of the device. Inside the mouse's housing are two rollers, one that senses vertical movement, the other horizontal. Infrared sensors determine the speed at which the mouse is moving. This information is transmitted to the mouse driver (a piece of software you install in your computer), which then tells the processor how to interpret the movements in the program you are running. An optical mouse uses reflected light, instead, to determine the movement of the mouse on almost any surface. Optical mice (Figure 4.2a) have no moving parts and do not have any openings in which dirt can enter, nor do they require mouse pads on your workstation. As with keyboards, mice can be connected to your computer by physical cables or infrared devices. Few, if any, computer workstations come without mice today. One notable exception is the notebook or portable computer, which has one of three pointing devices built into the keyboard area: the touchpad, the trackball, or the pointing stick.

  Touchpads (Figure 4.2b) are small, square, touch-sensitive panels that respond to the touch of a finger to move the cursor on the screen. **Trackballs** (Figure 4.2c) operate like a mouse ball, only the ball is facing upward. **Pointing sticks** (most commonly called TrackPoint after the IBM version of this device) are small eraser-like devices that respond to the user applying pressure in the direction the user wants the cursor to move. Like their mouse counterparts, these three devices have two buttons to perform left- and right-click functions.

  Depending on the industry you are in and the job functions you are required to perform, you might use other pointing devices. **Graphics tablets** (Figure 4.3a) are used extensively in graphic design applications. The user presses on a tablet that functions like a drawing board with a stylus (a pen-like stick with no ink). Another type of pointing device is the **touch screen** (Figure 4.3b) . Computer programs respond when users point to and touch various locations on the screen. A variation of this is the PDA, where users touch the screen using a stylus rather than their finger (due to size limitations) to enter text and select functions. Figure 4.4 summarizes the most common tasks performed on a computer and shows how they are performed using a keyboard or a mouse.

- *Scanning tools*. Many business environments have automated the entry of data using **scanning tools**. By eliminating the need to enter

digiknow

A Jerusalem-based hi-tech company has developed a virtual keyboard that can be projected onto a surface for data input. This device can detect keystrokes and input the data into PCs, PDAs, notebook computers, and other consumer information appliances. Follow the links on the *Business Connections* Web site to find out more about this and other exciting developments in keyboard technology.

Figure 4.2a
An Optical Mouse

Figure 4.2b
A Touchpad

Figure 4.2c
A Trackball

Figure 4.3a

Figure 4.3b

A graphic tablet (a) functions as a drawing board and is used with a stylus, while a touchpad (b) is a screen that the user touches to enter text and select functions.

data manually, error rates are reduced and data entry is quicker and more efficient. One of the earliest scanning methods was developed by the banking community to scan and enter the **MICR (magnetic ink character recognition)** numbers located at the bottom of cheques. These numbers, which represent the bank, the branch, and the account number, are preprinted on cheques according to strict specifications before the customer receives them. When the cheque is processed, the bank teller needs only enter the amount.

Another common scanning device is used with **bar codes** and **Universal Product Codes** (UPCs). The use of bar codes has led to the automation of many industries, with this code being the key to a sophisticated database management system for inventory, ordering,

Figure 4.4
Methods To Access Software Tasks

Task	Mouse	Keyboard	Menus
Select the Menu bar	Point and click once	ALT + underlined letter on menu	Nil
Open new document	Click on "new document" icon	CTRL-N	File/New
Save	Click on the "save" icon	CTRL-S	File/Save
Print	Click on the "print" icon	CTRL-P	File/Print
Select All	Click and drag	CTRL-A	Edit/Select All
Cut	Right-click and click on "cut"	CTRL-X	Edit/Cut
Copy	Right-click and click on "copy"	CTRL-C	Edit/Copy
Paste	Right-click and click on "paste"	CTRL-V	Edit/Paste
Undo	N/A	CTRL-Z	Edit/Undo
Offer spelling suggestions for a misspelled word (in Microsoft Office)	Right-click mouse while your cursor is on the misspelled word	F7	Tools/Spelling
Close a window	Click on the "X" in the top, right-hand corner	CTRL-F4	File/Exit
Maximize a window	Click on the box icon in the top, right-hand corner	ALT-F10	

Note: The commands listed under Menus can be accessed either by using a mouse and clicking on the menu and options presented, or by using the keyboard. If you use the keyboard, hold down the Alt key and press the underlined letter in each menu or menu item (e.g. Alt/F for File menu).

and delivery tracking. One example of the use of bar codes in delivery tracking is the Xpresspost service from Canada Post (see Figure 4.5). You will also notice a bar code on the back of this book. It is used by the publisher to manage inventory and order processing.

Other scanners work in conjunction with **optical character recognition (OCR)** software to convert printed documents into digital text that can be manipulated with word-processing software.

There are many other input devices that can be used for specialized applications and more are being developed all the time, including voice-recognition and handwriting-recognition devices and devices that rely on your senses of sight and movement to send instructions to the processor. What will they think of next?

digiknow

A variety of input devices can be used to perform the same task. Figure 4.4 illustrates how different input devices can perform identical tasks in a Windows environment.

There are many other shortcuts available for users in all operating environments. Develop a list of the "Top 10 Shortcuts" for your system and your future use.

Figure 4.5

GETTING IT

1. Define *input*.
2. Describe what takes place when you depress a key on a keyboard.
3. Describe the various pointing devices and where they are best used in different business settings.
4. Explain how graphics tablets and touch screens are used to input data.
5. Indicate where the following scanning technologies are utilized:
   a. MICR
   b. OCR
   c. UPC

4.1.2 Processing

Figure 4.6

This position of this silicon chip on the knob of a gearshift shows you how small a CPU is. A motherboard appears in the background.

Once you enter information using one or more of the input devices mentioned above, it is the processor's job to transform that input into some form of output you can utilize. The **CPU** (**central processing unit**, or, more commonly, "the processor") performs this function. The CPU performs all necessary calculations, executes instructions contained in programs, and communicates with all the other components of your workstation to perform tasks such as saving files, displaying output, and printing documents. Modern CPUs are extremely complex, executing millions of instructions each second. Their remarkably complex electronic circuitry is placed on a single silicon chip (see Figure 4.6), and this microprocessor is located on the motherboard along with other components in a typical workstation. There are numerous manufacturers of computer processors today, including Intel (Pentium® and Itanium® chips), AMD (Athlon®), IBM (PowerPC®), and Motorola.

4.1.3 Output

digiknow

The speed of a processor is measured in megahertz (MHz) or gigahertz (GHz). The faster the processor, the higher the number of GHz. A 2.0-GHz processor operates much faster than a 1.0-GHz processor, for example.

Once you have entered the information into the computer and it has been processed, it is not very useful unless you can see the results. "Output" refers to the visible results of the computer's processing operations. It can be worthwhile information or it can be unintelligible chatter, depending on what has taken place in the processing unit. You, as the computer user, must make that determination.

Output devices allow our senses of sight, hearing, and even touch to be engaged in the work produced. Hard copy output allows us to touch the finished product as with printed documents. Soft copy is seen on the monitor or stored on disk. Let us first look at the devices that allow us to view the output.

4.1.3.1 Monitors

Get Connected

Through the links at www.pearsoned.ca/businessconnections, locate the sites of chip manufacturers and investigate the advances being made in chip technology. Prepare a comparison chart of the features of the new processors that power today's computers.

Once the processor has dealt with the data and instructions, the data are sent through a video adapter (or video card/graphics card) on the **motherboard**—the computer's printed circuit board—where they are formatted for display on a monitor. This image is not a permanent record of the information; you need to print or save it to have it for future reference. There are two basic types of display units on today's computers: CRTs and LCDs.

CRTs (**cathode ray tubes**) look like small television sets (see Figure 4.7) and use similar technology to generate the image you see on the screen. A small electron gun at the back of the unit shoots a stream of electrons at the screen's phosphorescent surface. In a colour monitor, there are three guns, one each for red, blue, and green, which together make up all the colours you see. CRTs are inexpensive to manufacture, but use more electricity and take up lots of room on a desktop.

LCD (**liquid crystal display**) or flat panel monitors (Figure 4.8) are in more and more offices due to advances in technology and the reduced cost to purchase them. They are most common on notebook computers. LCD panels contain small liquid crystals sandwiched between two or more pieces of polarized glass. As electrical currents are applied to the crystals, they untwist, changing the angle of the light and forming the images you see on the screen. LCD panels use much less energy but are more sensitive to swings in temperature.

Monitors are compared in terms of their size, resolution, and image-processing capabilities. Typical workstation monitors range from 15" (38 cm) to 21" (53 cm) in size. This is measured diagonally, so the actual width of the screen is narrower than this. Those whose jobs require intensive graphic work tend to use larger monitors. Images on the screen are measured in pixels, or picture elements. The closer the pixels are placed together on the screen, the higher the resolution will be. Screen resolutions are described in terms of the number of pixels across by the number of pixels down, e.g., 1024 x 768. The dot pitch of a monitor is another measure of its image quality. Dot pitch indicates the diagonal distance between like-coloured phosphor dots on a display screen. Measured in millimeters, the dot pitch is one of the principal characteristics that determines the quality of display monitors. The lower the number, the crisper the image. A screen with a 0.28-mm dot pitch or less is considered good.

The refresh rate is another measure of monitor quality. The higher the number of times the image refreshes, or is redrawn by the computer, each second, the less flicker the user will see on the screen. The standard refresh rate for new monitors according to the Video Electronics Standards Association is 75 Hz (hertz) or 75 times per second (Webopedia).

Figure 4.8
An LCD Monitor

List the advantages and disadvantages of an LCD monitor.

Figure 4.7
A CRT Monitor

Indicate the advantages and disadvantages of a CRT monitor.

digiknow

The CRT you have on your computer system here in Canada operates in a different manner from those manufactured for sale in South America or any other nation in the southern hemisphere. The electron beams in a CRT monitor are pulled back and forth by the earth's magnetic fields: the North and South Poles. You can still use your monitor in the opposite hemisphere, but the colours and image will be affected slightly. (*Mirror Magazine,* 2002).

Get Connected

Extensive research has been undertaken to find new and exciting applications for liquid crystal display technology. Visit the *Business Connections* Web site at www.pearsoned.ca/businessconnections to find out more about this technology and where it might take us in the future.

IT In Action

Displays Get Skinny

Imagine walking into your local department store and seeing the poster advertising one of this week's specials change before your eyes. No, you don't need glasses. What you are seeing could be one of the new forms of display coming to a retail location near you. Flat panel displays, which look much like ordinary poster signs, have been developed by Gyricon, a Xerox company, in their Palo Alto Research Center in California, and by E Ink in Cambridge, Massachusetts. Gyricon expects to make inroads into the market that serves large department stores that typically spend thousands of dollars each year updating the posters gracing their walls and aisle displays. The e-paper signs can be updated electronically from remote computers (wirelessly!) and could, over time, save large organizations significant advertising costs. They are currently only available in black and white, but advances in research may see colour displays down the road.

The displays use significantly less energy than any other form of display in current use. Two AA batteries could power a display for more than a year. The technology is being developed to one day allow the displays to be rolled up or folded without damaging the systems that bring the images to life.

Both companies are using similar, but also different, technology to achieve the same results. E Ink's product has millions of tiny microcapsules containing positively charged white particles and negatively charged black particles. Depending on the electrical field applied to the different parts of the display, the white or black capsules face outward creating the image. Gyricon's SmartPaper™ uses tiny beads to achieve comparable results. Half of each bead is white; the other half black. Again, depending on the charge applied, the white or black half faces outward.

Will we see these being used with computer systems one day? Only when they become bendable and the price comes down, according to industry experts.

Questions

1. Explain the impact that this new technology will have on the computer hardware industry.
2. Describe other applications you can foresee for this technology.

Get Connected

Start at the *Business Connections* Web site www.pearsoned.ca/businessconnections to locate updated information on flat displays. Prepare a short summary of your findings to submit to your teacher.

4.1.3.2 Printers

To get a hard copy of the computer processor's output you can print it on one of many types of printers. Two basic forms of printer technology are used to create permanent records of output: impact printers and non-impact printers.

Impact printers form images by striking a hammer against a ribbon, which then hits the paper, transferring the ink to the paper surface in a manner that is similar to the one used by typewriters. Two forms of printers fall into this category: *line printers,* which print thousands of lines of text each minute and are usually connected to large mainframe computers; and *dot* *matrix printers* (Figure 4.9), which are smaller than line printers and create letters with tiny dots to produce "near letter quality" images. Both of these printers use continuous printer paper with tractor feed at the sides that may or may not be removed after printing. They are typically used in large-volume operations, where image quality is not the primary concern to the computer user and application involved (e.g., billing customers).

Non-impact printers have replaced most of the impact printers in today's workplaces. The two most common forms of non-impact printers in use today are *laser printers* and *ink-jet printers*. Laser printers (Figure 4.10) work much the same as a photocopier. Once the data are received from the computer processor, a laser beam is used to charge a rotating drum where the image is to appear. The drum picks up toner in these areas as it rotates past the toner bed. The paper in the printer is negatively charged, so it attracts the toner as the rollers carry it through. The paper and toner are then fused using heat and rollers, virtually stamping the image into the paper. The drum is cleaned or discharged after depositing the toner and the process repeats. Laser printers are ideal for high-volume copying. Colour laser printers are also available, and as technology improves and costs come down, they are becoming more economical to use for short runs where setting up printing presses is not feasible. New laser printers produce very high quality images and can produce up to 50 pages per minute, making them economical in large volume operations.

Ink-jet printers (Figure 4.11) are an economical alternative to laser printers and are ideal in situations where colour output is required. Ink-jet printers spray ink onto the paper as it passes beneath the toner cartridge in tiny dot patterns that are not discernible to the naked eye. They do not print as fast as laser printers (less than 20 pages per minute) but the up-front cost of acquiring an ink-jet printer is very low. Advances in technology have made it possible to use ink-jet printers to produce high quality photographic output at relatively low cost.

Some offices might use a **multifunction printer** where space is at a premium. These output devices combine printer, fax machine, and sometimes a scanner and copier into one unit. They are ideal for small or home office operations. In specialized engineering offices or where maps are the desired output, **plotters** are used. These devices produce large, wide-bed printed images using pens that can create the fine details necessary in drafting, blueprints, and map making.

Figure 4.9
A Dot Matrix Printer

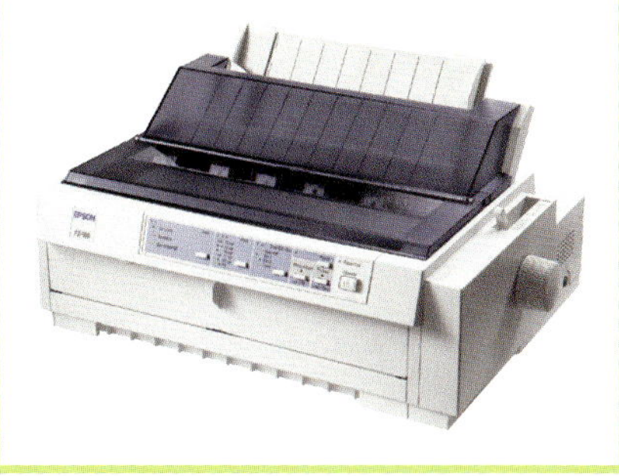

Figure 4.10
A Laser Printer

Figure 4.11
An Ink-jet Printer

4.1.3.3 Audio Output

The phrase "You've got mail" is almost a cliché in our culture. This is a form of audio output. Audio output may be used to hear the results of the

List three jobs that should be done on each of the printers shown in Figure 4.9, 4.10, and 4.11 and indicate why that particular printer would be used in each case.

data you have processed. Most PCs and computer workstations contain sound cards that process the output from the processor and send the signals to speakers. This would enable the user to collaborate with others using audio/video conferencing or Internet telephony, or to utilize speech recognition programs in the workplace. For more information on these forms of electronic communication, see Chapter 8.

GETTING IT

1. List the main functions of the CPU.
2. Explain how a CPU's speed is measured.
3. Explain why output devices are necessary.
4. Describe the function of a video card.
5. Define *pixels*. Explain how they affect image quality on display mechanisms.
6. Explain hard copy. Soft copy.
7. Where do impact printers fit in today's high-tech business environment?
8. Draw a diagram/flowchart to describe the process a laser printer uses to create images.
9. Compare the advantages of non-impact printers over impact printers.
10. Describe a multifunction printer.
11. Name two types of non-impact printers and explain how each functions.
12. Explain where a plotter is used.
13. Audio output is most often used in home PC systems. Explain how it can be used in a business setting.

4.1.4 Storage

To maintain a copy of the computer processor's work, you must store the data or they will be lost, regardless of whether you have a hard copy printout or not. There are wide varieties of storage devices on the market today and in many cases your choice of storage is contingent on the intended use of your data. Do you have to take it or use it anywhere or can it stay at the office? The size of the file(s) is also a factor. An overview of the most common storage devices and their use appears on p. 7 in Chapter 1 of this text. Take a moment to review those devices.

A typical workstation in a business environment may contain a floppy disk drive, a CD-/DVD-ROM drive, and a hard drive. Additional storage is also available on the network server for authorized users. (Newer Macintosh computers and some notebook computers do not have floppy disk drives.) The floppy and hard disk devices store data magnetically. Let us examine the process of storing files on these devices.

The magnetic disk inside the protective housing of a floppy disk and the surface of the platters inside a hard drive are polarized, enabling them to store encoded information. Each disk contains circular bands called tracks that are divided into sectors (Figure 4.12). Read/write heads hover over the surface of the disks as they spin in the disk drive. The heads move to a clear location on the disk where they write the data transferred from the computer's processor. The computer's operating system keeps track of the data on a disk by writing a virtual table of contents on the disk.

Figure 4.12
Anatomy of a Floppy Disk

In a standard Windows environment this table of contents is called a **FAT** (**file allocation table**). Hard drives contain numerous platters encased in hard plastic, each with two read/write heads (one for each side of the platter). They spin much faster and accept significantly more data than a floppy disk. They are also hermetically sealed and do not stop spinning between read/writes. It is very important to keep floppy disks free of dust and other particles that interfere with the read/write heads doing their job.

To protect the data on a floppy disk from being written over, you can open the write protect tab on the disk housing. When the disk drive attempts to write to the disk, the light shining through the tab will signal to the computer that this disk is protected.

To protect your floppy disks from damage, follow these simple guidelines:

- Do not touch the surface of the disk inside the housing. The oils and dirt on your fingers can damage the magnetic coating and your files.
- Avoid magnetic fields, such as the sensors used in library entrances/exits. These magnetic fields can erase or jumble your data.
- Avoid eating, drinking, or smoking around your workstation.
- Keep disks in a temperature- and humidity-controlled environment.
- Do not expose the surface of the disk to contaminants such as dust or skin cells.

ON THE CASE

Going, Going, Gone?

When you delete the files on your computer's hard drive, are they really gone? Not necessarily. Until you empty the contents of the Recycle Bin or Trash Can the deleted files are still contained in these folders. However, the original data are still on the hard drive and can be located and retrieved using the right software. When you erase a file, only the instructions, or "pointers," telling the operating

ON THE CASE (continued)

system where to find the file are erased, rendering the file "invisible." The data still exist, but the operating system is unable to find them because the space occupied by the file is labelled available.

The only way to completely erase data is to overwrite them. The operating system will eventually overwrite data on the hard drive that have no pointers associated with them. The longer the unpointed file remains on the hard drive, the greater the chance it will be overwritten. Software makers have developed utility programs that will permanently erase files by overwriting them, some as many as 70 times!

Questions

1. Explain why anyone would want to retrieve previously deleted files.
2. List the type of organizations (business, government, etc.) that would be involved in the retrieving of data.

IT In Action

Storage on a Keychain?

Remember the last time you had to make a presentation and the file you had was too large to load onto a floppy disk to carry to the presentation area? Or you did not have your own notebook computer to store the presentation on? Well, new advances in storage technology may make this frustration a thing of the past.

A number of manufacturers have taken the technology that allows us to store digital camera images on a flash card and extended it to the personal computer. These memory sticks plug into the USB (Universal Serial Bus) port of your desktop or notebook computer, where they are recognized as another disk drive by most operating systems. When you are ready to save the file, you simply copy it to the portable memory device on the USB port and away you go. Transferring the file to the next computer is just as easy — just plug, drag, and drop.

These devices are often referred to as "keychain" memory (because of the ability to carry them on your keychain). Although people use CDs to transport large multimedia presentations, memory sticks have brought the portability back to storage that we lost with trying to store large multimedia, presentation, music, or photo files on floppy disks.

Figure 4.13
Memory Stick Devices

Most workstations also contain a CD-/DVD-ROM drive that is primarily used for loading programs or viewing the contents of the disk that have been saved at the factory or by a CD writing device. Some workstations also have CD-RW drives that many people use for storage and backup purposes. Depending on the storage medium chosen, each sector of the disk can be written to once (CD-R) or multiple times (CD-RW). With the ability to save over 650 Mb of data, the CD is one of the most economical forms of portable storage per Mb.

GETTING IT

1. Explain how information is stored on magnetic (i.e., floppy/hard) disks.
2. Explain how the surface of a disk is divided for storage purposes.
3. Describe how you can protect the data on a floppy disk from being written over.
4. What other steps can a person take to ensure data on a disk are not erased or damaged?
5. Define *FAT*.
6. Describe the circumstances under which you would choose to use a floppy disk, a CD-R, or keychain memory as described in this chapter. For example, when would you save to a CD versus a floppy disk? Why would keychain memory sticks be a better choice? Be sure to consider all possible situations in your answer.

4.2 Connecting Computers Together

When companies, small and large, want to make the most of their human and computer resources, they look at networking their computers. A **network** links two or more computers so that they can exchange data, and share resources and peripheral devices such as printers and scanners. There are many advantages to connecting these devices and people together.

4.2.1 Why Network?

When computers, peripheral devices (such as printers or scanners), and people are connected together there are numerous advantages, which can be grouped into three main categories:

- *Reduced costs.* Computer networks enable companies to share expensive equipment and thus reduce costs. Rather than having printers and other devices connected to individual computers and users taking the data to their computers for further processing, networks allow people to access these devices regardless of their physical location (as long as the devices have been configured to accept jobs from that workstation!). Large geographically spread networks (WANs, which will be discussed in more detail later) allow users to access high-speed mainframe computing power and lightning-fast printers at a central location.

- *Sharing software and data.* Computer networks allow users to share data and software that have been loaded on a central file server or another computer on the network. Many programs can be purchased with network licences that allow all network users to have access to the programs without having to install them on each workstation. Other shared data, such as clipart libraries or documents that can be downloaded by all students in a class, can also be stored on a file server. This eliminates the need to provide copies to all users to load on their individual PCs or workstations.
- *Collaboration.* One of the most important facets of network communication is the ability for users to collaborate on projects. Special software called groupware, e.g., Lotus® Notes or Microsoft® Exchange and Centrinity FirstClass®, can be installed on the network that enables individual users to enter appointments on a group calendar so that they can schedule meetings when everyone is available. Other groupware enables users to collaborate on documents and other files, so that each member of the group can "have their say." As you will read in Chapter 8, networks have enabled users to take advantage of e-mail, instant messaging, and other collaborative tools that have increased productivity in many organizations.

GETTING IT

1. Define *network.*
2. Explain how networking can reduce corporate expenditures.
3. Describe how networks enable users to share data and software.
4. Describe a situation where collaborative software would be useful in a networked environment.
5. Discuss with a partner how networks enhance teamwork and communication. Share your thoughts with another set of partners.

4.2.2 Local Area Networks

Now that we have discussed why companies might consider networking their human and physical resources, a closer look at the various network types is required. A **local area network** (**LAN**) is a group of computers that are connected in a small geographic region, such as within the same office building. The organization's computers and peripheral devices (e.g., printers, scanners, and fax machines) are connected so that users can access these devices and share data resources. Each computer and peripheral device is a **node**, or connection points, within the network. When a PC is connected to a network, it is referred to as a workstation. Each workstation and peripheral device is identified separately on the network with a unique name and identifying number. Even the simplest network has data transfer rates of at least 10 Mbps (over six times faster than high-speed modems) and faster networks are becoming more common. Four factors need to be considered when putting together a network: the necessary hardware, the software, the number of people using the network, and the requirements of the users.

To network computers together, they must have the hardware to support the required connections. Each workstation must be equipped with a **network interface card** (**NIC**) (see Figure 4.14) attached to the motherboard. The NIC is a computer circuit board that allows an individual computer or workstation to be connected to a network. It controls the communication between the individual workstation's RAM and the network cable. It also works in conjunction with special network cabling to physically connect the devices. The type of NIC depends on the network being installed, but the most common type is an Ethernet card.

Figure 4.14
Network Interface Card

To physically connect the workstations to the LAN, network cabling is required. The cable creates the backbone through which all communications travel, like the central nervous system in your own spine. Network cable comes in a number of varieties (Figure 4.15).

- *Twisted pair cable.* This is similar to the type of wire used to connect your telephone to the local telephone carrier. Within the cable you find four pairs of insulated wires twisted together to reduce electrical interference when transmitting data and other communications. One of the best forms of twisted pair wiring, category 5 (cat-5), can handle data transmissions up to 100 Mbps.
- *Coaxial cable.* This is similar to the cable that brings television transmissions into millions of homes around the world. It contains a central wire surrounded by insulation and a layer of braided wire around that. Together they shield the wire from electrical interference.
- *Fibre-optic cable.* This is one of the fastest forms of data transmission. It transmits data along very thin fibres of glass using pulses of light. This form of cable can carry more data for longer distances than either twisted pair or coaxial cable.

Figure 4.15

a) Twisted pair cable

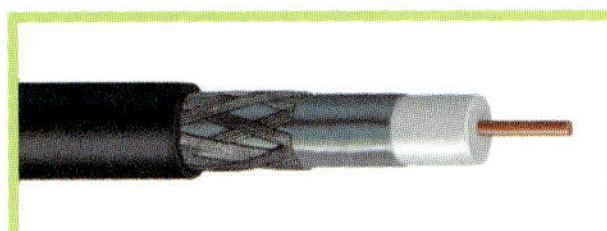

b) Coaxial cable

c) Fibre-optic cable

Networks are built on these physical media.

Some networks work without wires. These wireless LANs utilize infrared signals to transmit data to and from individual nodes on the network. The drawback to infrared signals is that the devices must be within "line of sight" — there must be nothing blocking the signal transmission or reception and they are limited to approximately 30 m to be effective. Other wireless networks use radio waves to transmit data. Because radio signals can be easily intercepted, most wireless LANs will use technology to spread the signal over a random series of frequencies to prevent interception and theft

> **Get Connected**
>
> Companies are continually striving to offer quicker, more powerful ways to transfer data and images over networks and the Internet. Investigate four advances in technology at www.pearsoned.ca/businessconnections. Record this information in your notes.

of data. Radio-based LANs have a range of approximately 300 m. Recent advances allow wire-free networks to utilize infrared light to transmit data and send signals up to 3 km.

Once the workstations and peripheral devices are connected together physically, are you ready to get networking? No. You still need to install the appropriate software to enable the devices to talk to one another over the system. Before discussing specific software requirements, you must first decide whether your network is a **peer-to-peer (P2P) network** or a **client/server network**.

P2P networks treat all computers as equals on the network. Each computer user determines what files and which peripheral devices they are willing to share with the other network members. P2P networks are very easy to set up. In fact, your computer's operating system (e.g., Windows® 95/98/NT/XP, UNIX, Linux, and Mac O/S) includes this option as a standard feature. One drawback to these networks is speed; they tend to slow down with increased traffic. Another drawback is lack of centralized control; individuals can make changes and each machine is then susceptible to tampering, i.e., the data are not secure. These networks are ideal for SOHO (small office, home office) operations or businesses that do not need to connect more than 10 or 20 computers.

Client/server networks are more common. In this configuration, one computer is designated as the file server from which all shared devices, files, and programs are controlled. A server is usually a high-speed unit with significant file storage space to house shared programs and user files. The server also has the **network operating system (NOS)** loaded on it to run the network. The NOS provides for the operation and management of the network.

Figure 4.16

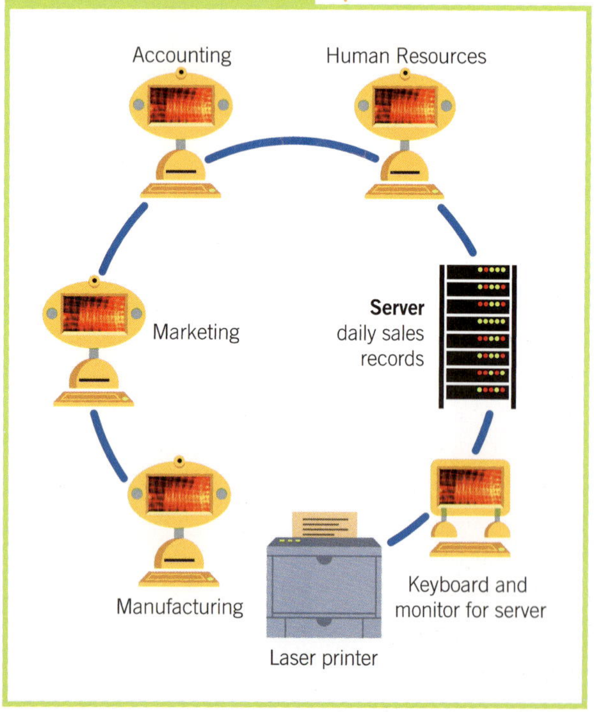

LANs transform individual computers into one gigantic computer system.

The clients are the individual workstations and peripheral devices (or nodes) that access the programs, files, and other networked devices through the file server.

In a client/server model, a NOS is required over and above the individual operating system loaded on individual workstations. Like your PC's operating system, the NOS determines which files to retrieve, where to send print commands, etc. However, it does this for many workstations and coordinates the communication between all devices. Examples of common NOS software are Novell NetWare and Microsoft® Windows® 2000 Server or Windows.NET® 2003 Server.

There is one more important distinction to make when discussing how LANs are configured. The network's **topology**, or physical layout, is also a decision a network administrator must make before the wiring is in place and the software installed.

4.2.2.1 LAN Topologies

All networks do not act the same way in carrying data from one location to another. A problem, called **contention**, occurs when two or more workstations try to access the LAN at the same time. This could result in a collision where data could be corrupted. The solution to this problem rests in the network's topology, or physical arrangement. There are four forms of LAN topology: bus, star, ring and tree. Each will be examined in more detail below and is shown in Figure 4.17.

Figure 4.17
Network Topologies

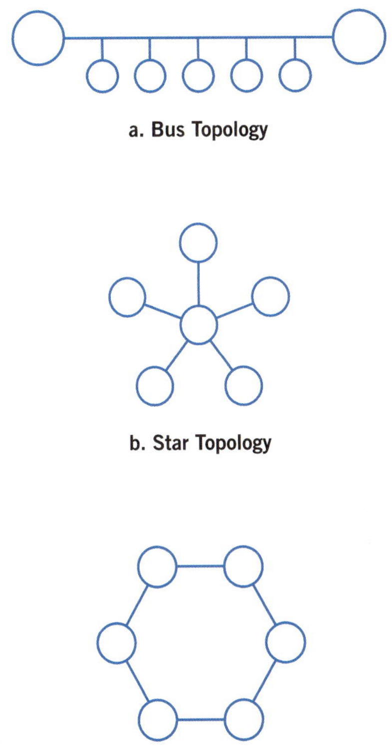

a. Bus Topology
b. Star Topology
c. Ring Topology

- *Bus topology*. A bus topology connects the server, the individual workstations, and the peripheral devices to the network along a single bus route in a "daisy chain" (think about the way Christmas lights are typically arranged). Information travels along the cable until it reaches its destination node. At the end of the bus, special connectors called terminators are attached. Contention is dealt with using special software that determines what is to take place if and when a collision occurs. One limitation of a bus topology is that it is difficult to add nodes along the route. Another limitation of this topology is that if there is a breach of connection anywhere along the way, the entire line goes down, so although they are very cheap and easy to set up, they are not very reliable.
- *Star topology*. In a star network configuration, a hub is inserted to which individual nodes are connected. The hub acts as a transfer station in that it takes a message from one node and passes it on to the desired node. To add users, simply run a cable from the hub to the node. Once the hub is filled, other hubs can be attached to increase the size of the network. Again, special software is used to manage collisions.
- *Ring topology*. Like a bus network, ring networks connect all the nodes in a daisy chain fashion. The difference is that they create a circle; the end of the chain is connected to the first node and there is no terminus point. To send data around the ring, a token travels along the backbone. As the token passes each node, instructions are either taken from the token or added to it to be transmitted to another node along the way. Only the node with the token can send/receive data. This can affect network efficiency, depending on where the token is and what data are being sent/received. When you look at a ring network, it resembles a star network in that all cabling is attached to a hub. The difference lies in how the data travel from node to node. Fibre-optic networks also work on this model and have

redundancy built in within a double ring, so if one goes down, the data are transferred onto the other ring.

- *Tree topology.* One of the most common configurations is a combination of the star and bus topologies. Within a network, stars are created linking nodes in specific areas. The hub of each of these stars is connected along a bus backbone to maximize flexibility. These are sometimes referred to as "tree" topologies because of the similarity to a "trunk" backbone as provided by the bus and the stars "branching" off the bus.

Figure 4.17 (continued)
Network Topologies

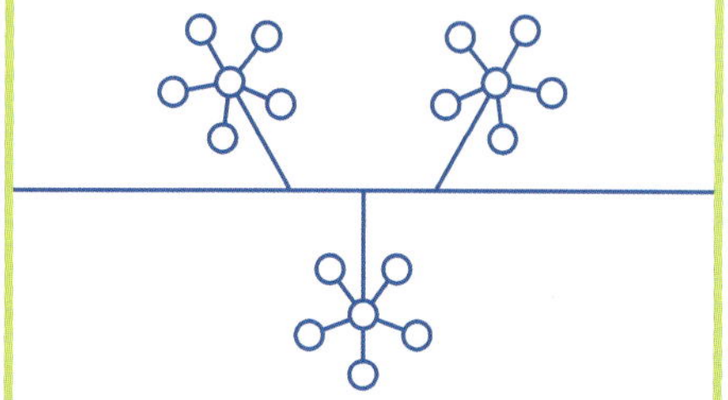

d. Tree Topology

In a business environment, LANs are ideal when you have one physical location to place all the workstations and peripheral devices. However, many organizations have multiple locations and individual LANs must communicate with each other over greater distances. This creates the need for MANs (metropolitan area networks) and WANs (wide area networks).

GETTING IT

1. Define *LAN*.
2. Explain what a node on a network is.
3. Define *NIC* and explain the function it performs on a networked workstation.
4. Describe the three main forms of network cabling in use today.
5. Explain how networks can work without wires.
6. What is the difference between a P2P and a client/server network?
7. Explain what is meant by "contention" on a network.
8. Describe where a daisy chain might appear in a LAN.
9. Describe what a hub does in a star network.
10. Create a document on common network topologies that describes the most common network topologies. Which is the most commonly used and why?

4.2.3 Metropolitan Area Networks and Wide Area Networks

A **metropolitan area network** (**MAN**) connects two or more LANs within a limited geographic region such as a city. Telephone companies typically provide the service to connect the locations using fibre-optic cable. For example, the London Metropolitan Network connects 33 university and college locations within the greater London, England, region. Beyond the scope of the MAN is the **wide area network** (**WAN**).

WANs use long-distance communication tools to link computers in widely dispersed regions. In a WAN each LAN is a node on the network. The backbone through which all communications occur is made up of fibre-optic cable and satellites — the elements of the standard telecommunications services around the world. WANs allow individuals within large corporations with global locations and governments to communicate easily with each other.

Today, we find LANs and WANs communicating with each other on a daily basis. In order to make this happen, bridges, gateways, and routers are employed. **Bridges** connect networks of the same type. **Gateways** connect networks of different kinds. And **routers** connect several networks, choosing the most efficient route for communications to travel. For example, Government of Canada employees located in offices across the country use computers connected to a LAN. They can access files located at another location through the WAN so that they do not have to duplicate all the files at each individual location.

4.2.4 Business Applications for WANs

As we conclude this discussion of networks, it is important to see where WANs are used in business to improve overall productivity while protecting the integrity of the data that are transmitted. Many corporations use WANs to enable their personnel to communicate with others in the organization in a secure environment. Collaboration on new product designs can be maximized, protecting the data from interception. With the increased speeds that telecommunications providers are installing via fibre-optic cable, users can send data files quickly and easily so as not to lose precious time developing new products and ideas.

WANs are also ideal for collecting data from scattered locations. As you check out of your local Wal-Mart, for example, the record of your purchases is sent via satellite to the central computers, so that inventory can be managed and sales analyzed. The cash register is really a point-of-sale terminal or computer that collects the data. This helps Wal-Mart to ensure that their stores are always stocked with enough items for your shopping convenience.

Another important business application for WANs is the electronic exchange of information between partner organizations using **EDI (electronic data interchange)**. Companies that choose to partner in this fashion conduct all business over electronic channels. For example, when the General Motors plant in Oshawa needs to buy spark plugs, they send the purchase order to their supplier electronically. The supplier fills the order and then transmits the invoice for the spark plugs electronically over the same network. Payment is also sent electronically from buyer to vendor through its bank. No "paper" ever changes hands. An electronic paper trail exists, however, to allow the parties (including their auditors) to track and verify orders and payments. This form of data interchange has reduced the cycle time for companies ordering and receiving critical components for production of goods and services in many industries. For more information on how business has changed with the introduction of information technology, refer to Chapter 10.

GETTING IT

1. Define a *MAN* and explain where it is best suited.
2. Define a *WAN*. What organizations are the biggest users of WANs?
3. Describe three business applications for WANs. Use your school board as one application.
4. Explain EDI and how it makes commerce more efficient.

4.3 System Software

When you start up a PC or network workstation, your primary concern should be that of using the applications, not whether the RAM memory is being utilized efficiently, or how the computer will process the instructions you send it to save, print, or copy the file. The system software looks after all these details and more. **System software** includes the operating system and the utility programs that enable you to manage your files and connect to peripheral devices, and that coordinate your use of the computer with other very important tasks.

4.3.1 Functions of the Operating System

Every computing device, from your PDA to supercomputing workstations, has an operating system (OS). Its job is to keep the hardware running efficiently and to allow communication with the hardware. Running continuously in the background, the OS performs the following functions:

- *File management.* As you start up or launch a program on your computer, the OS locates the files on your hard drive and loads them into RAM for your use. It performs the same function when you request a file, such as a report you are writing for school, from one of the disk drives.
- *Peripheral connections.* One of the most complex tasks the OS performs on your system is the coordination of tasks as your computer's processor makes requests of other devices. For example, displaying your work on a monitor or sending a file to print are basic but very necessary tasks, and it is the responsibility of the OS to ensure that they are carried out correctly.

- *Coordination of tasks.* A computer can only perform one task at a time. However, it can process millions of instructions each second, so it seems to the user that the computer is doing many things at once. When you multitask, you have numerous programs open and operating at one time. For example, you might be keying a document for class tomorrow, listening to a Web broadcast through your Web browser, and flipping over to a game of Scrabble from time to time to improve your word power. Each program is up and running, yet because the computer can only process one instruction at a time, the OS must coordinate what instructions to process and the order in which to process them.
- *Memory management.* When you open an application on your computer, it is allocated a particular portion of the RAM memory from which to function. The OS must ensure that, as you perform multiple tasks, the programs being used do not encroach on the space allocated to other programs or tasks. But computers only have a limited amount of RAM, you say. Correct. Your OS uses a trick called virtual memory to convince the computer that it has more memory than it actually has. **Virtual memory** is an area on the computer's hard drive that is set aside to increase the memory available to run programs. The OS divides the files into pages that can be swapped back and forth between the virtual memory area and RAM as needed, to perform the functions of the program that you request.
- *User management.* Another function of the OS is to authenticate users who attempt to access the computer or networked workstation. An OS can be configured to ask for a user name and password to prevent unauthorized access to the computer. Even a personal PC has this capability through its system software. This helps to protect the data that reside on the unit's hard drive or in the network space. Protecting your login name and password is vital to ensure program and data integrity.

4.3.2 Utility Programs

Utility programs are important for overall system maintenance and user interaction with software and peripheral devices. Many utility programs come with the OS, whereas others are purchased and installed separately. The most important and most frequently used utility programs will be discussed here.

- *File management.* As discussed in Chapter 1, you should organize your files into folders for ease of access and maintenance. The file management utility that comes with your OS enables you to do just this. In Windows 98, you would launch Windows Explorer to perform these functions. Newer versions of Windows (i.e., Windows XP) have incorporated Windows Explorer functions into My Computer to access files and folders (see Figure 4.18).

When you are in the file manager, you can easily see the individual folders and files designated by the application in which they were created. You can create new folders, move and copy files between folders and disks, examine the contents of files (e.g., photographs), delete files and folders, or even start programs.

- *Disk maintenance.* As discussed in Chapter 1, it is important to perform periodic maintenance on your computer to keep it running as efficiently as possible. Two disk utilities that are very helpful are disk scanning and disk defragmenting. Disk scanning will check the selected disk (floppy or hard drive) for errors and bad sectors that could interfere with saving and retrieving files. Many errors can be fixed automatically by this utility. The disk defragmenting utility (see Figure 4.19) rearranges the data on the disk so that it operates more efficiently. How is a disk fragmented? Every time you load a program, or save a file, the disk looks for the next available chunk of disk space on which to save the file. Many times, your files are saved in numerous bits on the disk and are reassembled when you call for them off the drive. By rear-

Figure 4.18
Windows XP

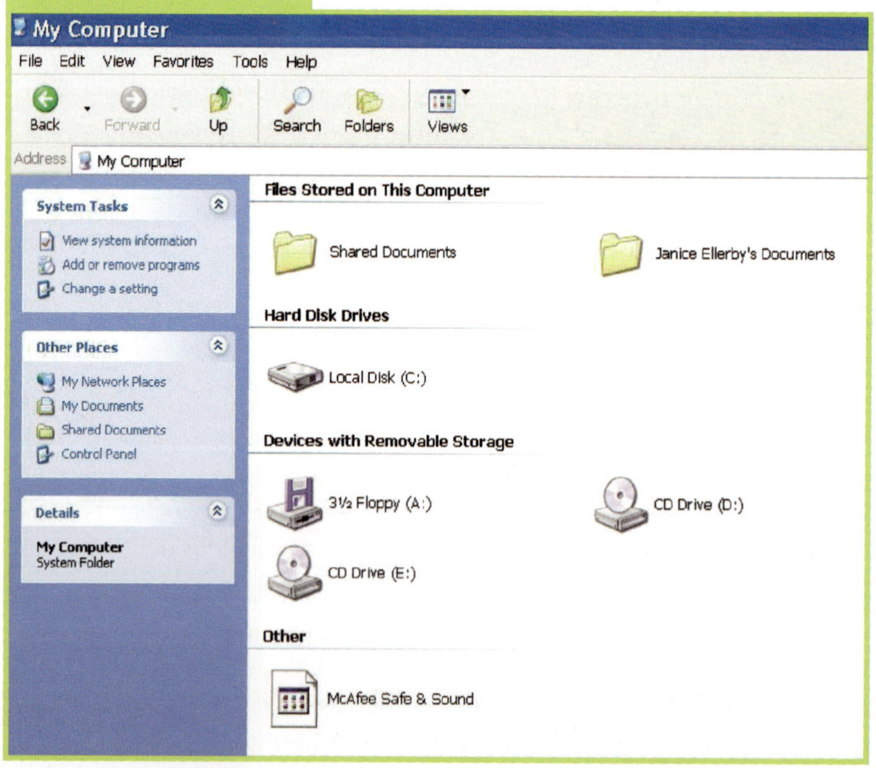

In newer versions of Windows, you access files and folders through My Computer.

Figure 4.19

Disk Defragmenter

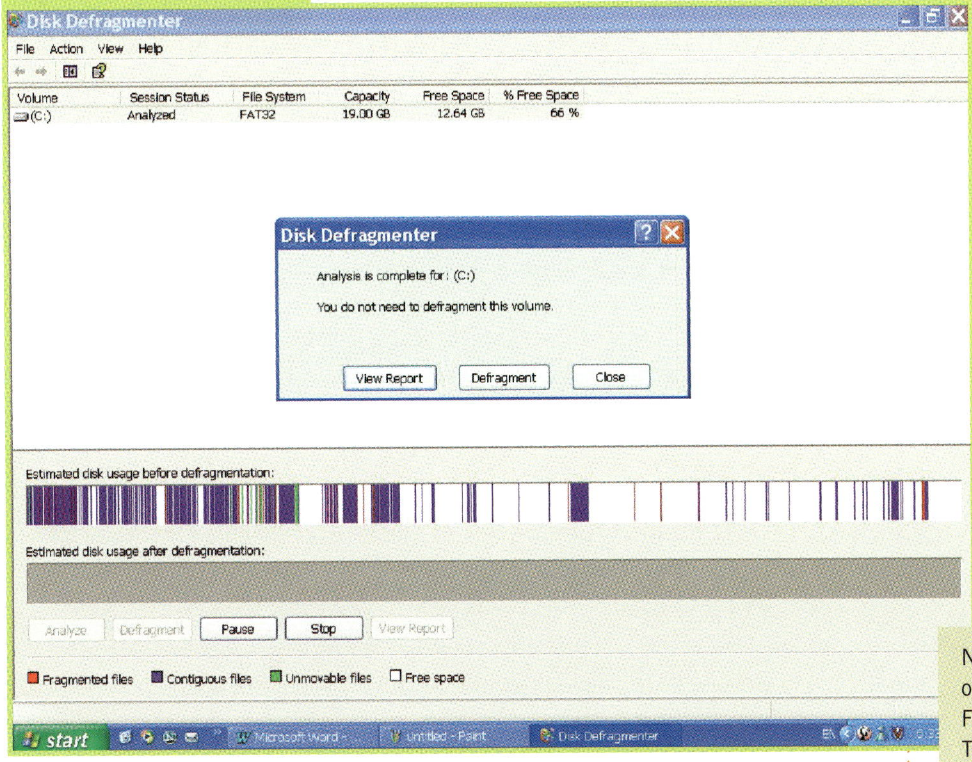

NEVER move or delete files or folders in the Program Files or Windows folders. This can compromise the system and some of your software may not function correctly.

ranging the files so that the bits are all together and eliminating any empty spaces created when you delete files from the hard drive, your disk operates more efficiently.

- *Backup.* A very important, yet infrequently used, utility is that of backing up your files. A full backup makes a "mirror image" of your hard drive, saved on another source, e.g., CD-RW (Figure 4.20), or magnetic tape, so that in the case of a system crash, the contents of your hard drive can be restored to the point where the backup was performed. Incremental backups copy only those files that have changed since the last full backup was performed. Businesses use this utility on a regular basis, because they cannot afford to lose important data due to a system failure or a hacking incident. You do not have to do a full backup to protect your files. It is also wise to copy your user files to CD or other disks from time to time. If a hard drive fails and all your files are on it, you could lose countless days or months of work.

Figure 4.20

System Backup

CD-RW disks provide full read/write capabilities so that the disks can be updated many times.

Figure 4.21
Norton Antivirus Program

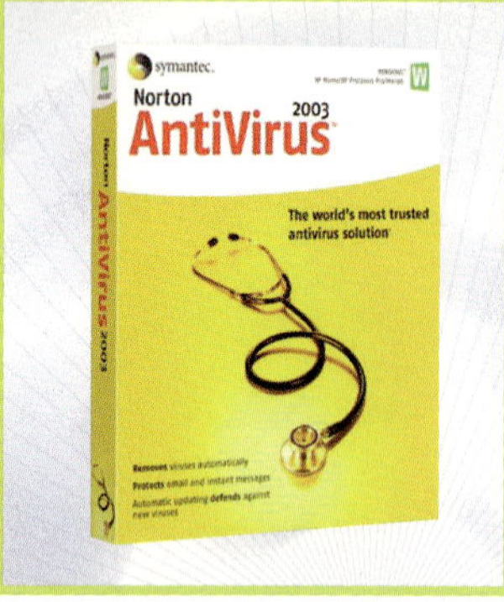

Virus protection software can only recognize viruses that are identified in its database. It is very important, therefore, to update your virus protection software on a regular basis.

- *Anti-virus programs.* One essential utility in today's wired world is anti-virus software. A virus is a program that can wipe out selected files or an entire system (more on this in Chapter 9). A business cannot afford to lose important files (everything from e-mail address lists to entire network contents) to a virus attack. Every minute an organization is unable to use its computer system costs the firm thousands, if not millions, of dollars in lost revenue. To detect viruses in files you create or download from other sources (e.g., Internet or e-mail attachments), anti-virus software (Figure 4.21) is used. This program examines files as they are saved, stored, opened, or executed, looking for code that identifies them as infected files. The software can only recognize those codes it has in its database, so it is important to update your software virus database on a regular basis.

GETTING IT

1. Create a notebook page on System Software on which you include answers to the following questions. Submit your note to your teacher for approval.
   a. What is an OS?
   b. What is the most complex operation the OS performs on your system?
   c. What is multitasking and how does the OS allow this to happen?
   d. How does virtual memory management assist in the process of multitasking?
   e. What security function is built into most OS software?
   f. What folders/files should not be moved or deleted? Why?
   g. What is the purpose of disk scanning?
   h. What does defragmenting a hard disk accomplish?
   i. How is a drive fragmented? How do you fix it?
   j. Why should you back up your files?
   k. What is the difference between a full backup versus an incremental backup of your hard drive?
   l. Why do businesses perform backups on a regular basis?
   m. How can anti-virus software protect your system?

4.3.3 Operating Systems: Windows, Mac O/S, Unix, Linux

The OS is either fully or partially housed in **ROM (read only memory)**, which is the built-in computer memory that contains the essential systems programs. If fully stored in ROM, the applications are immediately available at the time the unit is started. Only devices with small operating systems store the entire OS in ROM. PCs store only enough of the OS in ROM to get the unit up and running. Once this permanently stored portion is copied into RAM on startup, the system requests the rest of the OS from the hard drive to complete the booting or starting up process. When you use your computer, you are interacting with the OS and the way in which it works with the application programs. Many users find that the quality of this user interface will either enhance or detract from the overall computing experience. There are three basic forms of user interface: a command line interface, a menu-driven interface, or a graphical user interface.

- *Command-line interface.* Early versions of PC operating systems used a command-line interface (see Figure 4.22), where the user had to interface with the OS using keyed commands. These commands follow a specific format (syntax) that must be keyed exactly for the OS to understand what is required (e.g., copy, move, delete).
- *Menu-driven interface.* A menu-driven interface gives a choice of options at each screen the user encounters. Most systems require the user to select the option by scrolling down a list of them using arrow or cursor keys on a keyboard or other device. Cellular phone handsets, such as that shown in Figure 4.23, are examples of menu-driven devices.
- *Graphical user interface (GUI).* The Apple computer system was the first to develop and embrace a commercially available GUI. This interface controls every pixel on a screen and monitors the movement of the mouse. The screen, or desktop, contains icons that represent files, folders, or programs. A typical screen appears in Figure 4.24. When the mouse points to an icon on the screen, it can activate these programs or open files or folders. The desktop is designed to represent an individual's physical workspace in an office, with a "trash can" file folder, and projects he or she is working on. Within programs, the user can select from available options by clicking on icons on toolbars or by selecting options from drop-down menus that appear on the menu bar of a program. Other commands cause dialogue boxes to appear on the screen, containing a number of options for the user to choose among before the command is activated. Alert boxes also appear if you are asking the computer to perform a command such as deleting files, asking if you really want to perform that task. This gives you the option of declining if the action is not required. Although GUIs have improved the overall user satisfaction level with OS interfaces they are memory intensive, requiring more memory and processing power to perform the functions than their command- or menu-driven counterparts.

Figure 4.22
Command-Line Interface

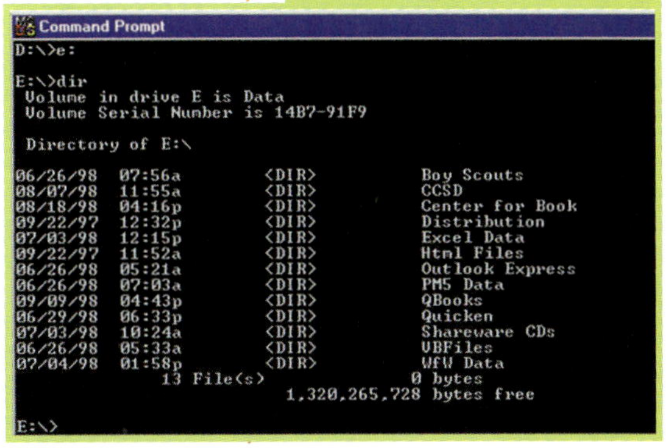

Figure 4.23
Menu-Driven Interface

Figure 4.24
Microsoft® Windows Interface

A Graphical User Interface (GUI) such as Microsoft's Windows interface contains icons representing files, folders, or programs.

User interfaces generally perform similar tasks. They all allow the user to gain access to the workstation or network through a user ID and password. They also allow the user to launch applications, manage disks and files, and perform a safe shutdown procedure when the user wishes to log off the computer. It is very important to use the OS to log out of a workstation; otherwise, you risk corrupting necessary system files or you leave scrambled data on the computer's hard drive, thus reducing the system's efficiency.

Many of the desktop elements are common among today's OSs, since all of them compete for a share of the personal computer and corporate workstation market. But there are subtle differences in how users access programs and what elements are on the desktop, as you will see.

- *Mac OS.* As mentioned previously, the Apple Macintosh was the first PC to have a GUI when it was released in 1984. It was based on ideas developed by Xerox, but that company had been unable to gain commercial acceptance for the system it launched in 1981. The Mac interface is considered to be one of the easiest to learn and operate, but it fell behind Microsoft's Windows product in the late 1980s. The Apple brand and OS were revitalized in 1998 by one of the founders, Steve

Jobs. With new releases of the Mac OS they have come back into the market, competing technically with the newest Windows products. The Mac OS uses a combination of pop-down menus and onscreen icons to allow access to programs and functions, such as shutting down and launching applications. A sample Mac OS X screen appears in Figure 4.25.

Figure 4.25
Mac OS X Interface

Mac OS X interface uses a combination of pop-down menus and onscreen icons giving the user access to programs and functions.

- *Microsoft Windows.* Microsoft originally developed the MS-DOS® disk operating system to work with the IBM PC, the first commercially viable personal computer on the market in 1982. This command-line interface had some severe limitations that prevented its development past its use with Intel® 386 processors. That, combined with demands for more user-friendly interfaces, prompted Microsoft to develop the Windows OS. At that time, Windows was merely a shell within which DOS was housed. Since the introduction of Windows® 95, the DOS foundation on which Windows was based rarely surfaces. Commands are more intuitive, relying less on knowledge of proper code and syntax, and more on what the user wants to do. The desktop features icons that enable users to access frequently used programs or files without going through the Start menu located at the bottom of the screen. These icons are called shortcuts because

Figure 4.26
The Evolution of Windows

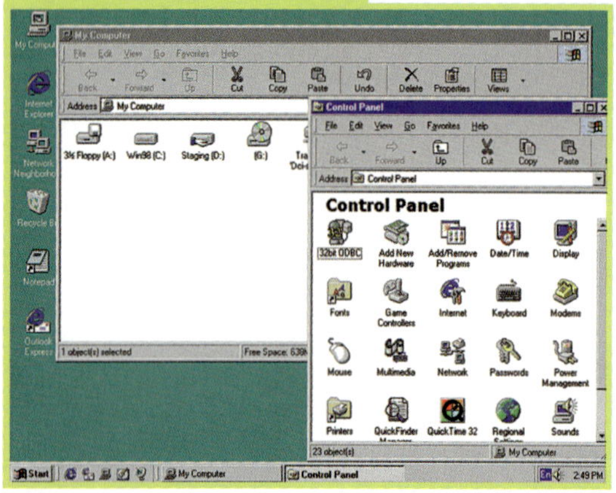

Windows 98 Desktop

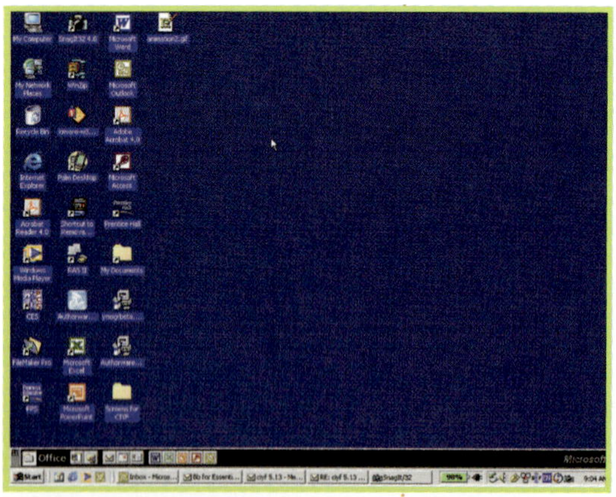

Windows 2000 Desktop

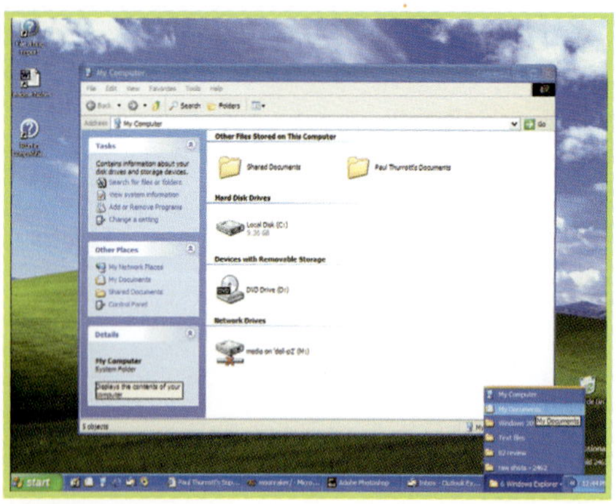

Windows XP Desktop

they allow you to take a shorter route to the destination program or file. The Start menu, however, gives the user access to all the programs that have been loaded on that unit. Figure 4.26 shows the evolution of the Windows desktop.

There are versions of Windows that help operate portable handheld computers and full network servers and workstations, as well as home and office PCs. Windows NT, for example, is specifically designed for client/server networks and offers the following benefits:

- security through restricted access (i.e., login and password controls),
- network administration from remote locations, and
- a Web server that enables organizations to make Web pages available to Intranet/Internet users.

- *UNIX*. The UNIX operating system was, and still is, one of the trailblazing OSs available on the market today. UNIX was the first to allow true multitasking and it was designed to work within a secure, centrally administered computing environment. The ability to organize files using folders and file pathways was another important development. Despite its superb features and capabilities, it was not popular because of its extensive reliance on command-line interface, which is challenging even for adept computer users to learn and memorize. To combat this market reluctance, recent versions of UNIX have been developed with a GUI interface, improving its market acceptance.

  UNIX is considered one of the best OSs in client/server computing and is one of the most common OSs in the corporate environment today (Figure 4.27). Its strength lies in the two programs that handle network traffic — the client program and the server program — the latter residing on high-powered central computers that all users can access (if cleared by the network administrator). The number-crunching ability of UNIX systems makes them the choice for many corporations.
- *Linux*. The Linux OS, created in 1991 by Finnish student Linus Torvalds, is based on the UNIX OS but is geared to the PC market. Linux contains features for PCs previously available only on more expensive UNIX systems.

Figure 4.27
UNIX Screen

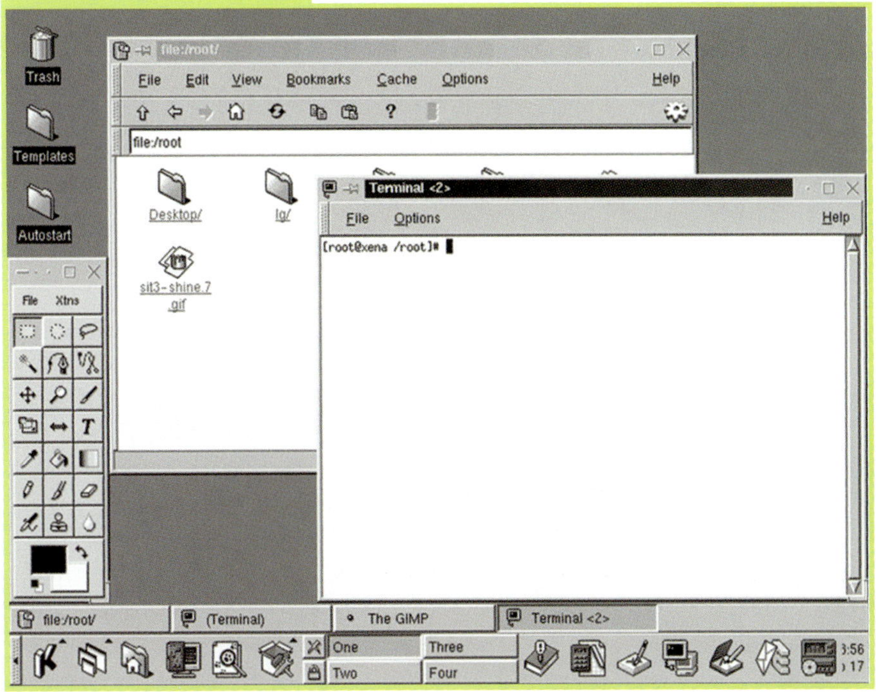

UNIX is one of the most common operating systems in the corporate environment.

It allows for multitasking, virtual memory, Internet support, and multiprocessor support, all in a user-friendly GUI. On this desktop interface, you access commands such as log out (or shut down) from a pop-up menu that resembles the Windows Start menu. Other tasks are accessed through shortcut icons on the desktop or the taskbar at the bottom of the screen. Figure 4.28 is a Linux screen.

The system was developed (and is still being developed) by computer experts around the world. The OS is posted online for people to download and tinker with and repost when they feel they have made improvements to it. It is therefore known as open-source software. It is free to anyone who wants to download it and install it on her or his system. The OS works not only on PCs but PDAs, notebook computers, and supercomputers as well. This approach has led to Linux being the fastest-growing OS for Intel-based PCs in the world (Pfaffenberger 2003). However, it will run only Linux applications, not Windows applications, so if you own Windows software you may need to consider the cost of new programs.

Figure 4.28
Linux Screen

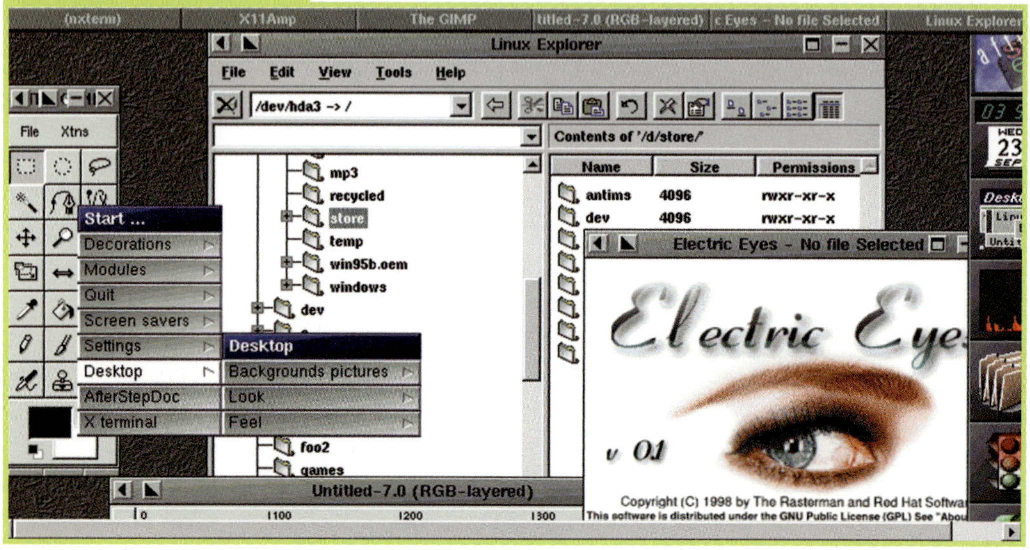

The Linux operating system contains features previously available only on more expensive UNIX systems.

GETTING IT

1. Use software to create a report titled "Operating Systems." Incorporate the answer to the questions that follow under appropriate subheadings. Submit your finished document to your teacher electronically.
   - a. Where is the OS for your computer stored?
   - b. What is an interface?
   - c. Describe the differences between a command-line interface, a menu-driven interface, and a GUI interface.
   - d. What tasks do interfaces help the user perform?
   - e. Why is it important to log out or shut down a workstation properly?
   - f. What OSs are in use today and what determines which one is on the system you are using?
   - g. What features are common among today's OSs?
   - h. State an advantage and a disadvantage to using an OS with a GUI.
   - i. Why are there different versions of the Windows OS?
   - j. State an advantage and a disadvantage to using the UNIX OS.
   - k. How was the Linux OS developed?

4.4 Interacting With Your Computer Environment

The shift in our workplaces from labour intensive to information intensive tasks has resulted in a fundamental change in the tools we use to get our daily jobs done. Many people find themselves in front of computer workstations or terminals for most of the workday. This shift has raised a number of concerns that organizations never had to deal with in the past. Companies and other organizations (like schools) have drafted policies that govern the use of information technology for their members. In the past, access to information was tightly controlled by the distribution of hard-copy data — no electronic versions existed.

Who should have access to information and how it can be controlled are issues for corporate executives to grapple with in today's IT environment. Likewise, concerns regarding the health and safety of employees have always been present but have focused more on industrial noise, chemicals, and job site safety — not the use of computer equipment. These issues, and more, highlight the need to better understand our new work environment.

4.4.1 Acceptable Use of Computer Equipment

When, as part of an organization, you gain access to a computer network, you are entrusted with the electronic assets of that organization. What comes with this tremendous opportunity is the responsibility to use the network correctly. Most organizations require their employees to sign an agreement that outlines the use of, and access to, the computer network and all the programs licensed to the organization and the results of the work of its employees. When you work for a company, the results of your work are the property of the company, not yours.

Most of these agreements (called **acceptable use policies** or **AUPs**) outline, but are not limited to, the following points:

- Use only your personal login and password to gain access to the network.
- Safeguard your password and files to prevent unauthorized access.
- Do not install any unapproved software on the network.
- Connect only approved equipment.
- Use files that have been scanned for viruses prior to opening them on the network.
- Report any known security breaches on the network to the appropriate personnel.
- Access only your personal files.
- Do not use the network for criminal, commercial, or frivolous purposes (e.g., games).

- Follow the rules for sending and receiving e-mail, including chain e-mail letters.

Violation of these policies can lead to dismissal from the organization. But why have such policies in the first place?

The safety of information on a network is vital to safeguarding individual privacy. Many systems house a significant amount of information on customers, employees, and other stakeholders. Suppose a disgruntled hospital employee gathers information about patients who are HIV positive and disseminates that information via e-mail to the media. Or suppose a person sends an e-mail message under another account holder's name to implicate that person in a criminal activity. If you were the only one who is supposed to have access to that e-mail account, you would have a hard time disproving your involvement.

Furthermore, if an organization's computer system is breached but no harm occurs, there are still many other things at stake. Network administration personnel waste time and effort investigating security breaches. After re-securing the system, they must then focus efforts on preventing future breaches. And while the system is shut down to investigate security breaches other personnel cannot do their jobs, which causes a loss in overall productivity. In business, time lost is money lost.

Many organizations are reluctant to report computer-related crimes because of the adverse publicity that comes with it. From their point of view, why advertise that the system is not secure? This only invites other hackers to try their hand at getting in and causing damage.

So, how can organizations restrict access to accounts? Our next section will investigate this issue.

4.4.2 System Safety and Security

As outlined above, many security problems stem from people who gain unauthorized access to computer networks and the data contained therein. To combat this problem, networks include processes that verify the identity of the person logging in. The simplest and most common authentication system is to assign users a login identification name and password. Many systems allow the user to select her or his own password and require the user to change the password from time to time. It is important to select passwords that are not easily guessed by other people, such as variations of your name or words that are easily connected to you. The best passwords are a combination of letters, symbols, and numbers at least seven or eight characters in length. The longer the password, the harder it is for someone to determine with a casual glance over your shoulder while you enter it.

Some computer systems require the user both to know something (e.g., a password) and to have something (e.g., an access card). This is commonly seen on ATM units or bank machines. **Smart card** technology is also used in some systems. Smart cards contain information about the user and, when used with a PIN number, can provide the requisite **authentication**. One of the most foolproof methods of authentication is **biometric security**, a system that uses a person's physical characteristics to allow access. Your fingerprint, your voice pattern, and a scan of your retina (the back of your eye) or face are three such methods used to allow access to computer networks because each characteristic can be measured. The most secure method is the retinal scan. The retina is the thin membrane at the back of the eyeball composed of layers of nerve tissue that senses light and transmits impulses to the brain. Tiny blood vessels located on the retina are unique to each person. Scanning devices measure the location of the blood vessels while a person looks into the device. Vessel patterns are compared with a database of eye scans to identify the person at the scanner.

IT In Action

Biometric Security Meets High Fashion

Prominent Canadian retailer Holt Renfrew, known for decades as a cutting-edge provider of the latest fashions, recently introduced cutting-edge technology in its upscale retail locations. Starting in 2002, all Holt Renfrew staff that use cash registers identify themselves with their thumbprint, a form of biometric security. Traditional cash registers required the cashier to enter an employee number, which could easily be "stolen" or guessed. This new system ensures that employees' privacy is maintained (since the only way one can gain access to a cash register is through a registered thumbprint).

A biometric system consists of three elements: a physical reader that scans the body part used for identification, software that translates the image, and a database where the identification data are stored. As a biometric device scans the body part (in this case, the cashier's thumbprint) with a small reader that looks like a tiny, thumb-sized scanner, it marks a number of specific points on the scanned image to serve as match points. Biometric software then converts those points into an algorithm (set of steps to solve a problem), and that data set is loaded into a database. When a user's thumb is later put into the reader, the match points on his or her thumbprint are converted into numbers and compared with the stored file using the algorithm created for that print. If they match, the employee gains access to the network and can proceed.

The software must be programmed to be able to account for biological changes as well. For example, your thumbprint can change up to 10 times in a day. Most high-security areas use at least two biometric scanners so that legitimate users don't get locked out of the system.

The system is in place at all Canadian Holt Renfrew locations.

Questions

1. Identify other forms of biometric security available for organizations to implement today.
2. Use the search tools on the Internet to investigate the various methods and prepare a summary of your findings for a class discussion.

Another form of protection for company resources is the use of **firewalls** on the network. These programs allow users to access resources on the Internet and World Wide Web, but restrict access to the company's resources from outside Internet connections. **Encryption**, yet another form of data security, scrambles the data so that, even if intercepted, they will be unintelligible. More information on encryption is found in Chapter 9.

Proper access to networks as well as the safety and security of data are two very important considerations in today's high-tech workplaces. Another equally important area for consideration is the health and safety of workers in a computer environment.

GETTING IT

1. Explain what an acceptable use policy (AUP) is and why organizations have instituted such policies.
2. Use your favourite search engine to locate AUPs in place at other high schools and compare yours with those you find.
3. Create a visual display that depicts the characteristics of a good password.
4. Explain what is meant by "authentication."
5. Describe four commonly used methods of authentication in today's computing environment.
6. Identify the three elements in a biometric system.
7. Describe biometric identification. What is the most secure biometric?
8. Describe a firewall and explain how it works to safeguard a computer.

digiknow

Not only can workers be injured physically working in today's technology-filled environment, but they can also be affected mentally. A phenomenon called "digital depression" has resulted from having a daily overload of technology. Workers are stressed because of the continual interruptions to their work day that prevent them from being able to work on one task continuously until they can complete it.

(Selix 2001)

4.4.3 Health and Safety: Ergonomic Considerations

As people spend more and more time using computers, the side effects are being seen on an increasing basis. Using a new technology, from workstations to notebook computers and PDAs, without understanding the health risks associated with it can increase your chance of injury. Some people are concerned about low-level radiation given off from computer monitors and cellular phones but, at the time of writing, there is no conclusive scientific evidence to support those concerns.

There is evidence, however, that increased computer use does contribute to the development of a wide range of **repetitive strain injuries** (RSIs) in computer users. Repeated physical movements that damage tendons, nerves, muscles, and other soft body tissue cause these injuries. Because computer keyboards were flattened to allow for lighter-touch, faster keying, the user's hands rarely leave a set position. The use of mice and other pointing devices adds to the strain, as users keep their shoulders and arms in static positions while dragging the mouse around the screen. Improper hand position that adds stress to the wrist is another contributing factor to RSIs, as is the lack of adequate breaks away from the workstation.

One of the most frequently cited injuries that falls into this category is carpal tunnel syndrome, a condition where nerves to the hand and fingers are compressed from repetitive strain to the wrist. This injury is only one of a myriad of possible repetitive strain injuries. All of these are serious, and in advanced cases can cause great pain and permanent disability.

Not only can prolonged computer use increase the risk of RSIs, it can also lead to eyestrain, headaches, and fatigue. How can we combat these potential sources of pain? Ergonomics can help. **Ergonomics** is the study of the interaction of people with their environment. Part of this science is designing workplaces that are safer for the people who use them. Figure 4.29 illustrates an ergonomic workstation. Experts in the field of ergonomics make the following recommendations for an ergonomic workstation:

Figure 4.29
An Ergonomic Computer Workstation

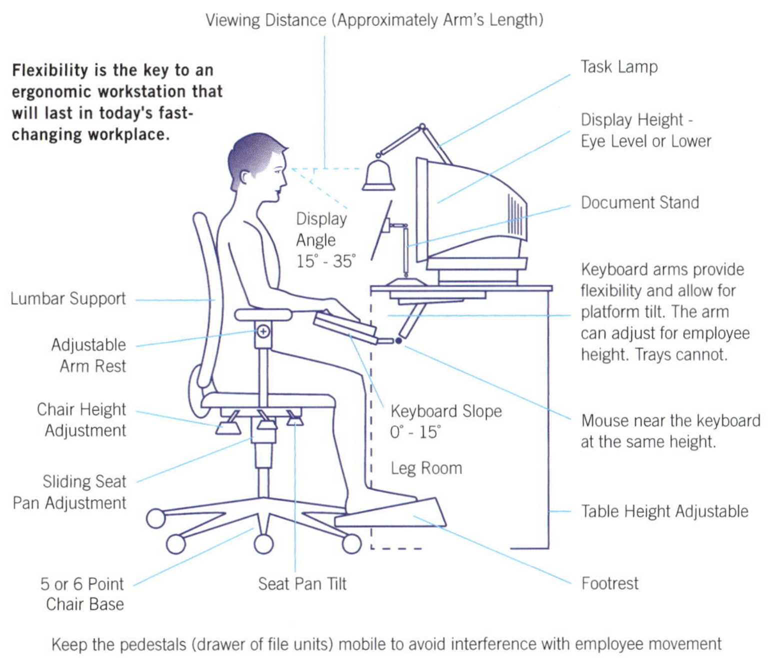

Choose five recommendations in this illustration and explain why they are important for a healthy working environment.

Get Connected

There are many sites on the Web devoted to the study of ergonomics and injuries that can be sustained using computers. Starting at www.pearsoned.ca/businessconnections, research the types of injuries that can be sustained. Prepare a chart in your notes to identify these injuries and suggestions and exercises that can help people avoid injury.

- *Chair*. Most experts agree that your chair is the most important factor in maintaining proper posture which, in turn, helps to reduce back injuries. You should be able to sit at the back of the chair, using the chair back for support. Lower back, or lumbar, support should be built into the chair, fitting comfortably into the small of your back. The chair should be high enough to allow your feet to be planted firmly on the ground. Use a footrest if necessary.
- *Desk*. Many desks on the market today have a fixed height, probably between 28" (71 cm) and 30" (76 cm). While this is a good height for writing, it is too high for a computer keyboard. The keyboard should be slightly below your waist so that your arms are not bent upward while using the keyboard. Where possible, a sliding, height-adjustable keyboard tray that is affixed to the bottom of the desk should be installed to position the keyboard at the proper height. If this is not an option, raise your chair so that you are at the correct height and use a footrest to support your legs.
- *Keyboard*. As mentioned above, the keyboard should be just slightly below waist height, allowing your arms to hang downward to reduce the strain on your shoulders. Ideally, the keyboard should be tilted away from you to avoid having to tilt your hands upward at the wrist. Avoid the use of the keyboard legs to reduce the upward angle of the keys as well.
- *Mouse*. Your mouse should be located close to the keyboard, within comfortable reach. You should be able to access the mouse while keeping your arms close to your side to avoid shoulder stress. Try to use other forms of pointing devices or even keyboard shortcut commands to reduce the number of times you have to reach for the mouse.
- *Monitor*. Keep the monitor directly in front of you to avoid having to turn your head while looking at the screen. Be sure to sit at least an arm's length back from the monitor to reduce eyestrain. Position the monitor so that you are looking down at the screen between 15 and 35 degrees from horizontal eye level (Canadian Standards Association 2000). If possible, position your monitor so that any light from windows in the room is not causing undue glare on the screen. Balancing the brightness of your monitor with your workplace light level also helps to reduce eyestrain and headaches.
- *Lighting*. Indirect lighting is the best for a workstation, i.e., light not shining directly on your computer or monitor. If you need to increase the amount of light on your station to see your work, be sure to have it to the side of your computer, shining on the documents not the screen.
- *Documents*. Wherever possible, place documents on copyholders or book stands. Trying to read documents that are lying flat on the work surface causes undue stress on your neck and eyes.

GETTING IT

1. Explain what RSI means.
2. Explain how the development of computer equipment contributed to the increase in RSIs.
3. Explain what digital depression is.
4. Define *ergonomics.*
5. Identify the most important consideration in designing an ergonomic workstation.
6. Describe how your keyboard should be positioned to reduce strain.
7. Describe the steps that can be taken to reduce glare from a computer monitor.
8. Describe the best location (ergonomically) for a keyboard.

4.4.4 Social and Ethical Concerns in the Age of IT

The age of technology has some people concerned about the breakdown of our society's structure. We see the results of automating the workplace all around us: lost jobs, overnight successes and failures in the corporate world, and an irreversible change in the way we function on a daily basis. On the positive side, we see advances in medicine that would be light years away without the use of technology to hasten their discovery and the forms of treatment to which they relate. As these and more technologies change the fabric of our society, we must consider the impact that information technology is having. Some of the concerns that have been raised include:

- threats to personal privacy, as databases of personal information abound and hackers increasingly get access to those storehouses of information;
- the definition of who owns what when information is so readily available;
- the cost to business if computer systems fail;
- the dehumanization of the workplace and the reduced need to interact with people when work can be done online from remote locations;
- the potential to use information as a political or economic weapon; and, of course,
- our dependence on technology.

As you read through the other chapters of *Business Connections*, you will find these and more concerns discussed in greater detail. The use of information technology has the potential to improve our lives, or harm them. By learning more about the various areas of concern, you can decide for yourself.

CAREER PERSPECTIVE

With the shift in our society from an industrial-based economy to one focused on information and computer technology, there has been a significant change in the types of jobs that students can pursue. This chapter has highlighted some of the advances in hardware and networking over the past few decades. In all cases, people have brought about these changes, from designing new pointing devices and flat screen technologies to linking computers to increase overall productivity.

Using the resources at your school, investigate the new jobs you could pursue that are related to the topics discussed in this chapter. Your Guidance counsellors should be able to provide you with print and electronic sources that will help you in your search. Prepare a summary that includes the following:

- Job title
- Description of the duties and responsibilities of individuals in these positions
- Preparation for employment (post-secondary programs or apprenticeships)
- Possible salary or wages
- Courses at high school to prepare you for these positions

IT's A Wrap

Key Terms in This Chapter

acceptable use policy (AUP) (p. 105)
authentication (p. 107)
bar code (p. 78)
biometric security (p. 107)
bridge (p. 93)
cathode ray tube (CRT) (p. 80)
central processing unit (CPU) (p. 80)
client/server network (p. 90)
contention (p. 91)
electronic data interchange (EDI) (p. 93)
encryption (p. 108)
ergonomics (p. 109)
file allocation table (FAT) (p. 85)
firewall (p. 108)
gateway (p. 93)
graphics tablets (p. 77)
impact printer (p. 82)
liquid crystal display (LCD) (p. 81)
local area network (LAN) (p. 88)
magnetic ink character recognition (MICR) (p. 78)
metropolitan area network (MAN) (p. 92)
motherboard (p. 80)
mouse (p. 77)
multifunction printer (p. 83)
network (p. 87)
network interface card (NIC) (p. 89)
network operating system (NOS) (p. 90)
node (p. 88)
non-impact printer (p. 83)
optical character recognition (OCR) (p. 79)
peer-to-peer (P2P) network (p. 90)
personal digital assistant (PDA) (p. 76)
plotter (p. 83)

IT's A Wrap *(continued)*

pointing stick (p. 77)
read only memory (ROM) (p. 98)
repetitive strain injury (RSI) (p. 108)
router (p. 93)
scanning tools (p. 77)
smart card (p. 106)
system software (p. 94)
topology (p. 90)
touch screen (p. 77)
touchpad (p. 77)
trackball (p. 77)
Universal Product Code (UPC) (p. 78)
virtual memory (p. 95)
wide area network (WAN) (p. 92)
workstation (p. 76)

1. Create a list of the competencies you have acquired through your work in this chapter.

2. Update your portfolio to include examples of work you have completed in this chapter.

Know It!

3. When most people think of scanners they think in terms of pictures. How else can scanners be used to input data and improve productivity?

4. Describe the differences in CRTs and LCDs in a chart, using the following headings: Physical Description, Image Creation, Size, and Price.

5. Of all the benefits of networking, which has the potential to give companies a competitive edge?

6. Which LAN topology would be best used in:
a. a small office with fewer than 20 computers?
b. the offices of a company with locations spread over three floors in an office building?

7. Explain the difference between your computer's OS and its utility programs.

8. Describe how you should use the file management utility to organize your files for your courses this semester/year.

Do It!

9. Talk to your school's network administrator or site technician and determine the hardware used in your school's LAN. Prepare a fully labelled diagram for your notes.

10. Organize your files using your computer's utility programs for this semester/year. Draw a flowchart that describes how you have organized them and why.

11. Go into the Help menu of your computer and locate the steps to defragment your hard drive. Write these down in your notes for future reference.

12. Search the Web for Linux and investigate its development further. Explain why you think computer manufacturers around the world have not embraced it.

13. Search the Web for RSIs other than carpal tunnel syndrome. In groups of two or three, choose an RSI and investigate its causes and treatment. Prepare a presentation to make to the class on your findings.

IT's A Wrap (continued)

Analyze It!

14. In groups, discuss the merits of using the keyboard as an input device in this age of information technology improvements. Share your group's findings with the rest of the class.
15. Discuss with your classmates the situations in a corporate environment where ink-jet or laser printers are best used.
16. In groups of four, debate the statement "Floppy disks are obsolete in today's computing environment." Use examples from the chapter and your own thoughts to support your position.
17. UNIX has long been considered the best OS by computing professionals. Explain why, then, it is not installed on all PCs and computer networks.
18. Analyze your school's acceptable use policy (AUP) document using the criteria set out within this chapter. Is it complete? Are there areas of the policy that require attention?
19. Privacy and security are of paramount importance in organizations. List and describe three possible abuses of data and information NOT outlined in this chapter. What are the potential results of such abuse?

CHAPTER

Office Productivity 1

5

On completion of this chapter, you will be able to:

- use word-processing software to create attractive documents;
- organize documents to take advantage of formatting features;
- work with others to create documents;
- create spreadsheets that incorporate formulas;
- sort data in a spreadsheet; and
- incorporate a spreadsheet in a word-processed document.

As you know, Canadian employers look for certain skills, abilities, and traits in prospective employees. One skill set that has become increasingly sought after is the ability to use computer technology and, specifically, office productivity software as tools in performing job-related duties. A basic understanding and demonstration of these skills is important to get your "foot in the door" in many organizations. This chapter will give you the opportunity to develop skills in these areas:

- Word Processing
- Spreadsheets
- Databases
- Emerging Software Practices in Business

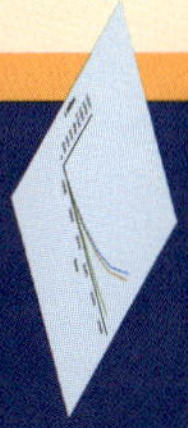

Ready, Set, Go!

Ready

- Use notes taken in this class, from a newspaper/magazine article, or from an article on a news site on the Web as the basis for a document. Create the document in your word-processing program with the following features:
  - 1.5" (3.75 cm) margins, left and right;
  - double spacing;
  - full justification;
  - landscape orientation;
  - indented paragraphs;
  - bulleted or numbered lists incorporated into the body of the text (single spaced); and
  - any additional features you have learned in previous experiences using word-processing software to showcase your skills and abilities.
- Spell check and grammar check the document.
- Save the document as "Ready Chapter 5" in your file space.
- Have a classmate proofread your document and edit as required, moving and copying text as indicated.

Set

- In your spreadsheet program, create a document that contains the following data:

Summer Earnings Analysis by [Your Name Here]	
Week 1	$ 89.58
Week 2	$108.44
Week 3	$145.99
Week 4	$122.87
Week 5	$187.49
Week 6	$137.45
Total	
Average Weekly Earnings	
Highest Earnings Amount	
Lowest Earnings Amount	

- Insert a formula to calculate the total earnings for the six-week period.
- Insert a function to determine both the highest and lowest earnings amounts and insert them in the appropriate cells.

(continued)

- Format the title attractively by increasing the font size, changing the colour of the font, and adding a background colour to the title area. Ensure the title spans both columns. Avoid excess formatting.
- Italicize the labels in the first column.
- Create a line chart to show the six weeks' earnings. Insert this chart below the spreadsheet data on the same sheet. Include titles on the two axes of the chart.
- Save this document as "Set Chapter 5" in your file space.

Go

- Use your database software to create a database that contains the names, full addresses (including street address and postal codes), and telephone numbers of five of your best friends.
- Sort the database alphabetically by last name.
- Generate a report of the database making sure it fits on one page for printing.
- Save this database as "Go Chapter 5" in your file space.

Introduction to Chapter Project

Recall that the Chapter Project is introduced at the beginning and is to be completed as you work through the chapter. Your teacher will provide you with assessment and evaluation criteria.

CHAPTER PROJECT

This chapter project is an extension of your major course project. Your project team should have developed a draft of your project plan to date. Using the skills developed in this chapter, your task is to complete the following:

- key and format your project plan;
- complete a budget for your project plan and incorporate the data, charts, and graphs into your plan; and
- develop a database of the resources you are using to complete your project and incorporate a report of the planned versus actual resources used in your project plan.

Your project plan should be a comprehensive report that demonstrates the use of advanced functions of each of the programs utilized (e.g., page numbering, headers, footers, etc.). To demonstrate your competence in these areas, be prepared, in an interview with your teacher, to describe the tools and software features you have used. Use the competency checklist provided by your teacher to guide your efforts.

5.1 Word Processing

The power of the computer was first realized because of its incredible ability to process large amounts of data and numbers in very little time. It was not considered an office productivity tool until the advent of smaller systems and more user-friendly software. Once this occurred, the personal and networked computer became an office essential.

The most frequently used application on a personal computer is **word processing**. Virtually all word-processing software on the market today gives users the ability to create clean copy, edit without having to recreate the entire document, and communicate effectively in writing in today's wired world.

All word-processing software allows you to perform the same basic functions:

- enter text;
- edit text;
- format text;
- verify the accuracy of text;
- save text; and
- print text.

Most computer users switch back and forth among entering, editing, and formatting text so freely that they do not see these steps as separate components.

This section will focus on some of the most frequently used formatting and editing features and tools of word-processing programs, which help to improve your overall productivity. As you enter text, think carefully about how you want it to appear when printed out. This will help you to determine the choice of font, the line spacing, and where many of the word-processing package's formatting features will be employed. One of the first decisions you need to make is how to have the text appear — in paragraph form, as tables, in columns, or in some other form. Let us examine these features first.

5.1.1 Tables, Columns, and Other Display Methods

Text does not always have to be presented in simple paragraph form. In order to assist the reader's comprehension and understanding, the creator of documents may choose to present information in any number of ways — in tables, columns, or lists. Figure 5.1 illustrates two very different methods of presenting information.

The paragraph in Figure 5.1 describes the five types of fonts in words, whereas the **table** shows the fonts themselves. The reader can refer to the table for a more visual representation of the information.

Type of Font	Example (12-point size)
Serif	Times New Roman Garamond
Sans Serif	Arial Avant Garde
Script	Palace Script MT Zapf Chancery
Display	Comic Sans MC **Impact**
Symbols	❁ ❒ ◗ ❄ ▲ ◗ ❁ Zapf Dingbats

Figure 5.1
Table versus Full Text Paragraphs

There are five basic font types. Your choice of font can change the "feel" of a document from very formal to informal, or even comic. Serif fonts such as Times New Roman and Garamond, with their small "tails" (called serifs) on each character, are the most formal. Sans (without) serif fonts, such as Arial and Avant Garde, have no "tails" on the characters and are much cleaner in appearance. Script fonts appear like handwriting, whereas display fonts such as Comic Sans MC or Impact allow you to match the look of the font to the mood or subject of the paper. Symbols are shortcuts that graphically display what would otherwise be difficult or lengthy to describe in words.

Most programs allow the user to determine the number of columns and rows in the table, to add borders around all or part of the table and its cells, and to add colour to the text and background to emphasize and highlight important information.

Another effective formatting option is the use of **columns** with text. Companies frequently create their newsletters for both internal and external audiences to look like newspapers. Articles are keyed in and the entire document is formatted for columns quickly and easily. As with newspaper columns, the paragraphs are fully **justified** to give the text clean lines on both left and right sides with no jagged edges. The program automatically adjusts the spacing between characters and words to create the appearance of paragraphs with no jagged edges. As you examine Figure 5.2, you will see how a document with normal paragraphs can be formatted with columns to create a more newspaper-like piece.

Figure 5.2
Columns in Documents

ENTERING AND EDITING TEXT

Entering Text
There are a number of fundamental differences between entering text in a simple text editor like NotePad and using modern word-processing software. The foremost difference is the word wrap feature.

When you enter text using a word-processing program, you do not have to press Enter until you want to start a new paragraph. The software automatically starts a new line as you come to the end of each line of text. The program determines if the words you are keying are going to go beyond the length of line you have set with the margin settings.

Editing Text
This feature will adjust your paragraphs as you edit your document as well. As you add words or even full sentences in the middle of text that is already keyed, the program will adjust the text accordingly. The same goes for text that is removed or cut to be placed elsewhere. The program will adjust the paragraph. If you press Enter at the end of each line, the program cannot make those adjustments as the word wrap feature only works within each paragraph. As soon as you press Enter, the program treats the next line as a new paragraph.

Many users of word-processing software find it helpful to set formatting features at the outset of a document so that they do not have to go back and change settings later. For example, if you want every paragraph indented, you can change paragraph settings to automatically indent when you press Enter. **Line spacing** is another setting that you can change at the beginning to have the program leave the required space between lines of text as you key. This is very handy when you key term papers and rough drafts of documents that require further editing.

GETTING IT

As you progress through this chapter, you are to develop a Personal Reference Manual that includes tips and step-by-step instructions to perform specific software tasks. Take the time to investigate the formatting tools contained in your word-processing program. The **Help menu** includes step-by-step instructions for performing the various functions in your program and can be of great assistance in this effort. For the software used in your school, write the steps necessary to complete the following:

- Create a table with 5 columns and 10 rows.
- Add colour/shading to the background of the first row.
- Create a three-column document like a newspaper, full-justified.
- Change line spacing from single to double.

digiknow

When selecting text by clicking and dragging the mouse in a Windows environment, you can alter the actions by holding down the Alt key in conjunction with the click and drag. Try it and see what happens to your commands!

5.1.2 Inserting Symbols and Special Characters

As you key documents, there are occasions when you need to enter text other than the letters, numbers, and symbols located on your keyboard. To do this, you need to access the symbols that are loaded as fonts in your word-processing software. A **font set** is the combination of typeface, size, style, and visual characteristics that make up a design set. Most font sets contain symbols that can be inserted into a document quickly and easily. As you can see in Figure 5.3, the Symbol screen for Times New Roman contains the entire regular alpha and numeric characters on your keyboard, plus many, many more. Many languages use characters that are variations on the characters used in the English language and these, too, are included for your use. There are also mathematical operators (e.g., x, ≤, ≈), currency symbols (e.g., ¢, £), and symbols used in the business community, such as Registered Trademark (®) and Copyright (©), both of which you will learn more about in Chapter 11 of this textbook. You can also insert special symbols into a text to add humour or to illustrate a point (e.g., ✪, ✎).

Many of the symbols have **shortcut keystrokes**. These are predetermined codes that represent a command to the software such as inserting symbol characters without the use of the mouse to access the Insert Symbol menu in your program. For example, by holding down the Alt key and pressing 0182

Figure 5.3
The Insert Symbol Screen

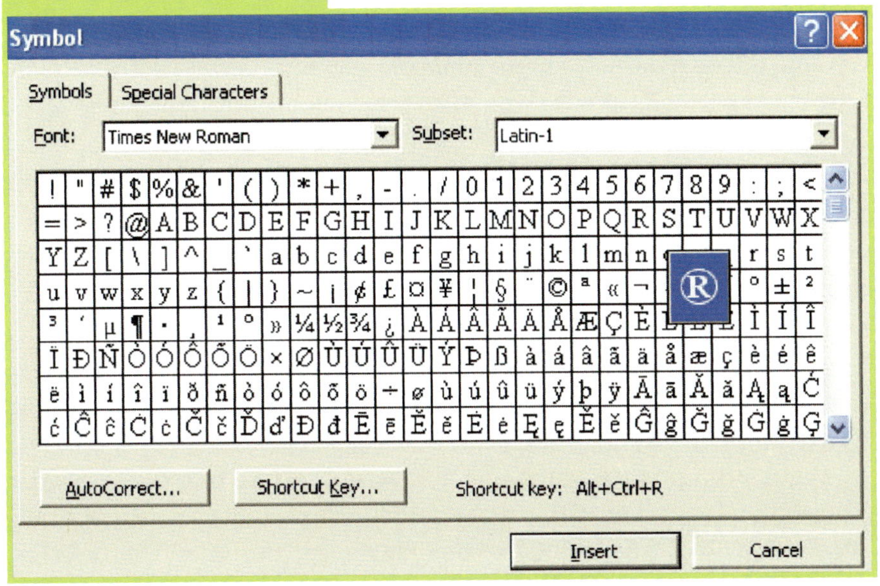

0182 on the numeric keypad of your keyboard, the paragraph symbol (¶) will appear. Alt/0182 is the ASCII code for that symbol. **ASCII** (pronounced ask-ee) refers to the ***American Standard Code for Information Interchange***, a code for representing characters as numbers. All characters have ASCII codes assigned to them, but a keyboard is used for the most common ones — the letters of the alphabet and numbers, of course. If you use a symbol frequently in your day-to-day keying, it is quicker and more efficient to assign a shortcut to that symbol so you are not always reaching for your mouse.

GETTING IT

1. What is the most frequently used office productivity application? Why?
2. Describe what word-processing software actually enables users to do.
3. Explain how and why columns and tables could be used to present information in a document.
4. Describe how automatic formatting features are useful in terms of efficiency and consistency.
5. Where are symbols located within your word-processing software? Describe how they can be accessed without using the pull-down menus.
6. In your Personal Reference Manual, list and describe the steps to perform the following tasks:
   a. Insert special characters and symbols into printed documents.
   b. Set up shortcut keys for symbols.

Get Connected

Are you tired of the same old fonts that came with the software you have installed on your computer? Fear not; there are countless sources for free fonts that you can download from the Web and install on your system at home. If you have never done this before, be sure to follow the instructions carefully! Investigate some of the fonts that you can download at www.pearsoned.ca/businessconnections or simply do a search in your favourite search engine for "free font downloads."

Pick three new fonts you especially like, print a sample (if possible), and explain when you might use each.

5.1.3 Using Breaks

When you are keying documents, it is more efficient to insert breaks where you want new pages or columns to begin, rather than hold down the Enter key until it forces the new page/column. As you know, each keystroke takes up room in a document when you save it. By holding down the Enter key to get to a new page, for example, you add unnecessary bytes to the document size. Not only that, if you later insert text into the "blank" areas it will force down the balance of the blank lines, throwing off your new page or column beginnings. The most efficient way to start a new page when you want one is to use a "forced page break" or perform a "**hard page break**" by holding down Ctrl/Enter or to insert a page break from the pull-down menu. If you have the hidden characters turned on within the program, you will see a dotted line with "Page Break" written across it. This allows you to find where your new page starts and edit as needed.

If you are using the automatic numbering feature or bullets and you want to start a new line within a paragraph, but not start a new item in the list, you can use a "**soft return**" by holding down Shift/Enter. This will start a new line under the same item number in the list. See point 2 in Figure 5.4 as an example.

Break What?

Many people get confused when the word "break" is mentioned in relation to word processing. Here is a handy guide:

Page break (press Ctrl/Enter) starts a new page in a document.

Section break divides a document into sections; may be continuous (on the same page) or start on the next page.

Column break starts a new column in a multicolumn document.

Hard return (press Enter) starts a new line or paragraph by pressing Enter.

Soft return (press Shift/Enter) starts a new line within a paragraph.

Get Connected

Many online tutorials are available to help you to improve your skills and competencies with office productivity software. To learn more about specific office productivity packages, visit three of the tutorial Web sites available at www.pearsoned.ca/businessconnections. Create a list of the topics each tutorial site offers users in the word-processing section. Select one of the tutorials and follow the steps contained therein. Write a short review of the tutorial that describes how easy it was to follow. Compare your findings with those of others in the class.

Figure 5.4
Using Soft Returns in Numbered Lists

HANDY FORMATTING FEATURES

1. Font Appearance: Within the formatting toolbar there are three frequently used font enhancement icons, namely Bold, Italic, and Underline.
   B (bold) allows the user to make the text appear with **more emphasis** without changing the font size.
   I (italics) will make the characters appear *slanted* on the screen.
   U (underline) will automatically insert a line below the text.
2. Justification: On the same toolbar we find paragraph justification icons. These allow the user to format paragraphs in four ways, namely left, right, centre, and fully justified.
   Text that is left justified has a jagged right edge with a straight left edge.
   Text that is right justified has a jagged left edge with a straight right edge.
   Centering a paragraph will result in all lines in the paragraph being centered around the midpoint of the line length chosen.
   Full justification creates paragraphs with both sides straight, and the program automatically adjusts the space between characters and words to achieve this effect.
3. Automatic Numbering: Inserting a list of items in a priority sequence is also a feature that is frequently used in word processing. By activating the automatic numbering, the inputter does not need to key the numbers, only the text that appears beside each number. There are numerous options for numbering, including Roman numerals and lettered items (e.g., a, b, c) as well as standard numeric sequences.
4. Bulleted Lists: A bulleted list is similar to a numbered list in that the word-processing software automatically inserts the bullets and the inputter needs only key the text that appears beside each bullet. Bullets can be formatted to appear as simple dots or you can select any character from a symbol set to appear as the bullet.

Long documents can benefit from the use of **section breaks**. This feature/command allows the author to divide the document into sections. For example, if you are keying a report with numerous chapters (like this text book), each chapter could be a section within the document. When you get to the end of a chapter and want to begin the next, insert a section break that forces the beginning of a new page. Section breaks also allow the writer to apply different formatting features within a document to individual portions by using continuous section breaks. The new section begins on the same page but has different settings applied to it. This can enhance the appearance of a document when you want to apply different features to different portions of your report. Another type of break starts a new page at the next odd or even page, allowing the author to always start a new chapter on the same side of the book, for example. Figure 5.5 shows some types of section breaks.

Figure 5.5
Section Break Screen

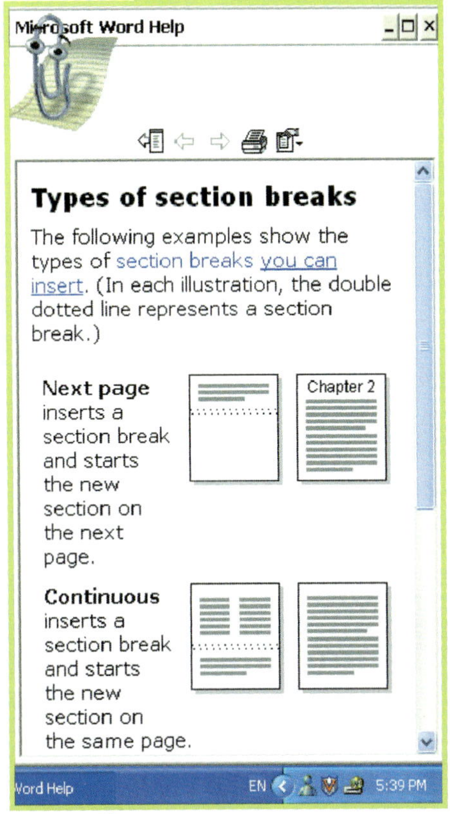

The final type of break allows the user to start a new column when the column option is being used. If you reach a point in your document where you want the text to appear at the top of the next column, you insert a **column break**, which instructs the software to force that text to begin at the top of the next available column.

GETTING IT

Investigate the section break options contained within your word-processing software by accessing the Help menu and looking under section breaks for more details. Summarize the steps to create the various breaks in your Personal Reference Manual.

5.1.4 Widows and Orphans, Headers and Footers

When keying in long documents, you must pay attention to where paragraphs and sections begin and end in order to keep pertinent information together. If you have ever seen a report with a section heading at the end of one page and the first paragraph of that section appearing at the top of the next page, you know what we are referring to. This is where Widow and Orphan protection comes in. A **Widow** occurs when either the section heading or the first line of a paragraph is left behind at the bottom of one page, while the balance appears at the top of the next. An **Orphan** occurs where all but one line of a paragraph appears at the bottom of one page and the last line sits all by itself at the top of the next page. See Figure 5.6 for an example of each problem. Widow and Orphan protection ensures that you will have at least two lines of text in a paragraph together.

Many word-processing programs have some sort of Widow and Orphan protection as an option. In WordPerfect, for example, you can select "Keep

Figure 5.6
Example of Widow and Orphan

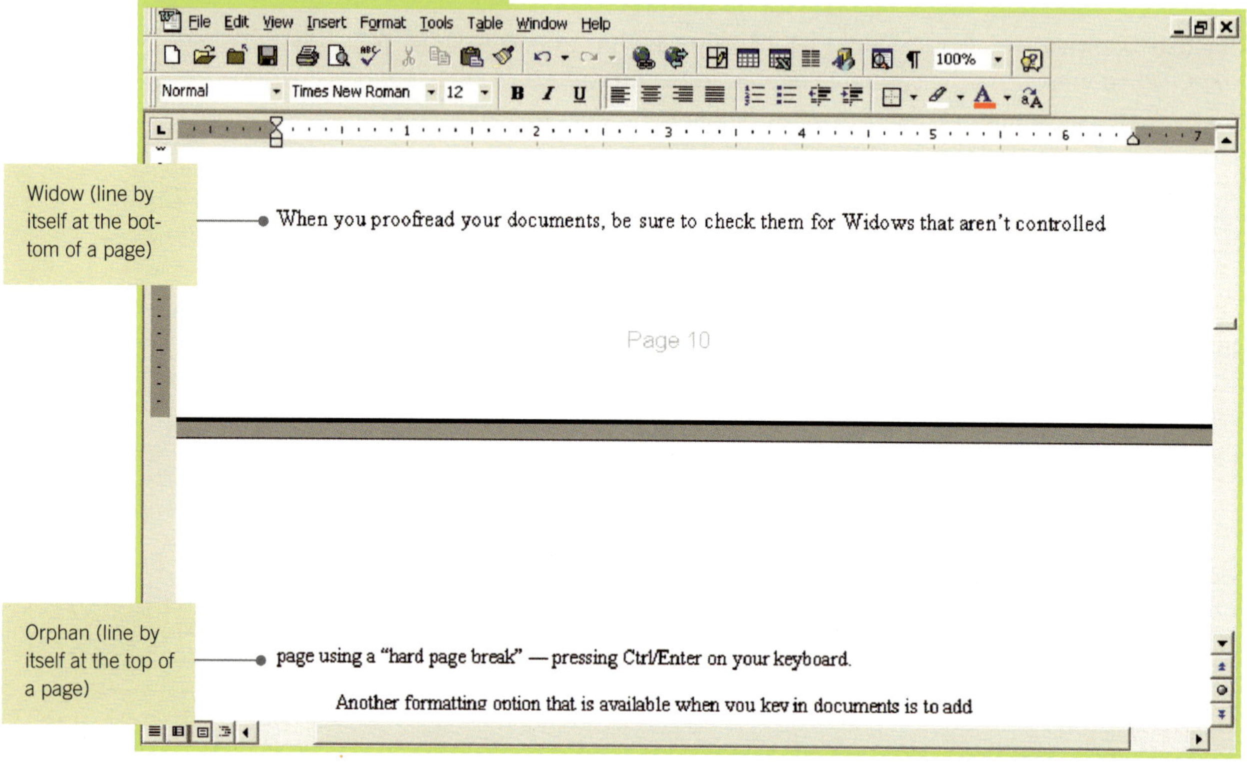

Text Together" from the Format menu for any paragraph that is split in this manner. Figure 5.7 shows the Widow and Orphan control option in Word.

When you proofread your documents, be sure to check them for Widows not controlled by the software. For example, the heading for a section might appear at the bottom of a page, while the first paragraph in the section is at the top of the next page. This requires you to manually adjust the text position by "forcing" the heading to the next page using a "hard page break" — pressing Ctrl/Enter on your keyboard.

Another formatting option that is available when you key in documents is to add Headers and Footers. Most word-processing programs allow you to reserve a portion of the page layout for information that is entered once but appears on all designated pages. A **Header** is the space reserved at the top of the page; the **Footer** is at the bottom. You can enter any type of information in the Header/Footer areas of the page — text, graphics, links, etc. Most programs allow you to specify whether the same header is to be used on all pages in all sections, or to set a different Header/Footer for each section, for odd/even pages, or even to customize the first page of the document to have unique settings.

Figure 5.7
Widow and Orphan Control Option in Word

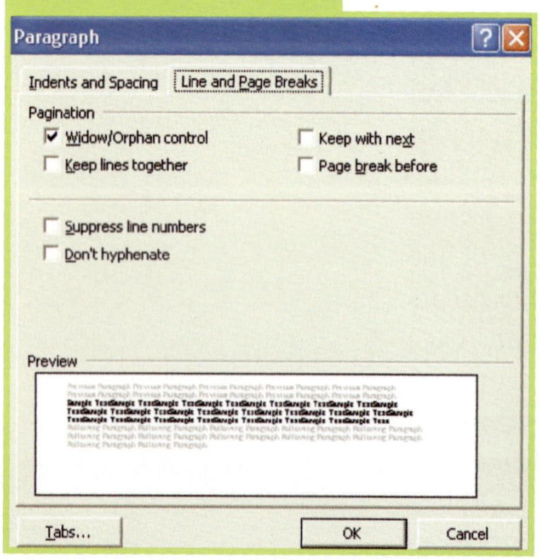

GETTING IT

1. Explain why you should use a hard page break when you start a new page in a document.
2. Explain section breaks and how they can be used in a document.
3. Describe the difference between page breaks and column breaks in a newsletter, for example.
4. What is a Widow? An Orphan? Explain how you can avoid their appearance in a document.
5. Describe how Headers and Footers are used in documents. Give three examples of information that could be entered into Headers and Footers in documents you create as a student.
6. Investigate the Help menu in your word-processing program and add the steps to perform the following tasks to your Personal Reference Manual:
   - Set a Header/Footer on all pages of a document.
   - Set a unique Header/Footer on the first page of a document.
   - Include the page number in a Header/Footer.
   - Include the date (using an automatic date function) in a Header/Footer.
   - Turn on the Widow/Orphan protection feature.
   - Change the options for Widow/Orphan protection.

5.1.5 Find and Replace Features

If you open an existing document and need only to replace, for example, the recipient's name and address in a letter, you simply scroll down and change the text. But, what if your document is 50 pages long and you have to change certain words to update the document? Manually scrolling through the text is problematic on two counts:

- It is time-consuming to find each place where the word appears.
- It is subject to human error and oversight.

Imagine, for example, that near the end of the editing processes the publisher of this textbook chose to change the name of the GET CONNECTED features to IT CONNECTS! There would be too many instances of this name used in the textbook to make the change manually. A quick way to complete this type of task is to use the Find and Replace or Search and Replace feature of a word-processing program. You enter the text or keying sequence you want the program to locate (GET CONNECTED) and what you want it to replace the text with (IT CONNECTS!), and instruct it to proceed. You can set the software to perform the task automatically without intervention, or you can review each case in which the words occur to ensure that the program replaces the text you want replaced. This is

digiknow

You can create a "**watermark**" in a word-processed document by inserting an image and changing the properties of the image so that it appears faintly behind the text on the page.

particularly helpful when the string of letters you have entered could appear in other words and you do not want them replaced as well. Figure 5.8 illustrates the Find and Replace function in Word 97.

Figure 5.8
Find and Replace dialog box

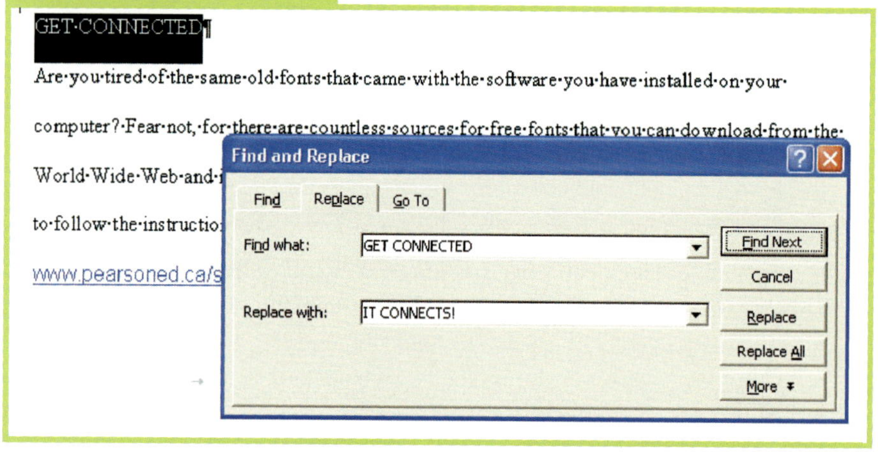

This function allows the user to specify which words to replace and with what. By pressing the Find Next button, the user can manually audit the changes to take place whereas the Replace All button instructs the program to proceed without user intervention.

5.1.6 Navigating Through Documents

When you create longer documents, subject headings should be consistent in both format and style. If, for example, you use the Style feature to denote subject headings as you key in your documents, you can use a feature called the **Document Map** in Word to help you navigate through your document. By selecting Document Map from the view menu, you will see a list of the headings in your document. To go to a particular section in your document, simply click on the heading and the program moves the cursor to the beginning of that section. You can see the main headings or all subheadings by expanding the Document Map-level buttons located beside the section heading. It is very similar to looking at your directory structure in My Computer where you see all the folders. If a folder contains subfolders, it will have a + symbol on the main folder. Clicking on the folder allows you to see the subfolders contained within.

How does the Style feature work? The Style pop-down box is located on the Format toolbar in your word-processing program. A **style** is a preset combination of font style (including enhancements such as bold and italics) and size. If, for example, you wanted to have all main headings in a report in Arial size 16, bold font, you could set that in the style menu under Heading 1. Then, as you key in your document, highlight the text to be formatted in this manner with your mouse or other pointing device and select Heading 1 from the Style menu. This would change the font, size, and enhancements to the style you have determined. Word-processing programs generally have these styles pre-programmed in each document template available for your use. They can, of course, be customized for the look you desire. See Figure 5.9 for an example of the style menu in Word and of the customization options in WordPerfect.

Figure 5.9
Styles Pop-Down Menu

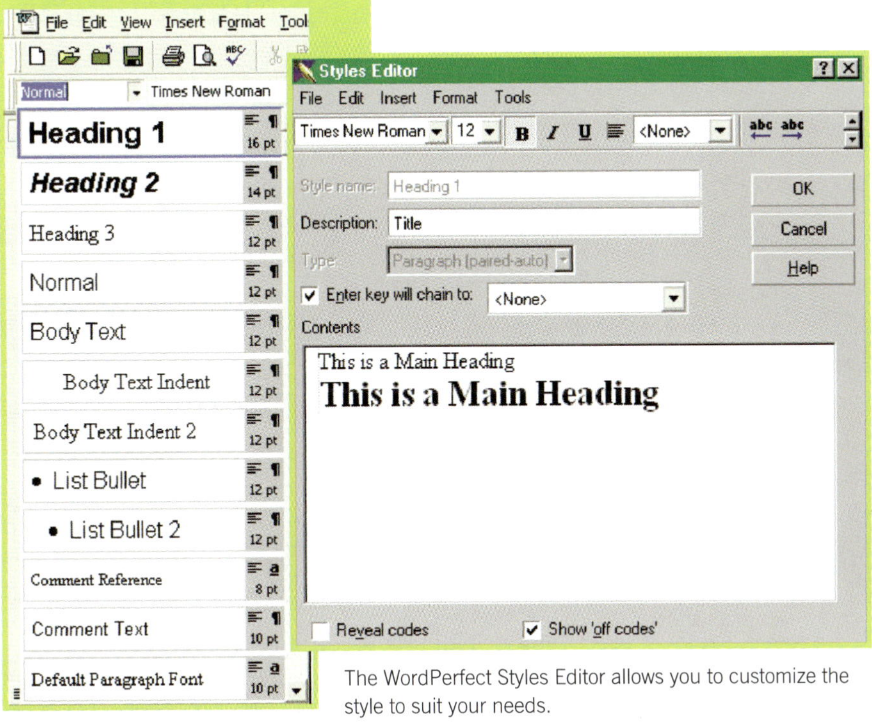

The Styles pop-down menu in Word 97 lists the various styles set for a particular document.

The WordPerfect Styles Editor allows you to customize the style to suit your needs.

Once your document has been formatted to meet your needs, you will be able to easily navigate through it using the Document Map feature.

GETTING IT

1. Describe how Find and Replace features can help to save time and improve accuracy in documents.
2. Describe how a Document Map can help when you are creating a long document.
3. Define *styles*. Explain how the use of the style feature can improve your efficiency in creating documents.

digiknow

Documents may soon be talking for themselves, according to futurist David D. Wienberger. He predicts that documents will not only provide information to their readers, they will customize their own contents depending on who is reading them. These "intelligent documents" will "add information, change graphics, or even determine what readers may or may not see."

(McCormick 1991)

4. Investigate the pull-down menus and the Help menu in your word-processing program and describe how to perform the following functions in your Personal Reference Manual:
   - Replace all instances of the word "but" in a document with the word "and."
   - Replace all places where the letters "on" appear (even if they are in another word) with "in."
   - Create a new style in a document.
5. Format the project plan for your Chapter Project, using the word-processing features and functions covered to date.

5.1.7 Collaboration in Creating Documents

In today's world of business, teamwork and collaboration are crucial to overall corporate success. Computers have given members of organizations the ability to collaborate on projects like never before. This textbook, for example, was created using the built-in functions of word-processing programs. In this way, the authors could work together to produce a seamless final product. This teamwork was assisted greatly by the Internet and the ability to send data files to the members of the team quickly and easily.

As you will read in the chapters on e-business, team members do not have to be physically located in the same office, or even the same city. Worldwide collaboration on new products, designs, and reports is common, where members rarely need to meet face to face. Let us examine some of the tools available to you for your group projects.

- *Highlight.* Just as in the pen-and-paper world, your word-processing program has a built-in **highlighter**—a feature that allows the user to emphasize changes using colour. If a partner were to create a document and you made changes, you could highlight the changes so that your partner could quickly and easily identify them. If, however, the original text were deleted, the author would have to go back to a copy of the original text to know what was there before, in order to determine if the changes were acceptable. The Track Changes feature, available on many programs, eliminates the problem of comparing two versions.
- *Track changes.* The Tools menu of Word contains the **Track Changes** feature. This allows one member of the team to edit the work of another, showing where the changes were made and also showing the text deleted. If the Track Changes feature is turned on, you will see the changes on the screen. It will show in another colour if a third member of the team edits the text as well. To help the author locate the changes easily, there is an additional visual clue: a vertical line appears beside the lines with the changes if Track Changes is activated. When you hold your cursor over the changed text, it indicates who made the change and the date it was changed. See Figure 5.10 for an example of this feature.

Figure 5.10

Track Changes Feature in Word

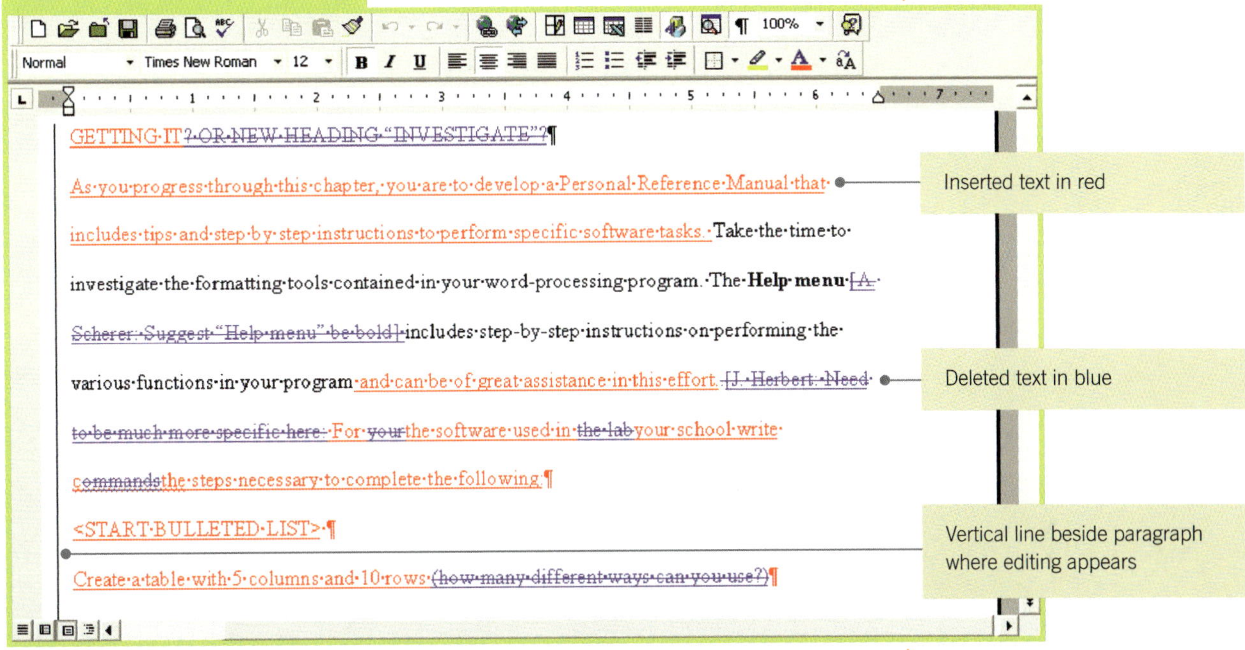

Once each member of the team has had an opportunity to provide input on the final product, the changes must be accepted or rejected. If accepted, the changes shown in colour disappear from the screen, leaving only the final text chosen for inclusion in the paper. See Figure 5.11.

Figure 5.11

Accepting Changes in the Track Changes Feature in Word

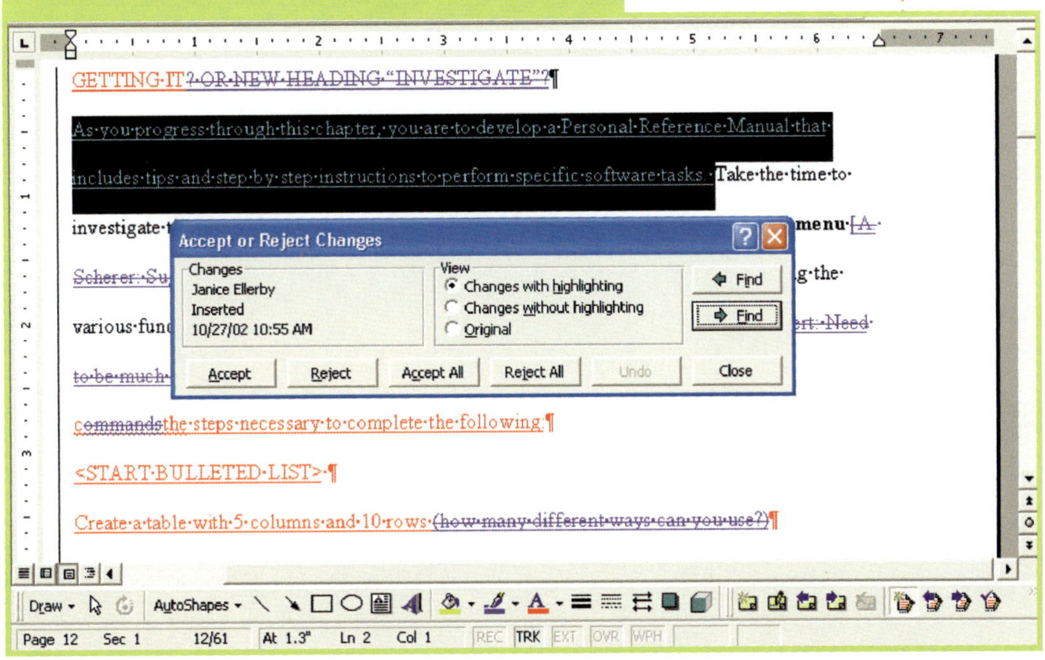

The author has the opportunity to accept each change, reject it, or move on without taking any action. This gives each team member the opportunity to add comments to the original document without creating the need to re-key the entire document.

- *Insert comment.* If a team member does not want to make changes to existing text, but has a **comment** to make about it, he or she can insert a comment into the document (see Figure 5.12). The person who receives the document back is alerted to the comment's existence by highlighted text with the initials of the comment maker as registered on their computer. The comment is hidden from view until the reader positions his or her cursor over the highlighted text. It will then pop up on the screen for review. Team members can save this document under a different name to keep both the original and comment versions separate if desired.

Figure 5.12
Comments Inserted in Text

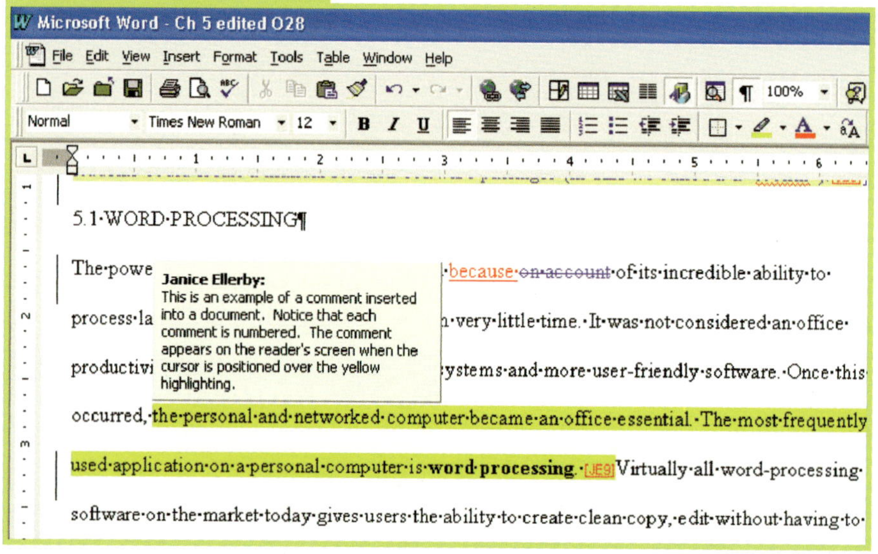

Comments inserted into text by reviewers of documents allow for input to be made without changing the actual words on the page.

These are but a few of the features of word-processing programs that will assist you in creating documents that look professional in your business and personal activities, particularly in team situations. Chapter 6 will examine more advanced functions that are used extensively in the business environment.

GETTING IT

1. Describe the difference between using a highlighter and tracking changes while editing a document.
2. Explain why you think an editor/team member would use the comment option versus the track changes option while reviewing a document.

CAREER PERSPECTIVE 1

A résumé that makes a good first impression can increase your chances of getting an interview. Follow the links at www.pearsoned.ca/businessconnections to research the features of a good résumé. Find examples of résumé templates in your word-processing software. Visit the Guidance or Career Counselling office in your school for information. Then, based on your research, reformat the résumé shown in Figure 5.13 incorporating your word-processing skills. Present your work to the class. Notice the variety of techniques your classmates used — they might come in handy one day.

Figure 5.13

RÉSUMÉ

Tammi Krisnik
25 King Street
Brantford, Ontario
N3T 3C4

Telephone: 519 555 3312

Education

High School	Brantford Central Collegiate
Graduation	June 2003
	High School Diploma (70% average)
Special Skills	Microsoft Office (Word, PowerPoint, Excel)
	Computer Graphics and Animation
	Simply Accounting journalizing

Work Experience

Brantford Health Centre, part-time receptionist for busy medical centre
OPC Credit Union, data-entry clerk during summer months (2 years)

Personal Interests

Squash, cross-country skiing, golf
Reading and writing poetry
Home decorating and baking

References

Will be supplied upon request

5.2 Spreadsheets

digiknow

Depending on the spreadsheet program you use, the names for the file and individual sheets within the file will differ. In Quattro® Pro, for example, the file is a notebook that is made up of 256 individual spreadsheet sheets. In Microsoft® Excel, the file is called a workbook and the individual sheets are referred to as worksheets.

As you know, computers were originally created to handle large quantities of numbers — everything from the Census to an organization's accounting and financial functions. The organization of today relies on computers and programs to handle numbers for a myriad of operations. A **spreadsheet** program allows the user to manipulate data in a two-dimensional matrix of columns and rows that resembles an accounting ledger sheet. Being able to use a spreadsheet is one of the most important competencies in today's business environment. This section will examine the uses of a spreadsheet to help improve office productivity.

5.2.1 The Spreadsheet Screen

A **notebook/workbook** is made up of a number of individual **worksheets** that can be treated separately or linked together for related information. All worksheets consist of a series of columns and rows (see Figure 5.14) in which the user enters information. That information belongs to one of three types:

- ***Values***: the numeric entries or data that are used to perform calculations;
- ***Labels***: the text that describes the data contained in the various cell locations; and
- ***Formulas and functions***: the commands that tell the software what to do with the cell content.

Labels are essential for you to understand the data contained in the spreadsheet and the results of calculations performed on the data. Rows and columns of numbers are meaningless without labels to help you make sense of them.

When the designer of a spreadsheet enters formulas using cell references into it, the power of the software is unleashed. From that point forward, when the values in the spreadsheet are changed, the formulas automatically recalculate the results. This allows for:

- the periodic updating of numbers;
- the reuse of spreadsheet templates for recurring applications; and
- the performance of "what if" analysis, where values can be changed and the results seen instantly!

"What if" analysis is particularly helpful when management needs to make decisions because the impact of such decisions can be measured prior to venturing into new areas. Organizations rarely venture into new business areas (e.g., products or services) unless it can be demonstrated that an

Figure 5.14
Quattro® Pro Spreadsheet

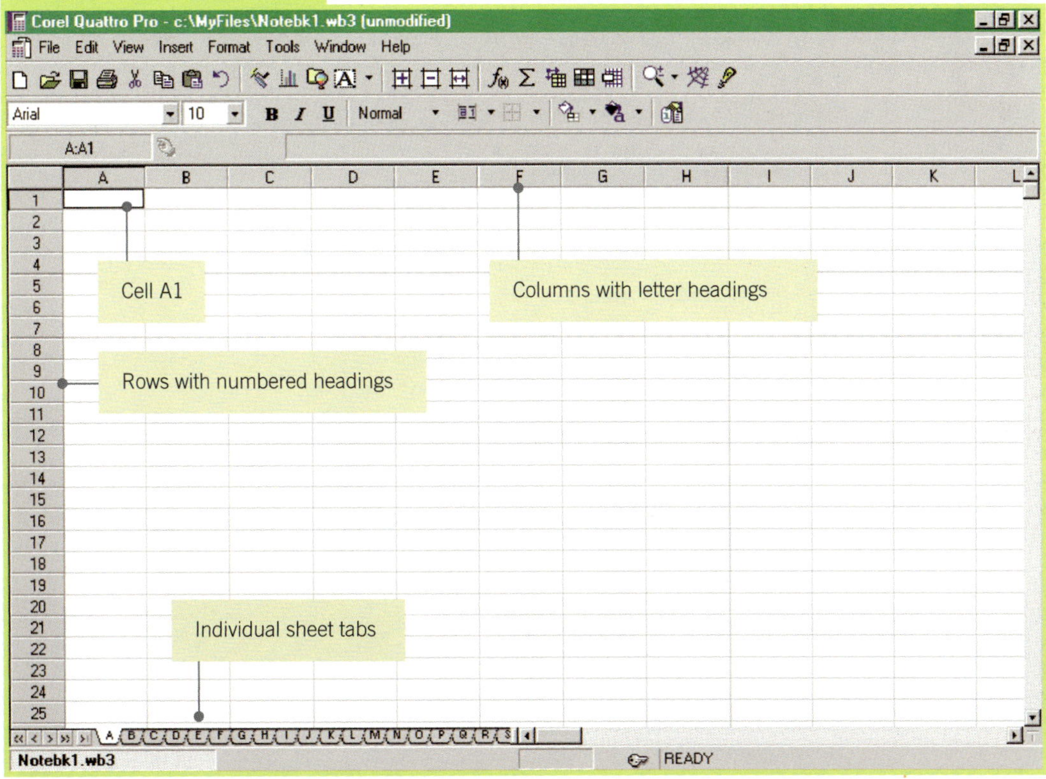

undertaking has the potential to generate revenue and profit. The tool to use for this type of analysis is the spreadsheet. For example, a product manager would forecast the potential sales for new software, then calculate the costs to bring the product to market and determine if it will be profitable based on this analysis. If the figures look positive, the company may go ahead with the new product.

It is very important for you to enter values into a worksheet cell without any formatting symbols (e.g., $ or ,) or spaces where commas would appear. Otherwise, the program will treat the values as labels or text and you will be unable to manipulate or perform calculations on the data in that cell. Instead, format the cell content using the toolbars and formatting menus (see Figure 5.15) as an aid to understanding. Examine the various formatting options contained in your spreadsheet program as you enter values in your worksheets. The numeric data in a worksheet can be formatted in a variety of ways:

- as currency;
- as percentages;
- as positive or negative values; and
- with or without decimal places.

Figure 5.15
Formatting Your Spreadsheet

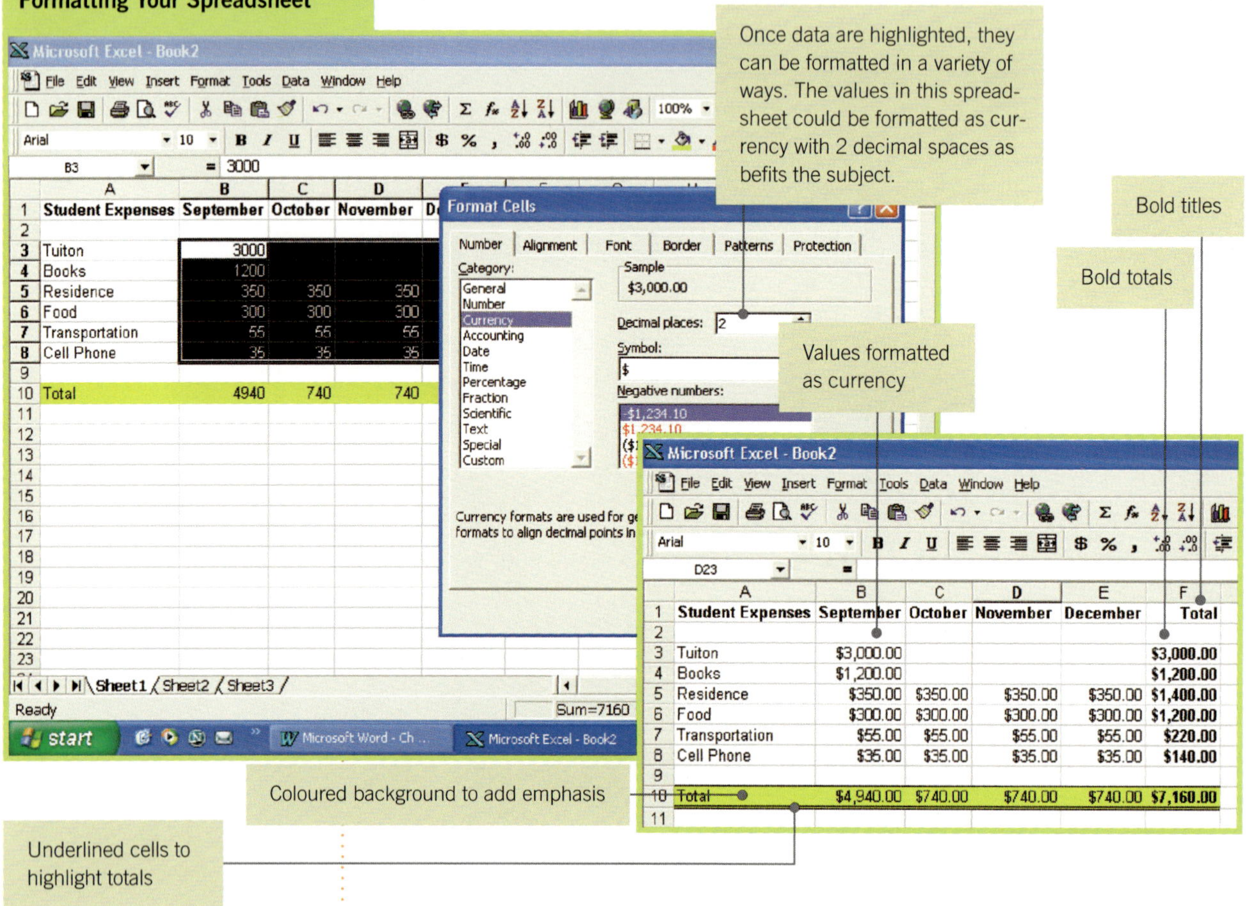

Other tools are available to enhance the visual appeal of the entire worksheet as well. Text and background colours can be changed to highlight information. The individual cells or a range of adjacent cells can be formatted with borders. And, just as in word processing, the text alignment can be changed for information in individual cells or groups of cells.

5.2.2 Working With Columns and Rows

As you create a spreadsheet, you might find that the content of a cell needs more width. Many programs can be set to automatically adjust the column width as you proceed. This is more efficient than skipping columns as your cell content spills over into adjacent columns.

If you find that you require an additional column between existing data or that you need to delete a column, you can easily make these changes. In most programs, you simply click on the column heading (alphabetical) and use either the Insert or Delete command as required. Once you have established the spreadsheet template and entered labels and values, you are ready to insert formulas and functions. Regardless of the changes you make to the formatting of your spreadsheet, it is important to make these changes *after* you have entered all necessary formulas and functions for the data. Adding more data or formulas to a formatted sheet may overwrite formatting, making it necessary to redo it.

GETTING *IT*

1. Explain what a spreadsheet is and who might use it.
2. Explain why the ability to use a spreadsheet is so important in today's business environment.
3. Create a comparison chart that shows the difference among labels, values, and formulas as they pertain to spreadsheets.
4. How does the use of formulas increase the functionality of a spreadsheet?
5. Explain why users must enter values in their "raw" format.
6. Use the Help menu in your spreadsheet software to determine the steps required to complete the following tasks. Summarize them in your Personal Reference Manual:
   - Change the font type and size.
   - Change the format of numerical data (values) to currency with two decimals.
   - Centre the heading of a spreadsheet across four columns.
   - Change the text colour or background colour of cells.
   - Add a border around spreadsheet data.
7. Explain why you think a user would insert or delete columns and rows in a spreadsheet.

5.2.3 Formulas and Functions

As mentioned previously, the power of the spreadsheet lies in its ability to perform calculations on numeric data quickly and accurately. To have the program perform these operations, you use formulas and functions. A **formula** is a step-by-step procedure entered into a worksheet cell following the order of operations learned in Math class. For example, the formula =(B2+B3+B4+B5)/B6 instructs the program to add the content of cells B2 through B5 (inclusive) and divide that result by the value in cell B6. Regardless of the values contained in these cells, the formula will always perform the same procedure. This allows the user to change the values in any of the cells B2 through B6 and determine the results quickly and accurately.

Depending on the software you use, the math operator at the beginning of the formula will be a symbol such as = (equal sign) or + (plus sign).

Most spreadsheet software is also pre-programmed to perform a variety of **functions** from simple to complex calculations on the values contained in its cells. Like the rounding button on your calculator, which increases or decreases the number of decimal places to which to round the results, the functions in a spreadsheet perform desired actions on the values identified. For example, the most commonly used function is SUM, which adds up the values specified. Functions allow the user to enter a range of numbers (cells that are adjacent to one another) or individual cells upon which the calculations are performed. The function =SUM(A4:A228,B5) will add up the values in cells A4 through A228 and cell B5 and display the result where the function is keyed.

Functions include frequently performed mathematical, statistical, financial, and engineering calculations among others. There are hundreds of functions built into most of today's spreadsheet programs, each allowing the user to calculate everything from the monthly payment for a loan to the computed value of a number raised to a power. Exercises using these functions will help you develop competency in this important business software.

> **Get Connected**
>
> Many tutorial sites on the Web help spreadsheet users increase their skill and productivity using this powerful software and its functions. To learn more about spreadsheet programs, visit two of the tutorial Web sites available at www.pearsoned.ca/businessconnections. Create a list of the topics each tutorial site offers users in the spreadsheet section. Select one of the tutorials and follow the steps contained therein. Write a short review of the tutorial describing how easy it was to follow. Compare your findings with those of your classmates.

GETTING IT

1. Explain the difference between a formula and a function.
2. Using the pull-down menus and Help menu of your spreadsheet software, determine the following and add the information to your Personal Reference Manual:
   - which operator is used at the beginning of formulas (e.g. +, =, @);
   - the function used to calculate the monthly payment for a car and the information needed to complete the function;
   - the function used to calculate the number of days between February 1 and August 5 in a particular year; and
   - the function used to find the average of the values stored in cells B6 through B12.
3. Create a budget for your Chapter Project using formula and function spreadsheet formatting techniques.

5.2.4 Time-Saving Features

As you enter data, you often find the information is repetitive or linear in nature. For example, if you are entering a formula to calculate the total of a series of rows in a worksheet, it is more efficient to enter the formula once and copy it down the column to calculate the total of each row. The **Fill Command** allows you to do that (see Figure 5.16). The same would be true for a formula or an amount you wish to copy across columns. You simply "grab" the Fill Handle at the bottom right corner of the cell with your mouse and drag it across/down until you reach the final cell location you wish to copy it to.

The Fill option also allows you to create a **series** of values or labels that follow a sequence. For example, if you wanted to enter the values 1 through 20 in a column, you need only enter the 1 in the first cell, highlight the cells with the fill handle, then access the Series command to specify the type of series you wish to create. You are not limited to numeric values either. For example, in Microsoft® Excel, you can create series for days of the week, months, dates, and times; you can even create a series that skips periods.

5.2.5 Sorting Data

It is always necessary to analyze the data created in a spreadsheet. But often the order in which data are entered into the sheet is not the easiest to analyze. For example, if you are the sales manager of an organization and you have 25 sales professionals reporting to you, their sales would most likely be entered into a spreadsheet in alphabetical order for each week or month. At the end of the year, however, you need to analyze their sales to determine such things as sales bonuses and the top salesperson that year. In this case, it would be more efficient to organize the sales data numerically, not alphabetically.

Fortunately, the creators of spreadsheet programs have anticipated this need and added **sorting functions** to the software. In order to preserve the original data, it is important to first copy the data to another sheet tab within the program. You can then take the original data as entered, highlight the columns you wish to sort, starting with the column that contains the primary sort data (e.g., total sales), and activate the sorting command. By starting with the Total Sales column and highlighting the other data after, the name of the salesperson stays linked with her or his total so that the data do not become scrambled. This gives an accurate gauge of the performance of your sales personnel quickly and easily.

5.2.6 Manipulating Worksheets

When you wish to copy an entire worksheet to another sheet tab in your document, as in the example above, the software can perform the operation in a few simple steps. First, access the Move or Copy Sheet menu (see Figure 5.17). If you simply want to move the worksheet, click on or enter the sheet tab you want to move it to and press OK. If you need a copy of the worksheet, click on the Create a Copy box and the location desired before you press OK in Microsoft Excel, or copy and paste the entire sheet to a new location in Quattro Pro. It is as simple as that! Then you can manipulate the data without disturbing the original information.

Figure 5.16
Using the Fill Command in a Spreadsheet

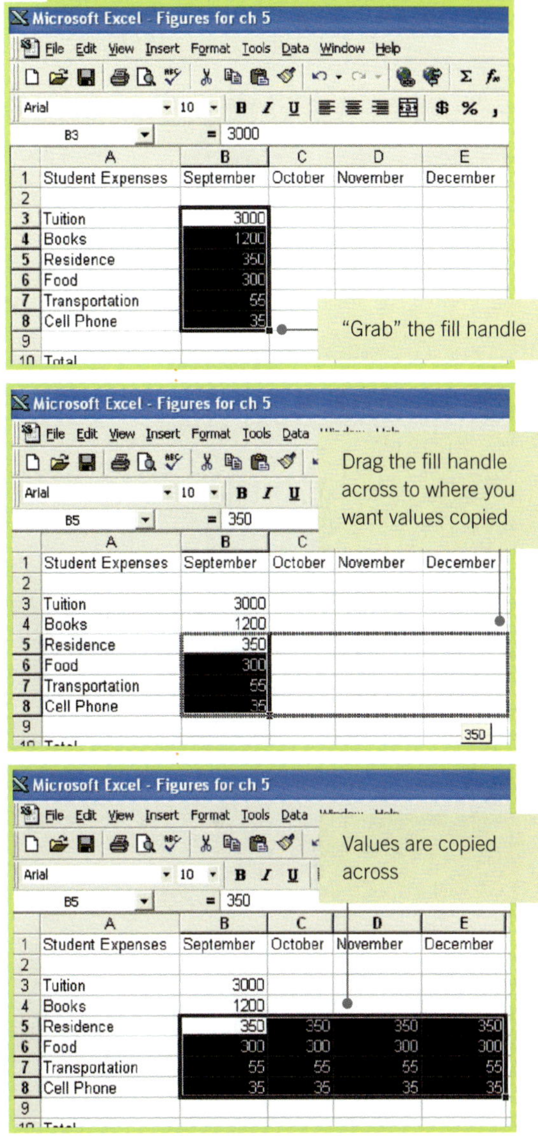

Figure 5.17
Move and Copy Worksheet Menu

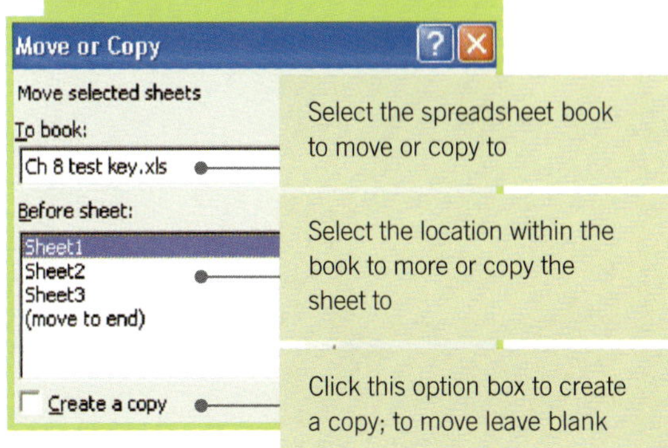

5.2.7 Linking Worksheets With Word-Processed Documents

Often, the results of your work in spreadsheet applications must be incorporated into reports that help management make decisions based on the numbers you have calculated. Today's office productivity software packages make this integration of applications possible. When you reach the point in your word-processed document where you want the spreadsheet data inserted, you **link** with the file that contains the desired data (see Figure 5.18). But what if you have to change the data in the spreadsheet? By linking the word-processed document with the spreadsheet file, the data in the document are automatically updated when changes are made to the spreadsheet. This creates a shortcut within the word-processed document to the source file in the spreadsheet program. Each time the source file is altered, the changes are reflected within the document.

Figure 5.18
Linking Spreadsheets within Documents

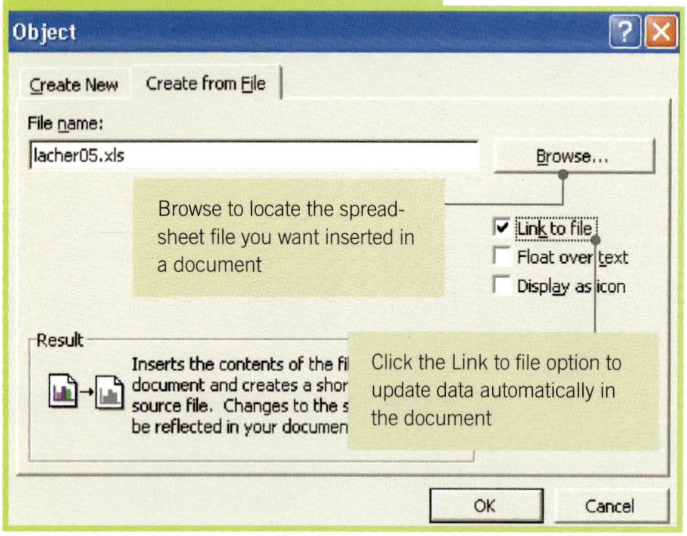

Spreadsheet software has long been used by organizations to increase their overall effectiveness and efficiency in working with data. These are but a few of the techniques you can use as you learn to unleash the power of this software. Chapter 6 will give you the opportunity to develop more advanced skills in this area. Another, even more powerful, application contained within office productivity packages is the database.

GETTING IT

1. Describe how the Fill Command works.
2. Give three examples where spreadsheet data would require sorting (other than the example in the text).
3. Explain how object linking between spreadsheets and word-processing software works.
4. Use the pull-down menus and the Help menu in your spreadsheet program to investigate and determine the steps to complete the following tasks. Summarize the steps in your Personal Reference Manual.
   - Copy a formula down a column, using the Fill command.
   - Create a series in a column — a list of the months of the year — using the Fill command.
   - Create a series in a row — numbers 1 through 30 — using the Fill command.
   - Sort data in a spreadsheet in ascending order, then in descending order.
   - Link a spreadsheet with a word-processed document so that the document automatically updates when you make changes to the spreadsheet file.

5.3 Databases

The transition to an information-based society has changed the way we do everything in both our personal and business lives. The amount of information that is "out there" is staggering. Computer technology, however, has led to the development of the tools to manage this information onslaught — database software.

A **database** program allows for the storage, organization, retrieval, and management of large quantities of data. Every day you interact with databases in all forms — from your PDA where you store your assignment due dates and personal contact lists, to the telephone directory, to Internet search engines that categorize and index Web sites for later retrieval.

To understand how database software works it is helpful to think of a filing cabinet (Figure 5.19). Within a filing cabinet you find files of related information; for example, student names and addresses in one file, grades in another file. Within each file you find individual records — in our example, one record per student in the school. Every student record is made up of individual pieces of information, such as last name, first name, telephone number, etc. Each bit of information is called a field.

The information contained in each field is determined by its **field** type. Names and addresses, for example, are **text fields**. A student's date of birth would be entered as a date field so that the program could do an age calculation. Other fields could be entered as **numeric data** to allow the program to perform mathematical calculations on records in that field. In a sales database, for example, the amount of the sale and related taxes would be entered as numeric data so that totals could be calculated and analyzed. **Computed fields** can also be included in a database that contains formulas similar to those discussed in the spreadsheet section of this chapter. This allows only raw data to be entered into the database and the program to perform the computations. Computed fields are similar to formulas and functions in a spreadsheet, containing instructions for the program to utilize. Figure 5.20 shows the steps and screens to create a database using Microsoft® Works Database software.

digiknow

Our society has moved from agricultural- to industrial- to information-based all within 200 years.

Figure 5.19
A Traditional Database

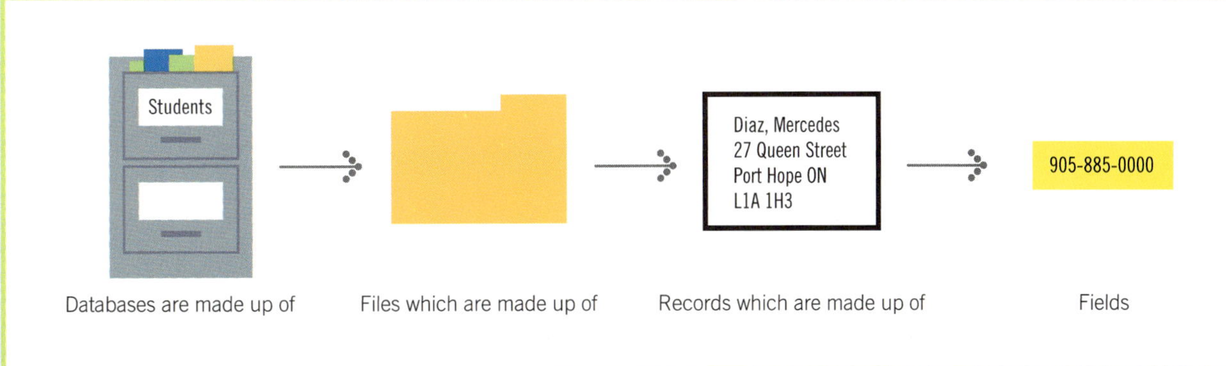

Figure 5.20

Building a Database

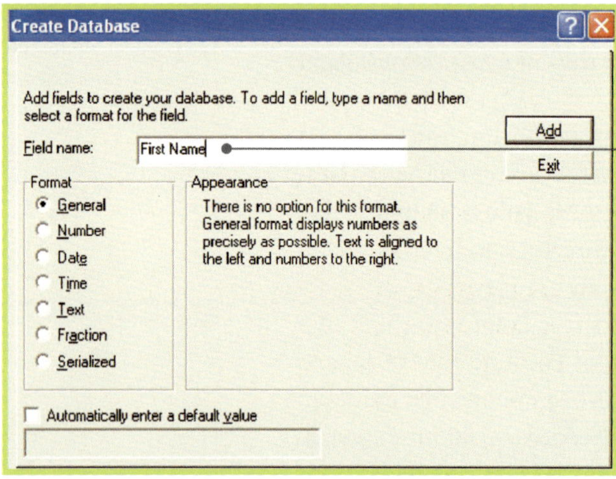

The first step in creating a database is to define the fields and the field types. In this Microsoft Works database, you specify the Field name and then Format. You can even enter a default value for information that remains constant.

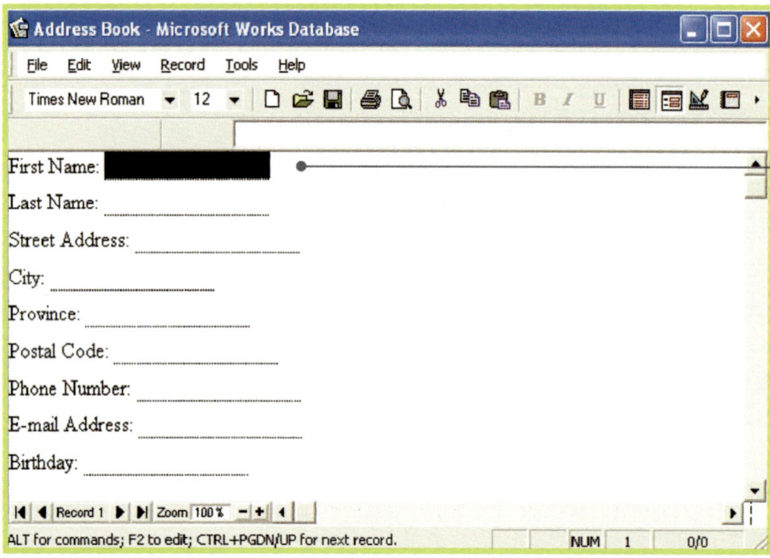

Most database programs allow for the creation of standard form-style data entry which may be easier to use to enter variable information.

GETTING IT

1. Describe how a file cabinet and a computerized database are similar. How are they different?
2. Explain why you think it is necessary to categorize the type of data entered into a database.
3. List and describe the advantages of using computerized databases.

5.3.1 Advantages of a Database

If we compare a computerized database to a standard filing cabinet, why go to all the bother of entering the data in a computer file? A database program offers several advantages:

- *Quantity*. If you only have two or three dozen customers, it is very easy to maintain a paper-and-pen database of sales and accounts. On the other hand, a database on two or three *thousand* customers is much harder to control. As volume increases, so does the demand for more efficient methods of keeping track of sales, returns, amounts owing and paid, and payments overdue.
- *Ease of retrieval*. Once the information has been entered into the database, the user can retrieve all, or only some of, the information quickly and easily. Customers will frequently call an organization with which they do business to ascertain the amount they owe at that moment. If this information is stored in a database, the answer can be retrieved within seconds, whereas in a paper-based file system the individual would have to pull all the sales records, payment records, and return records to calculate the amounts owing from all that related information.
- *Ease of organization*. Imagine, if you will, a doctor's office where all the files are stored alphabetically by patients' last name. If the office manager decided to assign each patient a number in an effort to streamline the storage and retrieval of files, all the files would have to be pulled and sorted manually to conform to the new filing system. In a computerized database, organizing the records in a different order is accomplished quickly and easily with a few keystrokes. If you don't like the new method, you can revert to the old one just as easily.
- *Flexibility in printing*. The information in a database can be retrieved and printed in a variety of ways. Names and addresses can be merged with a word-processed document to personalize letters, for example. Student names and homeroom allocations can be printed to let students know where to report on the first day of school. Report card data can be assembled for printing on official forms. Once the information is in a database, it can be printed in whole or in part depending on the requirements of the user.

The key to a successful database is to plan the information to be entered so that it can meet the needs of the users of the data. Consistency in data entry is also crucial to success. For example, if you enter the province as "ON," you must always enter it in this manner. Mixed entries (e.g., ON, ONT, Ontario) will lead to errors in data sorting and retrieval if you are trying to locate all addresses in that province.

5.3.2 Locating Information in a Database

Once the data have been entered into the database, you can perform a number of operations to locate and organize specific information. Browsing through records, performing queries, and sorting the data are three such operations that will be examined here.

> **Get Connected**
>
> Learning to use database software can be daunting. Fortunately, there are a number of online tutorials available to help you to become more adept at creating databases. To learn more about database programs, visit two of the tutorial Web sites available at www.pearsoned.ca/businessconnections. Create a list of the topics each tutorial site offers users in the database section. Select one of the tutorials and follow the steps contained therein. Write a short review of the tutorial to describe how easy it was to follow. Compare your findings with those of others in your class.

- *Browsing through a database.* There are a number of ways to find information in a database. The first is to **browse** through the records, scrolling down the screen manually looking for specific entries. This is not the most efficient way to locate records, because you might not see what you are looking for as the cursor scrolls past its location. It is more efficient to perform a database query.
- *Performing queries.* A **query** is a question you pose to the database. For example, "What is John Smith's telephone number?" or "What are the names and addresses of all customers who purchased PDAs in the last two weeks?" Performing a query, however, is not as simple as asking the question; it often requires that a special query language be entered into the program to produce the desired results. The way in which you perform a query depends on the program you use. Some programs have developed user-friendly interfaces to simplify this special process, using such familiar mathematical symbols as =, >=, <=, <, > to describe what is being sought. Once the query has been entered, the results can be printed out or displayed on screen.
- *Sorting data.* The data in a database are rarely useful to an end user in their raw form, so it is often helpful to organize the data in a specific order. For example, to generate class lists for every class in your school each period of the day, it would be important to sort the data by course code, then by last name and first name of each student in the class. Individual reports could then be generated to provide this information to your teacher. The Sort command in a database allows you to specify on which field(s) to sort the data to produce the desired result. You also have the option of sorting in ascending (e.g., A–Z) or descending (e.g., Z–A) order, depending on your specific needs.

GETTING IT

1. Why is consistency important in data entry?
2. Why is browsing through a database to find information inefficient?
3. What is a query and how does it work?
4. How can sorting add to the usefulness of database output?

5. Use the Help menu in your database program to determine the steps to perform the following tasks. Summarize them in your Personal Reference Manual.
   - Create the structure for a database.
   - Change the field type in a database from text to numeric with two decimal spaces.
   - Enter a computed field in a database to multiply the quantity field by the price field.
   - Perform a query to find the student record for Janet Simms.
   - Sort records in descending alphabetical order.

IT In Action

Keeping Track with the Blue Jays

Adapted from Ted Smalley Bowen, "IT scores a hit with baseball scouts," *The Globe and Mail*, Wednesday, July 10, 2002.

If you have ever been to a major league baseball game or watched one on television, you know that the scoreboards always post the players' stats on the giant screen and that the sportscasters are a wealth of information regarding the players' batting, RBIs, and earned runs, for example. But what about the players who are just being scouted by the big leagues? Major league teams, like the Toronto Blue Jays, employ a legion of scouts to watch the players in their amateur and minor league teams and make reports on the players they are keeping their eyes on. In the days leading up to the amateur draft, it used to be the norm to see executives shuffling through mounds of scouting reports on tables trying to get a handle on the talent that was out there, calling scouts in the field to get updates on the current situation.

Now, teams like the Blue Jays have embraced database technology to profile the up-and-coming players, entering the information into extensive systems that compile the players' every hit, run, and error, and the scout's judgment as to their future prospects. Now, with extensive intelligence reports at their fingertips, Blue Jays management enters the draft viewing digital videos of prospective players and scrolls through scouting reports on their laptops in conference rooms. Reports are up to date, synchronized daily with the main database in Toronto, so that everyone in the organization is working with the same data. They can perform extensive analyses on the players they are considering to determine the optimum mix in the organization.

The teams that have embraced this technology have cited speed and accuracy as two of the main benefits of automating the scouting system. They feel it improves their odds of getting the players they want and the most out of the players they have.

Questions

1. Explain how sports teams have employed database technology to help improve the teams' overall productivity.

2. List the statistics you think should be kept for such sports as baseball, basketball, and hockey to help scouts keep track of essential information on potential players. Explain how the data will be reported. Why do you think these statistics are important?

5.3.3 Data Retrieval

As mentioned above, once you have located the information you need to retrieve from a database, it is sometimes necessary to print the results of the query. The most common form of retrieval is the **report**, an organized printout of the records and fields in an easy-to-read format. Most database programs allow you to generate reports in a number of preformatted designs or to customize a report to suit your requirements. These preformatted designs are contained in the program as templates that can be accessed through the use of Wizards — programs within the software that direct you step-by-step to produce the desired report. Most reports arrange data in columns, with summary lines that contain calculated information such as totals or averages based on the records contained therein.

Organizations frequently export database information into a word-processing program to create mailing labels and to personalize letters. The word-processing program accesses the database fields and records and formats the data in its software to generate the documents. This is another example of how integrated software can help to improve overall office productivity.

Since the information in a database is organized in a manner similar to a spreadsheet, the data can be copied from a database table onto a worksheet by highlighting the desired records, then copying and pasting. The data can then be manipulated, organized, sorted, and even charted using the spreadsheet software tools. Many programs allow the user to save the data in another format so that it can be exported and used in that software. For example, the creator of a database in Microsoft® Access can export the file so that users of dBASE® or FoxPro® can use the data as well.

As you will read in the chapters ahead, businesses are utilizing the power of the database to cross-reference information and find out all they can about customer buying habits and trends in data that couldn't be found without the ability to analyze large quantities of information quickly and accurately. **Data mining** is this examination and extraction of information from databases. For example, retail stores examine the shopping habits of men and women to determine if there are differences and then tailor their marketing messages to appeal to different market segments. They also perform extensive customer analysis using customers' postal codes as the basis for establishing new store locations in areas where demand already exists. The information is out there — it takes a database and inquiring minds to locate its hidden jewels!

GETTING IT

1. Explain how database reports are used to retrieve information. Describe how you create a report in the database program used in your lab.
2. Describe how users can incorporate the contents of databases into other programs. Give two examples.

ON THE CASE

Data Mining for Gold in Northern Ontario

Based on Burke Campbell and Murray Conron, "Data under the scope: Mining corporate databases means even the smallest detail can turn up gold," *National Post*, January 14, 2002, National Edition, p. IT1/Front.

In the face of increased competition from providers of telephone, cellular, paging, mobile satellite, and high-speed Internet services, Northern Telephone needed to locate the "mother lode" or key to its future success in the mountain of data it had on hand. Within the records collected from all of its customers' calls, Northern Telephone needed to determine its most profitable services and customer groups and capitalize on these to meet emerging customer needs. No small task, to say the least.

This process, called data mining, is ideal for sorting through reams of customer data to identify and sort group users of products and services according to past use. For example, heavy telephone use between 3 p.m. and 6 p.m. each day suggests a household with teenagers whereas extensive use of telephone, fax, and modems between 8 a.m. and 4 p.m. might suggest business use. By identifying specific user groups, marketing campaigns to promote products and services to meet those customer needs can be more effectively developed and employed. For example, that household with teenagers in it might benefit from a call answering service so that important calls do not have to be interrupted!

Data mining has become even more popular in tight economic times when businesses are trying to maximize the sales to their existing customer base, because the cost to retain an existing customer is much less than that of attracting new customers. Many organizations are "striking it rich" with data mining, discovering relationships within their data that might not have been suspected before. New software allows data miners to ask very specific questions such as, "Which existing customers are most likely to buy our new product?"

The cost of implementing such a program is significant, but so can be the returns. Compared with mass marketing campaigns that take a "blanket" approach (sending out a message to everyone hoping it "covers" someone), data mining allows for a more targeted approach, increasing the customer purchase rate.

So, the next time your telephone provider calls asking if you are interested in a new product or service, chances are they suspect you will — the data told them so!

Questions

1. Explain how companies are using data collected in everyday operations to help them sell new products and services.
2. As you go through your next week or two, record all the times a retailer or other business/organization collects data on you. Consider bank card use, loyalty card use, telephone/cell/pager use, etc. From the data you have collected, write a paragraph that describes what a provider of new products or services could know about you. Identify other products/services you might be a good target for.

5.4 Emerging Software Practices in Business

The past decade has seen the emergence of a virtual plethora of software programs, from childrens' educational software to high-end specialized applications designed for specific customers and applications. As the personal computer has become established in the home, SOHOs, and, of course, the large corporation, the choice of software to use has been nothing less than overwhelming. New versions of software are being released before many users develop competencies in existing versions. The cost for an organization to upgrade to newer software versions is staggering as well.

One of the solutions that has emerged is the "rental" of software applications from **Application Service Providers (ASP)**, organizations that provide access to software applications via the Internet. These are important sources of software for smaller organizations and individuals with small technology budgets, and for large organizations as a form of outsourcing (i.e., hiring outside firms to perform specific functions). The software is kept up to date and is maintained by professionals at the ASP. The services are Web-based, so they are available from any Internet connection. For small businesses some software is prohibitively expensive, so renting from an ASP is the only way to afford its use. They usually charge minimal subscription fees to cover the cost of providing the software and any technical support required. This is not the solution for every organization and one should investigate it carefully before investing in it.

GETTING IT

In groups, use search tools to find information about other emerging hardware, software, and ergonomic practices in business. Select appropriate software (e.g., word processor, spreadsheet, database) on which to record the information you located. Share your group's findings with your class.

CAREER PERSPECTIVE 2

When applying for a job, a strong résumé and effective cover letter are essential. In preparation for future job searches, do the following:

1. Identify five organizations for which you would like to work. Create a database that has fields for the name of the organization, the person to whom résumés should be sent (if possible), and address fields.

(continued)

2. Use your favourite search engine to locate and bookmark two Web sites that provide advice on creating an effective résumé and writing cover letters. Prepare a summary of the information using word-processing software.
3. Use the advanced software features covered in this chapter as well as the information from your research to create a word-processed résumé for yourself.
4. Use word-processing software to create a cover letter to accompany your résumé. Use a template if available. Be sure to create fields with which to merge your employer database. Conduct the merge to create a set of customized letters.
5. E-mail the résumé and cover letter to your instructor.

IT's A Wrap

Key Terms in This Chapter

ASCII (American Standard Code for Information Interchange) (p. 121)
ASP (Application Service Providers) (p. 146)
browse (p. 142)
column (p. 119)
column break (p. 123)
comment (p. 130)
computed fields (p. 139)
database (p. 139)
data mining (p. 144)
Document Map (p. 126)
field (p. 139)
Fill Command (p. 136)
Footer (p. 124)
font sets (p. 120)
formula (p. 135)
function (p. 135)
hard page break (p. 122)
Header (p. 124)
Help menu (p. 120)
highlighter (p. 128)
justify (p. 119)
labels (p. 132)
line spacing (p. 120)
link (p. 138)
notebook (p. 132)
numeric data (p. 139)
Orphan (p. 123)
query (p. 142)
report (p. 144)
section break (p. 123)
series (p. 136)
shortcut keystrokes (p. 120)
soft return (p. 122)
sorting function (p. 137)
spreadsheet (p. 132)
style (p. 126)
table (p. 118)
text field (p. 139)
Track Changes (p. 128)
values (p. 132)
watermark (p. 125)
Widow (p. 123)
word processing (p. 118)
workbook (p. 132)
worksheet (p. 132)

1. Create a list of information technology competencies that you have acquired thoroughout your work in this chapter. Use a table with the headings Word Processing, Database, and Spreadsheet.
2. Update your portfolio to include examples of work from this chapter.

IT's A Wrap (continued)

Know It!

3. Explain why it is important to "plan" your documents prior to keying a single word.
4. Describe where tables are most effectively used in documents.
5. Explain the difference between a hard and soft page break. Hard and soft return.
6. "The Document Map doesn't list all the headings in my report!" Explain why you think this statement could be true. How could it be remedied?
7. Describe to a "newbie" the essential components of the spreadsheet screen and contents.
8. Explain how the use of functions can improve your efficiency in entering data into a spreadsheet.

Do It!

9. After you complete the project for this chapter, have another class member review your plan using the collaboration tools outlined in this chapter.
10. Analyze the different symbols available in the various font sets in your word-processing software. Create a chart that details the symbols you will use frequently and the font set they are located in for future reference.
11. Using a report or essay you have keyed and saved for another course, apply the styles in your word-processing program to it. Customize the styles as necessary to suit *your* style.
12. Develop a "Quick Reference Chart" for your spreadsheet software outlining commonly used formulas and functions for your notes.
13. Develop the structure for a database for:
    a. your CD/DVD collection
    b. your personal address book
    c. definitions of key terms you need to study from for any course

    Once you have the data entered, create a report to output the data in a variety of sorted orders.

Analyze It!

14. Many computer users rely solely on the mouse to perform software operations. Explain why you think this method is or is not the most efficient. What alternatives are there?
15. Explain how you think geographically dispersed work teams are utilizing collaboration tools in office productivity programs.
16. What options does your spreadsheet software at school have for the use of the Fill command? Describe where you think it can best be used and explain why.
17. Describe the necessary steps to perform a query in your school's database software.
18. Discuss the pros and cons of buying versus renting software through ASPs. List other arguments available for both options.

CHAPTER

Office Productivity 2

6

By the end of this chapter, you will be able to:

- create customized documents that incorporate elements from numerous software packages;
- key multipage business reports;
- use spreadsheets to develop financial plans for personal and business use;
- compile research in a database and analyze the results; and
- communicate with a variety of audiences using electronic tools.

Even though the computer was originally created to process numbers, it has been increasingly seen as a tool to process words and other data as well. Word processing, for example, has all but eliminated other methods of putting ideas on paper. Databases have become the tool of choice for handling large quantities of information that require frequent updating, are accessed on an ongoing basis, and are the basis of management reports. The spreadsheet is the backbone of the financial side of business.

This chapter examines some of the advanced functions and concepts that pertain to these three office productivity software packages. Key topics include:

- Advanced Word-Processing Techniques
- Creating Complex Spreadsheets
- Databases in Business

Ready,

Set,

Go!

This chapter deals with advanced concepts in word-processing, spreadsheet, and database software. To be prepared to embark on this learning, you should:

- retrieve from your portfolio examples of work that demonstrate your skills in these three areas to this point;
- review the skills and techniques required to produce these pieces; and
- be prepared to replicate the pieces for your teacher.

Specifically, your learning should reflect at least the following skills and techniques:

Word Processing	Spreadsheets	Databases
• doing basic data entry • formatting columns and tables • inserting section breaks • using symbols • setting headers/footers	• doing basic data entry • entering formulas and functions • using fill command options • linking spreadsheets with word-processed documents	• defining the structure of database tables, including field types/sizes • doing basic data entry • performing simple queries • generating reports; sorting and totalling data

Introduction to Chapter Project

Recall that the Chapter Project is introduced at the beginning and is to be completed as you work through the chapter. Your teacher will provide you with assessment and evaluation criteria.

CHAPTER PROJECT

One of the most frequent applications for many businesses is the collection and subsequent analysis of data in bringing new products to market. Your project for this chapter is to: develop a proposal for a survey to collect data on a specific product or idea, design the survey, collect the data, tabulate the data in a database that you design, and write an analysis of the data collected in a report. This data can also be used to assist you with your major course project. Specifically, your research must include the following components:

- a proposal that outlines the purpose for the data collection, e.g., to determine which brands of a certain beverage (could be soft drinks, water, sports beverages, etc.) are preferred by grade 12 students;

CHAPTER PROJECT (continued)

- a form designed electronically for the collection of the data from at least 25 respondents;
- a database designed to capture the results of the survey, including fields for text, numeric data, and at least one computed field;
- a spreadsheet of the data and a chart or graph that illustrates the results of your data;
- a report generated from your database program that captures the results of the surveys; and
- a word-processed report that includes:
  - a title page and table of contents (automated or hyperlinked),
  - an executive summary of your findings (a one-page overview of the purpose, findings, and conclusions),
  - the body/text of the report, including an introduction, the purpose of the study, and the findings, and
  - a conclusion that gives recommendations based on your findings.

6.1 Advanced Word-Processing Techniques

The ability to use word-processing software is a basic skill required in today's business and education environments. As discussed in Chapter 5, word-processing software incorporates a wide variety of features and options designed to help you produce professional-looking documents. Beyond the basics of data entry, formatting, and structuring a document into sections, numerous advanced features give the user the tools to produce highly sophisticated multipage and integrated documents. Word-processing software, like any of the components of office productivity packages, is designed to give the user the tools to improve his or her overall efficiency on the job. Let us examine some of these tools that can help you improve your productivity.

6.1.1 Macros

If you perform a task repeatedly in word processing, you can automate the task using a macro. A **macro** is a series of commands and instructions that you group together under a single command to accomplish a task automatically. That is, instead of manually performing a series of time-consuming, repetitive actions, you can create and run a single macro — a custom command — that accomplishes the task for you.

Here are some examples of typical uses for macros:

- *to speed up routine editing and formatting* (e.g., format titles using a specific font style and size, centred on the line);
- *to combine multiple commands* (e.g., insert a table with a specific number of rows and columns formatted in a specific manner); and
- *to automate a complex series of tasks* (e.g., create mailing labels from a data source used frequently).

To record a macro, start the macro recorder, perform a sequence of actions, then save the macro with a name. You can then run the macro whenever you need to perform this sequence. For example, if you often need to insert a specifically formatted table in your documents, you can record a macro that inserts the table with the correct borders, size, and number of rows and columns. In some programs it is necessary to record the macro using only keyboard commands — not the mouse!

After you have recorded the macro, you must name it; then it can be assigned to a toolbar, menu, or shortcut key (a series of keystrokes, such as Ctrl/851). Running a macro can be as simple as clicking on the icon or the option in a menu.

6.1.2 AutoCorrect

The **AutoCorrect** or **QuickCorrect** feature incorporated into most word-processing programs helps to speed data entry and improve overall accuracy, thus reducing the editing needed to produce final copy of any document. Within this feature:

- *You can instruct the program to substitute specific words or symbols for specific keystrokes entered.* For example, if you consistently misspell certain words, you can program them into the AutoCorrect feature to be corrected as you key in the wrong version.
- *You can correct errors committed by keying too quickly and misplacing spaces.*

You can also turn off this feature so that the words will not be corrected as you enter your text.

The AutoText or QuickWord option contained in the same menu allows you to enter frequently keyed phrases, so that when you start to key a phrase (e.g., "Yours truly" in a letter) a pop-up note appears on the screen with the rest of the phrase. If you want to accept the suggestion, simply press Enter and the text will appear on your screen.

GETTING IT

1. What is a word-processing macro? How is it created?
2. Explain the difference between a macro and AutoText.
3. List the options in your word-processing program that allow you to automatically insert text.
4. Explain the danger in overusing the automatic text entry features in a word-processing program.

6.1.3 Creating Complex Business Documents

As you embark on a large project with many components, one of the hardest things to do is to organize your thoughts so that the finished product is a cohesive, logical document. In the pen and paper world, we use techniques such as outlines and index cards with topic ideas written on them so that they can be organized into logical groupings. The designers of word-processing software have taken those concepts and automated them, giving users the tools to make this process more efficient and less painstaking.

The **Outline** feature in the Microsoft® Word View menu (see Figure 6.1) is one such tool that helps you process ideas and organize your work. This view allows you to arrange topics into different levels of importance (e.g., main headings, subheadings, sub-subheadings). If a subtopic is moved to a different section, its subtopics are automatically moved with it. As you complete research, individual sections can be collected, written, edited, and arranged in the outline. They can then be polished using standard formatting techniques discussed in earlier chapters.

Figure 6.1
Outline Feature in Microsoft® Word

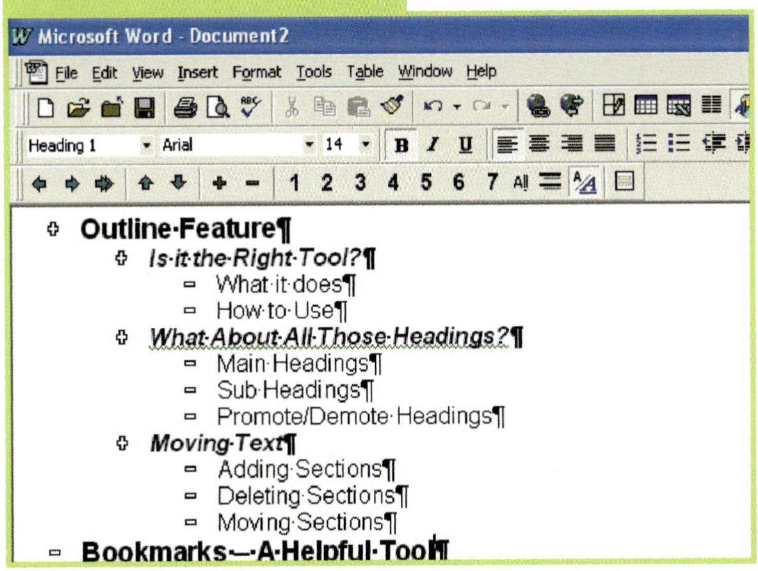

This feature allows you to organize and structure a document into distinct sections, each with associated formatting. Levels can be collapsed to show only the headings without the individual paragraphs or expanded to give starting lines in each section.

The font style and size can be customized for each level in your outline, so that the main headings and subheadings are easily identified by the reader of your report.

Another useful word-processing tool is the **Bookmark**. If you are working on a long document, such as a research paper, and you have to go back to a specific point to continue entering data after you do additional research, you can insert a bookmark at the exact location. If desired, you can set the viewing options in your word-processing program to insert a non-printing character to show the bookmarked locations on screen. These, however, are difficult to find when placed in a large body of text. It is much easier to use the Go To... feature when you are ready to go back to that point. By entering a descriptive name for the bookmark (e.g., "More e-commerce info") you can have the software find the bookmark once you select it in the dialog box. The program moves the insertion point to that exact location, saving you the time of finding where it was that you wanted to put the information.

As you create research papers, it is necessary to document your sources within the body of the text. As you will read in Chapter 11, there are a number of accepted methods of citing sources. A footnote or an endnote consists of two parts: a notation within the body or text that indicates to the reader that you are quoting or paraphrasing information found in another source (e.g., book, magazine, Web site). This notation can take the form of a superscript number or letter within the body and a full description of the source either at the bottom of the page (the footnote) or the end of the document (the endnote). (*Business Connections* places the author or source and date in parentheses within the text and provides the full reference at the end of the text in the Bibliography.)

When you need to enter a footnote, you access the feature through the Insert menu. Once you select the type of note required (e.g., footnote or endnote) and the notation type, the program inserts the notation and splits the screen horizontally, allowing for the entry of the footnote information. See Figure 6.2 for an example of a footnote entry screen. Be sure to refer to the appropriate style manual to ensure that you have all the required information for the note and for the bibliography or reference page that is required at the end of the paper. This will ensure that you are giving credit where credit is due — to the authors of the works you have referenced in your research. If you have not given such credit, you are stealing the intellectual property of another person or organization. More detail on this and other ethical and legal issues is found in Chapter 11.

One additional tool that can be utilized in the creation of long documents such as research papers is the automatic **table of contents** feature. A table of contents lists all the headings contained within your report and may also include the subheadings within each section (see Figure 6.3). The page number that the heading appears on is also a key component, so that

Figure 6.2
Footnote Entry Screen

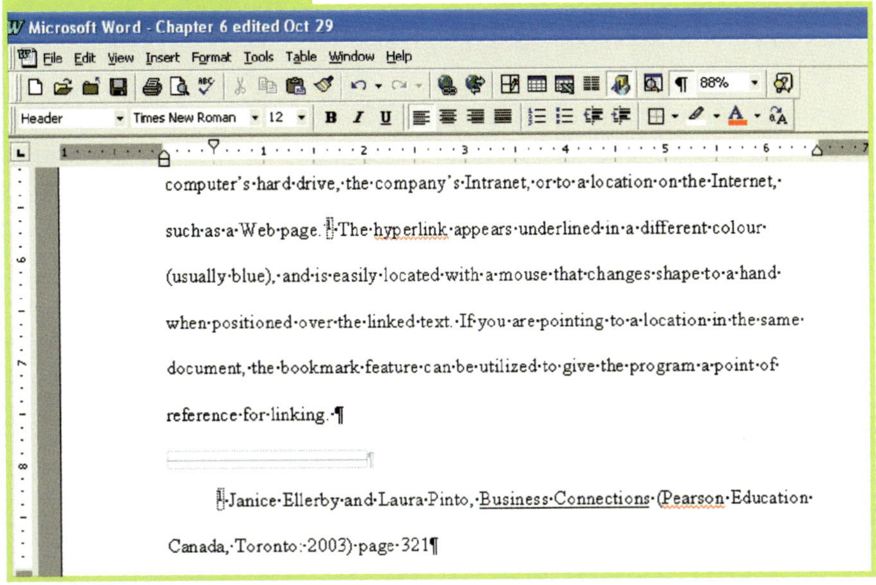

The software divides the page and inserts a dividing line to distinguish between the body/text and the footnote information.

the reader can quickly and easily go to the section he or she wants to read without having to browse through the entire document.

Some word-processing programs require that you apply the appropriate styles (see Chapter 5) to the headings contained throughout the report in order to generate the headings in the table of contents. Other programs require that text be marked for inclusion in the table of contents while that text is being created. Many programs offer a selection of preset formats or allow you to design your own format. Once you place the insertion point where you want the table of contents to appear, the program will search your document to locate the headings or markings and will build the table of contents, noting the page number on which each heading or marking appears.

Going to a particular section in the document is as easy as clicking on the page number in the table of contents. The word-processing program moves your cursor to the specific point selected, much as hyperlinks perform in a Web page.

Even if you have not applied the styles (e.g., headings, subheadings, page numbers) to your document, you can insert **hyperlinks** to do the job of the automatic table of contents feature. By inserting a hyperlink into a document,

Figure 6.3
Table of Contents

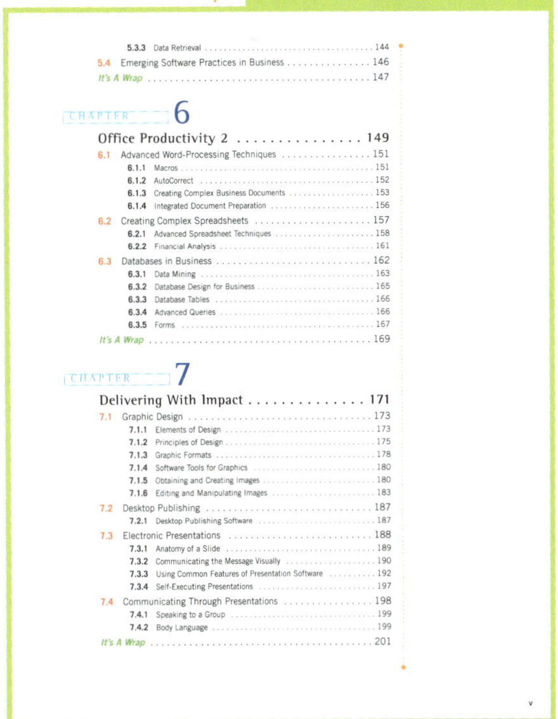

you can jump to a specific point in a document or be jettisoned to a Web page, to a file created in a separate document, or to open up sound or video files. These latter options require you to have the appropriate software on your computer to access the files you link to. The files the hyperlink points to can be located on a specific computer's hard drive, a company's Intranet, or a location on the Internet such as a Web page. The hyperlink appears underlined in a different colour (usually blue) and is easily located with a mouse, which changes shape to a hand when positioned over the linked text. If you are pointing to a location in the same document, the Bookmark feature can be used to give the program a point of reference for linking.

GETTING IT

1. Define *outline* and explain how it can be used to organize your work.
2. Define *Bookmark*. Give two examples of where the use of a Bookmark can be helpful.
3. Explain when footnotes are required. How do you enter a footnote into a document?
4. List the information that should appear on a table of contents. How is it organized?
5. Describe how you can use the features of your word-processing program to generate a table of contents automatically.
6. Explain how hyperlinks work. What can you link to?

6.1.4 Integrated Document Preparation

Most word-processing programs have a built-in **mail-merge** feature that allows for the production of mass mailings of the same document, customized and personalized, based on the entries in a database. Not only can the names and addresses be changed, but also the individual paragraphs in the letter can be tailored to match the characteristics of the individuals receiving the letter. For example, imagine a letter is being sent to recipients all over Ontario, but your organization wants to refer individuals to their local office for follow-up inquiries. In this case, the database would contain a field for the regional office containing the correct phone number. That phone number would be placed in the body/text of the letter. This process makes the letters appear to be custom generated, when in fact only the parts that change have been entered into the database.

The process of creating a form letter is twofold. First, the generic letter is created. This gives the designer the opportunity to determine what **variable information** needs to be inserted (e.g., name, telephone numbers, addresses). In the case of names, it is particularly important to determine if the name must be divided into separate fields (e.g., first name, last name, title) to allow for proper salutations in a letter (e.g., Dear Mr. Saleh). If the database is not designed properly, you could end up with a salutation like Dear Mr. Raul Saleh because the first and last names are entered in the same field. Once a draft of the base letter is written, noting the location of the variable text, the database is created. You can use an existing data source such as a file of names and addresses if all the necessary fields are present. Otherwise, it will be necessary to modify it in order to have all the necessary data input to personalize your mailing pieces.

The base letter must refer to the fields by their correct names in the database, otherwise the mail-merge will not work — the program will not know what information is required in that location. Most programs allow the user to point and click on the database field names to ensure that they have been referenced correctly.

The merged document can be saved in a separate file so that the original can be reused at a later date with a new data set.

Mailing labels and envelopes can be created in the same manner, where the document is created referencing the database fields. Once the form is created, it can be reused countless times, saving precious time and money for the organization.

GETTING IT

1. Explain the mail-merge function. Explain how you think this could be a useful tool for business.
2. Name the two files that must be created in order to generate form letters or mailing labels.
3. Explain what is meant by "variable information" in a database.
4. Prepare a list of warnings you would give to a person about to perform his or her first mail merge based on the information presented in this chapter.

6.2 Creating Complex Spreadsheets

Numbers are the heart of many functions within an organization, from the Purchasing department to Accounting and Payroll. Management decisions are often based on the numbers that are gathered and analyzed from corporate information systems. One of the key competencies in organizations today, therefore, is the ability to use spreadsheet software to perform analysis of financial data. This chapter examines some of the advanced functions built into popular spreadsheet programs that help to improve productivity in creating spreadsheets, the use of spreadsheets to assist in financial planning for individuals and organizations, and the techniques employed to analyze the financial performance of an organization.

6.2.1 Advanced Spreadsheet Techniques

Creating complex spreadsheets from "scratch" can be time consuming and difficult. Consequently, many programs have pre-designed **templates**—worksheets that contain labels and formulas and functions, but no values. You simply enter the values into the templates and the functions and formulas perform the required calculations. If the templates do not meet your needs, many third-party software providers sell templates that can be used for various business functions. There are even templates available on the Internet at many Web sites — some for free and others for a fee. Templates are available for such documents as invoices, purchase orders, income statements and balance sheets that report on the financial position of the business, and expense accounts that keep track of monthly expenses for sales professionals. If you find that you require customized forms, they can be programmed and saved as a template by professional programmers. Well-designed templates can save considerable time, effort, and frustration and increase your overall productivity: you spend time entering data rather than designing the template for use. Figure 6.4 provides a sampling of spreadsheet templates.

Figure 6.4
Spreadsheet Templates

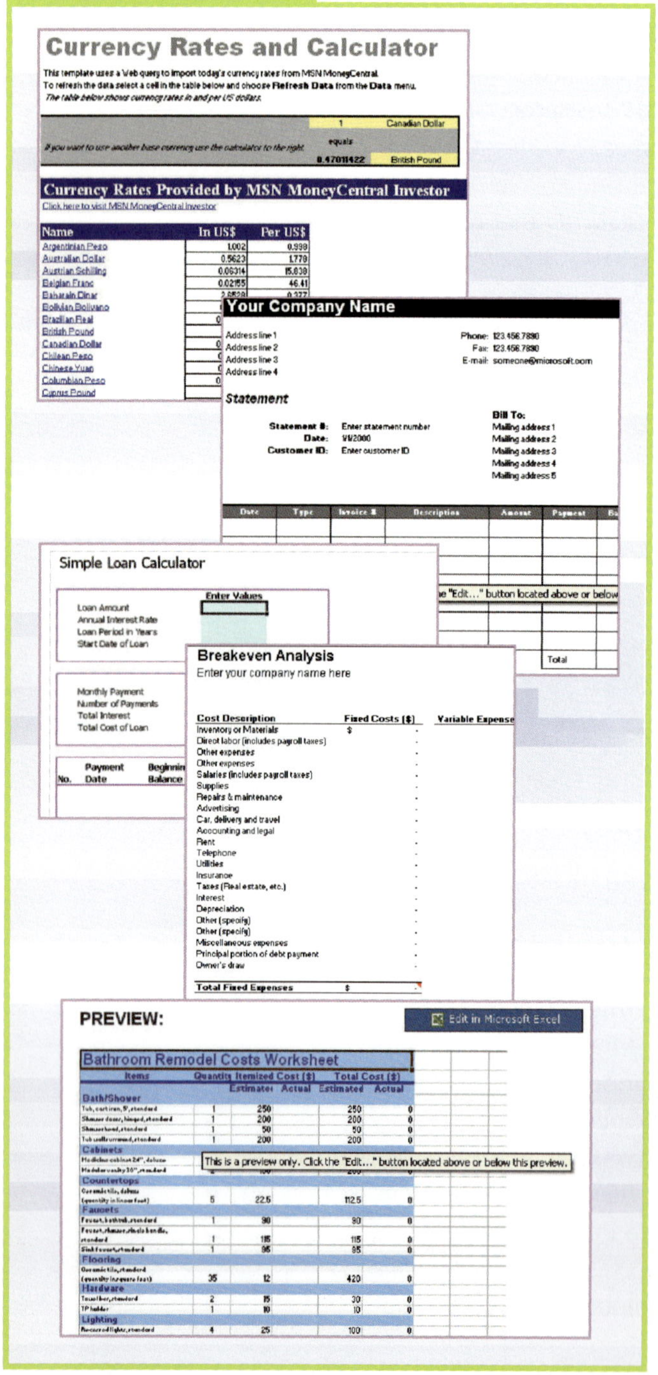

In Chapter 5 you were introduced to some of the tools programmed in spreadsheet software that automate popular operations, including data sorting and functions. These procedures are limited, however, to popular tasks. For situations where you require customization and these procedures are performed repetitively (e.g., weekly or monthly), a macro can be used. As defined earlier in the word-processing section, a *macro* is a series of operations or steps that are captured and recorded for use again and again. Some programs require you to enter the macro in a specialized language, whereas others have built in "recorders" that track each movement of the mouse and keyboard, allowing you to "play back" or repeat the operation within the spreadsheet each time it is required. It is important to record the sequence of instructions carefully. If you make a mistake and correct it during the recording operation, the macro will repeat those errors during playback.

After you have prepared your spreadsheet data, there will be times when others need to view the results. To protect the integrity of the data and ensure that the results are not tampered with, you should look at some of the built-in protection features in most programs. One of the easiest methods to protect the workbook is to save it as a read-only document, which indicates to the viewer that it is not to be tampered with. However, the viewer can save the file under a different name and then it is possible to make changes to the document.

The next level of protection is to save the file with a password protection feature. A viewer who does not know the password, will not be able to open or modify the file. You also have the option of password-protecting individual sheets within a document. Without the password, the viewer would be forced to open the file as read-only and save it under a different name. This would alert you to the fact that the sheet had been modified. This is, however, protection in a limited sense. It also lessens the usefulness of the document because it cannot be used as a template under these circumstances.

If the output required is a printed version of your document, there are a number of options you can activate and set to have your printed spreadsheets make more sense to the reader. The first option is to add a Header or Footer to the document (see Figure 6.5). As with word-processed documents, the information contained in a Header or Footer remains consistent from page to page. Using the automatic features within the program allows you to customize the information to change the font style and size, add page numbering, the date, or even the file name to either Header or Footer. To see the document as it would appear in hard copy when printed, you use the **Print Preview** feature.

Figure 6.5
Excel Header and Footer Options

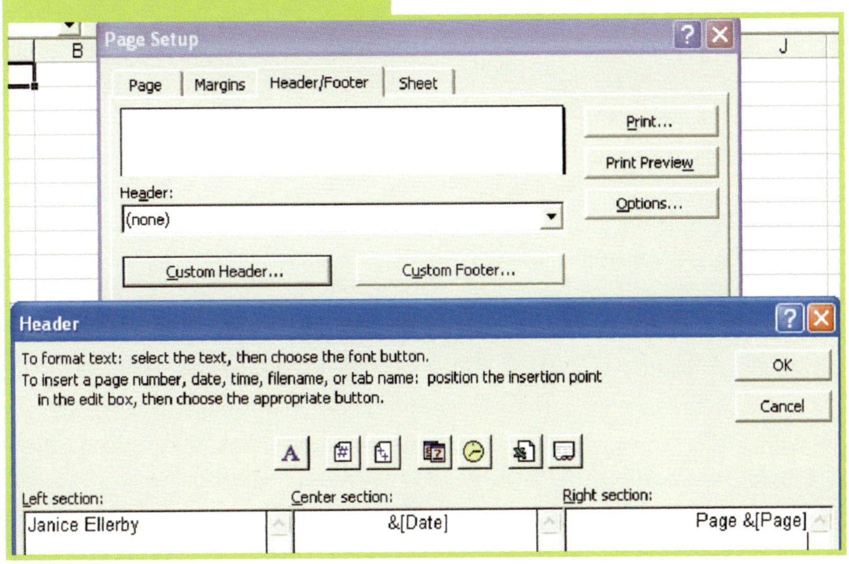

You can enter text directly into the custom header or footer area or choose from one of the automatic features such as page numbering, data, time, file name and location, and the sheet tab within the workbook providing maximum information to the reader.

When you set up a spreadsheet, you typically enter the column labels only once. On a printed version, however, it is helpful to the reader to have the column labels printed on each sheet. This eliminates flipping pages back and forth to determine what is in each column. You can achieve this by selecting file/page setup/sheet and putting your cursor in cell "rows to repeat at top." Then highlight the first row containing your heading information and click OK.

Another way to improve the readability of printed spreadsheets is to specify manually where pages should end by inserting page breaks into the document. This prevents page endings from breaking up the flow of ideas or concepts that should be kept together in the printed version.

GETTING IT

1. Define *template.* Explain how it can assist in the preparation of spreadsheet data.
2. Describe how a macro improves efficiency in using the same spreadsheet time after time.
3. Explain why you think protecting your document is so important when dealing with spreadsheets.
4. Describe two methods of protecting your spreadsheets.
5. List the printing options that are available to users of spreadsheets to increase the readability of printouts.

CAREER PERSPECTIVE

Financial Planning

Unless you are born into a very wealthy family or win a lottery, you will be faced with many difficult decisions about how and where to spend the money you earn during your life. If you are like most people, you need to make wise decisions about spending and saving to have the finances to do the things you want to do (e.g., buy a home or car, take a vacation). Many people turn to financial planners to assist them with their investments so that they can live "comfortably," free from the worry of running out of funds, and can achieve their life goals.

Professionally certified financial planners pass rigorous examinations to verify their competence in applying financial knowledge to actual situations. They take courses in the financial planning process, tax planning, employee benefits and retirement planning, estate planning, investment management, and insurance. A financial planner will work with you, the client, to determine what your financial goals are and an appropriate way of achieving them. Planners look at different types of investments (stocks, bonds, guaranteed investment certificates, insurance) and develop a number of "what if" scenarios so that you can make an informed decision.

(continued)

Developing a personal financial plan typically has four steps:

1. Determine your current situation.
2. Determine what situation you want to find yourself in three years from now.
3. Develop a plan to get there.
4. Review your plan on a regular basis.

The first step, determining your current situation, requires you to determine your net worth (what you own minus what you owe) and to look at your income versus expenses each month with a critical eye for where expenses can be trimmed. Knowing where you want to be financially in the future is key to planning, for without a destination in mind the route cannot be determined.

Financial planners can use automated tools to assist in their work for clients. The tool of choice for many financial planners is the computer and spreadsheet software, which makes the process of producing various scenarios quick and easy. They, or software specialists in their financial organization, develop sophisticated templates for use with client information. The planner just needs to enter the variable information (e.g., amount to be invested, time frame, and interest rate) to determine what the end result will be. This gives the client and planner the opportunity to look at different scenarios in a relatively short period of time — even over coffee at the kitchen table!

Questions

1. Explain the role of a financial planner and how one can be of assistance to an average person.
2. List the four essential steps in preparing a personal financial plan.
3. Use the tools provided by your teacher, or locate the information required from a search of the Web, to prepare a personal financial plan for the next three years.

Get Connected

Personal financial planning sites abound on the Web. You can get up-to-the-minute information on currency exchange rates if you are planning a vacation in another country or are involved in importing/exporting in your business. Up-to-the-minute stock prices on major stock exchanges worldwide are available, as are reports on investments such as mutual funds and rates on guaranteed investments. Investigate the resources that are available at www.pearsoned.ca/businessconnections and prepare a keyed summary of the planning tools you would recommend to a student who is planning to:

1. go to college or university next year
2. invest a $10 000 inheritance
3. buy a new car (or lease, for that matter)
4. take a school trip to Spain (check currency conversion)

6.2.2 Financial Analysis

Every day the stock exchanges in North America trade billions of shares representing ownership in thousands of corporations. How do people know which companies are good buying opportunities and which ones they should sell? In many cases, they rely on the recommendations of stockbrokers who, in turn, get their information from a bevy of financial analysts, who spend their working days evaluating the financial health of organizations.

Financial analysis is critical when you buy and sell shares in publicly traded corporations. Managers within companies, large and small, must be able to analyze the financial information prepared by accountants to assess the health of their companies and to make decisions on everything from cutting costs to launching new products. As explained in Chapter 5, careful analysis requires individuals to perform numerous calculations on the available data and to perform "what if" analyses to determine the best course of action for the future. For example, "what if" workers negotiating a contract are asking for a 6% increase over three years. Management can calculate the cost of this potential wage increase to determine how it will affect overall profitability.

Spreadsheets are the ideal tool for situations that require significant "number crunching." Most commercially available spreadsheet software allow the user to perform such tasks as:

- forecast everything from sales to expenses;
- examine overall profitability (return on investment or equity);
- perform standard accounting analysis using ratios to determine overall financial health;
- consolidate data (e.g., sales of each product type into one overall worksheet); and
- prepare budgets for current or future accounting periods.

Spreadsheet software has evolved amazingly since its introduction over 20 years ago. With today's tools, analysts can, with the click of a mouse, execute complex formulas, build elaborate functions, sort and filter data, perform "what if" analyses, and graph/chart the results. The end result is more accurate information on which to base business decisions.

GETTING IT

1. Write a brief paragraph to describe how financial analysis helps investors.
2. Explain how spreadsheet users employ "what if" analyses. How does this help business managers make decisions?

6.3 Databases in Business

Database software is a powerful application for businesses. Database software is used in every aspect of business — from financial management, to human resources management (to track employee information), to marketing (from Web-based applications to better understand customers), to sales and inventory management (processing transactions and tracking stock). Understanding how to use database software effectively not only saves time, thereby increasing productivity and profitability, but it also helps organizations gain a significant competitive edge.

6.3.1 Data Mining

With increased competition and expanded markets resulting from information technology, businesses have to understand and respond quickly to their customers' needs to survive. Two key database applications, data warehousing and data mining, help to achieve this. As shown in Figure 6.6, a variety of individual databases can be combined to create a **data warehouse**, which contains many types of information, often representing the habits, behaviours, and preferences of thousands or even millions of consumers. To make sense of this vast amount of information, a technique called **data mining** is used. In the data mining process, software containing formulas and procedures examines the data sets in the warehouse to find relationships, patterns, and connections between and among them. The end result is **knowledge discovery in databases (KDD)**, which is used to solve business problems and identify business opportunities.

Figure 6.6
Data Mining Process

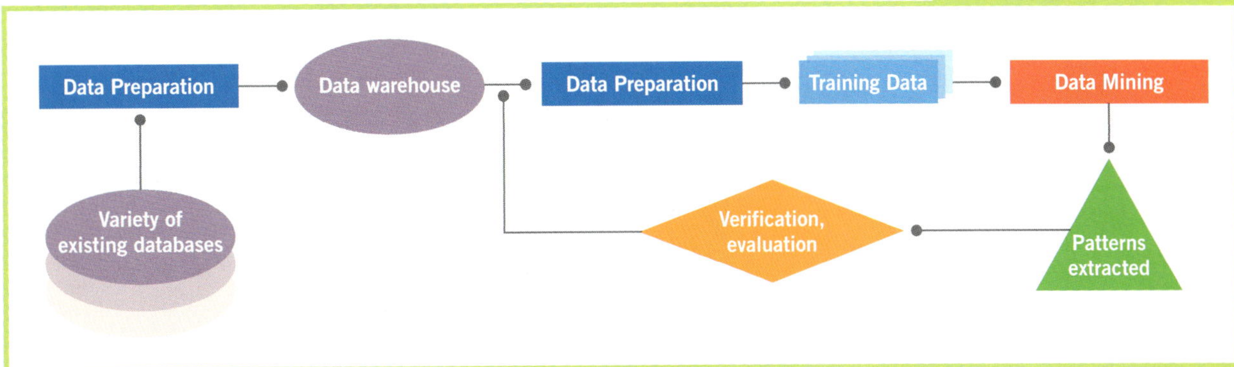

Adapted from Vipin Kumar and Mahesh Joshi, "Tutorial on High Performance Data Mining," http://www-users.cs.umn.edu/~mjoshi/hpdmtut/ (December 3, 2002).

IT In Action

Data Mining

Adapted from: Ted Kemp, "Customer Analytics At A Cost," *Internet Week*, December 11, 2001, at www.internetweek.com/story/ INW20011211S0002.

Looking to stretch their marketing dollars, companies are using software to analyze buying patterns and customer segments, both online and off. But organizing effective campaigns in this way is proving to be far more complex than many companies first realized.

Bank of Montreal, for instance, now conducts detailed analyses of consumer buying patterns and product preferences before it pitches new products via e-mail, phone, and regular mail. But getting to this point required the bank to consolidate information from many disparate company databases and information sources, says David Moxley, vice president of customer knowledge management.

IT In Action (continued)

Each of Bank of Montreal's products — from mutual funds and mortgages to chequing accounts — has its own legacy information store, so it's difficult to know offhand whether multiple customer records with similar names refer to the same person. The bank also gathers consumer data from information services such as Statistics Canada. In all, Bank of Montreal has to sift through data from 17 separate sources to compile its data warehouse.

To fully understand that data, the bank uses software from AB Initio to extract target data fields from its mainframes, transform those fields into a format that can be more uniformly analyzed, and load them into the bank's data warehouse.

Data mining software from Angoss Software Corp., IBM, and SAS Institute Inc. determine the true identity of a customer, presenting a complete picture of the individual and which products he or she already owns. For instance, the software might correlate partial names, initials, and postal codes to pinpoint multiple records of the same person in the data warehouse.

The bank then uses different software to cut its customer base into segments based on demographics, transaction frequency, account balance size, or whether the customer prefers banking through the Web site or branches. Phone-based market research reveals which products appeal to which groups. Only then are marketing campaigns crafted.

Bank of Montreal gathers more information on its Web site. Rather than monitor visitors' entire clickstream (i.e., every page on their Web site that the customer uses), the bank "flags" pages where transactions take place — for example, parts of the site that generate quotes for specific products. A record of the customer inquiry is then fed from the transaction engine to the data warehouse.

Looking ahead, the bank intends to use all this information to make quick, targeted pitches to consumers initiating contact with the bank's call centres, Web site, or branches. Early efforts in the bank's credit-card call centres, where phone agents make a particular product pitch based on the kinds of questions consumers ask, has tripled the percentage of customers who buy after receiving a pitch, Moxley says.

Moxley put the cost of deploying the customer analysis project at several million dollars. Ongoing costs amount to about $2 million annually.

Another example of data mining is seen in the gift and greeting card industry. Hallmark Co. created a "master repository" for customer information drawn each night from databases operated by various company units, such as Hallmark.com, Keepsake Ornament Club, and company loyalty programs. Hallmark then implemented a relational database within the master NCR Teradata warehouse that lets marketing staffers segment customer and transaction data through a Web interface. Hallmark spent about $10 million on the project, including implementing the software and linking the master repository with the separate business units' databases, says enterprise development manager Phil Skahan. The company also configured its Hallmark.com e-mail server so it can manage all of the business units' outbound customer e-mails.

Marketing professionals now can analyze data and design promotional schemes with minimal help from the IT department.

Questions

1. List the number of sources from which Bank of Montreal gets data for its data warehouse.
2. Explain how data mining is tied to marketing activities for the businesses discussed in the article.
3. Based on the article, record the methods that can be used to gather data about or from customers.

6.3.2 Database Design for Business

Chapter 5 introduced you to the concept of databases. When you create a database for a more complex business function (such as a database that will be used by third parties to input and maintain customer files), a number of elements must be incorporated. These elements should be designed keeping in mind they must all fit together (Figure 6.7)— information required for a report must be represented as a field. Similarly, if multiple tables are being set up, there needs to be a common field to tie them together; otherwise, they are useless. Some of the considerations in database design are shown in Figure 6.8.

Figure 6.7
Elements of a Business Database

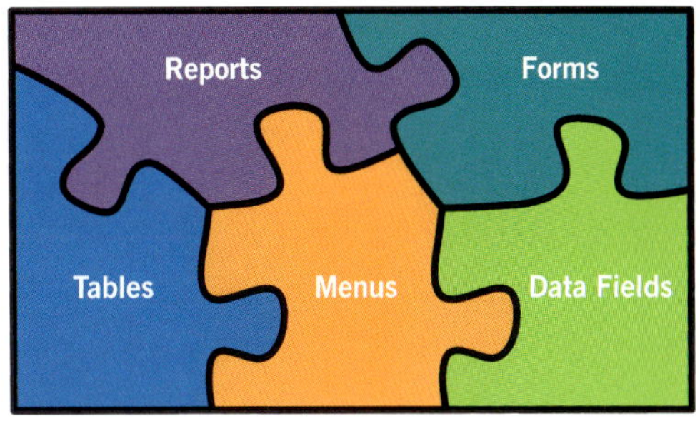

Figure 6.8
Considerations in Database Design

Element	Description
Report design	The required fields and overall appearance of reports (organized printouts) must be established. Existing templates can be used, or new forms can be created. In fact, reports can be designed in a word-processing program, with fields from the database merged in separately, allowing for more creativity in design.
Data design (fields)	The specific fields and the type of field (e.g., text, numeric, calculation) need to be established. A **key field** will be unique to each record (e.g., a student number) and should be included to prevent duplication. Most database software contains an icon or command that you can use to designate a key field.
Table design	The structure of the tables in which the database information is organized needs to be established. If several tables are to be used, then the relationships between and among them need to be established.
Form design	**Forms** are the pop-up boxes or GUIs (Graphical User Interfaces) that users see when they input or view records. In some cases, these are customized by the database developer to make them user friendly. Sometimes, they are incorporated into other applications, such as Web sites, for easy data gathering and/or retrieval.
Menu design	Customized menus can be created to help users understand the structure and options available when inputting or retrieving data. For example, entering provinces in an address menu would provide users with a list to choose from and help to ensure vital consistency in data entry.

6.3.3 Database Tables

Database information is organized in a **table**, which is a grid made up of fields (columns) and records (rows). Tables are simply a means of organizing data to ease other functions such as macros and form creation. All database applications have a command or interface that allows the user to create multiple tables. These tables should be created when the database is first developed and they represent specific sets of data that comprise selected fields. As mentioned earlier in this section, deciding on table contents in advance and in the context of the entire database will help you to avoid mistakes later. Keep in mind that tables are *not* reports. Printing the table will only give you the raw, unorganized data.

If you plan to perform multiple queries on the tables, be sure that a common field (e.g., a key field) exists between any tables that will be used together. For example, a retailer might want several tables: a customer information table, an inventory table, and an orders table. By creating these three and allowing them to communicate with one another, orders can be placed and automatic or timed inventory updates as well as customer profile updates can occur without further inputting.

6.3.4 Advanced Queries

Queries are commands that allow the user to view, change, and analyze data in different ways. Advanced queries can be made that sort, compare, or perform calculations among multiple fields or within ranges of adjacent cells. Figure 6.9 contains a standard list of operators to be used when you search for ranges.

Figure 6.9
Query Operators

Operator	Meaning
<	Less than
>	Greater than
<=	Less than or equal to
>=	Greater than or equal to
NOT	Exclude records that match the criteria after the word not
NULL	Blank fields
OR	Allows for more than one criterion

digiknow

Wildcard characters (such as * for one or more characters, ? for one character, and # for a numeric character) can be used to substitute unknown or unspecific information in a query. In a database, for example, to query for all people named Marie, Mary, Marco, and Marilyn who are aged 20 to 29, you would simply query "Mar* AND 2#."

To create a multiple table query, use the query command or button. Follow the prompts to get to a query dialog box that allows for options to be inputted (in some applications, it is the Design View selection). Where prompted, add the titles of the tables that need to be included in the query one at a time. Note that the key field(s) is the link between any two tables. For example, let us revisit the retailer example. Suppose a query was going to be done to determine if a piece of merchandise with the code number 22248P was in stock and not currently ordered by any customers. Both the order table and the inventory table would have to be queried. The field containing the code number would act as the primary key, linking those two tables and making the query possible.

Figure 6.10

Product Table

Product	Description
22248P	Table
22249P	Chair
22250P	Footstool
22300S	
22300T	

Inventory Table

Product	Qty in Stock
22248P	3
22249P	2
22250P	1
22300S	0
22300T	4

Orders in Process Table

Product	Orders
22248P	2
22249P	0
22250P	4
22300S	6
22300T	0

Using the Product Code as the primary key in all database tables you could determine that you have one table 22248P available for sale (quantity inventory – quantity reserved for customers).

Before the actual query can take place, the two tables need to be linked. This can be done in one of two ways, depending on the specific software. Some software allows linking by simply clicking and dragging the two fields. Other software requires the use of a menu or button labelled "link."

At this point, the query can take place, using the same process (described in Chapter 5) as for a single-table query.

6.3.5 Forms

Forms as described in Figure 6.8 are views of information based on underlying tables or queries. They can be entered, edited, displayed, filtered, and printed. Any information input into a form automatically updates the underlying table or query. Most database software have templates for forms (in Access, these are called AutoForms and are created through a Wizard). When creating a form, consider who the user is, why he or she will be using

digiknow

Structured Query Language (SQL) is the standard language and set of commands used to communicate with relational databases (which include Microsoft Access, Corel Paradox, and Oracle). SQL statements are used to perform tasks such as updating data on a database or retrieving data from a database. In most database software applications, however, the user does not have to know how to use SQL. When you use a dialog box (or other GUI) to make a query, sort, add, update, or delete records, an SQL command is triggered that actually makes the command happen. Advanced database users and developers use SQL to customize databases beyond the capabilities of GUIs.

Get Connected

To find out more about SQL and how you can use it to customize and retrieve data, visit www.pearsoned.ca/businessconnections. Create an SQL Information Sheet that defines the term and lists the commands that are possible based on the information presented on the site. Describe the user-friendliness of SQL.

digiknow

Advanced, customized forms are created using programming languages such as Visual Basic.

Get Connected

View some of the database tutorials available at www.pearsoned.ca/businessconnections. Is the software you use represented? Write a paragraph to describe how tutorials can help database users. Share your thoughts with a partner.

the form, and what type of information might be helpful to see. For example, if you are creating a form for use by cashiers at a gas station, the cashiers probably do not need to see detailed inventory fields that describe the snack foods in the shop. As well, the software requires you to specify information about the form, including:

- fields to be included;
- labels for fields;
- number of spaces available in each field for the end-user to key information; and
- other text, explanations, etc., for the end-user to see.

You have the option of formatting the form with such things as the height and width of the form or dialog box, font(s), Headers and Footers, and colours and lines.

Finally, automatic controls can be added to forms in most database software applications (using a format properties menu command or button). Let us again revisit the example of the cashier at the gas station. In this case, productivity and accuracy might be improved by adding an automatic calculation on the form to total purchases and adding PST and GST. Figure 6.11 compares a paper-based form and an electronic version of the same form.

Figure 6.11
Graphic Depiction of a Form

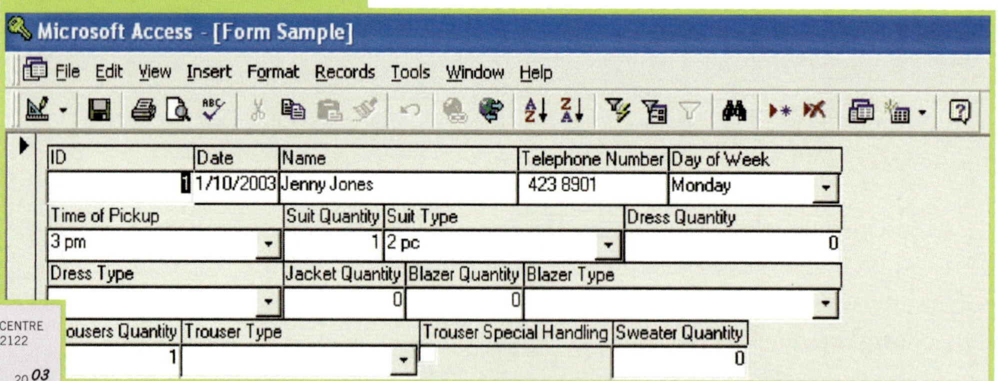

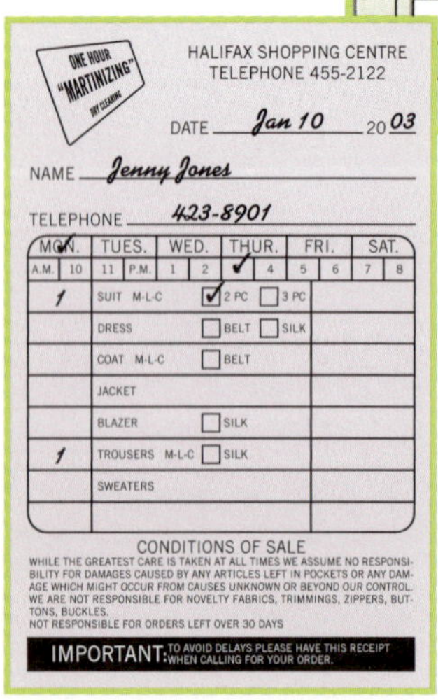

A computerized data entry form (above) automates the entry of many tasks in today's computer intensive business environment. Notice the menus for "Day of Week," "Suit Type," "Time of Pickup," "Dress Type," "Blazer Type," and "Trouser Type."

GETTING IT

1. Explain how data mining and data warehousing differ.
2. Explain KDD.

3. Indicate which of the following are examples of data mining results.
   a. 20% of customers are aged 13 to 17.
   b. Among the most profitable 5% of customers, the preferred method of purchasing is over the Internet with overnight shipping.
   c. 60% of all male customers shop weekly and spend an average of $73.12 per trip.
   d. The most commonly purchased colour among all items sold between 2003 and 2005 was red.
   e. The number of items purchased by Internet customers is 40% more than the number of items purchased by customers in the store, with sales per Internet customer at over $500 per year.
4. Describe in your own words the considerations in database design.
5. Using a database that you created previously, create at least two tables from the existing fields. Generate a query using a common field.
6. How would linking tables come into play in data warehousing?
7. Some people criticize data warehousing and data mining for being an invasion of personal privacy. Why might they say this? Do you agree or disagree? Explain.

IT's A Wrap

Key Terms in This Chapter

AutoCorrect (p. 152)
Bookmark (p. 154)
data mining (p. 163)
data warehouse (p. 163)
form (p. 165)
hyperlink (p. 155)
key field (p. 165)
knowledge discovery in databases (KDD) (p. 163)
macro (p. 151)
mail merge (p. 156)
mailing label (p. 157)
Outline (p. 153)
Print Preview (p. 159)
queries (p. 166)
QuickCorrect (p. 152)
Structured Query Language (SQL) (p. 167)
table (p. 166)
table of contents (p. 154)
template (p. 158)
variable information (p. 156)
wildcard characters (p. 166)

1. Create a list of competencies that you have acquired through your work in this chapter.
2. Update your portfolio to include examples of your work from this chapter.

Know It!

3. Describe the difference between text entry/editing and text formatting and give examples of each.
4. List the similarities between spreadsheet and word-processing programs.
5. Explain the difference between macros and functions.
6. Write a paragraph explaining how a database can be structured to help to minimize data entry errors by someone other than the designer of the database.

IT's A Wrap (continued)

Do It!

7. Prepare a guide for "newbies," giving specific instructions on how to use the features described in this chapter for the software in *your* school.
8. Design a brochure or newsletter to promote this course to students taking its prerequisite. Be sure to use the features learned in this chapter.
9. Develop a database structure for a personal information manager that will replace your PDA.
10. Develop a spreadsheet template that will help a student to track his or her grades in this course. Include functions and formulas to weight grades according to the course outline provided by your teacher.

Analyze It!

11. Identify the word-processing techniques in this chapter that are the most useful to you as a student. Explain why.
12. "The computer has put more emphasis on how text looks than on what is actually said." Do you agree with this statement? Explain why or why not.
13. People put more confidence into decisions that are based on computer simulations and programs, trusting the data because it came from a computer. Discuss with your class the dangers of relying on technology as the basis for decision making.
14. Explain to a classmate how errors in a spreadsheet template can go undetected, sometimes for months. Explain the consequences of undetected errors.
15. Often when dealing with large amounts of data it is difficult to know which program — database or spreadsheet — to use. Prepare a list of the criteria on which you would base your decision.
16. Prepare a summary of all the possible databases that might have information on you. Record the information a person might be able to find out about you from all the data collected from these sources.
17. "Discussions of privacy are often linked with databases." Write a paragraph to explain your thoughts about this statement.

CHAPTER 7

Delivering With Impact

By the end of this chapter, you will be able to:

- create and manipulate graphic images effectively;
- understand the fundamental concepts of desktop publishing;
- create an effective electronic presentation that is well sequenced and incorporates multimedia features (sound, graphics, animation); and
- demonstrate good presentation skills when you address an audience using information technology tools.

Technology has made it possible for communication to have an increased impact. Now, instead of just delivering a message with text, a message can be enhanced through visual images, pictures, and animation. The possibilities are endless. This chapter will provide you with the knowledge and skills to use software for graphics, desktop publishing, and presentations to better communicate your message. Topics to be covered include:

- Graphic Design
- Desktop Publishing
- Organizing Electronic Presentations
- Communicating Through Presentations

READY, SET, GO!

- Select appropriate software that will provide you with a slide design template that you think will best highlight your presentation.
- Create a presentation for other students entitled "Creating a Basic Presentation," based on your existing knowledge and without the use of outside references or tutorials. The content of your slides should include instructions that explain how to use presentation software and should be appropriate for your intended audience.
- Send this presentation electronically to your teacher for assessment purposes.

Introduction to Chapter Project

Recall that the Chapter Project is introduced at the beginning and is to be completed as you work through the chapter. Your teacher will provide you with assessment and evaluation criteria.

CHAPTER PROJECT

Create a slideshow that either:

a. explains the Elements and Principles of Design described in this chapter; *or*

b. treats an original topic of your choice approved by your teacher.

Present the slideshow to your class using effective communication skills for presentations. Your slideshow should include:

- an original presentation design;
- a logical structure that follows the guidelines in this chapter;
- graphics;
- sound; and
- animation.

7.1 Graphic Design

Graphic design is the process of creating visual media by combining text and graphics to effectively convey a message, usually for commercial purposes (such as marketing). Product packaging, logos, business cards, invoices, and books are all products of graphic design.

Effective graphic art serves the purpose intended by the designer and clearly communicates a specific message to the viewer. To do this, graphic design projects should begin with the following considerations:

- *Purpose of the design* (advertisement to get attention, brochure to inform the public, packaging to encourage purchase);
- *Characteristics of the audience* (culture, preferences, needs); and
- *Media to be used* (print, electronic).

7.1.1 Elements of Design

If you think about a graphic art project as though it is a recipe, then the **Elements of Design** represent the ingredients. The **Principles of Design** (discussed on pages 175–178) act as the recipe's instructions by explaining how to use each of these ingredients effectively. When elements and principles combine on a real or virtual page, the result is a composition. The principles and elements described on the following pages are relevant for both print and electronic (Internet and multimedia) composition. Use them as guides to create effective communication projects that are professional and pleasing to the eye.

7.1.1.1 Colour

Colour is a powerful component of design. It not only adds visual appeal, but is also important because of the message it sends.

When you select colours, consider their symbolism in relation to your desired audience. Reactions to colour are determined by a combination of factors: culture is one of them. If your audience includes people of a variety of cultures, make an effort to understand what meanings those cultures associate with colour. Figure 7.1 provides a chart describing the cultural significance of various colours.

Colours vary by **hue** (the shade or tint, e.g., red, green, yellow, violet, blue), **value** (the degree of lightness or darkness), and **intensity** (the strength of the brightness). Figure 7.2 on page 175 shows the colour wheel that graphic designers use.

Even with carefully selected colours for an electronic graphic design project, remember that what you see on your screen may not be what others see on their screens. To minimize problems caused by monitor display inconsistencies, it is important to understand the causes of those problems. If you use the 216 browser-safe colours, images will look good and will not dither, though this still does not guarantee that they will appear as intended

digiknow

Since prehistoric times, people have searched for ways to give visual form to ideas and concepts, to store knowledge in graphic form, and to bring order and clarity to information. Over the course of history, these needs have been filled by various people, including scribes, printers, and artists. It was not until 1922, when the outstanding book designer William Addison Dwiggins coined the term "graphic design" to describe his activities as an individual who brought structural order and visual form to printed communications, that an emerging profession received an appropriate name.

— Philip B. Meggs in *A History of Graphic Design*

Figure 7.1
Colour and Cultural Significance

Colour	Cultural Significance
Red	**China** — symbol of celebration and luck, used in many cultural ceremonies that range from funerals to weddings **India** — purity (used in wedding outfits) **Western cultures** — Christmas colour when combined with green; Valentine's Day when combined with pink; indicates stop (danger) at traffic lights **Eastern cultures** — signifies joy when combined with white
Yellow	**Asia** — sacred, imperial **Western cultures** — joy, happiness, or cowardice
Blue	**Western cultures** — strength, trust, serenity **China** — associated with immortality **Colombia** — associated with soap **Hindus** — the colour of Krishna **Jews** — holiness **Middle East** — protective colour ** Note: Blue is often considered to be the safest global colour.*
Orange	**Ireland** — religious significance (Protestant) **Western cultures** — inexpensive goods, Halloween (with black), indicates caution at traffic lights
Green	**China** — studies indicate this is not a good colour choice for packaging, green hats mean a man's wife is cheating on him **France** — studies indicate this is not a good colour choice for packaging **India** — the colour of Islam **Ireland** — religious significance (Catholic) **Some tropical countries** — associated with danger **Western cultures** — indicates go (safe) at traffic lights, environmental awareness, St. Patrick's Day, Christmas colour (red and green)
Purple	**Western cultures** — royalty
Gray	**Western cultures** — loneliness, lifeless and loveless times or settings
Brown	**Colombia** — discourages sales **Western cultures** — earth, home outdoors, simplicity
White	**Eastern cultures** — mourning, death **Japan** — white carnations signify death **Western cultures** — purity (used in weddings)
Black	**Western cultures** — mourning, death; or power, sophistication

Adapted from webdesign.about.com.

digiknow

Interesting facts about the use of colour in graphic design include:

- Colour visuals increase a person's willingness to read by up to 80 percent (Green 1984).
- Colour enhances learning and improves retention of presented information by more than 75 percent (Loyola University School of Business 1999).
- Colour advertising outsells black and white by 88 percent. (Loyola University School of Business 1999).

for all viewers. **Dithering** is an automatic process that approximates colour and shading (using the smaller, 216-colour palette) when software cannot display the full range of colours in an image.

7.1.1.2 Line

In graphic design, a **line** is a point in motion, with only one dimension: length. This definition may vary slightly from how a line is perceived in mathematics or science. As an element of graphic design, a line has both a position and a direction in space. Lines can be used within a graphic composition to separate or connect images and text.

Figure 7.2
The Colour Wheel

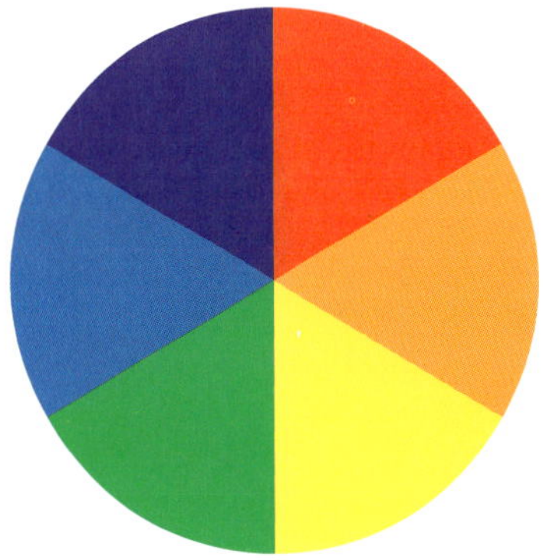

Complementary colours are opposites on the colour wheel, have drastically different wavelengths, and, consequently, have high contrast. **Analogous colours** are next to each other on the wheel. These colours share enough common attributes that they can work well with each other, but provide little contrast.

7.1.1.3 Shape

Shape refers to two-dimensional elements or objects that are formed by a closed line. Examples include circles, squares, text boxes, and free-form figures.

7.1.1.4 Form

Form refers to three-dimensional elements that incorporate length, width, and depth. Examples of forms include balls, cylinders, and boxes.

7.1.1.5 Texture

Texture is a technique used in two-dimensional design to replicate three-dimensional surfaces through various drawing and media techniques. On three-dimensional surfaces, it is experienced by touch or visually. The surfaces can be hard or soft, rough or smooth. Varying shading (and thereby creating different depths) is another technique that can be used to create texture.

7.1.2 Principles of Design

As discussed earlier, the Principles of Design provide instructions on how to use the Elements of Design effectively when you produce a graphic design composition. Though these principles are useful and generally lead to good design, sometimes creativity causes the traditional rules to be broken for a truly innovative composition.

7.1.2.1 Balance

Balance is the result of arranging elements in such a way that they equal each other in the viewing space; in other words, making good use of the space available. Balance ensures that elements are not "crowded" in one small area of the space available. Rather, balance is about arranging elements so that the space is filled relatively evenly. A lack of balance can lead to a lopsided composition.

Get Connected

To learn more about colour theory and how to use it in graphic design, visit www.pearsoned.ca/businessconnections. List specific information on the sites that is applicable to the development of graphic design projects for business. Use appropriate software to input an attractive, easy-to-read page for your notebook that includes at least one suitable graphic. Get teacher approval before you file your document.

Figure 7.3
CBC's Logo

Identify another logo that relies on symmetrical balance.

There are several types of balance. *Symmetrical balance* means that one side of a composition is the same as the other. For example, the logo of the Canadian Broadcasting Corporation (CBC) relies on symmetry (see Figure 7.3). *Asymmetrical balance* means that the composition has elements arranged in an unequal way (see Figure 7.4). The white (or empty) space serves as a balancing point for the graphic element used.

7.1.2.2 Contrast

Contrast creates visual interest by placing two different (or opposite) elements next to one another (see Figure 7.5). Contrast can be created by using complementary colours, opposite colour values (light/dark), different fonts, or opposite shapes in the same composition. As a rule of thumb, the major contrast should be placed in the middle of the composition.

7.1.2.3 Economy

Economy is about an understated approach to using elements, that is, ensuring that the composition is not "busy" and filled with many small elements that create visual chaos. It is especially important when dealing with clients,

Figure 7.4
John de Jong Jewellery Advertisement

This advertisement illustrates asymmetrical balance — notice how the three images on the left balance the single image on the right.

Figure 7.5
Microsoft Advertisement

This composition is an example of symmetrical balance, both vertically and horizontally. Note also the use of contrast between light and dark colours in each of the photographs for additional impact.

where their product or service is more important than the elaboration of design elements. To work toward economy, before adding an element the graphic designer should consider:

- whether it is necessary;
- what purpose it will serve;
- what would happen if it was not included.

See Figure 7.6 for an example of clutter and economy.

Figure 7.6
Clutter versus Economy

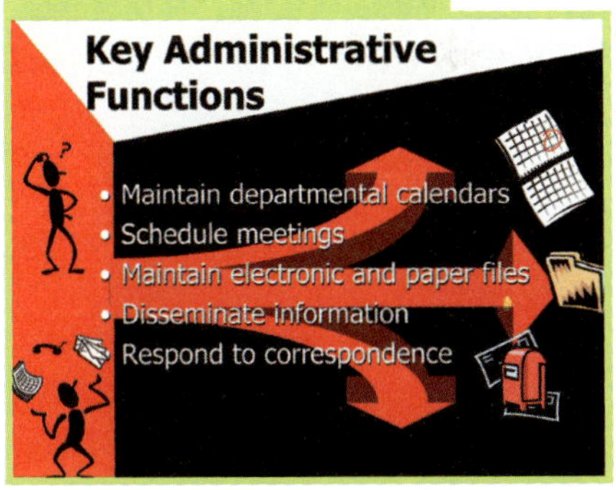

Though the images relate to the content of this PowerPoint slide, the clutter is distracting.

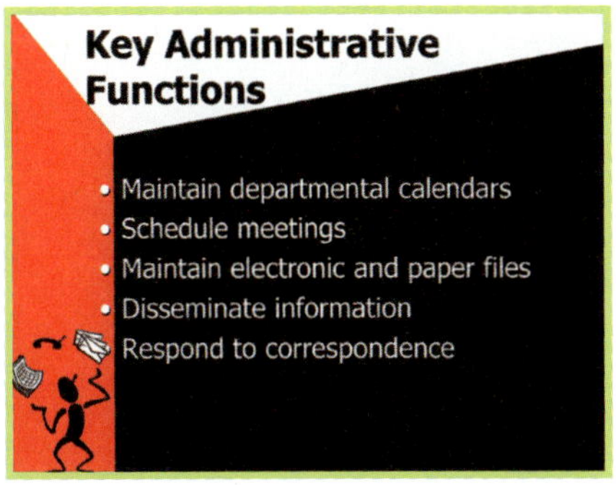

By exercising "economy," the composition of the slide is cleaner and easier to understand.

7.1.2.4 Emphasis

Also known as dominance, **emphasis** means placing one element in the forefront (such as a photo of a product), and minimizing the appearance of everything else (through white space or light colours if the dominant element is dark). This creates a **focal point** that draws the eye to one object, grouping, or shape, and takes attention away from other areas. Focal points need not be in the centre of the composition; they can appear anywhere, depending on the type of balance (i.e., symmetrical or asymmetrical) sought. When used effectively, emphasis can immediately draw viewers' eyes to a specific spot or image on a composition and create a natural, visual flow.

7.1.2.5 Consistency

Consistency helps your viewers feel at home by repeating Elements of Design throughout a composition or series of related compositions. One way of achieving consistency, or harmony, is to use the same colour palette throughout a composition or series of items. A general rule is that a maximum of two fonts should be used in any graphic composition.

7.1.2.6 Rhythm

Rhythm (see Figure 7.7) is the repetition of one or more elements within a composition to create a feeling of organized movement. This repetition creates a mood, similar to background music or dancing.

Figure 7.7
Hewlett-Packard Advertisement

This HP print ad creates rhythm through the repetition of a particular shape to express different elements. The elements together create a sense of unity, which is continued through all of their print and Web-based advertising.

7.1.2.7 Unity

The condition of completeness, with the use of all visual elements within a format, is called **unity**. This means that all elements work together. There is no single formula for unity, but one certainly notices its absence. Unity creates a sense of harmony and oneness, as illustrated in the Hewlett-Packard print ad (Figure 7.7). When unity is lacking, a composition looks unfinished, or elements of it "stick out" in an awkward way.

GETTING IT

1. The Elements and Principles of Design can be used for a variety of applications in this course. Using the most appropriate software for the task, create a table to summarize the Elements of Design and another table to summarize the Principles of Design. Have your teacher evaluate your work; keep a hard copy of it in your notebook for future reference.
2. The Elements of Design are said to be the "ingredients," while the Principles are said to be the "recipe." Obtain a hard-copy example of what you consider to be an effective composition on a Web site, a slide, or a print advertisement. Electronically create the "recipe" (including a list of ingredients) for how that example was achieved. Add this to your portfolio along with the hard copy.
3. Use the hard-copy example from question 2 to explain the way in which each of the principles applied was effective. Describe the improvements you could recommend based on what you learned in this section.

7.1.3 Graphic Formats

All images on a computer screen (from pictures to lines to letters) are made up of **pixels** — tiny dots of varying colours that are arranged in rows. Graphic software varies in the way it interprets graphic images. Two main types of graphic formats are used by various software packages:

- ***Object-oriented*** or ***vector-based graphics***: graphics stored as collections of lines, shapes, and other objects; and
- ***Raster***: bitmapped images that are maps made up of pixels, similar to what you see when you look at a newspaper photo under a strong magnifying glass. Each pixel carries with it a colour and a location. When hundreds or thousands of pixels are put together in the right

order, a graphic or photo appears. Raster takes more memory than object-oriented graphic format because detailed information about a number of pixels has to be stored.

Often, graphic images require a huge amount of storage space compared with text. To reduce the size of graphic (and other media) files, most software is able to **compress** files, that is, make files smaller using encoding schemes to save on disk space. Most commonly, compression/decompression algorithms known as **codecs** are used. In **lossless compression** the original file is compressed in a way that allows it to be completely restored. By contrast, in **lossy compression** the original file is processed during saving so that some unnecessary information is permanently removed, resulting in a small file size (but possibly less precision). The information that is removed is not perceptible to the human eye.

Figure 7.8 illustrates the more common formats that are used to save graphic images. The acronyms represent the file extension that appears when information is saved in that format.

Figure 7.8
Graphic Image Formats

Format	Description
BMP (Bitmap)	• Standard Windows bitmap image format on DOS and Windows-compatible computers, though images tend to be large
EPS (Encapsulated PostScript)	• Adobe® Photoshop® language file format supported by most illustration programs; in most cases, is the preferred format for these applications • Format intended for files that are to be printed • Tendency to large files • Format not readable by all applications
GIF (Graphics Interchange Format)	• Commonly used to display indexed-colour graphics (256 colours) and images in HTML documents over the Internet • A compression format designed to minimize file transfer time over phone lines • Ideal for simple images with large areas of solid colours
IFF (Interchange File Format)	• Used for working with Video Toaster® software and the Amiga™ system
JPEG/JPG (Joint Photographic Experts Group)	• Commonly used to display photographs and other continuous-tone images in hypertext markup language (HTML) • Unlike GIF, retains all the colour information (up to 16.7 million colours) • Uses a lossy compression scheme that effectively reduces file size by identifying and discarding extra data not essential to the display of the image • Image automatically decompressed when opened
MAC (Macintosh)	• Files created on Mac computers; tend to be monochrome

Figure 7.8 (continued)
Graphic Image Formats

Format	Description
PCX	• Established by Z-Soft® for its PC Paintbrush® software • Commonly used format for PCs • Popular due to its flexibility in handling colour, monochrome, and grayscale images
PICT	• Widely used among Macintosh graphics and page-layout applications as an intermediary file format for transferring files between applications • Especially effective at compressing images that contain large areas of solid colour
PNG (Portable Network Graphic)	• Developed as an alternative to the GIF format; like GIF, often used for displaying images on the Internet • Preserves all colour information and key features (e.g., transparency) of an image • Uses a lossless compression scheme to reduce file size
TGA (Targa Graphics Adapter)	• Designed for use on systems that use the Truevision® video board • Commonly used for colour graphics
TIFF/TIF (Tagged-Image File Format)	• Used to exchange files between applications and computer platforms • Supports lossless compression

7.1.4 Software Tools for Graphics

As mentioned earlier, a variety of software tools exist that can be used to create, edit, and manipulate graphic images. Figure 7.10 illustrates the types of software tools that are commonly used.

7.1.5 Obtaining and Creating Images

Figure 7.9

These "stringbean" clipart characters were created by Cathleen Belleville, a graphic artist who worked for Microsoft as a product planner between 1989 and 1995.

A number of options are available to obtain images that can be used for graphic and Web-based applications. Among the simplest to obtain is clipart (drawn objects such as cartoons) or photographs from galleries devoted to these types of images. Most office productivity and graphics software comes with a library of images. Alternatively, CD-ROMs can be purchased and Web sites are available that provide these images. However, copyright law (discussed in detail in Chapter 11) restricts the use of these types of images.

Another alternative is to create original images. Common methods for doing so are:

- Scanning images (such as original drawings or photographs) and saving them in digital format is one easy alternative. Be cautious: the creator of the image you are scannning owns the copyright, which restricts your use of it.

Figure 7.10
Software Tools for Graphics

Type	Description	Examples	Advantages	Disadvantages
Paint program	Allows the user to "paint" pixels on the screen with a pointing device	CorelPAINT Microsoft Paint	Mostly inexpensive and relatively easy to use	Limited capabilities for image editing; usually limited to BMP file formats
Image editor or image-processing program	Sophisticated version of a paint program; allows users to manipulate digital images (usually photographs)	Adobe Photoshop® Microsoft Picture It!® Paint Shop Pro® PhotoDeluxe®	Excellent for seamless modification to photos	Requires knowledge to use; many are costly to purchase
Draw program	Allows the user to create, modify, and combine two-dimensional vector graphics by creating independent lines and shapes	CorelDRAW Macromedia Freehand® Adobe Illustrator®	No inherent resolution in images created (unlike raster-based); can be resized easily	Does not always translate well to Web pages
3-D modelling or rendering software	Allows the user to create or edit three-dimensional graphics that can be rotated, stretched, and combined	Macromedia Shockwave® 3D Studio Max Strata 3Dpro™ LightWave®	Allows for creation of extremely sophisticated graphic images	Very complex to use; quite expensive to purchase

- Taking original photographs with a digital camera is a relatively easy and inexpensive way to create original images in digital format.
- Drawing images using the draw tools in office productivity software or using paint programs or draw programs allows you to create original graphics. An example of an object-oriented drawing appears in Figure 7.11.

Figure 7.11
Anatomy of an Object-Oriented Drawing

On the left, you see a piece of clipart in its normal state. That item is made up of dozens of lines and a few coloured shapes. Each of the lines and shapes was created individually, then all were selected and grouped to create the item. On the right, the object is shown ungrouped. The lines and shapes have been pulled apart to illustrate how they were drawn and assembled.

ON THE CASE

Using Draw Tools

Draw tools are relatively simple to use, but take some practice to get used to. Once you understand the "toolbox" that the software provides, you can very easily create anything from an abstract shape to a cartoon.

Figure 7.12 describes some of the most common buttons used for drawing (this is not an exhaustive list). Pictures of the buttons are not included since they vary from program to program.

By using the basic tools described above (as well as a few others), a graphic designer can create elaborate images. To "glue" all the tiny lines and shapes together, a technique called **grouping** is used. Grouping can be done in two ways. For a complex image, use the point tool and click and drag around the entire object to cause all parts to become selected. Then, they can be "grouped" with the click of a mouse on the group command or menu (depending on the software being used). The second method for grouping is to select individual objects, one at a time, by pointing and clicking once, but holding the Shift key down while doing so. All draw programs allow you to "permanently" keep these objects grouped. The command can be found in the menu and varies from program to program.

As you begin to use draw tools, you will notice that the most recently created object appears "on top" of all the others. When creating graphics, they are layered. Each program with draw features allows users to change the order of objects in the layers. A selected object can be brought to the front, to the back, one forward, or one backward (again, this varies depending on the software used).

Using these basic tools (in combination with unique ones available on your software application), you can create your own graphic. Follow the steps below Figure 7.12 to complete this activity.

Figure 7.12
Common Draw Tools

Button or icon looks like...	Name	Use it to...
White arrow	Point tool	select an object.
Semicircle with an arrowhead	Rotate tool	rotate an object.
Bucket	Fill	colour objects, change the fill, change effects by selecting the object, then clicking on the tool and following the prompts.
Paint brush	Line colour	colour or change the line around an object by selecting the object, then clicking on the tool and making a selection.
Letter "A" or "T"	Text	create a text box by clicking on the tool, then clicking and dragging the mouse on the drawing space.

ON THE CASE (continued)

Figure 7.12 (continued)
Common Draw Tools

Button or icon looks like…	Name	Use it to…
Magnifying glass	Zoom	zoom in or out by clicking on the tool, then clicking on the drawing space.
Solid square or rectangle	Square shape	create a square object by clicking on the tool, then clicking and dragging the mouse on the drawing space.
Solid circle or oval	Circle shape	create a circular object by clicking on the tool, then clicking and dragging the mouse on the drawing space.
Straight line	Line	create a straight line by clicking on the tool, then clicking and dragging the mouse on the drawing space.
Other shapes (star, polygon, triangle, etc.)	Basic shapes	create the shape of your choice by clicking on the tool, then clicking and dragging the mouse on the drawing space.

Activity

- Create a geometric composition by using draw tools. Be sure to create a variety of shapes and fill them with a variety of textures and colours. Play with the ordering of the layers.
- Group all objects together.
- Copy and paste your graphic composition into a slide presentation and add it to your portfolio, as an example of your personal growth and skills development.

7.1.6 Editing and Manipulating Images

Have you ever wondered how models in fashion and entertainment magazines manage to look so flawless? With image-editing software, a graphic artist achieves that. This section considers the basic tools and techniques used to edit and manipulate photographic images. The best way to learn the intricacies of this type of work is to practise with software features and functions.

Many image-editing programs are designed to correct common problems that amateur photographers often face. Common image correction features are:

- *Sharpening*: taking away fuzziness or blurriness in photos;
- *Brightness settings*: increasing or decreasing the intensity of the colours using a sliding scale; and

- *Contrast settings*: increasing or decreasing the distinctions between colours in an image using a sliding scale.

Image-editing software also contains more advanced tools and features that allow users to isolate and dismantle objects within photographs and do extensive manipulation to change features, colours, appearances, textures, etc. Understanding the basic tools will allow you to create your own unique edited images. Figure 7.13 provides instructions on how to use the items commonly found in image-editing toolboxes. You must click on each tool to activate it, then move the cursor to the image area to use the tool.

Figure 7.13
Common Image-Editing Tools

Tool	Description
Marquee tool	• This tool selects shaped sections for copying, cutting, or editing (available in other shapes in most image-editing software). • By holding the Shift key down in between shapes, they will be grouped together. • Once chosen with this or another tool, the selection can be cut or copied and pasted into another document.
Crop tool	• The crop tool selects and removes sections of the image.
Lasso	• This tool selects shapes by freehand clicking and dragging. • The lasso is often used for intricate work, such as cutting someone out of a photo and inserting him or her into another photo. • Several variations of the lasso are included in most software: – polygon lasso: uses straight lines instead of fluid lines – magnetic lasso: where a specific shape (such as a person's lips in a photograph) is to be selected, this lasso tool will gravitate and "stick" to the coloured pixels similar to those it started with (making intricate cutting easier)
Airbrush	• When clicked and dragged, this tool creates a "spray painted" line.
Rubber stamp	• This tool "clones" patterns (is used with the "Pattern Stamp," a hidden option that goes with this icon to transfer the pattern). • This tool is commonly used to correct flaws, for instance, to remove a blemish from a person's skin. The user would "clone" clear skin with the rubber stamp and then use the pattern stamp to cover the blemish with the clear skin.
Eraser	• This tool erases sections of the image over which it is rubbed.
Blur	• This tool blurs edges or sections over which it is dragged. • In some software, the hidden options of this icon allow sharpening of blurred or smudged pixels.

Figure 7.13 (continued)
Common Image-Editing Tools

Tool	Description
Pen or Path tool	• This tool draws paths (not graphic lines!) for adding, selecting, editing, and deleting sections of the image. • It works with "anchor points" — select the tool, then select a point on the image and click once to place an anchor. Next, with the mouse, create a path until the next desired anchor point is reached. Clicking the mouse once will establish a second anchor point. Continue until finished. To close the anchor path, click on the first anchor. • Several pen options are available with most software. The standard pen works with straight lines. Other forms of the pen include: – freeform pen: allows for freehand selection similar to a real pen or pencil – add/delete anchor pens: allow editing of an existing pen path – covert point pen: allows stretching or shaping of existing pen paths
Bucket	• This tool fills the selected area with colour.
Hand	• The Hand grabs and moves the selected image.
Move	• The Move tool moves a layer or selection.
Magic wand	• The Magic wand automatically selects similar-coloured pixels in a group after you point to the section and click once. For example, suppose you had a photo of someone holding a perfect green apple. If you clicked once on the apple with this tool, the whole apple would become selected. Though not as precise as the lasso tool, this is a quick way to select an image you need or want.
Paintbrush	• The Paintbrush paints freehand lines and colours (similar to draw and paint programs).
Pencil	• The Pencil draws freehand lines.
Dodge	• The Dodge tool allows for darkening or lightening of selected pixels.
Linear gradient	• The linear gradient tool creates colour blends along a spectrum.
Eyedropper	• The Eyedropper selects colours from an image to replicate.

Image-Editing Activity

Using either an image from www.pearsoned.ca/businessconnections, or your own photograph, test each of the tools available on the image-editing software you have in your lab. For your final product, cut out the subject of the photo and paste it onto a different background. Use the rubber stamp tool to change the surface of part of the image. Change the colour of at least one section of the image. You will compile the original and the image you edited into a single electronic document and provide a written description, electronically, of what you did. Include this in your portfolio.

GETTING IT

1. Now that you have had a chance to investigate software, hypothesize specifically how you think a graphic designer would use the Elements of Design and the Principles of Design in day-to-day work. Record your thoughts in your notebook.

2. Describe the specific ways that draw/paint applications and image-editing software differ. Name the common elements they share.

3. What specific image-editing tools do you think magazines and advertisers use? Create a three-column table that lists the tools, how they use them, and why they use them.

IT In Action

Creo Inc.

Based in Burnaby, British Columbia, Creo Inc. is a global company that develops imaging and software technology for the graphic arts field. It is the world's largest supplier of pre-press equipment for graphic design, leading the transformation of the graphic arts industry. Creo Inc. has been recognized as one of British Columbia's largest technology companies and is among Canada's 100 largest.

Creo Inc. manufactures more than 300 products, including professional digital cameras, colour and copy-dot scanning systems; inkjet and halftone digital proofers; workflow management tools; variable information workflow systems; computer-to-film and computer-to-plate devices; and colour servers for high-speed, print-on-demand digital printers.

Creo Inc. prides itself on its commitment to ethics through strong values and solid management philosophies. The company has been named one of the 50 best ethical stocks for Canadians and is considered one of Canada's top employers.

Keeping up with rapid changes in the graphic arts industry is a constant challenge for most companies. Research and development (R & D) at Creo Inc. begins with ideas — many originating from customers — and continues through product development, manufacturing, and service, ending with solutions that increase their customers' profitability. With hundreds of people working in R & D, they are able to develop a wide range of products and technologies at once. In fact, Creo Inc. files for a new patent about once a week, covering a wide range of activities from software to hardware.

Questions

1. With a partner or alone, brainstorm a list of the types of organizations or individuals who would be primary consumers of Creo Inc. products. Compare your list with another individual's or group's list. How are the lists similar and different?

2. The graphic design industry is constantly changing due to technology. Use your favourite search engine and the links available at www.pearsoned.ca/businessconnections to identify five emerging trends and issues in this field. Create a chart that includes a suitable main heading and these column headings: Trends/Issues, Description, Potential Use.

3. Describe two ways that these emerging trends would affect someone looking for a career in this field. Discuss your answers with a classmate.

7.2 Desktop Publishing

Desktop publishing (DTP) is the term that describes the process of using a desktop computer to produce documents such as newsletters, brochures, and books using specialized software. The term was first used during the mid-1980s when DTP software was introduced. DTP software lies somewhere in between graphic design and word-processing software. The key difference between these programs is that word-processing software focuses on text-based documents, whereas graphic design software focuses on design and artistic knowledge to produce visually appealing documents. DTP software combines these two purposes, serving as an application specifically designed to create visually appealing documents that have a lot of text.

Figure 7.14
Desktop Publication

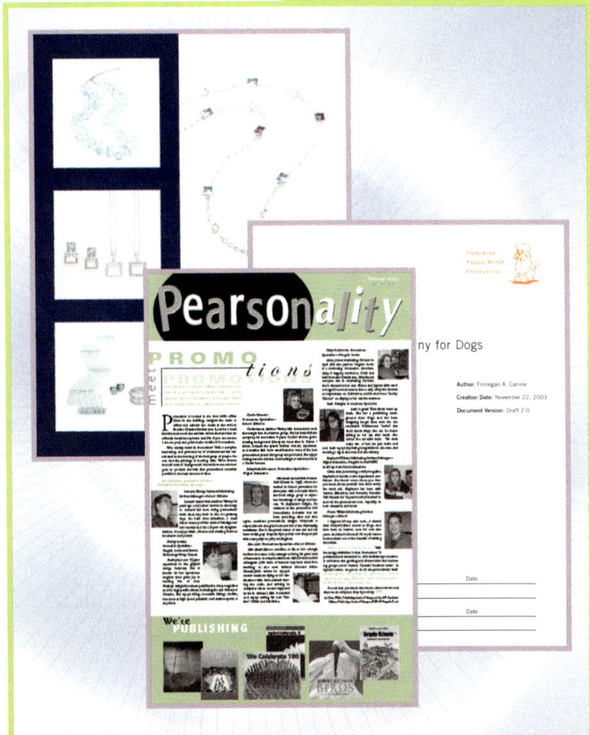

DTP software allows for the creation of many types of print items.

7.2.1 Desktop Publishing Software

DTP software allows the designer to rearrange text and graphics onscreen and to change typefaces with ease, and relies heavily on the use of templates that have predesigned formatting. Though highly specialized software exists for this purpose, most word-processing software incorporates DTP features in the form of templates, wizards, and features.

Common DTP programs include CorelDRAW®, Adobe® PageMaker®, QuarkXPress™, Broderbund™ The Print Shop® *Deluxe*, and Microsoft® Publisher. This software combines the text and graphic elements into an onscreen display that resembles a document page. This allows the user to see a draft of the finished product. These programs also can be used to further refine both text and graphics, including changing the size and style of the text and resizing or manipulating graphics. Finally, the finished document is either printed on a laser printer or saved to disk for later output.

DTP software ranges from simple to complex. PageMaker and QuarkXPress are the industry standards for larger, more complex documents such as newspapers, magazines, and newsletters. Simpler, less complex programs such as The Print Shop® *Deluxe* feature easy-to-use templates for commonly produced documents such as greeting cards, brochures, and newsletters.

Key features of DTP software include the ability to import text, graphics, and photographs, and to create documents with multiple columns and various formats. The software allows users to wrap text around odd-shaped graphics, to distort text and other elements to create bold graphics, and to produce colour separations for printing.

Get Connected

Many professions have a governing body or professional association that allows its members to connect. Visit the sites of professional design associations by following the links at www.pearsoned.ca/businessconnections. For the sites you visit describe how one can become a member. List three areas that the site is involved in. Compare your answers with those of another group. As a class discuss the benefits of joining such associations.

GETTING IT

1. Create, electronically, a chart with appropriate headings that compares the differences and similarities among DTP, word-processing, and graphic design programs.
2. Examine the templates, features, and functions of the word-processing software you usually use. What DTP elements or features does it include? What specific DTP templates are included?
3. Using the information gathered to answer question 2 above, create a two-column table that has the headings "Word processing" and "DTP." If possible, create the table electronically. In each column, list the templates and features available in each. Under the chart, make a list of those features and templates that are common to both. Check off the three templates that you would expect to use most frequently.

7.3 Organizing Electronic Presentations

Electronic presentations are now commonplace in most business environments. **Presentation software** allows users to create slide shows that incorporate text, graphics, animation, and sound to deliver a message with impact to the audience. Common forms of presentation software include: Microsoft® PowerPoint® (for Windows and Mac operating systems), Lotus Freelance, Corel® Presentations™, and HyperStudio.

Figure 7.15

In what type of presentations would using graphs be an effective way to convey information? Explain why.

Though presentation software is a powerful communication tool, a meaningful message in well-organized order is more important. Before getting to the software, it is crucial that you understand how to organize your thoughts into a message that is geared toward the needs of the target audience. Recommended steps in planning a presentation are:

1. Identify your target audience.
2. Determine why or in what context the audience is interested in the presentation.
3. State the purpose of the presentation (to provide an update? to teach skills?).
4. Select from one to three key messages that the audience must remember when they leave.
5. Identify what you hope to achieve by the end of the presentation.
6. Determine any time constraints (is there a limited amount of time allotted in which to present?).

Once those steps are completed, the content should be easier to organize. If a lot of information needs to be conveyed (or is available), prioritizing and editing is necessary. One effective framework is to draw a chart with the following headings:

- things the audience must know;
- things the audience should know; and
- things that are nice to know.

By placing all the available information into these headings, it becomes clear what should be used in the presentation and what can be left unused (or put in an appendix for further, independent reading).

Once the important information is identified, it needs to be organized into a logical sequence before it is translated into slides. A good presentation has a distinct beginning, middle or body, and conclusion. This can be done electronically or on paper. One method of ensuring a good flow is to create headings for all the intended slides, subheadings, and then bullets of information underneath each heading from your rough notes. Always refer back to your objectives and the needs of your audience to ensure that each point is relevant. Having a final slide that provides a very brief summary of your message is important to ensure that the key points "stick" with the audience.

Keep in mind that a slideshow is *not* a report, and therefore sentences and paragraphs are not usually used. Key words or phrases should be included, with detail to be filled in verbally by the presenter or speaker. A variety of suggested word limits have been proposed by many individuals and organizations. The consensus seems to be the fewer the words, the better. Generally, the following rules are recommended:

- a maximum of between 5 and 8 words per line
- a maximum of between 5 and 7 lines per page

Once this rough draft is complete, it is ready to be dressed up with software.

digiknow

Approximately 30 million PowerPoint presentations are delivered worldwide each day, which translates to 11 billion a year and 347 each second.

(Microsoft 2002)

7.3.1 Anatomy of a Slide

Slides contain several basic components (see Figure 7.16 on page 190) regardless of the software you use. Understanding what they are and how to use them is essential to using the software effectively.

- *Background*. The background is a setting that provides the colour or pattern behind all the objects that make up the slide. Presentation software offers a variety of backgrounds that vary from solid colours, to patterns, to textures. When a new background is chosen, it is applied to all slides automatically. For effect, you can also have one particular slide in the presentation appear with a different background colour or pattern.

Figure 7.16A
Anatomy of a Slide
Title Slide

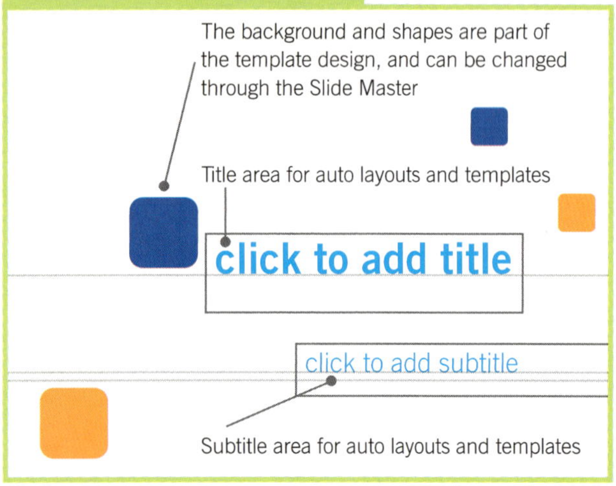

Figure 7.16B
Anatomy of a Slide
Standard Slide Layout

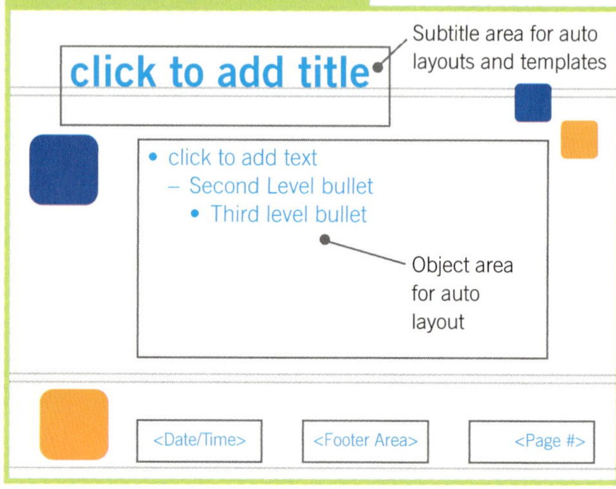

- *Design.* Though a slide's design usually includes a background, its design represents far more. The design refers to the entire "package" that defines the look of a presentation and includes fonts, borders, graphics, and the arrangement of these elements. Slide design is saved in the form of a template (as defined in Chapter 5). When a template is applied to a presentation, each slide will assume the properties of the template. Templates can be modified or created by using features such as Slide Master (located in the View menu) in PowerPoint.
- *Objects.* Each slide contains several (or sometimes many) objects. In slideshows, text comes in the form of text boxes — which are objects. Usually, a text object is used for the title, and another for the body. Other objects commonly included in a slide include drawn objects (arrows, geometric shapes, text art) and clipart. Users often rely on the "Draw" toolbox within the presentation software to create custom shapes to enhance the slideshow (see Section 7.1.5 on page 180 for further information about using Draw tools).

7.3.2 Communicating the Message Visually

One of the tricks to using presentation software effectively is knowing when and how to present information visually (i.e., using symbols and pictures instead of words). Remember that the Elements and Principles of Design (pages 173–178) apply to electronic slides. Before adding graphics, you should consider the purpose and tone of the presentation. A serious presentation should not contain bright colours or animated "cute" clipart. On the other hand, a presentation intended to energize and enthuse an audience should include animation, dynamic images, strong colours, and eye-catching graphics (see Figure 7.17).

Figure 7.17
Communicating the Message Visually

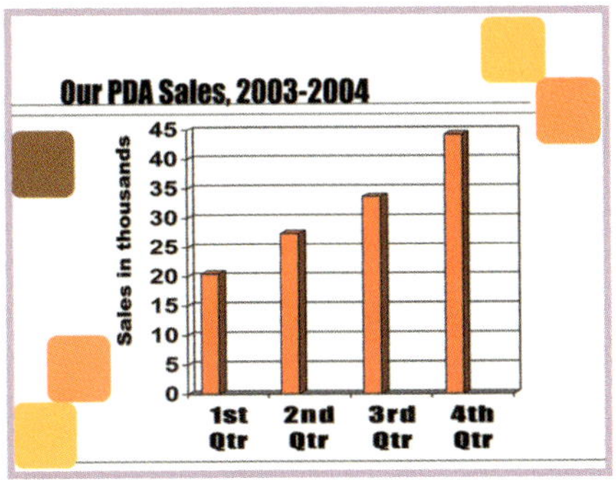

Instead of this…

Create impact through careful use of graphics to illustrate a point.

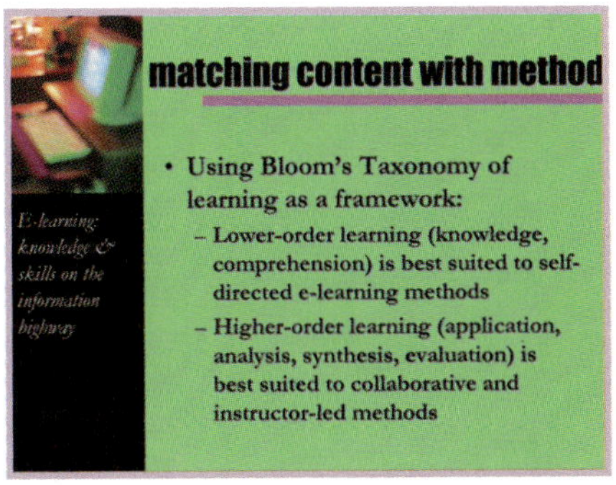

Instead of this…

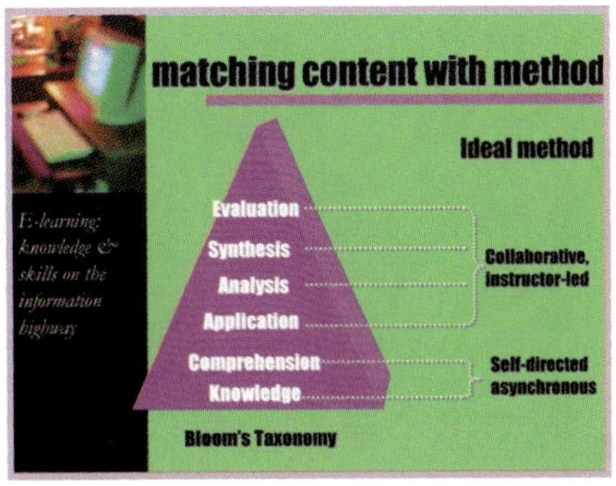

Use balanced shapes and colour to illustrate key concepts

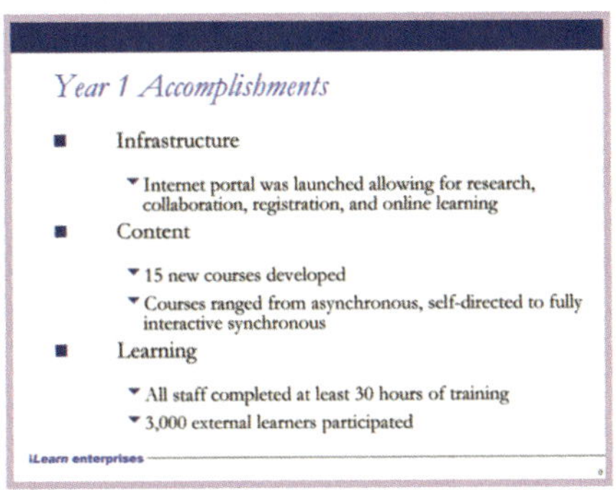

Both of these slides contain the same information. Which communicates the message more effecitvely?

Often, people simply create bulleted lists with a stylized background on each slide. Though bulleted lists can be appropriate and often are the best solution, using a variety of shapes can increase the impact of a message. The Draw tools available in each presentation software application, as well as clipart, provide solutions.

The following tips apply when you want to use graphics to communicate a message:

- Avoid too many shapes, colours, or objects on one slide. Too much creates visual clutter and loses the message.
- Ask yourself (or someone you trust) if the images with which you are experimenting make sense for the message in that particular slide. If they confuse you or another person, they will likely confuse your audience.
- Think about the actual information you are presenting. Does it bring any particular shapes or images to mind (either literally or metaphorically)? If so, can you find and use those images for the slide?
- When you see an effective slide or presentation, keep a copy of it for future reference. You may be able to adapt the layout or design style to meet your needs.

7.3.3 Using Common Features of Presentation Software

Presentation software opens up tremendous potential for effective and innovative communication. The sections below will illustrate how you can get the most from your software by using existing features and functions.

7.3.3.1 Adding, Moving, and Deleting Slides

When you use presentation software, slides have to be added individually. Almost all presentation software allows you to select preformatted slide layouts for specific purposes (e.g., slides with text only, with charts, with clipart, or a combination of those). Using an automatic layout feature (such as AutoLayout in PowerPoint), you can keep design elements within slides consistent. More importantly, the objects in the slides are tagged so that if you change the design template, the objects are automatically updated. Without AutoLayout, you have to manually change objects if a new template is selected.

Slides can easily be moved and deleted using the Slideshow view. While viewing all the slides on the screen, you can select a single slide (or a group of slides by holding down the Shift key), and move it using the mouse. Alternatively, you can delete a slide by selecting it and then using the "delete" key.

digiknow

The prototype for PowerPoint was created in 1981 with the original name "Presenter." It went on the market as PowerPoint 1.0 in April 1987.

7.3.3.2 Formatting the "Look"

Backgrounds. Backgrounds are similar to stationery that you might use in letter writing and comprise what appears behind the objects on every slide. Backgrounds can be added or changed automatically. Keep in mind that backgrounds need not be solid colours; all software allows for patterns, textures, and pictures to be placed.

Designs. A design refers to the overall combination of background, font(s), colour, and layout of objects. All presentation software comes with standard designs in the form of templates. These can be selected upon creating the presentation, or added or changed at any point in the presentation development process. They can be changed or edited (in PowerPoint, use the Slide Master view) to customize them. Alternatively, you can create your own templates (again, in PowerPoint use the Slide Master view for this). In a similar fashion to word-processing software (see Chapter 5), templates should be saved as such using the appropriate file extension (which varies from program to program).

Colour scheme. Most presentation software has the ability to provide a new colour scheme made up of a palette of visually appealing colours. Even when you use a design template, the colour scheme can be altered.

7.3.3.3 Speaking Notes

The majority of presentation software has a feature that allows speaking notes to be attached to each slide electronically. The speaking notes do not appear on the slide itself (and therefore the audience will not see them), but can be printed along with the slide. This is a very useful feature since it produces a document that can be used as a reference during a presentation.

7.3.3.4 Views

Normal. This view allows the user to edit individual slides, looking at only one slide at a time.

Slide sorter. This view provides thumbnails of all the slides in the presentation. They can be selected individually, then moved by cutting and pasting or dragging the mouse. As well, a slide can be copied in this view, then pasted into another application as a graphic object. Aside from moving entire slides, no editing is possible in this view.

Notes. This view allows you to see and/or input speaking notes to a slide. The area reserved for notes should be treated as if it is in a word-processing program.

Slideshow. This view is strictly for presenting the slides, and in this view the slide takes up the entire screen (and therefore the software window is hidden). No editing can be done. The Escape key can be used to terminate this view. Details on navigation can be found in Section 7.3.3.9.

7.3.3.5 Working With Objects

When you prepare to work with objects, it is beneficial to have the Draw toolbar on the desktop — it saves a great deal of time and allows you to see your options.

Inserting. Different types of objects are inserted in different ways. Generally, the Draw toolbar provides the quickest method by which to insert text boxes, shapes, lines, and graphics. To insert an object onto a slide, the appropriate menu or button is used.

Selecting. To select a single object, you click once while the cursor's arrow is over the object. To group multiple objects you hold down the Control (CTRL) key while pointing and clicking. This is similar to what is done in graphics programs.

Moving. To move objects, or groups of objects, click and drag or use the arrow keys if the objects are selected. Keep in mind that objects can also be rotated and tilted using the functions in the Draw toolbar.

Resizing. To resize an object, you select it and then drag one of the handles (little white squares around the object) to increase or decrease any of the object's dimensions.

Editing. To edit text objects, place the cursor inside the text box and then make changes accordingly. As well, you can change fonts manually for all or part of the text objects by selecting portions of the text, then using the Format Font menu or toolbar buttons. Graphic objects (such as clipart, shapes, and lines) are edited using the Format Auto Shape menu.

Layering. Layering refers to the order in which objects appear in a slide. Similar to what happens with paint and draw software, the most recently added object appears on top (sometimes hiding what is beneath). The order of the layers can be changed using the Draw toolbar or by right-clicking on the object in a Windows environment.

7.3.3.6 Adding Animation and Multimedia Effects

Before you add animation or other effects, be certain that they will make sense when your presentation finally reaches an audience. For instance, if you are going to speak about items in a bulleted list, make certain that the animations or sounds will not halt or slow down your discussion or distract from the tone of the message.

Animation. Animation can be added to individual objects or elements within a slideshow, such as:

- individual words, bullets, or text boxes; and
- graphic objects (e.g., clipart, pictures, shapes, lines, etc.).

Each presentation software application has a variety of available effects. Some common examples are: fly from the left, appear, zoom, flash, or dissolve. You can set the timing for these effects (from fast to slow) and add sounds to complement them. As well, you can set these effects to be "automatic" (i.e., they happen without prompting) or manual (usually upon mouse click).

When a presenter is speaking (as opposed to a stand-alone presentation), having animation activated by a mouse-click can help to ensure that the slide presentation keeps pace with the speaker. Keep in mind, though, that some speakers find it irritating to have to click to advance each bullet. Ensure that the person speaking is fully comfortable with the animation style and details.

Another important consideration is the order of animation. When animation is added, the top "layer" is animated first, followed by the second layer, and so on. The order of animation can be changed manually in the animation dialog box.

Having to animate every single object in every single slide is a time-consuming, frustrating task. Fortunately, the software allows you to modify the template (e.g., through Slide Master in PowerPoint), therefore making the animations that are selected on the master consistent for all slides in the presentation. This saves an enormous amount of time.

Sound. A variety of sound effects are available and there are several ways to incorporate sound into a presentation:

1. Sound can be linked to animation through the animation dialog box.
2. A pre-recorded sound file can be added with a button that appears on the slide. This will begin the audio clip when someone is viewing the show. To do this, a sound already available (either from a CD-ROM, a disk, the Internet, or the hard drive) needs to be inserted while the software is in slide view.
3. Original audio can be recorded and added to a slide in PowerPoint (provided the computer has a working microphone installed). The menu command path is: Insert/Movies and Pictures/Sounds/Record Sound. Whatever sound the microphone picks up when "Record" is clicked will be added to the sound file attached to the slide.

Slide transition. Slide transitions are the method by which one slide advances to the next. When no transition is set, slides simply appear on the click of a mouse. However, to add interest, a variety of animated slide transitions can be set. Examples include checkerboard, dissolve, uncover, and wipe.

The process for adding or editing slide transitions is similar to the one used in animations. The speed of the transitions can be set (from slow to fast) and the transitions can take place automatically (the user sets the time) or manually (upon mouse click or Page Up/Down key). Sound can also be added to the slide transition in the same manner it is to animation. Finally, slide transitions can be added manually to each slide or to the whole presentation through the design template.

The use of slide transitions is a personal choice. Some individuals prefer a single transition for all slides; others prefer one or two transitions only to be used for consistency, while others prefer a variety of transitions to be used. There is no single or standard rule for this.

Automation. A slideshow can be automated so that it runs on its own, with a pre-set animation and slide transition time. This is accomplished by setting timing for the entire template, or for individual slides. In most presentation software, this is done at the same time (and through the same dialog boxes) that you set animation. It can also be looped, so that once the last

digiknow

Saving to Web Sites

Most presentation software has features that allow slides to be uploaded to the Internet as Web pages (note that creating and uploading Web pages is covered in detail in Chapter 12). This can be achieved by saving the presentation as a Web page in the Save As dialog box.

slide is reached, the presentation returns to the first slide and continues running until you press the Escape (ESC) key.

7.3.3.7 Hyperlinks

Hyperlinks within a slideshow allow the presenter to "jump" to different spots in the presentation, or to other applications such as the Internet (usually for illustrative purposes). Action buttons are commonly used to create a point to click in order to initiate the jump. Presentation software allows you to select appropriate action buttons and to link them to slides or other applications.

7.3.3.8 Printing

All presentation software allows for a variety of unique printing options. The most commonly used options are:

- *full slides*: where one slide is printed on a page;
- *handouts*: where multiple slides are printed on a page; most software allows the user to edit the layout of handouts so that the number of slides per page (and the page layout) can be customized. Features such as Headers, Footers, and page numbers can be added to handouts; and
- *speaking notes*: generally used only by the presenter, the speaking notes feature prints each slide along with notes on one page.

7.3.3.9 Presenting Electronically

Liquid crystal display (LCD) projectors (see Figure 7.18) are peripheral devices used to present slideshows to groups. Somewhat similar to overhead projectors, they project the images that normally appear on a computer monitor onto a screen or wall. These projectors are connected to a computer using a cable (usually attached to the monitor output port).

While sometimes presenters bring their own portable computers with them, many venues have computers available for this purpose. To use the facility's computer system, however, takes planning:

- Ensure that the computer you will be using has the appropriate operating system and software installed to run your presentation (a self-executing file, described below, can solve this problem).
- Use only common fonts such as Times New Roman and Arial. Otherwise you run the risk that the fonts in the presentation (including bullets) may not be installed on the computer you will be using.
- Be sure to transfer the presentation to the computer's hard drive from your disk (or other storage device) before you begin the presentation. Sometimes, working from a disk can slow down slide transition or animation.

Figure 7.18
An LCD Projector

LCD projectors are often used to deliver presentations to groups.

To present a slide show to a group, the slide show view option must be selected so that the audience sees only the slide — not the editing tools and software GUI. If the slide show is not timed (i.e., the slides do not automatically advance), the speaker (or an assistant) has to manually advance the slides or animated objects. A couple of options are available:

Clicking the left mouse button will advance the animation or move to the next slide (right-clicking will allow options to reverse movement).

Using the Page Down key will advance the slide show, while the Page Up key will reverse it.

7.3.4 Self-Executing Presentations

Some presentation software has features that allow you to create a self-executing version of a slide show that can be played on any computer, even if the computer does not have that presentation software installed.

In PowerPoint, the Pack and Go feature allows this to happen. To "pack" a presentation, click on Pack and Go in the File menu and follow the wizard. Be sure to include the "Viewer" option to ensure that the presentation can be packed for viewing on a machine without PowerPoint installed.

In Corel® Presentations™, the Show On The Go™ feature is used. To use Show On The Go, in the file menu click Show On The Go. Then click Create and wait until the self-executing (.exe) file is complete.

GETTING IT

1. Name the features that make presentation software unique from other office productivity applications. How are they similar?
2. Describe the importance of planning a presentation.
3. Describe some of the features available in presentation software to make a slide show more interesting to the audience. Explain how you would use those features.
4. Name the print formats available for slide shows and describe how a presenter might use several of them.
5. Use the information from this section to prepare an outline for your Chapter Project and retain it to be submitted with the final project.
6. In your notebook, create a plan for the visual impact you hope to create for your Chapter Project. Specifically identify the Elements of Design you plan to use, and how you will use them.
7. Create a presentation template for your Chapter Project that incorporates the decisions you made in question 6. Share it with another student for feedback, and make changes accordingly.

7.4 Communicating Through Presentations

ON THE CASE

Tips for Effective Presentations

Adapted from "Remember Your Audience" by Doug Mollenhauer, *Marketing Magazine*, June 29, 1998.

"Each point you include in your presentation should run through a filter. Ask yourself: So what? What's in it for the listener?"

Get a handle on who you are talking to and what their needs are

Audiences respond best to messages that meet their needs and echo what they already believe. Abe Lincoln put it this way: "When I get ready to talk to people, I spend two-thirds of the time thinking about what they want to hear, and one-third of the time thinking about what I want to say."

Set an achievable objective

As they say, if you don't know where you're going, any road will get you there. Above all, not only be clear on what it is you want to achieve, but also be sure that this is consistent with what the audience wants to hear. Share an objective that addresses the issue you are presenting. One best practice is to start with a slide that reads "This presentation will...".

Structure your presentation so that it is easy to follow

Douglas MacArthur said "Tell 'em what you're going to tell 'em, tell 'em, and then tell 'em what you told 'em." It's not that people are thick, just generally inattentive and easily distracted. By previewing what you are going to cover, then covering material one point at a time, and then reviewing what you covered, you stand a much better chance of keeping the audience alert and on track with your message.

Use visuals selectively

Avoid the kind of "information dump" that results from using too many wordy slides. If you use slides, make them visual rather than verbal (charts, arrows, and the like instead of pure words). Keep slides clear and simple, creative and compelling. Whatever you do, never turn your back on the audience to read from the screen!

Engage the audience with genuine eye contact

Some presenters believe it's enough to shift their eyes back and forth across the audience as if they are running a radar screen. But that's bogus eye contact. You're there to talk to them, not at them. Genuine eye contact (looking at individuals in the audience throughout your presentation) is more personal and engages audience members.

Find the drama in your message

An audience tends not to care how much you know about a subject unless they know how much you care. Find something about your message that is urgent and compelling, something that will bring you to life. When you're wrapped up in your message, and especially when the message relates to the audience, you will likely speak more naturally and with more force than you would by rehearsing gestures.

Punctuate your presentations with pauses

Enthusiasm is one thing, but be careful not to let your train of thought become a runaway locomotive. Pause enough to ensure your audience is still with you, and have a look around to see if they are paying attention.

7.4.1 Speaking to a Group

Speaking before an audience can be very intimidating, so having a solid, informative electronic slideshow is a good start. However, communicating the message to a group also requires good verbal communication skills. Believe in your ability to deliver the presentation; speaking to a group is something that everybody can learn to do well.

Rehearsing is an excellent way to become comfortable with public speaking, particularly for those people who do not have a great deal of experience in speaking to groups. If possible, use either video (so that you can critique yourself) or a volunteer who will provide you with honest, constructive, and positive feedback. General tips for speaking to a group include:

Figure 7.19

An audience might comprise a large group of strangers, like this one, or a small group of familiar faces. Before which type of audience would you feel most comfortable speaking? Why?

- Practise losing your place in your presentation and come up with strategies to get back on track.
- Practise speaking clearly both at normal tones and at a higher volume.
- Try to give your presentation at different paces (speak quickly, then slowly) and decide which pace works best for you.
- Try to determine if you have any distracting mannerisms (e.g., moving your foot, using "hmm" or "like" in your speech) and work at minimizing them.
- Try to exude confidence in your speech — avoid phrasing statements as questions or speaking in a "sing-songy" manner.
- Pause briefly after you make an important point for impact.
- Repeat or rephrase important information.

7.4.2 Body Language

Body language is important in any communication exchange. As a presenter, you need to be aware of your own body language — and also be attuned to that of your audience. Keeping an eye on their non-verbal communication is important in gauging how the presentation is affecting them. Keep in mind, however, that the information contained in this section is specific to North American protocols. If you are speaking to an audience of a different culture, different rules apply.

As a presenter, you set the tone with your body language. We have all witnessed speakers who appear bored or nervous — and probably tuned out quite quickly ourselves. Ideally, the audience will perceive that you are alert, interested, and comfortable.

The first building block to achieving good body language is posture — keep your head high, shoulders back, and a relaxed stance. Slouching or speaking with your head down in your speaking notes is considered unprofessional. An added benefit to using good posture is that it will help you to project your voice more clearly. Try to move around, if possible, to engage the audience and to keep your eyes on them. As mentioned in *On the Case*, making genuine eye contact is an important component of effective communication (as well as a method of reading the audience's reaction).

While keeping an eye on your audience, be prepared to respond to their non-verbal cues. Things to watch for include:

- *watching or listening intently while leaning forward* (which is a sign of interest);
- *crossed arms* (which might be a sign of resistance to what you are saying);
- *quizzical expressions* (which might indicate that the person is confused or is considering a point made by the presenter); and
- *leaning back* (which might indicate lack of agreement or interest).

Keep in mind that there are no absolutes in interpreting body language — individuals have unique habits. However, if you sense that you are losing the audience, several strategies can be used to turn things around:

- Involve the audience through questions or solicit participation to re-engage them in your message.
- Inject humour (if appropriate) to win back the audience.
- If a section of your presentation is not working, summarize it as quickly as possible and move on (even if you have to skip some information).

As you make more and more presentations, you will develop your own unique communication style and discover strategies that help you overcome the inevitable bumps that presentations hit.

GETTING IT

1. In groups, brainstorm a list of the challenges of speaking to a group. For each challenge listed, write a sentence explaining what you can do to overcome it.
2. With a partner, prepare a skit that demonstrates why understanding body language is important to a presenter. Present your skit to your classmates.
3. List the steps you can take to improve your ability to present to audiences.
4. Develop a Reflection Sheet for your portfolio by drawing a line down the centre of a blank piece of paper. On the left side, list all the good presenter skills listed in this chapter. Put a checkmark beside each one you possess. On the right side, write a sentence stating what you need to do to acquire the skill needed for each point you did not put a checkmark beside.

CAREER PERSPECTIVE

More and more often at job interviews, organizations require applicants to prepare and give a presentation using presentation software. Select a local job advertisement using either the newspaper or the Internet. Research the job, the industry, and the company using resources available in your school and community. Retain your notes. Prepare a slide presentation to give at the interview that:

- identifies the skills, competencies, or knowledge you possess that qualify you for the job (remember to link these to the requirements of the job as described in the advertisement); and
- describes two projects you have worked on that demonstrate your eligibility for that job.

Be sure to consider the audience you will be presenting to and focus on clearly communicating your message in the shortest time frame possible. Refer to your portfolio for ideas. Use the information from this chapter to create a presentation that will "wow" a prospective employer.

IT's A Wrap

Key Terms in This Chapter

analogous colours (p. 175)
balance (p. 175)
codecs (p. 179)
complementary colours (p. 175)
compress (p. 179)
consistency (p. 177)
contrast (p. 176)
desktop publishing (DTP) (p. 187)
dithering (p. 175)
economy (p. 176)
Elements of Design (p. 173)
emphasis (p. 177)
focal point (p. 177)
form (p. 175)
graphic design (p. 173)
grouping (p. 182)
hue (p. 173)
intensity (p. 173)
line (p. 175)
lossless compression (p. 179)
lossy compression (p. 179)
object-oriented graphics (p. 178)
pixels (p. 178)
presentation software (p. 188)
Principles of Design (p. 173)
raster (p. 178)
rhythm (p. 178)
shape (p. 175)
texture (p. 175)
unity (p. 178)
value (p. 173)
vector-based graphics (p. 178)

1. Create a list of competencies that you have acquired through your work in this chapter.
2. Update your portfolio to include examples of your work from this chapter.

Know It!

3. Describe the Elements and Principles of Design and explain how they apply to presentation software.
4. Create a checklist, either electronically or in your notebook as advised by your teacher, to assess a graphic composition using the Elements and Principles of Design.

IT's A Wrap *(continued)*

Know It!

5. Describe three strategies that you or a colleague can use to organize ideas logically and effectively when planning an electronic presentation.
6. List the types of animation and multimedia effects available in the presentation software you will be using in this course. Explain how you will use them.
7. Identify the hardware you would want to have if you were making an electronic presentation.
8. Create a "top-ten list" of tips for making a presentation to a large group.
9. When presenting on someone else's computer, what should you do to ensure that things will work when it comes time to go "on stage"?

Do It!

10. Sometimes, breaking the rules of design can be effective. On the Internet or in a print source, locate an example of a graphic design item that breaks a rule. In your notebook, describe which rule is broken and why it is effective. Share your work with another student. Did that person agree or disagree with your opinion that breaking the rule was effective? Why or why not?
11. With a photograph that you can easily acquire, use image-editing software to improve or change features of the subject based on the techniques described on pages 183–185. Prepare an electronic comparison sheet on which you paste the original photograph and your altered version. Below the images, describe the changes you made. Explain which photo you think is better and why.
12. Using any graphic image and the "save as" command, save the image in a variety of file formats. Investigate how the file size changed, as well as whether the image itself changed. Record what you observed each time you changed the file type in your notebook.
13. Obtain a simple piece of clipart. Ungroup the objects that make up that piece of clipart, modify them, and then regroup the clipart. Save each stage of this process, and create a final printed page that illustrates each of the steps you took.
14. Use DTP software to create a one-page newsletter for a friend or family member to describe what is new in your life. After receiving teacher approval, send the newsletter, electronically if possible, to the intended receiver.

Analyze It!

15. Locate an advertisement either on the Internet or in a print publication. Analyze it using the Principles of Design. Record your analysis in your notebook.
16. In your notebook, describe an effective presentation you have seen. Explain what made it effective and the techniques the speaker used to hold your attention. Share this information with your teacher.

CHAPTER

Got the Message? Electronic Communication

8

By the end of this chapter, you will be able to:

- demonstrate your understanding and use of electronic communication tools;
- describe potential negative consequences of using electronic communication tools;
- explain how business adapts to changing communication customs, cultures, and environments;
- describe the services provided by Internet Service Providers; and
- demonstrate appropriate ways of communicating in the workplace.

Not long ago you would write a letter, use the telephone, or even go in person if you wanted to speak to someone. Our world today is filled with new and marvellous ways for people to keep in touch and to communicate, such as e-mail, voice mail, and cellular phones. This chapter will examine electronic communication methods that are in common use by business today and will cover the following areas:

- The Communication Process
- Telecommunications Technology
- Communication Tools: Using the Telecommunications Backbone
- The Internet as a Communications Medium
- Wireless Communications: Cellular Phones
- Wireless Communications: Wireless LANs (WiFi) and Bluetooth Technology

Introduction to Chapter Project

Recall that the Chapter Project is introduced at the beginning and is to be completed as you work through the chapter. Your teacher will provide you with assessment and evaluation criteria.

CHAPTER PROJECT

Consultants are often required to prepare submissions for consideration by clients. As you work through the chapter, develop a communications strategy for a small business located in or near your town or city. Use local ISPs (Internet Service Providers) and wireless communications providers as primary sources of information for product availability and pricing. Create your strategy and highlight it in a presentation or a portfolio format that you might give to the small business you are focusing on.

Picture this scenario. You are on the job at a construction site near Sault Ste. Marie, Ontario. Your boss approaches you to find out the status of a shipment of windows from your supplier in Calgary. He asks you to contact the supplier to determine if delivery is still scheduled for next Friday. You take out your voice-enabled PDA, check for the supplier's phone number in the handheld database, and dial the number on its portable handset. The supplier, on location in Canmore, picks up his cellular phone and dials into his corporate Intranet from his laptop computer using WiFi wireless connections to the Internet. Within minutes you have the answer to your question and can confirm delivery details with your boss.

Does this sound far-fetched? It shouldn't. The technology described here is being used now by businesses and individuals alike, and new advances in communications technology are being made daily. Before we examine the wide range of communication tools available to businesses today, let us first examine the process of communication.

8.1 The Communication Process

Communication involves giving or exchanging information. The key elements in the communication process are:

- *the sender* (who determines the verbal and non-verbal message to be sent);
- *the communication channel* (the means by which the message is sent);
- *the receiver* (who interprets the meaning of the message); and

- *feedback* (the return message to the sender to confirm the original message was understood as intended).

See Figure 8.1 for a graphic depiction of the communication process.

Figure 8.1
The Communication Process

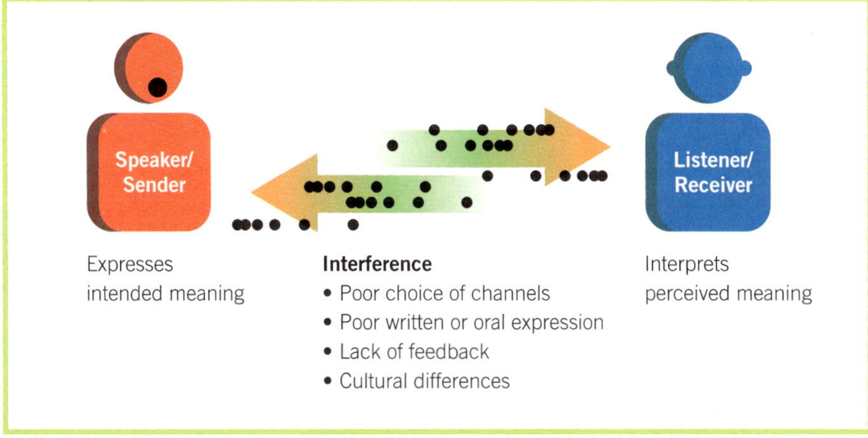

The communication process is subject to many outside influences that can make it difficult for both the sender and the receiver to understand the message in the same way.

There are two basic communication channels: written and verbal. Generally, written communication is best used when the messages:

- must be specific;
- will be easily understood;
- require quick distribution; and
- must be kept for future reference.

E-mail and message boards are two common forms of written communication.

Verbal messages are used:

- when convenient in real time; and
- where immediate feedback is required.

Telephone and cellular phone are verbal message options available in today's business environment (as well as face-to-face communication, of course).

Communication is effective when both the sender and receiver of the message understand the message in the same way. Efficiency is achieved when the cost (in terms of time and money) of the communication is kept to a minimum.

Communication channels are considered "rich" when effectiveness is maximized. Figure 8.2 illustrates communication channels organized along a spectrum. A channel is "rich" when it provides the opportunity for personal interaction and immediate feedback. At one end of the spectrum we find impersonal, mass-distributed messages such as postings and e-bulletins sent through the corporate Intranet. At the other end, we find face-to-face meetings. There is, however, an inherent trade-off. With increased richness, the speed or effectiveness of the channel is compromised, increasing the overall cost of communicating in any form. As a result, we see that it is difficult to achieve both effectiveness and efficiency in any one communication channel. However, advances in technology are improving the effectiveness of communication while maximizing efficiency as well (Schermerhorn 2002).

Figure 8.2
Richness of Communication Channel

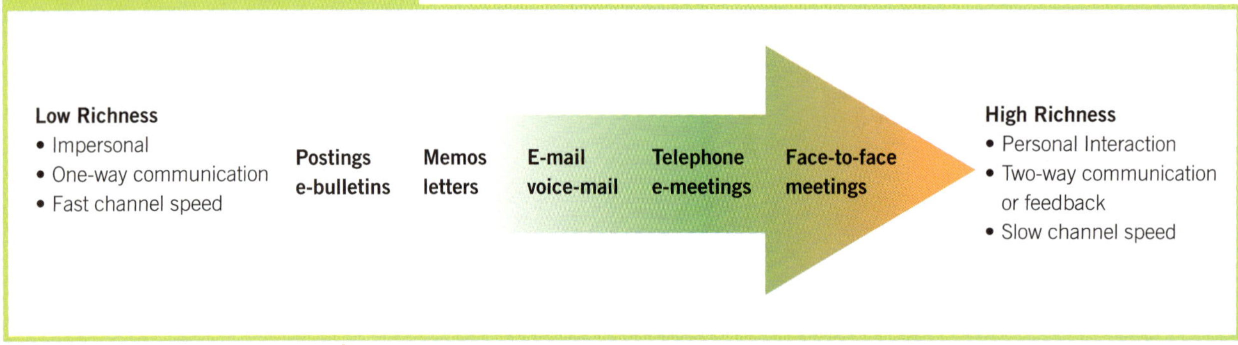

This chapter focuses on the available choices in terms of communication channels or methods of getting messages from sender to receiver in today's fast-paced business environment. Although much of the media attention is focused on mobile and wireless communication, it is important to look at some more traditional methods that utilize telecommunications technology, which is still the backbone of much organizational communication today.

GETTING IT

1. List and describe the main elements in the communication process.
2. Explain the meaning of a "rich" communication channel.
3. Can communication channels be both effective and efficient? Explain why or why not.

8.2 Telecommunications Technology

Traditionally, the term "telecommunications" refers to the transmission of voice or data over telephone lines. Much of today's organizational communication relies on this technology. To understand the devices that connect to this system, let us first examine how the telephone system works.

Local telephone service is provided by companies, also called **telcos**, that connect homes and offices via landlines and satellite. When you make a telephone call (see Figure 8.3), the analog signal from your phone (a continuously changing electrical signal) travels over a wire from the telephone to the telephone box located outside your home. This box, or **subscriber loop carrier (SLC)**, connects upward of 100 subscribers with twisted-pair copper cable. The copper wires are twisted to reduce electrical interference or noise from electrical circuits. This group of subscribers is known as the **local loop**.

Once the signal is received, the SLC converts the analog signal to digital. This signal is then sent along high-capacity cables (usually fibre-optic cables) to the local exchange (which connects all the phones in a relatively small geographic area). Fibre-optic cables transmit data along thin strands of glass by pulses of light. Calls are then connected to central exchanges and from there to other central exchanges or international exchanges, depending on the destination of the call. International calls are routed via satellite or underwater cables. Cellular phone transmission will be discussed on pages 226–227.

Figure 8.3
Transmission of a Phone Call

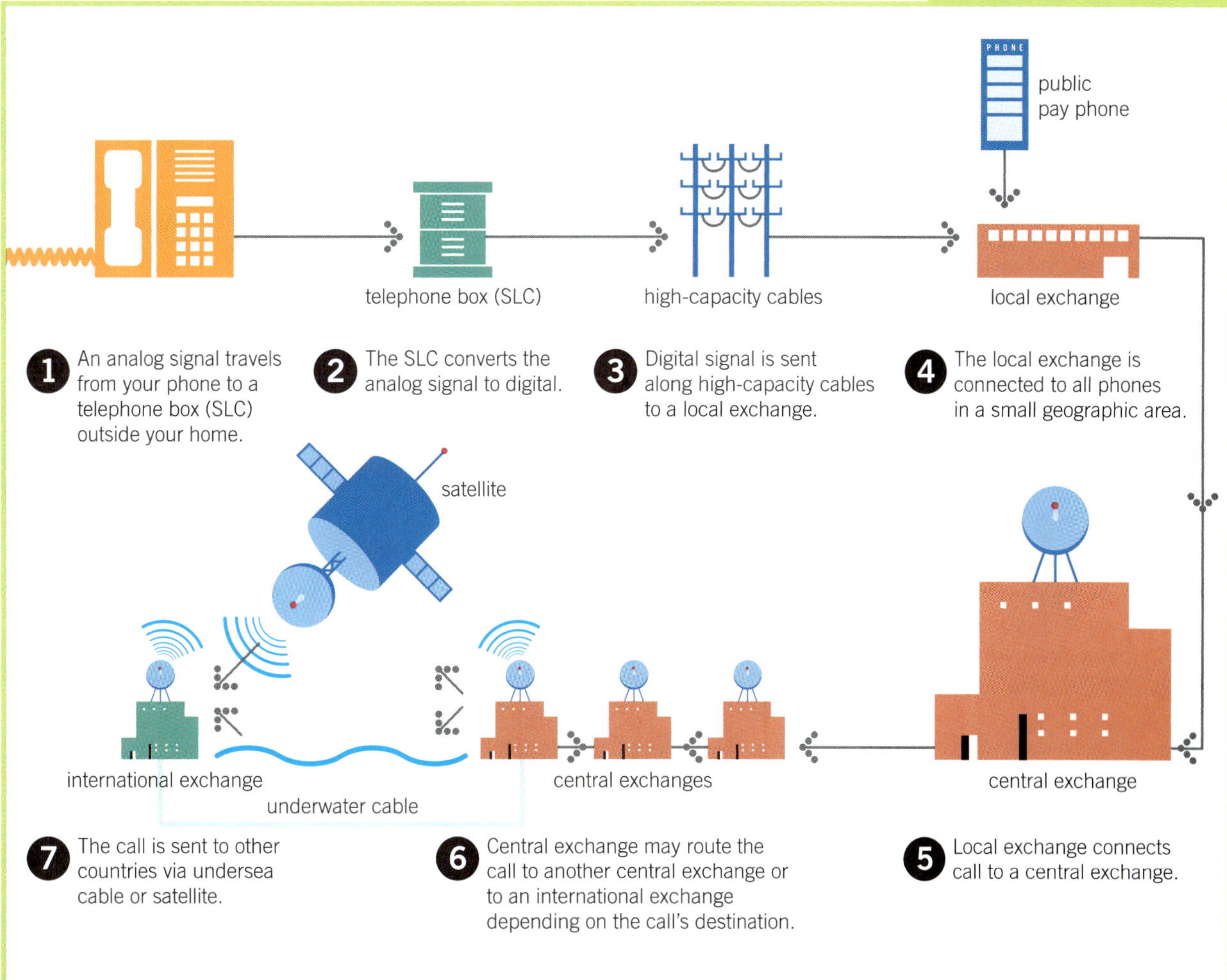

IT In Action

Coming to a Blimp Near You

Adapted from "Goodbye Phone Satellites, Hello Blimps," Reuters News Agency, June 25, 2002.

Look up into the sky over some major cities over the next few years and you might be surprised at what you see. Huge solar-powered airships, or blimps, are being developed that will sit in the stratosphere (11–55 km above sea level) and act as providers of telephone and Internet services. The blimps will keep their position static, making use of solar-powered propellers and the characteristics of weather in inner space. By staying in one position, they might be used to transmit data that satellites currently convey, at a fraction of the cost. While the telecommunications technology is currently available, there are concerns about the use of solar power and the launching of such vehicles into inner space. Tests being performed by Britain's Meteorological Office on monster helium balloons being sent to the edge of space are expected to determine if these commercial balloons can be launched successfully.

The first cities to be served by the blimps will be those nearest the tropics, such as Singapore and Los Angeles, where the weather in the stratosphere is more predictable.

The use of such equipment to transmit both voice and data might revolutionize mobile communications networks, broadband, and Internet services in the near future and alleviate concerns regarding the installation of communication towers near homes and offices.

Questions

1. Write a short summary of the reasons why organizations are looking for new methods of data and voice transmission.
2. Describe how a blimp can be a more effective and efficient means of conveying data.

digiknow

Bandwidth is the speed at which a given technology can transmit data. It is measured in kilobits per second (Kbps), megabits per second (Mbps), or gigabits per second (Gbps). How much bandwidth you need depends on what you are transmitting (and how patient you are). Straight text can be transmitted efficiently with a slow modem (56 Kbps), whereas Internet Web surfing is much less frustrating at 128 Kbps. High-quality video conferencing, however, requires a minimum of 10 Mbps or 10 000 Kbps, the standard speed for a local area network.

There are limitations to both the effectiveness and efficiency of the telephone network as a communication tool. Analog connections are susceptible to noise or static in the transmission of both voice and data. They are also limited in terms of their ability to handle any more than 56 Kbps for dial-up services such as the Internet. Although much of the telephone system has been converted to fibre-optics, there is still the "last-mile problem": twisted-pair copper wire, or analog service, makes up the final short distance that connects the SLC to your home or office. Why not replace all the twisted-pair cable to improve efficiency or speed of delivery? Cost. An estimated $325 billion worldwide, to be specific (Pfaffenberger 2003). Wireless technologies, which may one day replace the need for landlines as a delivery method, are also being developed.

To address the last-mile problem, telecommunications companies have developed two strategies that utilize existing twisted-pair copper wiring to increase speed of communication delivery:

- *Integrated Services Digital Network (ISDN).* This technology was the first to provide the user with digital telephone and data service.

Through a digital modem or router, the user is able to transmit data at up to 128 Kbps over the telephone lines. When a call comes in, the service cuts back to 64 Kbps to allow for simultaneous computer and telephone use. High-speed Internet services offered by the telcos use this technology. A new service, DSL, may eliminate ISDN lines in the near future, however.

- *Digital Subscriber Line (DSL)*. This technology is similar to ISDN in that it too uses existing copper wire to transmit both voice and data. DSL, however, is much faster, operating at speeds up to 1.5 Mbps for downloads and 256 Kbps for uploads. The technology itself is capable of much higher speeds, but the local loop again limits the rate of transmission. Users of this service must connect with a DSL modem to their existing phone lines, install noise filters on telephones in the house to eliminate interference with data transmission, and subscribe to the service through their local phone carrier. This service is only available within 5 km of your local exchange so it is not available to rural subscribers, a problem in a country such as Canada with a geographically diverse population.

Twisted-pair technology is likely to be with us for many years to come. As a result, we should be familiar with the communications tools that rely on the telephone network to relay both voice and data between individuals and organizations.

digiknow

To better appreciate the difference between twisted-pair copper wire and fibre-optics, consider this. Copper wire (a T1 connection) can handle up to 24 voice calls simultaneously, or up to 1.544 Mbps of computer data at one time, whereas one fibre-optic cable (a T3 connection) can handle 672 voice calls or 43 Mbps of computer data at one time.

(Pfaffenberger 2003)

GETTING IT

1. Define *telecommunications*. Investigate the organizations that provide telco services in your region.
2. Describe the differences between transmitting messages along twisted-pair wire and fibre-optic cable.
3. What unit of measurement is used to measure bandwidth? Create a chart that describes the various Internet connection methods and the speed at which each method connects.
4. Describe the "last-mile" problem associated with telecommunications.
5. Compare and contrast ISDN with DSL.

8.3 Communication Tools: Using the Telecommunications Backbone

To send both voice and data messages over telephone lines, information must first be converted to analog signals that can be transmitted through the local loop to the SLC, which then converts them back to digital signals.

The device that completes this task is the **modem**, and the process is called **modulation**. When messages are received, the reverse takes place. Analog signals are converted to digital signals through a demodulation process. Hence the name modem — short for modulator/demodulator. The invention of the modem initiated the development of numerous communication devices such as the fax machine.

8.3.1 Fax (Facsimile) Machines

Fax machines started to gain widespread acceptance as a business communication tool in the early 1980s, as companies saw the benefits of quick, accurate transmission of printed documents. Modern fax machines work in the following way. The sending machine scans the image to read the data. In actual fact, the scanner only looks for contrast between the ink and the background as it scans each line on the paper. The fax machine contains a small fluorescent light that shines on the paper for maximum contrast. The black dots picked up by the sensor are encoded in digital language, or digitized. The message is then sent via the fax machine's modem through the telephone lines. The receiving fax machine decodes the dots on the page and prints them out on either plain paper or special thermal fax paper.

Computers equipped with a fax modem can also send and receive facsimiles. Documents created in office productivity programs like Word, Excel, or Publisher that have built-in fax capabilities can be sent to a fax machine and printed out. If you want to send a hard copy document through your computer fax modem, you must scan it in first on a scanner before it can be transmitted. When you receive a document through your computer fax modem it can be viewed on screen or printed out on your computer printer. It cannot be edited on screen, however, without being converted using special OCR (optical character recognition) software.

IT In Action

Fax Machines Fight Back

Adapted from Scott Cullen, "Frugal Faxing," *Office Solutions*, April 2001, v. 18, i. 4, p. 38.

When e-mail use soared in the 1990s, some skeptics considered the fax machine to be on its deathbed. Not so. In fact, fax technology has been constantly improving to meet the demands of users. Fax machines are smaller, faster, and much more efficient than in the past and have features built into them to improve overall office productivity and efficiency. Figure 8.4 provides an overview of some of the time- and money-saving features of modern faxes.

Figure 8.4
Time- and Money-Saving Features of Modern Faxes

Feature	Description/Benefit
Dual access	• allows you to program a document into memory while the machine is receiving other transmissions
Dual lines	• accommodates two telephone lines; can be configured to use one line for incoming calls and one for outgoing calls, or both lines can handle incoming and outgoing transmissions
Internet faxing	• has built-in capabilities that allow you to send faxes over the Internet; requires an account with a local ISP • can save hundreds of dollars in long-distance costs for companies that send a large volume of faxes to long-distance and/or international destinations • can also send documents over regular telephone lines
Batch sending	• used if a company sends a number of faxes to the same destination each day, and the messages are not time sensitive
Quick scan	• scans document into fax machine's memory before transmitting • results in quicker process than other machines that scan and send at the same time • allows employees to get back to work quicker, rather than waiting for the document to go through
Speed dial	• eliminates the need to enter long numbers each time you send to a frequently dialed location
Speed of transmission (Super Group 3 fax machine)	• sends at speeds up to 33.6 Kbps, over twice as fast as older 14.4 Kbps models; important when sending a high volume of faxes long distance

Regardless of the type of fax machine you have, there are a couple of steps you can take to reduce faxing costs:

- *Watch ink density.* The more heavy ink there is on your documents, the longer they will take to scan and transmit (not to mention the cost of the ink for printing the document out on the receiving end).
- *Look at consumable costs.* The cost of toner cartridges for fax machines can vary significantly from supplier to supplier. Shop around and compare prices to find the best deals.

Just because you have a fax machine doesn't necessarily mean that you are maximizing your overall efficiency. Take advantage of the features your machine has to offer and see how your organization can reap the benefits and savings!

8.3.2 Voice Mail

"Thank you for calling Nantyr Shores Secondary School. If you know the extension of the person you are trying to reach, you can enter it at any time. To reach our reception desk, please press 0."

digiknow

A 1998 study on voice mail system use in the United States found that approximately 40% of people who dial in to organizations using voice mail systems automatically hit the 0 for an operator or other human being. This is the exact opposite of what systems like this were designed to do in the first place!

(Ashbrook Nickell 2001)

Voice mail systems have been implemented by organizations worldwide to streamline voice communications. Callers can leave messages for individuals in their mailboxes by selecting the appropriate option from the choice presented by the software. Individuals in the organization can dial the phone system and enter their mailbox numbers and passwords to retrieve messages and respond to them, forward them to other individuals, and delete them.

Voice mail systems are particularly attractive for small business owners who are not always available at the office. Many voice mail systems, even small digital answering machines, allow for various options to be given to callers. The initial voice message should give the caller a variety of options from which to choose, including leaving a message. Other options might include calling a pager or cellular phone number for immediate assistance, or listening to a list of your services and other contact information such as mailing address information (Spaeder 2002).

However, in spite of the attractive features and growing popularity of voice mail systems, both callers and users complain about them. Menus give too many options, people don't always check their voice mail on top of e-mail and mailboxes (for hard copy mail), and it is time consuming to record an outgoing message and check for messages throughout the day.

8.3.3 Computer and Internet Telephony

One way to combat the multitude of mail services an employee must check during a working day is to use computer telephony technology. Software is available to link your computer with your telephone in an effort to improve overall efficiency. Many PCs are equipped with the hardware that enables them to act as speakerphones, answering machines, and complete voice mail systems. **Computer telephony** systems connect to the phone system through modems equipped to handle voice conversations. When people telephone, your computer system picks up the calls, directs them to the correct voice mailbox, and records the messages for retrieval at your own workstation. Open Text Corporation (formerly Centrinity), a company located in Markham, Ontario, makes computer telephony software.

Internet telephony is a variation of computer telephony that directs your calls through the Internet to a telephone at another location. This technology is not as effective as standard telephone lines; voices are frequently garbled and the sounds echo. Congestion on Internet services can lead to delays in sending messages, also reducing overall efficiency. However, as with most technologies discussed here, Internet telephony is rapidly improving.

8.3.4 Video Teleconferencing

Companies with multiple offices across the country, around the world, or with employees who need to meet with suppliers or customers but cannot be there in person can use video teleconferencing as an alternative. Each location in a video teleconference is equipped with a video camera, a microphone, and a television monitor. Video signals are sent via telephone lines or the Internet so that each participant can see and hear everything the others are saying and doing. Groups who meet too often to justify the cost of travel use this form of communication most frequently.

Web cams can also be used for audio/visual communication between parties who have these cameras connected to their PCs or laptop computers. Using high-speed Internet services, callers can see each other on their monitors and can share documents at the same time through their e-mail systems. The images are rather disjointed, but advances in technology are leading to improvements in this area.

The above devices rely on the Internet to convey voice and data transmissions. But just how does the Internet work and how has its development revolutionized corporate communications?

GETTING IT

1. Describe the function a modem serves in communicating data.
2. Create a simple "How To" guide to describe to a new employee how fax machines work. Include tips to save time and ideas to reinforce what specific jobs fax machines are best used for.
3. Describe five ways productivity can be maximized using a fax machine.
4. Based on your readings, describe how voice mail systems can improve communications effectiveness and efficiency.
5. Explain the difference between computer and Internet telephony.

8.4 The Internet as a Communications Medium

The **Internet** is a global network, decentralized by design, that connects millions of computers in over 100 countries, allowing exchanges of information, news, and opinions. And yet despite these numbers, we are still in the early phase of Internet development. How did we reach this level of use so quickly?

8.4.1 The Origins of the Internet

The Internet as a communications medium has been around since 1969 when the Advanced Research Projects Agency (ARPA), an agency of the United States Department of Defense, linked large mainframe computers in select locations in the United States. Their mandate was to develop a communications network that would allow for the sharing of resources to "improve and increase computer research productivity." The intended byproduct of the communications network was valuable research results that could be used by the military. The development of the ARPANET gave rise to some of the most important principles on which today's Internet is based. **Protocols** or conventions were developed that allow sending and receiving computers to understand the messages being transmitted, regardless of the type of systems being used. The open approach to project development is another concept that has been one of the fundamentals of the Internet (Hauben).

As the decades progressed, ARPANET was replaced by a newer, faster high-speed network (the NSFNet) created by the National Science Foundation (NSF). The objective of NSF was to design a system to connect supercomputing centres so that they could access each other's resources and exchange information. At this point, however, these supercommunications networks were reserved for use by the academic and scientific community. The development of the personal computer in the early 1980s and its widespread use in both personal and business environments increased the demand for access to information "anytime, anywhere." Telecommunications companies saw the opportunity to market a service to these user groups and developed new networks that would give these groups the capability to communicate using essentially the same protocols that the NSFNet utilized.

> **Get Connected**
>
> View the original plan for the World Wide Web at www.pearsoned.ca/businessconnections. Write a paragraph explaining the purpose behind the development of the Web and how hypertext was supposed to help people link ideas.

The Internet is now a global network that connects millions of computers and storage devices. One aspect of the Internet is the World Wide Web.

8.4.2 The World Wide Web

The **World Wide Web** is a system of Internet servers (computers with mass storage capabilities) that allow users to access and view specially formatted documents using special software known as a browser. The Web was developed by Tim Berners-Lee while working at the CERN research centre in Switzerland in the late 1980s. The documents are formatted in a scripting language known as **HTML (hypertext markup language)** that allows the display of text, visual images, video, and audio files. One of the key features of HTML pages is the ability to link them to other pages within a site or to pages on other Web servers by clicking on hyperlinks. **Hyperlinks** are words or pictures that have been formatted to instruct the browser to locate a specific page and display it on the screen. The browser (e.g., Internet Explorer, Netscape Navigator) is programmed to display pages using a set of protocols known as **HTTP (hypertext transfer protocols)**. HTTP are conventions that determine how messages are formatted and transmitted and enable computers of all types to display the data in a consistent manner. Figure 8.5 provides a sample Netscape screen.

Figure 8.5
Netscape Screen Capture

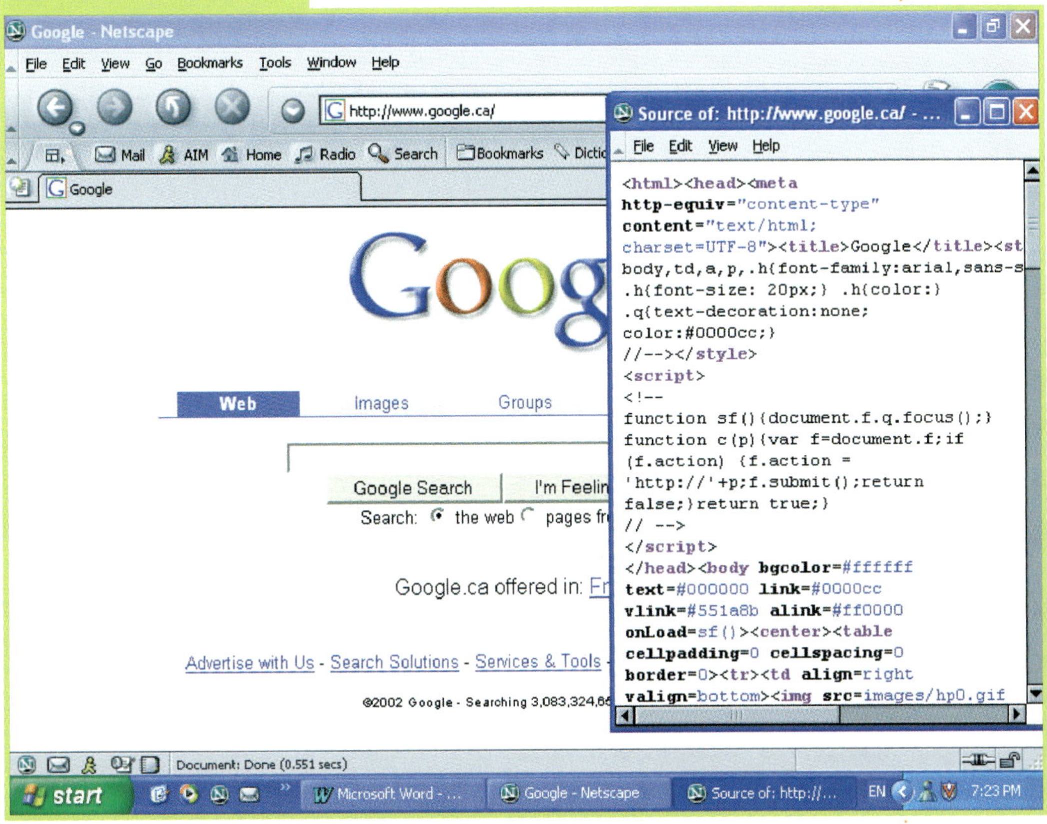

Web pages are created using HTTP (hypertext transfer protocols), which enables computers of all types to display data in a consistent manner. This image illustrates the HTML code used to create the Google.ca home page.

Web pages are identified by an address, known as a **URL (Uniform Resource Locator)**. Addresses that begin with http:// indicate to the browser that they are to use HTTP protocols to view the page.

URLs can be broken down into three main parts: the transfer protocol, the domain name, and the path (folder) and/or file name. See Figure 8.6 below.

Figure 8.6
Parts of a URL

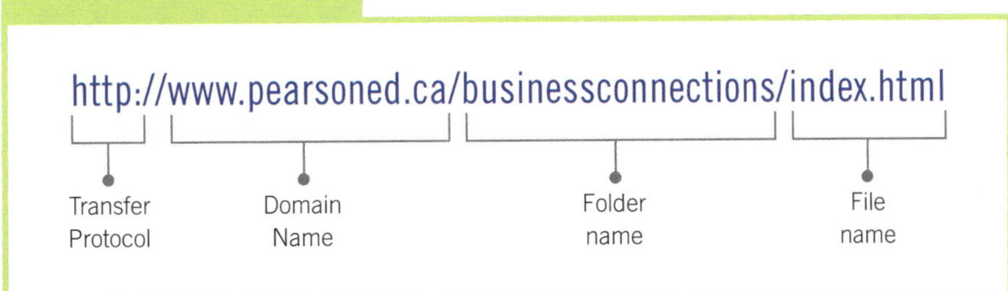

Choose a Web page that you visit frequently and identify the transfer protocol, the domain name, and the path and/or file name of the URL in your notebook.

The domain name portion of the URL has three distinct components:

- *Host name*. The www at the beginning of the domain name indicates that this program is a World Wide Web document and is hosted on a Web server. Variations on this include www1, Web, **ftp** (**file transfer protocol**), or nothing at all. File transfer protocol is a standard set of rules and procedures used to upload and download files between two devices.
- *Second-level domain*. This part of a URL indicates the organization that hosts the Web site on their server. For example in the URL www.pearsoned.ca, pearsoned refers to Pearson Education Canada Inc.
- *Top-level domain*. Every domain name has an extension or suffix that indicates to the viewer the type of organization that posted the site. Sites commonly end with such top-level domains as .com, .ca, .org, .edu, and .net.

digiknow

A survey conducted in April 2002 revealed that the .ca top-level domain is used exclusively by 38% of Canadian companies. According to the Canadian Internet Registration Authority, companies consider the .ca an advantage in terms of customer recognition.

(*Toronto Star* 2002)

The path (folder) and/or file name gives the user an indication of the location on the host computer where the file they are requesting is stored. For example, on the Pearson Education Canada Web site, there is a folder for all files relating to Business Connections and a home page called "index.html" for users to reference.

8.4.3 TCP/IP: The Standard for Communications

To send information over the Internet, whether it was a World Wide Web page or other data, transmission protocols had to be developed. **TCP/IP (transmission control protocol/Internet protocol)** was developed as the standard for transmitting information over the Internet. It was distributed freely at no cost and its widespread use has helped to fuel the increase in the use of the Internet as a communications medium throughout the 1990s and up to today. How does TCP/IP work?

Communications protocols determine how the data are formatted for transmission and receipt. The three elements a protocol must contain are:

- the rate of transmission (speed);
- whether the transmission is to be synchronous (in a steady stream) or asynchronous (at any time in irregular intervals); and
- whether the data to be sent will be in half-duplex (one way) or full-duplex (two-way) mode.

Protocols can also include ways to detect and recover from transmission errors and to encode and decode the data. Most Internet traffic is sent in asynchronous, full-duplex mode.

Internet messages and Web pages are divided into evenly sized packets before being sent over the Internet. Each packet is labelled with the information it needs to reach its destination in the message header — the sender's

IP (Internet Protocol) address, the receiver's IP address, the number of packets being sent, and the number of this one individual packet. Each packet also contains a footer that indicates that the end of the packet has been reached.

When the message has been divided into packets and the appropriate information has been applied to the packet's header and footer, the packets are all sent over the Internet to their destination via the best available route. Not every packet follows the same route, which makes the sending of data more efficient. If there are "traffic jams" on part of the network, the router chooses an alternate route by which to send the data. Once the packets reach their destination, they are reassembled into the original message or Web page by the TCP/IP at the other end.

One of the most frequently used applications on the Internet today is e-mail, with users coming online at a faster rate than the rate of growth of the total Internet market. Let us examine this important aspect of modern communication more closely.

digiknow

Every machine that is connected to the Internet has a unique IP address, a four-part number divided by periods (e.g., 123.451.100.4). Because people remember words easier than numbers, the Internet has developed the **domain name system (DNS)**, whereby each Web site is assigned a corresponding IP address. You key the URL in the browser's address bar and the domain name server at your ISP looks up the corresponding IP address to connect you to that site. The DNS is constantly updated so that you can always find the IP address, even if it has been moved to another Web server.

GETTING IT

1. Explain the vision of the Internet's creators.
2. Define the acronym *URL* and describe all its parts.
3. Prepare a note for a classmate that explains packet transmission and its role in sending e-mail over the Internet.
4. Explain the difference between transmission protocols and communication protocols. Use examples to support your ideas.

8.4.4 E-Mail

When you sign up for e-mail access through a local Internet Service Provider (ISP) or through your employer or school, you are assigned a user name (or login name) that identifies you as the individual at that organization who holds the e-mail account. A typical e-mail address, seen in Figure 8.7, is comprised of three parts:

1. *User name*: simply.aberfoyle
2. @: separates the user name from the host name. This allows for multiple addresses at the same host.
3. *Host name*: naturalsprings.ca This is the name of the organization that is hosting the e-mail server, a machine that handles incoming and outgoing e-mail messages.

Figure 8.7
A Typical E-Mail Address

simply.aberfoyle@naturalsprings.ca

To send an e-mail message, you need to first compose it on an e-mail client. This is a program that allows you to compose messages and send them, view a list of the messages that have been received and not yet deleted, and read messages that have been sent to you. Common examples of e-mail clients are Netscape, Microsoft Outlook, and Eudora. A sample Outlook composition screen has been provided in Figure 8.8.

Figure 8.8
Outlook Composition Screen

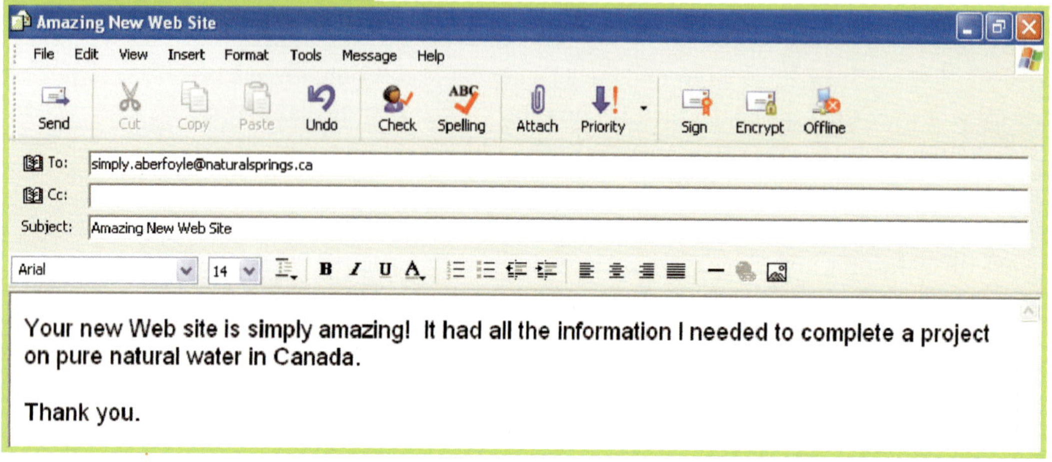

E-mail client programs such as Outlook Express allow users to compose, edit, and send messages.

digiknow

58% or 14 million Canadian adults use at least one e-mail address.

(Hamilton 2002)

The next thing you need in order to send your message is a connection to an e-mail server. An e-mail server is a software application that runs on the host computer that you log into in order to access your e-mail account. This application runs constantly on that computer, waiting for people or other computers to contact it. The e-mail server maintains a list of all the e-mail accounts currently active on the server. It also maintains a text file for each account on the list. As the e-mail server receives e-mail messages, it adds the messages to the text file that it has for each user. When you log into the e-mail server to get your messages, your client formats each message into separate entries on your screen, when in actual fact it is one large text file. See Figure 8.9 for a picture of multiple entries in a text file converted into individual messages on an e-mail client.

That is what happens to the message when it arrives, but how does the message get sent over the Internet? Each e-mail server contains two different applications — the **POP3 (Post Office Protocol)** server application that handles the incoming mail, and the **SMTP (Simple Mail Transfer Protocol)** application that handles the outgoing mail. Once you have composed an e-mail message and you click the Send button on your screen, your e-mail client connects to the SMTP server to handle the outgoing message. The SMTP server does the following:

1. It examines the e-mail address to determine if it is destined for the same or another e-mail server. If the message is to another user at the same domain, the SMTP server will simply give the message to the POP3 server to be appended to the recipient's text file. For recipients at another domain further steps are necessary.
2. The SMTP server requests the IP address of the other domain from the Domain Name Server.

Figure 8.9
E-Mail Client's Individual Messages

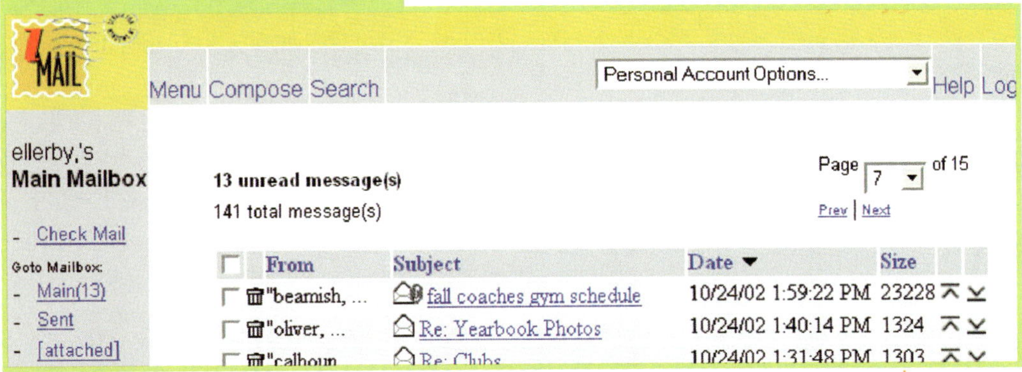

E-mail client screens organize text files into individual messages on your screen, showing the sender, the subject, the file size, and whether attachments are included with messages. When you select a message header on the screen, the client program displays only that message.

3. Using the IP address provided by its own DNS, the SMTP server contacts the SMTP server at the other domain for delivery at that domain.
4. The SMTP server at the receiving end examines the user name to determine if there is such a person at that domain. If there is, the message is handed to the POP3 server at the receiving domain to be added to the recipient's text file. If the account has been closed, the message will be returned to the sender as undeliverable.

Figure 8.10 shows the steps in sending an e-mail message in graphic form.

Figure 8.10
Steps in Sending an E-mail Message

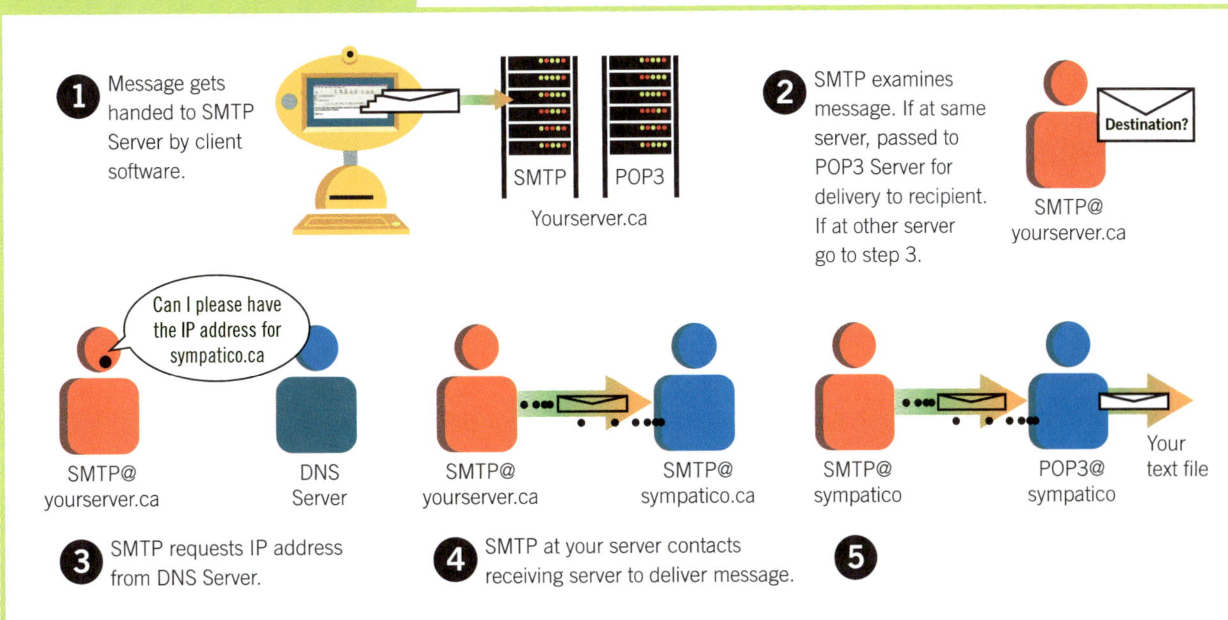

If for any reason, there is "no answer" at the receiving server (system is down or there are network problems), the sending SMTP server will continue to try to send the message every 15 minutes for four hours. If there is still "no answer," you will receive a message saying that the message was undeliverable.

8.4.4.1 Advantages of E-Mail

E-mail has been embraced as a form of communication for a number of reasons:

- *Speed.* E-mail is a fast form of communication; from composition to sending it takes only minutes. The speed of e-mail delivery has improved the efficiency of much organizational communication. This speed has also led some people to refer to the traditional postal system as "snail mail."
- *Accessibility.* Depending on the type of e-mail you use, you can access it from a variety of locations. Web mail services abound where you can log into any Internet-enabled computer to access your mail (e.g., Hotmail). Many POP e-mail services also provide access to users from Internet-enabled computers so that they can retrieve messages while away from their homes or offices. The messages stay on the POP server until the user logs in from the usual e-mail client location.
- *Collaboration.* An e-mail message to a group of people is no more difficult or costly to send than a message to one person. Most e-mail clients allow for the creation of mail groups that send the same message to every e-mail address designated as part of that group. The messages can also be edited and sent back to the originator for further work.
- *Timing.* Retrieving e-mail is done when you have time to access the computer and log in, as compared with telephone calls that can interrupt your workday. Senders of messages can do so when it is convenient for them, as well. When you receive an e-mail, there is no urgency to respond immediately either. You can think about your response before you reply.
- *Focus on the message, not the messenger.* When you receive an e-mail, you are more likely to concentrate on what has been written rather than on the gender, race, voice, or other mannerisms that can impede face-to-face communication.

8.4.4.2 E-Mail Concerns

As much as e-mail has revolutionized the communication process in many organizations, there are some concerns about its use and potential abuses.

Just What Are You Agreeing To?

When you sign up for e-mail and Internet access, your ISP requires you to agree to their terms of service. Did you really read that document? Or were you in such a hurry to activate an e-mail account that you readily clicked on the "I Accept" button? Many people fall into this latter category. In order to protect yourself and your e-mail account from improper use, you should always read fully the contents of the Acceptable Use Agreement at your ISP. Go back to the site where you activated your e-mail account and look up the Agreement. Just what does it contain? Whose interests is it protecting? Write a brief synopsis of the terms and conditions contained in the agreement.

digiknow

Many Internet e-mail client programs allow users to configure them so that the clients can pick up and send e-mail from multiple POP servers at one time. All you need to know is the POP3 server domain name or IP address of your ISP or e-mail service, your login name, and your password. Unfortunately, with increased access to messages come a few catches. See Section 8.4.4.2.

- *Too much!* It is so easy to send an e-mail message that people overuse it. Individuals can receive hundreds of messages a day. The sheer volume of messages, and reading them to determine which ones require immediate attention, is time-consuming and potentially time-wasting. Some organizations have implemented e-mail-free days to allow employees time to catch up on other work.
- *Who are you?* It is so easy to send e-mail to large groups of people that many receive messages from people they do not know who got their address from another source. Some of these messages are for a good cause (e.g., charities), but much of it is unsolicited, fraudulent, or aimed at getting people to part with their money. This junk e-mail is called **spam** and has many people very concerned (see On the Case: Do You Want Spam With That? on page 222).
- *Privacy.* The content of traditional mail is very private. Unencrypted e-mail, however, is not. The organization that gives you e-mail access is entitled to read your e-mail messages to ensure that you have not violated any of the terms to which you agreed when you signed up for the account (e.g., misuse, criminal activity). Furthermore, some clever hackers have determined how to "sniff" the lines that transmit e-mail to intercept e-mail messages and compile e-mail addresses. This raises some serious concerns about individual privacy.
- *Identity of sender.* There is no guarantee that the name on the bottom of an e-mail message belongs to the sender of the message. Anyone who gains access to a user's account can assume his or her identity and send messages under the account-holder's name.
- *Get my message?* E-mail systems are only as effective as the people who use them. If people do not check their inboxes regularly, messages can go unanswered for days or weeks. If you are awaiting critical information, business opportunities can and will be missed.
- *Dehumanization of communication.* The proliferation of wired and wireless devices that are used to communicate today require the careful choice of words, both verbal and written, to convey a message. When you take the face-to-face interaction out of communication, you lose non-verbal clues as to the meaning of the words (e.g., body language, inflection, tone of voice, etc.) and the opportunity for chance meetings that can get important issues resolved.

Netiquette

Just as there are rules for polite human interaction, there are rules that govern proper behaviour on the Internet, in e-mail, on instant messaging services, and in online discussion groups. Consider the following:

- In e-mail, avoid SHOUTING or the use of ALL CAPITAL LETTERS.
- Subject lines should be short and concise, not misleading.
- Use emoticons (smileys, e.g., :) or :() to convey meaning and emotions when you write — many words in the English language have double meanings and your message might not come across as intended.
- Don't ramble. E-mail by its very nature is quick to write and read. Don't waste the time of others unnecessarily.
- When replying to a message, refer to the appropriate parts of the original message.
- Keep business e-mail on business-related topics; use home e-mail for personal messages.
- Avoid sending chain e-mail. It only clutters inboxes.
- Before joining an online discussion, monitor it to determine how people "speak" to one another.
- Don't use an online discussion group to publicize your personal pet peeves.

ON THE CASE

Do You Want Spam With That?

Adapted from Rachel Ross, "Spam! Spam! Spam!" *Toronto Star*, April 8, 2002, pp. E1, E2.

Delete. Delete. Delete. Does this sound like you when you open your e-mail inbox only to find countless junk mail messages or spam, as they are more commonly known? You are not alone if such is the case. According to studies that measure the amount of e-mail that travels through networks around the world, the amount of spam grew by 340% over a six-month period from September 2001 to April 2002 — more than triple the rate for e-mail overall. Estimates suggest that 20% of all e-mail is spam, which is enough to seriously affect the efficiency of most e-mail networks due to its overwhelming volume.

Marketers have found spam to be an easy and inexpensive form of direct-mail marketing, but have taken it to the extremes! The difference between spam and legitimate e-mail marketing is permission. When you sign up for e-mail newsletters and other correspondence, you expect it to land in your inbox. With spam, you have no idea where they got your address. E-mail addresses can be purchased at low cost and many spammers don't care where the address lists came from as long as they can use them.

One of the most notorious scams is the fake unsubscribe feature in an unsolicited e-mail message. By clicking on the unsubscribe link in the message you are really telling the spammer that your e-mail address is active. This, in turn, can cause a virtual torrent of messages to head your way as these folks sell the list of active accounts to other spammers.

There are, however, methods of combatting spam. Governments, ISPs, and software developers worldwide are developing solutions as we speak. One such company, Brightmail, Inc., based in San Francisco, has created a clever approach. This software sets up dummy e-mail accounts to lure spammers. It sprinkles these decoys around the World Wide Web: at Web sites, at chat rooms, and on Internet bulletin boards. It then sits back and waits for the spammers to take the bait. Once spammers have been identified, it instructs client servers to block similar messages coming into their e-mail customer base. One company that has installed this program with great success is Bell Sympatico, which estimates that over 80% of the spam intended for customers is blocked before it ever reaches their inboxes. Customers are more satisfied, not having to spend hours wading through the spam, and their systems run much more efficiently with the reduced volume to deal with.

Questions

1. Explain why e-mail users are inundated with spam.
2. List the methods that spammers use to get and validate e-mail addresses.
3. Describe how Brightmail, Inc., has combatted this problem.
4. Identify spam that you have received. Decide where you think it came from and what you can do to prevent the spammer from sending you more.

GETTING IT

1. Using your own (or a fictitious) e-mail address, label and describe its elements.
2. Write a paragraph to describe the advantages of e-mail as a communications medium.
3. Prepare a brief (5 min or less) speech to explain why e-mail is said to be dependent on the individuals who use it. Present your thoughts to your class.
4. Create a diagram in your notebook that illustrates the way an e-mail message is sent from one address to another (at different servers).

8.4.5 Mailing Lists (List Servs) and Online Discussion Groups

Once you have access to e-mail, you might wish to join one or more mailing lists or list servs. A mailing list allows people with common interests to communicate with each other via e-mail. When you send a message to the list serv (mailing list) the message goes to everyone on the list. Anyone in the group can respond to the message. Businesses use list servs to facilitate discussion among workgroups whose members may be located across the hall or across the country. Messages are delivered to the individual's e-mail inbox for easy retrieval. Collaboration regarding product development or even the building of a new school can be facilitated in this manner.

A variation on the mailing list is the online discussion group. Again, people with common interests can enter into discussions on topics posted online, or begin new discussions under a new "thread." Unlike mailing lists, the user must log into the Web site where the discussions are taking place to engage in the conversation. Messages are posted at the site rather than being sent to individual e-mail inboxes. This reduces the volume of e-mail that an individual receives and the various "threads" stay together so that the participants can follow the development of ideas as messages are posted.

Get Connected

Follow the links at www.pearsoned.ca/businessconnections and investigate the information that is available to assist Canadians with e-mail issues such as fraud, scams, and spam. Describe at least three of the suggestions made to reduce unwanted e-mail. Compare your list with those of your classmates. If you are missing an important point, add it to your list.

8.4.6 Instant Messaging

One of the most exciting uses of the Internet for communication today is the use of instant messaging to facilitate group discussions and workgroup collaboration. Instant messaging allows each person to create a "buddy list" of individuals who have Internet e-mail addresses and determine when each person is online. You can start an online conversation with anyone on your buddy list (or the whole group). Conversations take place in "real time" and you eliminate the need for telephone calls or personal meetings.

To ensure that conversations are secure in a networked environment, enterprise instant messaging (EIM) packages have been developed. Once installed, password entry protects unauthorized access to restricted data.

IT In Action

Enterprise Instant Messaging Takes Off

Adapted from Jonathan Angel, "What RU marketing tonight? *Adweek Magazine's Technology Marketing*, Dec. 2001, v. 21, i. 11, p. 10(1); and "LinqWare Links Employees Via EIM" *Client Server News*, July 1, 2002.

"How RU?" "OK. Did you get that joke?" "LOL."

If you understand this cryptic conversation, you probably use instant messaging (IM) online. And not just at home, either. Instant messaging as a conversation medium has taken off. According to Forrester Research, "almost half of the online population uses IM once a week, while "intense" users have six or more conversations per day." The most popular IM clients are AOL's instant messaging feature and Yahoo! instant messaging.

But business IT managers have concerns about the use of such consumer IM clients in a networked environment. Once consumer IM clients are downloaded and installed on networked computers without IT authorization, controls vanish. There is no way to track messages, ensure that conversations are secure, or manage who uses IM in the corporate environment. As a result, some software manufacturers are developing EIM (enterprise instant messaging) clients. These client packages cut down on time delays for communication when installed and integrated with other network systems. New EIM clients require secure login and password entry to protect client data and confidentiality, which also helps to prevent unauthorized access to restricted information. Administrative personnel in the IT department monitor how many conversations are happening and who is having them — not the content of the messages themselves! New users can be added quickly and easily. Companies benefit from increased collaboration on projects as a result of IM interactions. So, what RU waiting 4?

Questions

1. Create and complete, electronically, a chart similar to the one below for at least three Enterprise Instant Messaging packages.

Enterprise Instant Messaging		
Type	Advantages	Features

2. Write a paragraph to explain how EIM addresses the concerns of corporate IT departments.
3. Describe how you would go about installing and setting up IM on your home computer.

GETTING IT

1. Describe how mailing lists and online discussion groups can help to improve organizational communication and collaboration on projects.
2. Explain why you think instant messaging has grown in popularity.

8.5 Wireless Communication: Cellular Phones

The scene is familiar: people walking along a crowded sidewalk, seemingly talking to no one in particular. Then you spy the handset held up to their ear, or a cord running from their ear to the handset in their hand. Our world has embraced wireless communication in a big way. How does wireless communication work? What features are available on today's handsets? And, where is this technology headed?

8.5.1 Cellular Phone Technology

When you make a call on a cellular phone you are using a very sophisticated radio. The drawback to radio signals is that they lose their strength as you get farther away from the transmitting unit. Early mobile radio communication relied on large communication towers in various geographic locations and radios that had transmitters big enough to carry the signal up to 70 km away. Needless to say, these early devices were large and bulky. Another problem was that the towers could handle a minimal number of calls, making it difficult to connect due to the limited channel availability.

The solution was to divide a large geographic region into smaller zones called cells. Within each cell a repeating transmitter (called a cell site) is installed that broadcasts signals throughout its area. As the caller moves from one cell zone to another the new transmitter picks up the signal and the conversation carries on. All cell sites are connected to a **Mobile Telephone Switching Office (MTSO)** that controls all cellular activity in the region and relays calls to the regular telephone system. Figure 8.11 on page 226 shows cellular phone transmissions. Each cell site covers approximately 26 square kilometres. As networks convert their cell sites from analog to digital transmission, the number of calls that can be handled increases.

Cellular phones are configured to allow for true two-way communication, unlike walkie-talkies or CB radios where only one person at a time can talk.

digiknow

The number of mobile phone subscriptions is set to surpass the number of fixed landline subscriptions. In 2001 mobile phone subscriptions grew by a record 40% worldwide. The market for mobile phones in Western Europe has almost reached the saturation point, whereas the markets in China and India offer the greatest room for growth. Growth in Canada and the United States is being held back by subscription plans that charge both the initiator of the call and the receiver.

(M2 Communications Ltd. 2002)

8.5.2 Wireless Handset Features

The lines between what is and is not a cellular device have been blurred in recent years. Manufacturers of cellular phones now regularly incorporate Web browsing and e-mail features into their handsets. Wireless pagers such as the RIM BlackBerry shown in Figure 8.12 on page 226 now enable users to send voice and radio dispatches. The BlackBerry also functions as an electronic organizer, scheduler, and address book and can run countless applications based on the popular Java programming language.

Figure 8.11
Cellular Phone Call Transmission

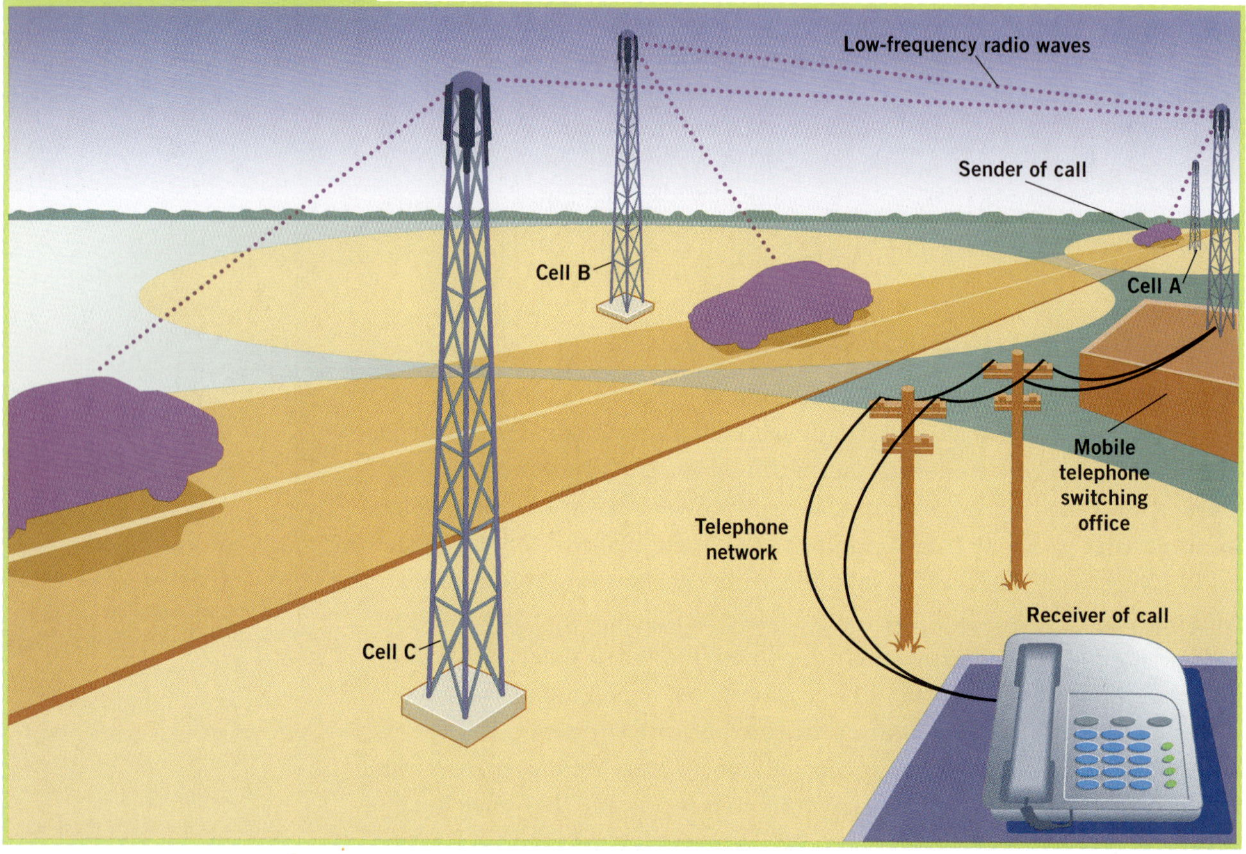

As a caller moves from one cell zone to another, the new transmitter picks up the signal and the conversation goes on.

Figure 8.12
RIM BlackBerry

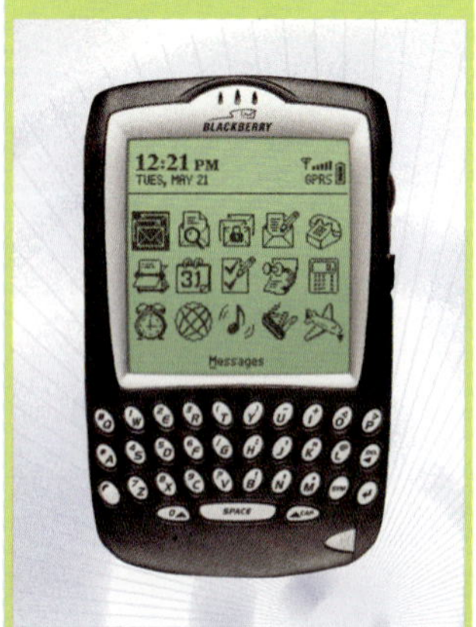

Cellular phones have progressed through a number of generations. Here is an overview.

- *1st Generation.* These large, clunky devices were the first cellular phones to be introduced in the early 1980s. They transmitted messages over analog networks, using radio waves, and were subject to signal interference.
- *2nd Generation.* These phones and networks were introduced in the early 1990s and featured digital technology, commonly known as PCS (personal communications services). Data are converted to digital signals for transmission and, as such, are not as susceptible to interference or to the lack of security relative to 1st generation technology. The conversion to digital allowed access to the Internet and other digital services.
- *2.5 Generation.* As communications providers move toward true 3G (3rd Generation) technology, a number of 2.5G devices have been

developed. These handsets are always turned on, making sending and retrieving e-mail more effective. You can check messages when they arrive, rather than when you remember to dial in. Connecting your laptop or handheld computer to the Internet provides service roughly equivalent to dial-up access. Some 2.5G devices allow you to connect to digital cameras so that you can e-mail pictures as well.

- *3rd Generation*: 3G handsets and networks are expected to address many of the concerns of current users of cellular technology. Changes in the system will see packet technology being used for voice and data transmission. That means you will be able to access and view streaming video data on your cellular handset and access networks at faster speeds. Widespread use of 3G technology in North America is not expected until at least 2004.

8.5.3 Wireless Communication Concerns

As the use of wireless communication devices grows, so do the concerns relating to their use. The wireless market is still in its youth compared with more mature forms of communication such as the telephone. And, like the Internet, as new technologies develop, so do the fears surrounding their use. How secure are wireless transactions?

Secure Internet transactions rely on a number of steps being taken to ensure safe transmission of data: users need to be authenticated, data must be encrypted for transmission, and the data need to be secure from tampering. (More details on this are covered in Chapter 9.) Wireless devices that use **WAP (wireless application protocols)** run what are called microbrowsers. They use a special form of cryptography where users authenticate themselves by entering a PIN number and data are encrypted for transmission. But because the handheld device carries the only encryption key, the assumption has to be made that the person who makes the call is the "real" person. Some organizations are developing other encryption methodologies to deal with this concern. The real key to dealing with security issues is consumer education about the risks and concerns regarding cellular use for secure transactions. Credit card details and other personal data should never be given out without careful consideration.

GETTING IT

1. Describe how cellular technology overcame the limitations of radios as communications devices.
2. Create a timeline that helps to describe the evolution of cellular telephones. Be sure to include the dates and a description of the technology at each phase.
3. Explain what you think the concerns are surrounding the use of cellular phones.

Get Connected

Through the links at www.pearsoned.ca/businessconnections, investigate the wireless services available in Canada provided by such carriers as Rogers AT&T Wireless and Bell Mobility. Electronically, create a comparison chart of the wireless products and services that are currently available from each company, including wireless PDAs and handsets and their features.

digiknow

Young cell phone subscribers put more emphasis on the handset that comes with the cellular package than on other factors. The size of the screen, the possibility to change faceplates, MP3 capability, and the overall look and feel of the handset are the primary considerations.

(Stone 2001)

digiknow

In 2001 China surpassed the United States as the largest and fastest-growing market for cellular handsets. However, users are not necessarily interested in the features and functions of 2.5G and 3G technology. They are more concerned with becoming wireless than in potential cutting edge features.

(Romanelli 2002)

IT In Action

Coming to a Wal-Mart Near You

Adapted from Ephraim Schwartz, "MVNOS on the Move – Media, Retail Giants Explore New Model to Expand Services to Cellular," *Infoworld*, June 17, 2002, v. 24 i. 24, p. 41.

In spite of a cellular phone market that has seen significant declines in the number of handsets shipped and new subscribers, some of North America's largest brand names are poised to enter the cellular phone provider network. These organizations will be known as **MVNOs (mobile virtual network operators)**. They will purchase bulk minutes for voice and/or data communications on other operators' networks and resell them to customers like you and me through their extensive operations.

Companies such as Wal-Mart, Best Buy, and AOL are considering this move in the near future. All have loyal customer bases at which to target such a product and may be able to attract customers that might otherwise not consider cellular phone use.

A B2B (Business to Business) model might also emerge for organizations with offices across the country and/or around the world. Businesses that own their own wireless networks could benefit through reduced costs as bulk airtime is purchased.

Questions

In small groups, discuss the following questions. Present your group's analysis to the class.

1. Based on the information presented, what market segments are MVNOs targeting in the consumer marketplace?
2. Why might they succeed in signing these customers up for cellular service when other companies have failed?
3. What benefits might a B2B (Business to Business) network reap by having its own network for corporate communications?

8.6 Wireless Communication: Wireless LANs (WiFi) and Bluetooth Technology

Adapted from Roger O. Crockett et al., "All Net, All the Time," *BusinessWeek online*, April 29, 2002.

Wireless handsets and PDA-type devices are fine for some types of communication and mobile applications, but many technology users want more. They want to be able to use their notebook computers to access networks to become true mobile users of technology. One of the newest advances in this area is called **WiFi** or (**wireless fidelity**). This client/server technology allows multiple users to log into a wireless network as long as they are within a small geographic area (a few hundred square metres). Although not as fast as a typical LAN or WAN Ethernet connection, WiFi can easily handle large e-mail attachments and multimedia Web downloads. These networks are becoming increasingly popular for home use and at other "hot spots" in offices, in coffee shops, and on university campuses.

As the popularity of WiFi networks increases, so do the applications that support them. Microsoft is building alarms into its operating systems that let users know when they are within range of a WiFi network. Dell, Apple, and Hewlett Packard/Compaq are building WiFi radios into their notebook computers and handheld PCs. Experts expect almost half of the business notebooks to be WiFi-enabled by 2004.

The potential for increased productivity has businesses excited about the installation of WiFi networks. Employees can take their notebook computers to meetings, the lunchroom, or the warehouse. Studies suggest that people stay online an additional 105 minutes per day, which adds to overall productivity. Printers can be hooked up to the wireless network as well to receive commands from workers on the move. Fewer data lines need to be installed, which frees technical support workers for other services.

In spite of its growing popularity there are some security concerns. The radio signals that enable WiFi networks to operate easily penetrate the walls of businesses and homes that have them installed. Wireless transmissions can be sniffed out by hackers who then log into the network without authorization. In response, network hardware suppliers are working on systems that build in encryption keys, which change for every session and every user, and authentication features that require logins and passwords.

Another development in the wireless arena is **Bluetooth** technology, which allows communication between all forms of cellular phones, handheld computers, PDAs, and PCs regardless of their operating systems. Bluetooth uses radio technology similar to WiFi networks, but the range of transmission is limited to about 10 metres. By installing Bluetooth chips into electronic devices, individuals can create personal area networks that link all forms of wireless devices.

By all accounts, Bluetooth and WiFi technologies will complement one another in the marketplace. It is expected that WiFi will be used for wireless network access while Bluetooth will be a cable replacement to create personal area networks.

digiknow

By the end of 2002, more than 24 million Bluetooth-enabled mobile phones will be in use worldwide. TDK Systems Europe predicts that by 2006 Bluetooth chip manufacturers will sell as many products in one week as WiFi specialists ship in one year.

(*Database and Network Journal* 2002)

GETTING IT

1. Explain WiFi technology. How is it affecting Internet use?
2. Describe how Bluetooth and WiFi technologies are working to improve access to communication for users.

IT In Action

Inukshuk Builds Canadian Wireless Network

Adapted from Tyler Hamilton, "Inukshuk a Wireless Beacon," *Toronto Star*, May 20, 2002, p. E1.

Inukshuk Internet Inc. of Montreal is working toward building a high-speed wireless communication network across Canada. Inukshuk is building their broadband service using MCS (multipoint communication systems) technology, which operates on a radio-based frequency band designated by the Canadian government for two-way high-speed broadband Internet services.

The attraction to this system comes from Internet users who cannot currently sign up for high-speed Internet access from their cable or telephone provider because their areas are currently not served or are underserved. Communities outside of major metropolitan areas in Canada are such markets.

Inukshuk is experimenting with products from IP Wireless Inc. in California that could provide data transmissions at 9 Mbps — more than five times the speed of current DSL or cable-modem services. All you need to do is plug the wireless modem into your notebook computer and go! Imagine sitting in a coffee shop and surfing the Net while waiting for your business partner to arrive. The modem would find the network and log in under your account. It has the potential to be faster and more economical than any DSL or cable modem technology available today.

Questions

1. Describe the challenges of building a wireless network in Canada as compared with other countries.
2. Explain the attraction of wireless data transmission for this new national communications network.
3. In small groups, brainstorm the potential uses for wireless computing. Where would you like to be able to "hook up" and why? Present your group's ideas to the class.

IT's A Wrap

Key Terms in This Chapter

bandwidth (p. 208)
Bluetooth (p. 229)
computer telephony (p. 212)
domain name system (DNS) (p. 217)
fax machine (p. 210)
ftp (file transfer protocol) (p. 216)
HTML (hypertext markup language) (p. 214)
HTTP (hypertext transfer protocols) (p. 214)
hyperlink (p. 214)
Internet (p. 213)
Internet telephony (p. 212)
local loop (p. 207)
modem (p. 210)
modulation (p. 210)
MTSO (Mobile Telephone Switching Office) (p. 225)
MVNO (mobile virtual network operators) (p. 228)
POP3 (Post Office Protocol) (p. 218)
protocols (p. 214)
SMTP (Simple Mail Transfer Protocol) (p. 218)
spam (p. 221)
subscriber loop carrier (SLC) (p. 207)
telcos (p. 207)
TCP/IP (transmission control protocol/Internet protocol) (p. 216)
URL (Uniform Resource Locator) (p. 215)
WAP (wireless application protocol) (p. 227)
Web cam (p. 213)
WiFi (wireless fidelity) (p. 229)
World Wide Web (p. 214)

1. Create a list of the competencies you have acquired through your work in this chapter.

2. Update your portfolio to include exemplary work you have completed in this chapter.

Know It!

3. Explain whether or not you think fax machines are the "dinosaur" of the modern office.

4. Create a chart comparing the similarities and differences between the Internet and the World Wide Web.

5. Explain how TCP/IP helped to fuel the growth of the Internet.

6. Describe the function of the following e-mail components and add the information to your notebook or list of key terms.

a. client
b. server
c. SMTP
d. POP3

7. Describe the differences in process between a telephone call being handled by the telecommunications system and a cellular phone call.

Do It!

8. Contact three local ISPs in your area. Electronically create a comparison chart that provides details on the products and services offered and the prices charged for their services. Below the chart, include a paragraph where you recommend a service. Explain why.

IT's A Wrap (continued)

Do It!

9. Contact a local business or one you can access on the Internet, and investigate the communications tools they use most frequently. Prepare a short presentation to make to the class on your findings.
10. Assess your school's Acceptable Use Policy. Prepare a three-column point-form list of what the policy covers and does not cover and indicate improvements you would make.
11. Research on the Internet, or interview an office manager, to find the keys to leaving successful voice mail messages. Electronically create a short set of guidelines that might be published for students to help reduce the frustration of leaving messages. Ensure that your guideline is easy to read and attractive.

Analyze It!

12. In small groups, discuss how video conferencing can help organizations improve collaboration and lower costs on projects. Come to a group consensus on the answer and share it with the rest of the class.
13. Of all the concerns surrounding the use of e-mail, which has the potential of becoming the most dangerous? Explain why.
14. Write a short essay on the impact of WiFi, Bluetooth, and MCS technologies on traditional ISPs and Internet service in general. Input your essay using appropriate software and send a copy to your teacher for assessment.

CHAPTER

9

The Internet and E-Commerce

By the end of this chapter, you will be able to:

- explain how e-commerce works;
- identify good e-commerce sites and the elements of a good site;
- explain the impact of e-commerce on how a business operates; and
- explain the impact of e-commerce on competitors.

B2B, B2C, P2P. Just what do all of these have to do with business? This chapter will explore the world of electronic commerce or the use of the Internet and the World Wide Web to conduct business transactions. To introduce you to this emerging business method, the following topics will be explored:

- What Is E-Commerce?
- Major Business Models for B2C E-Commerce
- E-Commerce Payment Systems
- E-Commerce Security Threats
- Protecting Organizations from Security Threats
- Getting Your Company Ready for E-Commerce
- Web Sites that Work
- The Impact of E-Commerce on the Competitive Environment

Introduction to Chapter Projects

Recall that the Chapter Projects are introduced at the beginning and are to be completed as you work through the chapter. Your teacher will provide you with assessment and evaluation criteria.

CHAPTER PROJECT 1

Create a business plan that describes a design for an e-commerce Web site for a business that does not currently sell its products or services on the Web.

- Describe the features you intend to incorporate into the site, the structure of the site from home page to final purchase page, and how a customer would navigate through the site to make a purchase.
- Use flowcharts to describe the navigation.
- Design the home page for your new business venture using the Web authoring tools you will be using for this course.
- Present both your business plan and the home page to your class.

CHAPTER PROJECT 11

Locate two e-commerce sites from the same industry that provide similar products and services (e.g., two banks). Based on what you study throughout this chapter:

- Develop criteria to evaluate and compare the sites.
- Analyze the two sites using your criteria, and create a report to describe your analysis and conclusions.
- Include recommendations for improvement to the sites if applicable.
- Present your report to the class using appropriate technology.

9.1 What Is E-Commerce?

Industry Canada defines **e-commerce** as "commercial activity conducted over networks linking electronic devices (mainly computers)." Stated simply, e-commerce is conducting business on the Internet and the World Wide Web. E-commerce has fueled a business revolution in recent years that is having a profound impact on the way business sells products and services to consumers and other businesses. These impacts will be discussed further in the next chapter. For now, let us take a look at the difference between e-commerce and e-business.

9.1.1 The Difference Between E-Commerce and E-Business

There is no universal agreement about what constitutes "e-commerce" and "e-business." However, in most instances, experts agree that e-commerce has three basic features:

1. an exchange of goods or services of some value between parties;
2. an exchange of payment for those goods and services; and
3. transactions that are conducted through digital technology, on the Internet and World Wide Web in most cases.

Therefore, exchanges of goods or services within a company, where there is no exchange of payment for those services, would *not* qualify as e-commerce. Rather, these exchanges would be examples of **e-business**.

To illustrate this concept, let us look at two departments in a typical company. The Accounting department maintains extensive records of all sales transactions, invoices outstanding for the company's customers, and data that help to create profit and loss statements during the year. If the Sales department requests, and receives electronically, monthly sales reports by region from the Accounting department, these reports would be e-business transactions. No payment between departments is required.

You might ask where the data for those reports came from in the first place. In fact, all data originate from the commercial transactions of the organization. The Accounting department's infrastructure and systems support both e-commerce transactions with the company's outside customers and suppliers and e-business transactions with their internal customers.

Now that we have established the distinction between e-commerce and e-business, let us examine the different types of e-commerce.

9.1.2 Types of E-Commerce

When we think of e-commerce, we tend to think of consumers like you buying the latest CD from HMV's online site, or ordering flowers to be sent to your grandmother across the country for her birthday. In fact, this is but one of the four main types of e-commerce. In all four, the people involved in the transactions usually define the different types of e-commerce. Let us look at each one in turn.

9.1.2.1 Business to Consumer E-Commerce

Business to Consumer (B2C) is the most commonly discussed form of e-commerce, where a business sells goods and services to consumers for their personal use and consumption. However, in the world of e-commerce B2C accounts for only a small percentage of the sales conducted through the Internet. B2C sales in Canada rose 59% to \$2.3 billion in 2001 from

Get Connected

The Canadian economy is filled with new and innovative success stories in e-commerce. Follow the links at www.pearsoned.ca/businessconnections to find out more about companies that have been successful in the world of e-commerce.

Choose two or three of the businesses (preferably those you have not heard of) and prepare a short summary that highlights what their sites have to offer Canadian consumers.

$1.45 billion in 2000. Although this sounds significant, it constitutes only a small percentage of manufacturers' and retailers' revenue sources. Furthermore, only 22% of all Internet sales in 2001 were to households or consumers as compared with other businesses (Statistics Canada 2002).

Figure 9.1 graphs worldwide e-commerce revenues, while Figure 9.2 graphs Internet sales to consumers by industry for 2001.

Figure 9.1
Worldwide E-Commerce Revenue

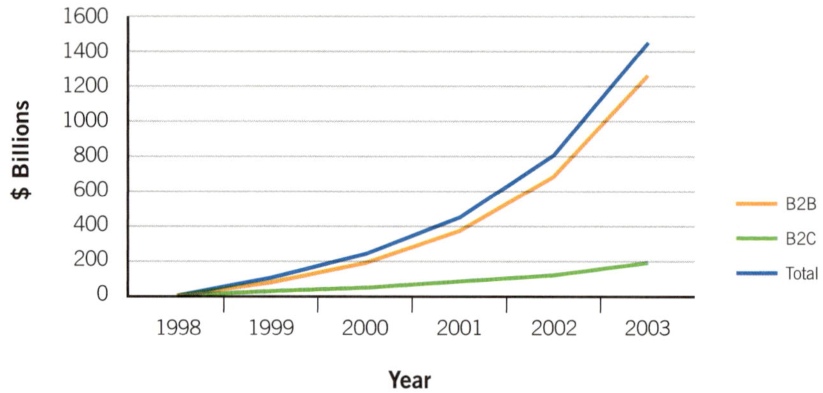

Source: http://e-com.ic.gc.ca/english/research/inter/interb2b/sid001.htm (February 6, 2002).

Figure 9.2
Internet Sales to Consumers by Industry, 2001

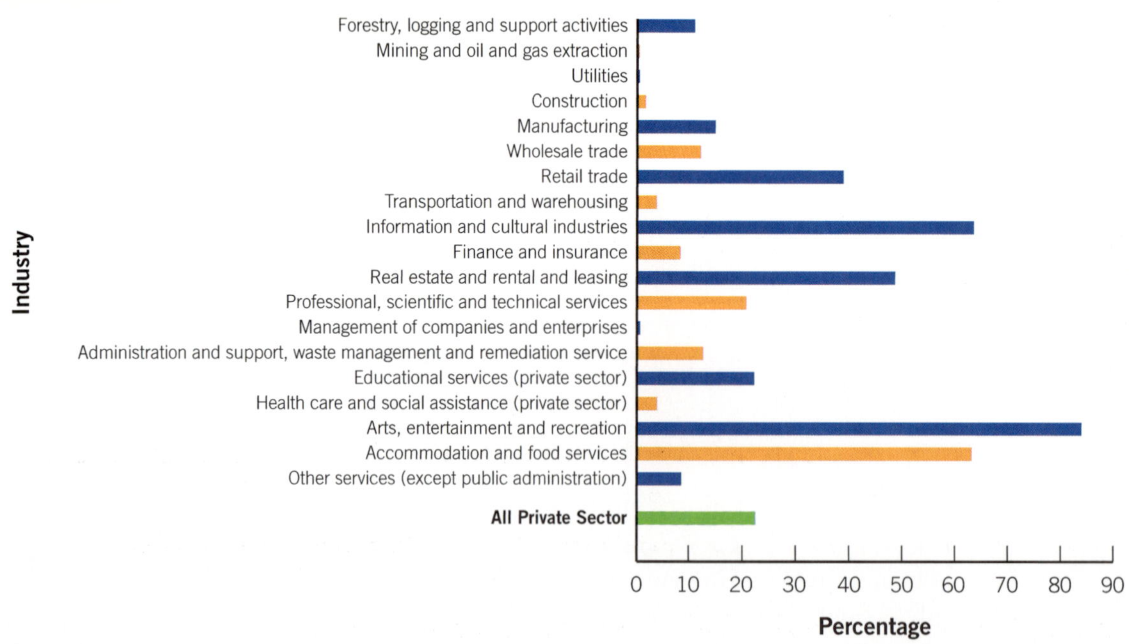

Source: Statistics Canada, *The Daily*, April 2, 2002.

B2C marketing has grown significantly since its inception in the mid-1990s and there are many different business models an online business might adopt. These will be discussed in greater detail in the next section of this chapter.

9.1.2.2 Business to Business E-Commerce

Business to Business (**B2B**) e-commerce focuses on transactions between businesses — everything from purchasing office supplies from Grand & Toy's secure Internet Web site, to electronically processing purchase orders for manufacturing components such as automotive parts. In Canada, the growth of online procurement — or purchasing goods and services needed in an organization — has grown steadily in recent years from 13.8% of businesses in 1999 to 22.4% in 2001, with medium-sized and large organizations embracing the technology more extensively than smaller ones (Industry Canada 2002).

Recent surveys indicate that businesses are using the Internet to procure the types of goods and services listed in Figure 9.3.

Figure 9.3
Types of Goods and Services Purchased by Businesses Using the Internet

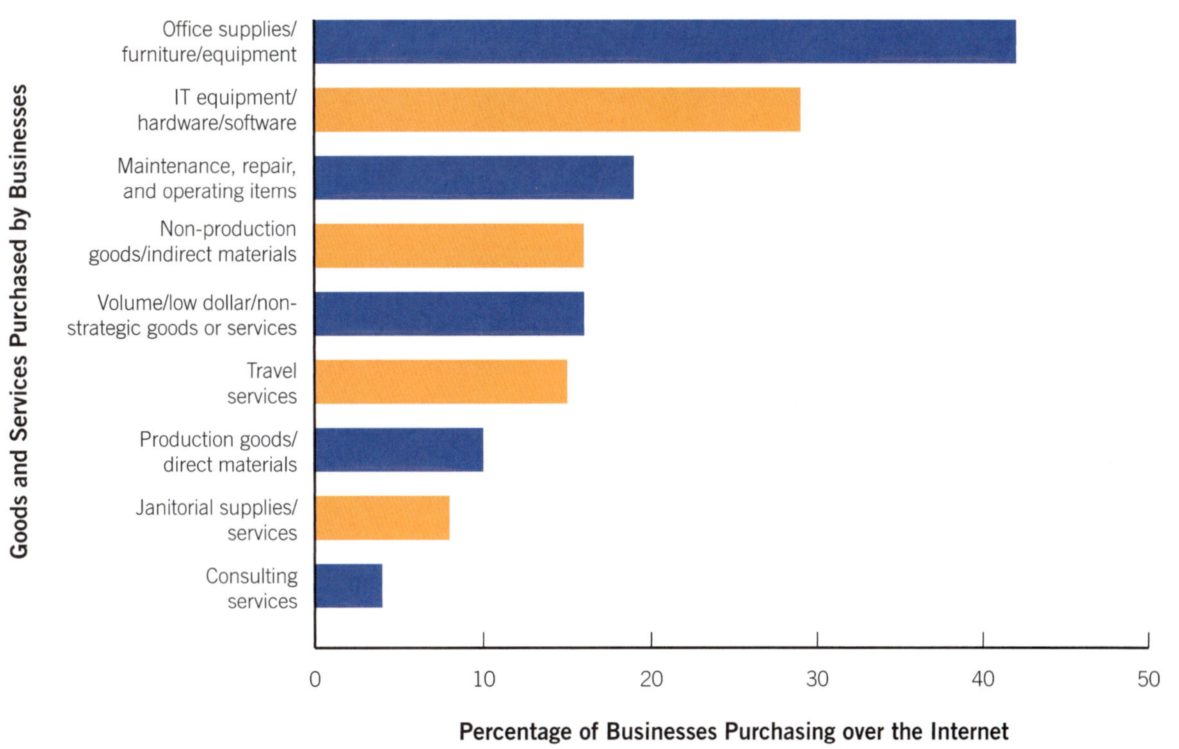

Source: Industry Canada, *Electronic Commerce in Canada,* updated February 6, 2002. Available at http://e-com.ic.gc.ca/english/research/b2b/procurement/sld002.htm.

IT In Action

Amberhill Collection Inc.

What do you get when you combine a love for horses and a keen sense of business? Just ask Kristy Dukelow of Guelph, Ontario, the founder and driving force behind Amberhill Collection. After 15 years on the Canadian show jumping circuit, Kristy "retired" from the competitive ring (at age 27!) and started her company, which produces and sells equestrian, golf, pet, and fashion accessories. She saw an opportunity to fill a market "niche" — a gap between low-end, poorly made products and high-end, very expensive products such as Burberry and Hermès. The Amberhill product line ranges from key fobs and hair barrettes ($12 to $15) to handbags ($180 to $300), all the way up to a large tack trunk ($1600). The designs are based on hunter-jumper horses, polo, fox hunting, thoroughbred racing, and golf. Her Paw Prints line of pet accessories features sets of leather dog collars and leashes studded with tiny sterling silver dog bones and hearts.

Dukelow just loves the Internet and what it has done for her business. She ships products around the world — to 50 U.S. states, Italy, Spain, Austria, Japan, and the United Kingdom. Customers can browse the product lines and order through her secure Web site (see Figure 9.4). "The Internet is a tremendous tool because retailers can order online," says Dukelow.

Figure 9.4
www.amberhill.com Web Site

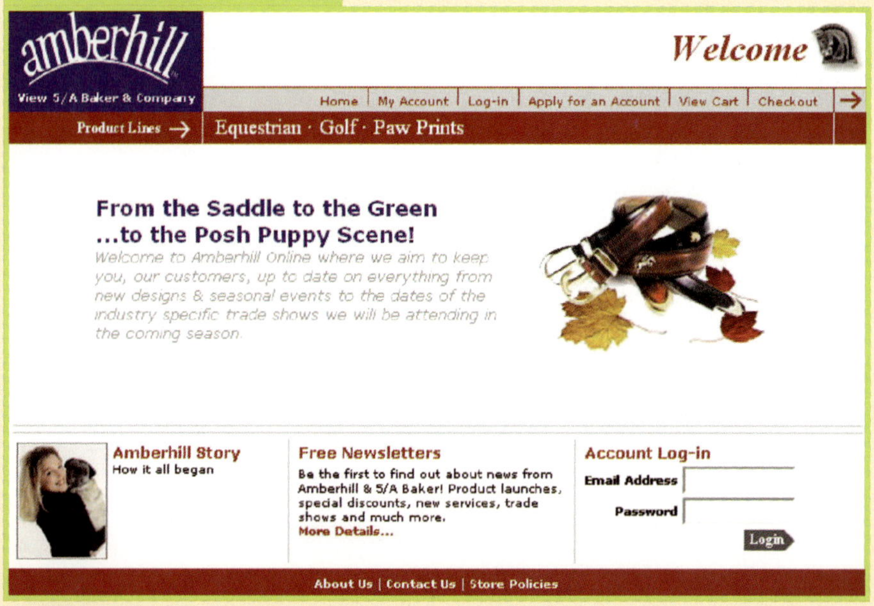

Follow the links at www.pearsoned.ca/businessconnections to the Amberhill Collection and similar sites.

Questions

1. Describe how Amberhill Collections or another online retailer is using the Internet as a source of competitive advantage in this specialized market.
2. List and describe three other products or services that could benefit in the same manner.

9.1.2.3 Consumer to Consumer E-Commerce

Consumer to Consumer (C2C) e-commerce gives individuals an opportunity to sell items to others using an intermediary, such as eBay.ca, to facilitate the sale. The seller is responsible for preparing the goods for sale, placing the ad for the product at the online auction or trading site, and shipping the goods. The market intermediary is responsible for maintaining the site, including the search engine through which buyers locate the product for sale, and processing the payments, both from the buyer and to the seller. This market has been rapidly growing in popularity. In fact, more than 37 000 apparel (clothing) items are sold daily on eBay according to the U.S. company's figures (Black 2002).

Auction sites are only one form of C2C activity. Some sites allow the sellers to set a fixed price for the goods rather than putting them up for bid. These sites charge a commission for each sale.

9.1.2.4 Person to Person E-Commerce

Person to Person (P2P) technology allows users of the Internet to share files and computer resources directly, without going through a Web server. However, since the file sharing is supposed to be provided free of charge, the challenge is to make enough money to keep the P2P site operating. The most famous P2P file-sharing site in recent history is Napster.com. This site at one time enabled users to find MP3 music files located on other users' computers and download them directly from their systems. In this way, they bypassed the Web servers that traditionally host files for downloading.

9.1.2.5 M-Commerce

M-commerce refers to mobile commerce, or the use of wireless digital devices to conduct business over the Web. These devices are discussed in greater detail in Chapter 8, Electronic Communication. In essence, people can use their wireless devices, such as a Palm PDA, RIM BlackBerry, and more and more cellular phones, to connect to a wireless network, to order movie tickets, or to do banking or any of a myriad of transactions. The advantage of this wireless service is that it provides access in any place. With more people worldwide using cellular phones, the potential for this type of commerce is huge.

9.1.3 Variations in B2C and B2B

Whether your organization provides goods or services to consumers or business customers, you have to generate revenue in some way; otherwise, business failure is imminent. You can generate this revenue in the following ways:

- *Sales*. If your company has a product or service to sell, you have adopted a sales strategy. Purchasers may buy books (e.g., chapters.indigo.ca), book holiday travel (e.g., Travelocity.ca), or pay for the results of research conducted on trends in information technology (e.g., EKOS.ca).

- *Advertising*. Many **Web portals** (e.g., Yahoo.ca) have adopted an advertising strategy to generate revenue. They sell space on their Web sites to advertisers who pay for their ads to be shown to site visitors. Sites that have a high rate of return-viewers are able to generate significant revenue, since the ads will be seen repeatedly by visitors to the site.
- *Subscriptions*. Web sites that offer information or content for a fee are called **subscription sites**. Numerous research sites, including Electric Library, offer access to full-text newspaper and magazine articles, radio show transcripts, and television transcripts on a subscription basis to students and teachers alike.
- *Transaction fees*. Web sites that charge a commission or fee for each transaction that you perform online are employing the transaction fee strategy for generating revenue. Examples of this type of site are eBay.ca, which charges the seller of the merchandise, and companies that build and host your e-commerce Web site and process your transactions on your behalf (a popular option for businesses that do not possess the time or technical expertise to build their own site).

GETTING IT

1. Define *e-commerce*.
2. List the three basic features of an e-commerce transaction.
3. Explain the difference between e-commerce and e-business.
4. List and briefly describe the four main types of e-commerce Web sites.
5. If a site has adopted a sales strategy for generating revenue, where does the money come from? An advertising strategy? A subscription strategy? A transaction fee strategy? Give examples to help explain your answers.

ON THE CASE

No More Something for Nothing!

Based on Katherine Harding, "From free to fee," *Toronto Star*, July 1, 2002, p. D4.

Two of the most popular Web portals, Yahoo! and Hotmail, have slowly but surely converted free e-mail services to subscription services — something that caught many loyal users by surprise.

Many users of the popular Web-based e-mail services utilized such features as mail forwarding and the free mail storage space, and have come to expect these services always to be available. Mail forwarding allows customers to have e-mail redirected to another e-mail address, thus avoiding the advertising that helps to generate the revenue for the service provider. And advertisers are not pleased. As a result, both ISPs instituted subscription fees in the $30 U.S. range for customers to have these services continued.

File storage space is another issue. Although file storage is a relatively inexpensive commodity, Web-based e-mail providers have had their systems taxed to their limits. The result has been one of two approaches: either delete e-mail files that are over the "free" limits, as Microsoft has done with the Hotmail system, or reduce the storage capacity of free accounts, as in the case of Yahoo!

How willing are Canadians to pay for formerly free services? Not very, but it appears that people are adjusting to the idea. A study by ComQuest Research Inc. in Toronto during 2002 indicated that many respondents said they would find "premium content or services valuable." They also ranked "enhanced Web-based e-mail service" highest among their choices. A slightly smaller number indicated they would pay for access to content-based services on the Web.

The world of the Web is constantly changing and its users must be prepared to see product and service offerings change along with it.

Questions

1. In small groups, discuss whether the conversion of free services to fee services is forcing people off the Web. What are the social implications relating to this "stripping" of services? Come to a group consensus and report your thoughts to the class.
2. **a.** Write a paragraph that describes the advantages in having messages forwarded to another e-mail address.
   b. Explain whether you think it is right to do so.
3. Brainstorm, as a class, to develop a list of free Web-based e-mail service providers. Select three from the list and electronically create a chart that compares the products and services they offer clients, both for free and on a subscription basis. Present your findings to the class.

9.2 Major Business Models for B2C E-Commerce

Within the B2C category of e-commerce sites, businesses adopt a number of different strategies to entice consumers to purchase products and services on the Web. This section will examine the major business models used in the B2C area, describe the characteristics of each, and look at the revenue-generating strategies employed at those sites.

1. ***Portals.*** These sites offer Internet users a full-service package, such as searching, news, e-mail, chat, downloads, video streaming, and calendars. Their goal is to be the first site that users log into in order to maximize their presence on the Web. Examples of portals include Yahoo!, Sympatico, and MSN. They earn revenue through advertising, subscriptions, and transaction fees for various services, such as e-mail forwarding or expanded file space. Some portals are also ISPs, so they are able to generate revenue through monthly access fees paid by their customers. According to Search Engine Watch, the top 10 sites gather more than 90% of search engine traffic due to their brand recognition among Internet users.
2. ***E-tailers.*** These online retail sites range in size from small one-person shops with Web sites for customers to purchase products to the large traditional physical stores that also have a Web presence (known as "clicks and mortar" or "clicks and bricks"). There are online versions of direct-mail catalogues (e.g., Mountain Equipment Co-Op), online malls, and online sites that offer products direct from the manufacturer. This is a highly competitive business, but the barriers to entry have been lowered with Internet technology. Now, small retail operations can compete on an equal basis with the large e-tail sites. The challenge is differentiating their store from the others in terms of product offering or price to entice you to buy their products. Those companies that develop a successful "niche" strategy (see *IT in Action Amberhill Collection Inc.*) stand the best chance of success. The revenue strategy for this model of B2C business is obviously the sale of goods to customers. Although many consumers use such sites for comparison shopping, the hope is that looking will lead to buying.
3. ***Content providers.*** These types of B2C sites provide information and entertainment to potential customers. News, sports, how-to directions, special interest stories, and other up-to-date data are examples of the type of information consumers are willing to pay for. In fact, more Internet users go online to get information than to purchase products, and content provision is the second-largest source of revenue for e-commerce B2C sites (Laudon and Traver 2001). Content

providers generate revenue through subscriptions. Examples of content providers are e-zines (online magazines) and newspapers.

4. *Transaction brokers*. These types of e-commerce sites process consumer transactions that would normally have been handled in person, by mail, or over the telephone. Online stock trading services, travel agents, and job placement services are all transaction brokers, which generate revenue through fees charged for use of their services.
5. *Market creators*. These B2C sites create an electronic marketplace for buyers and sellers to meet, and for buyers to view products and establish the prices they are willing to pay for them. Examples of these sites in 2002 were eBay.ca and Priceline.com. The key to their success is providing the structure within which buyers and sellers feel confident that their transactions will take place in a secure environment. Each sale generates a fee for the service the site provides from buyers and sellers alike.
6. *Service providers*. Time demands on people's lives have given rise to these types of B2C sites, whose value resides in providing services that free people to do other things. Examples include grocery shopping and delivery to your door, or florist delivery across town or to another province or country. Revenue is generated at these sites through the sale of their services.
7. *Community providers*. These B2C sites are digital "places" where people with similar interests can come together to interact, transact (buy and sell goods), and receive information related to these interests. The idea of a community is not new; the Internet and World Wide Web have eliminated the need for people to physically "go" to the meeting place. Advertising revenue is generated from companies whose products and services are of interest to people visiting the sites. Check out the forums available from your local ISP or on national service providers for examples of these special interest sites.

GETTING IT

1. Electronically create a chart titled "B2C E-Commerce" and use the following column headings:

Type of B2C Site	Description	Revenue Strategy

2. Summarize the features of the seven B2C site types in this chart. Include this chart in your notes once it has been approved by your teacher.

Get Connected

Canadian E-Tailers

Often, Canadian shoppers get frustrated looking for e-tailers that ship to Canada or, when they do find one, they suffer from "sticker shock" when they get the final bill after foreign exchange, shipping charges, GST, and Canada Post's handling fee. Go to www.pearsoned.ca/businessconnections to find a number of truly Canadian shopping sites and directories. Select three sites from the list and compare them in terms of privacy protection, user-friendliness, number of products offered, and delivery charges. Create a shopping comparison chart for budget-conscious Canadian consumers.

9.3 E-Commerce Payment Systems

Once you find the site you have been looking for and make your purchase decision, it is time to finalize the purchase. On many B2C and B2B Web sites, you click on the merchandise you want and the item is placed in your virtual shopping cart. When you have finished adding items to your cart, you proceed to the checkout just as you would in a traditional shopping environment. Then it is time to pay for your purchase. To understand online payment options, let us first summarize the various methods of paying for products and services in the physical world:

- ***Cash.*** Each country in the world defines some form of **legal tender** to represent value to its citizens. Cash is instantly convertible into other forms of value without an intermediary being involved. You simply hand over the required amount and you get the desired goods or services. Private organizations can also produce a private form of "cash" known as scrip that can be instantly redeemed for goods in their stores. Canadian Tire money is an example of this and is used to develop loyalty from customers who purchase goods at Canadian Tire retail outlets. Cash is still one of the most popular forms of payment because of its convenience, instant acceptance, and the lack of transaction fees for its use.
- ***Cheque.*** A cheque is a draft written against the balance in your account at a bank or other financial institution. Once the draft is presented to the merchant from whom you buy the goods, it must clear your account. This means it must go through the banks' **clearing system** to transfer the amount from your bank account to the merchant's bank account. As such, you cannot use cheques without the aid of a third party, that is, the banks in conjunction with their clearing system. If you wish to use a cheque, most merchants require two forms of identification to ensure that you are the person whose name is on the cheque. This also gives the merchants information by which to trace you should there be insufficient funds in your account to cover the purchase. Due to their inconvenient nature and the growth of the debit system in Canada, cheques have declined somewhat in popularity and use.
- ***Debit card.*** This looks like a credit card, but works in a very different manner. When you use your debit card at a participating merchant, the amount of the purchase is immediately transferred from your bank account to the merchant's bank account. This very popular method of payment in Canada is available at stores of all sizes. The cost for each debit transaction depends on the type of account you have and the number of free debits you are allowed each month in your service package.

digiknow

Canadians are the world's most frequent users of debit cards. Compared with consumers in the United States, Canadians have more than twice the number of debit card transactions per year. According to the Interac Association, in 2002, Canadians used the direct payment system over 2.2 billion times at over 328 000 participating merchants!

(Interac 2002)

- *Credit card.* This method of payment allows purchasers to buy items and defer payment until later. Credit cards are accepted around the world and offer consumers the opportunity to make large purchases without immediately having the funds in the bank to pay for them. Merchants benefit from this form of payment in that consumers tend to make much larger purchases; however, merchants pay anywhere from 2% to 4% to the credit card issuers for each transaction.

These payment methods are all options for traditional retail purchases, but what about in the online world?

Figure 9.5 shows how an e-commerce transaction takes place. Payment methods vary. In 2000, 95% of all online purchases in the United States were made using credit cards (Laudon and Traver 2001). Online e-tailers prefer this method of payment for a number of reasons. To get a credit card, you typically have to go through an extensive application process that indicates to the issuing bank or financial institution that you are a good credit risk — you pay your bills. When online merchants process orders using a credit card for payment, they obtain authorization from the issuing bank. Authorization means that:

- the buyer's account is not over its set spending limit;
- the card has not been reported as stolen; and
- the buyer's account is up to date in respect of payments.

digiknow

More than 60% of Canadian consumers do the majority of their banking through electronic channels — ATMs, telephone, and Internet.

(Interac 2002)

Figure 9.5
An E-Commerce Transaction

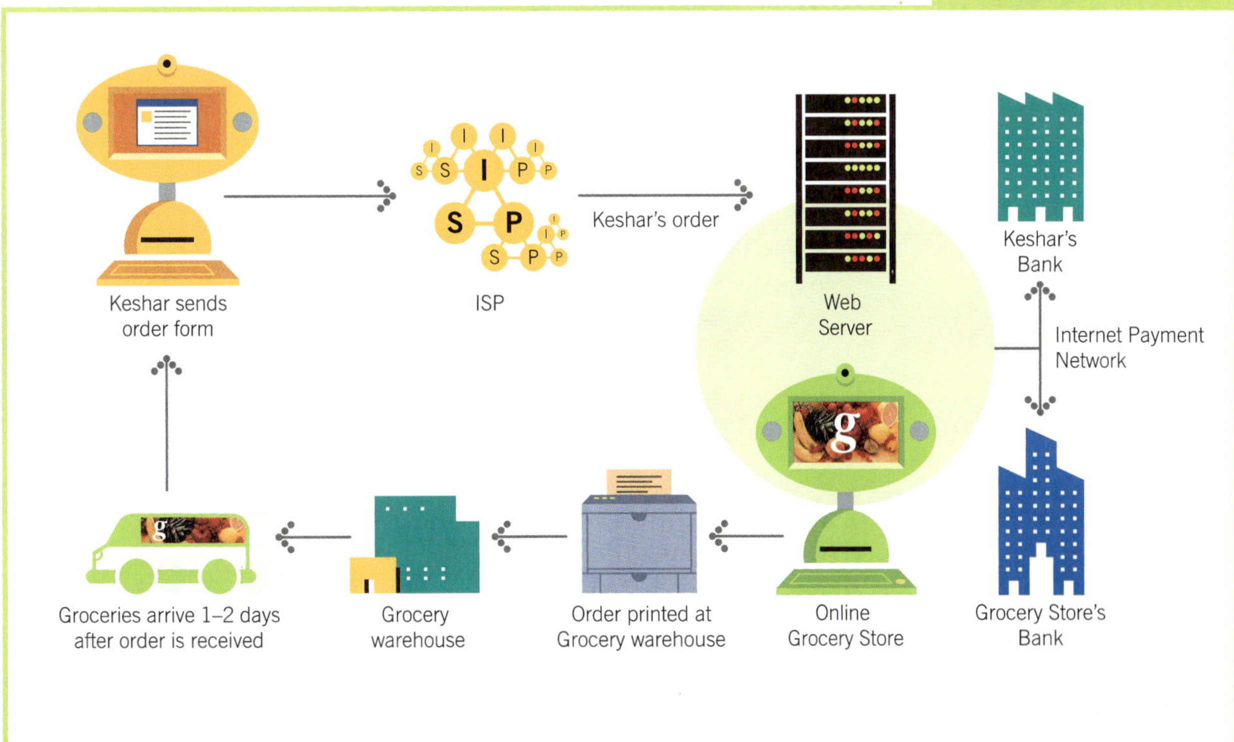

Which traditional method of payment do you think would be the most convenient to use for e-commerce transactions? Explain why.

Since online merchants never obtain a signature from the purchaser, this authorization minimizes their risk that buyers may dispute the fact that they ordered the goods.

A number of new and unique payment methods are emerging in the digital world. Let's take a look at them.

- ***Digital wallet.*** Like a physical wallet, a digital wallet contains identification information — debit card and/or credit card information you access when you purchase online. The advantage of using a digital wallet is that you do not have to fill out forms every time you want to make a purchase from a site. The digital wallet contains all your identification, billing, and shipping information, and it is installed as a plug-in to your Web browser. Purchasers have to use a password to access their digital wallets and make purchases, thus increasing the security of using such a tool. Merchants like digital wallets because they reduce transaction costs, make purchasing easier from their sites, and may reduce fraud. This form of payment is in its infancy and there are still many details to work out.
- ***Digital cash.*** Also called e-cash, digital cash was one of the first forms of payment developed for online purchases. Early versions of digital cash required the development and adoption of entirely new standards and practices, and therefore did not gain wide acceptance. The newest forms of digital cash are based on P2P (person-to-person) platforms and are expected to explode onto the scene in Canada in the coming years. (See *IT in Action CertaPay Taps E-Cash Potential.*) The growth of online auction sites has created a need for payment systems that would allow individuals (as opposed to businesses, which can take advantage of the credit card systems) to send money to each other to pay for items purchased at these sites. PayPal, one of the first P2P systems in the United States, has become so popular with users of their site that eBay has purchased the company. These P2P systems require an intermediary to process the payments, and both the sender and the receiver of the payments require an e-mail account to notify them of incoming payments.
- ***Stored value.*** An online stored value system allows purchasers to transfer funds from their own bank accounts to an account that is held at another site for use in making online purchases. When purchases are made, the amounts are taken out of this online account. Some online merchants require the user to download a digital wallet (see above) in order to have the funds stored in that location. Some online stored value systems are aimed at the teen market, because teenagers have large disposable incomes and many do not possess credit cards.

IT In Action

CertaPay Taps E-Cash Potential

Adapted from Tyler Hamilton, "Cash is in the e-mail," *Toronto Star*, February 11, 2002, p. E1.

Canadian consumers have always embraced electronic payment systems — first it was the ATM (automated teller machine), then debit cards. Get ready for P2P!

Canada's major banks — Bank of Montreal, Scotiabank, CIBC, and TD Canada Trust have launched a new service that will make online shopping and payments even easier than before. Their P2P (person-to-person) payment system works this way. You first log into your online banking service and select the e-mail money transfer option at that site. You complete the form, specifying who to send the money to using their e-mail address as an identifier, the amount to be transferred, and the account it is to come from. You are also required to add an expiry date, so the person has to "cash" the payment by that date or lose out on the chance to get the funds! An additional layer of security is provided by adding a security question to the transfer and you can also include a personal message to the recipient (e.g., "Bob, here is the $20 I owe you. Thanks for the loan."). The recipient gets the e-mail notification, which contains hyperlinks to their choice of bank so that they can deposit the money online. The transfer is completed instantly for recipients who bank online. The money does not travel over e-mail, but through the existing bank system.

What do you do if you don't bank online? The sender of the money must bank online for this transaction to occur. The recipient, however, does not have to. In this case, the recipient would go to the CertaPay money transfer site and specify in which bank and account number the funds should be deposited. This transfer takes three to five banking days to complete.

The real power of this system is in the IT infrastructure that comprises the Canadian banking system. Canada has a very tightly knit banking system. To illustrate this cooperation, in the United States there are 12 ATM networks; in Canada there is one (**Interac**). This increases the level of trust with the average consumer, because we are used to the Interac system. It is expected that Canadians will transact $2.2 billion in bank-based e-mail payments within a year of the introduction of this system.

Experts in e-commerce expect Canadians to embrace this form of payment in the future. The expectation is that Canadian retailers will begin to install point-of-sale terminals with e-mail access to allow for e-mail payments at traditional stores. They also expect ATM use to drop off as the need for having ready cash is reduced.

How does this affect e-commerce? Many consumers are hesitant to make online purchases because of concerns regarding the theft of personal credit card information. Consumers concerned with credit card security will see this as a positive step and will be more inclined to make those purchases online, because no personal banking or credit card information is required. There are also a number of individuals in our society (under 18 years of age and those with poor credit ratings) who do not have credit cards and are effectively locked out of the world of e-commerce. In order to expand their customer base, sites that currently offer only credit card payments will have to look seriously at this new payment system. Online merchants will also benefit from the instant transfer of funds to cover purchases and will reduce their cost of doing business due to the reduction of fraudulent purchases and non-payment.

IT In Action (continued)

Get Connected

Check out a P2P Web site at www.pearsoned.ca/businessconnections. Determine the top nine reasons to use e-mail money transfers. Use appropriate software to prepare a summary of each reason for your notebook.

Questions

Create a note page that answers the following questions on the P2P payment system. Insert the completed note page into your notebook upon approval from your teacher.

1. What does the acronym P2P stand for? What is a P2P e-mail transfer?
2. Describe how the P2P payment system works.
3. Explain why it is expected that Canadians will adopt this form of payment system when other systems have failed in the past.
4. Explain the implications of this new form of electronic payment for e-commerce sites.

One example of this is Rocket Cash in the United States. Major credit card companies, like VISA and MasterCard, are also launching stored value cards that act like credit cards and are accepted at e-commerce Web sites. The online merchant does not know if the card number is for a credit card or a stored value card. This card has money "loaded" onto it from either the user's bank account or that of another person (e.g., a parent), and users are able to make purchases as long as enough money is loaded onto the card to cover the cost of the items.

Get Connected

To find out more about all forms of electronic cash, visit the site at www.pearsoned.ca/businessconnections, where you will find an extensive list of the companies that offer these services in both Canada and the United States. Prepare a summary of services provided by three companies on the list. Compare your findings with those of your classmates.

GETTING IT

1. Explain what scrip is and how it can be considered to be cash.
2. Why is cash still one of the most frequent forms of payment for goods and services?
3. List some of the reasons for the increase in popularity of debit card payments, as compared with cheques, in Canada.
4. Credit cards are a popular form of payment for purchases in both the online and offline world. Why? What are the costs and risks to a retailer/e-tailer of accepting credit card payments?
5. Describe how a digital wallet works.
6. Explain why a person might say that P2P payment systems are like debit cards for e-commerce.
7. Describe how stored value cards enable more people to make online purchases.

9.4 E-Commerce Security Threats

The Internet has opened up a whole new world for individuals and businesses worldwide. Most users of Internet e-commerce and the Web are law-abiding citizens. However, there is an element in our society that looks for new and unique ways to steal from others. The Internet has created a very profitable way to do just that. For criminals, the lure of the Internet is that it is very difficult to trace theft committed online. The way that e-commerce transactions occur hides peoples' identities from the online merchant; placing fraudulent orders is quick and easy. The cost of such crime has increased the cost of doing business online for both consumer and provider and must be addressed.

This section will take a look at the security threats in the e-commerce arena and the ways that organizations can protect their sites from such attacks and crime.

To understand the risk of a security breach in e-commerce, we must first examine a typical e-commerce transaction (shown in Figure 9.5).

The customer connects to the Internet, completes an order form, and sends it to the online merchant. This is sent via the Internet through his or her ISP to the Web server, where the online merchant's site is located. The transaction is paid for through the payment network chosen (usually a credit card) and the order is sent for processing at the merchant's warehouse. The merchandise is then readied for shipment and sent via public carrier (e.g., Canada Post) to the customer. Transactions are vulnerable at three points: at the client (home or business computer), at the server of the ISP, merchant, or bank, and along Internet communication channels. Each point is subject to different types of attack. These types of attack will be discussed individually.

9.4.1 Virus Attack

A **virus** is a computer program that makes copies of itself (replicates), spreads to other files, and delivers a "payload" or another program that can do anything from displaying a harmless message when activated to destroying files, reformatting computer drives, or causing programs to malfunction.

The **macro virus** is the most common and affects the program for which it is written, e.g., Microsoft Word, Excel, or PowerPoint. When you open the document containing the macro virus, the virus copies itself to the templates in the application so that when new documents are created they will be infected as well. The **file virus**, also common, infects executable files (programs) so that when they are launched the file can be copied to your system. Both of these types of virus usually spread via e-mail attachments.

Script viruses are written in JavaScript or VBScript (Visual Basic) and overwrite other file types, eliminating the files in their original form. These viruses are activated by double clicking and opening an infected *.vbs or

*.js file. One famous example of this type of virus was the Melissa or "I LOVE YOU" virus, which overwrote *.jpg and *.mp3 files. Virus attacks are a threat to both the client and the server in the e-commerce transaction. A virus attack can bring down an entire e-commerce site, preventing customers from using it. These attacks are rare; viruses typically attack more at the client level and are limited to that one computer.

> **digiknow**
>
> Hackers fall into one of three categories:
>
> - *White Hats*: do-gooders who are paid to break into systems to pinpoint weaknesses;
> - *Black Hats*: those who break into systems with the intent to cause harm; and
> - *Grey Hats*: those who break into systems and reveal system flaws because they feel they are doing the right thing.

9.4.2 Hacking

A **hacker** is someone who attempts to gain unauthorized access to a computer system. Among hackers, the term "**cracker**" is used for those whose purpose in gaining access is to steal or corrupt data. However, most people use the terms interchangeably.

Regardless of whether you call them hackers or crackers, they take advantage of the features of the Internet to break into corporate and government Web sites. Those who do so with criminal intent destroy files, steal data, and/or disrupt service. There are, however, those who break into servers to do good deeds. Some corporations use hackers to try to break into their own systems in order to pinpoint weaknesses that can then be secured. There are those, however, who break into systems without prior authorization and then try to sell the information to the organization or publish the security flaw for others to take advantage of.

As you can see in Figure 9.6, hackers cause the most harm at the server point of an e-commerce transaction.

9.4.3 Credit Card Fraud

The number one deterrent to making online purchases is the possibility of credit card information being stolen. In traditional retail transactions, the threat to consumers is that their cards will be physically stolen. However, there is protection for consumers in that they are only liable for the first $50 of charges after reporting the theft. In e-commerce, the threat is much greater. Seemingly secure e-commerce sites have been the target of hackers who steal the customer databases along with all their credit card information. With this information, criminals can assume new identities — yours — and establish new credit for their own purposes, with you potentially left to pay the bill.

Credit card fraud is most likely to take place at the merchant server level or during the transmission of data to the server over the Internet from the client to the merchant.

The online community is very concerned about this due to the negative impact it has on potential sales. They are looking closely at new identity verification methods to decrease the risks associated with credit card fraud.

9.4.4 Spoofing

When hackers assume a fake identity or attempt to falsify their identity through fake e-mail addresses, they are **spoofing**. This can also involve redirecting Web traffic to a site different from the one the consumer thought he or she were going to. Once an unsuspecting consumer places an order at the spoof site, the hacker can alter the order (e.g., increase quantities or alter items purchased) and then send it to the true Web site for processing. This leads to very dissatisfied customers and disrupted business operations. This latter form of spoofing takes place during Internet communications as seen in Figure 9.6.

digiknow

Credit card fraud amounted to about $173 million in Canada in 2000, with 13% of that amount attributed to fraud committed without the actual use of a card (e.g., on the Internet).

(Royal Canadian Mounted Police 2002)

Figure 9.6
Vulnerable Points in an E-Commerce Environment

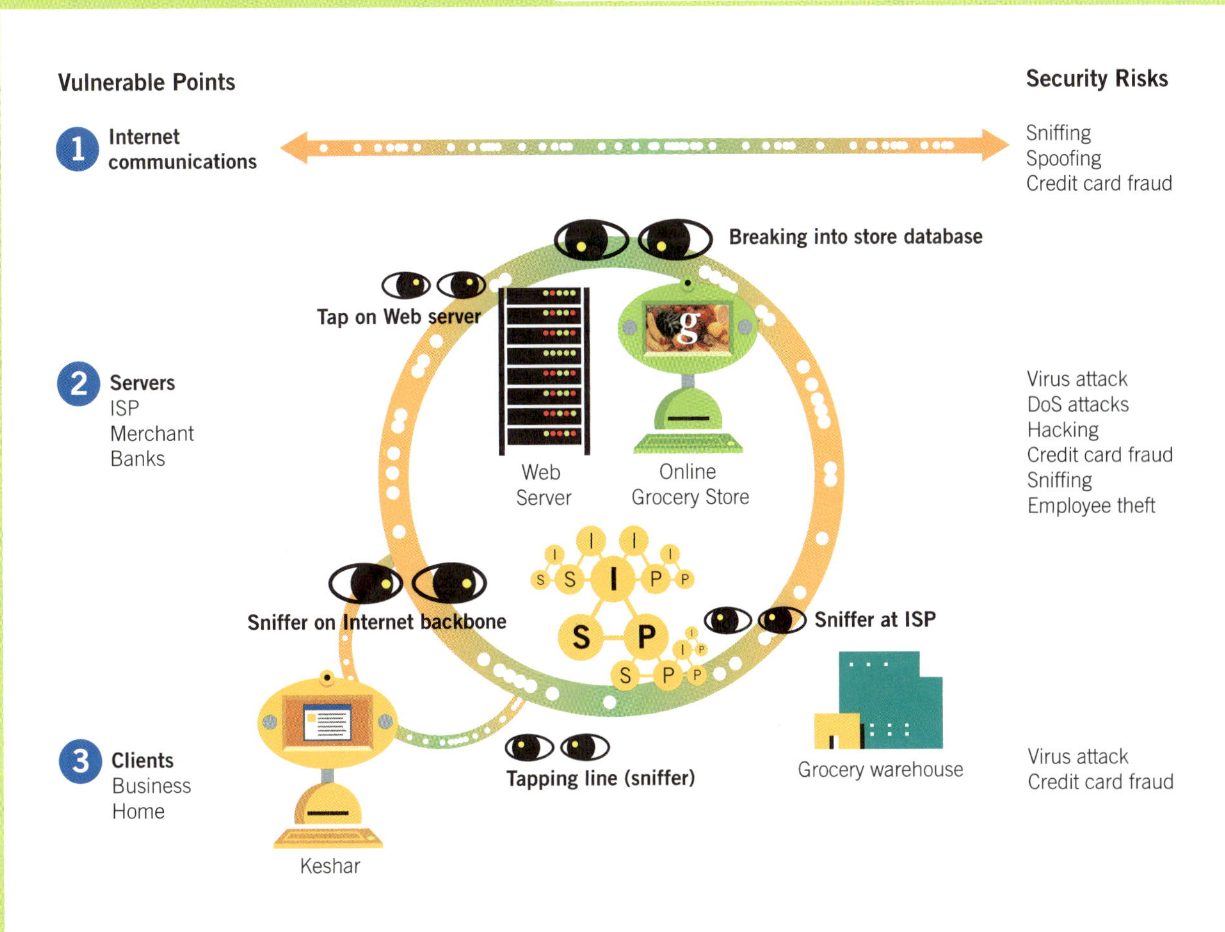

There are five vulnerable points in e-commerce transactions: The link from the client to the ISP, the ISP, the Internet backbone, the Web Server, and the store database.

9.4.5 Denial of Service Attacks

In a **Denial of Service** (**DoS**) attack, a hacker floods the e-commerce site with traffic, overwhelming the merchant's network. This effectively shuts down the server, stopping the merchant from handling real transactions from genuine customers. Again, customers get frustrated by not being able to send in orders and may look elsewhere for the desired products.

9.4.6 Sniffing

A **sniffer** is a program and/or device that monitors data travelling over a network. Sniffers can be used for legitimate purposes or, in the case of e-commerce crime, to enable hackers to steal information from anywhere on that network — from e-mail messages, databases, or company reports. They are one of the favourite tools of hackers because they are virtually impossible to detect and can be inserted anywhere.

Sniffing takes place at any point in the e-commerce cycle where information is being transmitted from one party to another.

9.4.7 Company Employees

Although we like to think that all employees are honest and loyal to the organization, much crime takes place from inside the company. Employees have access to information that would be very difficult to obtain from outside the company, they know the security systems that are in place, and they are usually able to enter restricted areas of the company without detection by others. Internal theft takes place at the server level of the e-commerce process.

GETTING IT

Create a guide in brochure or newsletter format that introduces consumers to e-commerce concerns. Address each of the following questions in your guide:

1. Name the five points along an e-commerce transaction that are vulnerable to attack.
2. What is a virus? Explain the difference between a macro virus and a script virus.
3. Write a paragraph that describes where virus attacks are most likely to occur in an e-commerce transaction.
4. Define the term *hacker*, and explain how you can tell the difference between a "good" hacker and a "bad" hacker.
5. Name the number one deterrent for potential e-commerce customers.
6. List the two methods of spoofing described in this text. At what point in the e-commerce transaction would spoofing occur?
7. Describe how a Denial of Service attack works.

8. Describe how a sniffer works and explain why it is one of a hacker's favourite tools.
9. List two reasons why employees can be considered a risk in e-commerce.

9.5 Protecting Organizations From Security Threats

Now that we have identified the major threats to an e-commerce transaction, we need to examine the ways that transactions can be protected, starting with encryption.

9.5.1 Encryption

In very simple terms, **encryption** is translating data into a secret code. Encryption is the most effective way to ensure that the data you send, receive, and/or store are secure. To read an encrypted file, you must have access to a key or password that enables you to decrypt the message or put it back into a language you can understand. Unencrypted data are called *plain text*; encrypted data are called *cipher text*.

There are two basic forms of encryption: symmetric and asymmetric (also known as public-key encryption).

Symmetric encryption (see Figure 9.7) uses the same key to encrypt and decrypt the data that are being transmitted. Symmetric encryption was used extensively in World War II and is still being used in some Internet applications.

Symmetric ciphers suffer from some serious flaws. Both sender and receiver must know the key, so in all likelihood it must be sent over insecure

Figure 9.7
Simple Form of Symmetric Encryption

BUSINESS → SSENISUB

Spelling the word "business" backwards is a simple form of symmetric encryption.

digiknow

The Enigma machine (see Figure 9.8) used by the Germans in World War II followed a system of symmetric encryption. The machine combined two forms of ciphers to code messages: *substitution cipher*, where letters in the alphabet are substituted for others (e.g., b = e), and *transposition cipher*, where letters were switched within words in some systematic way. The Germans changed the cipher daily so that the Allies could not break the code in a timely fashion. However, the Allied forces captured several Enigma machines and analyzed their function. Eventually, when codes were broken, the Allies were able to intercept and act on German military and diplomatic messages.

Figure 9.8
Enigma Machine

Create a code using symmetric encryption and encrypt a sentence from this page. See if a classmate can break your code.

Get Connected

To learn more about encryption methods, visit www.pearsoned.ca/businessconnections and follow the links.

channels. Also, each party you interact with would need its own unique key. Imagine having 100 000 customers, each with a key!

Asymmetric encryption overcomes these concerns by having two keys: a public key and a private key. The public key is known to both the sender and the recipient and is used by the sender to encrypt the message. The private key is only known by the recipient and is used to decrypt the message after it has travelled over the Internet. Each public key has only one private key associated with it, but it is next to impossible to figure out the private key because of the digital encryption methods used today. This method secures transmission of data so that, even if "sniffed" out by a hacker, the information would be useless. E-commerce usually uses 128-bit encryption; it would take tremendous computing power and time to crack the code.

9.5.2 Digital Envelopes

Asymmetric encryption of lengthy documents is time consuming at both the sending and receiving ends. One solution is to create a **digital envelope** by using two layers of encryption — symmetric and asymmetric — to protect the message as shown in Figure 9.9. First the message is encoded using symmetric encryption. Then the recipient's public key to decode the message is encrypted. The recipient first uses his or her private key to decrypt the symmetric key. Then the recipient uses the symmetric key to decrypt the message.

Figure 9.9
The Creation of a Digital Envelope

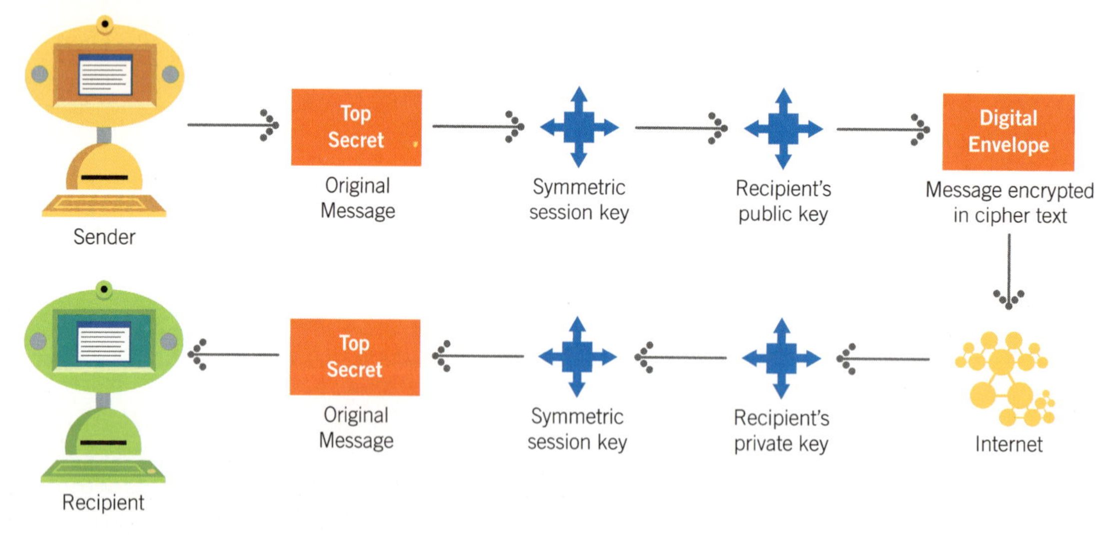

Digital envelopes provide a secure way to send and receive confidential information over the Internet to facilitate financial transactions.

9.5.3 Digital Certificates

Once the message has been encrypted using symmetric encryption and the key encrypted using public-key encryption, how does the recipient really know who sent the message? In a physical (bricks and mortar) store, a merchant might ask for several pieces of identification before accepting a cheque for payment of a purchase. But in the digital world, is there a way to know who is sending in an order and if online merchants are truly who they say they are?

Figure 9.10
A Digital Certificate

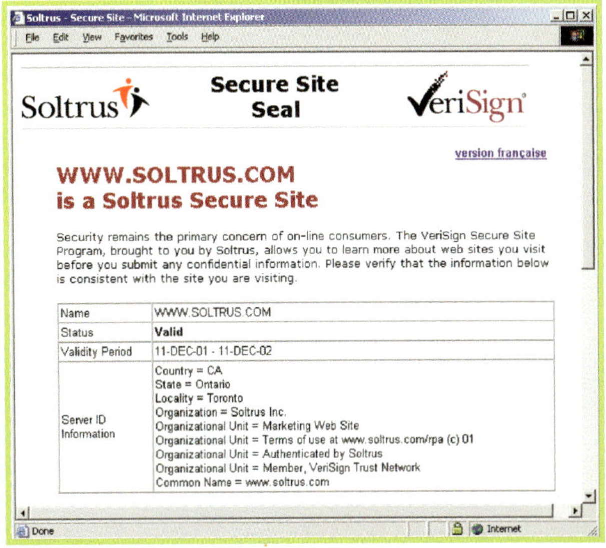

One method used today is the **Digital Certificate** (see Figure 9.10 for an example). This is a document (digital, of course) issued by a **certification authority (CA)** upon request by the sender of a message. A certification authority is a trusted third-party organization that issues digital certification verifying the identity of the individual granting the certificate. The certificate contains the sender's name, the public key, and other identification. The recipient uses the CA's public key to decrypt the message, ensuring that the CA issued it, and retrieves the sender's public key and identification so that he or she can send an encrypted reply. Once the session is over, the keys are discarded and the process has to start again.

9.5.4 Secure Sockets Layer

The most common method of securing the channels of communication for Internet messages is **Secure Sockets Layer (SSL)**, which combines encryption, digital envelopes, and digital certificates in each session to provide maximum security.

Figure 9.11
Security Padlock

When you connect to a Web site that has a secure server, you are entering a secure, negotiated session in which all information exchanged is encrypted. Your first indication that you are entering a secure site may be a dialog box that appears on the screen with the message "You are now entering a secure Internet connection. Continue?" depending on how your browser has been configured. When you have entered a secure site:

- the padlock at the bottom of the screen closes and turns yellow in colour (see Figure 9.11); and
- the http at the beginning of the URL changes to https (see Figure 9.12).

Figure 9.12
Address Line of a Secure Web Site

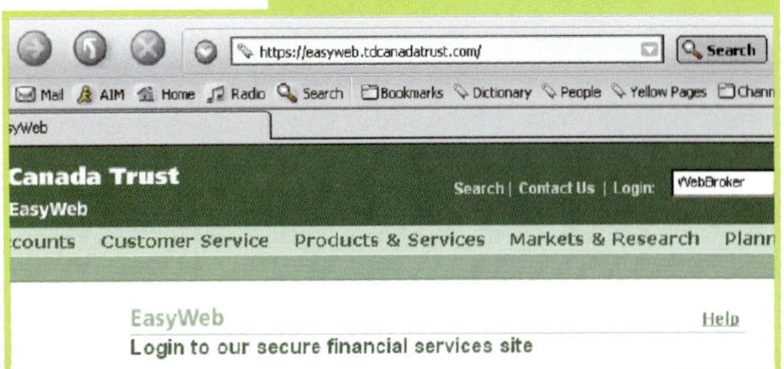

The URL of a secure site usually begins with https:// indicating that you have entered the secure portion of a server.

Your browser and the site server exchange digital certificates to authenticate each other's identity. They then determine if they have a strong enough level of encryption (typically in Canada, 128-bit encryption is required for secure transactions). On your client machine, this level of encryption is programmed into your Web browser; if you do not have strong enough encryption, you can download an upgraded version of your browser from Microsoft or Netscape. A session key is generated for that one session (after which it is discarded), then the transaction takes place (see Figure 9.13).

Figure 9.13
Secure Session Using SSL

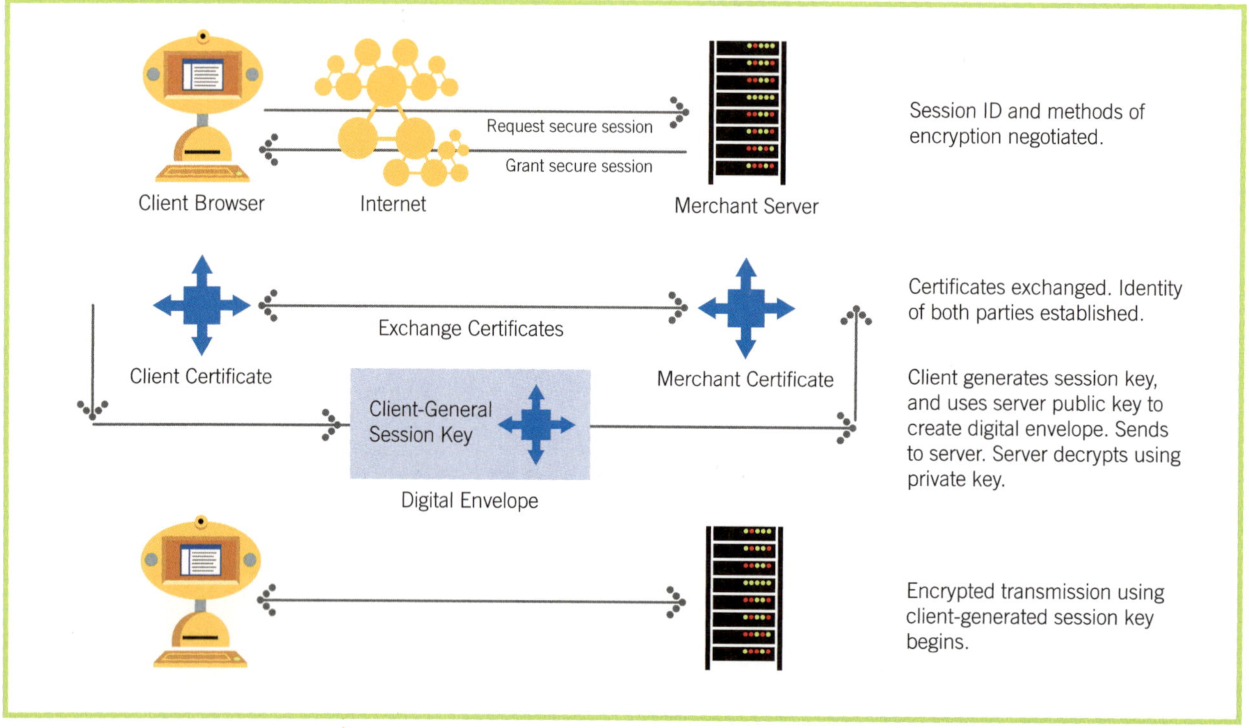

Certificates play a key role in using SSL to establish a secure communications channel.

Most reputable e-commerce sites will have a privacy policy available for customers to read. Most sites in Canada state that their servers and all transactions are protected by SSL technology to reassure customers of their privacy and security.

9.5.5 Firewalls

So far, we have only examined methods to secure the transmission of data from one party to another. As discussed earlier, one of the most vulnerable parts of an e-commerce transaction is at the server of the merchant and possibly that of the bank. A **firewall** is a software application that is designed to prevent unauthorized users from accessing your computer network. In the case of e-commerce, a firewall is put in place to prevent Internet users from gaining access to the Web server, which processes customer orders and maintains a database of valuable information. All messages entering or leaving the network are examined to ensure that they meet the security standards set by the organization before they are allowed in.

There are a number of methods used by firewalls to protect the server. **Packet filters** examine each packet entering or leaving the network to determine if they are destined for prohibited areas on the network. This method is, unfortunately, susceptible to spoofing (see Section 9.4.4) because it does not attempt to verify the identity of the sender.

Application gateways are another method a firewall can employ, where the message is filtered based on the application being requested rather than on the area of the network requested. This can improve system security but it may also slow down system performance.

Proxy servers intercept all traffic coming into and leaving a computer network. They are mainly used to limit Intranet users from accessing specific external Internet sites, but can act as a firewall as well by prohibiting access to a company's internal network.

9.5.6 Passwords

To further protect systems from unauthorized access, most networks require the entry of a user ID and a password (see Figure 9.14). The network then checks these against a database of all authorized users. If either the user ID or the password does not match the file, you are denied access to the system.

Figure 9.14
Network Login Screen

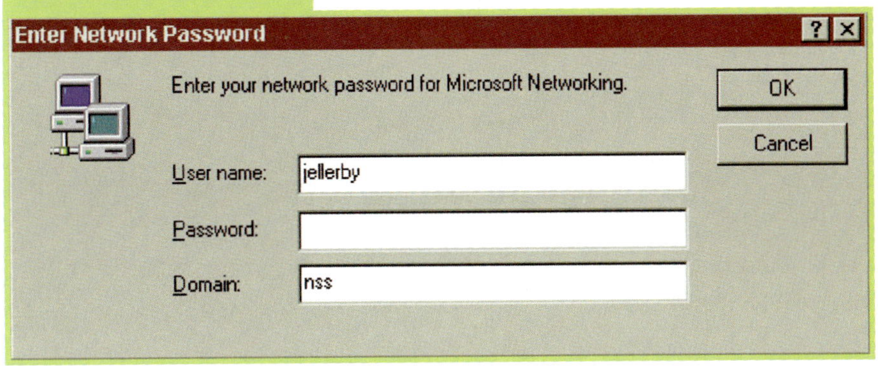

Network security is enhanced by requiring the user to enter his or her user name and password.

9.5.7 Anti-Virus Software

A very easy and relatively inexpensive way to protect both clients and servers from virus infestation, discussed in Section 9.4.1, is to install **anti-virus software** on your system. These programs scan files as they are downloaded from the Internet and as they are executed or opened on your computer and can be used to scan files that have been stored on your system to check for bugs that are not yet activated. The most common programs (see Figure 9.15) are made by McAfee and Symantec (Norton AntiVirus) and can be updated quickly and easily to ensure you have all the latest virus definitions loaded on your system.

Developing "safe" computing habits will prevent many possible mishaps from occurring. Be sure to scan all disks for potential viruses prior to use, especially if they are from an unknown source.

Figure 9.15
McAfee and Norton Anti-Virus Software

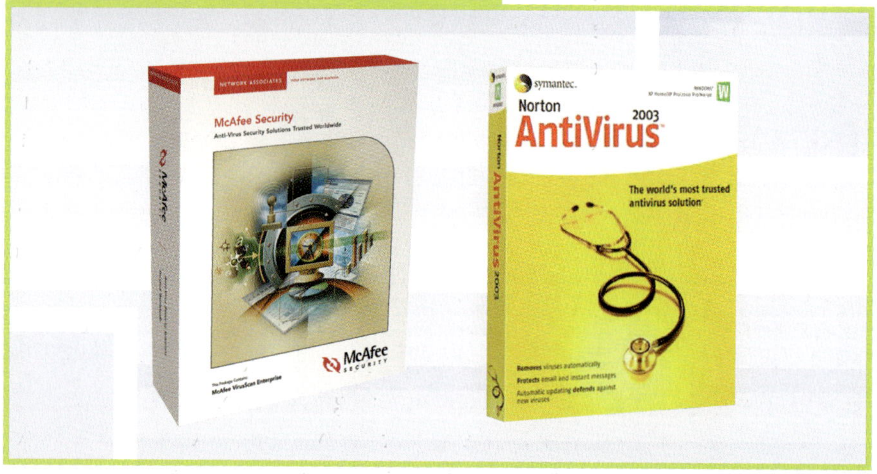

GETTING IT

1. What is the difference between plain text and cipher text as it relates to encryption? How would you recognize each type of text?
2. Write a paragraph to describe the difference between symmetric encryption and asymmetric encryption. Give examples to support your answer.
3. Describe two ways in which asymmetric encryption overcomes concerns related to symmetric encryption.
4. What is a digital certificate? Describe how a digital certificate helps an e-commerce site to confirm the identity of a customer and vice versa.
5. Describe the two ways to know you have entered a secure Web site.
6. Write a paragraph to describe how each of the following can help to protect your company from attacks:
   a. firewall
   b. proxy serve
   c. anti-virus software

9.6 Getting Your Company Ready for E-Commerce

Once you decide to offer goods or services on the Web, you have some organizational decisions to make. In-house? Outsource? Build your own? Hire designers? This section will examine these issues and look at the software and human resources you will need to get wired and get going.

9.6.1 Building a Web Site

To create a Web site that works, you will need an array of skilled people — designers, programmers, graphic artists, and management personnel — to oversee the production of the site. If you own a small business, or are new in the e-commerce arena, you most likely do not have this kind of talent in-house. Large organizations that have IT departments may, on the other hand, have skilled personnel available to perform those tasks.

You will also need the hardware and software to create the site. There are a number of excellent Web authoring tools available to help you to build sites from scratch. Alternatively, you can choose software packages that have pre-programmed templates that make it easy to get started by filling in the variable information that pertains to your company. You will have the opportunity to try some of these Web authoring tools yourself in Chapter 12.

There are positive and negative aspects of building your own Web site. On the positive side, you have control over the design and features that are built into the site and can add personal touches that give your site a distinctive flavour. However, there are also drawbacks to creating your site in-house. The cost of development can be substantial, depending on the features you decide to incorporate (e.g., shopping carts, credit card authorization and processing, inventory management, and so on). Some of these features may already be available. If your employees lack the necessary skills, you might be faced with the risk of errors and delays in entering the market, which translates into a loss of potential sales. You need to evaluate the positive and negative factors carefully.

9.6.2 To Host or Not To Host

"Hosting" an e-commerce site refers to the location and ultimate responsibility of operating a site on a Web server. When a company operates its own e-commerce site, it is taking the responsibility of operating the Web server, ensuring that the site is up and operating 24-7 (24 hours a day, 7 days a week), maintaining the communication lines, and updating the site as needed. This is a huge undertaking and requires your technical staff to perform these functions.

digiknow

How would you choose a Web host? In surveys conducted to determine the most important criterion for choosing a Web host, 71% of companies stated that customer service was most important. Although cost (50%) and flexibility (45%) are also important. A company is more likely to switch e-commerce hosts due to a lack of customer service or the Web host not being able to respond to the needs of the customer in a timely and accurate fashion.

(*Information Age* 2002)

Many organizations will **outsource**, or hire another company to provide, hosting services. Hundreds of companies have developed the expertise to host e-commerce sites, from small ISPs to large organizations (e.g., IBM). The larger hosting firms establish huge "server farms" in key locations around the country that host Web sites for thousands of companies. These hosting firms combine their technical expertise with the hardware required to ensure that your site is up and running at all times. One of the key factors in choosing a Web host is its ability to grow with you as your e-commerce needs expand. Many businesses start off small and choose their Web hosts accordingly. However, a Web host must be able to accommodate the needs of the company as orders increase and it expands its site to include more features.

The compromise solution sometimes chosen by e-commerce companies is to co-locate or purchase the Web server and locate it at a Web host location, thereby giving the companies control over the hardware and site contents. The Web host maintains the facility and communication lines, ensuring "anytime access" for customers.

9.6.3 Testing, Implementation, and Maintenance

Many people think that once the site has been designed and located on a Web server, the difficult tasks have been completed. This is not so. Extensive site testing must take place to ensure that the customer's experience is trouble free. Every possible choice the customer has at the site must be tested and examined for bugs; if problems are found, reprogramming is necessary. This requires the company to have systems analysts on site and computer programmers available to perform the task.

Once the site has been tested, it is time to go live. During the life of the site, extensive maintenance is required for breakdowns and repairs. The site needs to be continually checked, tested, and, where bugs are found, fixed. Also, with continual changes to product lines, prices, and site sponsors/advertisers, e-commerce sites are always in a state of flux. As a result, an organization needs the systems and technical personnel readily available to keep the site functional.

On the marketing side, a dedicated team of personnel is required to monitor the site, respond to customer feedback, ensure all links are functioning, update pages as necessary, and check prices. Monitoring of the competition is also needed to ensure that the organization is competitive in pricing and product offering compared with other e-commerce firms. The Web has given customers a greater opportunity to do price comparisons, so if your site is not reflecting the competitive environment, you will lose sales.

Jobs in an e-commerce environment are very different from those in their "bricks and mortar" counterparts. There is no such thing as the store being closed — with e-commerce, orders are being placed and processed any time of day. Many large e-tailers have orders being filled in their warehouses 24 hours a day, with personnel working on a shift basis at those locations. Smaller e-tailers, who also have physical retail locations, may process orders, as they are received, at the store during traditional business hours.

All of these advances mean that personnel must be more computer literate. They must be able to interact with the e-commerce system, send e-mail to customers, and keep up to date with technical advances as they occur in their organization. This may require extensive retraining of personnel when a company decides to "go digital," and this has the effect of adding stress to many employees as they adapt to the new working conditions. A more thorough examination of how computers have changed the conditions of work for employees will be covered in Chapter 10.

GETTING IT

Use appropriate software to create a bulletin board display on Frequently Asked Questions and Answers about E-Commerce Web sites. Incorporate all of the questions below and your answers. Add any additional questions that you think are important.

1. What factors should you take into consideration when making the decision to design your own e-commerce Web site?
2. What does hosting a Web site involve?
3. What is outsourcing? What are the key criteria when choosing a company to host your Web site?
4. What is the most important phase of a Web site's development and why?
5. How can an e-commerce site be compared to a living being?
6. Describe some of the necessary job skills for employees to possess in an e-commerce environment.

9.7 Web Sites that Work

Regardless of whether you have decided to design your own Web site or outsource its design, what must you take into consideration to get it up and running? In the early days of the Internet and e-commerce, just setting up a home page was enough. Not so today. Today's sites are interactive, personal, and keep the customer coming back to make more purchases. So, how do you make your site sizzle?

9.7.1 Top 10 Ways to Make Sites Sizzle

1. *Plan, plan, plan.* Well-planned Web sites will help an organization succeed online. Decide what you want your Web site to be able to do:

Provide information? Handle e-mail questions? Allow customers to order online/offline? Process credit card transactions? Think of your customers from an online perspective. What do your customers know, or what do they need to know when they log into your site? How are you able to help them find it? A Web site should be more than a static, unchanging marketing brochure; it should be an interactive, living vehicle for product information, prices, and services. Once you have your plan, stick to it in terms of Web site design.

2. *Integrate your online and offline strategies.* A successful e-commerce site will help the organization meet its overall business objectives. As such, the Web site must be seen to be part of an integrated strategy, not a stand-alone operation. This means that the e-commerce site is a joint responsibility of IT and Marketing. By tying together your online and offline activities, you make it possible for shoppers who use multiple channels to make purchases (i.e., buy at both your "bricks" and "clicks" locations). It has been shown that customers who use multiple channels spend up to 36% more than those who use single channels (*Computer Weekly* 2002). For example, you might consider having an online kiosk in your stores to answer routine customer inquiries regarding product availability in order to free up sales personnel to assist customers with other needs. This integration will help you to get more value from your online presence.
3. *Involve users in site development.* Your customers are your best source of feedback regarding the design and usability of a site. Have representatives from your target audience test your site and watch their reactions carefully. E-commerce sites cannot afford to be confusing, boring, or frustrating. Once the site is operational, survey your test group to determine how satisfied they are with their shopping experience. Use these data to improve your site in order to retain that important customer base.
4. *Keep it clean and navigable.* E-commerce sites that are clean and uncluttered in appearance and easily navigated are more user friendly. Many consumers will immediately reject sites that have poor service or design. Be sure to write for the Web. An e-commerce site should:
   - have limited text on any one screen;
   - have clear links to pages for those who need them;
   - use correct grammar and spelling (always, always, always do grammar and spelling checks!);
   - be simple — blinking text, busy backgrounds, repetitive animations, and glaring graphics are a turn-off to many would-be purchasers;
   - be consistent in terms of design; all pages of the site should look like they are related (use fonts, graphical elements, colours, buttons, and menus to achieve this consistency);

- be easy to use; visitors should know within a few seconds how the site works (using common terms and buttons, e.g., About Us, Contact Us, will help); and
- use hyperlinks instead of pull-down menus wherever possible, since menus are difficult for some people to navigate.

ON THE CASE

Is Your Site Truly Accessible?

Based on Paul Bonner, "And Web Sites for All," *PC Magazine*, May 7, 2002.

Many users of technology face obstacles that most of us wouldn't think about — but Web site designers must in order to ensure that their site is accessible.

For the visually impaired computer user, navigating Web sites can be a challenge. Those who use screen-reader-equipped browsers to surf the Web have the number of links announced verbally to them when they go to a site. The Amazon.com home page, for example, has 189 links, each with a different set of keyboard commands. The user would have to listen for the link they want and press the associated keys to go there. How frustrating would that be?

The number of links is only one impediment for Internet users who have disabilities. Pop-up windows also present a challenge to a user who is unable to see because they interfere with the user's screen reader. Colour-blind users are unable to navigate sites that require the user to click on colour-coded links/buttons and may have difficulty distinguishing between text and background. Visually impaired visitors to sites, who need to increase font sizes are limited by sites that specify absolute font sizes in their layouts. And, hearing-impaired visitors are frustrated by sites that have audio content but provide no captions or transcripts, and by sites that give only audio instructions to indicate what visitors have to do to use the site.

There are devices available to assist users with physical disabilities: screen magnifiers, audio e-mail, talking browsers. Unfortunately, many sites incorporate features that make these technologies hard to use.

Creating a Web site that takes these factors into account is the "right" thing to do. Many individuals whose mobility is limited have found that the Internet and Web have allowed them access to the world outside again, and given them the ability to interact with businesses and government agencies on the same level as people without disabilities.

Questions

1. This case discusses many issues regarding "accessibility." Explain how accessibility is defined as it relates to Internet browsing.
2. Describe four challenges a visually impaired Internet user faces when browsing the Web.
3. According to the case, describe how the Internet has "levelled the playing field" for users with physical disabilities.

Get Connected

Analysis tools are available to assess the accessibility of your Web site. Visit www.pearsoned.ca/businessconnections to learn more about these services. Create a list of the types of tools available. Compare your list with a classmate's.

> **Get Connected**
>
> Search engines come and go, but you can assess available search engines by going to www.pearsoned.ca/businessconnections. Select three search engines from the list provided and perform a search for "e-commerce." How many hits did your search produce? Upon closer inspection, how many of the first 10 hits are for commercial sites? How much overlap is there between search engines on the first 10 hits? Compare your findings with those of your classmates. What conclusions can be drawn from this exercise?

5. *Keep new technology in mind.* As discussed in earlier chapters, new technological advances are making Internet use available from a wide variety of devices. PDAs, cell phones, and all other forms of mobile communication devices are hooking up to the Web in droves. If your site does not work for these mobile users, they will just leave. Web site designers must consider the different device sizes, screen displays, speed, etc. in their development plans.

   Another technological issue is that of Web searching. E-commerce businesses recognize that many Web searchers only read the first one or two pages of hits in a search. After researching your target audience's Web searching habits (search engines and directories), you should develop a description that best matches your company and submit it to relevant search engines for inclusion in their index. It pays to be in the right location.

6. *Not too much, not too little.* Information, that is. But how much is just right? You must ensure that there is enough product information on the site to make customers feel comfortable buying online.
   - Reduce the number of screens a customer has to go through to check out, offer more than one payment option (see e-commerce payment systems in Section 9.3), and be sure to give customers a final sales receipt that can be printed for future reference, indicating the total amount of the purchase.
   - Always be sure to check any facts or figures you publish online. Accuracy is of the utmost importance for building customer confidence in your site.
   - Always include contact information — e-mail addresses, phone and fax numbers, and the address of your physical location. This, too, builds customer confidence that your company really does exist.
   - A technical consideration relating to content is how much you put online that requires broadband (high speed) Internet services. Much of the online world is still operating on narrow band (dial up) services that take longer to load pages if they are too graphic intensive.

7. *Personalize your site.* **Personalizing** not only means recognizing customers when they log in, but having a site that can react to the customer's choices and offer built-in guidance based on those choices. For example, if shopping for a motorcycle online, the customer might select a particular model. The site would then offer only the options that apply to that model, thus reducing the time needed to browse the options and make a selection. Many customers abandon complex transactions on the Web before completion.

8. *Test, test, test.* As stated earlier, having customers involved in the design stage is a must. So is having their input during the testing phase. They will tell you if your site is working well or not. This test phase is not one event, but an ongoing process. You should test, tune

up, and monitor your site from all angles and locations — both inside the firewall and outside as well.

9. *Make sure goods get to your customers.* Check addresses entered by customers against postal databases to ensure correct street names and postal codes have been provided. These databases are readily available for use in the e-commerce community. Also, make sure the address matches the one you already have for repeat customers, so that your customer database is as accurate as possible.
10. *Measure your site's effectiveness.* How many new customers is the site attracting? What are people doing at your site: browsing or buying? How many hits are you getting and are they going elsewhere without looking beyond the home page? These and more questions must be answered to determine if your site is doing its job attracting the traffic and whether the right people are using the site.

GETTING IT

Use appropriate software to create a notebook page on "Web Sites that Work." Record each question below and your answer to it. Once your teacher has approved the page, file it in your notebook.

1. What does it mean to integrate your online and offline strategies in e-commerce?
2. How can you involve potential customers in the development and testing of your Web site?
3. List and describe five ways to keep your site clean and navigable.
4. How are new mobile devices affecting the design of e-commerce sites?
5. How do you know you have the right amount of information on your site?
6. What does personalizing your site involve?
7. How can you measure your site's effectiveness and why is this important?

ON THE CASE

How Easy Is Your Site to Use?

Based on "Simplicity is priceless," *Information Age*, April 2002.

Internet usability guru Jakob Nielsen has critiqued the home pages of 50 of the best known e-commerce sites, looking for positive aspects and those that could be improved upon with careful planning. Here are two of his critiques:

Amazon.com:

- The site categorizes a vast selection of products while still maintaining an uncluttered appearance on home page.

ON THE CASE

(continued)

- It uses examples of its best sellers to draw users into a particular product area.
- Help is located in the top right-hand corner — a location where customers tend to expect it to be.
- The site is optimized for personalization — in other words, when you are a registered Amazon customer, your preferences are retained in a "cookie" when you log in, so the site "speaks" to you by name. This is great for returning customers, but can be confusing to new users.

Microsoft.com:

- The site has an attractive, clean layout.
- It is very easy to navigate, so users don't get frustrated trying to find their way around.
- The site lacks a single "voice" and "tone" — the way in which it speaks to the customer varies depending on which of the company's products or technologies you click on, causing confusion.
- The text is too technical and serious, aimed at the technology professional — some visitors, such as game enthusiasts, might feel alienated.

Questions

1. Using the *Top 10 Ways to Make Sites Sizzle* (in Section 9.7.1) as a guide, evaluate at least three Canadian e-commerce sites that you locate on the Web. Create a chart (see headings below) listing the 10 criteria down the first column and create a column in the chart for each site you evaluate. Rate each criterion on a scale of 1 to 5, with 1 being poor and 5 being excellent.

Criteria	E-Commerce Site 1	E-Commerce Site 2	E-Commerce Site 3

2. Compare your findings with those of your classmates to compile a list of the Top 5 Canadian E-Tail Sites, based on their ease of use.

9.8 The Impact of E-Commerce on the Competitive Environment

To understand how e-commerce has changed the competitive landscape in business, we must first examine the **forces of competition** (see Figure 9.16) in the traditional business environment.

Imagine you are the owner of a retail clothing store in your town, offering fashions specifically geared to the teen market. You will face five possible threats to the success of your store (Porter 1980).

1. *Threats from existing competitors.* All other retail clothing stores that have product lines appealing to teens will be **direct competitors.** The number of direct competitors will depend in part on geography, that is, how easily your target audience can get to your store. For example, the geographic scope for a retail shop may be much larger in Vancouver, with its mass transit system for people in the suburbs, than in Swift Current, where customers are largely dependent on personal motor vehicles for transportation.
2. *Threats from substitute products.* All other retail clothing stores and department stores that sell a variety of clothing products sell substitutes for your specialized line of clothes. Also, new styles and trends in clothing are threats if you do not change your product lines with the times.
3. *Threat of new entrants to the market.* How many stores like yours are in the area? Is the market big enough to support other players? How difficult is it to set up business in your area? Are suppliers available to support another store? And, how loyal are your customers to your store? If other companies come into your region, you will face stiffer competition. In this scenario, prices tend to be driven down to meet the competition, thus reducing potential profits.
4. *Power of buyers.* Your target audience (i.e., teens) will be more price sensitive and will purchase elsewhere if your product is not unique, if it is expensive in relation to their incomes, and if quality and durability are not particularly important to them.
5. *Power of suppliers.* The companies that supply the clothing you sell can exert power over you with threats to raise prices or reduce the quality of the goods and services you buy. If you don't want to raise your prices, they have, in effect, the power to squeeze profits out of your operation. This group tends to have more power if there are few other companies from which to choose and the products are unique.

Figure 9.16
Porter's Five Forces Model of Competition

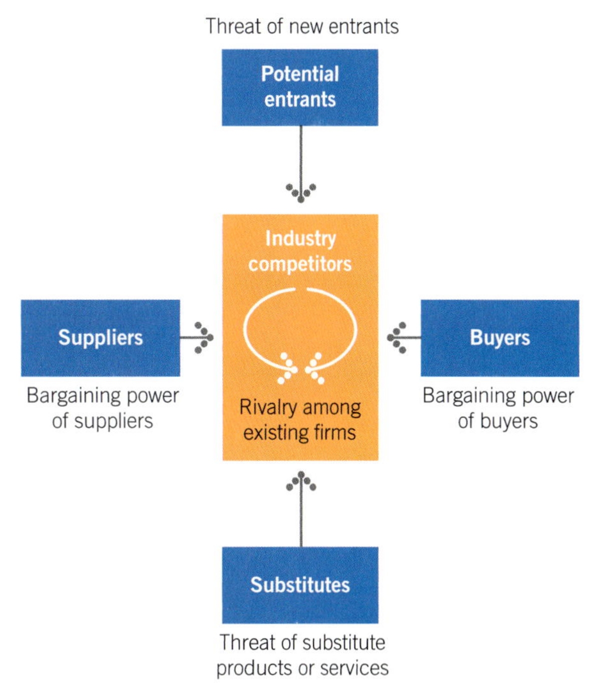

The Internet and e-commerce have had a significant impact on this traditional model of competition. Let us examine some of these changes.

- *New market entrants via e-commerce.* Some industries have seen e-commerce providers enter the market and completely bypass traditional channels of distribution. For example, the music industry has been affected negatively by Web sites that allow users to download music directly to their PC — no CD has changed hands!

  Other forms of electronic media have had even more disastrous effects on current players in the marketplace. Sales of printed encyclopedias, for example, have suffered greatly from the introduction of CD-ROM versions, for which parents will gladly pay $75 compared with $2000 for a set of hardcover books.
- *E-commerce can level the playing field for new entrants.* Size matters less in the world of e-commerce. A company's Web site is an online brochure. The better it looks, the better your company will be perceived by the buying public. Small players have as good a chance of being noticed as large e-tailers in the online world.
- *E-commerce and the world as its market.* Geographic boundaries no longer define competitive markets in the world of e-commerce. Consumers now have global access to information regarding products and prices and are better informed. This effortless "comparison shopping" has increased price competition among e-tailers and retailers alike. Consumers can also save on provincial sales taxes if their purchases are made in one province and shipped to another.

  On the other hand, the Internet has allowed e-commerce providers to differentiate their products and services from others and to get that message out in a very cost-effective manner.
- *Power of B2B buyers is increased.* Using the Internet, manufacturing firms in industrial markets have collaborated to combine their purchases for greater quantity discounts and to increase their bargaining power. As a result, suppliers who increase prices risk the wrath of a number of buyers.

Businesses use the Internet and its associated technologies to differentiate their products and services and offer more high-value products to gain a competitive edge. For example, chapters.indigo.ca uses the Internet to offer a wider array of books, at lower costs, than traditional bookstores. The value-added part of their Web site is the reviews and the personalization of the site, in terms of showing other books that might appeal based on the shoppers' choices during the visit.

Other firms that specialize in limited product lines can use the Internet to get their message to consumers through search engine listings, directory listings, and by getting involved in online forums that appeal to particular market segments. Being small once meant that your product appealed to a very minor segment of the population. Now, the Internet provides the e-tailer the opportunity to appeal to countless times their previous market potential.

Businesses are just starting to tap into the potential of the Internet and e-commerce. As the Web matures and businesses build their strategies to combine both online and offline product offerings, consumers can only benefit.

ON THE CASE

Beyond Borders

Based on "Simplicity is priceless," *Information Age*, April 2002.

As mentioned throughout this chapter, e-commerce opens up virtually limitless possibilities to do business with customers and suppliers from anywhere in the world. When engaging in international business activities, organizations need to be aware of customs regulations and international trade agreements enforced by the governments of countries in which business is taking place.

Duty (a specific tax imposed on imports by the customs authority of a country) affects the cost of goods imported or exported and is usually paid for by the receiver of the goods. Duties are based on the value of the goods and/or the weight or quantity and can differ based on the type of item being imported.

Traditionally, countries that trade many goods and services regularly have developed trade agreements to allow business to flow more quickly across borders. Usually, trade agreements are limited to specific types of goods. Canada, the United States, and Mexico, which have strong trading relationships, have such agreements in place including the **North American Free Trade Agreement (NAFTA)**. In 2001, Canadian customs and tax rules increased the number of free-trade zones. These zones allow foreign companies to bring goods into Canada, perform work to transform those goods, and then ship them to other countries without paying duty or tax on the components. Only the final customer pays taxes to the Canadian government.

Questions

1. Using the Internet, determine what regulations and duties would affect the following transactions. Use appropriate software to create a two-column answer sheet that lists the statements below and the regulations/duties you located.
   - A Canadian consumer purchases a live iguana from an exotic pet e-commerce site in Florida.
   - A consumer in the United States purchases a novel from a small book e-tailer in Victoria, BC.
   - A database development company in Calgary employs a programmer in Vilnius, Lithuania, to create source code, with all work to be conducted via the Internet.

Get Connected

To find out more about exporting goods to other countries, visit www.pearsoned.ca/businessconnections. Create a list of the types of information the sites listed there recommend you investigate if you plan to conduct international transactions.

GETTING IT

1. Describe the five forces of competition in any market.
2. Explain the impact that e-commerce has had on direct competitors.
3. Describe how geographic boundaries have changed with the entrance of e-commerce product and service providers.
4. Explain how you think small e-tailers can compete with the larger counterparts in the world of e-commerce.

IT's A Wrap

Key Terms in This Chapter

anti-virus software (p. 257)
application gateways (p. 257)
asymmetric encryption (p. 254)
Business to Business (B2B) (p. 237)
Business to Consumer (B2C) (p. 235)
cash (p. 244)
certificate authority (CA) (p. 255)
cheque (p. 244)
clearing system (p. 244)
community provider (p. 243)
Consumer to Consumer (C2C) (p. 239)
content provider (p. 242)
cracker (p. 250)
credit card (p. 245)
debit card (p. 244)
Denial of Service (DoS) (p. 252)
digital cash (p. 246)
Digital Certificate (p. 255)
digital envelope (p. 254)
digital wallet (p. 246)
direct competitor (p. 267)
duty (p. 269)
e-business (p. 235)
e-commerce (p. 234)
e-tailer (p. 242)
encryption (p. 253)
file virus (p. 249)
firewall (p. 256)
forces of competition (p. 266)
hacker (p. 250)
hosting (p. 259)
Interac (p. 247)
legal tender (p. 244)
macro virus (p. 249)
market creator (p. 243)
m-commerce (p. 239)
North American Free Trade Agreement (NAFTA) (p. 269)
outsource (p. 260)
packet filter (p. 257)
Person to Person (P2P) (p. 239)
personalizing (p. 264)
portal (p. 242)
proxy server (p. 257)
script virus (p. 249)
Secure Sockets Layer (SSL) (p. 255)
service providers (p. 243)
sniffer (p. 252)
spoofing (p. 251)
stored value (p. 246)
subscription site (p. 240)
symmetrical encryption (p. 253)
transaction broker (p. 243)
virus (p. 249)
Web portal (p. 240)

1. Create a list of competencies you have acquired through your work in this chapter.
2. Update your portfolio to include examples of your work from this chapter.

Know It!

3. Electronically create a chart that compares and contrasts the five main forms of e-commerce.
4. Explain how Web portals have had to change, in terms of the products and services they offer, in order to remain competitive.

Know It!

5. What is meant by "bricks and clicks" in terms of e-commerce? Explain why these players are so successful in the market.
6. What payment method has the most potential for growth? Explain why.
7. List the positive and negative aspects of designing and hosting your own e-commerce site.

Do It!

8. Use the Internet search strategies learned in this course and the information provided in this chapter regarding e-commerce sites to locate three vendors of the same model of DVD player. Rate their sites in terms of:
   a. ease of use **b.** payment options **c.** amount of information about the DVD player
9. Locate three articles from online newspapers or magazines that discuss the issue of hacking. Summarize these articles in terms of the three "hats" hackers could wear.
10. From your readings in this chapter, electronically create two flowcharts that depict the process of using symmetric and asymmetric encryption in an e-commerce transaction.
11. Research the features of mobile devices that can perform e-commerce transactions and electronically prepare a chart to compare their features. This chart should be of assistance to a Web site developer in designing a site that works for those devices.
12. Use appropriate software to develop a list of five guidelines to follow if you plan to conduct e-commerce internationally.

Analyze It!

13. In small groups, discuss whether the following statement is true: "The Internet has made it possible for more people to purchase goods and services online than ever before." Come to a consensus on your answer and report your ideas to the rest of the class.
14. Visual impairment is one accessibility issue for Internet users. Identify three other accessibility issues and research them on the Web. Present your findings orally to the class.
15. Of the four main revenue-generating strategies open to e-commerce sites, which one is poised to make the biggest gains in the future and why? Input your answer in paragraph format.
16. In small groups, debate the need for all the security measures that e-commerce sites incorporate into their operation.
17. E-commerce sites that maximize personalization have created massive databases that contain all your personal information. Use appropriate software to prepare an essay that focuses on the privacy issues this raises.
18. Identify at least three products or services that will not face stiff competition from online counterparts and give the reasons for your choices. Share your answers with your classmates.

CHAPTER

Business in a Wired World

10

On completion of this chapter, you will be able to:

- explain how business functions (production, human resources, sales, and marketing) can be affected by information technology;
- explain operational terms related to information technology;
- identify and describe emerging management information technologies and systems;
- forecast trends in conducting business electronically;
- discuss social, economic, ethical, and political implications of the use of information technology; and
- identify and describe ways that e-business has changed the way we work.

The introduction of technology into the business world has had a dramatic impact. Every facet of a modern organization is touched in some way by information technology. This chapter will explore the impact of information technology on business operations and look specifically at the following areas:

- Product Development and Design
- Production of Goods
- Electronic Marketing
- Marketing Communication the IT Way
- Distribution
- Pricing
- Accounting for Business
- Managing the Business
- The Human Factor: Assessing the Impact of Technology on People

Introduction to Chapter Projects

Recall that the Chapter Projects are introduced at the beginning and are to be completed as you work through the chapter. Your teacher will provide you with assessment and evaluation criteria.

CHAPTER PROJECT I

After completing the exercises in this chapter, you should have a better understanding of the role of technology in the workplace. Revisit your *Information Technology Growth Plan* or *Education Plan* created in Chapter 1 and revise it to reflect this new information.

CHAPTER PROJECT II

Select one of the following sectors: manufacturing, banking, retail, or government. Use the Internet and personal interviews with family or friends to create a slide presentation that compares the way this sector operated 20 years ago with the way it operates today as it relates to information technology. In your presentation, describe how individual jobs have changed, as well as how the structure of organizations has changed. Use visual images if available. Cite all sources used, including interviews.

For thousands of years, people have made goods and provided services, first in exchange for other goods and services (barter) and then for money. Producing goods or providing a service for sale involves a number of *steps* in a business organization. Over the years, little has changed in the steps involved (see Figure 10.1).

Figure 10.1
Steps in the Business Organization

Design the product* → Produce the product → Market the product → Account for the cost to produce and sell the product → Manage the process and the people → Repeat

*The product can be a good or a service.

Which of these steps in the business organization do you think would be the most interesting one to be involved in? Why?

What has changed is the *way* that we perform the tasks in each of the steps outlined in Figure 10.1 and *where* each task is performed. We are moving, in many ways, toward the creation of **virtual enterprises** in which e-business customers, distributors and suppliers of goods and services, and staff work on a specific job or project from a number of different locations and as members of different organizations. Organizational structures and jobs are changing along with this new, more project-oriented approach to doing business.

As explained in Chapter 9, e-business involves electronic transactions within a company that do not involve an exchange of payment. Examples of such transactions include internal employee communications and automated inventory control systems. This section will examine the new world of e-business and how it has affected each of the steps in the business cycle.

10.1 Product Development and Design

Competitive pressures in the 21st century have manufacturers vying to be the first to bring new products to market. Product development time has shrunk from years to months and the biggest reason for this decrease has been the use of **Computer Aided Design (CAD)** programs. CAD allows designers to create 3-D models (see Figure 10.2) and simulations that possess the "physical" characteristics of life-size products (e.g., weight, volume) and can be rotated and viewed from any angle. Simulations can apply imaginary pressure to a model from various directions to determine how the actual item will withstand it. For example, engineers can determine how strong the beams need to be to keep a tall building standing in the event of a natural disaster.

Figure 10.2
3-D CAD Model

Identify two other products not mentioned in the text that might be improved by using CAD programs in their design and explain why.

And automobile designers can test the crash resistance of new models before they ever leave the designer's PC.

CAD technology, which has improved in capability and has decreased dramatically in price, can now be installed on the newer generations of PCs, reducing the hardware costs as well. Today, small- and medium-sized businesses can realistically afford to purchase the technology — a must in today's competitive marketplace.

The benefits of using CAD technology are clear to large manufacturers. According to Hawkes Ocean Technology, a manufacturer of submarines, the use of CAD software has "cut our design costs by one-third. And we have literally bypassed the prototype stage. Our products have gone straight into service. That's quite extraordinary" (Salkever 2002). The use of CAD programs has also allowed designers to "think outside the box" and work with shapes and models that would have been very difficult when using the 2-D methods of old. Just look at the curvy Colgate brand toothbrushes (see Figure 10.3) at your local drugstore.

Figure 10.3
Curved-Style Colgate Toothbrush

Explain how Colgate designers would use a CAD program to develop a toothbrush like this one.

CAD's major impact has been in the area of collaboration. In the past, either extensive travel was required to bring interested stakeholders to where the designs were created, or the drawn designs had to be sent to the stakeholders. By having the design team members collaborate via their respective workstations, errors are caught in the early stages and costly production retrofits (that is, changes to address problems or needs that arise) are avoided. Geographic location is also no longer a barrier to the members of work teams in the Internet age and in virtual enterprises. By having Web-enabled design tools, designers can outsource parts of the design process when local talent is not available and multidiscipline teams can collaborate efficiently in the creation and use of designs.

One of the technical impediments to collaborating on projects in the past was the inability to send huge files over inadequate networks. Increased bandwidth and wide area networks (WANs) have changed all that. Security was also a concern. If a company's designs were intercepted by a competitor, the company could lose its advantage. Today's methods of encryption and digital signatures (see Chapter 9) have reduced such concerns.

Overall, the use of technology in the design process has dramatically reduced the product development cycle and the time to bring a product to market. Using the Internet in all phases of the product life cycle, and involving manufacturers, suppliers, and customers in the process, can also help with producing better-quality customized products that meet the specific demands of individual customers and get those products to market more quickly.

IT In Action ▸▸

Rex: The New Breed of Electronic Organizer

Source: Rob Walker, "Time to ditch the old development recipe," *Electronic Engineering Times*, May 4, 1998, n. 1005: p. 49(1).

The Rolodex Rex is a credit card-sized personal information device that holds up to 3000 names, addresses, and telephone numbers. It also has an appointment book and notebook function.

The features of this device are not so unique; personal digital assistants have been around for years now. What makes this product unique from a design standpoint is the collaborative process undertaken to produce it. A small software company by the name of Starfish Software in California came up with the idea and application. Citizen Watch Co. of Japan contributed the advanced display mechanism and handled the high-volume manufacturing of the product's hardware components. And finally, Franklin Electronic Publishers of Burlington, New Jersey, markets the product under the highly respected Rolodex brand within their established channels of distribution.

Small players in many markets lack the funding, marketing, manufacturing, and distribution channels necessary to bring their innovative ideas to market. Larger companies sometimes lack the entrepreneurial spirit that champions new ideas like the Rex. When small and large companies collaborate on innovative ideas, new products have more opportunity to be launched in the marketplace.

Questions

1. Describe the functions and features of the Rex.
2. Explain the reasons for the collaborative approach to product development in this case. In particular, what competencies did each partner bring to the process?

It is difficult, however, to quantify the impact on an organization's bottom line or profit as a result of implementing this technology. Yes, sales representatives are able to tell customers about future new products with more certainty as to their look, feel, and durability. Is this a guarantee of sales? Not necessarily. It depends on how fast competitors are moving as well.

10.1.1 Impact on People

As we will see in the pages to follow, the introduction of CAD technology into the operation of a business has a tremendous impact on its employees. Hawkes Ocean Technology, referred to earlier, reduced its engineering staff from 10 to 3 people while maintaining overall productivity in terms of the number of designs produced (Salkever 2002).

With fewer people to complete the actual design work, dramatic shifts take place in the design process. Design teams can now involve a wider variety of people who often do not work in the same area of the company. Intranets and other forms of electronic communication allow the lines of communication to be kept open among team members — often one of the most difficult tasks in teamwork.

GETTING IT

1. Explain what CAD has done for companies vying for market position.
2. Describe how 3-D CAD can help bypass steps in the development of new products.
3. Explain how CAD has levelled the competitive playing field for big and small companies alike.
4. Describe the three ways technology has reduced the geographic barriers faced by companies with regard to designing better products.
5. Describe the technical impediments faced by product designers in the past. Create a document that illustrates how these compare with the new ways that they do business today.
6. Describe the shift in personnel involved in the product design process now compared with the past.

ON THE CASE

Building Better Buildings

Source: Jane Black, "Stronger, Smarter Buildings in Less Time," *Business Week Online*, July 16, 2002.

When most people think of Computer Aided Design (CAD), they think in terms of the use of computer software to design goods destined for the consumer or industrial marketplace. What about real estate?

Architects have been using computers to design buildings for over 30 years. Early versions of design and drafting software allowed architects to create drawings previously completed by hand. The introduction of the PC into engineering departments in the 1980s expanded this process exponentially. The latest generation of PCs and software that renders 3D designs has revolutionized the process once again.

"Drawings of a simple four- to five-storey building might total 200 to 300 documents 2 feet by 3 feet [60 cm by 90 cm] each. There are a lot of opportunities for someone to make a mistake," says Huw Roberts, an architect and marketing director for an American software company. The power of CAD software lies in the coordination of drawings;

where links are established, a change made on one drawing will be reflected on others.

By having designs created digitally, developers can make better plans for the delivery and placement of supplies during the construction phase, thus reducing costly delays. Sir John Egan, chairman of a British government task force on construction, estimates that "30% of the cost of any building could be reduced or eliminated by avoiding what should be foreseeable inefficiencies during construction."

From a marketing perspective, CAD has facilitated the promotion of products before they ever leave the drawing board. For example, Ford Field, the new home of the Detroit Lions in the NFL, used 3D simulations in their sales presentations; the simulations "demonstrated" the view from each and every seat in the house. As a result, Skyboxes sold out in record time.

Architects played a pivotal role in saving lives in the September 11, 2001, attack at the Pentagon. Rescuers used sophisticated 3D models created for the contractors who had recently remodelled that section of the building, to avoid walls and passages that had been damaged in the attack. Over 50 architects, engineers, and planners were involved in the rescue effort.

Today, architects are creating lifelike, interactive models of buildings. In fact, the new buildings slated to be built on the former World Trade Center location in New York City have been created in 3D, so that all interested stakeholders can visualize the development prior to the start of the construction.

Questions

1. Describe the ways that building designers and contractors are using technology to build better buildings.
2. Look around your school. Identify areas where you could use CAD technology to improve it.

10.2 Production of Goods

Once a product such as the toothbrush shown in Figure 10.3 has been designed using one of the many CAD programs available today, the results are fed into a **Computer Aided Manufacturing (CAM)** program. CAM software controls the manufacture of the components that make up the final product. This software also helps to solve the tolerance and layout problems of manufacturing equipment and plant design to make for more efficient manufacturing of the components. In the manufacture of electronic parts, for example, CAM software takes the design and translates it directly into a template for etching circuits onto a chip.

IT In Action

Giving Sports a Winning Edge

Alex Salkever, "Sports Gear Goes Geek," *BusinessWeek Online*, July 16, 2002.

What do golf, cycling, tennis, and running have in common? Technology, of course. Many sporting goods manufacturers use technology to design products that give their users a competitive edge. Look at the 2002 Tour de France, for example. Cyclist Lance Armstrong competed, with a myriad of high-tech gear in his arsenal, for his fourth title in this gruelling month-long event. On his wrist was an altimeter made by Seiko and Nike that comprised a digital compass, a military-grade altimeter that measures distance travelled uphill and altitude, a temperature sensor, and a temperature alarm, all encased in a titanium-urethane cover and wristband for comfort. His sunglasses (by Oakley), designed specifically for him, were precision molded to thousandths of an inch for maximum aerodynamics. Let us not forget his bike, built with a super strong carbon fiber-epoxy bicycle frame designed to minimize wind resistance with teardrop shaped tubing. The frame weighed only 2.27 pounds (just over 1 kg).

Product designers and engineers use CAD and CAM to manufacture such high-tech products. The technology available today allows engineers to design a product and create a precision prototype in much the same way as we print pages from a word processor. These wax or light plastic models can be tested and feedback programmed into the computer, all within one working day — not the three to four months it used to take for the same process not many years ago.

By producing such quick turnaround, companies are becoming more efficient and this is good news for their overall profit picture. Greater product variety as a result of introducing many new product models to the market helps to generate increased sales. There is always something new coming out on the market.

Questions

1. Explain how technology is giving athletes a "winning edge."
2. Explain how the product development and design process has been shortened and what edge it gives companies that employ CAD technology.

Robots also play an important role in modern manufacturing facilities. The word **robot** was taken from the Czech word *robota*, meaning forced labour; it expresses what we have primarily used these mechanical devices for in manufacturing facilities: to perform repetitive manual tasks. This computer-controlled machine responds to sensory input (visual images, sounds, touch, heat) or other external control devices, processes the input through a CPU (central processing unit), and sends its output to its joints, arms, fingers, sensor controls, wheels, etc., to complete a task programmed in its memory. In essence a robot is a computer; its four main components are input, processing, storage, and output. Industrial robots can be designed to react to infrared light, to rotate their joints 360 degrees, and to perform other tasks that are not humanly possible.

From a managerial perspective, robots offer many advantages. In spite of their high initial cost, robots work 24 hours a day, 7 days a week (24/7) without breaks, food, or sleep. They also never go on strike. Robots can improve overall productivity and product quality because they can perform repetitive tasks without getting tired, bored, or careless. As a result, companies have been quick to make the investment to have robots perform such tasks as welding and painting. Costs can be reduced significantly in factories that are 100% automated, where lighting is used only for security purposes. Furthermore, robots can be used in situations that could put people in danger (Figure 10.4): cleaning up wreckage from hazardous chemical spills or performing underwater salvage operations, for example.

The automated factory of today has Web cameras positioned at strategic locations along the assembly process to enable managers and production personnel to monitor production and inventory from a remote location — across the building or across the continent! These automated factories increase overall efficiency for the firm in two ways:

- Automated scheduling can help to reduce "downtime," the time that machines sit idle waiting for parts.
- Automation results in less waste in terms of raw materials, labour, or physical space utilization. For example, the manufacture of blue jeans is fully automated, with the cutting process controlled by computer to reduce waste in material and to keep the cost of production down.

Get Connected

To find out the latest news on personal and industrial robotics, robot competitions, and other developments in this area, go to www.pearsoned.ca/businessconnections. Create a document (e.g., a short report or chart) titled "What's New in Robotics" to summarize the information obtained on this site. Enhance your document using appropriate visuals (e.g., clipart, pictures, graphics). Send your document electronically to your teacher for approval.

Figure 10.4
Robots Perform Tasks in Laboratories

Scientists who work with chemicals and deadly viruses often use robots to perform dangerous procedures. Identify three industries where robots might be used to perform hazardous tasks. Be specific.

IT In Action

Coming to a Citrus Grove Near You

Source: Kevin Bouffard, "The Citrus Department is paying for a study on the feasibility of robotic harvesting," *The Ledger Online*, July 18, 2002.

We most often think of robots on a factory assembly line performing repetitive tasks from a stationary platform or location. But imagine robots travelling up and down rows of orange and grapefruit trees harvesting ripe fruit. In 2002, the Florida Citrus Commission commissioned a study to determine the feasibility of robotic harvesting of their most famous export. The study, which is expected to take one year to complete, will help them to determine if the Department of Citrus (a government agency) should commit the financial resources, expected to be in the millions of dollars, to develop robotic harvesting machines.

A European company has developed a machine that takes approximately 3.5 seconds to locate, pick, and handle a single piece of fruit on a tree. This speed is too slow. The Florida Commission is looking for speeds of less than one second to compete with their human counterparts. (See Figure 10.5 for a picture of conventional harvesting methods.) "The first challenge is to sense every fruit on the tree, no matter where it is, whether it's behind a limb, branches, or leaves," said Galen Brown, the Department's harvesting program administrator.

The robot must be able to harvest the fruit without damaging it so that it can be sold fresh. Bruised and damaged fruits are destined for juice production.

Who knows? Next time you head south for vacation, you might see strange creatures in the orange grove as you pass by.

Figure 10.5
Conventional Harvesting

Questions

Electronically create a notebook page titled "Robotics" on which you input the answers to the following questions:

1. Describe the new technology the Florida Department of Citrus is investigating.
2. Explain how quickly a robot must harvest fruit to be competitive with its human counterparts.
3. Identify what factors must be improved to make robot use feasible in the harvesting of fruit.
4. Describe the risks associated with automating the harvest.
5. Name another task in each of the areas below that might be automated by the use of robots and describe how automation might improve the results of the task:

   a. in your school **b.** at home **c.** in the community **d.** in industry

10.2.1 Impact on People

Although organizations are rapidly automating factories, robots still cannot compete with human beings in performing tasks that require fine motor skills or doing jobs that require complicated analysis before actions are taken. What they do threaten, however, are the positions that require manual labour. Even though many people in the labour force perform unpleasant, menial, or repetitive tasks, they still earn their living doing so.

The introduction of technology into the manufacturing environment has created new jobs in the design, building, programming, selling, running, and repair of all the computers, robots, and networks. However, many of the people whose jobs are replaced by technology lack the education and skill level required to take on these new, challenging positions. These displaced workers must often take lower-paying jobs, if they can find a job at all. The impact on people and job quality will be examined in section 10.9.

GETTING IT

1. Describe the difference between CAD and CAM.
2. Explain the similarities and differences between a robot and a computer.
3. Identify areas where robots are most frequently employed. Describe the kinds of tasks they perform best.
4. Write a short essay to answer the following:
   a. How does automation in a manufacturing environment improve overall corporate performance?
   b. In what areas are robots not acceptable substitutes for people and why?
5. Prepare and input a position paper that discusses how technology has increased the gap between those who have post-secondary education and those who do not. Use evidence to support your position.

10.3 Electronic Marketing

Information technology has had an enormous impact on the way that businesses market products. All four aspects of the **marketing mix** have been affected, from marketing research and product development, to promotion strategies, to product distribution, and pricing. Marketers have had their traditional notions of what constitutes a market challenged by new technology. They have responded with new and creative strategies to get consumers and businesses alike to purchase their products and services.

Entire courses are dedicated to electronic commerce marketing concepts and strategies. This section will highlight some of the changes the marketing arena has undergone and what we can expect in the future.

10.3.1 Knowing Your Customer

Traditionally, marketers have relied on demographic data to identify their markets. **Demographics** are statistics that profile segments of the population by factors such as age, gender, income, marital status, family status, and so on. However, marketers must now consider a new factor when looking at consumer behaviour, namely how consumers travel on the Internet, known as their **clickstream behaviour**.

Electronic marketers know more about you from your clickstream behaviour than their "bricks and mortar" counterparts ever dreamed of knowing.

Every Web server maintains a detailed **transaction log** that records user activity at that particular site. This capability is built into Web server software that helps to run the e-commerce facility. An e-commerce provider can combine data from these sources:

- the transaction log with registration forms that you fill out during your visit to their site;
- the information contained in their shopping cart database (containing the items purchased and payment information); and
- product forms, chat groups, or e-mails sent inquiring about products or services.

These data sources provide invaluable information about the customer base and can be of help to answer such questions as:

- Where do shoppers go most frequently after the home page?
- What are specific individuals interested in?
- How can we personalize our message to potential consumers?

While transaction logs provide some information, the real power of the data is revealed when we combine this information with data from two other technologies — cookies and Web bugs. A **cookie** is a small text file with an identification number that Web sites place on the hard drive of the user's computer to allow the user to interact with the site efficiently. A cookie allows a Web site server to recognize the user during a communication. Through the use of cookies, marketers have a quick means of identifying customers and can monitor their use of the Web site. Marketers are able to know if these are new or repeat customers and how often they visit the site.

Web bugs are tiny one-pixel graphic files embedded in e-mail messages and on Web sites. They are used to transmit information about the user and the pages being viewed to a server that monitors such traffic. They are not visible to the user.

Many privacy advocates are concerned about the use of these technologies to track online behaviour. They suggest that when marketers combine the information from these data sources, they end up knowing too much about the consumer, who has no option but to have the data tracked.

digiknow

The more time people spend online, the more likely they are to purchase products and services online.

(Laudon and Traver 2002)

10.3.2 Just What Do Marketers Do With the Data?

One complaint of marketers over the years has been that they are unable to get a clear picture of just who is buying their products and what products will best meet the customers' needs. The data available to marketers today can help them to answer questions like these.

The information from transaction logs, cookies, Web bugs, and other sources is loaded into enormous databases for further analysis. By compiling the data in offline **data warehouses** that do not affect the day-to-day transactions of the firm, marketers can get answers to many questions. A data warehouse compiles information from numerous sources across the enterprise for analysis by management. For example, data from Web site transactions, shopping carts, cash register scanner systems, warehouse inventories, and sales reports, plus financial data can all be compiled to give a complete picture of the organization at any point in time. Managers can determine the most profitable product lines, products that should be removed from inventory, how efficient a Web site is, and so on.

digiknow

The most popular online consumer purchases are books, music, clothing and accessories, software, and toys. Each product category shares some common characteristics:

- low purchase price (involves less risk for the purchaser);
- physically small items (low shipping costs);
- high profit margins for retailers (retailers quickly recover cost of initial investment in online service)

(Laudon and Traver 2002)

Managers and marketers can also engage in **data mining** — the analysis of databases or data warehouses in order to identify the behaviour patterns of Web shoppers and browsers alike, based on the behaviour of millions of visitors to the site. If a customer typically enters a financial site and checks on the performance of his or her mutual fund portfolio, marketers can target that customer by tailoring the advertising to contain banner ads that appeal to mutual fund buyers.

Marketers can also compile information from offline services the company has (1-800 numbers, telephone call centres, automated telephone response systems, mobile devices, and sales representatives) to develop **Customer Relationship Management** (**CRM**) systems. Typically much of this information was stored in separate areas and the relationship between one set of data and another was rarely ever known. For example, if a cell phone company had a television advertisement listing an 800-number to call for more information and you went to the Web site instead, chances were the company would never know that you had seen the phone number in the television advertisement. New CRM systems track all the ways a customer interacts with a firm, and give marketers better information from which to judge the success of their efforts. By cross-referencing information in separate database files, companies can now track the success rate for programs such as advertising campaigns.

IT In Action

GM Wants To Get To Know You Better

Source: Bob Wallace, "Data Warehouse to Drive Online Marketing at GM; Central repository will pull customer data from all car, truck, financial units," *Computerworld*, July 5, 2002, p. 6.

General Motors, one of the world's largest automobile manufacturers, is using data warehousing to help improve relationships with customers. The warehouse combines data from its car and truck divisions, car leasing, home mortgage, and credit-card divisions in a central database with links to all international divisions as well.

The information compiled will help GM managers to better understand their customers and will help them to satisfy those customers' needs in the future. The project was initially conceived to help to give their BuyPower online car shopping service a boost and to cross-sell customers on GM financial services. **Cross-selling** is the process of encouraging customers to purchase additional products that go with products already selected. In this case, GM wants customers to finance their automobile purchase through GM financial services.

The challenge is bringing together huge amounts of data stored in many different locations, deciding how to use the data, and then figuring out how to turn it into marketing opportunities using both the GM Web site and e-mail to reach customers. This is not an easy task.

Questions

1. Create a list of the data General Motors is bringing together in their data warehouse.
2. Explain cross-selling.
3. Forecast what marketing opportunities you can see for GM in the data they are compiling. Explain your choices.
4. Give an example of how GM would use the information they have gathered.

10.3.3 Impact on People

As a result of the heavy reliance on data collection and statistical analysis, people looking to get into marketing must be very comfortable with data collection, data manipulation, and data analysis — traditionally data analysis was not considered part of the marketer's job. University and college programs in marketing now include far more courses in these areas to prepare students for the new world of e-commerce data collection. A thorough understanding of the mathematical field of statistics is an advantage for prospective marketers.

GETTING IT

Using appropriate technology, create a summary of this section that answers the following questions. Have your teacher approve your summary prior to filing in your notebook.

1. Define *demographics* and explain how marketers use this information.
2. Define *clickstream behaviour.* Explain what it "says" about you.
3. Explain why e-commerce sites gather and analyze clickstream data, information from registration forms, and shopping cart data. What do all these tell them?
4. Define *cookies* and explain the value they represent to marketers.
5. Describe a Web bug and the information it transmits.
6. Describe a data warehouse and explain how marketers utilize the information it contains.
7. Define *data mining.*
8. Describe how marketing jobs have been affected by technology.

10.4 Marketing Communication the IT Way

Once marketers have a identified their target group, they must design appropriate **marketing communications** to get their message to the intended group. Marketing communications serve two basic purposes:

1. to increase consumer awareness of the company's brands and the features that make their products unique; and
2. to promote sales of those brands.

Traditional forms of marketing communication include television, radio, print (magazines, newspapers), outdoor (billboards), transit advertising, direct mail, and telemarketing. The Internet has opened up an entire range of new ways marketers can reach their intended target groups. In fact, the Web itself can be viewed as a communications tool.

digiknow

Web site advertising in Canada has increased over 400% from $24.5 million in 1998 to over $110 million in 2000.

(Internet Advertising Bureau of Canada and MultiMediator Strategy Group 2000)

10.4.1 Online Advertising

Of all the communications tools available to the modern marketer, advertising is the most common and familiar to viewing audiences. When compared with traditional forms of advertising, online advertising applies to only a very small portion of the total market, but it is rapidly increasing. Currently there are four main forms of online advertising: banner ads, paid search engine inclusion and placement, sponsorships, and affiliate relationships.

10.4.1.1 Banner Advertising

This form of advertising was the first to develop on the Internet and World Wide Web. A **banner ad** displays a promotional message in a square or rectangular box on a Web page. It is similar to a print advertisement but with some distinct differences. If Web site visitors click on the banner ad, it transports them to the advertiser's Web site by opening another browser window or opening the site in the current window. Often banner ads are not static images; rather, they utilize animated GIF technology to change the message frequently while the viewer is at the site, to attract his or her attention. The Internet Advertising Bureau of Canada has established a number of common sizes for banner advertisements, stipulating the width, height (in pixels), and maximum file size allowable for an advertisement, to ensure that they do not take too long in loading on a Web site. Figure 10.6 provides some common banner ad formats for you to examine.

Figure 10.6
Samples of Common Banner Ad Formats

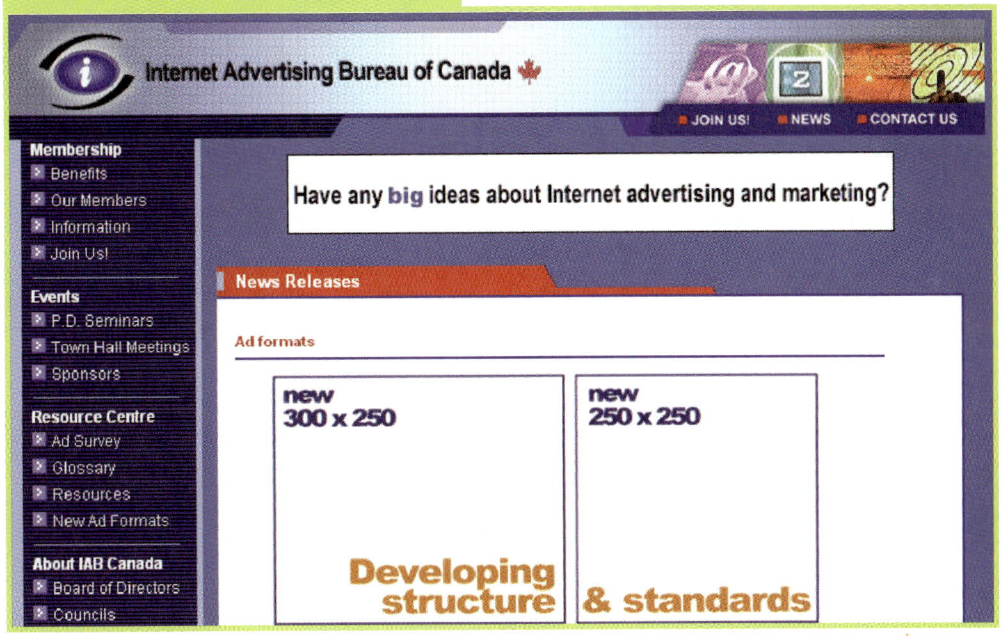

The Internet Advertising Bureau of Canada, as part of its drive to "develop structure and standards to lead the industry," has established standard ad formats. Visit www.pearsoned.ca/businessconnections and follow the links to view the full range of standard ad formats.

Two new varieties of banner ads to surface in recent years have been the **pop-under ad** and the **rich media ad.** Pop-under ads open a new browser window under the current window, so that it is not visible until the viewer closes the current browser window; the ad remains on the desktop until the viewer closes it. These ads are seen by many as nuisances. Rich media ads are an emerging ad type using Flash, DHTML, and Java technology in an attempt to involve the viewer more actively in the advertising process. These ads use 3-D imagery to show all aspects of a product, and their use is expected to increase.

Get Connected

Internet Advertising

The Internet Advertising Bureau of Canada is a non-profit association whose members are publishers, advertisers, and advertising agencies. IAB Canada provides marketers with a forum to evaluate and provide input on the direction of Internet advertising in Canada. Work with a partner to locate more information on Internet advertising. Go to www.pearsoned.ca/buisnessconnections. Create a list of 10 examples of the types of information found. Share your findings with your classmates.

10.4.1.2 Search Engines and Pay for Show

Even though banner advertising is thought of as the most common form of Internet advertising, it is not. Research indicates that more firms will pay to have their Web sites appear in search engine directories and indexes (**Pay for Show**), in order to have their sites found more frequently by Internet searchers. Since 1998, search engines have been converting their services to a form of online Yellow Pages where firms pay for placement. Previously, search engines had scoured the Web, looking for sites that met specific criteria (key words) and included the sites found in the index that searchers subsequently accessed to find information. Today, most search engines charge for preferred placement. Overture.com charges firms for listing their sites. The higher in the list the merchant wants to be, the more they will pay for the placement. Every time a user clicks on the site, the merchant is charged an amount shown on the search engine page beside its listing. Each search engine has different criteria and rates for its services. Figure 10.7 shows Google.ca's Web page advertisement for its online placement service.

Paid search engine inclusion is by far the most effective form of Internet advertising because of the sheer numbers of people who use search engines to locate information about available products and services. Small businesses that cannot afford full-fledged advertising campaigns can have their products and services found for a fraction of the cost by using this method.

Figure 10.7

Google.ca's Web Page Advertisement

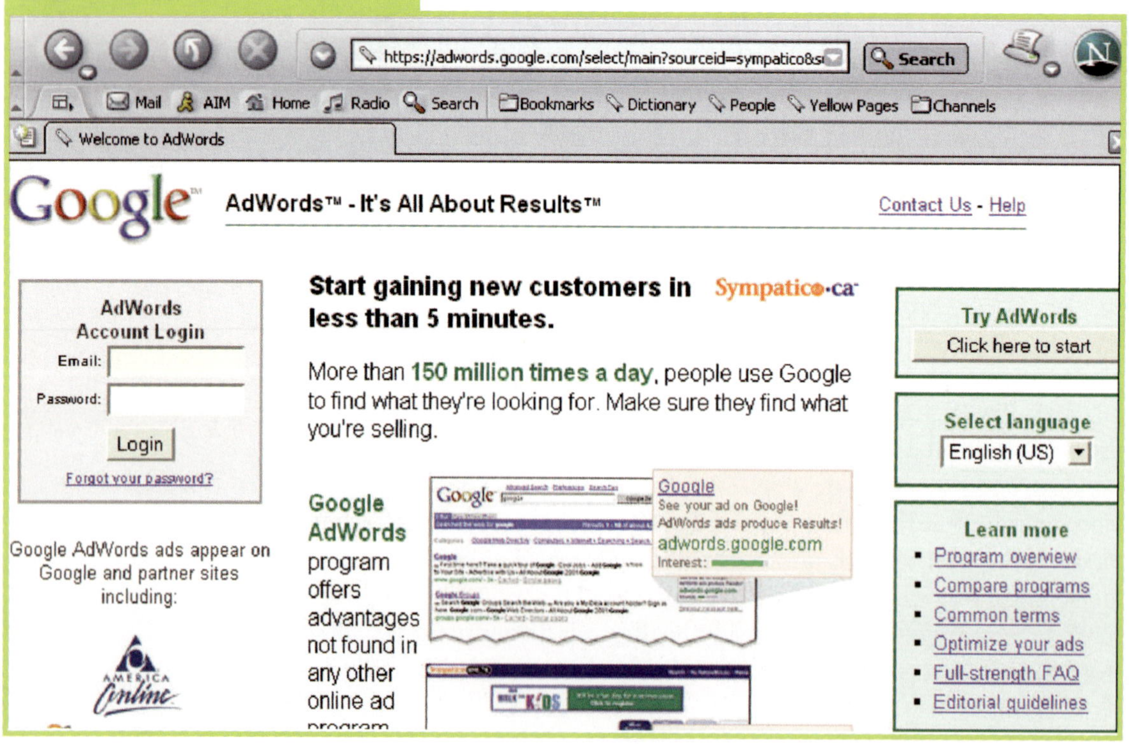

10.4.1.3 Sponsorships

Sponsorships are similar to paid advertising, but the sponsor's goal is to have their name and that of their products and services associated with a particular site or event. Much online sponsorship takes the form of "advertorials," where the content of a site is "brought to you by...." For example, Crayola, makers of crayons and markers, sponsors an arts and crafts column at a parenting resources Web site (not all the art projects are created with crayons!). Their goal is to increase brand awareness and desire for their products, but not by purchasing banner ads on the site.

10.4.1.4 Affiliate Relationships

Some online merchants or sites enter into partnerships with other firms to allow each other to advertise on their respective sites without charge. This is known as an **affiliate relationship**. You see this type of advertising on the sites of companies that all share the same corporate parent; Bell Canada is an example. All affiliate sites (Bell Mobility, Bell Canada, Bell Sympatico) feature affiliate ads from their corporate siblings (see Figure 10.8).

Figure 10.8
www.bell.ca

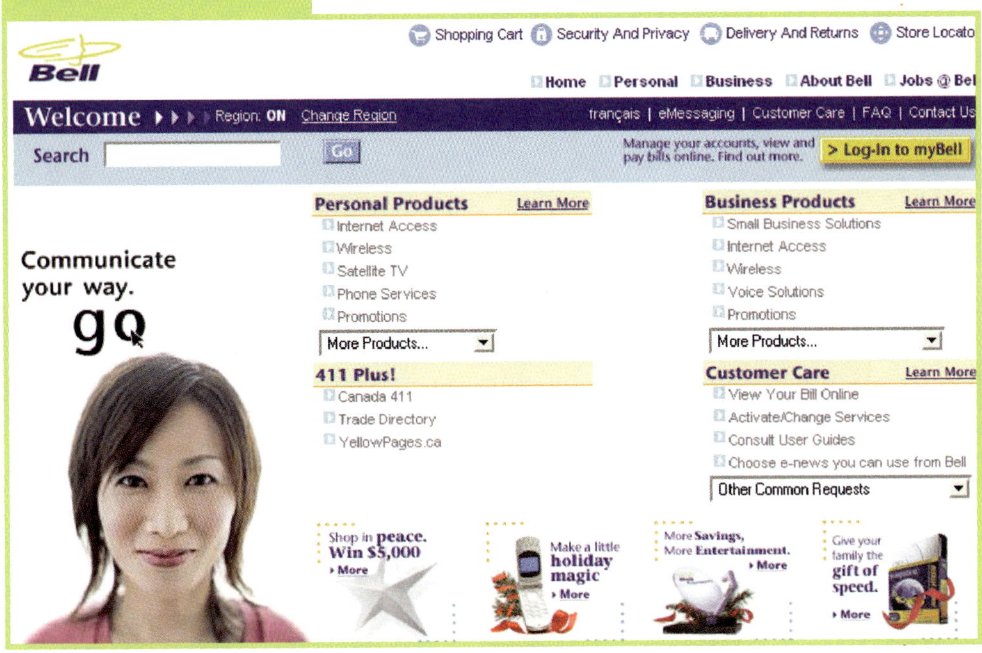

The affiliate ads are shown on the bottom of this Bell Canada Web page.

10.4.1.5 Direct E-Mail Marketing

Unlike spam, which is unsolicited e-mail advertising, **direct e-mail marketing** is sent to people who sign up for e-mails because they are interested in the topic or product. This approach allows marketers to direct their message to specific individuals. For example, purchasers of Janome sewing machines can sign up for a newsletter (see Figure 10.9) featuring new sewing projects and techniques that, of course, utilize the features of Janome sewing machines and sergers.

Figure 10.9
Janome Direct E-Mail Newsletter

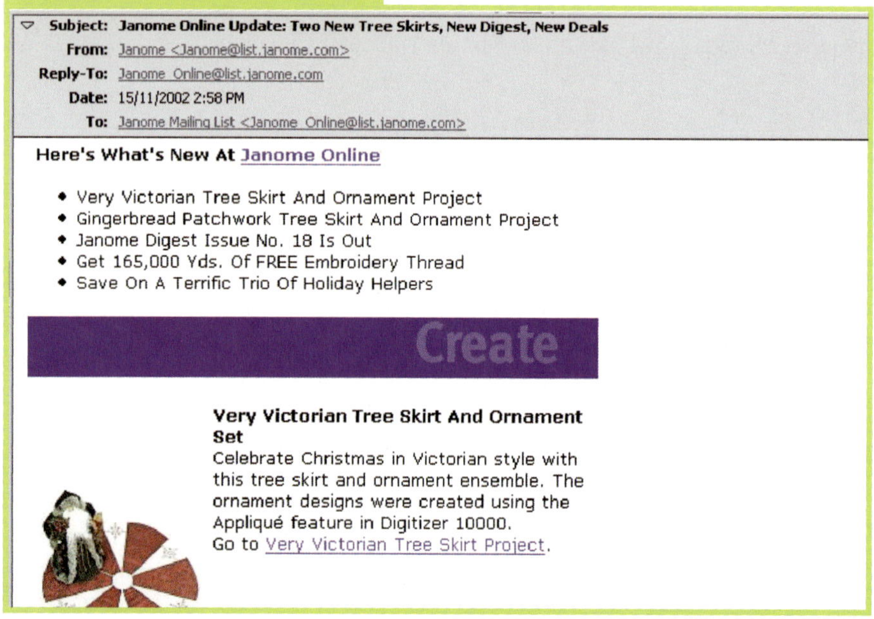

The cost of this form of advertising is quite low, with the major expense being the assembly of the mailing list. At 15 to 50 cents per name, it still costs less than printing a postcard or letter and mailing it through the traditional postal system. Customers tend to respond more favourably to this form of advertising, since they were the ones who requested the information in the first place.

10.4.1.6 Online Catalogues

From the earliest days, catalogue sales have been very popular with Canadian consumers. The Eaton's catalogue was one of the major marketing breakthroughs for Canadian consumers.

Goods like those advertised in the 1899–1900 catalogue (Figure 10.10) were available for shipment across Canada. With Canada's expansive geography, people could not always travel to major centres where the stores were located to make purchases. Catalogue shopping meant that Canadians no longer had to do without certain goods. Beam yourself into the 21st century and you will see that some things have changed. We still have people spread throughout this country, but now technology allows us to view catalogues online and order through the Internet. Shipment takes days or weeks, not months. **Online catalogues** (see Figure 10.11) allow purchasers to view the merchant's wares, see colour availability, and access up-to-date pricing information, all at the click of a mouse. Simple catalogues comprise HTML pages combined on one merchant's site. New technology allows for the creation of dynamic catalogues, whose pages are generated from a massive database that allows for frequent updates to products and prices. Catalogues are becoming one of the most popular forms of online e-commerce for consumers and businesses alike to purchase all forms of goods (see Chapter 9).

Figure 10.10
The 1899–1900 Eaton's Catalogue

Timothy Eaton became one of the world's outstanding retail merchants. Products in the catalogue included everything from butter churns to Bibles to ostrich feathers.

10.4.1.7 Public Relations

Unlike paid advertising, **public relations (PR)** uses the news media to boost awareness of the organization by informing audiences about new events, new products and services, and activities the firm undertakes. Traditional PR uses hard-copy newspapers and magazines to channel their messages to audiences. Online PR consists of using Web sites and e-mail to communicate messages to lists of individuals who can get the word out (e.g., newspaper columnists). Free online press release services also exist on the Web, where companies can send and distribute press releases at no charge.

All these forms of online advertising give companies a wider variety of tools to reach potential customers. Many of them have

Figure 10.11
Sears.ca Web Site for an Online Canadian Catalogue

digiknow

Of the various forms of online advertising, search engine inclusion and placement is the most popular. The overall ranking is as follows:

1. Search engine inclusion and placement;
2. Online public relations and press releases;
3. Buttons and hyperlinks;
4. Reciprocal ads and links (trading banner ads on pages);
5. Affiliate programs; and
6. Paid banner advertising.

(Laudon and Traver 2002)

the advantage of being able to target advertisements to narrow segments of the whole market and to track the effectiveness of the ads through click-stream data. Online ads also allow for more direct communication with target audiences — direct e-mail, for example. If the target audience responds to the ad by clicking on the hyperlinks in your e-mail communication, you have engaged them in a two-way "conversation," something traditional forms of advertising lack. The disadvantage of online advertising is the total cost as compared with its benefits; the effectiveness of this form of advertising is difficult to measure (Laudon and Traver 2002). Different online advertising methods yield substantially different results. Banner ads produce less than a 1% response (click through) rate on average, but direct e-mail advertising can return up to a 15% response rate (Internet Advertising Bureau of Canada 2002). The goal, therefore, is to use the advertising method that best fits with the goals of the promotion.

10.4.2 Web Sites as a Communications Tool

Online advertising can help to get your name out there, but the ultimate destination for any advertisement is the company's Web site. By combining an appropriate URL or domain name with effective content and search engine placement, a site can be considered the ultimate online advertisement for your company.

The criteria for a good domain name include:

- memorable;
- short;
- easy to spell, difficult to misspell; and
- unique in the market.

Good domain names are connected directly to the brand names that a firm has spent years imprinting in the minds of consumers. Many firms use the new domain name extensions (e.g., .ca, .tv, .biz,) to better identify their sites to consumers. To be found more frequently by search engines, companies can employ the following strategies:

- register with as many search engines as possible;
- write a site description with as many key words as are typically used by searchers in looking for a similar site; and
- link the site to as many other sites as possible through advertising and entering into affiliate relationships with other companies.

By employing the above strategies in a corporate marketing plan, organizations can potentially improve their online marketing effectiveness.

GETTING IT

Using appropriate technology, create a summary of this section that answers the following questions. Have your teacher approve your summary prior to filing it in your notebook.

1. Explain the term *banner ad*. Create a list of the standards that have been established for banner ads.
2. Compare and contrast traditional marketing strategies with those used through the use of the Internet.
3. Explain why search engine inclusion and placement is the most popular form of Internet advertising.
4. Electronically create a document that clearly illustrates the difference among advertising, sponsorship, and public relations.
5. Explain how corporate affiliates benefit from the use of Internet advertising.
6. Describe direct e-mail marketing. Why is this not the same thing as spam?
7. In small groups, discuss why consumers are comfortable with online catalogues as a means of making purchases. Share your thoughts with the rest of the class.
8. Describe two strategies that can be employed in using your Web site as a communications tool.

10.5 Distribution

One aspect of marketing that is crucial to ensuring complete customer satisfaction is getting the goods to the customer, i.e., the entire **distribution** process. Information technology has had as much of an impact in this area as on product development and marketing communications. One of the earliest uses of information technology for distribution was in order fulfillment. For example, bakeries, bottled water companies, and snack food distributors started using handheld computer systems to monitor sales to their extensive customer base by the sales representatives and delivery personnel in the trucks. These **direct store delivery** systems give them information about each customer's buying history and about products that are selling that week as detailed in the inventory analysis done at the time of the sales call. This up-to-date information gives a clearer picture of what should be ordered at that precise moment so that the sales rep can fill the order from the back of the truck. Some systems allow the sales rep to generate a line-by-line invoice at a customer's site, providing even more detailed information in the database about buying habits and needs.

The Internet has highlighted the importance of distribution for companies small and large. Accenture (formerly Andersen Consulting) estimated that

40% of online shoppers had a problem with their Christmas 1999 shopping experience. Problems ranged from selecting items only to find out that they were out of stock or delivery would be too late — often too late for the holiday itself (Craig 2000). What these problems, at arguably the busiest time of year for all merchants, emphasize is that all your business processes must work smoothly. Products must be picked out from the warehouse, assembled into packages for shipment, packed, shipped and billed to the correct person at the correct address, and payments must be processed. IT systems must also be in place to handle customer returns, reshelving, order tracking, and billing errors. This is no small task.

Information technology has also had an impact on warehousing. Canadian Tire's massive warehouses in Brampton, Ontario, for example, are fully automated. Products are picked from the warehouse's multistorey shelves by robots, which scan the bar codes on the shelves to locate the products required for each shipment.

On the B2B side, e-commerce has made it easier for small companies to become suppliers to large organizations. In the past, large companies demanded that suppliers be connected electronically to them through **EDI (electronic data interchange)**, a very expensive system to implement, therefore blocking out smaller suppliers. The openness of the Internet has made it easier for both buyers and sellers of products and services to begin and end supply relationships that do not have high capital costs associated with them. In fact, many large business operations are outsourcing supplies and services previously done by internal departments, where it makes economic sense. The Purchasing Management Association of Canada (2002, Supplement) surveyed their membership and found some interesting trends related to online procurement of products and services. In this study they found that:

- 73% of products and services are obtained from Canadian sources.
- Online procurement constitutes only 5% of the 2001 total, but it is expected to increase to 14% in 2002 and 35% by 2005.
- 73% of companies have/will have within two years online purchasing capabilities for frequently purchased items, such as office supplies and furniture.
- 94% of companies use the Internet to locate potential suppliers.
- 90% use the Internet to communicate with suppliers.
- 89% use the Internet to view electronic catalogues.

Security concerns and system compatibility are the two most frequently cited reasons for not purchasing online. Nonetheless, companies are looking at e-commerce as a real alternative to traditional buying methods in an effort to keep costs down and remain competitive. Any business wanting to participate in B2B activity will need to carefully consider online options.

IT In Action

Batter Up!

Source: Mark Zwolinski, "Jays' high-tech ticket pitch." *Toronto Star*, April 4, 2002, pp. A1, A20.

When we think of the impact technology has had on marketing, people tend to gravitate to the Internet and e-commerce. However, technology has had even more impact on the way products and services are sold. Look at the Toronto Blue Jays. This American League baseball club has created a team of "cyber-sellers" who take ticket selling out on the streets, bringing the product to the customer, instead of waiting for the customer to come to them at the ticket office. These ticket agents are armed with wireless credit card verification equipment to instantly process the transaction when they approach potential customers outside SkyDome. The cyber ticket allows the customers to proceed directly to the admission gate instead of having to pick up tickets at the ticket office first. The Blue Jays' marketing and sales group wanted to give fans better value for their money and give them an option to buying tickets from scalpers on the street. Paul Allamby, Senior VP of marketing and sales, indicated, "We didn't want people to have to stand in line so we equipped our staff with wireless equipment....They could swipe credit cards and just go to a fast-track window. Now, we're offering a bar-coded coupon so fans can just go right to the gate." Rogers Communications, owners of the team, provides the high-tech gadgets that make this all possible.

Questions

Electronically create a summary sheet that includes the answers to the following questions. Have your teacher approve your summary prior to filing it in your notebook.

1. Describe the technology that is being used by the Toronto Blue Jays' ticket sellers.
2. Explain why they have implemented this approach to selling tickets before the game.
3. Discuss with a partner how you think fans will react to this approach. Share your thoughts with the rest of the class.
4. Identify another business where this type of technology would be useful and explain why.

10.6 Pricing

The final element in the marketing mix is product pricing. In the offline world, companies typically look at the cost of producing or providing the product or service (including advertising, administrative and support functions, and distribution) and add appropriate markups to generate a profit. The amount added will vary depending on the demand for the product and the competition the company faces in that particular market.

Pricing goods on the Internet has caused confusion among both buyers and sellers. For a company that is in the business of providing information (e.g., *National Post*, one of Canada's national newspapers), the cost of producing that same information for distribution over the Internet is close to zero. This is why many information Web sites offer content at no cost to Internet viewers. News stories, stock quotes, weather reports and forecasts, articles, pictures, and editorials are already produced for their print products. The cost of archiving that information, however, is passed on to the consumer in the form of subscriptions to enable the Web viewer to access historical content.

The Internet has also enabled merchants to offer **dynamic pricing** to customers. Auctions (e.g., eBay) allow for flexible pricing of products, with bidders determining the price. Another form of dynamic pricing is called **yield management**, where the company determines the price of their product or service based on the quantity they have in stock. For example, airlines often discount available seats closer to the date of departure in an effort to attract customers, instead of leaving the seats empty and getting nothing for them. Snack food companies use this technique to keep products moving off the shelves to avoid stale products. Yield management pricing requires the company to have extensive database management and monitoring systems in place. Perishable products that vary in demand, in highly competitive markets where conditions change rapidly, are good contenders for yield management systems.

GETTING IT

Electronically create a summary sheet that includes the answers to the following questions. Have your teacher approve your summary prior to filing it in your notebook.

1. How do route delivery salespeople use technology to help them sell the right products to their customers (e.g., small variety stores)?
2. How is e-commerce making it easier for smaller suppliers to engage in B2B transactions?
3. Why are some products free on the Internet? Find or name one such product. Why do you think it was it offered without charge?
4. What is dynamic pricing and how has the Internet enabled more use of this pricing technique?

10.7 Accounting for Business

The accounting side of business has been automated since the first computers were installed in large organizations. The very nature of accounting made it a likely candidate for automation, due to its large quantities of similar information. Every day hundreds, if not thousands, of entries for sales, purchases, money received on account, and payments to suppliers are processed in accounting departments. In the early computing days, large mainframe computers processed these batches of transactions at the end of each business day, when the entries were keyed into computer tapes by keypunch operators after being assembled by the accounting staff. The tapes were then fed into the computer systems overnight and reports were generated detailing the transactions that were processed. However, only large organizations or institutions were able to take advantage of these processes due to the significant hardware, software, and personnel costs associated with them.

Microcomputers and PCs changed all that. With the PC came the development of countless software packages for all parts of an organization, with accounting being no exception. Today, programs such as Simply Accounting allow all kinds of companies to manage the accounting process in an effective and efficient manner. New versions are constantly being produced to reflect changes in accounting procedures from the Canadian Institute of Chartered Accountants and changes in tax laws from Canada Customs and Revenue Agency. The programs are actually databases of information entered by the small business owner or accountant. Once the entries are made, the program sorts and classifies data, calculates account balances, and generates a variety of reports that comply with the Generally Accepted Accounting Principles (GAAPs) that guide accountants in Canada. Many of the programs available today are integrated to allow the company to automate most aspects of the accounting function, from purchasing to payroll.

Accounting personnel must still understand the entire accounting cycle and the rules that govern accounting in Canada. What has been added is the need to be able to function in an automated accounting environment, whether it be on a PC or on mainframe computers in a large organization. This skill can be developed both through courses that prepare an accountant for employment and on the job, where specific system details are taught.

10.8 Managing the Business

We have seen the impact of information technology on a number of departments within an organization. But what about the management of those departments? More and more, management is seen as a science where data and information are required inputs to managerial decision making. As a result, computer systems are considered vital to the health of the modern organization.

As discussed in earlier sections, the Internet and information technology have enabled companies to compile massive databases that collect all kinds of information about customer buying habits, payments, online movements, questions asked via e-mails, and other communication logs. It is the manager's job to take the data, analyze them, and make decisions for the firm, ranging from which products to discount or eliminate from the product lines to which warehouses to close due to declining sales in particular regions. On the positive side, they can take the same data and make decisions regarding increased product offerings in particular markets or even where they need more staff to deal with the increase in demand for products and services. These **management information systems (MIS)** are designed to allow for maximum flexibility in what information to extract, depending on the needs of the individual managers involved.

Another variation on the MIS is the **decision support system (DSS)**, which allows managers to ask "what if" questions and develop simulations based on historical data. The data warehouses described earlier allow for that type of analysis without disrupting the day-to-day operations of the business, by working with data offline.

Chapters 2 and 3 of this text have also described in greater detail the project management software that is available for managers to handle complex projects. This software allows for the coordination, scheduling, and tracking of complex work projects that are broken down into deliverables, tasks, and personnel responsible for the delivery of each project component.

Another addition to the management toolkit is Enterprise Resource Management (ERM) — software that enables the manager to manage all of the company's assets and resources. It generally includes basic accounting applications such as the General Ledger, Accounts Payable and Accounts Receivable, as well as manufacturing, inventory, and human resources software applications.

One component of this complex set of programs is the Human Resources Management (HRM) software such as that developed by PeopleSoft or SAP. These programs enable businesses to manage every facet of their human resources from recruiting to training and development to employee compensation. They also give managers the tools to determine the contribution of their human resources to overall profitability. Automating the Human Resources functions allow HR employees to spend their time on more analytical and strategic efforts than on the paperwork associated with the management of people in an organization.

All in all, the job of a manager is still to manage people and tasks. The tools with which managers perform their jobs may have changed, but they are still responsible for the overall performance of the organization.

GETTING IT

Electronically create a summary sheet that includes the answers to the following questions. Have your teacher approve your summary prior to filing it in your notebook.

1. Explain why accounting was one of the first business processes to be automated.
2. Describe how accounting software packages work.
3. Define *MIS.*
4. Explain how a decision support system (DSS) differs from an MIS.

10.9 The Human Factor: Assessing the Impact of Technology on People and Jobs

We have already examined the impact of technology on product development, design, and manufacturing in this chapter. However, a number of other factors must be considered when looking at the use of technology in the workplace:

- The people who must use technology do not always welcome it.
- Management may be reluctant to use new technology to solve problems because they lack an understanding of how technology can benefit the firm.
- Technically skilled employees can be frustrated by an organization that uses old or inadequate technology.

As a result, the overall quality of employment can be affected as jobs are redesigned in organizations. To better understand the impact technology has on overall job performance, we will first examine the nature of job design.

10.9.1 Job Design and Satisfaction

The challenge modern management faces in terms of human resources is designing jobs so that overall job performance, or total quality and quantity of task accomplishment, does not suffer, yet employee satisfaction is maximized at the same time. Add to this puzzle the fact that all human beings are unique and what satisfies one person may not satisfy another, and you have a difficult task to say the least.

All jobs vary in terms of job scope, job depth, and task specialization. **Job scope** is the number and variety of tasks a person has to perform, whereas **job depth** is the extent to which a person has responsibility for planning her or his workday and ensuring tasks are performed correctly. **Task specialization** is another way of looking at the division of labour to complete a whole job. For example, on an assembly line in an automobile manufacturing plant, an individual may only be responsible for installing the steering wheel in the unit as it passes by his or her workstation. This is a highly specialized task. The introduction of automation or information technology into a job has a tremendous impact on all three of these areas. The challenge lies in designing jobs that "use technology to their best potential while still treating people with respect and allowing their human talents to be applied to their fullest potential." (Schermerhorn 2002).

There are three basic job design strategies that managers can employ in the quest to maximize employee potential and output. Figure 10.12 compares Job Simplification, Job Rotation and Enlargement, and Job Enrichment in terms of job scope, depth, and specialization.

Figure 10.12
Three Basic Job Design Strategies

	Job Simplification (e.g., assembly-line work)	**Job Rotation and Enlargement** (e.g., retail store employee handling customers, check-out, and inventory)	**Job Enrichment** (e.g., member of product design and development team)
Job Scope	• very narrow • few tasks performed • low skill required • easy to train	• moderate • more tasks performed on rotational basis or combined in one job • linear tasks (performed one after another) • increased skill required	• broad • wide variety of tasks performed • not all tasks linear • higher skill levels required
Job Depth	• limited • tasks mandated • highly supervised	• limited • tasks mandated • highly supervised	• extensive • job incorporates planning and evaluation of tasks • work teams common in enriched environments • individual sees "whole picture"
Task Specialization	• highly specialized due to narrow scope	• increased load of specialized tasks • lower division of labour, but not responsible for entire process	• low specialization • less division of larger jobs into small tasks

The rationale behind moving jobs from highly simplified to enriched lies in the satisfaction of employees on the job. Frederick Herzberg, in his studies of motivation, theorized that people are more highly motivated to do a good job when they are involved in it. His studies of people on the job indicate that there is no sense in simply giving them more tasks to do if they are still highly specialized, highly supervised, and they lack meaning in terms of the finished product. Highly simplified jobs frequently result in workers becoming bored and feeling alienated, resulting in low satisfaction and higher rates of absenteeism and errors.

As a result of studies like Herzberg's, many organizations introduced robotics into jobs that were highly simplified, such as in manufacturing assembly plants. This is the ultimate form of simplification, while eliminating people from the job. The rationale is that managers are using the capabilities of their human resources to their fullest potential by having robots complete the meaningless, repetitive jobs. By introducing robots into the work environment, however, management is changing the way work flows throughout the organization and the skill sets that are required by their human resources. Companies must be prepared to engage in retraining their personnel in order to increase their comfort in the changing nature of their jobs. On the other hand, jobs that are automated may reduce the skill levels required by employees. This "up-skilling" and "de-skilling" of jobs is of great concern to managers and workers alike.

10.9.2 Up-Skilling and De-Skilling

As information technology is introduced into work environments, the nature of the jobs that people are required to perform can be changed dramatically. As dedicated word processors and eventually PCs were brought into office environments, clerical staff were required to learn how to operate the equipment in order to produce the documents they previously created on typewriters. Now, as companies adopt databases, integrated office productivity software, Internet connectivity, Intranets, e-mail systems, and other such technology, workers face additional challenges as their jobs are **up-skilled**. Many people feel ill-prepared to use new technology, never having been trained in its use. Others see the new tools as challenges that they welcome on the job.

The way in which employees receive the training has changed dramatically as well. In virtual enterprises, employees who work off-site use Web-based employee orientation materials and interactive video to achieve classroom-like experiences. Companies also provide traditional training courses for employees both in-house and off-site. As people are retrained and acquire the requisite job skills, they frequently see these changes reflected in job descriptions and paycheques as well. However, many jobs have been **de-skilled** over the past decades with the implementation of technology. The job of a fast-food clerk has been greatly simplified with the introduction of point-of-sale terminals that require staff only to press the item on the screen (e.g., large coffee).

Total sales and change are automatically calculated, requiring less thought and information processing by the clerk. Office jobs have suffered similar de-skilling. Entry-level jobs requiring minimal skills, where a person could work their way up to higher-level positions with experience and training, are threatened. These individuals have been moved to jobs entering data into computer systems — mindless, repetitive work where productivity is measured in keystrokes and monitored electronically by the computer system. The transition to more simplified jobs has had the predicted results: higher job dissatisfaction, higher absenteeism, and higher error rates. This electronic monitoring of employees has become one of the more controversial aspects of the modern work environment.

ON THE CASE

E-Learning

To keep up with the demands of their jobs, employees need to have the tools to do their best. Knowledge is increasingly one of the most important tools in today's economy. Many organizations now leverage the impact and immediacy of technology to help to get valuable information to their employees in innovative ways.

One success story in this area is Canadian Tire. In 2001, Canadian Tire launched an online, e-learning program for all their retail staff to help them to acquire the product knowledge they need to effectively serve their customers. Self-directed, Internet-based modules that look somewhat like animated video games were designed for different areas of the business. For example, a module set up to look like an auto racing game was developed to teach employees about the types of tires available in the store, so that staff would be better equipped to answer consumer questions and recommend an ideal product. Because Canadian Tire provides self-directed modules, employees are able to log onto the Internet whenever it is convenient for them (day or night) and complete their learning at their own pace. Canadian Tire continues to update existing modules and develop new ones to ensure that their staff continue to provide excellent customer service.

Questions

Electronically create a document (e.g., report, table, poster) titled "E-Learning." Include appropriate sections based on the questions below. Send your finished product to your teacher electronically.

1. The approach to e-learning followed by Canadian Tire was clearly successful in the retail industry. What applications for e-learning can you see in the following industries:
   a. automotive manufacturing?
   b. restaurants?
   c. government?
   d. schools?
2. Explain how you would design and implement an e-learning system for organizations that operate in these industries. How would this benefit the employees?

10.9.3 Electronic Monitoring of Employees

Many organizations have installed **automated monitoring systems** (see Figure 10.13) to keep track of employees and their productivity. Often, these systems do not give the employee an indication that their performance is being monitored at the time it is taking place. Some examples of automated employee monitoring include:

- measurement of keystrokes at a computer data terminal while the employee enters information;
- length of time computer systems sit idle;
- scan rates of grocery store clerks (items scanned in any one grocery order and the speed at which they are scanned);
- employee phone records monitored for calls made and duration;
- e-mail systems tracking people e-mailed and the content of messages;
- Internet searches and browser history files to determine sites visited;
- network software that allows a manager to see on his or her monitor what is on an employee's monitor at that moment; and
- employees being videotaped on the job.

Figure 10.13
Electronic Surveillance Equipment

Electronic surveillance equipment can be used to monitor activity from remote locations. Give two additional examples of how an organization might use electronic surveillance in its business activities.

This electronic surveillance highlights some important issues in the modern workplace. First and foremost is the threat to individual privacy. People may feel threatened by the existence of job monitoring, the amount of data that an employer can gather on any one person in the organization, and the possible outcomes (e.g., firing) if wrongdoing is suspected. On the other hand, if you are doing your job, what is there to fear?

The second aspect of this type of monitoring is the stress and anxiety it creates in some people. Employees cannot tell when and where they are being watched and this can have a negative impact on overall morale. Management is viewed as non-trusting and this, in turn, can create a great divide between employees and management. People who should be working together to attain overall corporate goals can be divided by the use of such technology.

The third aspect for consideration is the devaluation of other skills an employee might possess. Just because one grocery store clerk does not scan products as quickly as another does not mean that he or she is not a great customer service representative. Interacting with customers is also an important skill to possess and employ in such an environment.

The final aspect is that of overall effort expended by employees. Some employees may adopt the attitude that if something does not "count" toward the assessment of their performance on the job, then it is not important. This is similar to an academic environment, where students do not consider it important to engage in classroom activities if they do not "count" toward their final grade in a course. They miss out on valuable learning experiences by adopting such an attitude.

ON THE CASE

Looking in on "Junior"

Source: Tyler Hamilton, "Candid cameras," *Toronto Star*, March 4, 2002: pp. D1 and D3.

A number of progressive day-care centres in the Southern Ontario region are experimenting with a type of technology that permits parents to access a secure Web site and look in on their children during the day. The strategically placed cameras and password-protected Web sites appeal to many working parents who are anxious about the safety and well-being of their children while they are at work. Being able to look in on them from time to time also helps to relieve the guilt about leaving them with others to care for them. According to Statistics Canada, over 700 000 children under the age of six attend day-care regularly, where persons who are not related are charged with their care. On average the children spend nine hours each day in this outside care.

The Web site developers bundle the service for the day-care centres to provide them with their own Web site as part of the package. The video cameras that are installed have a built-in Web server running over a Linux operating system, which makes it possible for the service provider to control each camera from its remote location. Cameras send 15 images per second that simulate full motion video for viewing parents.

Day-care workers, however, are concerned about the installation of such systems. Sandra Griffin, executive director of the Canadian Child Care Federation, points to growing distrust of day-care facilities and the constant scrutiny that workers will be under as areas for consideration.

Questions

Write a discussion paper on *Looking in on "Junior"* that addresses the following questions. Submit this paper to your teacher for approval.

1. What privacy issues does the installation of day-care surveillance systems bring to light?
2. How might teachers and students in day-care facilities react to the installation of video cameras? Will this be positive or negative for all parties involved?
3. Are the rights of the parents more important than the right to privacy of the day-care workers? Discuss your thoughts with your classmates and add this information to your paper.

Get Connected

To find out more about Web accessible day-care facilities go to www.pearsoned.ca/businessconnections. Prepare a summary of your findings and submit it electronically to your teacher for approval.

10.9.4 Electronic Sweatshops

Computer monitoring of employees is common in call centres and data entry environments, where hundreds of employees sit at computer terminals performing repetitive tasks on a daily basis. In *The Electronic Sweatshop: How Computers Are Transforming the Office of the Future into the Factory of the Past*, Barbara Garson examines how the implementation of technology has dehumanized many aspects of jobs. With attention focused on how quickly a person enters data into computer systems, prepares fast foods, handles calls from incoming customers, or even processes clients in social service offices, companies have forgotten that it is people who perform these tasks.

The very nature of technology has allowed companies to move such centres to locations where they can take advantage of lower wages, in regions where unemployment is higher. The customer has no idea if data are entered into corporate databases or if calls are answered in Saint John, NB, or Swift Current, SK. Many governments offer tax holidays to companies that locate their premises in their regions, in order to attract employment even though it may only be low-paying data-entry jobs. This strategy is popular from a political perspective. Government officials can boast of employment creation when organizations establish operations in their region. As technology improves, however, such electronic ghettos may eventually become extinct. **Optical Character Recognition (OCR)** software that allows text to be scanned from a printed page into a digital text file and voice programs are improving, so that less human intervention is required to enter data into systems. Over time, the very technology that brought about the sweatshops may allow for total mechanization of the jobs.

As jobs move through the spectrum from simplification to enrichment, the key factor will be training and development of our human resources. Newspaper articles highlighting the need for skilled workers in the new millennium abound. Apprenticeship programs, college and university curricula, and on-the-job training programs are all being revamped to handle this shift in our economy. Will you be ready for it?

GETTING IT

1. Describe what is meant by *job scope, job depth,* and *task specialization.*
2. Explain why companies have automated many simplified jobs.
3. Describe the differences between up-skilling and de-skilling.
4. List and describe five ways employees are monitored electronically.
5. Describe the four concerns that electronic surveillance of employees brings to light.
6. In small groups, discuss what we can do about the loss of privacy at work and in the community. Share your thoughts with the rest of the class.

7. Explain what an electronic sweatshop is and describe where these sweatshops are found today.
8. Name three personal experiences you have had with electronic monitoring. How did these make you feel? Why?

IT's A Wrap

Key Terms in This Chapter

affiliate relationship (p. 289)
automated monitoring system (p. 303)
banner ad (p. 287)
clickstream behaviour (p. 283)
Computer Aided Design (CAD) (p. 274)
Computer Aided Manufacturing (CAM) (p. 278)
cookie (p. 283)
cross-selling (p. 285)
Customer Relationship Management (CRM) (p. 284)
data mining (p. 284)
data warehouse (p. 284)
decision support system (DSS) (p. 298)
demographics (p. 283)
de-skilled (p. 301)
direct e-mail marketing (p. 289)
direct store delivery (p. 293)
distribution (p. 293)
dynamic pricing (p. 296)
electronic data interchange (EDI) (p. 294)
job depth (p. 299)
job scope (p. 299)
management information system (MIS) (p. 298)
marketing communications (p. 286)
marketing mix (p. 282)
online catalogue (p. 291)
Optical Character Recognition (OCR) (p. 305)
Pay for Show (p. 288)
pop-under ad (p. 287)
public relations (PR) (p. 291)
rich media ad (p. 287)
robot (p. 279)
sponsorships (p. 289)
task specialization (p. 299)
transaction log (p. 283)
up-skilled (p. 301)
virtual enterprises (p. 273)
Web bugs (p. 283)
yield management (p. 296)

1. Create a list of the competencies that you have acquired through your work in this chapter.
2. Update your portfolio to include examples of work you have completed in this chapter.

Know It!

3. Explain what happens to people when jobs are automated.
4. Analyze whether online shoppers always save money. Explain why or why not.
5. Electronically create a visual that illustrates why there are concerns regarding cookies, Web bugs, and other forms of Internet tracking.
6. Explain why companies are building Customer Relationship Management systems. What do they hope to achieve in doing so?
7. Make a list of the new forms of Internet advertising that have developed with new technological advances.
8. Prepare a document that shows the advantages and disadvantages of online advertising.

IT's A Wrap (continued)

Know It!

9. Summarize the differences between jobs that are simplified, enlarged/rotated, and enriched.
10. Write a paragraph describing what companies should do/provide for employees when they automate jobs.
11. Explain the difference between de-skilling and simplifying a job.

Do It!

12. Investigate how technology has had an impact on your favourite sport or after-school activity (e.g., band). Prepare a presentation for your classmates to illustrate your findings.
13. Locate articles in your local newspaper or on the Internet at newspaper Web sites that profile new product designs. Write a short report on how technology has enabled the development of that product.
14. Visit a local business and interview personnel to see how automation has influenced the creation and delivery of their products or services.
15. Visit five Web sites in different categories — portals, e-tailers, information providers, etc. — and investigate the different forms of Internet advertising at the sites. Prepare a chart that compares the different forms found at each site.
16. Working with three classmates, log into your favourite Web portal (e.g., Sympatico.ca) and determine in how many different ways you can get to a specific part of their site. Document each potential "clickstream" for discussion and demonstration for the rest of the class.

Analyze It!

17. Describe the impact CAD has had on the overall design process for new product ideas.
18. "There is not a job that cannot be automated in some shape or form." Debate this statement with information gathered from this chapter and other sources.
19. Analyze the statement "There is a strong correlation between Internet use and online purchasing." Prepare an argument explaining why you do or do not believe this to be true.
20. Investigate current trends in products and services purchased over the Internet. How do these compare with the list presented in the chapter (e.g., books, CDs)? Explain the conclusions you draw from your research.
21. "You can have the slickest Web site and the coolest products, but ultimately it is old-fashioned delivery that ensures customer satisfaction." Do you agree or disagree with this statement and why?
22. Prepare arguments to support or refute the right of an employer to utilize electronic means to monitor employees. Discuss your arguments with your classmates. Summarize the arguments presented by others to add to your own.

CHAPTER

11

Research and Ethical Issues

On completion of this chapter, you will be able to:

- understand why research is important in business;
- differentiate between primary and secondary data;
- use a variety of electronic methods to gather data;
- evaluate research with respect to validity, bias, confidentiality, currency, etc.;
- learn to cite sources properly; and
- describe a variety of ethical and legal issues related to information technology.

"When you take stuff from one writer, it's plagiarism; but when you take it from many writers, it's research."

—Wilson Mizner (1876–1933)

Our increasing reliance on information, coupled with the effortless availability of it from a variety of electronic sources, opens up a Pandora's box of issues related to fair and appropriate use of information. Both consumers and producers of information are faced with dilemmas ranging from how to gather information, to what can and should be done with it, to how to know which information should be used for what purposes. This chapter will help you make your way through some of the murky issues related to making good decisions about when to gather information and how to use it in fair and legal ways. Topics that will be covered in this chapter include:

- Research
- Citing Your Research Sources
- Ethical Issues
- Legal Issues

Ready, Set, Go!

Using your favourite search engine:

- Locate 10 Internet-based electronic resources that can be used to find or monitor financial information in Canada.
- Bookmark or record the URLs and names of these sources for future use.

Using either the Internet, a library, or resources from other courses you have taken:

- Record definitions for the following terms in a word-processed document: *investment, principle, mortgage, debt, interest, mutual fund, GIC, savings bond, stock, compound interest, return on investment.*
- List the sources from which you got each of these definitions. Submit your definitions to your teacher for approval before filing them in your notebook.

Introduction to Chapter Projects

Recall that the Chapter Projects are introduced at the beginning and are to be completed as you work through the chapter. Your teacher will provide you with assessment and evaluation criteria.

CHAPTER PROJECT 1

A close friend or family member has asked you for advice on how to invest a $50 000 inheritance. To help this person, complete the following tasks:

- Use the Internet or other electronic sources to investigate the types of available investment options (include mutual funds, stocks, GICs, and savings accounts) and what the associated rates of return are. Evaluate each electronic source used with respect to its validity, bias, confidentiality, currency, appropriateness, and accuracy.
- Use a spreadsheet to calculate the projected return on a $50 000 investment for time periods of one year, three years, and five years for at least three investment options.
- Use word-processing software to prepare a report that includes the following:
  - definitions of each of the types of investments researched;
  - analysis of each investment option (advantages, disadvantages, risks, ethical issues related to each form of investment);
  - a recommendation for a full investment strategy (which may include spreading the money across several investments) with a rationale for this choice; and
  - proper citation and description of all sources used and how each can be used in the future for this investor to monitor his or her investment.

CHAPTER PROJECT 11

You have been hired as a consultant to help a local company, Sparkle-Dot-Com, to determine the best course of action to take financially, given recent developments. Sparkle-Dot-Com has $90 000 in cash reserves that it does not foresee a need to use. The owner and CEO of Sparkle-Dot-Com, Veronica Meliukstis, is considering several options for these funds:

- Purchase a building using all or part of the $90 000 as a down payment. Sparkle-Dot-Com currently pays $2500 per month for rent (including utilities) for a space that is approximately 100 square metres. Instead, that monthly amount could be used for mortgage payments, utilities, and property taxes.
- Continue renting space and invest the $90 000. Ms. Meliukstis has thought about stocks in other companies, mutual funds, and GICs but is not sure which is the best alternative. She is concerned with ethical investments and will sacrifice high returns to make sure her money is used fairly by companies or governments.

Prepare a report for Sparkle-Dot-Com using word-processing software and an integrated spreadsheet in which you propose and describe options for the use of this money. Use the Internet to research prices for local real estate and rates of return for relevant types of investment. Your report must contain the information listed below:

- the options available for investing the $90 000 (including purchase of a local space). Include details such as specific pieces of real estate available for purchase, specific investment options, current interest rates, etc.;
- advantages and disadvantages of each option described;
- projections for total return on investment for time periods of one year, three years, and five years;
- a recommended course of action for Sparkle-Dot-Com; and
- an annotated bibliography with proper citations that mentions the results of your evaluation of sources used (e.g., validity, bias, accuracy, etc.).

11.1 Research

Businesses collect data in various forms and for a number of reasons. Valid information, gathered from research, is essential to making good business decisions. Before launching a new product or service, an organization would at the very least need to research the following:

- what, if any, competition exists and how competitors are positioned in the marketplace;

- what, if any, laws (both domestic and international) affect the new product or service;
- the types and cost of resources (people, facilities, equipment, raw materials, packaging, distribution) needed to create the product or service;
- the size of the market and likely reaction of consumers to the new product or service;
- types and cost of marketing or advertising that would be necessary;
- financial data, including cash flow, needed to launch the product and to estimate when it would generate a profit; and
- potential risks of entering the market.

Research may also be done to improve or modify products or services to better meet consumer needs, or to improve the organization itself. Examples of issues that organizations may seek to address include: Web sites or content, response to advertisements, opinions about a company, employee satisfaction, or employee learning needs. The reasons for engaging in research are countless. The challenge is getting the right information to solve business problems.

11.1.1 Primary and Secondary Research

Information collected directly "from the source" through surveys, interviews, or experiments is known as **primary data**. Information that has already been gathered by other individuals or groups and is available through a published source is known as **secondary data**.

Researchers virtually always begin by identifying secondary research to avoid duplicating someone else's work. Sources of secondary data include:

- printed sources, such as books, magazines, and newspapers;
- e-publications, such as e-books and online magazines and journals;
- newsgroups, listservs, and discussion groups;
- CD-ROMs;
- information from marketing research companies such as Ipsos-Reid; and
- databases.

Creating a research plan is important if you want to use time efficiently and obtain the type of information needed. Recommended steps are:

1. State the research problem as clearly as possible.
2. Identify the specific types of information needed to solve the research problem (e.g., current mortgage rates, average monthly expenditure on food for a Canadian household of four members).

digiknow

When you conduct a search using an Internet search engine, you receive a number of "hits" that match the keywords you selected. As you learned in Chapter 10, many search engines "sell" keyword results to advertisers. In that way, if you search the term "modem" the first group of results you find may have been purchased by companies that sell modems. Do you think that this is fair? Explain.

3. Identify the types of secondary sources that will be investigated to attempt to solve the research problem. For each, identify keywords that will be used if a search is necessary. Using a thesaurus can be helpful in this step.
4. Identify the types of primary research necessary (if applicable) to solve the problem (e.g., survey, observation).
5. If primary research is necessary, design an instrument to collect data. This could be an observation sheet, a questionnaire, or an online form.
6. Ask an "expert," such as a teacher, professional researcher, or librarian to look at the research strategy and suggest improvements or sources.
7. Begin researching.

When very specific information is needed that has not been gathered by others, a researcher designs a method for collecting primary data. Some common methods of primary data collection for business purposes include:

- telephone, face-to-face, e-mail, or Internet-based surveys;
- focus groups in which a small number of individuals are brought together by a researcher and asked to offer their opinions on a product sample, advertisement, or topic; and
- observation of individuals' habits in certain environments (e.g., in a shopping mall).

Get Connected

To look at one of the systems that enables blogging, go to www.pearsoned.ca/businessconnections. Then, describe how you can go about getting a "blogspot." Make a list of the requirements. Describe the type of information you would want to contain in your own blog.

digiknow

Blogs

Through **blogs** – online journals or diaries – people share ideas, views, and favourite sites. Blogs can be found that cover a variety of topics – from current events, to education, to music. The activity of updating a blog is *blogging. Bloggers* combine personal writing, online diaries, and Weblogs, or lists of links, meant to facilitate the connection, communication, and collaboration among people with similar interests or views. Because bloggers collect relevant links and provide them to visitors to their site, a researcher can view a variety of sources on a particular topic, rather than having to perform multiple electronic searches as a starting point. Remember though, the sources are only as good as the blogger is adept at evaluating them.

ON THE CASE

Surveys: Your Ticket to Primary Data

Just about everyone has, at one time or another, participated in a survey. Surveys are usually in the form of questionnaires (either telephone, paper-based, or online). Respondents answer a series of questions that provide a researcher with information for a specific purpose.

Creating a Survey

Have you ever found yourself filling out a survey, only to discover that you have no idea what the questions are getting at? Constructing an effective survey takes practice and a basic understanding of how to write effective surveys.

Start with objectives or a purpose for the survey. Ask yourself:

- How will the survey data be used?
- What types of information are needed?
- Who would be the best group of people to ask?
- How many people need to be surveyed to get enough responses to draw a conclusion?

All the questions in a survey should be linked to its purpose and objectives. Below are some tips to help you to construct a useful survey.

- Write questions that each person will interpret in the same way. A good question is short and straightforward. Only through careful writing, editing, review, and rewriting can you create a good questionnaire.
- Start with a cover letter (if the survey is going out by mail) or a brief explanation (for telephone or online) so that participants know the source of the survey, why it is being conducted, and how the results will be used.
- The questionnaire should be as short as possible. When writing questions, determine what is essential to know, what is useful to know, and what is "nice" to know. In general, only keep the questions that are essential. If the answer to the question is not important enough to include in your report, the question should be eliminated.
- Survey recipients may have a variety of backgrounds, so use simple language. For example, "What is your frequency of travel to school in the last 30 days?" is better understood as, "About how many times in the last 30 days have you travelled to school?"
- Use closed-ended (sometimes called "selected response") questions rather than open-ended questions. Closed-ended questions should have a fixed number of response categories, similar to multiple choice. An open-ended question is one for which respondents are given blank space to write whatever they wish. Closed-ended questions are useful because the respondents clearly know the purpose of the question and are limited to a set of choices where one answer is right for them. This also makes tabulating responses easier. However, when using closed-ended questions, keep the number to a minimum to avoid overwhelming those completing the survey.
- Arrange simple easy-to-answer questions in a logical order. For example, you might start with a set of questions that tell you about the person responding (e.g., age, education, occupation, income). A separately marked section might contain a group of questions about the respondent's use of or attitudes/preferences

about a particular product (e.g., Do you have a computer? How often do you use your computer? How many hours per week do you spend on the Internet?).

- Pre-test your survey with a small group of people to ensure it makes sense before you start your research.

Tabulating Survey Results

Appropriate software makes tabulating survey results manageable. Special statistical software (such as Statistical Package for the Social Sciences™ often called SPSS) is used for complicated, large-scale studies that require complex calculations. For simple questionnaires, spreadsheet software is quite effective.

The number of each type of response to each question should be reported. Then, results are calculated. The type of calculation depends on the type of data collected, as well as how those data will be used. Most commonly, percentages and averages (usually in the form of means) are calculated.

The way to tabulate the results of a survey with multiple choice answers is to determine the percentage that each possible response is of the total number of responses to a given question. For example, you might ask 50 people "Do you have access to the Internet at home?" Let us assume you record 35 "yes" and 15 "no" responses in the software. Next, you would calculate what percentage of the total each response represents; using the example above, (35/50 x 100% = 70%), so 70% of all respondents have Internet access at home.

In some cases, different calculations are necessary. For example, you might ask "How many hours do you spend on the Internet per week?" For a range of data like this, you might wish to calculate the average (or mean). This way, you could report that the average respondent spends *x* hours per week on the Internet.

Questions

1. Locate two online surveys using your favourite search engine. Create a table or chart to compare them using the tips listed above as criteria. Which survey did you think was more effective? Why?
2. Suppose that you are the manager of a small retail clothing store thinking about starting an e-commerce site. You decide to create a survey to find out what customers would want on a Web site for your business. Complete the following:
   - State the objective(s) of the survey in your own words.
   - Determine to whom you would distribute the survey.
   - Create a one-page survey using the tips provided above.
   - Pilot your survey with at least three people in your class.
   - Use the most appropriate software available to you to tabulate the results of the pilot.
   - Create a brief word-processed report (maximum one page) that summarizes your findings. Hand in the results and the survey to your teacher.

IT In Action

Online Research Tools

Source: Peter Key, "MBA candidate's idea melds into iNetSurvey," *Philadelphia Business Journal* [online], January 11, 2002.

Where should an organization start if it needs to collect primary data? One relatively inexpensive and fast option is to use self-serve Internet-based surveying tools. iNetSurvey is a successful provider of software that can be used by students or companies to gather information via the Internet.

The concept for iNetSurvey was formed by Jitendra Lulla while he was working on his MBA at Rutgers University in 1999. He realized that companies were spending huge amounts of money conducting research, then paying employees to enter the data gathered into spreadsheets. His vision was to create software that would allow those being polled to enter their answers into any Web browser, and then have those results automatically transferred into a spreadsheet and provide real-time results in any form the researcher wanted (e.g., numbers, bar graphs).

Mr. Lulla's vision is now a reality. Upon subscribing to the service, your possibilities are limitless. iNetSurvey's customers create their own surveys or use one of the predefined surveys available online. The survey can be hosted on iNetSurvey's Web site or on the researcher's own site. The software can even ensure that each respondent completes the survey only once through the use of cookies. Most importantly, though, iNetSurvey allows for easy interpretation of all the numbers the survey collects. Results can be viewed online or downloaded in a variety of formats, including a variety of graphs, cross-tabulation (comparing responses for one question with another), and many other features.

iNetSurvey's clients use the surveys for a variety of purposes — from employee satisfaction surveys, to customer satisfaction surveys, to investigation of customer interests in new products. John Vairo, the Vice President of Sales and Marketing for iNetSurvey, summed up the prospects for this company: "The concept is fairly new, but the market is very, very large."

Questions

1. Through the links at www.pearsoned.ca/businessconnections, visit the iNetSurvey site or a similar site to view samples. Electronically create a document that shows the advantages and disadvantages of these samples over paper-based, face-to-face, and telephone surveys.
2. Describe the strategies that can be used to ensure that these forms of surveys are getting the intended audiences to respond.
3. Describe two problems you might encounter in getting people to respond to these sorts of surveys.

11.1.2 Classifying and Assessing Research

Gathering information is the just the beginning. Volumes and volumes of data are readily available through a variety of sources and can be gathered relatively easily. The challenge to any researcher is to sort through data and select what should be used to solve the research problem.

- ***Relevance*** refers to the degree to which information is applicable to the research problem. An effective researcher ranks the relevance of data found from most important to least important, and uses the information accordingly. Irrelevant information should not be used.
- ***Appropriateness*** refers to how suitable the information is to the research question or problem being addressed. Interesting information may be available, but it may be superfluous or unnecessary to the research being conducted.
- ***Validity*** is a word used to describe how truthful, logical, and trustworthy information is. When doing research, it is important to use valid information to ensure that your work is as correct as possible. When evaluating a secondary resource, look at the validity of the author, the publisher, and the facts. Where the author and/or publisher are well known for their tendency to publish factual and balanced work, the data are likely to be valid. Unknown sources can be investigated to determine their reputation. Another method of determining validity is to cross-check any facts, numbers, statements, and so on to see if they are accurate. Look to see how the information was gathered and whether the methods make sense. Were the right people asked? Were the questions appropriate?
- ***Accuracy*** refers to how exact the information is. Accuracy can be determined by cross-checking facts and numbers with other sources, by employing common sense, and by reading the "fine print." For example, data from a survey conducted by a polling organization (such as Ipsos-Reid) will usually indicate how exact the findings are by describing the margin of error. Alternatively, checking Web sites of reliable organizations, such as Statistics Canada, can provide insight into the accuracy of statistics and information.
- ***Bias*** describes information that expresses a particular viewpoint or is incomplete for a specific purpose. For example, some tobacco manufacturers might omit facts about the dangers of tobacco in a document about cigarettes in order to protect their image or to sell their product. This type of prejudiced information is biased. Researchers need to be extremely wary of sources and to try to determine what, if any, bias the author or sponsoring organization might show. Another strategy to identify bias is to compare and contrast similar information from several sources and to identify bias based on the differences.

By looking at a variety of different sources, a more balanced view might be evident. When assessing secondary data, consider what questions were asked, to whom they were asked, and in what context. If questions are phrased in a certain way, sometimes respondents are led to answer in a certain way.

- *Confidentiality* is the degree to which information is for private use. Before using data and/or information, a researcher should be certain that use of them will not infringe on anyone's privacy. Usually, information published in online magazines or newspapers or in many reputable databases is intended for public consumption and is not an infringement on confidentiality. If data or information are provided from a person to the researcher, the researcher should check with the source to ensure that they may be used. When collecting primary data, confidentiality is an issue. As described in the section on Privacy later in the chapter, there are legal implications to gathering information from individuals.
- *Currency* refers to how current or up-to-date information is. If a source or Web site does not provide a publication or "last updated" date, the currency may be impossible to determine. In most cases, more recent information is preferable to older information.

GETTING IT

1. Identify a company familiar to you (either through the media or as a customer). Suggest a research problem the company might face. Explain how the company should go about gathering data to solve the research problem.
2. If somebody gave you an article from a Web site to help you with a research project, what steps would you take to assess the document? Identify the criteria that would lead you to use it in your project.
3. Give a specific example in which currency would not be necessary for assessing data (*hint*: think of examples of assignments or articles that require very old information).

digiknow

An **editorial** is a piece of journalism (such as an opinion article) in which the writer is paid by a publisher or by the entity that runs a particular publication. Most magazines and newspapers have editorials in which staff are paid by the newspaper (not by an advertiser) to write about a topic. An **advertorial** is a piece of journalism that looks like an article, but is paid for by an advertiser of the publication in which it appears. For example, an article in a fitness magazine about the benefits of a particular protein supplement is an advertorial if it was placed by the manufacturer. **Stealth sites** are Internet sites that appear to be traditional and credible journalism (such as an independent newspaper or newsletter), but are actually advertisement sites that do not mention that they are sponsored and run by a commercial organization. These sites are used by companies to provide biased information to individuals researching a particular topic related to a company's products or services. It is extremely difficult to detect a stealth site because advertisers cover their tracks extremely well.

IT In Action

Ipsos-Reid Canada

Sources: Ipsos-Reid Corporation, "Company Profile," "About Us," and "Canadian Homepage" all available online.

Ipsos-Reid is practically a household name in North America. This organization is frequently referred to in the media (and in books like this one) because it provides frequent and reliable information about the opinions and behaviour of Canadians.

With offices worldwide, Ipsos-Reid works with a network of over 3000 researchers and offices in 11 North American cities to collect data. This organization conducts a variety of types of research. They are known for their **omnibus surveys** (large-scale surveys that look for general opinions, attitudes, or types of behaviour not specific to any one company), but they can be hired to conduct customized research for organizations. Some examples of their ongoing surveys include the Canadian Ipsos-Reid Express, a weekly omnibus survey for Canadian opinions on a variety of issues; Ontario Reid Express, a bi-monthly public opinion omnibus survey that provides the results of telephone interviews with 1000 Ontarians; and the Alberta Reid Express and BC Reid Express omnibus surveys, each conducted monthly. Though some research results are available free of charge and highlights are often distributed to the media and public through press releases, much of Ipsos-Reid's work must be purchased.

In addition to traditional data collection methods, Ipsos-Reid has an online division, NPDOR, which has a database of Canadians from which to gather very specific information on behalf of specific clients (such as companies, governments, or associations). The advantage to this is that information can be gathered and tabulated very quickly using electronic channels.

Several decades ago, researchers could not have imagined the volume of data they would be able to gather in such short periods of time. Organizations like Ipsos-Reid have grown and thrived based on their ability to harness the capabilities of technology to perform these types of tasks.

Questions

Through the links at www.pearsoned.ca/businessconnections, visit a public opinion research site and investigate some of the data available.

1. Identify the types of data that are available free of charge.
2. Make a list of the types of reports that are available for purchase. Give an example of one, including the price.

11.2 Citing Your Research Sources

When producing documents, ensuring that the ideas of others are acknowledged is not only fair, but required to prevent plagiarism. In fact, most schools have policies in place to prevent plagiarism, in some cases with severe consequences.

11.2.1 Style Manuals

Countless ways exist to express the same information. In an attempt to standardize the way that information is presented in reports, essays, publications, and other documents, writers and publishers over the years have developed **style manuals**. Style manuals are guides that prescribe ways for writers to organize their work and cite sources of quotations and information. They also provide information on grammar, punctuation, preferred spelling, hyphenation, and citation format.

Though life as a student or writer would be simpler if there were only one set of standards, a wide range of style manuals exist. This section will provide you with tips on how to adhere to the conventions of the three most common manuals: *MLA Handbook for Writers of Research Papers* published by the Modern Language Association of America, *The Chicago Manual of Style*, and the *Publication Manual of the American Psychological Association*. Generally speaking, publications for the social sciences (e.g., psychology, business, sociology, education) follow the APA style, the humanities (e.g., philosophy, theology, arts) follow MLA style, and history publications follow Chicago style.

digiknow

Some of the other style manuals that are used include those developed by the American Medical Association (AMA) for medical publications and by the Institute for Electrical and Electronics Engineers (IEEE).

11.2.2 Embedded Citations, Footnotes, and Endnotes

Embedded citations, footnotes, and endnotes serve the same purpose: to identify the source of a quote or an idea contained in the body of a document. Different style manuals prescribe different ways of citing sources within a document (as illustrated in Figure 11.1 on page 320). One important point is that any source cited in an embedded citation, footnote, or endnote must appear in the bibliography at the end of the document.

The difference among these formats lies primarily in their location.

- **Embedded citations** appear within the text in brackets and cite the author's last name, and sometimes additional information, such as year of publication or page reference. These appear immediately before or after the information being cited.
- **Footnotes** appear at the bottom of the page; they are identified by a number or symbol that corresponds to a number or symbol that appears immediately following the quotation or idea being cited. Footnotes usually contain more information than embedded citations (such as the name of the publication, the place and year of publication, and, in the case of books, the publisher).
- **Endnotes** are also identified by a number or symbol within the text, but their information appears at the end of a chapter or document rather than at the bottom of each page. Word-processing programs have built-in functions that make footnotes easy to insert.

Figure 11.1
Citing Sources in a Document

Style Manual	Form	Example
MLA Handbook for Writers of Research Papers	Embedded citation	The progress of the Information Revolution mirrors that of the Industrial Revolution. (McKeown). (*Note*: a page number would be included if this was a direct quote.)
The Chicago Manual of Style	Footnote or endnote	[1]Robert McKeown, *The Information Age* (Toronto: Lily Press, 1999): 432.
Publication Manual of the American Psychological Association	Embedded citation	The progress of the Information Revolution mirrors that of the Industrial Revolution (McKeown 1999). (*Note*: a page number would be included if this was a direct quote.) According to McKeown (1999), the progress of the Information Revolution mirrors that of the Industrial Revolution.

11.2.3 Bibliographies

A **bibliography** is a list of sources used in the preparation of a document (such as a report or a book). Bibliographies appear at the end of the document and ought to follow the same style as the rest of the document in terms of the format of citations. Entries are organized alphabetically by the authors' last names. Sometimes, bibliographies are categorized by subheading to indicate the types of sources used. Subheadings often used to organize bibliographies include: books, magazine articles, journal articles, Web sites, interviews, and so on. When citing electronic sources, the date on which the item was retrieved is often included. Figure 11.2 compares the styles for bibliographic citations of three major style guides.

Figure 11.2
Bibliographic Citations

Source	MLA Style & Chicago Style	APA Style
Book	Pinto, Laura and Janice Ellerby. *Business Connections*. Toronto: Pearson, 2003.	Pinto, L. & Ellerby, J. (2003). *Business Connections*. Toronto: Pearson.
Article from a database	Lucas, Tim. "The Effects Of E-Learning On Schools." Journal of Applied Education, 21 May 2003: 78, 443-449. EduArtS Database. 26 May 2003 <http://www.Eduarts.com>.	Lucas, T. (2003). The effects of e-learning on schools. *Journal of Applied Education, 78*, 443-449. Retrieved May 26, 2003, from EduArtS database.
Stand-alone Internet document (e.g., Web site), no date, no author	"WWW User Survey." 1 Apr. 2003. <http://www.lp.edu//surveys/survey1-10/>.	*WWW user survey.* (n.d.). Retrieved April 1, 2003, from http://www.lp.edu//surveys/survey1-10/

Figure 11.2 (continued)
Bibliographic Citations

Source	MLA Style & Chicago Style	APA Style
Internet article based on a print source	Doe, Jason. "Varsity Team Wins." Provincial High Newsletter. May 2002: 1. 23 June 2003 <http://phn.ca/23_09>.	Doe, J. (2002). Varsity team wins [Electronic version]. *Provincial High Newsletter,* May 2002, 1.
Document available on corporate or educational Web site	Badikonis, Karl. "Dog Acceptance of Multimedia Stimuli." CyberDog Web Site. 24 August 2004 <http://www.cydog.net/papers/new.html>.	Badikonis, Karl. (2004). *Dog acceptance of multimedia stimuli.* Retrieved August 24, 2004, from CyberDog Web site: http://www.cydog.net/papers/new.html
CD	Encyclopedia Britannica. (2003). The World Wide Web. Retrieved from *Encyclopedia Britannica* CD-ROM, Fall 2002 release.	Encyclopedia Britannica. (2003). The World Wide Web. Retrieved from *Encyclopedia Britannica* CD-ROM, Fall 2002 release.
E-mail	Baird, Elle. "Convergent Technology" e-mail to the author. 23 November 2003.	Baird, E. (personal communications, November 23, 2003).
Listserv	Libby, Margaret. "RE: Digital Media." Online Posting. 20 March 2004. TechEd. 1 April 2004 <http://TechEd.lt>.	Libby, M. (2004). *RE: Digital Media.* Online posting. TechEd Listserv. Retrieved April 1, 2004 from http://TechEd.lt.

An **annotated bibliography** is one that provides additional information about the source, such as a brief summary of the contents. Usually, annotations appear in paragraph form directly below each citation. For example, an annotation following the citation for this book might read "*Business Connections: Information Technology in Action* covers a variety of topics ranging from project management and computing and software basics, to e-commerce and e-business, research and ethical issues in IT, and multimedia applications."

GETTING IT

1. Summarize your school's policy on plagiarism.
2. Describe why style manuals are useful. Explain who might use them.
3. Carefully compare the different types of bibliographic citations. There are differences in capitalization and punctuation. What are they?
4. In many cases, style manuals require citations to include the date when electronic sources were accessed. Why do you think that is?

Get Connected

You can explore a number of style guides at www.pearsoned.ca/businessconnections. Prepare a summary of your findings that includes the tips the sites provide and how you might use this as a student. As an employee.

11.3 Ethical Issues

Initially, the Internet was used primarily for information exchange among individuals, governments, and educational bodies. The type of information transmitted electronically (from the Internet and other sources) has evolved to include information, entertainment, and commerce. As the lines between these types of information have become blurred — and more and more information is readily and quickly exchanged through the course of e-business — a variety of ethical issues have emerged. Figure 11.3 provides some guidelines for the ethical use of electronic research on the Internet.

Figure 11.3
Guidelines for Ethical Use of Electronic Research in E-Business

Ethical Issue	Description	Ask Yourself...
Confidentiality	The degree to which information is for private use	• Did the sources of information know that data were being gathered and did they give consent? • Are those people or organizations aware of how you plan to use the information? • Is there any threat to the privacy, safety, or reputation of the sources if you use the information?
Validity	How truthful, logical, and trustworthy information is	• Are you confident that the information you are using is valid (i.e., genuine, well-founded, authentic)? • Is the information factual? What data are used to support statements? • Can you verify background information through other sources?
Credibility	How believable the information is	• Was the information collected using proper data collection methods? How do you know? • What sources were used to gather facts or numbers? Do you trust them?
Integrity	How honest and unbiased the information is	• Why was the information published and for what audience and purpose? • Is the author's point of view objective? • What is the source of the information? Check the publisher or URL; do they have any reason for bias? If the source is a Web site, are you certain it is not a "stealth" site? • Is the author qualified? How do you know? What are her or his credentials? • Will the way you present the information be in any way misleading to readers? • Are you being careful to ensure a balance of points of view in the sources you select?

A simple definition for **ethics** is a set of principles or rules that a person follows regarding what is good and bad and right and wrong. If something is "ethical," it does not necessarily mean that it is legal, and vice versa. This is partially because ethics are "subjective" — that is, each person's ethics are unique to that individual. It is this subjectivity, and the fact that ethical and legal are not always the same thing, that make ethics so tricky to understand.

Here is an example to help you understand. Geri donated her computer software to the community bazaar to raise money for the Breakfast for Kids fund. Geri believes this action is ethical because it is for a good cause. However, she is also aware that it is illegal because it violates the licensing agreement and that there are consequences to breaking the law. The computer software company may not see Geri's action as ethical.

The most common factors that form a person's individual ethics are described below. Keep in mind that ethics are highly personal, so the influences may vary from one person to the next.

- *Family influences.* People tend to develop beliefs about ethics and morals from their parents, brothers, and sisters based on observing their behaviour and/or receiving punishment for doing things that the family perceives as "unethical."
- *Peer influences.* Classmates and others in a person's social network can shape ethics. Peer pressure, for example, can help to determine how much a person is willing to engage in questionable activities like shoplifting, lying, hacking, etc.
- *Past experiences.* Often, the consequences of previous behaviour condition a person to feel comfortable with certain ethical standards. For instance, if a salesperson lies to a customer to make a sale and then is reprimanded by the manager, he or she would likely perceive lying as undesirable and unethical behaviour. On the other hand, if the person makes the sale and is rewarded by the manager, lying may be perceived as desirable and ethical behaviour.
- *Religious affiliation.* Generally, a person's religious beliefs may shape what that person perceives as right and wrong.
- *Situational factors.* People adjust their ethics to suit certain circumstances. For example, Mike, who works in an office as a data-entry clerk, is opposed to stealing. However, he often takes home boxes of pens, paper clips, markers, and masking tape to give to his nieces and nephews. He is taking supplies that belong to his employer without permission, which can be considered stealing. He feels comfortable taking these items from his employer in this situation, though he would never steal from a store.

11.3.1 Ethical Frameworks

An **ethical framework** is a system that a person can use to help to make a decision when faced with a dilemma. Below are two frameworks: deontology and utilitarianism. Either one can be employed when trying to make a decision that involves an ethical dilemma — there is no one correct framework to use. The framework chosen to guide a decision will always depend on the situation and on the individual feelings of the person faced with the problem.

Deontology is the belief that there are some things that a person should do ("right"), and others a person should not do ("wrong"). People should try to do the things they believe are right (such as being honest), and refrain from doing the wrong things (such as stealing), regardless of what the consequences are. This can cause problems, if doing the right thing has a negative consequence. For example, if you are honest about the whereabouts of someone who has been wrongly accused and is being sought by the police, the consequence is that an innocent person will be arrested. Another problem with deontology is that no clear method exists by which to classify behaviour and actions as absolutely right and absolutely wrong. Deontological arguments are based on adhering to sets of rules.

Utilitarianism suggests that an ethical decision results in taking action that will result in the greatest good for the greatest number of people. The result or outcome is the key factor in deciding what to do. Looking again at the example above, a utilitarian would argue that you should not disclose the location of the wrongly accused person to the police because it would cause more harm than good to a greater number of people. You would harm the wrongly accused person (incarceration) and family members who depend on the accused for financial support. By not saying anything, nobody would be harmed, thus creating the greatest good for the greatest number of people.

ON THE CASE

Association for Computing Machinery Code of Ethics and Professional Conduct

Adapted from George Beekman, *Computer Confluence: Exploring Tomorrow's Technology.* Upper Saddle River, NJ: Pearson Education/Prentice Hall 2003: pp. 465–467.

Many organizations and associations have implemented codes for ethical behaviour in recent years. The intent of such codes is to help employees and members to make ethical decisions that contribute to the well-being of themselves, the organization, and others. The Association for Computing Machinery (ACM) is no exception. This organization for technology professionals has developed a code of ethical professional conduct for its members. It consists of four sections:

- General moral imperatives;
- Specific professional responsibilities;
- Organizational leadership imperatives; and
- Policy for compliance with the code.

ON THE CASE (continued)

Very briefly summarized, ACM members are expected to adhere to the following general moral imperatives:

- Contribute to society and human well-being.
- Avoid harm to others.
- Be honest and trustworthy.
- Be fair and take action not to discriminate.
- Honour property rights, including copyrights and patents.
- Give credit for intellectual property.
- Respect the privacy of others.
- Honour confidentiality.

Questions

1. Identify the ACM moral imperatives that are based on deontology and those that follow the principles of utilitarianism.
2. Explain why you do or do not agree with some or all of the imperatives.

ON THE CASE

The New Meaning of Loyalty

Sources: Jane Hadley, " 'Loyalty' cards cause griping over swiping," *Seattle Post-Intelligencer* [online]; CASPIAN, "Is Big Brother in your grocery cart?" www.nocards.org (January 4, 2003).

In order to create new products to meet consumer needs, to increase demand for products, and to advertise more effectively, companies gather enormous amounts of data in the form of market research. Types of information useful to companies include customer preferences, buying habits, and reading, radio, and television habits. Traditionally, market research took the form of surveys — conducted either by mail, by telephone, or in person. As anyone who has received a telephone survey request at an inopportune time can tell you, not all consumers are interested in taking the time to provide information to researchers! This problem has posed a challenge to researchers for decades.

During the early 1990s, advances in technology led to the creation of "loyalty cards." Similar in appearance to credit cards, loyalty cards are swiped by a merchant at the time of purchase (or a number is keyed in for electronic transactions) to transmit purchase information. Examples of loyalty cards include AirMiles Reward Miles, Shopper's Optimum, and HBC Rewards. Loyalty cards present a twofold opportunity to companies. First, they encourage a consumer to use a particular business in order to gain rewards. Second, they allow the company that distributes the cards to track information about where the consumer shops, how often, what she or he purchases, and so on. For example, AirMiles Reward Miles can provide a "portrait" of a consumer's brand preferences at a variety of retailers in Canada, their financial habits (Bank of Montreal and American Express allow for AirMiles on their financial services), what their leisure preferences are based on how they redeem rewards (e.g., travel, movies, etc.), and opportunities to contact them (through their statements).

Consumers Against Supermarket Privacy Invasion and Numbering (CASPIAN) is a U.S. group that opposes the use of loyalty cards, because they record purchase information that could potentially be used against the cardholder. For instance, a loyalty cardholder could be rejected for health coverage through an insurance agency because she or he has a heart condition and her or his grocery store records show that she or he has been purchasing potato chips and rich desserts. One of CASPIAN's fears has already become a reality in the United States — after persisting in a lawsuit over an injury in the parking lot of a shopping mall, a cardholder's record of excessive alcohol purchases was introduced as evidence, implying that the person was an alcoholic and was therefore personally responsible for the injury.

Questions

1. Identify the members of your family who have loyalty cards. Prepare a list of the types of information that is recorded on the cards.
2. In your opinion, is it a fair exchange to receive loyalty rewards in "payment" for this type of information? Explain.
3. Do you have any privacy concerns about loyalty cards? Explain.
4. Was the use of loyalty card information in the lawsuit described above ethical? Explain.

GETTING IT

1. Give an example of an ethical problem or dilemma that you might encounter while doing research, and while conducting e-business.
2. Describe the benefits for an organization of having a code of ethics.
3. Describe a scenario that would demonstrate the potential damage of using information that:
   a. lacks confidentiality
   b. is not valid

digiknow

Seemingly harmless, Internet **hoaxes** and chain letters (those messages that you find in your inbox with subject lines such as "Safety Tips for Young Women" or "Help a Sick Child") can wreak havoc on servers and cost companies a great deal of money in employee time spent reading and sending these messages. The Computer Incident Advisory Capability (CIAC) Internet Hoax Information site estimates that by the sixth generation of a hoax e-mail (that is, the sixth set of recipients that mail it to their distribution lists), a million e-mails are sent, having the potential to cause mail servers to slow down.

Hoax generation	1st	2nd	3rd	4th	5th	6th
Number of times forwarded	10	100	1000	10 000	100 000	1 000 000

More importantly, the CIAC suggests there is evidence that spamming businesses create some hoax e-mails in order to harvest e-mail addresses to use for unsolicited advertisements. (CIAC 2002)

11.4 Legal Issues

Most of us, at some point, have experienced that unique sense of frustration when an idea that we had was used or effectively put into action by someone else. More often than not, this type of situation is simply a coincidence. But what if someone actually knowingly stole your idea? As information becomes increasingly valuable in our society, greater legal emphasis is being placed on the recognition and protection of original work.

Intellectual property is a broad term used to describe a variety of creative endeavours (see Figure 11.4) in the following areas: patents, trademarks, industrial designs, confidential information/trade secrets, integrated circuit topography, and copyright.

Figure 11.4
Intellectual Property Law

Area of Intellectual Property	Type of Works Protected	Example
Patent Law	- apparatus - article - composition - process	- pocket-sized cassette or CD player
Trademark Law	- picture - symbol - word	- Walkman
Industrial Design	- design - shape - pattern	- design of headphones
Confidential Information/Trade Secrets	- idea - research information - concept	- idea to improve the CD player
Integrated Circuit Topography	- microchips	- microchip in the Walkman
Copyright Law	- artistic works - dramatic works - literary works - musical works	- instruction booklet and written warranty

Source: Blair, Annice et al. *Law in Action: Understanding Canadian Law Teacher Resource.* Toronto: Pearson Education Canada Inc., 2003, p. 486.

The constant flow of information over electronic channels has created new challenges for those who produce intellectual property, as well as lawyers and governments that struggle to keep up with new and unforeseen problems.

The sections that follow describe key Canadian laws related to the use and protection of creative work, ideas, and information.

11.4.1 Copyright

Whether you write a paper, an article, a book, Web content, a song, or some other original piece of work, you probably want protection so that nobody can steal it. In Canada and other countries, copyright law protects authors from this form of theft.

11.4.1.1 Copyright and Ownership

In Canada, when an individual creates an original work (such as a literary work or a musical composition), legislation gives the creator of a work the **copyright** that is the exclusive right to reproduce, publish, or perform the work. If the work is created while in the course of employment or the creator was paid/commissioned to do the work, the copyright generally belongs to the employer who commissioned the work, unless a written agreement signed by both parties states otherwise. Canada's *Copyright Act* says that no one can reproduce or use the work created by another person without permission from the holder of the copyright. There are exceptions, which you will read about in Section 11.4.1.4.

Copyright owners should mark their works with their name, the year in which the work was first published, and the copyright symbol ©. Using the symbol ensures the work will be protected in other countries that adhere to the Universal Copyright Convention, and where such a requirement is mandatory. The copyright symbol is a reminder to others that the work is copyright protected.

In Canada, compliance with copyright law is monitored by one of several copyright bodies that look after that particular form of media. For example, an organization called Access Copyright (formerly CANCOPY) monitors print and some digital written media, while a separate body, SOCAN, monitors music.

11.4.1.2 Duration of Copyright

Copyright generally exists for the life of a creator plus 50 years after the end of the calendar year of the creator's death. However, there are some exceptions to this rule, including the following:

- *Crown works* (government publications);
- *Posthumous works* (meaning they were not published during the lifetime of the author); in this case, copyright extends from the date of publication, performance, or delivery in public, until the end of that calendar year and 50 years thereafter;
- *Works by an unknown author* (copyright for either the remainder of the calendar year of first publication plus 50 years thereafter or the remainder of the calendar year of the making of the work and 75 years after, whichever comes first); and
- *Works created through joint authorship* (These hold their copyright for the lifetime of the author who dies last and 50 years after).

Once the copyright expires, the work is said to be in *public domain* and may be copied freely without permission.

11.4.1.3 Printing and Copying

Contrary to popular myth, libraries and educational institutions *cannot* make multiple copies of Web site content, articles, parts of books, or articles for student use. Production of multiple copies requires the consent of the copyright holder, which may be obtained through a licensing agreement with a copyright body (such as Access Copyright, which governs print material) or directly with the copyright owner. However, Canada's *Copyright Act* does allow printing and copying by individuals of parts of works for private study or research. Such copying should be minimal. This exception falls within the "fair dealing" section of the Act.

11.4.1.4 Fair Dealing

Fair dealing is the use or reproduction of a work for private study, research, criticism, review, or news reporting without permission from the copyright holder. It is not a law, but a set of principles or guidelines that are used to interpret the law. Fair dealing was created to allow research, news, and certain educational activities to use parts of copyrighted work without the permission of the author. Four factors are considered to determine fair dealing:

1. *What is the character of the use?* The scales tip in favour of educational use, and away from commercial use.
2. *What is the nature, content, or topic of the work to be used?* Factual information and published material tip in favour of use, while unpublished or creative materials tend not to be covered under fair dealing.
3. *How much of the work will you use?* Generally speaking, the smaller the amount used, the more likely that fair dealing is in place.
4. *What effect would this use have on the market for the original or permissions if the use were widespread?* This factor is highly dependent on the outcomes and nature of the previous three. It refers specifically

to the potential to lose income as a result of your use of the copyrighted material. For example, photocopying a *Toronto Star* article so that you can refer to it as background for your work is fair dealing. Photocopying it for classmates in a course is not (unless the organization offering the course is an Access Copyright member). Any actions that would damage the commercial potential of the copyrighted work (such as saving an e-mail's content from a subscriber-based Web site so that others would not have to pay subscriber fees) would not be allowed. Figure 11.5 offers a list of dos and don'ts with respect to copyrights.

Figure 11.5
Copyright Dos And Don'ts

Dos	Don'ts
• Reference sources of quotes and original ideas in your work through embedded citations, footnotes, or endnotes. • Provide lists of resources suggested for further reading, including relevant Web sites instead of copies of content. • As a courtesy, inform Webmasters if providing links to their sites. • Use clipart if you have read the licence and can comply with it. • Contact the appropriate media body or copyright holder if you have questions.	• Do not save content from digital media (e.g., Web sites) and share it with others. • Do not take images, sounds, or animation from the Internet unless explicit permission to use it for your intended purpose is granted. • Do not show a rented video/DVD or one purchased for your private collection to a group (such as a class or online Webcast). The copyright on these types of multimedia are for personal use only. A special licence (obtained at the time of purchase) is needed to show a video to a group in a formal setting, such as a classroom.

11.4.2 Trademarks and Patents

Similar to copyright, trademarks and patents protect ownership of nonwritten work. **Trademarks**, symbolized as ® or ™, protect intellectual property in the form of words, phrases, or images. Unlike copyrights, which are automatic, trademarks must be registered with governments and are costly to acquire. Nike is an example of an organization that relies on trademarks; they have trademarked their name, the *swoosh* logo, and the phrase "just do it!" This prevents competitors or other people and organizations from using these pieces of intellectual property without Nike's permission. A Web site that contained the *swoosh* logo without Nike's permission would be in violation of the trademark and could face a fine. Similar to trademarks, **patents** can be registered to protect intellectual property in the form of processes, articles, and inventions. As with a trademark, registering a patent can be a costly and lengthy process.

11.4.3 Fraud

Fraud is a crime in which individuals or groups knowingly deceive or misrepresent themselves to gain personal benefit. Examples of fraud include false businesses, identity theft (posing as someone else), or selling a product or service as something it is not. Not surprisingly, the Internet and other digital media open up the floodgates for a variety of fraudulent activities. Because it is quite easy to mask one's identity (or worse yet, take someone else's identity), Internet fraud has steadily grown over the past decade. Figure 11.6 provides interesting data on this issue for 2001.

Figure 11.6
Top Internet Frauds in 2001

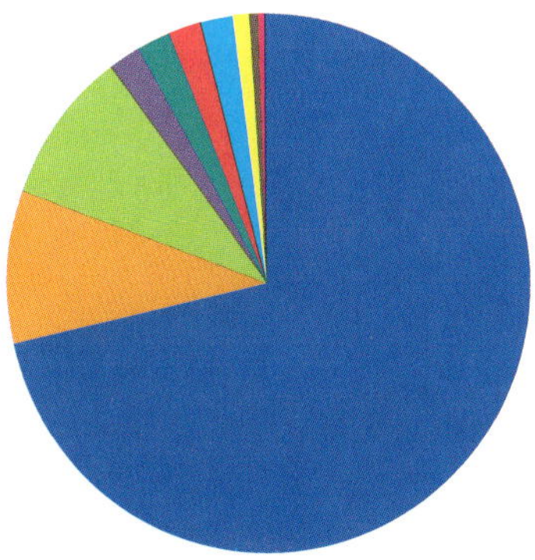

- Online auctions ($411)
- General merchandise sales ($730)
- Money offers that suggest if you "loan" money to a person, you will receive a high payback in the future ($5957)
- Computer equipment or software sales ($1048)
- Internet access services ($535)
- Information services ($209)
- Work-at-home offers ($121)
- Advance-fee loan offers ($1121)
- Credit card offers ($309)
- Business opportunities or franchises ($10 147)

Note: Figures in parentheses represent the average loss per person or business. All amounts are in U.S. dollars. Data specific to Canada are not yet available.

Source: National Fraud Information Centre at www.fraud.org/internet/2001stats.htm (November 15, 2002).

ON THE CASE

Fraud On Purpose

Dan Clements, a fraud expert who runs the anti-fraud Web site CardCops.com, wanted to find out just how long it takes for stolen credit-card details to find their way around the world. He posted fake card data online and put links to the information in a few Internet chat rooms. Within 15 minutes, 74 "carders" from 31 countries viewed his page. After one weekend, more than 1600 potential thieves had viewed the page. With his tracking software, Mr. Clements determined that they came from 75 countries, with the top three being Indonesia, the United States, and Romania (Sandoval 2002).

Questions

1. Describe the legal issue involved in Dan Clements's experiment.
2. Identify one ethical implication of putting "fake" credit card information online as Dan Clements did. Explain.
3. Describe two implications of this experiment for a company that engages in e-business through online transactions.

11.4.4 Licensing

A **licence** is a contract through which the owner of a piece of intellectual property permits another individual or organization to make, use, or sell that piece of intellectual property in exchange for some form of compensation. The licence allows the owner to maintain his or her ownership of the intellectual property — it does not surrender ownership to the licensee. With respect to the digital age and e-business, Davidson and Bryant (2001) identify three forms of licensing:

1. **Content licensing** refers to the ownership and sharing of any type of information in digital form (including databases, articles, Web content, videos, clipart, fonts, stock reports, music) through a contract. In 2000, interesting cases (such as the digital music site Napster) were reported regarding ownership and sharing of content. In such licences, the owner of the copyright provides the user with permission to use the information for specific purposes and usually for a specific fee. Problems arise when this type of information is exchanged beyond the terms of the licence, or without a licence at all.
2. **Technology licensing** refers to permission to use processes or actual software applications. For example, individual and corporate users purchase software licences to use most commercially produced software (such as Microsoft products). For individual users, the licence is part of the purchase agreement. Organizations often purchase a specific number of licences that allow a certain number of employees to use that particular software application. If additional employees install and use the software, the licence agreement has been violated.
3. **Advertising and cross-branding** refers to agreements among businesses (and sometimes individuals) to use one another's names and logos to increase business. Problems arise when intellectual property is used without a licence (such as a Web site that has a company's logo displayed without permission next to a link to their site) or logos are not properly displayed as per a licence agreement. For example, suppose that Kristen and Keegan have a Web site on which they evaluate recent innovations in information technology. Beside each product they review they put the logo of the manufacturer on the site without the manufacturers' permission. This is the use of intellectual property without a licence. Now suppose the manufacturers give Kristen and Keegan permission to use their actual logos. However, Kristen decides to change the colours so they will look better against the background of the Web site. This means she has not properly displayed the logos, which could cause the manufacturers to take action against Kristen and Keegan.

Get Connected

The National Fraud Information Centre (NFIC) is dedicated to tracking, investigating, and reporting on fraud perpetrated all over the world. Visit their Web site or a similar site by following the link on www.pearsoned.ca/businessconnections. Explain how the site can be of use to an Internet user. Create a list of the specific Internet fraud activities currently described on the site.

digiknow

Business Software Alliance (an organization formed in 1988 to tackle software piracy issues) reports that 40% of all new software installed by businesses around the world in 2001 was obtained on the black market, up from 37% in 2000, just as illicit software became widely available on the Internet. Eastern Europe and Latin America had the highest levels, with piracy rates of 67% and 57%, respectively. North America, where the copyright infringement laws are toughest and awareness is the highest, had the lowest rate of piracy.

(http//www.bsa.org/usa 2002)

ON THE CASE

Record Giants May Sue Individuals

Excerpt from: Reuters News Agency, "Record giants may sue individuals," Globeandmail.com, Thursday, July 4, 2002.

LOS ANGELES. The music industry is adding more firepower to its arsenal in the fight against online piracy, planting "decoys" on free peer-to-peer services and considering lawsuits against individual song-swappers, sources say.

Many large record labels have resorted to what is known as "spoofing" by hiring companies to distribute "decoy" files that are empty or do not work to frustrate would-be downloaders of movies and music.

"Spoofing is just one example of a lawful and appropriate self-help measure available to the labels to respond to the growing problem of peer-to-peer network piracy. It also happens to confirm the adage 'you get what you pay for,' " said a spokesman for the Recording Industry Association of America, the trade association for the big labels.

Additionally, sources said the RIAA, which represents music giants like Bertelsmann AG BMG, EMI Group, AOL Time Warner, Vivendi Universal and Sony, is considering taking a new tack by suing individuals who use the services, rather than the companies that host them.

"They're talking about suing individual users. It's one of many options to stop declining sales, but they haven't agreed yet whether to go forward or not," said a record executive.

Questions

1. Do you think the actions of the record companies are ethical? Explain why or why not.
2. Downloading music without paying for it is *illegal* because it infringes copyright. However, do you think the actions of those downloading music without paying for it are *ethical*? Explain why or why not.
3. Are the actions of the record companies illegal or fraudulent? Explain why or why not.
4. Write a paragraph in which you describe what you see as a reasonable solution to the problem that record companies are facing.

11.4.5 Privacy

With the volume of information changing hands electronically, many organizations (from the government, to health-care providers, to companies with whom you do business) and individuals have information about you on their databases. Use and misuse of this information can lead to problems as benign as annoyances from telemarketers, and as dangerous as identity theft or disclosure of information meant to be kept private. What is available to protect the privacy of Canadians in the digital information age?

The Government of Canada enforces a law entitled the *Personal Information Protection and Electronic Documents Act*, aimed at ensuring that organizations in Canada use information about individuals responsibly. According to the Privacy Commissioner of Canada, this piece of legislation contains five key requirements of organizations:

1. Organizations must obtain the consent of Canadians when collecting, using, or disclosing personal information.
2. A product or service cannot be withheld from a person if that person refuses to disclose personal information, *except* when that information is essential to the transaction (e.g., providing a driver's licence in order to purchase a vehicle).
3. Information must be collected in fair and lawful ways.
4. Personal information policies that are clear and understandable must be made available.
5. Personal information that is no longer needed for the purpose for which it was collected should be destroyed or made anonymous.

ON THE CASE

Freedom of Information and Privacy

According to the federal government, Canada is one of approximately 20 countries that have freedom of information (FOI) and approximately 40 that have data protection legislation. As described in Section 11.4.5, the federal government is responsible for privacy legislation.

However, each province has jurisdiction over FOI. FOI legislation and policies provide individual citizens with specific information and privacy rights for information collected or controlled by public bodies (such as governments). This allows individuals and organizations to obtain certain types of information, and forbids the release of other types of information that might compromise an individual's privacy.

Questions

1. Following the links at www.pearsoned.ca/businessconnections, select two provinces or territories and explore their FOI policies and legislation. Prepare a chart or table that specifically compares:
   - the role of the privacy commissioner;
   - how each province defines the audience;
   - key features of the policy or legislation (i.e., roles, responsibilities, and penalties); and
   - processes for requesting or obtaining information.
2. Prepare a brief (less than one page) word-processed summary of your findings.

Get Connected

Take the Government of Canada's privacy quiz available on the Privacy Commissioner of Canada's site available at www.pearsoned.ca/businessconnections. Record your score in your notebook. Identify anything that surprised you. Explain why.

GETTING IT

1. Explain what intellectual property means.
2. As a student, you are protected by intellectual property legislation. Describe the specific protection you have.
3. Think about a time (either at school or in your personal life) when you were faced with copyright infringement. You may not have been aware of it at the time. Describe the situation and how you handled it.
4. Differentiate between copyrights, patents, trademarks, and licences. Use examples.
5. Provide an example of how licensing affects a product or service that you use in your everyday life.
6. Do you think that your privacy is adequately protected by Canadian law? Explain.

CAREER PERSPECTIVE 1

Putting the Ethics in E-Business

By Zachary Tobias

Excerpt from *Computerworld*, November 6, 2000. Accessed on November 15, 2002, at www.computerworld.com.

Ethics Consultant

- Name and title: Tom Shanks, ethics consultant
- Nature of work: In workshops and meetings, he advises executives on setting ethical guidelines for day-to-day business practices. He also meets with employees and conducts surveys to find out where the hurdles are in meeting guidelines.
- Skills required: Communication, training and facilitating skills are key, as well as a theoretical background in ethics. Business knowledge is helpful, too. "At some point, you have to get real-world experience with how these things work in a business that has to make money," says Shanks.
- Training needed: Many begin with either a master's degree or a Ph.D. in philosophy, with an emphasis on ethics.
- Job and salary potential: Ethics consultants can earn as much as $5000 to $8000 per workshop at corporations, or $175 000 to $200 000 as full-time employees.

As technology in general and the Internet in particular become a more important part of how virtually all companies do business, many are finding themselves faced with new ethical dilemmas.

(continued)

Take for example when New York-based Internet advertising company DoubleClick Inc. made plans to share customer information with an off-line marketing firm last year. Consumer advocates were up in arms that DoubleClick would betray such "confidential" information. The controversy not only tarnished the company's name, but also raised a host of Internet privacy issues that e-commerce companies could no longer avoid.

Examples like this explain why some firms are hiring people like ethics consultant Tom Shanks. Some companies, such as insurance firms, have long relied on the advice of professional ethicists to sort out thorny ethical problems that, if not nipped in the bud, can cause legal and financial disasters later. Now an increasing number of companies are seeking the expertise of a new brand of ethicist — one who can apply abstract principles to quickly changing technologies.

E-commerce firms, for example, might call on an ethicist like Shanks to help sort out issues like the ones that plagued DoubleClick: Just what limits should there be on how online businesses use the information they gather about their customers? And what responsibility do companies have to publicly disclose their data mining practices?

Or if a company is considering using software to monitor its employees' computer use, an ethicist can help gauge whether it's a legitimate way to ensure productivity or a violation of employees' privacy.

One thing is for sure: The Information Age will continue to pose new problems for experts like Shanks to grapple with.

Since he started ethics consulting in the early '90s, he's had plenty of experience dealing with the conundrums technology can create.

Recently, Shanks has begun regular consulting at San Jose, California-based e-commerce applications vendor Propel Software Corp. Propel is Infoseek founder Steve Kirsch's fourth start-up company.

Kirsch, one of the best-known philanthropists in Silicon Valley, had already written a list of 12 "core values" to guide business practices at Propel before Shanks joined the company. The values included maxims like "give back to the community" and "play to win-win" — the notion that the company should strive to do business in such a way that all parties involved benefit.

Based on interviews with the company's 60 employees, Shanks suggested ways to refine the guidelines to make them more realistic. He continues to meet regularly with a "values committee," made up of 12 employees drawn from all levels of the company, to discuss how to put the core values into practice.

One of the main ethical problems in the e-commerce arena centres on the controversy over data mining — the selling of consumer information by e-commerce merchants to online advertisers. "If you're creating e-commerce applications and your customers want your product to have data mining capabilities, what is your responsibility?" asks Shanks. "That's the kind of thing we're sorting through."

(continued)

The first challenge in working with his clients is forming a common language that employees can use to talk about ethical issues, Shanks says. And as deadlines near, ethical guidelines can end up on the back burner. This is especially true at fast-paced start-ups. "When there are 110 other things taking up people's time, there's some convincing that has to be done to show employees that they should be paying attention to ethics and values more than they are," explains Shanks.

Questions

1. Explain what an ethics consultant is. Describe what one has to do to become an ethics consultant.
2. Would you consider this career for yourself? Explain why or why not.
3. Describe three ways in which a company can benefit from using the services of an ethics consultant.
4. Describe two barriers that might prevent a company from using an ethics consultant.

CAREER PERSPECTIVE 2

Researching a New Technology

Locate an article from a magazine, a newspaper, or the Internet about a Canadian company that describes a new technology product or service they are launching. Based on what you read, answer the questions below.

Questions

1. What is the new product or service? Where will it be available?
2. What types of primary or secondary data would you recommend the company collect before launching the product? Why?
3. To launch the new product or service, what types of jobs will the company have to create?
4. What types of skills will members of the project team need to make this come to life? For each skill you list, explain why you have identified it.
5. Imagine that you were applying to join the project team. What skills or competencies do you possess that you could contribute? Explain.

IT's A Wrap

Key Terms in This Chapter

accuracy (p. 316)
advertising and cross-branding (p. 332)
advertorial (p. 317)
annotated bibliography (p. 321)
appropriateness (p. 316)
bias (p. 316)
bibliography (p. 320)
blog (p. 312)
confidentiality (p. 317)
content licensing (p. 332)
copyright (p. 328)
currency (p. 317)
deontology (p. 324)
editorial (p. 317)
embedded citations (p. 319)
endnotes (p. 319)
ethical framework (p. 323)
ethics (p. 322)
fair dealing (p. 329)
footnotes (p. 319)
fraud (p. 331)
hoaxes (p. 327)
intellectual property (p. 327)
licence (p. 332)
omnibus surveys (p. 318)
patents (p. 330)
primary data (p. 311)
relevance (p. 316)
secondary data (p. 311)
stealth sites (p. 317)
style manual (p. 319)
technology licensing (p. 332)
trademarks (p. 330)
utilitarianism (p. 324)
validity (p. 316)

1. Create a list of competencies that you have acquired through your work in this chapter.
2. Update your portfolio to include exemplary work from this chapter.

Know It!

3. Identify the electronic sources available in your school or local library to gather research. Name the ones you have used.
4. Differentiate between primary and secondary data, and provide examples of each.
5. Identify five sources of information that you consider reputable (that is, you would trust the information provided).
6. Define the term *ethics.*
7. List the key influences in your personal ethical beliefs.
8. Define *integrity.* Identify the specific steps you can take to maintain integrity.
9. Sometimes, actions that are legal are not ethical. Give an original example of this that specifically relates to information technology. Create a table with four quadrants to record your responses: Legal/Not Legal/Ethical/Not Ethical.
10. Define *intellectual property* and explain why this is a growing field.
11. Provide three examples of materials for which you hold the copyright.
12. Explain how the *Personal Information Protection and Electronic Documents Act* affects researchers.
13. List the Canadian laws that affect intellectual property.

IT's A Wrap (continued)

Do It!

14. Design one checklist or rubric to assess primary research, and one to assess secondary research. Include detailed criteria.
15. Using your favourite search engine, perform a search on the phrase "Canadian Internet use statistics." Using your checklist from the previous question, evaluate and rank the first four hits. Record the URLs.
16. Design a worksheet or form to help students develop research strategies.
17. Using either MLA or APA style, create annotated bibliographic citations for the Web sites you retrieved in question 15.

Analyze It!

18. Organizations collect vast amounts of information about people through research. Describe two possible scenarios that illustrate misuse of research data.
19. Give an example of a time when you used deontology to solve an ethical problem and an example of a time when you used utilitarianism to solve an ethical problem.
20. Draft a code of ethics (with a minimum of five imperatives) for use by you as a student.
21. Describe the importance of protecting intellectual property. In your description, discuss the measures currently in place to do so. Do you think more protection is needed? Explain.

CHAPTER

12

Creating Web Sites

On completion of this chapter, you will be able to:

- identify and describe the elements of good Web design;
- plan a Web site for a specific audience and objectives; and
- create a Web site using authoring tools.

Web sites have become an important tool for individuals and organizations to communicate information and ideas. The ability to create an effective Web site is, therefore, a valuable skill to possess. Designing and creating Web sites requires knowledge about how to organize information for the medium and how to use available technological tools efficiently to realize the Web site's vision. This chapter will address the knowledge, skills, and competencies you need to create a basic Web site. Topics that will be covered include:

- Web Design
- Markup Languages
- Authoring Tools
- Planning and Designing Your Web Site
- Production: Putting It All Together
- Evaluating and Testing
- Going Live

- Review and reflect on your work from Chapter 7. Describe, in paragraph format, how you incorporated the Elements and Principles of Design into your work, and how they translate into Web design.
- Use your favourite search engine to locate sites that are examples of good Web design. Locate three sites that you personally think are particularly well designed and bookmark them or write down the URLs. Look at the various pages and links.
- Electronically create a note page on which you provide the answers for each of the following:
  - Describe how the three sites were set up.
  - List the features that you used to help you navigate around the sites.
  - Record the criteria you used to determine that the sites were well designed.
  - List the attributes of each site that convinced you it was well designed.
- Also, locate three sites that you think are poorly designed.
  - Record the criteria you used to come to your decision.
  - List the specific attributes that made their design poor.

ReAdy,

Set,

Go!

Introduction to Chapter Project

Recall that the Chapter Project is introduced at the beginning and is to be completed as you work through the chapter. Your teacher will provide you with assessment and evaluation criteria.

CHAPTER PROJECT

Create a Web site that includes a home page along with at least two sub-pages, using appropriate authoring tools. The topic must be mutually agreed upon by you and your teacher. Your finished product, when submitted, must include:

- a table, created electronically, that provides a detailed explanation of the site's objectives, audience, and how these will be addressed through the content and structure;
- an explanation, in electronic format, of how you incorporated Elements and Principles of Design into your site;
- a flowchart that uses the appropriate symbols, illustrating the structure of the Web site; and
- a live site that includes animation, authored and uploaded, using the appropriate software. Once completed, archive all the files associated with your site.

12.1 Web Design

Effective Web sites are the result of careful planning and the application of the best practices for good Web design. This section will provide you with an understanding of how to go about planning a Web site, and things to consider to ensure the design is appealing and effective for users.

12.1.1 Web Sites and Design

digiknow

A **Web ring** is a collection of pages linked by a common theme (such as poetry, parakeets, gardening, or any other topic). It helps people interested in a particular topic to find sites and also helps those who own the Web sites to get more exposure.

The terms *Web site* and *Web page* are often used interchangeably. There is a difference, however. A **Web page** is a single document viewed via a browser at one time. Individual Web pages comprise files, words, visuals (e.g., pictures, animation, graphics), colour, and links. A **Web site** is a linked series of pages (usually a main point of entry called a **home page** and many **sub-pages** that follow by links), programs, sounds, databases, documents, and/or images that are found at one domain name.

Web design refers to how a Web site is organized, how it functions, and how it looks. Figures 12.1, 12.2, and 12.3 provide examples of home page and sub-page layout and are labelled to illustrate some common features.

Figure 12.1
The Pearson Education Canada School Site, 2003

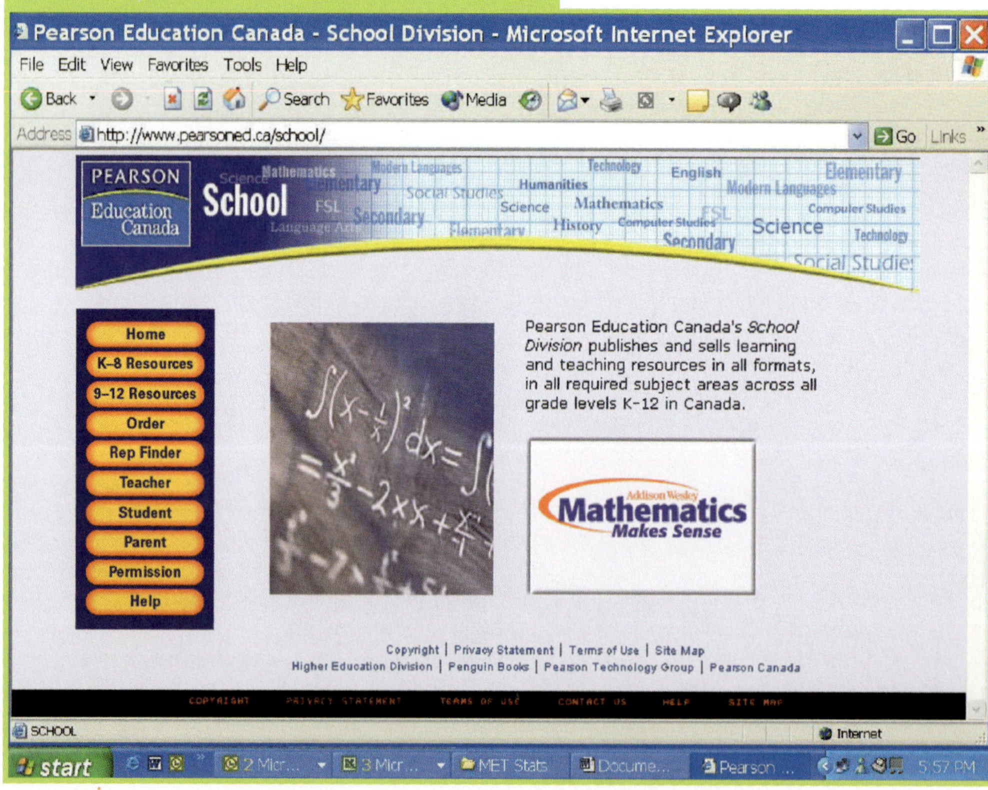

Figure 12.2

The Home Page for the Gavin Crawford Show, 2002

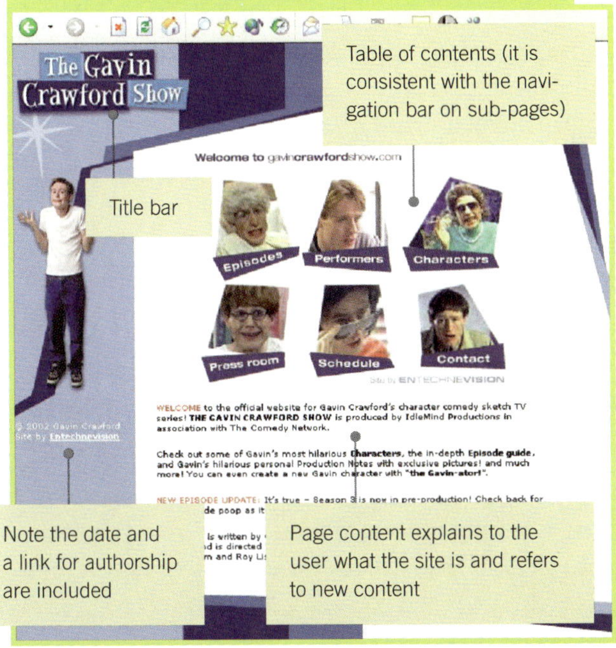

Figure 12.3

Sub-page Layout for the Gavin Crawford Show, 2002

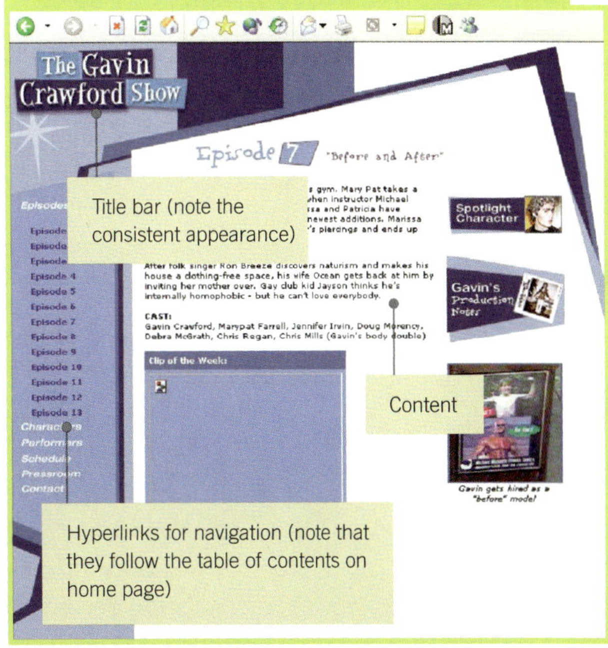

Effective Web design incorporates a variety of criteria. A great deal of important usability research indicates that most people absorb information from Web sites in a manner different from what they do from printed materials (Hewitt 1998). Therefore the look, organization, features, and content have to be put together in a way that is suitable to the medium.

digiknow

On the Web, people tend to browse or scan information, rather than really "read" it the way they would read a book or traditional print document (Hewitt 1998). In fact, Crawford Kilian (2001) cites a study by Jakob Nielsen that found only one-third of a site's visitors read an entire article; the rest focus on headlines, summaries, and captions. Kilian suggests the following for preparing Web content to address the habits and preferences of visitors:

- "Jolt" visitors using sensory stimuli, such as pop-ups, links, buttons, etc., to get them hooked.
- Keep blocks of information on a page to 100 words or less, and avoid scrolling. Where more information is needed, provide a link.
- Provide links to other pages on every page (including the home page), in case visitors enter the site on a sub-page or users investigating the entire site want to return to something they saw before.
- Use short sentences, fragments, or phrases ("Sometimes." "Not always." "It works." "Great!") to make reading on the monitor simpler and more "punchy." For example, a 3000-word analysis of the impact of computers on students' lives in the late 20th century would be difficult to read online, given the amount of information in paragraph form and the scrolling involved. Suppose you converted that 3000-word essay into 50 proper sentences, each sentence being approximately two lines long. Though better, this would still require a great deal of scrolling and reading. Now suppose you cut that further to bullets with sentence fragments. Though a lot of content would be lost, the text would be much easier and more inviting to read. Keep in mind that the full-text essay could be available as a downloadable text document.

A five-step process is generally used to create Web sites and other multimedia projects.

1. **Planning,** the most important step, involves determining the objectives of the Web site, the content it will include, the intended audience, how the audience will use the site, and when and how the site will be finished. This step is investigated in detail in Section 12.4.
2. **Designing** a Web site involves making decisions pertaining to each of the elements of Web design (as per Figure 12.4). This is also further investigated in Section 12.4.
3. **Producing** a Web site involves bringing the plan and design to life, either by coding or using specific software. Section 12.5 illustrates how to use these tools to create your own Web site.
4. **Evaluating and testing** a Web site occurs before it is accessible through the Internet, to ensure it meets the original objectives and that all the components work. Follow the checklist outlined in Section 12.6.
5. **Delivering** the Web site is simply putting it "out there" for people to access via the Internet. Section 12.7 walks you through the process of going live.

Figure 12.4
Elements of Effective Web Design

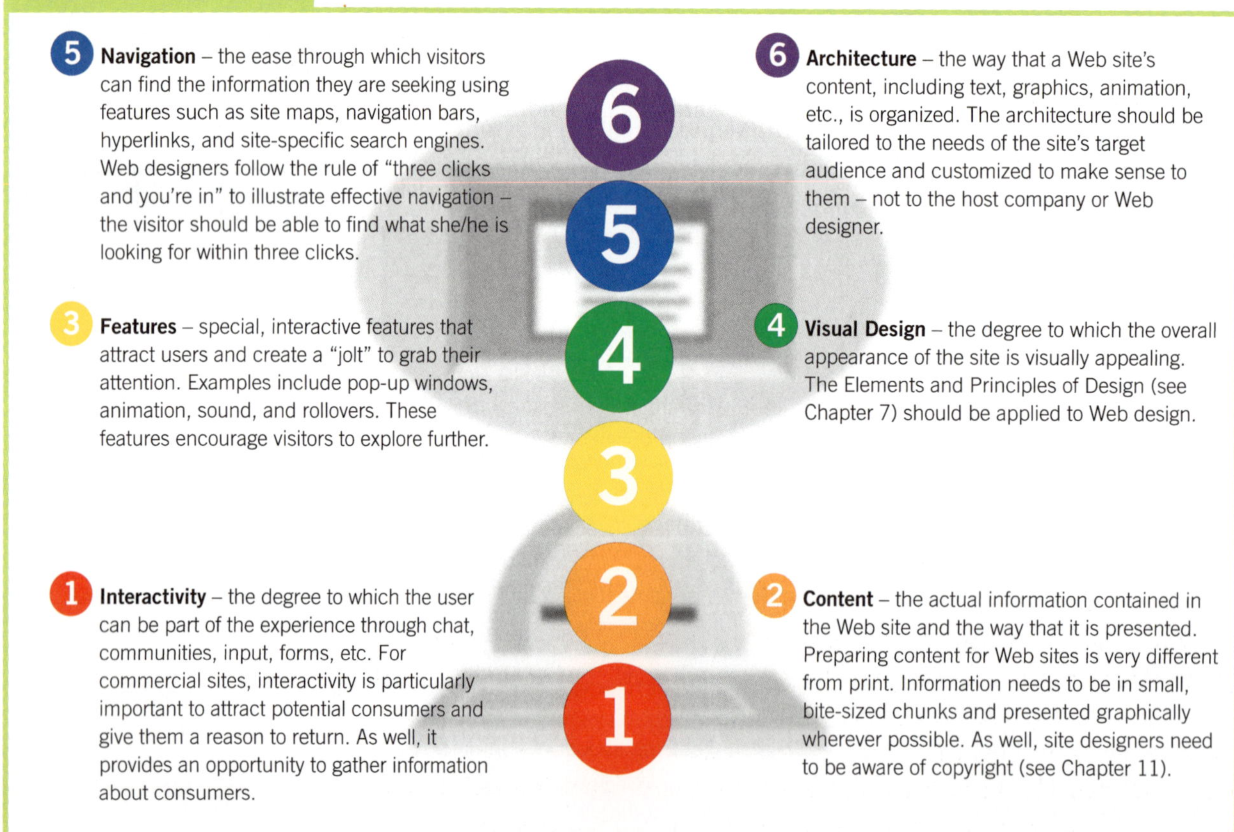

All the elements of Web design need to work together to create a unified, logical, and easy-to-use Web site that appeals to users.

12.1.2 The Tools You Need

The most important piece of hardware needed to create a Web site is a computer with Internet access. The computer is used to construct the Web site, while Internet access allows the site to be posted for visitors to view. Next in importance are the storage media (both online and remote) required to maintain all the electronic files that will be included in the Web site.

Software is also needed to create a Web site. In some cases, a single software application will do (e.g., as an authoring tool or an office productivity application, such as word-processing software with Web functions). Alternatively, Web pages can be created in a text-editing program (such as Notepad) by entering a markup language. Sometimes, additional software applications are necessary to get information up on the Internet.

Finally, a Web address and space to host Web page data are necessary to get a Web site up and running for visitors. Many Internet service providers (ISPs) offer a certain amount of space and an address as part of the account package. However, this does not allow for a customized address (such as www.pearsoned.ca), though specific domain names can be registered and purchased (see Get Connected). Additional storage space can also be purchased for a monthly fee from hosting services for particularly large amounts of data.

Get Connected

Different organizations allow you to register domain names. For example, InterNIC administers all domain names ending in .com. Follow the links at www.pearsoned.ca/businessconnections to determine what organizations administer domains for .ca, .org, and .net. What do you have to do to register a name with each of these? Compare your answers with those of another student. Are there any differences?

GETTING IT

1. Explain the difference between a home page and a sub-page.
2. Identify and describe the elements of Web design that need to be considered when you plan a Web site.
3. Write a paragraph describing how the behaviour of someone visiting a Web site differs from that of someone who is reading a book or an advertisement. Read your paragraph to a partner to see if she or he agrees with you.
4. Identify the hardware, software, and services you currently have available to you to begin Web design.

12.2 Markup Languages

Using a system of codes, **markup languages** define the format, layout, and structure that tell a browser how to display a Web page. A **source document** contains all the content that you want to display, as well as markup language instructions (called tags). The markup language takes care of how information is displayed (e.g., bold, italic, heading, bullets, alignment), while the content is what is displayed. The source document is either created "from scratch" by keying all the instructions in the markup language in text-editing software (such as Notepad), or by Web authoring software (discussed later). Most browsers allow you to view the **source code** (the markup language contained in the source document) by clicking on Source in the View menu.

Markup languages differ from programming languages. Whereas programming languages provide commands that tell a computer what to do, markup languages only tell the computer how to present text-based items. Markup languages work on *any* computer and are, therefore, called **cross-platform** standards. Knowledge of how markup languages work is important because it allows you to modify or adapt Web pages to suit your preferences.

The most common language is **hypertext markup language (HTML)**. It describes specifically how a Web browser should arrange text, images, and buttons on a Web page using tags among content. **Tags** are markup language instructions that surround a unit of text and define what it is supposed to be (e.g., a heading). They are made up of beginning and ending angle brackets (< >) called delimiters and have a word or symbol between the brackets. The tags explain how to arrange the information, but not what type of information it is (e.g., a number, an address). Because of this limitation, HTML does not allow for any additional functions, such as e-mailing information, making decisions, or searching. Some common HTML tags are shown in Figure 12.5, while Figure 12.6 shows how source code appears on your screen.

Figure 12.5
Common HTML Tags

Tags	Function
<B> </B>	Text displayed in between these two tags is boldface.
<BLOCKQUOTE> </BLOCKQUOTE>	Indents the body of the text between the two tags.
<BODY> </BODY>	Marks the start and end of the Web page's content.
<CENTER> </CENTER>	Centres the text between the tags (note the American spelling of "center").
<FONT> </FONT>	Enables specification of the text's font, colour, and size.
<H1> </H1>	Specifies heading text (that can be set H1 through H6). H1 is the largest heading size.
<HTML> </HTML>	Indicates the start and end of an HTML document.
<IMG SRC= "xxx.xxx">	Displays an image, where the "xxx.xxx" would contain the file name of the image to be retrieved.
<LI> </LI>	Indicates a bulleted list.
<P> </P>	Indicates the start and end of a paragraph.
<TITLE> </TITLE>	Indicates the Web page's title that should appear in the browser's title bar.

Figure 12.6
Source Code

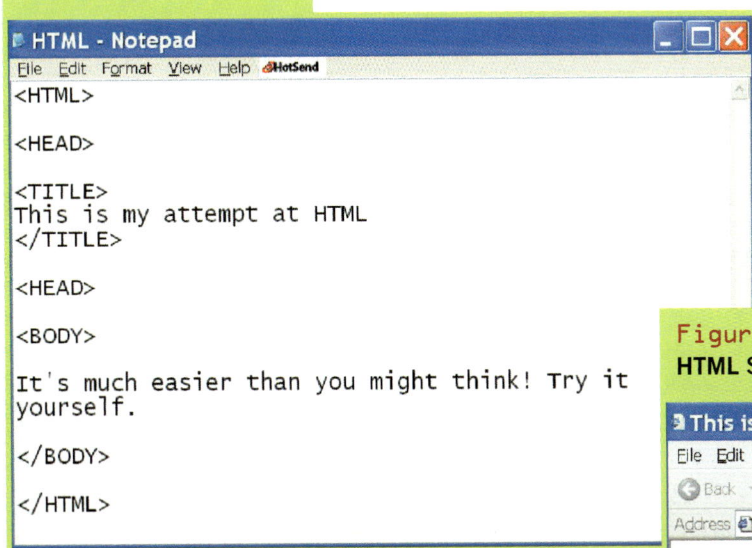

The source code, as entered in Figure 12.6, looks very different when viewed through a browser as shown in Figure 12.7.

Figure 12.7
HTML Source Document

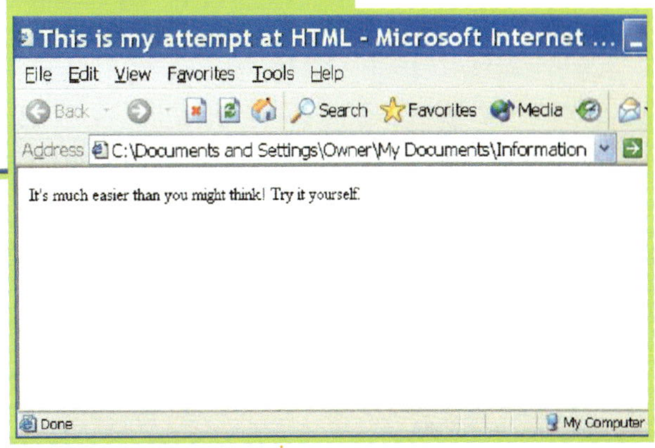

Extensible Markup Language (XML), which was developed in 1998 by the World Wide Web Consortium (W3C), was designed to make information self-describing (Alesso 2000). In other words, unlike HTML tags, which only explain how to arrange the information, XML tags tell the browser what type of information is found within the tags. This is similar to the way that databases recognize certain types of fields within a record, such as price, size, quantity, etc. In XML, tags always come in pairs (like quotation marks) and surround the text to which they apply. Several layers of tags can be applied to provide a variety of information about the type of data contained within them.

A **style sheet** is a form of HTML template, or pattern, that ensures consistency in Web design. **Cascading Style Sheets (CSS)** are created by keying specific tags that describe the design of the sheets (e.g., colours, margins, line spacing, fonts, etc.) into a text editor. The file must be saved with the extension .css. This file then needs to be linked to the Web site (through the HTML or XML source document) as one would normally treat a hyperlink. It would look something like this in HTML:

```
<html>
<title>Linked Style Sheets</title>
<link rel="stylesheet" href="whateveryoucalledit.css"
type="text/css">
<body>
```

Experiencing HTML first-hand will help you to understand how Web sites are developed. Being able to create tags will even allow you to customize templates! Use text-editing software to create your own HTML document and view it through a browser, using the tags above and Figure 12.8 as a guide.

Get Connected

The W3C is an international organization that establishes standards for Internet publishing. Among many documents they have produced that provide guidelines and standards are CSS guidelines and online hypertext rules and etiquette. Through the link at www.pearsoned.ca/businessconnections, view an Internet standards document. How is this useful to Web developers? What type of information does it contain? Electronically create a Guideline for Web Developers that explains why this information is useful to Web developers and list the type of information it contains.

digiknow

The term "JavaScript" is often confused with a couple of other similar terms. **Java**, a more complex programming language, is often used to build systems that interact over networks and is different from JavaScript. Jscript is a separate code created by Microsoft to perform functions similar to those performed by JavaScript.

Linking style sheets not only saves time, but also allows a Web site to have a uniform format. With a style sheet, updating is much easier and quicker because things need to be changed only in one file, should the look need to be changed. Recall the Pearson site (www.pearsoned.ca) that you viewed earlier in the chapter. Suppose Pearson wanted to change the colour scheme and navigation for the entire site. Without a style sheet, Pearson staff would have to change each page on the site individually (there are many!). If a style sheet were used, Pearson would simply change the style sheet once and all the pages would change automatically once the new style sheet was applied.

Synchronized Multimedia Integration Language (SMIL) (pronounced "smile") is a markup language that is an application of XML used specifically to coordinate multimedia elements (such as audio and video) within a Web application. Functioning in a similar fashion to HTML, SMIL files (with the extension .smil) can be created in any text file using tags unique to this language.

Another markup language, **PHP (PHP: Hypertext Preprocessor)**, is a general-purpose scripting language that is suited for complex interactive Web development and can be embedded into HTML. The goal of PHP is to allow Web developers to create complicated Web pages far more quickly than is possible with other markup languages. It is used by many e-commerce site developers because it allows them to easily, quickly, and effectively connect databases to Web pages.

At this point, it is worth mentioning **JavaScript**. Though not a markup language, JavaScript is a scripting language that works with HTML to enhance Web pages and make them more interactive. **Scripts** are short programs used to create animated pictures, sound effects, games, chat, **rollovers** (onscreen buttons that visibly change when a pointing device hovers over them), and other similar features. JavaScript code is usually embedded into HTML code.

Figure 12.8
Rollovers

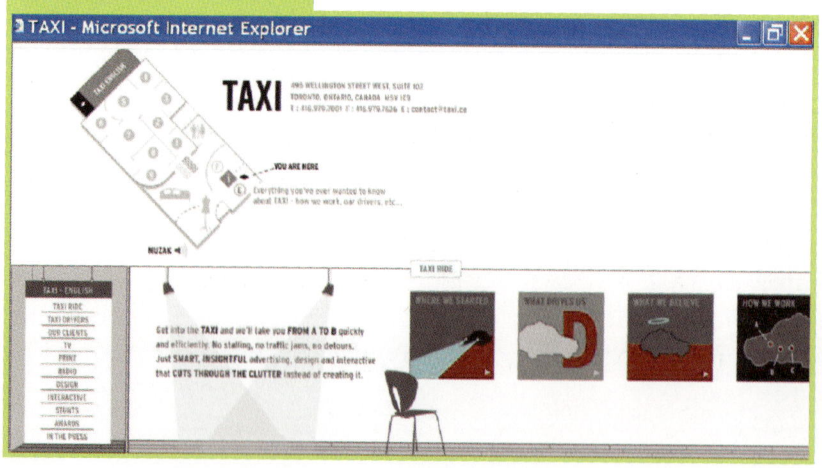

Taxi, a Canadian advertising company, uses rollovers in their Web site. As you move the cursor over the floor plan (as shown in the screen capture), information appears about each of the spaces.

ON THE CASE

Getting Recognized by Search Engines

Just because you get your Web site online does not mean that it will be recognized automatically by search engines. There are several ways to be recognized by search engines:

1. Use specific software designed to automatically submit your site to hundreds of search engines. Though very easy, the software tends to be expensive.
2. An inexpensive, but time-consuming, option is to submit to each search engine manually.
3. A third option is to use <META> tags in the Web site's source document. A <META> tag provides instructions to search engines about what keywords the Web site addresses. The <META> tag is placed between the <HEAD> tags and contains information about the site — either to describe the content, or to provide keywords for search engines, or to do both. Examples of how these might appear are:

```
<META NAME="description"
CONTENT="Information about online
learning and instructional design can
be found here.">

<META NAME="keywords" CONTENT=
"e-learning, online learning, curriculum
design">
```

Question

Using the feature to view source code through your browser, visit three sites from your list in the "Ready, Set, Go!" activity at the beginning of the chapter and look at the tags. In each case, determine whether the site creators used <META> tags. If so, describe what the tags say.

GETTING IT

1. What is the most commonly used markup language? Create a two-column chart that lists the advantages and disadvantages of this language.
2. Explain how a markup language is different from other programming languages.
3. Explain tags. Describe how they are used.
4. Identify the type of software you need to create a markup language source document.
5. Explain what style sheets are and why they are used.
6. Describe JavaScript.

7. Create a guide for Web site developers that explains steps they can take to ensure their site is recognized by search engines. With teacher approval, post this guide in the classroom.

8. What are <META> tags? Describe how you would use <META> tags in your own Web site.

12.3 Authoring Tools

Authoring tools are software applications that facilitate the creation of Web sites using a graphical user interface (GUI) that makes the process similar to desktop publishing (DTP). These tools usually provide templates and layouts that can be used or adapted by Web designers. Using specialized software to create Web pages and sites has both advantages and disadvantages, as illustrated in Figure 12.9.

Figure 12.9
Advantages and Disadvantages of Authoring Tools

Advantages of Using Authoring Tools	Disadvantages of Using Authoring Tools
• Authoring tools have familiar, easy-to-use GUIs. • Authoring tools tend to be faster to use, since original code and layout templates do not have to be keyed in. • Many authoring tools have special effects, such as rollover buttons and search pages, that would be too difficult to code manually. • Most authoring tools do not require any knowledge of markup languages. • Some authoring programs contain features such as site management, in which automatic hyperlinks between pages occur as updates happen.	• Authoring tools tend not to be efficient in the use of code, resulting in longer downloading time. • The Web site may lack originality, since other people using the same authoring tool may use the same templates and features. • Sometimes, authoring programs contain bugs.

digiknow

With most Web authoring software, viewers can only see Web pages in the fonts already installed on their computers. Therefore, it is important for the developer to use common fonts, so that what a viewer sees is what the developer of the Web page intended. Examples of fonts installed on most computers are: Tahoma, Times New Roman, and Arial.

More sophisticated Web authoring software (such as Dreamweaver®) make fonts appear as graphic objects, so that they are consistent regardless of the font collection on the machine of the person viewing it. Be mindful of this when designing your Web site!

A variety of software options exist to create Web sites. As mentioned in Chapters 4, 5, and 7, many office productivity applications have the functionality already built-in to create Web sites. For instance, Microsoft® Word and Microsoft® PowerPoint allow users to adapt Web page templates and use Wizards to create pages. These types of features are of great advantage, since they require little additional knowledge of Web authoring software and no knowledge of markup languages.

For more complex sites (and when other applications are not available), there are specific authoring tools dedicated to the creation of Web sites. Two of these, **WYSIWYG** (pronounced "whizzywig"), which stands for What You See Is What You Get, and **quasi-WYSIWYG** share a few basic functions that you will learn more about in Section 12.5. Figure 12.10 summarizes how the three main categories of authoring software work with examples.

Figure 12.10 Categories of Web Authoring Software

Category	Description	Examples
Pure WYSIWYG	The GUI used to build the Web page resembles a DTP software application.	• NetObjects Fusion™ • Macromedia Drumbeat 2000™
Code-Based	The software allows the user to build Web pages by entering raw HTML tags and programming JavaScript.	• HTMLed Pro® • Macromedia HomeSite™ • HotDog Professional
Quasi-WYSIWYG	Most tasks are completed in a WYSIWYG GUI, but can be switched to a source code view to modify the markup language.	• Microsoft FrontPage® • Dreamweaver® • QuickSite • Claris Home Page

Deciding whether or not to use an authoring tool depends on a few factors:

- What other options do you have available for Web site creation (e.g., word-processing software, presentation software, etc.)?
- Will those options allow you to create the type of Web site that you want? If not, what functions do you need, and which authoring tools can provide them?
- Do you need the ability to go in and edit HTML code to customize your site?

The answers to these questions will help you to determine your software needs and help you to select the most appropriate application for your purpose.

GETTING IT

1. Determine the Web authoring options that are available to you at the present time. For each, electronically create a chart that lists its advantages and disadvantages. Compare your chart with the charts of two classmates.
2. Describe the advantages and disadvantages of the software you will use for your Chapter Project.
3. Select any two quasi-WYSIWYG authoring tools (either from the examples above, or others familiar to you). Research and develop a comparison chart listing the similarities and differences between them, as though you were thinking of purchasing one. Be sure to consider system requirements, costs, and any other relevant aspects you consider important for creating your Web site.

12.4 Planning and Designing Your Web Site

The saying "fail to plan, plan to fail" is most applicable to Web developers. Consider that building a Web site is similar to building a house — without a blueprint, the task can be complicated and important things can be overlooked. This section will walk you through the steps of creating your own Web site blueprint.

12.4.1 Planning

Every good project begins with a plan. When creating a Web site, your plan should include answers to the following questions:

- What is the purpose of this Web site (e.g., to inform people, to showcase work/accomplishments, to sell a product or service)?
- What are the specific objectives of this Web site (e.g., to inform, to entertain, to sell, to persuade opinions)?
- Who is the audience? What are they like? How do they use the Internet? How do they like to find information?
- What specific content needs to be included (breadth, depth, format, topics)? What content would be nice to include? Does any of it need copyright permission in order to be included?
- Based on the content and purpose, what is the tone of the site (serious, fun, happy, etc.)?
- Given the tools I have available to create this site, what features and functions can I include in my site (navigation, graphics, interactivity, etc.)?

Identifying a site's target audience and developing a site design and content that will attract and serve the target market is the most important part of planning. Keep in mind that people visit sites for specific reasons: if they do not find what they want quickly (or at all), they will simply click elsewhere.

Determining the scope of content (and how much information is to be included) is also necessary in order to proceed with designing a site. The Web designer needs to be able to estimate how many pages a site will comprise, what the table of contents will include, and the best way to present the information. As well, the type of information may influence the look and tone of the site.

12.4.2 Designing

The Web designer must focus on the "big picture" while organizing all the small details to create an effective Web design. Designing involves making a lot of decisions about look, organization, and features. One advantage of the Web today is that it offers designers many options for presenting diverse types of information, as well as various levels of detail. For example, a graphic may explain a concept better than a thousand words. Or, if information gets too long, it can be appended to a separate page that a user can click on to see more.

This is also where the Web designer becomes an architect. Taking all the pockets of content, as well as features, graphics, and navigation tools, and organizing them into a plan that will eventually be developed into a Web site can be a monumental task.

Flowcharting (see Section 12.4.3) is one of the best ways to create a blueprint for a Web site. The top of the flowchart should begin with the home page, and then subsequent options, pages, and features will flow from that starting point. As well, features that appear on each page (such as Navigation tools or hyperlinks) should be included.

Ideally, the design should include a **site map**, a dedicated sub-page that identifies the entire contents of the Web site through clickable links. The site map functions in a way similar to the index of a book: it allows the user to go directly to a specific area without having to navigate through a series of menus.

Best practices suggest that the following items should be included in all Web pages:

- a title bar that indicates the name of the site, including a logo (if it is a commercial site and a logo is available);
- hyperlinks to get to the home page and site map, preferably in the form of a navigation bar; and
- the date of posting or when last modified.

Get Connected

For practice purposes, examine the way in which the Pearson Education Canada School Division site is organized at www.pearsoned.ca/school/. View the site map. Describe the way that navigation is set up.

12.4.3 Flowcharting

Flowcharts are visual representations of the flow of data, the structure, and/or the process of an organization or a project. They serve as a valuable planning tool for laying out the architecture of a Web site (see Figure 2.8 on page 37) or the flow for any electronic project. The flowchart serves as a blueprint: all requirements, actions, and steps are laid out in a logical order. The flowchart needs to be clear, neat, and easy to follow so that the individuals providing approval for the project, as well as those working on it, can understand what will happen. There is no room for ambiguity or mixed messages.

Usually (but not always), flowcharts follow a top-to-bottom or left-to-right direction; the arrows direct the viewer where he or she should go next. The draw tools of most office productivity software applications allow you to create the symbols necessary to make a flowchart (see Chapter 7, pages 182–183 for a refresher). Microsoft Project also allows for flowchart creation.

Alternatively, for large projects or complex flowcharts, flowcharting software is available. Examples of dedicated flowcharting software include: iGrafx FlowCharter, Tension Software's Flowchart Maker PPC , Microsoft's Visio®, and Kivio (a freeware product). Figure 12.11 summarizes the flowchart symbols and their use.

Figure 12.11
Flowchart Symbols and Their Use

Symbol	Name	Use
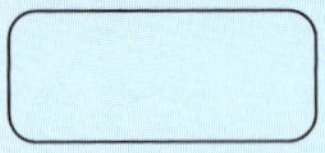	Terminator	This is used at the start or end point of a system; usually, "start" or "end" appears in the oval.
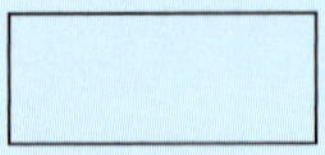	Square or rectangle	This denotes computation, action, or processing that represents a single step.
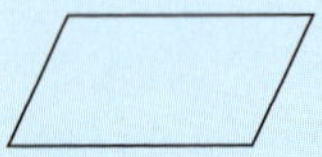	Input/output	This represents material or information entering or leaving the system (e.g., customer order is input, a product is output).
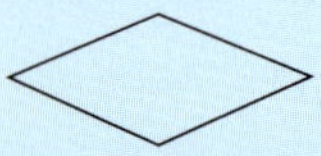	Decision	This symbolizes decision or branching out.
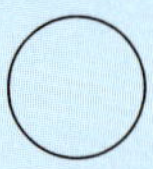	Connector	This is an indication that the flow continues on another page where the matching symbol has been placed.
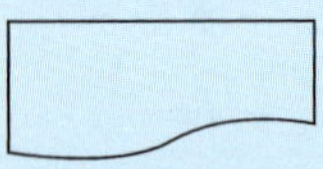	Document	This represents a printed document or report that will be generated.
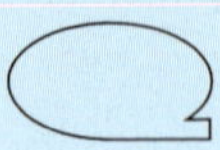	Magnetic tape	This denotes storage, saving, or archiving.
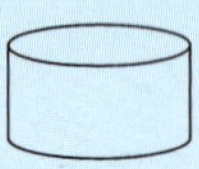	Magnetic disk	This symbolizes a database function.
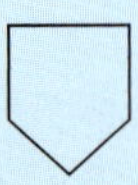	Off page connector	This shows that information or functions are not part of the page.
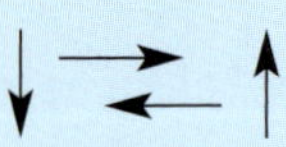	Arrows	This denotes a flow of action.
	Annotation	This indicates an explanation or added information.
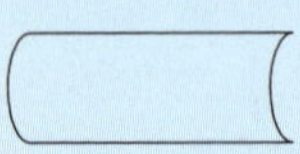	Display	This shows what is displayed to the user.

GETTING IT

1. Explain why identifying a Web site's audience is so important.
2. Identify the target audience for your Chapter Project. Who are they? What are their preferences? What type of information would they seek on your site?
3. Create a list of the things you can do to make your Web site more attractive to your target audience.
4. Create a flowchart using the appropriate symbols for your Chapter Project.

IT In Action

Entechnevision

ENTECHNEVISION web development solutions

Entechnevision, a Montreal-based marketing and multimedia firm, provides a range of services for clients who need a Web presence. Because a Web site is a powerful multimedia business tool that can potentially reach millions of consumers, Entechnevision focuses on providing comprehensive services to ensure clients get a high-impact Web presence. Their services include:

- Web site hosting and management;
- research into the site's target audience and target market;
- site hierarchy and architecture to ensure ease of access;
- translation of content into multiple languages, text copywriting;
- optimization of site for high search engine rankings;
- testing across all major browsers and operating systems (PC and MAC), all major monitor resolutions, and speed of download at 33.6K, 56K, and broadband to ensure download within the 8- to 9-second average expected download rate;
- multimedia components, such as streaming media, video, audio, etc.;
- development of a GUI that is clear and easy to navigate;
- design of customized navigational aids, including animations and button effects;
- logo re-branding optimized for the Internet; and
- custom scripting that involves the development of unique tools to transfer data, incorporation of relational databases into Web sites, or creation of electronic site content management systems.

The expertise of Entechnevision's staff allow them to provide complex and specialized functions that an individual or a non-multimedia company would otherwise be unable to supply. Entechnevision also has the hardware and software to provide Web solutions that are simply not financially feasible for most organizations to achieve on their own.

Questions

1. Explain why an individual would or would not use Entechnevision's services.
2. Revisit the Web sites you identified in the Ready, Set, Go! activity at the beginning of this chapter and locate the answers to the following questions:
   - If the information is available on the site, identify who created it. Determine whether it was a multimedia firm, an individual, or the company itself.
   - Explain how a firm like Entechnevision would be able to add to those sites.

12.5 Production: Putting It All Together

Once all the pieces are in place, they need to be assembled into a Web site. This section will explore ways to put all the pieces together into a coherent Web site, either manually or using one of the tools available to you.

12.5.1 Using the Tools

Now that a design has been established and a blueprint is set, production of the Web site can begin. A good starting point is to set up folders in which you will save all the files that will eventually be used in your site. Figure 12.12 provides an example of how you might want to organize your work.

If you are coding the markup language manually, all you need is a text-editing program and a comprehensive list of markup tags (in addition to those in Figure 12.5). Remember that each page is a separate document saved with the extension of that markup language (e.g., .html or .xml).

Figure 12.12
Organizing Your Files for the Web

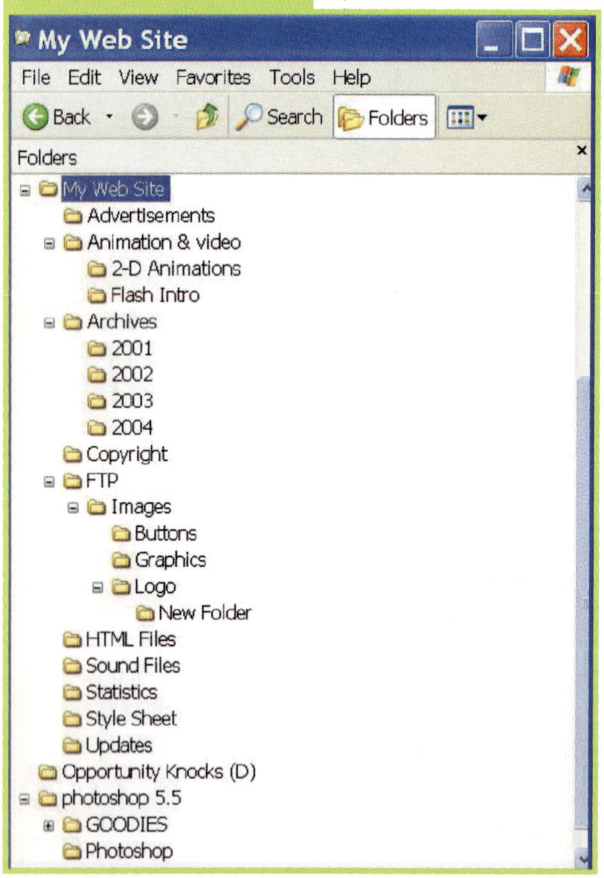

The figure above provides an example of how to organize files for a Web site. Notice the hierarchy. The root directory, My Web Site, contains all the files associated with the site. All images are in an image folder so that they can be accessed easily.

If using the Web page functionality of an office productivity application (see Figure 12.13 for an example of a Wizard), simply follow the prompts to get the page started. Then, edit the contents as you normally would in that software application, until you have created all the pages with the necessary colours, layout, hyperlinks, and graphics. Alternatively, some software applications have the option "Save As Web Page" in the File menu that can be applied to any document.

If using authoring tools, the key is to understand the basic functions of these programs. Though the fundamental elements are roughly the same, some authoring tools allow more complex functions, like setting up forms, adding scripted applications, and so on. WYSIWYG programs allow users to see what a Web page would look like if it were live as they are working. A few basic functions shared by WYSIWYG and quasi-WYSIWYG authoring tools are:

- A Browse or Preview view or mode allows you to see what the page looks like on a browser, while the Edit or Normal view or mode is available to make changes to the document.
- A Toolbar or buttons allow you to identify different types of text objects. When using this form of software, text needs to be identified as a certain type, such as paragraph, heading 1, heading 2 (and so on), bulleted lists, numbered

lists, etc. The authoring tool specifies formatting for each of these types of text objects (e.g., font, size, colour). You can edit the default settings for these. Keep in mind that, as in HTML, headings are identified in descending order; heading 1 is the highest (and usually the largest typeface), followed by heading 2, etc.

- Pictures, images, and clipart are added using a button.
- The background colour, texture, pattern, or image can be set for all pages in the Web site using the menu bar; some applications allow for different settings for home and sub-pages.
- Navigation buttons can be added using the appropriate button or menu. In some authoring tools, these are called Hover Buttons.
- To create a hyperlink, select the text or picture that you want to act as the link, then click on the Link button. The GUI will ask you to identify the name of the file or URL to which you want to link. The software will then create the link, but the path or URL will not be visible to the viewer.

Figure 12.13
Web Page Wizard

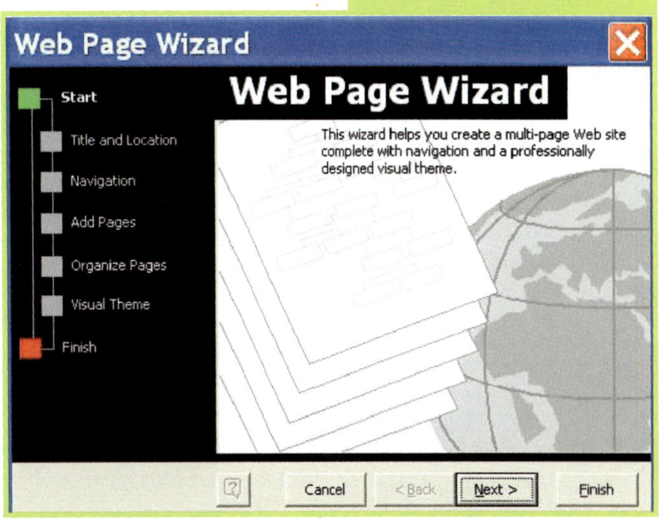

Microsoft's Web Page Wizard (this one is in Word) walks you through the process step by step.

12.5.2 Using Tables to Organize Your Site

Tables with invisible rows and columns are frequently used as alignment tools in Web design. Navigation tools, graphics, text, and other elements can be nestled into cells, keeping them lined up regardless of the browser used to view them and the screen size and resolution. Web authoring and office productivity software applications allow you to insert tables with ease. The lines and borders can be made transparent, so that visitors to the site cannot see them. Next, you can determine the cell properties (height, width, alignment). The final step is to fill the cells with navigation tools, graphics, or text.

GETTING IT

1. Use the "Save As Web Page" command if available in your word-processing software on a document that you have already created. Describe what happens.
2. View your saved document (from question 1) through your browser. Explain what happens to its appearance.
3. Explain how the tables are used to organize data.

12.6 Evaluating and Testing

Evaluating and testing Web sites before going live on the Internet is crucial. Otherwise, the site could go live, but visitors may not be able to use features and functions or even see all the fruits of your labour on their screen!

Evaluating a Web site involves assigning a level of quality to the end product. Evaluation should always focus on the original objectives for the site. When evaluating, use this checklist:

- Does the site meet its objectives in my opinion?
- Does the site meet its objectives based on the opinions of members, or the needs (or requirements) of the target audience?
- Do all the elements of the site work properly?
- Do all the elements of the site (architecture, visual design, navigation, features, content, interactivity) work together to create an effective Web experience for a visitor? Using testers, determine whether the "three clicks and you're in" principle applies to your site.

Suggestions for testing include:

- Use several different browsers (e.g., Internet Explorer, Netscape Navigator, Opera, etc.) to ensure all visitors are able to view the site as it was intended to look.
- Use different monitor sizes and settings to ensure that colours appear as they were intended and that users can see all the aspects of the pages that are necessary.
- Use different modem speeds to ensure that the site loads in a reasonable amount of time.
- Have people with varying degrees of computer literacy (from Internet novices to veterans) test the site and provide you with feedback on ease of use.
- Test all links to make sure they work.
- Test all features and buttons to make sure they do what they are supposed to.
- If possible, test the site on a computer other than the one with which the site was created, to ensure that fonts appear as intended and graphics upload properly once the site goes live.

digiknow

A number of electronic "bells and whistles" can be added to Web sites to increase their functionality and interest. Some, though relatively easy to do with the latest authoring tools, are beyond the scope of this chapter. However, you may wish to investigate these on your own:

- Helper applications (such as RealPlayer, Shockwave, Flash, and QuickTime) allow for certain complicated multimedia elements to be included in Web sites.
- Online forms allow for individuals to respond to questions or send information to the Web site's owner by filling in a series of fields and submitting them electronically. Some authoring tools, such as Microsoft FrontPage®, have built-in forms features.
- Database-driven Web sites allow for automatic changes to page and site content based on a live database. Examples of these are online library catalogues and e-tailers. These can be created by linking a database to the source document.

GETTING IT

1. Electronically create a list of tests that should be performed before a site goes live. Include any additional useful tests that have not been mentioned in this chapter.
2. List the steps you can take during development to minimize the errors or problems that might arise during final testing.
3. Evaluate and test your Chapter Project.

12.7 Going Live

After much planning and hard work, your Web page is finally complete! However, only someone with access to your computer can see it. To debut your masterpiece, you need to ensure it goes live on the Internet. This section will help you get your site in cyberspace for the world to admire.

12.7.1 Getting Your Site Online

Uploading is the process of copying files from a personal computer to a server. Regardless of which transfer method you use, you need to have several pieces of information handy when you are ready to upload your Web site:

- the name(s) and location(s) of the files and/or folders you want to upload;
- the path and directory to which you want to upload the files and/or folders;
- the host address or the specific address of your server;
- the username to access your server space; and
- the password to access your server space.

Once you are confident that you are ready to go live, you must select a transfer method to upload files. Figure 12.14 provides a summary of options available for uploading. Depending on the resources and software you have available, select the most appropriate method for your circumstances.

Figure 12.14
Transfer Methods for Uploading

Transfer Method	Description
FTP programs	FTP applications (such as CuteFTP and Fetch) allow you to drag and drop files from one window to another to upload them. To create an FTP connection, input the information into the correct fields of the GUI. Next, connect to the Internet, activate the FTP connection, and proceed to upload the pages. When using this process, follow a logical order and do not change file names. Remember that any change to folder or file names will confuse browsers (i.e., they will not be able to locate graphics for your Web page).
Web publishing wizards	Wizards provide a series of dialog boxes that walk you through the uploading process. They are extremely simple to use and a good alternative to FTP applications for beginners.
ISP interfaces	These tools are hybrids of FTP programs and Web publishing wizards that are provided by ISPs. Because they are unique to each ISP, their user-friendliness varies from provider to provider.

Figure 12.14 (continued)
Transfer Methods for Uploading

Transfer Method	Description
HTML editor function	Also hybrids of FTP programs and Web publishing wizards, some HTML-based authoring programs (such as Microsoft FrontPage®) offer built-in uploading features. These are very convenient tools to use and tend to be very user friendly, walking you through a series of questions to obtain the necessary data.
Browsers	Some browsers (such as Internet Explorer) can act as FTP clients to upload files and folders. Be aware that some hosting services do not support this feature; test to be certain. The method to upload through a browser is: **1.** Use the address bar to display the contents of your server folder in this format: ftp://username:password@ftp.domain.com. **2.** Drag files from local folders on your computer into the server folders that you see in the browser window.

GETTING IT

1. Create a note for a classmate to explain what is involved in the process of uploading a Web site.
2. This section described several options for uploading. Determine which of those are available to you on your school computer. If you have a computer at home, determine that information for your home computer as well.
3. Upload your Chapter Project.

12.7.2 Updating and Archiving

Web sites are living documents that are never truly "finished." Having a regular schedule for updates (e.g., weekly or monthly) is good practice, since it forces you to re-examine the site on a regular basis. It also helps site users to know when to return for new information. Reasons for regularly updating a Web site include:

- to add new information about the topic or organization;
- to encourage or entice new traffic/visitors;
- to improve the usability of the site based on experience;
- to promote new and upcoming events, issues, or causes;
- to correct problems or errors, such as removing hyperlinks that no longer exist; and
- to reflect changes in the site's ownership (particularly if it is a business).

Many authoring tools allow you to edit "live" sites (i.e., edit online). Generally, updating live is not recommended; it could result in visitors seeing half-finished work. A more effective system is to work, one page at a time, from the previous version locally on your hard drive. Then, preview the changes in your browser. If satisfied with the preview, proceed to update the site. Archiving, described below, is recommended.

Archiving refers to saving past versions of a Web site that is being updated. When updating, it is a good idea to save the "old" version in case you need the information, text, graphics, or other elements in the future. Archiving versions of a Web site is similar to archiving any other document. They can be stored online (if your ISP or Web host allows ample storage space), on your hard drive, or on a removable storage device.

The old files should be archived *before* the new files are uploaded, so that nothing accidentally gets lost. Ideally, the process should go like this:

1. Complete your updated Web page and set it aside before you upload, to minimize disruption when you take the pre-updated version down.
2. Create a folder called "Archive" in your storage destination. Copy the original set of files from your Web page into that folder. Be sure to include the date in the file name for easy organization.
3. Delete the original file from your Web site's main directory.
4. Upload the new file into the directory.

GETTING IT

1. Write a paragraph explaining how you can tell if and when a Web site you visited has been updated.
2. Thinking about the Web site you are creating for this course, how often would you recommend it be updated?
3. Explain why Web pages should be archived.
4. Archive your Chapter Project.

CAREER PERSPECTIVE

Each member of a Web design team has a specific area of expertise. A Web team generally includes:

- A **Webmaster**, who manages or coordinates all aspects (design, content, and technical aspects) of the Web site's creation. The Webmaster ensures that when all the parts come together, the original vision for the site is intact. Understanding the roles of the other members of the team is essential for the Webmaster to ensure that she or he is able to understand what is realistic and feasible, and to make constructive suggestions for improvement. Diplomacy is important in a Webmaster, since this role is often a link between the team and outside clients.
- An **information architect**, who organizes the content and tests the site's usability. This person ensures that the site is clear and logical so that users are able to access the information they need. The information architect needs to understand the target audience, their needs, and their preferences to effectively organize the site.
- A **designer**, who creates the overall look for the site. This person generates graphics, animation, and other elements. In addition to having a strong understanding of effective graphic design, the designer should also have a good grasp of HTML.
- A **programmer**, who writes the code (HTML, XML, etc.) and develops additional scripts and applications for the site. Often, the programmer also has to customize and link databases for more complex Web sites.
- A **system administrator**, who monitors and maintains the servers (including hardware and software) to keep the site running problem free.
- **Writers**, who prepare the content for a Web site. Sometimes, in a larger organization, information to be included in the Web site is provided by subject matter experts (SMEs). Writers then translate that information into easy-to-digest pieces that are written with a Web audience in mind.

Specific projects may require other experts. For example, setting up an e-learning site would require online instructional designers who understand how to apply learning principles to a Web-based environment.

Questions

1. Locate an advertisement for a Web-related position. Explain how the position in the advertisement differs from the description above. How is it similar?
2. Through working on your Chapter Project, you have experienced some of the roles that members of a Web team can play. Which did you like? Why? Which did you dislike? Why?
3. Use your favourite search engine to locate information about preparing for job interviews. Compose and input a paragraph that explains what you could do to prepare for an interview for the job in the advertisement you found for question 1.

IT's A Wrap

Key Terms in This Chapter

archiving (p. 361)
authoring tools (p. 350)
cascading style sheet (CSS) (p. 347)
cross-platform standards (p. 346)
delivering (p. 344)
designer (p. 362)
designing (p. 344)
evaluating and testing (p. 344)
Extensible Markup Language (XML) (p. 347)
flowchart (p. 353)
home page (p. 342)
hypertext markup language (HTML) (p. 346)
information architect (p. 362)
Java (p. 348)
JavaScript (p. 348)
markup languages (p. 345)
PHP (PHP: Hypertext Preprocessor) (p. 348)
planning (p. 344)
producing (p. 344)
programmer (p. 362)
quasi-WYSIWYG (p. 350)
rollovers (p. 348)
scripts (p. 348)
site map (p. 353)
source code (p. 346)
source document (p. 345)
style sheet (p. 347)
sub-pages (p. 342)
Synchronized Multimedia Integration Language (SMIL) (p. 348)
system administrator (p. 362)
tags (p. 346)
uploading (p. 359)
Web design (p. 342)
Webmaster (p. 362)
Web page (p. 342)
Web ring (p. 342)
Web site (p. 342)
writer (p. 362)
WYSIWYG (p. 350)

1. Create a list of competencies that you have acquired through your work in this chapter.
2. Update your portfolio to include examples of your work from this chapter.

Know It!

3. Describe what a Web site is.
4. Name and describe the elements of Web design.
5. Given that Web authoring tools are so easy to use, explain why a person would bother learning about markup languages. In a table, summarize the advantages and disadvantages of using Web authoring tools versus coding in HTML.
6. Describe to a partner the format in which graphic images for the Web are found.
7. List the elements that should be included in all Web pages.

Do It!

8. Select a Web site from this chapter's Ready, Set, Go! activity. Analyze it and record your analysis using the elements of Web design discussed in Section 12.1 as the criteria. Select a Web site that you often visit (it might be one from this chapter's Ready, Set, Go! activity). Create a flowchart that illustrates how that site is organized.
9. Create a rubric to evaluate a Web site before it goes live.
10. Create one brief page of Web content, including graphics, using a table and another page without a table. View these two documents through a browser. Create a list of differences you see.

IT's A Wrap (continued)

Analyze It!

11. With a partner, discuss the ways Web design is similar to more traditional, print-based publishing. How is it different? Compare your answers with those of another set of partners.
12. Compose and input a paragraph to explain the ways you can incorporate the Elements and Principles of Design into Web sites.
13. Commercial Web sites have evolved as the Internet has grown. Describe this evolution and how it relates to Web design.
14. Research one code-based authoring tool and one quasi-WYSIWYG or WYSIWYG authoring tool. Electronically create a comparison chart that shows how they are similar. How are they different?

CHAPTER

Multimedia Projects

13

On completion of this chapter, you will be able to:

- create a multimedia product that incorporates a variety of elements including text, graphics, sound, and animation; and
- present your finished product to an audience.

Multimedia communication is quickly becoming the norm in our society. New and affordable technology enables us to present information in dynamic and exciting ways. A variety of interactive formats allow recipients of the information to take an active role in communication. This chapter focuses on enabling you to incorporate text, images, sound, video, and animation to communicate a message. Topics that will be covered include:

- What Is Meant by Multimedia?
- Planning Your Project
- Elements of Multimedia
- Authoring Tools
- Putting It All Together

ReAdy, Set, Go!

- Review your work from earlier in this course *or* in the course you took prior to this one.
- Ensure that you still remember how to create an electronic presentation, work with graphics, create a flowchart, and use Web authoring tools. If you need a refresher, review Chapters 7 and 12.
- Locate two examples of rich multimedia applications (you may wish to read the definition for multimedia in Section 13.1). One should be in the form of a CD-ROM, and the other an Internet site.
- Answer the questions below in table format as they pertain to your examples.
  1. Who was the intended audience?
  2. What was the purpose?
  3. Who created the application?
  4. When was it created?
  5. What text, animation, video, and/or audio elements are included in this multimedia application? How do they interact?
  6. In your opinion, is this an effective multimedia application? Why or why not?

Introduction to Chapter Project

Recall that the Chapter Project is introduced at the beginning and is to be completed as you work through the chapter. Your teacher will provide you with assessment and evaluation criteria.

CHAPTER PROJECT

Create an interactive multimedia product that includes text, animation, graphic images, and sound using the appropriate authoring tools. The topic and publishing media (e.g., Web-based or CD) must be mutually agreed upon by you and your teacher. Examples of types of multimedia solutions may include an interactive Web site, an e-learning module, an interactive résumé, or an informational presentation. Your teacher may assign you a project from the Project Bank. Your finished product must include:

- a project plan;
- a detailed explanation of the product's objectives and audience and how the objectives will be achieved through the content and structure;
- a flowchart and storyboard illustrating the structure of the product (refer to Chapter 12 to refresh your flowcharting skills); and
- a presentation of your finished product using appropriate presentation techniques, as discussed in Chapter 7.

13.1 What Is Meant by Multimedia?

Traditionally, information was transmitted to recipients through a single medium and path, such as text. The transmission was a non-interactive, one-way process (see Figure 13.1a). With the advent of media technology, recipients began receiving information through passive multiple media, such as television and videos (see Figure 13.1b). Today, information is presented using a variety of media along many paths.

The term **multimedia** relates to any presentation that involves two or more of text, sound, graphics, animation, or video. The number of media available in one source is referred to as its **multiplicity**. Multimedia presentations are rich in information and apply to multiple senses and/or emotions through the integration of media elements.

Multimedia that invites the user to choose what they want to see and hear is known as **interactive multimedia.** Users can choose their own paths through the information (see Figure 13.1c). The degree to which the user has a choice in the flow of information is referred to as **interactivity**.

Interactivity is usually quite high when multimedia is blended with the Internet to create **hypermedia**, giving users the opportunity to navigate through a variety of media and materials over many paths (see Figure 13.1d).

Figure 13.1
Information Transmission

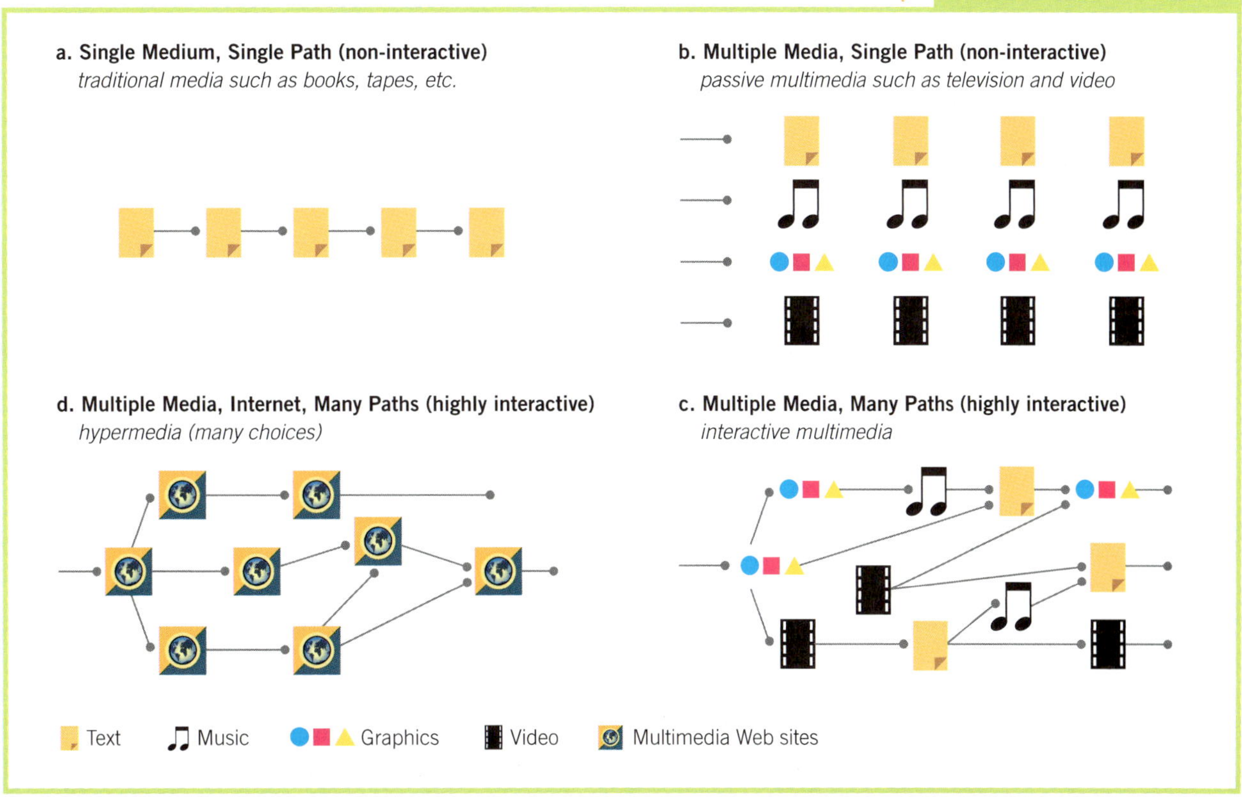

In a chart, indicate the interactivity and multiplicity for each of the four examples shown. Adapted from George Beekman, *Computer Confluence: Exploring Tomorrow's Technology,* 5th edition (Upper Saddle River, NJ: Prentice Hall, 2003), p. 200.

digiknow

For a long time, businesses and individuals have been providing basic information about themselves (company name, contact name, address, and how to contact them) on paper to clients, colleagues, and acquaintances. Now technology has caused the birth of the business card CD-ROM — a CD in the same shape and size of a business card that contains digitized information. In many cases, this new form of business card is printed with the same information found on a regular business card, but when inserted into a computer's CD drive, it usually contains a multimedia show that describes the business or person who distributed it. Though obviously more costly to produce, this new technology opens up tremendous promotional opportunities that the traditional business card cannot provide.

A variety of approaches are available for multimedia projects, as illustrated in Figure 13.1. These approaches would be reflected in the flowchart used to plan the multimedia product. The linear structure shown in Figure 13.2 allows the user to navigate in a certain direction. Each box in the flowchart may represent several media elements (e.g., text, animation, video, or a combination). The hierarchical structure, common to many Web sites, also limits the direction in which users can navigate. The non-linear structure allows users to navigate freely through content, while the composite structure contains elements common to two or more of the other structures.

Figure 13.2
Types of Multimedia Navigational Structures

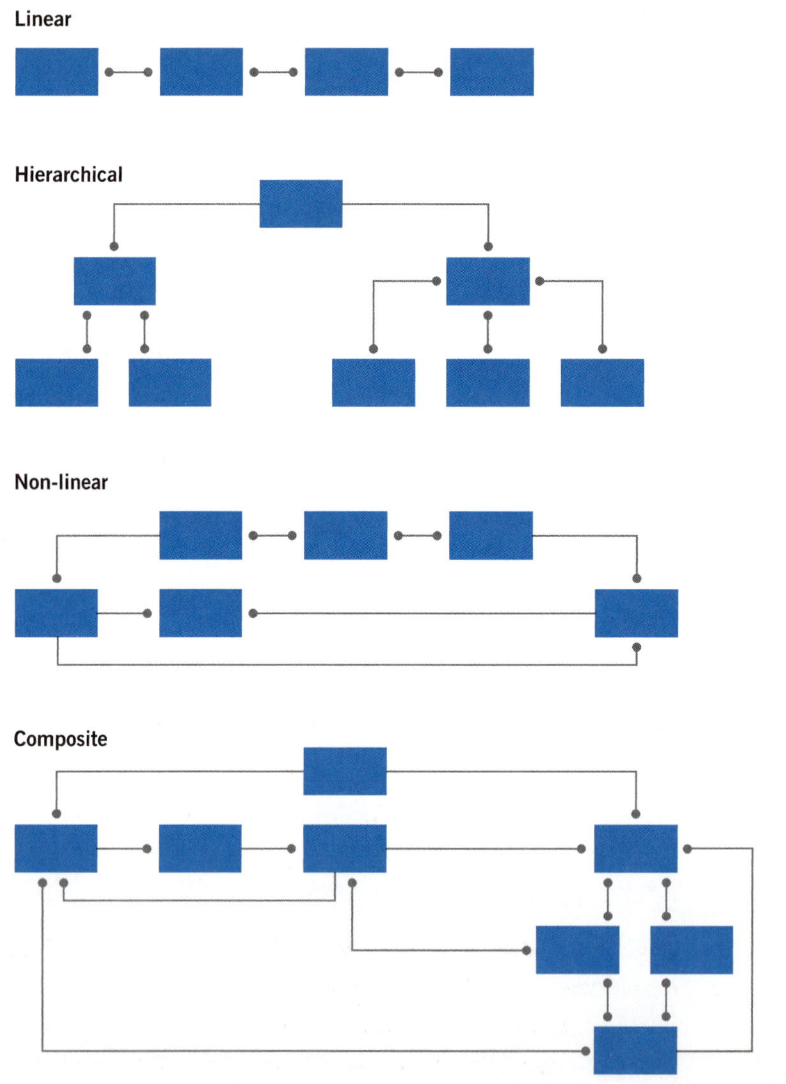

Adapted from Tay Vaughan, *Multimedia: Making IT Work* (Berkeley, CA: Osborne Publishing, 1998), p. 465.

13.1.1 Interactivity

Interactivity defines the degree to which users have input into the direction and flow of information. Good interactivity achieves several things:

- **Motivation.** Interactivity motivates users to participate by giving them options that are clear and easy to follow.
- **Independence.** Interactivity makes possible a unique and interesting journey that the user can navigate independently.
- **Control.** Interactivity gives users control over their experience.

A wide spectrum of interactivity can be achieved, as illustrated in Figure 13.3.

Figure 13.3
Interactivity

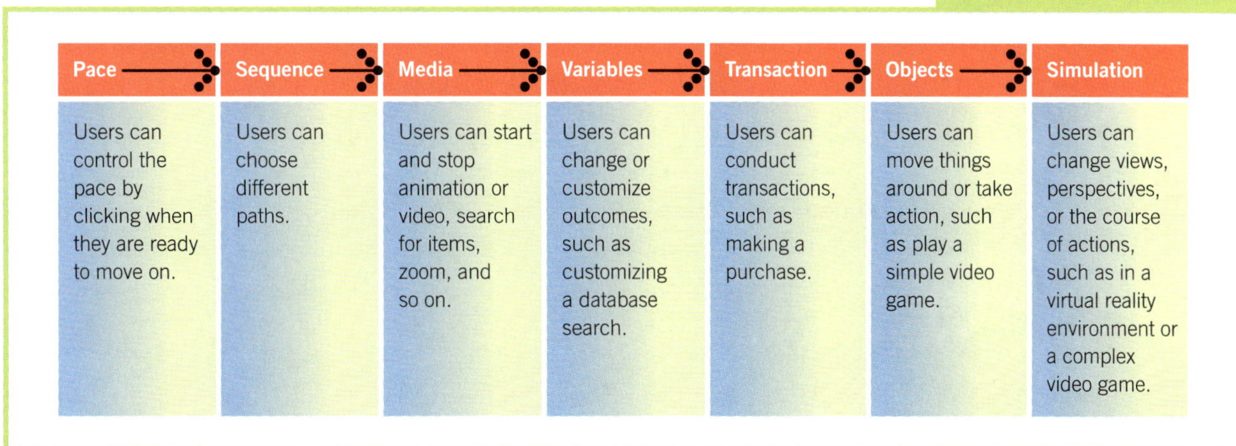

Adapted from Ray Kristof and Amy Satran, *Interactivity By Design: Creating and Communicating with New Media* (Mountain View, CA: Adobe Press, 1995), p. 37.

To provide users with a multimedia experience that they can effectively manage (without frustration), a good navigation system is important. The methods by which to interact, whether they be buttons, hyperlinks, or other features, need to be intuitive, so that the user can get to a destination easily. Alternatively, clear and unobtrusive instructions should be readily accessible to help the user to determine how to interact.

13.1.2 Multimedia in Business

Organizations harness the power of multimedia for a variety of applications. When we think of multimedia possibilities, the first that comes to mind is marketing and promotion. Multimedia definitely lend themselves to reaching customers — whether through highly interactive Web sites, CD-ROM advertisements and information packages, or information kiosks (see the Digi Know on page 370 for more information about kiosks). Multimedia,

digiknow

Information kiosks are gaining popularity as multimedia applications for businesses. Essentially, an information kiosk is a stand-alone, automated presentation system that can be viewed and used by consumers. They can be found at trade shows, on college and university campuses, and even at shopping malls.

however, have far more applications. Consider the possibilities to train employees through multimedia. Many organizations employ computer-based training (CBT), interactive CD-ROM training, and other e-learning solutions to educate their employees.

Multimedia applications are also used to facilitate transactions. Some automated banking machines (ABMs) walk customers through financial transactions using multimedia elements. In other cases, companies use multimedia to walk employees through internal transactions, such as selecting their health and dental benefits.

Clearly, companies using multimedia will continue to reinvent the way they conduct business. And increasingly, customers and employees will come to expect more sophisticated multimedia applications to make learning, understanding, and doing business easier and more fun.

13.1.3 Hardware and Software

Multimedia can only be created and viewed if appropriate hardware is available. Remember that multimedia applications contain many elements — sound, images, movement, video — and therefore need the correct peripheral devices for input and output. How could one create a voiceover without a microphone, or hear it without speakers? As well, success in uploading and viewing multimedia depends on processor speed and the type of Internet connection.

Ideally, a computer intended for multimedia use should include a sound card, a video card, appropriate storage media (CD-ROM or DVD), speakers, a microphone, a high-speed Internet connection, and a fast processor. Of course, less complex multimedia require fewer components.

Though sometimes specific software is not necessary to view certain types of multimedia (such as self-executable files), in many cases there are software requirements. Some software used to create multimedia products (e.g., Flash or presentation software as described in Chapter 7) requires that a user have that same software on his or her computer to view the product.

Get Connected

Follow the links at www.pearsoned.ca/businessconnections to view examples of dynamic multimedia Web sites created by businesses. Electronically create a comparison chart that illustrates what these sites have in common and their strengths and weaknesses.

GETTING IT

1. Define *multimedia* and give an example of a multimedia product that made an impact on you. Describe what the impact was and why that multimedia product was so successful.
2. Define *hypermedia* and give an example of hypermedia that you have used.
3. Describe three ways that businesses use multimedia.
4. Identify three advantages to interactivity in multimedia.
5. Create a list of hardware and software considerations you need to think about before you get started on your Chapter Project.

13.2 Planning Your Project

Before you begin any project, it is important to carefully plan the various aspects of its development. Not only will preplanning contribute to your success, it will also help you avoid unnecessary problems. Drawing on the project management framework introduced in Chapter 2, this section will help you to understand how to plan your Chapter Project or any other multimedia project you may undertake in the future.

13.2.1 Stages of Multimedia Project Development

Because of the complexity of multimedia projects, thorough understanding and application of the project management methodology are important for successful project completion. A project plan (as described in Chapter 2) lays the foundation for what the end product will look like, who will be responsible for completing what, and the deadlines that need to be met.

Some important aspects need to be considered and addressed in the project plan. They are described in Figure 13.4.

Figure 13.4
Multimedia Project Considerations

Aspect	Considerations
Audience	• Who is the intended audience? • What is their skill level in using multimedia? • What hardware and software does the audience have available to access or view the multimedia product? • What is the purpose of the multimedia product? What message or information does it hope to convey?
Technical Specifications	• In what format will the product be available (Web, CD-ROM, other)? • What restrictions does that format have (size of files, length, etc.)? • Are there bandwidth (transmission speed) issues if this is to be viewed over the Internet? • What hardware and software are available for developing the multimedia project? • What features does the software have? • What restrictions does the software have? • Are there any plug-ins (helper applications) required for viewing (e.g., Flash)?

Figure 13.4 (continued)
Multimedia Project Considerations

Aspect	Considerations
Design and Development	• What is the deadline for completion? • How long does the multimedia product need to be? • Who will work on the project? • What type of navigational structure will be used? What interactivity features are necessary? • What look or feel will the project have? • What pace will the finished product have (e.g., fast, slow)? • How interactive will it be?
Testing	• How will the final product be tested to make sure it works? • What criteria will be used to evaluate its effectiveness? • Is it possible to have a member of the intended audience test the product to make sure it meets the audience's needs?

Addressing these considerations is only part of the planning process. In addition, a structure for the site needs to be detailed. One of the best ways to illustrate structure is to create a flowchart (see Chapter 12, pages 353–354) to illustrate how the different sections of the multimedia project interact. Another useful tool that can complement a flowchart is a storyboard. **Storyboards** provide sketches of how each page or section of a multimedia document will look. Usually, storyboards are hand-drawn, and provide instructions for what multimedia elements appear. They can be used by the developer in the project and help that person understand what needs to happen and in what place. Figure 13.5 on page 373 provides an example of a storyboard for a simplified animated presentation. Note the descriptions beneath each storyboard panel.

13.2.2 Content for Multimedia

When planning a multimedia project, keep in mind that content needs to be presented in a succinct way. People viewing multimedia presentations do not want to be bogged down with large amounts of text. Sentences should be kept short and effective. Wherever possible, try to represent things visually and use clickable icons — whether through charts, tables, graphics, animations, or video — to keep things interesting and interactive. Viewing examples created by others is one way to get ideas for information presentation (as well as to see what does not work).

Figure 13.5
Storyboarding

Animation: women talking

Sound: discussion about product as shown in sync with animation

Image – fade in: "Try this" man

Sound – voice-over: try this

Pop-ups: appear as shown and stay for 4 seconds each

Animation: mail carrier walks across screen as shown by arrow (total time, 5 seconds)

Sound: happy, retro walking music

Sound: voice-over as shown

Image: flash in, stay for 3 seconds, flash out

Sound: bell ringing in sync with the flash in

Animation: fade in, man reading book; his finger will move across page and eyebrows go up and down

Sound: voice over as shown

Animation: fade in, man in suit speaking; fade out when his statement is over

Sound: voice over in sync with animation

Animation: flash in "that's all" graphic for 2 seconds; flash out

Get Connected

Review the project management Web sites at www.pearsoned.ca/businessconnections and create a list of the things you need to do to plan your own multimedia project. Use a checklist to assess your progress as you work through your project.

GETTING IT

1. Respond to each of the multimedia project considerations in Figure 13.4 as they relate to your multimedia project. Add any points to your checklist that you may have missed in *Get Connected*.
2. Create a flowchart for your multimedia project (refer to Chapter 12, pages 353–354, for a refresher).
3. Create a storyboard to represent your vision for your multimedia project.
4. List three suggestions that will help you to develop effective content for multimedia that you could share with someone new to this type of project.

13.3 Elements of Multimedia

A number of components are necessary for multimedia to happen. In multimedia, **elements** are the pieces (text, images, sound, animation, and video) that make up a multimedia product. Each of these is created and then organized, using special authoring software (described in Section 13.4).

A complex multimedia project can become overwhelming; consider that all images, buttons, graphics, sounds, and animations are separate electronic files. A large project can have hundreds or even thousands of files. See Figure 13.6 for a list of some of the possible file types you could gather in a multimedia project. Keeping these organized is key to ensuring that the entire project is on track. More importantly, transferring the entire multimedia project to a storage medium is much easier when every file is in its place.

Figure 13.6
Common File Types for Multimedia Projects

File Type	Extension	File Type	Extension
Text files		***Image files***	
Pure text (usually from a text editor)	.txt, .rtf	Tiff	.tif
Microsoft Word	.doc	***Audio files***	
Adobe Acrobat	.pdf	Musical Instrument Digital Interface (MIDI)	.mid
WordPerfect	.wpd	AIFF	.aif
PostScript	.ps	Wave	.wav
Image files		MP3 (MPEG Audio Layer Three)	.mp3
MAC Pict file	.pic	***Animation files***	
Joint Photographic Expert Group (JPEG)	.jpg	Gif	.gif
Gif	.gif	Moving Pictures Experts Group (MPEG)	.mpg

Figure 13.6 (continued)
Common File Types for Multimedia Projects

File Type	Extension	File Type	Extension
Animation files		***Video files***	
Flash	.swf	Audio Video Interleaved (AVI)	.avi
Video files		***Multimedia authoring files***	
QuickTime	.mov	HyperStudio	.stk
Windows media file	.wmg	HTML-based authoring	.htm
MPEG	.mpg	Self-executing program	.exe
RealAudio/RealVideo	.ra, .rm, .ram	Director	.dir, .dcr
Vivo	.viv		

Here are a few tips to keep things organized:

- Keep your files organized from the moment you start a multimedia project.
- Set up one folder for each multimedia project you work on.
- Organize sub-folders by type of medium (as illustrated in Figure 13.7).
- Create a naming system for files that makes sense to you and is descriptive of the file contents.

Figure 13.7
Folder Organization for a Multimedia Project

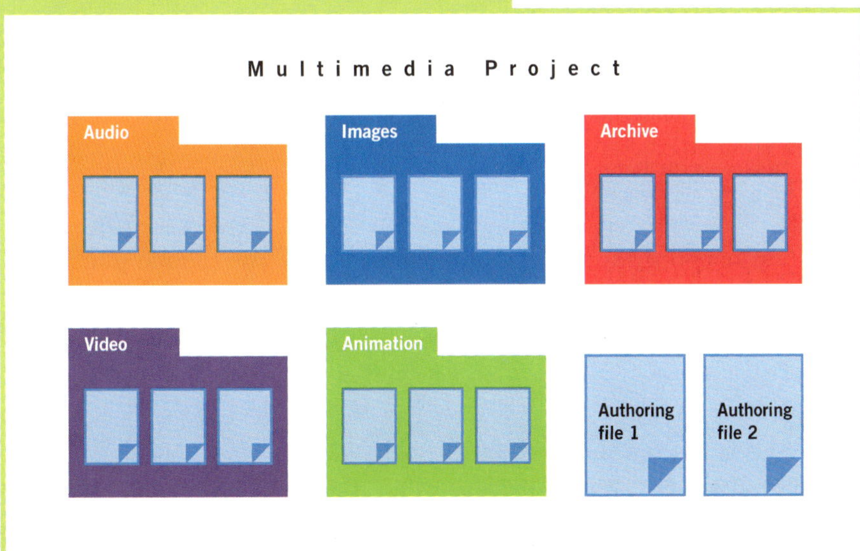

13.3.1 Text

Text refers to the written components of the multimedia project. Ideally, text should be keyed in with word-processing software first, then edited and finalized before being incorporated into a multimedia presentation. The reason for this is that software designed for text makes revisions easier; word-processing software allows for specialized functions, such as spell check, thesaurus, and grammar check. Remember that, to be effective, text written for multimedia follows similar rules to that in Web design: it needs to be brief, effective, and suit the tone and theme of the other multimedia elements.

When putting text into a multimedia product, the following decisions need to be made:

- If the text does not fit on a page (or screen), will users have to scroll or will it be split into two pages (or screens)?
- Will hyperlinks be used to jump between text sections?
- What fonts and colours will work best to make the text readable and attractive?

13.3.2 Images

Images can be in the form of clipart, graphics, or photographs and can originate from a variety of sources. They can be used as part of the content, graphic design (e.g., clickable icons), or both. For a refresher on the graphic images and how to create and manipulate them, refer to Chapter 7. Be certain to adhere to copyright law when using images.

13.3.3 Sound

Sound, or audio, can be in a variety of formats — from music, to sound effects, to narration or voiceovers. It can be a "stand alone" element (such as introductory music) or synchronized with other elements (such as voices for animated characters that are conversing). As such, sound can be very powerful in communicating a message and setting a tone for a multimedia product.

A few key points to think about when incorporating sound into a multimedia product are:

- In a digital audio file, silence takes up the same amount of space as sound. Therefore, sound files should contain *only* sound. Instead of having one large file with silence in between speaking, music, or sound effects, several separate files should be created. **Trimming** is done to remove blocks of silence. This is accomplished using commands with names such as Cut, Clear, or Erase, depending on the software being used.

- Volume adjustments are usually necessary if using pieces of audio from different sources. When they come from different sources, sounds can be too loud or too soft in relation to one another. **Normalizing** creates a consistent volume level. The easiest route to normalization is to select all the data in the audio file, and then raise or lower the overall volume by a certain amount. Try to adjust all sound clips in a presentation to the same level to avoid the users having to make ongoing volume adjustments.
- **Looping** means setting a sound file to play over and over. This is commonly done with small music files, so that it sounds like an endless song playing in the background. When done well the result is seamless. Certain music clips lend themselves to this. Most sound editing software contains tools for looping. (Video and animation files can also be set to loop.)

Sound files can originate from many different sources. Many digitized sound files are available in a format similar to clipart — that is, they are created for individual use without copyright infringement. Other digitized forms, such as MP3s, are also available. Alternatively, sound files can be created. Audio from other sources (such as tapes, video, etc.) can be digitized with special software or hardware. Original sounds can be created using a microphone. Finally, music can be created via digital keyboards and/or special software. For instance, Midisoft® Studio for Windows can be used to create original music in the form of MIDI files. Always remember that sound files created by others are subject to copyright ownership by the author. Refer to Chapter 11 for a refresher on legal use of audio.

Once you have a source of audio, editing is the next stage. Using most sound-editing software is relatively straightforward. Programs like Sonic Foundry's Sound Forge™, Opcode's AudioTrack, Macromedia® Deck, and Macromedia SoundEdit™ allow you to capture and process sound. Common file formats for sound include MIDI, MP3, Sun/Next (AU) Sounds, and WAV.

When you add sound to a multimedia product, consider:

- How will the sound start and end (automatically or user-driven)?
- How much control will users have over the sound? Can they stop it or re-start it? If they are able to re-start it, will it start again from the beginning?
- If users have control, how will it work?

digiknow

Waveforms are digital audio sounds that were recorded live.

digiknow

The **sampling rate** determines the frequency makeup of the recording, measured in kilohertz (kHz). Sampling at higher rates more accurately captures the high-frequency content of sound. Higher sampling rates result in larger file sizes, which may affect the speed of the operation of the presentation transitions. The **audio resolution** determines the accuracy with which sound can be digitized.

13.3.4 Animation

digiknow

Animation works via a biological phenomenon called persistence of vision. The human eye's retina remains imprinted with an image for a split second after seeing it. When the eye sees a series of images that are changed very quickly and very slightly, they blend together to create an illusion of movement. Consider that television works by transmitting 30 still images per second.

However, for computer animation, frame rates as low as 4 frames per second can be used to simulate movement (though it will not appear as realistic).

(Vaughan 1998)

Animations are series of graphic images assembled using software to provide the appearance of movement. Though animation is often thought of as cartoons, many more types of animation exist. Transitions between screens or pages, such as wipes, zooms, fade-ins and fade-outs, are all forms of animation, as are words or images moving across a screen. Animation is an ideal way to add interest to an otherwise static Web site. Good animation can add emphasis or create a visual bridge to help to make the transition from one part of a multimedia product to another. Examples of animation software include GIF Builder (freeware), SWiSH, GIF Construction Set, Macromedia® Flash™, and 3d studiomax™. Certain types of animation require helper applications called **plug-ins** (such as Macromedia® ShockWave®, Flash™, or QuickTime) that must be downloaded by users in order to view the animation.

To create, edit, and use animation, some key concepts need to be understood. There are four main categories of animation:

- flip-book;
- sprite-based;
- path-based; and
- vector-based.

Flip-book animation works in a similar way to the traditional form of animation: each page of an animation book contains a drawing that is slightly different from the previous one. (A flip-book is shown in Figure 13.8.) When the pages are flipped quickly, the picture appears to move. Using this concept, electronic flip-book animation displays a series of still graphic images referred to as **frames** for animation purposes. Each frame is slightly different from the previous one and is displayed quickly to simulate movement. GIF animation files use this principle. **Server-push** is also a technique that uses Common Gateway Interface (CGI) scripting language to create flip-book animations (by "pushing" a series of graphics on the screen) in JPEG or other formats.

Figure 13.8
Flip-book Animation

Flip-book animation has been used for decades as a simple animation technique.

Sprite-based animation (sometimes called cast-based animation) works by creating a bitmap object, called a sprite, that moves independently over a still background. A sprite could be a chipmunk, a word that spins, or a ball that rotates. This form of animation is more efficient and creates smaller files than flip-book animation, because the software used to create it only updates the *portion* of image that appears to be moving, not the whole picture.

Path-based animation is a sub-set of sprite-based animation. A sprite is attached to a **motion path** (a line drawn across the viewing area or background) along which the sprite travels. When motion paths are created from a series of lines (to create a jagged or bumpy path), they are called **splines**.

Macromedia Flash is an example of software that uses sprite- and path-based animation, as illustrated in Figure 13.9.

Figure 13.9
Spline-Based Editing in Flash

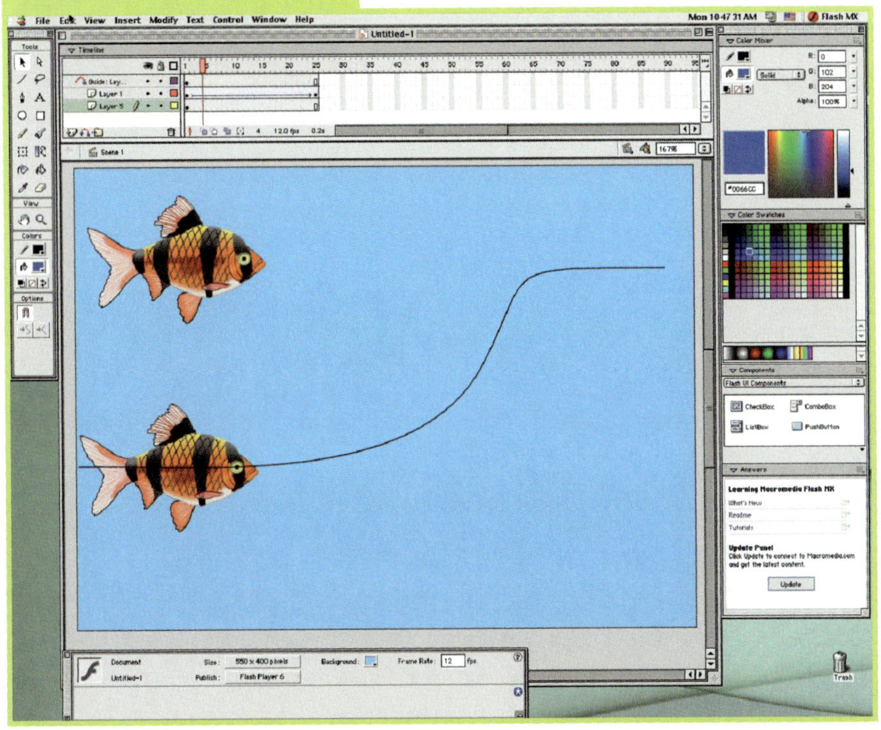

The line represents a spline-based motion path along which the fish graphic will travel.

Vector-based animation works in a similar way to sprite animation, except that mathematical formulas (instead of pixels in a bitmap image) are used to create and describe sprites. Sophisticated animation software, such as Sizzler and FutureSplash, use this form of animation.

Figure 13.10 on page 380 presents some common animation techniques and describes how they work.

13.3.4.1 Animation Software

When using animation software, keep the following in mind:

- Usually, animations have to be fully downloaded to be viewed if the source is Web-based. This can cause problems for users if an animation file is large. Use compression (as discussed in Chapter 12) to reduce the size of animations whenever possible. When estimating the download time, keep in mind that users with 28.8 bps modems can only download at a rate of about 2.5 kb per second.
- Some animation and authoring programs allow for **streaming.** This technology sends audio, animation, or video over the Internet as a continuous stream. This allows users to view or listen to files before

Figure 13.10
Common Animation Techniques

Technique	How It Works
Scrolling	Moves the object from the top to the bottom of the screen
Fading (e.g., fade in, fade out)	Makes the object materialize or disappear slowly, as though it is disintegrating
Easing (e.g., ease in, ease out)	Gradually slows down or speeds up animated objects to mimic a real-life pace
In flight or zoom in, zoom out	Makes the object fly quickly across the screen Changes the perspective of the object
Looping	Sets the animated object to continue the motion over and over
Morphing	Changes the size, shape, weight, or other characteristics over time
Path or arc	Has objects follow an invisible curved line or path (set by the developer) across the screen
Exploding	Makes the animated object appear to break apart and fly away
Stretch and squash	Distorts the rigidity and mass of the object
Onion skinning	Layers all the frames in a flip-book animation to see how the movement will appear
Cut-outs	Cuts out one portion of the object (e.g., cut a hand from the arm) that will be moving and animates only that cut-out item
Hierarchies or hierarchical motion	Links or attaches two or more animations or animation loops so that they move together (e.g., an animated solar system)

the entire file is downloaded as the data begins playing almost immediately when it is received. The use of streaming, if available, can usually alleviate the problems associated with long download times. However, users may still experience delays during times when the streaming server is being heavily used.

- A file can be made smaller by reducing the frame rate of an animation or reducing the colour depth (see Figure 13.11 on page 381).
- Some of the more sophisticated sprite-, path-, and vector-based animation software use timelines for animation. This is particularly helpful when many objects are animated and the animations need to occur in a certain order. **Key frames** are main poses or actions that make up the animation. For example, two key frames would be used to show a person blinking: one frame with the person's eyes open and one with

the person's eyes closed. These key frames are placed along a timeline that resembles a spreadsheet. This timeline coordinates what happens at what time and in which order. **Tweening** is the process of creating intermediate frames between key frames. Animation software automatically tweens intermediate frames for the animator.

Figure 13.11
Colour Depth

Colour Depth	Description
1-bit	Any 2 colours (usually black and white)
4-bit	16 colours, poor quality
8-bit	256 colours (good enough for graphics)
16-bit	Thousands of colours
24-bit	More than 16 million colours, fully realistic, the highest level that can be achieved

The colour depth represents the palette of colours used. The smaller the palette, the less storage space a file will take. Note that most monitors use the 8-bit depth.

digiknow

According to Macromedia, Flash 3 players are installed on over 96% of browsers, Flash 4 on 92%, and Flash 5 on over 60% (Ryder n.d.). When designing multimedia presentations, this needs to be considered. Take, for example, the fact that a multimedia product that needs to be viewed in Flash 5 would only be accessible to just over 60% of people.

(Macromedia 2001)

IT In Action

3-D interface draws praise from digital animators

By Grant Buckler

Excerpt from *The Globe and Mail* [online], Thursday, August 22, 2002.

A diagram of a three-dimensional object seems to float in space on a computer screen. A digital animator wants to alter the object's shape, rotate and move it in three dimensions, even program a flight path to move the object through space.

Currently, the standard way to do this is to select various parameters — the *x*, *y*, and *z* axes — from menus and make various awkward movements with a mouse.

But what if you could just hold a hand out and twist as though actually manipulating the object with your fingers?

That's the idea behind a novel computer interface aimed at speeding up the often painstaking process of 3-D digital animation and design. The interface, called HandGear, is made by Montreal-based DSI Datotech Systems Inc. It looks like one of those old Etch-a-Sketch drawing pads but works more like an oversized laptop-style track-pad, sensitive to the movements of not just one, but two or more fingers at a time.

The number of fingers touching the pad can determine how movements are interpreted. Place the thumb and index finger on the pad and twist and the object

IT In Action (continued)

rotates in two dimensions. Twist three fingers, and the object spins around in three dimensions.

Meanwhile, the user's other hand works the mouse or keyboard to do things such as selecting which object to work with or choosing colours and textures. "Think of a sculptor holding an object in his left hand and doing painting or deformations with his right hand," says Tim Heaney, DSI's vice-president of marketing.

A series of programmable buttons provides further control — for instance, locking the size of an object or its position in any dimension.

Some early test users are enthusiastic. "We already see some major improvement in our work flow," says Luc Larouche, president of Side City Studios Inc., a Montreal-based video game development company with international clients stretching from Hollywood to England. "We were looking for a way to accelerate the process without sacrificing quality."

Mr. Larouche, whose company has been testing two prototype HandGear units, has placed an order for seven commercial models and believes the technology will eventually come standard with graphics animation workstations. "That's what we all think, that it will be dominant in the industry," he added.

Questions

1. Explain how this interface is innovative or different from others.
2. Describe why a 3-D animator would want to have access to HandGear.
3. Mr. Larouche predicts that this technology will become an industry standard. Explain why you agree or disagree with this statement.

13.3.5 Video

When used well, video can add a great deal to a multimedia product. Like all multimedia elements, it should be used only when it makes sense to the product as a whole. Video can be particularly effective when:

- The multimedia product needs to communicate how something works or how to do something.
- The multimedia product needs to show an object from different perspectives (e.g., front, back, side, etc.).
- The video makes sense as an artistic addition to the product as a whole.

Video can be captured using a video recorder or film, and then digitized (converted to electronic format, so that it can be viewed on a computer) using special hardware. Alternatively, it can be recorded using a digital camera and used in that format.

Digital video quality varies significantly. Better quality video requires more storage space, while poorer quality video files can be very small. For

Figure 13.12
Windows Media® Player

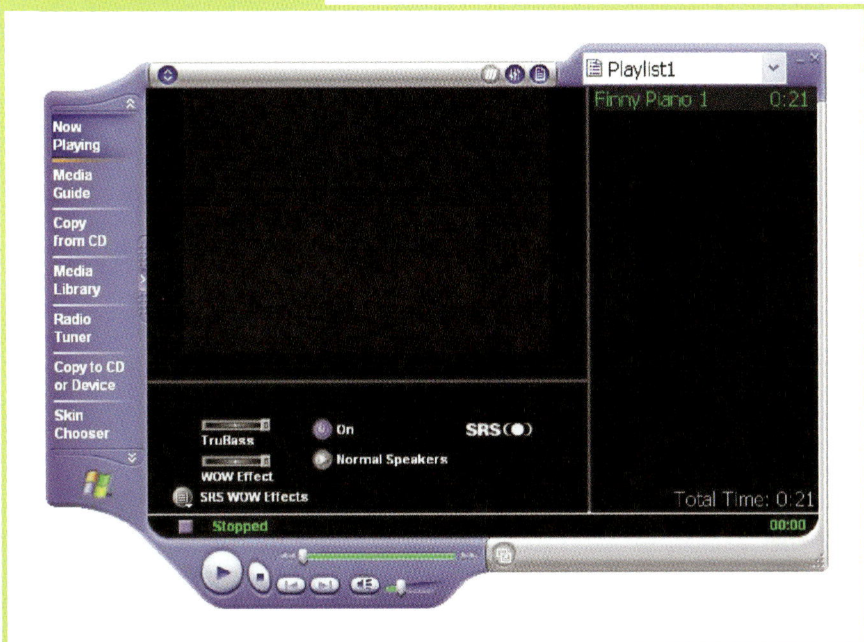

Windows Media® Player is one example among media players available.

instance, broadcast quality video (i.e., a full screen in high quality) exists when each frame is 640 pixels wide by 480 pixels tall, where each pixel has a colour depth of 24 bits and frames advance at a rate of 30 per second (this is called the **frame rate**—the higher the frame rate, the better the quality). Video of this quality would require approximately 28 megabytes of storage per second (Estrella n.d.).

These programs allow you to modify digitized videos through a video capture board. Segments can be cut or resequenced (edited), transitions can be added, and files can be compressed. File formats commonly used include MPEG, QuickTime, RealVideo, and Vivo. Common software used to capture and edit video includes QuickTime, Avid Cinema™, Trinity, Adobe® Premiere®, and Media 100®. In order to view video, software such as Media player (for Windows or MAC) or QuickTime player is needed.

To reduce the size of video files, several things can be done using editing software. First, the size of the grid can be reduced (320 by 180 and 160 by 120 pixels are common). Second, the frame rate can be reduced (15 or 20 frames per second is reasonable quality). Third, colour depth can be reduced to as low as 16 bits. Fourth, video files can be compressed in a way similar to image files (as discussed in Chapter 7, page 179). Finally, some new digital cameras can capture video in a form that is already compressed, so that it can be incorporated directly into a multimedia presentation.

When adding video to a multimedia product, consider:

- How large will the video window be?
- How will the video start and end (automatically or user-driven)?
- How much control will users have over the video element? Can they stop it or re-start it? If they are able to re-start it, will it start again from the beginning?
- Will users be able to rewind, pause, or fast forward?
- Will the video add impact or value to the presentation?

Get Connected

Examine the links at www.pearsoned.ca/businessconnections to learn more about digital video editing. Create an appropriate document that will clearly illustrate the things you discovered and the things you would like to learn more about.

GETTING IT

1. Create a list of multimedia elements. For each element, explain if you will include it in your Chapter Project, and if so, how.
2. Select one of the multimedia elements and describe how it can be used, what software it requires, and common file formats for it.
3. Describe the relationship between the colour palette used for an image and its file size.
4. Multimedia elements can sometimes be large (in terms of file size). Describe strategies that can be used to reduce the file size of images, video, and sound.
5. Determine video or multimedia players you have available to you. List them electronically or in your notebook.
6. Describe how you could use streaming in your Chapter Project. Identify the advantages and disadvantages of this.
7. Using your favourite search engine, locate a Web site that has animation. Bookmark it or write down the URL in your notebook. For that site, describe the type of animation using the content in this section. Also, describe how it contributes to (or detracts from) the effectiveness of the site. Compare your findings with those of another student.
8. Either use the resources available in your school or your favourite search engine to locate two sound files of similar sounds (e.g., both music) that are different formats (e.g., .mp3 and .wav). Listen to them. Then, record the similarities and differences you notice. Also, record both the length and file size of each. Is there a difference in the time/size ratio? Why or why not?

13.4 Authoring Tools

Multimedia authoring systems are programs that coordinate all multimedia elements (e.g., text, sound, animation, video, audio) to create a unified multimedia product, even if they were created with other applications. We will refer to them as authoring tools. Unlike presentation software, authoring systems offer greater branching possibilities for complex structure, device control (so that many peripherals in addition to a mouse can be used to prompt action), and the potential for totally original and highly innovative graphical user interfaces (GUIs).

Figure 13.13
Types of Authoring Tools

Type	Description
Card- or page-based tools	• Elements are organized as pages of a book or a stack of cards. • These tools are ideal when content consists of elements that are to be viewed independently. • Each element is sequenced like a page in a book, but hyperlinks (buttons) allow jumping. Each button takes the user to a new card in the stack. • Examples include Apple HyperCard, HyperStudio, Multimedia Toolbook, and MetaCard.
Icon-based, event-driven tools	• Elements and events are organized as objects in a structural framework that cues action. **Events** are actions or changes in the state or appearance of the multimedia product, or triggers for an element to appear, disappear, or change. They could be automatic (such as a sound timed to happen at a certain point) or externally generated (such as a mouse-click by the user). • These tools allow for a structure that appears like a branching path. • Examples include Authorware and Icon Author.
Time-based and presentation tools	• Elements and events are organized along a timeline that is set up with a GUI similar to a chronological spreadsheet. • The metaphor of a movie is sometimes used in this type of software (e.g., elements are called the cast, the background is called the stage, etc.). • These tools are best to use for a linear project structure, since things are triggered by timing. • Navigational elements allow for interaction and jumping. • Examples include Macromedia Director and Action!
Object-oriented tools	• Multimedia elements become objects in a hierarchical order. • Messages passed among the objects order them to do things according to assigned properties (e.g., in a video game, if the user clicks on a laser beam and hits an asteroid, the element known as the asteroid disintegrates based on the property associated with a laser beam reaching it). • This type of authoring tool is primarily used for games and simulations. • Examples include Gain Momentum and MAEstro.

A well-designed multimedia project should result in the user not knowing what authoring tool was used — the presentation should be seamless, original, and highly interactive. Using this technology, the end product can be published on the Internet or burned onto a CD-ROM or DVD.

Without these authoring tools, the instructions for how the project uses elements and events would have to be programmed using a **scripting language** (a type of programming language that is used for multimedia), such as JavaScript. Using these tools allows for the same end product in a fraction of the time (though in some cases it may sacrifice a degree of control). Specifically, this type of software specifies how to display the elements in relation to one another, how long to display them, and how to enable the user to interact with them.

Figure 13.14 shows a HyperStudio® editing screen and Figure 13.15 shows a Macromedia® Director® editing screen.

Figure 13.14
HyperStudio® Editing Screen

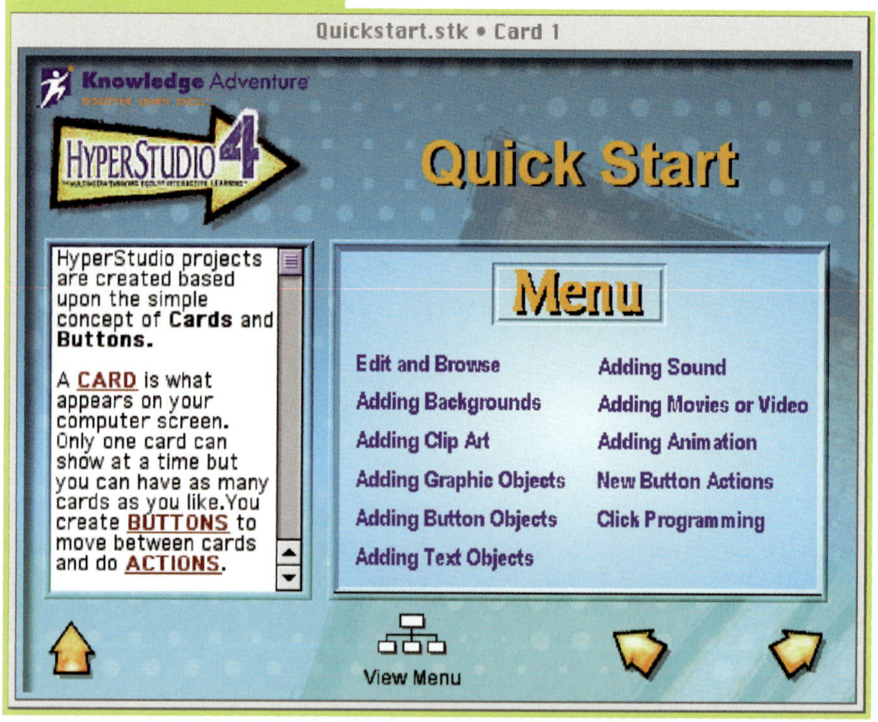

Figure 13.15
Macromedia® Director® Editing Screen

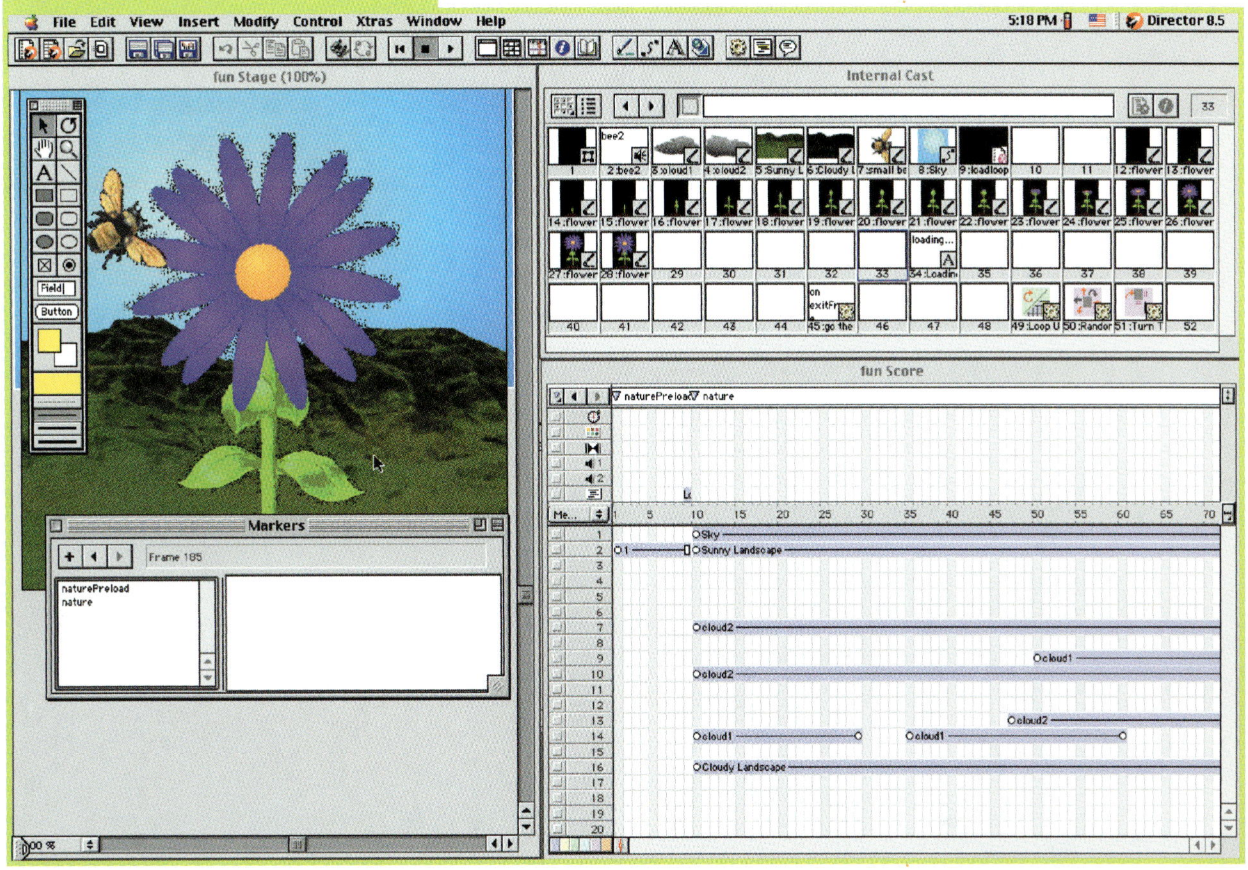

GETTING IT

1. Define *authoring tools* and explain how and why they are used.
2. Discuss at least three benefits of using authoring tools.
3. Describe the basic categories of authoring tools and identify the key features of each.

13.5 Putting It All Together

You have all your multimedia elements ready to go. Your flowchart and storyboard accurately illustrate your vision. You have your authoring tool open. Now what? To bring your multimedia project together, follow the steps below:

1. Import all elements (in the form of files) into the authoring tool.
2. In the authoring tool, position all elements. If needed, re-size or make changes.

Get Connected

Investigate authoring systems by viewing two tutorials. To do this, visit www.pearsoned.ca/businessconnections. Create a table and identify what these programs have in common, how they are different, and whether each is easier or more difficult than you expected. Post your table in the classroom so that it can be used by other students.

3. Create interactivity among the media elements using the features and functions in the authoring software. Set all timings and do a practice run. Take extra care to ensure that all elements are sequenced as you intend them to be, and that elements are properly synchronized (i.e., that the sound, images, and text work together).
4. Insert interactivity tools and navigational elements (e.g., buttons, hyperlinks).
5. Insert transitional effects between and among sections of the multimedia product. Determine if the intended impact was achieved. If it was not, make revisions.
6. Test, test, test and make the necessary repairs.
7. Publish the multimedia product either by uploading to the Internet (see Chapter 12, pages 359–360 for a refresher) or burn a CD (see On the Case, below).

ON THE CASE

Burning Your Multimedia Product onto a CD

CD burners are available in a variety of speeds. They will have a notation such as 8X/4X/24X. This means they write at 8 times normal speed, re-write at 4 times speed, and read at 24 times speed. For example, at 8X, a CD burner would usually finish burning a full CD of music files in about 12 minutes, and at 4X it would take about 20 minutes.

Before you burn a CD, make sure all the necessary files and documents are contained in a single folder — this will ensure that nothing gets omitted and will speed up the process, since only the folder will need to be dragged to the CD.

Unlike saving to a 3.5" disk, putting data onto a CD involves the use of special software, such as Adaptec's Easy CD Creator for Windows and Toast for MACs. This software uses GUIs to walk you through the process. Blank CDs come rated at certain speeds representing the top recommended burn speed. The CD's speed should be the same as that of the CD burner.

Once all of this is set, launch the software for CD burning. Follow the software's wizard or GUI windows to complete the process. Most software will follow a process similar to this:

- The drive will prepare the CD for burning.
- The software will require you to identify the data to be burned.
- The software will ask you to verify or select the speed at which it is to be burned.
- The CD will be burned.
- The session will be closed.

Before burning, close all unnecessary programs and check for any resident programs (such as a virus scanner) that run in the background. Disable your screen saver. As well, the more RAM

ON THE CASE (continued)

the computer has, the higher the success rate of burning. When burning a CD, do not use the computer for any other tasks. When you are working on a network, it is recommended that you transfer the file(s) to be burned to the local drive (usually C:). This will ensure that the CD will be burned more quickly, and reduces the risk of failure.

Questions

1. Explain how saving data to a CD is different from saving to other storage media.
2. List the factors that affect the success rate of burning a CD.

GETTING IT

1. Create a flowchart that illustrates the process of assembling a multimedia product.
2. Explain the methods that are available to publish your multimedia product.

CAREER PERSPECTIVE

What can you do to increase the odds of success when you're just starting out?

By Bob Rosner

Excerpt from www.workopolis.com, Thursday, April 19, 2001. [Cited October 2002.]

Dear WW: I'm going to graduate from college this spring and I'm starting to look for a job. I know what it takes to be successful at school, any advice on what I'll need to know to face the job?

— *THE GRADUATE*

Dear GRADUATE

Let's start with a quiz. Remember when you studied Darwin in your biology class? Which answer best sums up Darwin's theory?

- **a.** Only the fittest survive
- **b.** Only the strongest survive
- **c.** Only the smartest survive
- **d.** Only the most adaptable survive

(continued)

According to one Darwin expert, being fit, smart and strong all matter, but the species that thrive are the ones that are the most adaptable.

It's no different at work. The following tips will help. Also check out "The Complete Idiot's Guide to Cultural Etiquette" (Alpha 1999).

Can you be on time? No one cared if you got to class 15 minutes late. But your coworkers will care A LOT if you show up late for meetings. So give yourself plenty of time to get where you need to go, call ahead if you're running late, and if morning meetings are a problem — get more sleep.

Can you dress appropriately? It's tough to give up jeans for a business suit. I learned how to deal with that from my friend Danny. Before Danny interviewed for his first "real" job, he cut his signature shoulder length hair. Shocked, I asked him why. "Clothes, hair, they're just costumes," he said. "This is my work costume."

Can you use proper business language? You know, there are a lot of people in business who won't appreciate it if you can't, like, make it through a sentence without, you know, using a lot of, like, vulgarity and even, like, slang. Make an effort to write and speak well and opportunity will come knocking at your door.

Are you discreet? Have you ever been burned by telling something to someone in confidence only to have them blab it all over? How inclined were you to share more secrets with this person? Honour people's confidences in you. Yes, there may be times when it will seem like violating a confidence can score you points, but over the long haul you'll be better off being discreet.

Are you courteous, pleasant and positive? There's something to be said for being the kind of person that people want to work with. I'm not saying that you have to have a smile plastered on your face at all times, but being courteous, pleasant and positive will go a long way to keeping people on your side.

Are you concerned with others, not just yourself? Go out of your way to do a favour for people you work with and most of them will return the favour — and then some.

Don't monkey around, be adaptable and follow the tips above and you'll prove Darwin right: you'll be the species that will thrive at work.

Questions

1. Do you agree with the advice given to "The Graduate" by Bob Rosner? Explain why or why not.
2. Describe what you would add or change to Mr. Rosner's response.
3. List the steps you can take to improve your own ability to get a job.

IT's A Wrap

Key Terms in This Chapter

animation (p. 378)
audio resolution (p. 377)
elements (p. 374)
events (p. 385)
flip-book animation (p. 378)
frame rate (p. 383)
frames (p. 378)
hypermedia (p. 367)
interactive multimedia (p. 367)
interactivity (p. 367)
key frames (p. 380)
looping (p. 377)
motion path (p. 378)
multimedia (p. 367)
multimedia authoring system (p. 384)
multiplicity (p. 367)
normalizing (p. 377)
path-based animation (p. 378)
plug-ins (p. 378)
sampling rate (p. 377)
scripting language (p. 386)
server-push (p. 378)
splines (p. 378)
sprite-based animation (p. 378)
storyboard (p. 372)
streaming (p. 379)
trimming (p. 376)
tweening (p. 381)
vector-based animation (p. 379)

1. Create a list of competencies that you have acquired through your work in this chapter.
2. Update your portfolio to include examples of your work from this chapter.

Know It!

3. Describe how multiplicity and interactivity are related to multimedia.
4. Explain how the terms *multimedia* and *interactive multimedia* differ.
5. Describe why and how organizations use information kiosks.
6. Explain the ways organizations can use multimedia to help employees to learn. Provide a specific example for each.
7. List the ideal hardware requirements of a computer in a multimedia environment.
8. Create a list of planning steps for a person who wants to create a multimedia product.
9. Explain how flowcharts and storyboards are similar. How do they differ?
10. Describe the elements of multimedia.
11. Compare and contrast the four types of animation.
12. Describe what you can do to reduce the size of a sound file.
13. Create a "checklist" that identifies the steps required to burn a CD.

Do It!

14. Using one of the items you found in the Ready, Set, Go! assignment at the beginning of this chapter, create a flowchart that represents its navigational structure. Based on the flowchart, identify the type of multimedia structure.
15. Using the multimedia product from the previous question, sketch a very rough storyboard to illustrate any three panels or pages.

IT's A Wrap *(continued)*

Do It!

16. Locate an animated GIF on your favourite clipart Web site. Identify how you think it was created. Identify the frames that it comprises and draw them in storyboard format.

17. From www.pearsoned.ca/businessconnections, obtain a video clip. What is the file format? If you have video-editing software available, cut and resequence the clip.

Analyze It!

Analyze each of the questions below. Then prepare a brief report that summarizes your analysis.

18. Describe the ways that a variety of elements used together enhance multimedia.

19. Re-examine the authoring tool tutorials you viewed. Describe how presentation software can be used to mimic an authoring tool.

20. Identify the advantages of an authoring tool over presentation software.

21. Describe the advantages and disadvantages of using a CD instead of publishing a multimedia project over the Internet.

Glossary

acceptable use policy (AUP) a signed agreement between an organization and an employee/system user that outlines the use of, and access to, the computer network and all intellectual property it contains

accuracy the degree to which information is error-free or exact

active listening hearing a message and clarifying the information by asking questions to fully appreciate what is being said

advertising and cross-branding agreements among businesses to use one another's names and logos to increase business

advertorial a piece of journalism that looks like an article, but is paid for by an advertiser of the publication in which it appears

affiliate relationship an arrangement between online merchants or sites to allow each other to advertise on their respective sites without charge

analogous colours colours that share common attributes but provide little contrast to one another

animation a series of graphic images assembled using software to provide the appearance of movement

annotated bibliography a list of sources used in the preparation of a document with a brief summary of their contents that is organized alphabetically by the authors' last names at the end of the document

anti-virus software programs designed to scan files as they are downloaded from the Internet and files stored in the computer system to check for virus infestation

application gateways a method of firewall protection that filters messages based on the application being requested rather than on the area of the network requested

appropriateness the suitability of the information to the research question or problem being addressed

archiving saving past versions of a Web site that is being updated

ASCII stands for American Standard Code for Information Interchange — a code for representing characters as numbers

ASP (Application Service Providers) organizations that provide access to software applications via the Internet

asymmetric encryption translating data into a secret code using two keys: a public key, known to both the sender and the recipient, used by the sender to encrypt the message and a private key, known only to the recipient, used to decrypt the message

audio resolution the accuracy with which sound can be digitized

authentication a computer network's safeguard that requires the input of personal information for access to the network

authoring tools software applications that facilitate the creation of Web sites using graphical user interface (GUI)

AutoCorrect a feature in a word-processing program that automatically corrects keystroke errors for words that are often misspelled (or words specified by the user); sometimes called QuickCorrect

automated monitoring system a method of keeping track of employees and their productivity using electronic surveillance

balance in graphic design an arrangement of elements so that they equal each other in the viewing space

bandwidth the speed at which a given technology can transmit data

banner ad a promotional message in a square or rectangular box on a Web page

bar code a printed set of lines encoding price and inventory data that can be scanned electronically

baseline a snapshot in time of a project plan made up of the tasks, deliverables, and milestones against which project progress can be measured

basic input/output system (BIOS) essential programs that contain the instructions to start the computer and facilitate the transfer of data and control instructions between the computer and other hardware, such as a printer or monitor

bias information that expresses a particular viewpoint or is incomplete for a specific purpose

bibliography a list of sources used in the preparation of a document that is organized alphabetically by the authors' last names at the end of the document

bidding attempting to secure available work by submitting a quote for the fee expected to the organization that has posted the work

biometric security a type of authentication that uses a person's physical characteristics to allow access to a computer system

blogs online journals or diaries where people share ideas, views, and favourite sites on a variety of topics of interest to them

Bluetooth technology that allows communication between all forms of cellular phones, handheld computers, PDAs, and PCs regardless of their operating systems

Bookmark a feature in a word-processing program that allows the user to mark a specific point in the document making it easier to find later

bridge software that connects networks of the same type in local area network and wide area network communication

browse scroll manually through a document

bureaucratic/hierarchical structure a vertical organizational structure with a very formal, layered system of authority and a very specific chain of command for decision making and request approval

Business to Business (B2B) a form of e-commerce involving transactions between businesses

Business to Consumer (B2C) a form of e-commerce involving transactions between a business and a consumer

byte a unit of measurement for computer storage; one byte is equal to one character, number, or letter

cascading style sheet (CSS) a number of linked style sheets created by keying specific tags that describe the design of the sheets into the text editor

cash a form of legal tender that can be converted into other forms of value such as goods or services

cathode ray tube (CRT) a monitor that looks like a small television set and uses similar technology to generate the image on the screen

central processing unit (CPU) a computer's internal processor that transforms input into a form of output

centralized structure an organizational structure in which power and control for decision making are at the top levels of the organization (e.g., at the level of president or vice-presidents)

certificate authority (CA) a trusted third-party organization that issues digital certification verifying the identity of the individual granting the certificate

cheque a draft written against the balance in an account at a financial institution

clearing system the process that involves the transfer of money from one account to another account in a financial institution

clickstream behaviour the way consumers travel on the Internet

client/server network a network configured to designate one computer as the file server to control all shared devices, files, and programs

codecs compression algorithms used to reduce the size of graphic files

column a formatting option that allows the user to present information similar to newspaper text

column break a feature that allows the user to force the text to begin at the top of the next available column

comment highlighted text containing a statement about the document, which is numbered and initialed

communication an interpersonal two-way process that involves sending a message and receiving one

community provider Business to Consumer Web sites that provide digital places where people with similar interests can interact, transact, and receive information

competencies characteristics, such as skills, behaviours, and traits, that employers expect employees to have to perform successfully

complementary colours colours that have drastically different wavelengths and, consequently, have high contrast; opposites on the colour wheel

compress make files smaller using encoding schemes to save on disk space

computed fields a field in a database that contains the results of an expression or calculation rather than stored data

Computer Aided Design (CAD) software that allows designers to create 3-D models and simulations that can be rotated and viewed from any angle

Computer Aided Manufacturing (CAM) software that controls the manufacturing of components to overcome tolerance and layout problems for more efficient manufacturing

computer telephony hardware that enables computers to act as speakerphones, answering machines, and complete voice mail systems

conflict differences of opinion or ideas that can cause tension between individuals or team members and reduce a team's productivity if not dealt with quickly and constructively

confidentiality the degree to which information is for private use

consistency harmony created in a composition or a series of compositions by repeating the same components

Consumer to Consumer (C2C) a form of e-commerce involving transactions between individuals using an intermediary

content licensing ownership and sharing of any type of information in digital form through a contract

content provider Business to Consumer Web sites that provide information and entertainment to potential customers

contention a problem that occurs when two or more workstations try to access the local area network (LAN) at the same time

contrast the placement of two different or opposite elements next to one another to create visual interest

cookie a small text file with an identification number that a Web site places on the hard drive of a user's computer to allow the user to interact with the site efficiently

cooperative a shared workspace maintained by a group of independent individuals, often entrepreneurs

copyright the right to reproduce, publish, or perform a work given to the owner of that work through legislation

corporate workplace setting a central location where employees of an organization come together to work

cracker a person who gains unauthorized access to a computer system to steal or corrupt data

credit card a method of payment that allows purchasers to buy items and defer payment until later

cross-platform standards markup languages that work on any computer

cross-selling the process of encouraging customers to purchase additional products that go with products already selected

currency the degree to which information is up-to-date

Customer Relationship Management (CRM) a system that allows marketers to track all the ways a customer interacts with the organization and to judge the success rate of particular strategies

database a program that allows for the storage, organization, retrieval, and management of large quantities of data

data mining the examination and extraction of information from databases in a data warehouse to locate relationships between and among data sets

data warehouse offline storage of information from numerous sources across the enterprise for analysis by management

debit card a method of payment that immediately transfers funds from the purchaser's bank account to the merchant's bank account

decentralized structure an organizational structure in which power and control are delegated to lower levels of the organization, giving employees or teams authority to make decisions

decision support system (DSS) a variation of management information systems that allow managers to ask "what if" questions and develop simulations based on historical data

defragmenting the process of reorganizing the files on the hard drive so that unnecessary gaps are eliminated in the storage area

delivering the process of going live with the Web site

deliverable specific outcomes that can be measured to satisfy the requirements of managers or end users

demographics statistics that profile segments of the population by factors such as age, gender, income, marital status, and family status

Denial of Service (DoS) a hacker attack that floods an e-commerce site with traffic to overwhelm the merchant's network

deontology a belief that there are some things that a person should do ("right") and others that a person should not do ("wrong") regardless of the consequences

designer the person who creates the overall look of a Web site, generating such elements as graphics and animation

designing the process that involves making decisions pertaining to each of the elements to create an effective Web design

de-skilled the implementation of new technology to perform tasks previously done by employees making the job less demanding intellectually

desktop publishing (DTP) the process of producing documents such as newsletters, brochures, and books using specialized software using a desktop computer

digital cash a payment system used online to send payment person to person; also called e-cash

Digital Certificate a digital document issued by a certification authority upon request by the sender of a message to verify the identity of the sender

digital envelope a method of decrypting a message by first decrypting a symmetric key using a private key, then decrypting the message using that symmetric key

digital wallet an online wallet installed as a plug-in to your Web browser that contains identification information so that a person can make a purchase on site

direct competitor a business that targets the same audience

direct e-mail marketing advertising and promotion e-mail requested by people who are interested in the product or topic

direct store delivery a system that gives information about each customer's buying history and about products that are selling that week to salespeople so that they are prepared to fill orders from their trucks

disclosure communicating information about yourself that is relevant to a particular situation

distribution the stage in the marketing mix of getting the goods to the customer

dithering an automatic process that approximates colour and shading when software cannot display the full range of colours in an image

division-/department-based organization an organizational design in which departments operate on their own as business units and work without much interaction across divisions or departments

Document Map a feature in Word that allows the user to view the list of headings in the document

DNS (domain name system) a system that connects the URL address with the appropriate four-part numbered IP address to locate the requested Web page

duty a specific tax imposed on imports by the customs authority of a country

dynamic pricing a system of flexible pricing of products that allows the bidders to determine the price

e-business transactions that are conducted over networks linking electronic devices that do not involve an exchange of payment

e-commerce commercial activity conducted over networks linking electronic devices (mainly computers)

economy the use of elements in graphic design to achieve a composition that is not too "busy"

editorial a piece of journalism (such as an opinion article) written for a publication and paid for by the publisher rather than an advertiser of that publication

electronic data interchange (EDI) a system that allows companies to exchange information electronically to facilitate procedures such as ordering and paying for supplies

electronic portfolio a collection of materials maintained online through a Web page or stored on a CD-ROM that showcase an individual's skills and talent over time

elements the various pieces, i.e., text, images, sound, animation, and video, that make up a multimedia project

Elements of Design the various components used in graphic design analogous to the "ingredients" of a recipe

embedded citations source information (author's last name and year of publication) that appears within the text in parentheses immediately before or after the information being cited

emphasis the placement of an element in the forefront to minimize the appearance of everything else in a graphic design

encryption a form of data security that translates data into a secret code so that they are unintelligible if intercepted

endnote source information (author's last name, name of publication, place and year of publication, and the name of the publisher) that appears at the end of the chapter or document and is identified by a number or symbol that corresponds to a number or symbol that appears immediately following the information being cited

ergonomics the design of workplace computers, machines, and tools, based on the study of the interaction of people with their environments, to make the equipment safer for people who use it

e-tailer a company that sells merchandise online

ethical framework a system that a person can use to help make a decision when faced with a dilemma; see also **deontology** and **utilitarianism**

ethics a set of principles or rules that a person follows regarding what is good and bad, right and wrong

evaluating and testing the process of ensuring that a Web site meets the original objectives and that all the components work before the site becomes accessible through the Internet

events actions or changes in the state or appearance of a multimedia product, or triggers for an element to appear, disappear, or change

Extensible Markup Language (XML) a markup language that uses pairs of symbols (tags) to tell the browse what type of information is found within them that allows authors to capture specific types of data by creating their own elements

extension an identifier determined by the application in which the file was created that is added to a file name

fair dealing the use or reproduction of a work for private study, research, criticism, review, or news reporting without permission from the copyright holder under circumstances identified in the fair dealing criteria

fax machine a machine that transmits and receives printed documents through telephone lines

field a single piece of information entered into a database record

file allocation table (FAT) a table of contents that the operating system uses to locate files on a disk in a standard Windows environment

file management the process of organizing your work in files so that it can be located later

file name a unique name assigned to work to identify it for later retrieval

file virus a computer program that infects executable files so that when they are launched the file can be copied to your system

Fill Command a command that allows the user to enter a formula once and copy it down (or across) the column

flip-book animation a book that contains different drawings on each page so that when the pages are flipped quickly the picture appears to move

firewall a form of protection that allows users access to the Internet but restricts access to the company's resources from outside the Internet connection; a software application designed to prevent unauthorized users from accessing a computer network

flowchart a visual representation, or blueprint, of the flow of data, the structure, and/or the process of an organization or project; a valuable planning tool for laying out the architecture of a Web site that clearly shows the requirements, actions, and steps that need to be included in the site

focal point the attention-getting element in a graphic design that attracts the eye

Footer the space reserved at the bottom of the page where information can be entered to appear in the same way on some or all pages in a document

footnotes source information (author's last name, name of publication, place and year of publication, and the name of the publisher) that appears at the bottom of the page and is identified by a number or symbol that corresponds to a number or symbol that appears immediately following the information being cited

font set the combination of typeface, size, and visual characteristics that make up the design set for different characters

forces of competition possible threats to the success of a business in a traditional environment

form a pop-up box or Graphical User Interface that users see when they input or view records; information viewed is based on underlying tables or queries that can be entered, edited, displayed, filtered, and printed; three-dimensional elements in graphic design that incorporate length, width, and depth

formula a step-by-step procedure entered into a worksheet cell following the order of operations

frame rate the speed at which each image advances to create movement; the higher the frame rate, the higher the quality of a video or animation file

frames a series of still graphic images used for electronic animation

fraud crimes in which individuals knowingly deceive or misrepresent themselves to gain personal benefit

ftp (file transfer protocol) a standard set of rules and procedures used to upload and download files between two devices

function predefined formulas that perform simple to complex calculations

gateway software that connects networks of different protocols in local area network and wide area network communication

gigabyte one billion bytes

graphic design the process of creating visual media by combining text and graphics to effectively convey a message

graphics tablet an input pointing device used extensively in graphic design applications to give the computer commands

grouping a technique used in graphic design to "glue" tiny lines and shapes together

groupware software that can have more than one user collaborating on a particular document or project simultaneously

hacker a person who attempts to gain unauthorized access to a computer system

hard page break forcing a new page in a document by holding down Ctrl/Enter or inserting a page break from the pull-down menu

Header the space reserved at the top of the page where information can be entered to appear in the same way on some or all pages in a document

Help menu a list of step-by-step instructions for performing various functions in a software program

hierarchy a system of arranging and saving computer files in folders within folders to make finding files quicker and easier

highlighter a built-in feature of a word-processing program that allows the user to emphasize changes using colour so that they can be quickly and easily identified

hoaxes messages sent over the Internet that seem harmless but can cause servers to slow down

home page the main point of entry in a Web site

horizontal structure an organizational structure in which many individuals report to one supervisor, but with fewer layers of management than a hierarchical structure

hosting assuming the location and ultimate responsibility of operating a site on a Web server

HTML (hypertext markup language) a scripting language used to describe how a Web browser should display text, visual images, video, and audio files

HTTP (hypertext transfer protocols) conventions that determine how messages are formatted and transmitted and the actions to be taken by Web servers and browsers on the World Wide Web

hue shade or tint of colour, e.g., red, green, yellow, violet, blue

hyperlink an element in an electronic document that takes the user to another document, a place within the same document, or another file

hypermedia presentations that blend multimedia with the Internet giving users the opportunity to navigate through a variety of media and materials over many paths

hypertext markup language (HTML) a scripting language used to describe how a Web browser should display text, visual images, video, and audio files

impact printer an output device that forms images by striking a hammer against a ribbon, which then hits the paper, transferring the ink to the surface of the paper in a manner similar to the process used by typewriters

information architect the person who organizes the content and tests a Web site's usability

Information Revolution a shift from manual labour to information processing caused by the introduction of information technology

information technology all aspects of managing and processing information including the use of electronic tools and the input of people using those tools to manage the information

initiator a team member who initiates discussion by contributing knowledge of facts, experiences, or opinions

intellectual property the term used to describe creative endeavours in the areas of patents, trademarks, industrial designs, confidential information/trade secrets, integrated circuit topography, and copyright

intensity strength of the brightness of colour in graphic design

Interac the association responsible for the development of Canada's national network of shared cash dispensing machines and direct payment/debit system

interactive multimedia presentations that allow users to choose what they want to see and hear

interactivity the degree to which the user has a choice in the flow of information

Internet a global network that connects millions of computers and storage devices by cables and/or satellite

Internet telephony a variation of computer telephony that directs telephone calls through the Internet to a telephone at another location

Java an object-oriented programming language often used to build systems that interact over networks

JavaScript a scripting language that works with HTML to enhance Web pages and make them more interactive

job depth the extent of responsibility an employee has for planning his or her workday and ensuring tasks are performed correctly

job scope the number and variety of tasks an employee has to perform

justify to create a clean line appearance on both left and right sides of paragraphs with no jagged edges

key field information unique to each record that is included in a data design to prevent duplication

key frames main poses or actions that make up the animation

kilobyte one thousand bytes

knowledge discovery in databases (KDD) finding unnoticed patterns or connections among data sets to solve business problems and find business opportunities

labels the text that describes the data contained in the various cell locations in a spreadsheet

licence a contract through which the owner of intellectual property permits another individual to make, use, or sell that intellectual property in exchange for some form of compensation

line a point in motion in graphic design with only one dimension, that being length

line spacing a setting that allows the user to leave a required space between lines of text as the text is keyed

link join two files so that data in one file is automatically updated when changes are made to the second

liquid crystal display (LCD) a flat panel monitor most commonly seen on notebook computers; LCD displays utilize two sheets of polarizing material with a liquid crystal solution between them

listening hearing and concentrating on understanding a message being received

legal tender currency designated by law as acceptable payment

local area network (LAN) a group of computers connected in a small geographic region, such as within an office building

local loop a group of 100 or more subscribers connected to the subscriber loop carrier

looping setting a sound, video, or animation file to play over and over

lossless compression a process that reduces the size of an original file in a way that allows it to be completely restored

lossy compression a process during saving that permanently removes some unnecessary information to reduce the size of an original file

macro a series of commands and instructions grouped as a single command to accomplish a task automatically

macro virus a computer program that infects the program for which it is written

magnetic ink character recognition (MICR) a scanning method developed for use in the banking community to electronically enter data from the numbers preprinted on the bottom of cheques

mail merge a feature in a word-processing program that allows for the production of mass mailings of the same document, customized and personalized, using entries in a database or table that are linked to fields in the word-processed document

mailing label a form containing addresses created referencing the database fields that can be reused countless times

market creator Business to Consumer Web site that creates an electronic marketplace for buyers and sellers to meet

management information system (MIS) a massive database containing a variety of information that management can analyze to make decisions for the organization

marketing communications methods used to increase consumer awareness and to promote sales

marketing mix the four elements – market research and product development, promotion strategies, product distribution, and pricing – that make up a company's marketing program

markup languages a system of codes that tell a computer how to format, lay out, and structure text-based items

matrix-/project-based organization an organizational design in which employees belong to more than one department and move from project to project to perform their specialized tasks as the need arises; characterized by employees reporting to more than one manager or supervisor

m-commerce the use of wireless digital devices to conduct business over the Web; mobile commerce

megabyte one million bytes

metropolitan area network (MAN) a system that connects two or more local area networks within a limited geographic region such as a city

milestone an important event that gives feedback to the project team on the progress of the project

minutes notes taken at a meeting that summarize the discussion that took place

modem a device that converts voice and data messages to analog signals and then converts them back to digital signals

modulation the process of converting digital signals to analog signals

motherboard the computer's printed circuit board containing connectors to which additional boards are attached to determine the computer's capabilities

motion path a line drawn across the viewing area or background on which a sprite is attached in path-based animation

mouse an input device that gives the computer commands to respond to prompts from software or to position the cursor on the screen

MTSO (Mobile Telephone Switching Office) a transmitter that controls all cellular activity in the region and relays calls to the regular telephone system

multifunction printer an output device that combines printer, fax machine, and possibly a scanner and copier into one unit

multimedia presentations that incorporate two or more of text, sound, graphics, animation, or video

multimedia authoring system programs that coordinate all multimedia elements to create a unified multimedia product

multiplicity the number of media available in one source

network a system that links two or more computers to allow the exchange of data and the sharing of resources and peripheral devices

network interface card (NIC) a computer circuit board that allows an individual computer or workstation to be connected to a network

network operating system (NOS) an operating system on a network that provides for the operation and management of the network

node a connecting point within a computer network

non-impact printer an output device that forms images either by laser, ink jet, or thermal technology

North American Free Trade Agreement (NAFTA) a trade agreement signed by Canada, the United States, and Mexico that came into force on January 1, 1989

normalizing adjusting volume levels from different sources to create a consistent volume level

notebook the name for the file and individual sheets in Quattro® Pro spreadsheet documents

numeric data a field classified as numeric information to allow a database or spreadsheet to perform mathematical calculations on records in that field

object-oriented graphics graphics stored as collections of lines, shapes, and other objects; also known as vector-based graphics

omnibus surveys large-scale surveys that look for general opinions, attitudes, or types of behaviour not specific to any one company

online catalogue a Web site that allows consumers to view a merchant's wares, see colour availability, and access pricing information

operating system (OS) a computer's master control program that keeps the hardware and software running efficiently and allows the user to communicate with the hardware

optical character recognition (OCR) software that converts printed documents into digital text that can be scanned electronically

organizational design the decisions and assumptions that lead to a specific organizational structure, including processes for how parts of the organization work together, ways that information flows, and how technology is integrated

organizational structure the pattern of responsibilities, authorities, and relationships that control how people perform their functions and how they interact with one another within an organization

Orphan the last line of a paragraph sitting alone at the top of a page

Outline an organizational feature in the View menu of a word-processing program that allows the user to arrange topics into different levels of importance

outsource to hire another company to provide services

packet filter a method of firewall protection that examines each packet entering or leaving the network to determine if they are destined for prohibited areas on the network

patents intellectual property in the form of processes, articles, and inventions

path-based animation a sub-set of sprite-based animation in which the sprite is attached and travels along a motion path

Pay for Show payment made to a search engine to have a Web site appear in its directory and index so that Internet searchers will find the site more frequently

peer-to-peer (P2P) network a system that treats all computers as equal on the network

Person to Person (P2P) technology that allows users of the Internet to share files and computer resources directly, without going through a Web server

personal digital assistant (PDA) a hand-held device used to store information such as appointments and addresses; newer PDAs have networking features

personalizing a Web site feature that recognizes customers when they log in, reacts to their choices, and offers built-in guidance based on those choices

PHP (PHP: Hypertext Preprocessor) a general-purpose scripting language that can be embedded in HTML and is suited to complex and interactive Web development

pixels tiny dots of varying colours that are arranged in rows

planning the first step in creating a Web site, which involves determining the objectives of the site

plotter an output device that produces large, wide-bed printed images using pens that can create fine detail used in drafting, blueprints, and map making

plug-ins helper applications that can be downloaded for special purposes, such as viewing animation

pointing stick a small, eraser-like device that has left- and right-click function buttons and responds to the user applying pressure in the desired direction of movement

pop-under ad an advertisement that appears in a new browser window under the open window and remains on the desktop until the viewer closes it

POP3 (Post Office Protocol) the server application that handles incoming mail from the Internet

portfolio a collection of materials that showcase an individual's skills and talent over time

portal an Internet site that offers users a full-service package, such as searching, news, e-mail, chat, downloads, video streaming, and calendars

presentation software software that allows users to create slides that incorporate text, graphics, animation, and sound to deliver a message with impact to an audience

primary data information collected directly from the source through surveys, interviews, or experiments

Principles of Design guidelines for using components and elements in graphic design analogous to the "steps" prescribed in a recipe

Print Preview a feature in a word-processing program that allows the user to see the document as it will appear in hard copy when printed

producing the process of bringing the plan and design of a Web site to life, either by coding or using specific software

productivity the efficient use of resources, including time and technology, by individuals and teams

programmer the person who writes the code (markup language) and develops additional scripts and applications for a Web site

programs application files stored on a computer's hard drive or on a file server

project a process undertaken to achieve a specific goal that has a defined scope and outcomes, can be accomplished within a specific time frame, utilizes human effort and a limited set of resources, and is characterized by a sequence or activities

project management the approach used to manage non-repetitive work within the constraints of time, cost, and performance targets

project manager the person responsible for meeting the performance, schedule, and cost constraints of a project

project team a specific group formed to plan and execute projects

protocols a set of rules and procedures, or conventions, developed to allow sending and receiving computers to understand the messages being transmitted

proxy server a method of firewall protection that intercepts all traffic coming into and leaving a computer network to prohibit access to a company's internal network

public relations (PR) creating an awareness of an organization by informing audiences through the news media about new events, products and services, and activities the firm undertakes

quasi-WYSIWYG a type of authoring tool or Web site creation that allows users to switch between WYSIWYG and code-based views to allow authors to easily modify the markup language tags

queries commands that allow the user to view, change, and analyze data in different ways

QuickCorrect a feature in a word-processing program that automatically corrects keystroke errors for words that are often misspelled (or words specified by the user); sometimes called AutoCorrect

random access memory (RAM) a computer's main memory

raster bitmapped images that are maps made up of pixels that carry colour and location with them

read only memory (ROM) built-in computer memory that contains essential systems programs allowing the user to "boot up" or start the computer

relevance the degree to which information is applicable to a research problem

repetitive strain injury (RSI) damage to a body part that develops due to repeated movements over a long period of time

report an organized printout of the records and fields of a database in an easy-to-read format

responder a team member who listens to the discussion and responds by evaluating and/or commenting on the information

rhythm organized movement in graphic design created by the repetition of one or more elements of design

rich media ad an advertisement that uses 3-D imagery to involve the viewer more actively in the advertising process

robot a mechanical device that performs some of the tasks previously done by humans

rollovers onscreen buttons that visibly change when a pointing device hovers over them

router software that connects several networks, choosing the most efficient route for communication to travel

sampling rate the frequency makeup of a recording, measured in kilohertz (kHz)

scanning tools technology used to enter data electronically

script virus a computer program written in JavaScript or VBScript that overwrites other files, eliminating the files in their original form

scripting language a type of programming language used to create small programs quickly, commonly to create multimedia products

scripts short programs used to create animated pictures, sound effects, games, chat, rollovers, and similar features written in scripting languages

secondary data information that has been gathered previously by others and is available through a published source

section break a feature that allows the user to divide long documents into sections and apply different formatting features to individual portions in the document

Secure Sockets Layer (SSL) a method of securing the channels of communication for Internet messages that combines encryption, digital envelopes, and digital certificates in each session

series values or labels that follow a sequence, such as days of the week, months, dates, and times

server-push a technique that uses Common Gateway Interface scripting language to create flip-book animation by "pushing" a series of graphics on the screen

service providers Business to Consumer Web sites that provide services to free people to do other things

shape in graphic design, two-dimensional elements or objects that are formed by a closed line

shortcut keystrokes a predetermined code that represents a command to the software such as inserting symbol characters without the use of the mouse to access the Insert, Symbol menu

site map a dedicated sub-page that identifies the entire contents of the Web site through clickable links and allows the user to go directly to a specific area

smart card information about the user that can provide authentication when it is used with a PIN number

SMTP (Simple Mail Transfer Protocol) the server application that handles outgoing mail over the Internet

sniffer a program and/or device that monitors data travelling over a network; a favourite tool of hackers

soft return starting a new line within a paragraph (but not a new paragraph) by pressing Shift/Enter

SOHO (small office, home office) space within a private residence used for business/commercial purposes

sorting function a command that allows the user to sort information based on the content of a specified field or fields for analysis

source code the markup language instructions contained in the source document

source document the document that contains all of the content for the Web page and the markup language instructions

spam junk e-mail

splines motion paths created from a series of lines to suggest a jagged or bumpy path

sponsorships associating a name and product or services with a particular Web site or event as a way to increase brand awareness

spoofing assuming a fake identity through fake e-mail addresses

spreadsheet a computer program that allows the user to manipulate data in a two-dimensional matrix of columns and rows that resembles an accounting ledger sheet

sprite-based animation the appearance of movement created by a bitmap object, called a sprite, that moves independently over a still background

stealth sites Internet sites that appear to be traditional and credible journalism, but are actually advertisement sites that do not mention their connection with a commercial organization

storage a hardware compartment that allows the user to save and retain files so they can be retrieved later

stored value an online system that allows purchasers to transfer funds from their bank accounts to an account that is held at another site for use in making online purchases

storyboard hand-drawn sketches with instructions illustrating the proposed look of each page or section of a multimedia document

strategic plan a document that serves as a roadmap by identifying where an organization wants to be in the future and the specific steps necessary to achieve that objective

streaming a technology that can be used to deliver audio, animation, or video over the Internet as a continuous stream, allowing the user to view or listen to files without having to download an entire file

Structured Query Language (SQL) the standard language and set of commands used to communicate with relational databases

style a preset combination of font style and size

style manual a guide that prescribes ways for writers to organize their work and cite sources of quotations and information and provides information on grammar, punctuation, preferred spelling, hyphenation, and citation format

style sheet a form of HTML template that ensures consistency in Web design

sub-pages a linked series of pages that make up a Web site and are found at one domain name

subscriber loop carrier (SLC) a telephone box located outside your home that connects 100 or more subscribers with twisted-pair copper cable

subscription site a Web site that offers information or content for a fee

symmetrical encryption translating data into a secret code by using the same key to encrypt and decrypt the data being transmitted

Synchronized Multimedia Integration Language (SMIL) a markup language that is an application of Extensible Markup Language (XML) used specifically to coordinate multimedia elements (such as audio and video) within a Web application

synergy a situation where the combined output of a group is greater than the sum of the output of the individuals that compose the group

system administrator the person who monitors and maintains the servers, including hardware and software, to keep a Web site running problem free

system software the operating system and utility programs used to manage files and connect peripheral devices

table a visual presentation that lists information in categories; also a means of organizing data with fields (columns) and records (rows) to facilitate other functions

table of contents a feature in a word-processing program that lists all the headings and subheadings in a document with their page numbers so that the user can quickly go to the section he or she wants by clicking on the page number

tags markup language instructions that surround a unit of text and define what it is suppose to be; made up of beginning and ending angle brackets (< >) called delimiters with a word or symbol between the brackets

task an activity or event that has a well-defined start and end or duration and produces a measurable result or end product

task specialization the number of tasks an employee performs in the whole job

TCP/IP (transmission control protocol/Internet protocol) standard conventions developed for transmitting information over the Internet

team a collection of people who regularly interact in pursuit of a common goal

technology licensing permission to use processes or actual software applications granted as part of the purchasing agreement

telcos companies that provide local telephone service by connecting homes and offices via landlines and satellite

telecommute to work from home rather than in the employer's corporate workplace setting

template a format used to create standardized documents; also a pre-designed worksheet in a spreadsheet program that contains labels and formulas and functions, but no values

text field information entered into a database requiring no mathematical manipulation, such as last and first names

texture a technique used in two-dimensional design to replicate three-dimensional surfaces through various drawings and media techniques

terabyte one trillion bytes

topology the physical layout of a network

touch screen an input pointing device that gives commands to the computer when the user points and touches various locations on the screen

touchpad a small, square, touch-sensitive panel that responds to the touch of a finger to move the cursor on the screen

Track Changes a feature in the Microsoft® Word Tools menu that allows one member of a writing team to edit the work of another, showing where the changes were made and any text that was deleted

trackball an input device that has a ball facing upward, which is moved to give the computer commands to respond to prompts from software or to position the cursor on the screen

trademarks intellectual property in the form of words, phrases, or images that has been registered

transaction broker an e-commerce site that processes consumer transactions that would normally be handled in person, by mail, or over the telephone

transaction log a compilation of the activity at a particular Web site

trimming removing blocks of silence from a digital audio file using software commands

tweening the process of creating intermediate frames between key frames done automatically by animation software

two-minute rule actions that require less than two minutes to complete should be done immediately

unity condition of completeness in graphic design

Universal Product Code (UPC) a bar code printed on consumer products indicating product classification, price, and other data that can be scanned electronically

uploading the process of copying files from a personal computer to a server to put a Web site online

up-skilled the introduction of new technology as tools for employees to use to do their jobs requiring additional skills/training on the part of employees

URL (Uniform Resource Locator) an address having three distinct components used to identify a Web page

utilitarianism the belief that a person should do what will result in the greatest good for the greatest number of people

validity the degree to which information is truthful, logical, and trustworthy

value degree of lightness or darkness of colour used in graphic design

values the numeric entries or data that are used to perform calculations in the spreadsheet

variable information data to be inserted in a generic document that changes with each document, e.g., names, addresses, and telephone numbers in a letter

vector-based animation the appearance of movement created by a bitmap object that is created and described by mathematical formulas

vector-based graphics graphics stored as collections of lines, shapes, and other objects; also known as object-oriented graphics

virtual enterprises organizations equipped with information technology that enable customers, distributors and suppliers of goods and services, and staff to work on a specific job or project from a number of different locations

virtual memory an area on the computer's hard drive set aside to increase the memory available to run programs

virus a computer program that replicates, spreads to other files, and delivers a "payload" or another program that can create havoc in your computer system

WAP (wireless application protocol) special cryptology used to ensure safe transmission of data over wireless communication devices

watermark an image that appears faintly behind the text on a page

Web bugs tiny one-pixel graphic files that are embedded in e-mail messages and on Web sites to monitor the behaviour of the user visiting the site

Web cam a camera connected to a PC or laptop computers used for audio/visual communication between users

Web design how a Web site is organized, how it functions, and how it looks

Web page a single document that comprises files, words, visuals, colour, and links viewed via a browser at one time

Web portal an Internet site that offers users a full-service package, such as searching, news, e-mail, chat, downloads, video streaming, and calendars

Web ring a collection of pages linked by a common theme

Web site a linked series of pages, programs, sounds, databases, documents, and/or images that are found at one domain name

Webmaster the person who manages or coordinates all aspects (design, content, and technical aspects) of the Web site's creation

wide area network (WAN) a connection of computers over distances greater than those serviced by the local area network (LAN)

Widow a section heading or the first line of a new paragraph left at the bottom of a page

wildcard characters symbols used to substitute unknown or unspecific information in a query

WiFi (wireless fidelity) client/server technology that allows multiple users to log into a wireless network within a small geographic area of a few hundred square metres.

word processing a computer application that allows the user to create clean copy and edit it without having to recreate the entire document

workbook the name for the file in Excel

workplace setting the location where employees conduct their day-to-day work

worksheet the name for the individual spreadsheet sheets in Microsoft® Excel

World Wide Web a system of Internet servers that allow users to access and view specially formatted documents using special software known as a browser

WYSIWYG (pronounced "whizzywig") a document view that allows the user to see the results of formatting on the monitor; in Web authoring software WYSIWYG programs allow users to see what a Web page would look like if it were live as they work

writer the person who prepares the content for a Web site

yield management a form of dynamic pricing in which a company determines the price of its product or service based on the quantity in stock

Bibliography

Chapter 1

Beardsley, David (1998). "Four tricks that save time." *Fast Company* issue 14, April, p. 66.

Covey, Stephen R. (1989). *The 7 habits of highly effective people.* Copyright Stephen R. Covey, FranklinCovey Co. Available online at **www.franklincovey.com**.

Ipsos-Reid (2001). Software Experimentation and Learning. Public Release, May 31.

Kapica, Jack (2001). "Survey reveals motivation behind IT job hoppers." *The Globe and Mail*, September 4. Available online at **www.globeandmail.com**.

Livingstone, D. W. (2002). "Working and Learning in the Information Age: A Profile of Canadians." Discussion Paper No. W/16. March. Available online at **www.cprn.com**.

National Association of Professional Organizers (NAPO) (2002). *Chi Ro Newsletter*, March 8.

Weber, Terry (2002). "Rebound could spell worker shortage for Ontario's IT sector: Study." *The Globe and Mail*, May 6. Available online at **www.globeandmail.com**.

Chapter 2

Matson, Eric (1997/1998). "Project: You." *Fast Company* issue 12, p. 192. Available online at **www.fastcompany.com/online/12/projectyou.html**.

Project Management Institute (2000). *A guide to the project management body of knowledge.* Newton Square, PA: Project Management Institute.

Chapter 3

Busby, Bonnie (2001). "But you need experience to get experience!" *The Globe and Mail*, May 28. Retrieved from **www.workopolis.com**.

Hampton, John J., ed. (1994). "10 Commandments of Good Communication." *AMA management handbook.* New York, NY: American Management Institute.

Gebauer, Judith, and Arie Segev (1998). "Assessing internet-based procurement to support the virtual enterprise," *VoNet: The Newsletter @* [online], vol. 2, no. 3: p. 31. Retrieved August 2002 from **www.virtual-organization.net**.

Hardwick, Martin, et al. (1996). "Sharing manufacturing information in virtual enterprises." *Communications of the ACM*, vol. 39, no. 2: pp. 46–54.

Ipsos-Reid (2001). "Working in Teams." Public Release, May 31. Sponsored by Microsoft.

Kazmierski, Jack (2000). "Wanted: a good personality. Experts say IT skills rank second to good business skills." *Computing Canada*, September 29, vol. 26, no. 20: p. 28.

Kline, Theresa (1999). *Remaking teams: The revolutionary research-based guide that puts theory into practice.* San Francisco, CA: Jossey-Bass/Pfeiffer.

Maddux, Robert B. (1995). *Successful negotiation* (3rd ed.). Menlo Park, CA: Crispo Publications Inc.

Plesman Staff (2001). "Sharpening one's soft skills." *Computing Canada*, August 24, vol. 27, no. 18: p. 25.

Skyrme, David (1995 and 1999). The Virtual Corporation. Retrieved August 2002 from **www.skyrme.com/insights/2virtorg.htm**.

Van Fleet, David D. (1988). *Contemporary management.* Boston, MA: Houghton Mifflin, p. 271.

Chapter 4

Marxhausen, Paul (2002). "Computer-related repetitive stress injury." Retrieved September 2002 from **www.engr.unl.edu/eeshop/rsi.html**.

"Office ergonomics — ergonomic setup tips." Retrieved September 2002 from **www.healthycomputing.com**.

"Refresh Rate." Retrieved September 2002 from **www.webopedia.com**.

Selix, Caset (2001). "Diagnosis: Dreaded digital depression." *Pioneer Planet*, June 13. Retrieved September 2002 from **www.gulasgroup.com/diagnosis.shtml**.

"Static electricity and computers... Beware!" *Mirror Magazine.* Retrieved August 2002 from **http://sundaytimes.lk/020721/mirror/1.html**.

Chapter 5

Bowen, Ted Smalley (2002). "IT scores a hit with baseball scouts." *The Globe and Mail*, July 10. Available online at **www.globeandmail.com**.

Campbell, Burke, and Murray Conron (2002). "Data under the scope: Mining corporate databases means even the smallest detail can turn up gold." *National Post*, January 14, p. IT1/Front.

McCormick, John (1991). "Interleaf: Documents will soon talk for themselves." *Newsbytes*, July 23.

Chapter 6

Kemp, Ted (2001). "Customer analytics at a cost." *Internet Week*, December 11. Available online at **www.interweek.com/story/INW20011211S0002**.

Kumar, Vipin, and Mahesh Joshi (2002). "Tutorial on high performance data mining." December 3. Available online at **www.users.cs.umn.edu/~mjoshi/hpdmtut/**.

Chapter 7

Green, Ronald E. (1984). "The persuasive properties of color." *Marketing Communications*, October.

Hewlett-Packard (1999). *Advisor*, June. Available online at **www.hpadvisor.com**.

Meggs, Philip B. (1983). *A history of graphic design*. New York, NY: Van Nostrand Reinhold.

Mollenhauer, Doug (1998). "Remember your audience." *Marketing Magazine*, June 29.

Chapter 8

Angel, Jonathan (2001). "What RU marketing tonight?" *Adweek Magazine's Technology Marketing*, December, vol. 21, i. 11, p. 10 (1).

Angel, Jonathan (2002). "LinqWare links employees via EIM." *Client Server News*, July 1.

Ashbrook Nickell, Joe (2001). "To voice mail hell and back." Retrieved July 2002 from **www.business2.com/articles/mag/0,1640,14861,FF.html**.

Crockett, Roger O., et al. (2002). "All net, all the time." *BusinessWeek online* April 29.

Cullen, Scott (2001). "Frugal faxing." *Office Solutions*, April, no. 8, i. 4, p. 38.

Database and Network Journal, 2002.

Ellerby, J. L., L. E. Pinto, and V. E. Brady (2001). *Insights: Succeeding in the information age*. Toronto, ON: Irwin Publishing Ltd.

Hauben, Michael (n.d.). "The 'Open' History of the ARPANET/Internet." Retrieved July 2002 from **www.dei.isep.ipp.pt/docs/arpa/html**.

M2 Communications Ltd. (2002). "Mobile phones to outstrip fixed lines this year." *EuropeMedia*, February 8.

Romanelli, Alex (2002). "2G is still king: 3G important, but older technology won't go away." *Electronic News* (1991), January 1, 48, 1, p. 7 (1).

Ross, Rachel (2002). "Spam! Spam! Spam!" *Toronto Star*, April 8, pp. E1, E2.

Schermerhorn, John (2002). *Management*, 7th ed. Toronto, ON: John Wiley and Sons.

Spaeder, Karen E. (2002). "Make voice mail work for you." Retrieved July 2002 from **www.Entrepreneur.com/article/0,4621,296533,00.html**.

Stone, Martin (2001). "Young wireless users choosy about handsets." *Newsbytes*, July 31. Available online at **www.newsbytes.com**.

Toronto Star (2002). "Web domain 'dot-ca' begins to catch on," May 29.

Webopedia (2002). "Internet." Retrieved July 2002 from www.webopedia.com/TERM/I/Internet.html.

Chapter 9

Black, Debra (2002). "Why clothes click." *Toronto Star*, February 11, p. C1.

Bonner, Paul (2002). "And web sites for all." *PC Magazine* [online], May 7. Retrieved August 2002 from www.pcmag.com/article2/0,4149,2986,00.asp.

Computer Weekly (2002). "How to keep Web customers coming back." April 18, p. 40.

Hamilton, Tyler (2002). "Cash is in the e-mail." *Toronto Star*, February 11, 2002, p. E1.

Harding, Katherine (2002). "From free to fee." *Toronto Star*, July 1, p. D4.

Industry Canada (2002). *Electronic Commerce in Canada* [online]. February 6. Available at http://e-com.ic.gc.ca/english/research/b2b/procurement/sld005.htm.

Information Age (2002). "Customer service is key decider for Web hosting," [online] May. Available at http//infoconomy.com/pages/information-age/group.

Information Age (2002). "Simplicity is priceless," [online] April. Retrieved August 2002 from http://infoconomy.com/pages/information-age/group44399.adp.

Interac (2002). *Statistics*. Available online at www.interac.ca/statistics.html.

Laudon, Kenneth C., and Carol Guercio Traver (2001). *E-commerce: Business, technology, society.* Boston, MA: Addison-Wesley.

Porter, Michael E. (1980). *Competitive strategy: Techniques for analyzing industries and competitors.* New York, NY: Free Press.

Royal Canadian Mounted Police (2002). *Counterfeiting and credit card fraud.* Updated October 1, 2002. Available online at www.rcmp-grc.gc.ca/scams/ccandpc.htm.

Statistics Canada (2002). *The Daily*, Tuesday, April 2. Available online at www.statcan.ca/Daily/English/020402/d020402a.htm.

Webopedia (2002). Available online at www.webopedia.com/TERM/s/sniffer.html.

Chapter 10

Black, Jane (2002)."Stronger, Smarter Buildings in Less Time," *BusinessWeek Online*, July 16.

Bouffard, Kevin (2002). "The citrus department is paying for a study on the feasibility of robotic harvesting," *The Ledger Online*. Available online at www.theledger.com/top_stories/18citr.htm.

Craig, Robert (2000). "E-commerce and fulfillment." *ENT*, August 16, 5, 13: p. 32.

Garson, Barbara (1988). *The electronic sweatshop: How computers are transforming the office of the future into the factory of the past.* New York, NY: Simon & Schuster.

Hamilton, Tyler (2002). "Candid cameras." *Toronto Star*, March 4, pp. D1, D3.

Internet Advertising Bureau of Canada and MultiMediator Strategy Group (2002). *Canadian internet advertising 2000: A message for the medium* [online], March. Retrieved July 2002 from www.multimediator.com/publications/write040.shtml.

Internet Advertising Bureau of Canada and PriceWaterhouseCoopers (2001). *Canadian internet advertising report 2000 & 2001 Q1 results: Summary* [online], September. Retrieved July 2002 from www.iabcanada.com/resources/resource_centre.shtml.

Laudon, Kenneth C., and Carol Guercio Traver (2002). *E-commerce: Business, technology, society.* Boston, MA: Addison-Wesley.

Purchasing Management Association of Canada (2002). "The strategy of managing your bottom line: A virtual vision." PMAC Advertising Supplement in *Canadian Business*, March 4.

Salkever, Alex (2002). "Stronger, smarter buildings in less time." *BusinessWeek Online*, July 16.

Salkever, Alex (2002). "Sports gear goes geek." Special Report: Engineering Digital Era. *BusinessWeek Online*, July 16.

Schermerhorn, John (2002). *Management* (7th ed.). Toronto, ON: John Wiley & Sons, Inc.

Walker, Rob (1998). "Time to ditch the old development recipe," *Electronic Engineering Times*, May 4, no. 1005: p. 49 (1).

Wallace, Bob (1999). "Data warehouse to drive online marketing at GM: Central repository will pull customer data from all car, truck, financial units." *Computerworld*, July 5, p. 6.

Wintrob, Suzanne (1996). "Small fry overhauls IT after snack food takeover." *Computing Canada*, March 14, vol. 22, no. 6: pp. 1 and 4.

Zwolinski, Mark (2002). "Jays' high tech ticket pitch." *Toronto Star*, April 4, pp. A1, A20.

Chapter 11

American Psychological Association (2001). *Publication manual of the American psychological association*, (5th ed.). Washington, DC: American Psychological Association.

Beekman, George (2002). *Computer confluence: Exploring tomorrow's technology.* Upper Saddle River, NJ: Prentice Hall.

Blair, Annice (2003). *Law in action: Understanding Canadian law teacher resource.* Toronto, ON: Pearson Education Canada Inc.

Computer Incident Advisory Capability (2002). "The risk and cost of hoaxes." Retrieved September 2002 from **http://hoaxbusters.ciac.org/HBHoaxInfo.html#risk**.

CASPIAN (Consumers Against Supermarket Privacy Invasion and Numbering) (nd). "Is big brother in your grocery cart?" Retrieved October 2002 from **www.nocards.org**.

Davidson, Stephen J., and Daniel M. Bryant (2001). "Licensing issues in the new economy." *Journal of Internet Law*, October.

Gibaldi, Joseph (1999). *MLA handbook for writers of research papers.* New York, NY: Modern Language Association of America.

Hadley, Jane (2002). "'Loyalty' cards cause griping over swiping," *Seattle Post-Intelligencer* [online], May 11. Retrieved October 2002 from **http://seattlepi.nwsource.com/local/70072_loyal11.asp**.

Ipsos-Reid Corporation (2002). "About us," "Canadian homepage," and "Company profile." Available online at **www.ipsos-reid.com**.

Iverson, Cheryl, et al. (1998). *American medical association manual of style: A guide for authors and editors (AMA),* (9th ed.). Baltimore, MD: Williams & Wilkins.

Key, Peter (2002). "MBA candidate's idea melds into iNetSurvey," *Philadelphia Business Journal* [online], January 11, 2002. Retrieved October 2002 from **http//philadelphia.bizjournals.com/philadelphia/stories/2002/01/14/newscolumn5/html**.

Reuters News Agency (2002). "Record giants may sue individuals." *The Globe and Mail*, July 4. Available online at **www.globeandmail.com**.

Sandoval, Greg (2002). "Why hackers escape: organized, well-financed criminals stay a step ahead of the law," *CNET News.com* [online], May 14. Retrieved October 2002 from **http://news.com.com/2009-1017-912708.html**.

The Chicago Manual of Style, (14th ed.). (1993). Chicago, IL: The University of Chicago Press.

The Institute of Electrical and Electronics Engineers, Inc. (2001). *IEEE standards style manual.* Available online at **http://standards.ieee.org/guides/style/**.

Tobias, Zachary (2000). "Putting the ethics in e-business." *Computerworld*, November 6. Retrieved November 2002 from www.computerworld.com.

Chapter 12

Alesso, H. Peter (2000). *Producing internet video as broadband technologies converge.* Boston, MA: Addison-Wesley.

Hewitt, Perry (1998). "Evolution of corporate web sites" [online], January 6. Retrieved August 2002 from www.contentious.com/articles/1-3/guest1-3.html.

Kilian, Crawford (2001). "Effective web writing." *New Architect* [online], February. Retrieved August 2002 from www.webtechniques.com/archives/2001/02/kilian.

Chapter 13

Beekman, George (2003). *Computer confluence: Exploring tomorrow's technology,* (5th ed.). Upper Saddle River, NJ: Prentice Hall.

Buckler, Grant (2002). "3D interface draws praise from digital animators." *The Globe and Mail* [online]. Retrieved October 2002 from www.globeandmail.com.

Estrella, Steven G. (n.d.). "Multimedia basics: Understanding moving images" [online]. Retrieved September 2002 from www.stevenestrella.com/IWP/multimediabasics/movingimages.html.

Kristof, Ray, and Amy Satran (1995). *Interactivity by design: Creating and communicating with new media.* Mountain View, CA: Adobe Press.

Rosner, Bob (2002). "What can you do to increase the odds of success when you're just starting out?" Retrieved October 2002 from www.workopolis.com.

Ryder, Shawn (n.d.). "Flash 5: Good for business based web sites?" Available online at www.webryder.com.

Vaughan, Tay (1998). *Multimedia: Making IT work.* Berkeley, CA: Osborne Publishing.

Index

Numbers and Symbols

A

B

C

D

F

G

H

I

N

O

P

Q

R

S

T

U

V

W

Y

Z

Credits

Photographs

p. 1 (left): Dell Corporate Communications; p. 1 (middle): Nokia Products Ltd.; p. 1 (right): Research In Motion Limited; p. 7 (left): firstlight.ca; p. 7 (middle): Todd Gaul, Computer Science UNC—Chapel Hill; p. 7 (right): firstlight.ca; p. 15 (left): firstlight.ca; p. 15 (middle): PhotoDisc\Ryan McVay; p. 15 (right): Comstock; p. 36: Microsoft Project is a registered trademark of Microsoft Corporation in Canada and other countries; p. 41 (top left): Courtesy of Microsoft Canada; p. 41 (bottom right): Sure Trak is a registered trademark of Primavera Systems, Inc.; p. 47: Digital Vision; p. 49: PhotoDisc\Ross Anania; p. 50: PhotoDisc\Skip Nall; p. 58: Stone\Jon Riley; p. 64: Stone\Charles Thatcher; p. 74: Chuck Savage\Corbis\Magma; p. 76 (top): Courtesy of Microsoft Canada; p. 76 (middle): Research In Motion Limited; p. 76 (bottom): Courtesy of Think Outside, Inc.; p. 77 (top): Courtesy of Microsoft Canada; p. 77 (middle): EyeWire Collection; p. 77 (bottom): Courtesy of Logitech Canada; p. 78 (left): WACOM Technology Corp.; p. 78 (right): Courtesy of Micro Touch Systems, Inc.; p. 79: Image Produced Courtesy of Canada Post; p. 80: Photo Courtesy of IBM Corp.; p. 81 (top left and bottom right): Courtesy of ViewSonic Corp., Walnut CA 91789; p. 83 (top): Courtesy of Epson Canada Ltd.; p. 83 (middle): Courtesy of Brother International Corp. (Canada) Ltd.; p. 83 (bottom): Courtesy of Epson Canada Ltd.; p. 85: Copyright ©2002 HowStuffWorks, Inc. All rights reserved; p. 86: Photo provided by Sony; p. 89: Courtesy of 3M Corp.; p. 91: David Cheung, David Cheung Designs; p. 96: Windows XP is a registered trademark of Microsoft Corporation in Canada and other countries; p. 97: Corbis\Stock Market\Michael A. Keller; p. 98: Courtesy of Symantec Corp.; p. 99: Nokia Products Ltd.; p. 100: Microsoft Windows is a registered trademark of Microsoft Corporation in Canada and other countries; p. 101: Macintosh OS X is a registered trademark of Apple Computer Inc. in Canada and other countries; p. 102: Windows 98, Windows 2000, Windows XP are registered trademarks of Microsoft Corporation in Canada and other countries; p. 103: UNIX operating system is a product of Sun Microsystems, Inc.; p. 104: Linux operating system is a product of Sun Microsystems, Inc.; p. 109: Courtesy East Carolina University Environmental Health and Safety; p. 123, 127, 129, 130: Microsoft Word is a registered trademark of Microsoft Corporation in Canada and other countries; p. 133: Quattro Pro is a registered trademark of Corel Corporation in Canada and other countries; p. 134, 137: Microsoft Excel is a registered trademark of Microsoft Corporation in Canada and other countries; p. 140: Microsoft Works is a registered trademark of Microsoft Corporation in Canada and other countries; p. 149: SuperStock Inc.; p. 153, 155: Microsoft Word is a registered trademark of Microsoft Corporation in Canada and other countries; p. 168: Microsoft Access is a registered trademark of Microsoft Corporation in Canada and other countries; p. 171: Pearson Canada\Alex Li; p. 176 (top): Canadian Broadcasting Corporation; p. 176 (bottom left): Courtesy of JDJ Jewellery; p. 176 (bottom right): Courtesy of Microsoft Canada; p. 178: Courtesy of Hewlett Packard; p. 186: Creo Inc. www.creo.com; p. 188: V.C.L.\Taxi; p. 196: Courtesy of Sharp Electronics Corporation; p. 199: David Young-Wolff\PhotoEdit, Inc.; p. 203: Research In Motion Limited; p. 215: Google.ca is a trademark of Google.com in Canada; p. 226: Research In Motion Limited; p. 230: Mike Grandmaison\firstlight.ca; p. 233: Charles Gupton\Corbis\Magma; p. 238: Courtesy of Amberhill Collections; p. 253: Science Museum London/Science & Society Picture Library; p. 255: Soltrus Inc., Leading Provider of Internet Security Solutions in Canada. VeriSign's Canadian Affiliate; p. 258 (left): Courtesy of McAfee Security, Network Associates, Inc.; p. 258 (right): Courtesy of Symantec Corp.; p. 272: Taxi\Meikle John; p. 274: Ed Kashi\Corbis\Magma; p. 275: Reprinted with the permission of Colgate-Palmolive; p. 280: Bill Varie\Corbis\Magma; p. 281: Image Bank\Francesco Ruggeri; p. 287: Courtesy of Internet Advertising Bureau of Canada; p. 288: Google.ca is a trademark of Google.com in Canada; p. 289: Used by permission of Bell Canada; p. 290: Janome Online is a service of Janome America, Inc.; p. 291 (top): Eaton's Catalogue page from Commonwealth Imaging; p. 291 (bottom): Used by permission of Sears Canada; p. 303: Axis Communications, www.axis.com; p. 343: The Gavin Crawford Show is produced by IdleMind Productions in association with The Comedy Network; p. 348: Taxi, www.taxi.ca; p. 386: HyperStudio is a registered trademark of Roger Wagner Publishing Inc., a Sunburst Technology Company; p. 308: Craig Smallish\Artville; p. 340: Digital Vison; p. 357: Microsoft Web Page Wizard is a registered trademark of Microsoft Corporation in Canada and other countries; p. 365: Ian Mckinnell\Taxi; p. 378: Courtesy of Pocket Videos.com; p. 383: Windows Media Player is a registered trademark of Microsoft Corporation in Canada and other countries; p. 387: Macromedia Director is a registered trademark of Macromedia, Inc.

Extracts

p. 11: (Figure 1.9) From *The 7 Habits of Highly Effective People* © 1989, Stephen R. Covey. The Time Management Matrix phrase and model are trademarks of Franklin Covey Co., www.franklincovey.com. Used with permission. All rights reserved.

p. 56: (Figure 3.4) Adapted from *Contemporary Management,* David D. Van Fleet (Boston, MA: Houghton Mifflin, 1989), p. 271.

p. 60: (Figure 3.7) From information in *Remaking Teams: The Revolutionary Research-Based Guide That Puts Theory Into Practice*, Teresa Kline (San Francisco, CA: Jossey-Bass/Pfeiffer, 1999).

p. 70: (Figure 3.11) Adapted from *Successful Negotiation*, 3rd edition, Robert B. Maddux (Menlo Park, CA: Crisp Publications Inc., 1995), p. 68.

p. 90 (Figure 4.15) From *Computer Influence* p. 258 and *Computers in Your Future 2003*, Bryan Pfaffenberger (Upper Saddle, NJ: Prentice-Hall, 2003) Figures 9.3 and 9.4.

p. 90 (Figure 4.16) Adapted from *Computers in Your Future 2003*, Bryan Pfaffenberger (Upper Saddle, NJ: Prentice-Hall, 2003) Figure 10.7

p. 99 (Figure 4.22) From *Computers in Your Future 2003*, Figure 5.8.

p. 104 (Figure 4.28) From *Computers in Your Future 2003*, p. 516.

p. 163 (Figure 6.6) Adapted from "Tutorial on High Performance Data Mining," Vipin Kumar and Mahesh Joshi <www-users.cs.umn.edu/~mjosh/hpdmtut> (December 3, 2002).

p. 174 (Figure 7.1) Adapted from webdesign.about.com

p. 205 (Figure 8.1) Adapted from *Management,* 7th edition, John Schermerhorn (Toronto, ON: John Wiley and Sons, 2002) p. 447.

p. 206 (Figure 8.2) From *Management*, 7th edition, p. 453.

p. 226 (Figure 8.11) Adapted from *Computers in Your Future 2003*, Figure 9.7.

p. 245 (Figure 9.5) From *E-Commerce: Business, Technology, Society,* Kenneth C. Laudon and Carol Guercio Traver (Toronto, ON: Addison-Wesley, 2001), p. 238.

p. 251 (Figure 9.6) From *E-Commerce: Business, Technology, Society,* p. 239.

p. 254 (Figure 9.9) From *E-Commerce: Business, Technology, Society,* p. 254.

p. 256 (Figure 9.13) From *E-Commerce: Business, Technology, Society,* p. 259.

p. 267 (Figure 9.16) From *Competitive Strategy: Techniques for Analyzing Industries and Competitors*, Michael E. Porter (New York, NY: Free Press, 1980).

p. 327 (Figure 11.4) From *Law in Action: Understanding Canadian Law Teacher Resource,* Annice Blair, et al. (Toronto, ON: Pearson Education Canada Inc., 2003) p. 486.

p. 331 (Figure 11.6) From National Fraud Information Centre at <www.fraud.org/internet/2001stats.htm> November 15, 2002.

p. 367 (Figure 13.1) Adapted from *Computer Confluence: Exploring Tomorrow's Technology*, 5th edition, George Beekman (Upper Saddle, NJ: Prentice-Hall, 2003), p. 200.

p. 368 (Figure 13.2) Adapted from *Multimedia: Making IT Work,* Tay Vaughan (Berkeley, CA: Osborne Publishing, 1998), p. 465.

p. 369 (Figure 13.3) Adapted from *Interactivity By Design: Creating and Communicating with New Media,* Ray Kristof and Amy Satran (Mountain View, CA: Adobe Press, 1995), p. 37.

Literary

p. 5: (Figure 1.1) Adapted from www-ist.massey.ac.nz. Reprinted with permission; p. 13: © Ipsos-Reid, May 31, 2001; p. 17: Reprinted with permission from *The Globe and Mail*; p. 32: Reprinted with permission of *Fast Company Magazine* through the Copyright Clearance Center; p. 52: David Skyrme; p. 59: © Ipsos-Reid, May 31, 2001; p. 65: *Computing Canada* IT Business Group, Transcontinental Media; p. 72: © Jack Kazmierski; pp. 109–110: HealthyComputing.com, Inc.; p. 143: © Ted Smalley Bowen; p. 145: © Burke Campbell and Murray Conron; p. 163: Copyright 2001 CMP Media LLC. Reproduced from InternetWeek.com with permission; p. 186: Creo Inc. www.creo.com; p. 198: Doug Mollenhauer, Quantum Leap Learning; p. 210: © Scott Cullen; p. 222: Reprinted with permission — The Toronto Star Syndicate; p. 241: Reprinted with permission — The Toronto Star Syndicate; p. 247: Reprinted with permission — The Toronto Star Syndicate; p. 263: © Paul Bonner. Originally published in *PC Magazine*; p. 281: *The Ledger* in Lakeland, Florida; p. 295: Reprinted with permission — The Toronto Star Syndicate; p. 302: © Canadian Tire Corporation, Limited; p. 304: Reprinted with permission — The Toronto Star Syndicate; p. 318: Ipsos-Reid; pp. 325–326: Copyright © 2002, *Seattle Post-Intelligencer*. Reprinted with permission; and CASPIAN, http://www.nocards.org; p. 333: Reprinted with permission — Reuters; p. 389: Bob Rosner is the author of Working Wounded (Warner, 1998), a speaker and founder of the award-winning http://workingwounded.com.